SO-ADX-484

EASY REFERENCE

IRISH-ENGLISH
ENGLISH-IRISH

DICTIONARY

FOCLÓIR

GAEILGE/BÉARLA
BÉARLA/GAEILGE

ROBERTS RINEHART PUBLISHERS
Boulder, Colorado

Published by
ROBERTS RINEHART PUBLISHERS
6309 Monarch Park Place
Niwot, Colorado 80503
TEL 303.652.2685
fax 303.652.2689
www.robertsrinehart.com

Distributed to the trade by Publishers Group West

First published by The Educational Company of Ireland and Talbot Press, Walkinstown, Dublin 12

© 1998 The Educational Company of Ireland and Talbot Press

ISBN 1-57098-165-5 cloth
ISBN 1-57098-184-1 paperback

Library of Congress Catalog Card Number 98-86395

Printed in the United States of America

10 9 8 7 6 5 4 3 2 1

Cover Design: Ann W. Douden
Cover Photograph © 1998 Tom Kelly

Contents

GRAMMATICAL ABBREVIATIONS / NODA GRAMADAÍ

adj	adjective
adv	adverb
aut	autonomous (form)
cond	conditional mood
conj	conjunction
def art	definite article
excl	exclamation
f, fem	feminine (noun)
fut	future (tense)
gen	genitive
hab (H.)	habitual
impr	imperative
indef art	indefinite article
indic	indicative
interj	interjection
m, mas	masculine (noun)
n	noun
neg	negative
nom	nominative
num adj	numerical adjective
part	particle
pl	plural
poss adj	possessive adjective
prep	preposition
pres	present (tense)
rel part	relative particle
rel pron	relative pronoun
subj	subjunctive
v	verb
v adj	verbal adjective
vn	verbal noun
voc	vocative
voc part	vocative particle

GENERAL ABBREVIATIONS / NODA GINEARÁLTA

AGM	CGB	Cruinniú Ginearálta Bliantúil
AIDS	SEIF	Siondróm Easpa Imdhíonachta Faighte
a.m.	r.n.	roimh nóin
bc	r.c.	roimh Chríost
c/o	f/ch	faoi chúram

c.o.d.	í.a.s.	íoc ar sheachadadh
EC	CE	An Comhphobal Eorpach
e.g.	m.sh.	mar shampla
ECU	AAE	Aonad Airgeadra Eorpach
EFTA	LSE	Limistéar Saorthrádála na hEorpa
EGM	CGU	Cruinniú Ginearálta Urghnách
EMF	CIAE	An Ciste Airgeadaíochta Eorpach
EMS	COAE	An Córas Airgeadaíochta Eorpach
ESB	BSL	Bord Soláthair an Leictreachais
ESF	CSE	Ciste Sóisialta na hEorpa
etc	srl	agus araile
EU	AE	Aontas Eorpach
HIV	VEID	Víreas Easpa Imdhíonachta Daonna
h.p.	f.c.	fruilcheannach
IDA	ÚFT	An tÚdarás Forbartha Tionscail
i.e.	.i.	is é sin
IOU	DDU	dlitear duit uaim
GAA	CLG	Cumann Lúthchleas Gael
GDP	OTI	Olltáirgeacht Intíre
GNP	OTN	Olltáirgeacht Náisiúnta
IMF	CAI	An Ciste Airgeadaíochta Idirnáisiúnta
inch(es)	orl.	orlach/orlaí
Lower	Íocht.	íochtarach
Ltd.	tta	teoranta
m.p.h.	m.s.u.	mílte san uair
NATO	ECAT	Eagraíocht Chonradh an Atlantaigh Thuaidh
no.	uimh.	uimhir
page	lch.	leathanach
PAYE	ÍMAT	Íoc Mar a Thuillir
plc	ctp	cuideachta theoranta phoiblí
p.m.	i.n.	iarnóin
p.o.	o.p.	ordú poist
PRO	OCP	Oifigeach Caidrimh Phoiblí
PRSI	ASPC	Árachas Sóisialta Pá-Choibhneasa
RTC	CTR	Coláiste Teicniúil Réigiúnach
St.	N.	Naomh
St.	S.	San
UN	NA	Náisiúin Aontaithe
Upper	Uacht.	Uachtarach
VAT	CBL	Cáin Bhreisluacha
VHI	ASS	Árachas Sláinte Saorálach
vol.	iml.	imleabhar
w.p.m.	f.s.n.	focail sa nóiméad

A

a¹ *voc part* go raibh maith agat, a Thomáis thank you, Tomás, a chroí my dear, a asail! you ass!

a² *part (with numbers)* a haon, a dó, a trí, a ceathair, srl. one, two, three, four, etc.

a³ *prep* doras a dhúnadh to close a door

a⁴ *poss adj* his, her, its, their, a charr his car, a carr her car, a gcarr their car, a ainm his name, a hainm her name, a n-ainm their name

a⁵ *rel pron, rel part* that, which, who an bronntanas a fuair sé the present he got, an leaba a chóirigh mé the bed that I made, (gach) a bhfuil ann all that is there

a¹ *part* how a fheabhas, dhonacht atá sé how good, bad he/it is

á² *excl* ah!

á *poss adj (as object of vn)* him, her, it, them á cur putting her/it, á chur putting him/it, á gcur putting them

ab *m3* abbot

abair *v* (see *irregular verbs*) 1. say abair le tell 2. speak 3. sing abair amhrán sing a song

abairt *f2* sentence

ábalta *adj* 1. able-bodied duine ábalta able-bodied person 2. able, capable

ábaltacht *f3* strength, ability

abar¹ *m1* bunker (*golf*)

abar² *m1* boggy ground san abar in a difficulty, in difficulties

abhac *m1* dwarf

abhaile *adv* home, homewards chuir mé abhaile air é I persuaded him of it

abhainn *f* river rud a chur leis an abhainn to get rid of something

ábhalmhór *adj* huge, enormous

ábhalscaird *f2* jumbo-jet

abhantrach *f2* river basin

ábhar *m1* 1. topic, subject 2. material, matter ábhar múinteora student teacher, ní bhaineann sé le hábhar it doesn't have any relevance 3. cause ábhar bróin cause for sorrow, ábhar machnaimh food for thought 4. pus rinne sé ábhar it festered

ábharachas *m1* materialism

ábhartha *adj* relevant, material

abhcóide *m4* advocate, barrister, counsel

abhlann *f2* wafer, altar-bread, host

abhras *m1* 1. yarn 2. handiwork

abhus *adv, adj* on this side, here thall agus abhus here and there

acadamh *m1* academy

acadúil *adj* academic

ach¹ *prep, conj* 1. but, except níl ann ach cluiche it's only a game 2. provided that éireoidh leat ach an obair a dhéanamh you will succeed provided you do the work

ach² *excl* ah! ugh!

achainí *f4* plea, request, petition

achainigh *v* petition achainigh ar dhuine petition to somebody, implore somebody

achar *m1* 1. distance, area 2. duration

achasán *m1* insult, slur ag caitheamh achasáin le duine taunting somebody

achoimre *f4* summary, outline, synopsis

achoimrigh *v* summarise, shorten

achomair *adj* 1. near 2. brief, concise go hachomair in brief, in short

achomaireacht *f3* 1. abstract 2. brevity, conciseness

achomharc *m1, v* appeal

achrann *m1* 1. strife, **ag achrann** quarrelling 2. tangle

achrannach *adj* 1. quarrelsome 2. intricate, complicated, entangled 3. rocky, rugged

acht *m3* 1. act 2. condition **ar acht go** on condition that

aclaí *adj* 1. agile, supple 2. skilful, dexterous

aclaigh *v* 1. exercise 2. flex

aclaíocht *f3* 1. exercise 2. dexterity

acmhainn *f2* 1. means, resource(s) **acmhainní nádúrtha** natural resources 2. ability, potential, capacity **acmhainn grinn** sense of humour, **acmhainn iomaíochta** competitiveness

acmhainneach *adj* 1. wealthy, well-off 2. capable, endurable, seaworthy

acra[1] *m4* acre

acra[2] *m4* tool **acraí** utensils

acrach *adj* handy, convenient

acrainm *m4* acronym

adamh *m1* atom

adanóidí *pl* adenoids

ádh *m1* luck, success, good fortune **bhí an t-ádh orm** I was lucky, **ádh mór (ort)!** good luck! goodbye!

adhain *v* 1. inflame 2. ignite 3. kindle

adhaint *f2* 1. inflammation 2. ignition 3. kindling

adhair *v* 1. worship, adore 2. idolise

adhairt *f2* head-rest, pillow

adhaltranas *m1* adultery

adharc *f2* horn **in adharca a chéile** at loggerheads, fighting

adharcach *adj* 1. horned 2. horny

adharcáil *v* gore, horn

adharcán *m1* tentacle, feeler

adhartán *m1* cushion

adhlacadh *m* burial

adhlacóir *m3* undertaker

adhlaic *v* bury

adhmad *m1* 1. timber, wood 2. substance **adhmad a bhaint as rud** to make sense of something, to get substance from something

adhmadóireacht *f3* carpentry, woodwork

adhradh *m3* worship, adoration

ádhúil *adj* lucky, fortunate

admhaigh *v* 1. admit, acknowledge 2. confess, declare

admháil *f3* 1. admission, acknowledgement 2. receipt

aduaidh *adv, prep, adj* from the north **ag teacht aduaidh** coming from the north, coming south, **an ghaoth aduaidh** the north wind, **teacht aniar aduaidh ar dhuine** to take somebody unawares

aduain *adj* 1. strange, unusual 2. lonely, eerie

ae *m4* liver

aeistéitiúil *adj* aesthetic

aer *m1* air **aer úr, glan** fresh, clean, air, **amuigh faoin aer** in the open air, outdoors, **brú aeir** atmospheric pressure

aer- *prefix* air-, aerial **aerbhuama** air bomb

aerach *adj* 1. light-hearted, carefree **duine aerach** gay, light-hearted person 2. airy **áit aerach** airy place

aeráid *f2* climate **téamh aeráide** global warming, warming of climate

aeráil *f3* ventilation, (act of) airing, **prios aerála** hot press *v* ventilate

aerálóir *m3* ventilator

aerárthach *m1* aircraft

aerasól *m1* aerosol

aerdhíonach *adj* airtight

aerfhórsa *m4* air force

aerfort *m1* airport **Aerfort Chorcaí** Cork Airport, **Aerfort na Sionainne** Shannon Airport

aerionad *m1* airbase

aerlíne *f4* airline

aerlínéar *m1* airliner

aerlitir *f* air letter

aer-obach *adj* airtight

aeróbach *adj* aerobic **aclaíocht aeróbach** aerobics

aeróg *f2* aerial **aeróg tharchuir** transmitting aerial

aeroiriúnaigh *v* air-condition

aeroiriúnú *m* air-conditioning

aeróstach *m1* flight attendant

aerpháirc *f2* airfield

aerphíobán *m1* breathing tube, snorkel

aerphost *m1* airmail

aer-ruathar *m1* air raid

aerscuab *f2* airbrush

áfach *adv* however

Afracach *adj, m1* African

Afraic, an *f2* Africa **an Afraic Theas** South Africa

ag *prep* (*pron. forms* **agam, agat, aige, aici, againn, agaibh, acu**) 1. at, by, with **tá sé ag obair** he is at work, he is working, **ag am lóin** at lunch time, **níl sé léite agam fós** I haven't read it yet (it hasn't been read by me yet), **fág agam é** leave it with me 2. (shows possession with verb **bí**) **tá cailín agam** I have a girl-friend, **an bhfuil Spáinnis agat?** can you speak Spanish? **duine acu** one of them, **bíodh ciall agat** have sense, cop on, **is mór aige thú** he has a great regard for you, **an baile s'againne** our village, town, **punt a bheith agat ar dhuine** to owe somebody a pound

aga *m4* 1. distance 2. period of time **má bhíonn aga agat chuige** if you have the time for it

agair *v* 1. plead 2. sue 3. (with *prep* **ar**) avenge

agallaí *m4* interviewee

agallamh *m1* interview **agallamh le haghaidh poist** interview for a job, job interview

agallóir *m4* interviewer

aghaidh *f2* 1. face, front, aspect **aghaidh a thabhairt ar dhuine** to face up to someone, **aghaidh a thabhairt ar áit** to set out for a place 2. (in phrases with *preps*) **ar aghaidh** ahead, forward, **ar aghaidh leat!** carry on! go on! **leanúint ar aghaidh le** to proceed, carry on, with, **in aghaidh** against, **chuir sé i m'aghaidh** he opposed me, **in aghaidh na bliana** yearly, *per annum*, **ceithre chúl in aghaidh a náid** four goals to nil, **le haghaidh** for, **le haghaidh béile** for a meal

agó *m4* condition **gan aon agó** without a doubt

agóid *f2* objection, protest

agóideoir *m3* objector, protester

aguisín *m4* appendix (*in book*)

agus *conj* and **breis agus céad bliain ó shin** more than a hundred years ago, **agus a bhfuil déanta aige** considering all he has done, after all he has done, **bíodh agus go ...** granted that ..., although ..., **tuairim agus deich gcinn acu** about ten of them

agús *m1* 1. qualification 2. reservation, clause

áibhéalach *adj* exaggerated

áibhéil *f2* exaggeration

aibhinne *m4* avenue

aibhleog *f2* live coal, spark **aibhleoga (dearga)** embers, **aibhleoga dóite** cinders

aibhsigh *v* highlight (*with highlighter*)

aibí *adj* 1. mature, ripe 2. clever

aibíd *f2* habit (*dress*)

aibigh *v* mature, ripen

aibítir *f2* alphabet

Aibreán *m1* April

aibreog *f2* apricot

aice *f4* nearness, proximity **in aice na scoile** near the school, **in aice leis an áit** in proximity to the place

aiceann *m1* accent (*grammar*)

aicearra *m4* short cut

aicíd *f2* disease

aicme *f4* 1. class, genus 2. clique

aicmeach *adj* 1. class 2. generic

aicmigh *v* classify

aicmiú *m* classification

aicmiúchán *m1* classification

aicsean *m1* action **scannán maith aicsin** a good action film

aidhleanna *pl* oilskins

aidhm *f2* purpose, aim **d'aon aidhm on purpose**

aidhmeantúil *adj* volatile **go haidhmeantúil óg** young and volatile

aidhnín *m4* fuse (*of explosive*)

aidiacht *f3* adjective

aidréanailín *m4* adrenaline

aife *f4* ebb **taoide aife** ebbing tide

aiféala *m4* 1. remorse, regret **aiféala a bheith ort faoi rud** to be sorry about something 2. embarrassment, shame

aiféalach *adj* 1. regretful 2. embarrassed

áiféis *f2* 1. nonsense 2. exaggeration

áiféiseach *adj* 1. nonsensical, ridiculous 2. exaggerated

aifid *f2* aphid

aifir *v* 1. reproach, rebuke 2. punish

aifirt *f3* reproach, rebuke

Aifreann *m1* Mass

aigéad *m1* acid

aigéadach *adj* acid(ic) **báisteach aigéadach** acid rain

aigéadacht *f3* acidity

aigéadú *m* acidification

aigéan *m1* ocean **an tAigéan Ciúin** the Pacific Ocean

aigéanach *adj* oceanic

aigeanta *adj* spirited, merry, cheerful

aighneacht *f3* submission (*in writing*)

aighneas *m1* 1. argument, discussion 2. dispute

aighneasach *adj* argumentative

aigne *f4* 1. mind, disposition **ná himíodh sé as d'aigne!** don't forget it! don't let it out of your mind! 2. intention **bhí sé ar aigne agam é a dhéanamh** I intended to do it 3. cheerfulness **bheith faoi aigne** to be cheerful

aigneolaíocht *f3* psychology

áil (used with the copula **is**) desire, liking, wish **mar is áil léi** as she wishes, **níorbh áil leat é** you didn't care for it

ailbíneach *adj, m1* albino

ailceimic *f2* alchemy

áiléar *m1* 1. gallery 2. attic, loft

ailgéabar *m1* algebra

ailgéabrach *adj* algebraic

ailibí *m4* alibi

ailigéadar *m1* alligator

ailínigh *v* align

ailiúnas *m1* alimony

aill *f2* cliff, high rock, precipice **thit sé le haill** he fell off/down a cliff

áilleacht *f3* 1. beauty 2. delight

ailleadóireacht *f3* rock-climbing

áilleagán *m1* 1. toy, doll 2. trinket

ailléirge *f4* allergy

ailléirgeach *adj* allergic

ailp *f2* 1. knob 2. lump, chunk

ailse *f4* cancer **ailse cíche** breast cancer

ailseach *adj* cancerous **fás ailseach** cancerous growth

ailt *f2* steep glen, ravine

áilteoir *m3* joker, trickster

áilteoireacht *f3* playing pranks, joking

ailtire *m4* architect

ailtireacht *f3* architecture

áiméar *m1* opportunity, chance

aimhleas *m3* detriment, harm

aimhleasach *adj* detrimental, harmful

aimhréidh *f2* entanglement *adj*
1. entangled, untidy, dishevelled
2. uneven

aimhréireach (le) *adj* repugnant (to)

aimhrialta *adj* irregular, anomalous

aimhrialtacht *f3* anomaly

aimhriar *f2* 1. disobedience
2. incongruity

aimiréal *m1* admiral **aimiréal dearg** red admiral

aimitis *f2* amethyst

aimléis *f2* misery **bhí sé in umar na haimléise** he was in a terrible/ miserable plight

aimlithe *adj* 1. enfeebled, deformed
2. wretched

aimlitheacht *f3* feebleness, deformity

aimnéise *f4* amnesia

aimpéar *m1* ampere

aimpligh *v* amplify

aimplitheoir *m3* amplifier

aimrid *adj* sterile, barren

aimride *f4* sterility, barrenness

aimridigh *v* sterilise, make barren

aimsigh *v* 1. find, discover 2. hit
3. aim 4. attack

aimsir *f2* 1. weather **aimsir bhreá** lovely weather, **drochaimsir** bad weather 2. time, season, period of service **aimsir na Cásca** Eastertide, **caitheamh aimsire** hobby, pastime, **ar, in, aimsir ag duine** in service with, **cailín aimsire** servant girl 3. tense (*grammar*) **an aimsir chaite** the past tense

aimsitheoir *m3* 1. finder 2. marksman

aimsiú *m4* 1. hit (on target) 2. aim
3. attack

ain- *prefix* 1. over-, intense **in ainmhéid** overgrown, of huge proportions 2. in-, un-, not **aineolach** inexperienced 3. bad, unnatural **ainghníomh** atrocity

ainbhios *m3* ignorance

ainbhiosach *adj* ignorant

ainbhiosán *m1* ignorant person, ignoramus

ainbhreith *f2* unjust judgement

aincheart *m1* injustice, wrong

ainchleachtadh *m1* inexperience

ainchreideamh *m1* unbelief

ainchreidmheach *adj* unbelieving
m1 unbeliever

ainchríonna *adj* rash, imprudent

aincis *f2* 1. peevishness 2. malignancy

aindiachaí *m4* atheist

aindiachas *m1* atheism

aindiaga *adj* ungodly, impious

aindleathach *adj* unlawful, illegal

aindlí *m4* lawlessness, tyranny

áineas *m3* 1. delight 2. sport

ainéistéiseach *adj, m1* anaesthetic

aineoil *adj* strange, unknown

aineolach *adj* 1. inexperienced
2. ignorant

aineolas *m1* 1. inexperience
2. ignorance

ainfheoil *f3* granulation tissue (white flesh around a wound)

aingeal *m1* angel

ainghníomh *m1* evil deed, atrocity

aingí *adj* 1. fretful 2. malignant

aingiallta *adj* irrational

aingíne *f4* angina

ainglí *adj* angelic

ainglis *f2* goitre

ainimh *f2* disfigurement, blemish

ainligh *v* guide, manoeuvre, steady a boat

ainm *m4* 1. name **in ainm a bheith** supposed to be, **ainm comhaid** file name, **ainm úsáideora** user name 2. reputation **tá drochainm ar an bhfear sin** that man has a bad reputation 3. noun (*grammar*)

ainmchlár *m1* (street) nameplate

ainmfhocal *m1* noun

ainmhéid *f2* overgrowth, hugeness

ainmheasartha *adj* immoderate, intemperate, excessive

ainmheasarthacht *f3* immoderation, intemperance, excess

ainmhí *m4* 1. animal 2. brutish person

ainmhian *f2* lust, passion

ainmhianach *adj* lustful, passionate

ainmhíoch *adj* brutish, animal

ainmneach *adj, m1* nominative (*grammar*)

ainmní *m4* subject (*grammar*)

ainmnigh *v* name, specify

ainmníocht *f3* nomenclature

ainmnitheach *m1* nominee

ainmniúchán *m1* nomination

ainmniúll *adj* 1. well-known, noted 2. nominal

ainneoin, d'ainneoin, in ainneoin notwithstanding, despite, in spite of

ainnír *f2* young woman, maiden

ainnis *adj* miserable, wretched

ainniseoir *m3* miserable person, wretch

ainriail *f5* 1. lack of discipline 2. anarchy

ainrialaí *m4* 1. anarchist 2. undisciplined person

ainrialta *adj* 1. undisciplined 2. anarchical

ainrianta *adj* unbridled

ainriocht *m3* bad state, pitiful plight

ainscianta *adj* uncontrolled, wild, furious

ainseal *m1* **ag dul in ainseal, ag dul chun ainsil** becoming chronic

ainsealach *adj* chronic

ainspianta *adj* 1. abnormal, disproportionate 2. grotesque

ainspiantacht *f3* 1. abnormality 2. grotesqueness

Ainspiorad *m1* **an tAinspiorad** the Devil

ainsprid *f2* 1. evil spirit 2. hothead **is é an ainsprid é** he is a terrible hothead

aintiarna *m4* tyrant

aintiarnas *m1* tyranny

aintiarnúil *adj* tyrannical

aintín *f4* aunt

aintiún *m1* anthem

aíocht *f3* 1. hospitality 2. lodging **teach aíochta** guest-house

aipindic *f2* appendix (*in body*)

aipindicíteas *m1* appendicitis

airc *f2* 1. want 2. great hunger, voracity, greed

áirc *f2* ark

airceach *adj* 1. needy 2. voracious, greedy

aird[1] *f2* direction, point of compass

aird[2] *f2* 1. notice 2. attention **níor thug sé aon aird orm** he didn't pay any attention to me, **rud gan aird** insignificant thing

airde *f4* height, altitude, level **deich dtroithe ar airde** ten feet in height, **in airde** up, on high, **d'imigh sé leis ar cosa in airde** he left galloping, at a gallop

airdeall *m1* watchfulness, alertness

airdeallach *adj* watchful, alert

aire[1] *f4* 1. attention, care **tabhair aire duit féin** take care of yourself 2. heed **aire chugat!** look out!

aire[2] *m4* minister (*government*) **an tAire Sláinte** the Minister for Health, **aire stáit** minister of state

aireach *adj* 1. vigilant 2. attentive, careful

aireachas *m1* 1. vigilance 2. attention

aireacht *f3* ministry

aireachtáil *f3* perception

aireagal *m1* 1. ward (*in hospital*) 2. oratory 3. **ceol aireagail** chamber music

áireamh *m1* 1. arithmetic, number 2. counting, reckoning, enumeration **agus gach rud á chur san áireamh** including, counting, everything

áireamhán *m1* calculator **áireamhán in-ríomhchláraithe** programmable calculator

airéine *f4* arena

airgead *m1* 1. money **airgead tirim** cash, **fear mór airgid** rich man 2. silver

airgeadaí *m4* financier

airgeadas *m1* finance **an tAire Airgeadais** the Minister for Finance

airgeadóir *m3* cashier, teller

airgeadra *m4* currency **airgeadra eachtrach** foreign currency

airgeadúil *adj* 1. financial 2. silvery

áirgiúil *adj* 1. spacious 2. well-appointed

airí¹ *m4* characteristic, sympton

airí² *f4* desert **ba mhaith an airí uirthi é** she deserves it well

áiria *m4* aria

airigh *v* 1. feel **níl mé ag aireachtáil go rómhaith** I'm not feeling too well 2. hear **ar airigh tú an scéal?** did you hear the news? 3. perceive

áirigh *v* calculate, count; reckon **ag áireamh** calculating, counting; reckoning

airíoch *m1* caretaker

áirithe¹ *f4* 1. certain quantity **ní raibh ann ach an áirithe sin daoine** only that (exact) number of people were there 2. portion, allotment **áit a chur in áirithe** to book a place 3. certainty

áirithe² *adj* particular, certain **ach go háirithe** anyway, **go háirithe** especially, in particular

áirithigh *v* ensure

áirithint *f2* booking **rud a cur in áirtithint** to reserve, book, something

airleacan *m1* loan, advance **thug sé airgead ar airleacan dom** he gave me an advance of money

airne *f4* sloe

airneán *m1* sitting up late (at night), night-visiting, working late (at night)

airnéis *f2* 1. goods, equipment 2. chattels, cattle 3. lice, fleas

airteagal *m1* article

airtéiseach *adj* artesian

airtléire *f4* artillery **lámhach airtléire** artillery fire

airtríteas *m1* arthritis

ais¹ 1. **ar ais** back, again **droim ar ais** reversed, back to front, **ar ais arís** back again, **ar ais nó ar éigean** at all costs 2. **le hais** compared with, beside

ais² *f2* axis **ais chothrománach, ingearach** horizontal, vertical, axis

ais-³ *prefix* re-, back **aisfhilleadh dúbailte** double return (*keyboard*)

áis *f2* 1. facility, device **tá áiseanna iontacha ag an gclub sin** that club has great facilities, **ní haon áis dom é** it is of no use to me, **áiseanna closamhairc** audiovisual aids 2. convenience, favour **an ndéanfá áis dom?** would you do me a favour? 3. **ar áis!** at ease!

aisce *f4* 1. **in aisce** for nothing, **turas in aisce** wasted journey, a journey in vain 2. gift, favour

aischothú *m4* feedback

aiseag *m1* 1. vomit 2. restitution

aiseal *m1* axle

aiseipteach *adj* aseptic **teicníocht aiseipteach** aseptic technique

aiséirí *m4* 1. resurgence 2. resurrection

aiséirigh *v* rise again

aiséiteach *m1* ascetic

aiséitiúil *adj* ascetic

aiseolas *m1* feedback

aisfhilleadh *m* return **aisfhilleadh dúbailte** double return (*keyboard*)

aisfhreagra *m4* retort, back answer

aisghair *v* repeal, abrogate

aisghairm *f2* repeal, abrogation

aisig *v* 1. vomit 2. restore

aisíoc *m3* repayment, refund, restitution **aisíoc cánach** tax refund *v* repay, refund

áisiúil *adj* handy, convenient

áisiúlacht *f3* utility, handiness, convenience

aisléim *f2* recoil (*of spring*) *v* recoil

aisling *f2* vision, dream, vision poem

aislingeach *adj, m1* visionary

aislingeacht *f3* day-dreaming

aispeist *f2* asbestos

aistarraing *v* withdraw, pull back

aiste[1] *f4* 1. essay, composition 2. scheme **aiste (chothrom) bia** (balanced) diet 3. peculiarity, condition **gach duine agus a chuld aisti féin air!** everybody has their own strange ways!

aiste[2], **beidh aiste ar an iasc** the fish will rise (and take the bait)

aisteach *adj* 1. strange, peculiar, odd, droll 2. surprising

aistear *m1* 1. roundabout way, inconvenience **turas in aistear** wasted journey, a journey in vain 2. journey

aisteoir *m3* actor

aisteoireacht *f3* acting

aistreach *adj* 1. transitive (*grammar*) 2. roving, unsettled (*of person*), inconvenient (*of place*)

aistreán *m1* inconvenience, out-of-the-way place

aistreánach *adj* 1. migratory 2. inconvenient, out-of-the-way

aistrigh *v* 1. translate 2. move, transfer **ag aistriú tí** moving house

aistritheach *adj* movable **daonra aistritheach** shifting population

aistritheoir *m3* 1. translator 2. remover

aistriú *m4* 1. translation 2. removal, transfer

aistriúchán *m1* translation

ait *adj* 1. odd, queer, funny, comical 2. fine, pleasant

áit *f2* place, position, room **áit dhúchais** native place, **áit seasaimh** standing room, **muintir na háite** the local people, **dá mbeinn i d'áitse** if I were in your position, in your shoes, **in áit** in place of, instead of, **cá háit?** where?

aiteacht *f3* oddness, queerness

aiteal *m1* juniper

aiteall *m1* spell of good weather between showers

aiteann *m1* furze, whin, gorse

aiteas *m1* 1. odd sensation 2. fun, pleasantness

aiteasach *adj* joyful, delightful, pleasant

áiteoireacht *f3* argumentation, arguing

áith *f2* kiln

aitheach *m1* churl

aitheanta *adj* accepted, recognized

aitheantas *m1* 1. identification **cárta aitheantais** identification card 2. acquaintance, recognition **lucht aitheantais** acquaintances, **thug sé aitheantas dom** he acknowledged me

aitheasc *m1* 1. exhortation, homily 2. address, lecture *v* exhort

aitheascal *m1* oracle

aithin *v* 1. acknowledge 2. recognise, know 3. command, bid **d'aithin mé ar/de Sheán é a dhéanamh** I bade Seán do it

aithinne *f4* spark, firebrand

aithis *f2* 1. disgrace 2. reproach, slur

aithiseach *adj* 1. shameful, disgraceful 2. defamatory

aithisigh *v* defame, slur

aithne[1] *f4* 1. recognition **tá sí imithe as aithne orm** she has changed beyond recognition 2. appearance **aithne bisigh ag teacht ar dhuine** somebody showing the

appearance/signs of improvement
3. acquaintance **tá an-aithne agam air** I know him very well

aithne² *f4* precept, commandment **na Deich nAitheanta** the Ten Commandments

aithnidiúil *adj* well-known, familiar

aithreachas *m1* regret, repentance **aithreachas a bheith ort faoi rud** to regret something

aithrí *f4* repentance, penance **aithrí thoirní** sudden repentance, **ag déanamh aithrí** doing penance

aithríoch *adj* penitent *m1* penitent

aithris *f2* 1. imitation, mimicry 2. narration, reciting *v* 1. imitate, mimic 2. narrate, recite

aithriseach *adj* mocking, imitative

aithriseoireacht *f3* mimicry, recitation

aithriúil *adj* paternal, fatherly

áitigh *v* 1. argue 2. occupy, settle down to 3. **áitigh ar...** persuade..., **bhí sé á áitiú orm** he was persuading me of it

áitithe *adj* practised, (well) established **rógaire áitithe** a right, confirmed, rogue

áititheach *adj* persuasive

áititheoir *m3* 1. arguer 2. occupier, resident

áitiúil *adj* local **rialtas áitiúil** local government

áitreabh *m1* 1. premises 2. dwelling, habitation, abode

áitreabhach *m1* inhabitant

áitrigh *v* inhabit

áitritheoir *m3* inhabitant

ál *m1* litter, brood

ala, ar ala na huaire on the spur of the moment

alabhog *adj* lukewarm, tepid

alabhreac *adj* piebald, pied **capall alabhreac** piebald horse

áladh *m1* 1. lunge **thug an madra áladh orm** the dog grabbed, snapped, at me 2. wound

álainn *adj* 1. delightful 2. beautiful

aláram *m1* alarm **clog aláraim** alarm clock

Albain *f5* Scotland **ceol, muintir na hAlban** the music, the people, of Scotland/the Scots, **ó Albain a tháinig sé** he came from Scotland, **Gaeilge na hAlban** Scots Gaelic

albam *m1* album

albatras *m1* albatross

alcaileach *adj* alkaline **substaint alcaileach** alkaline substance

alcól *m1* alcohol **alcól eitile** ethyl alcohol (ethanol)

alcólach *adj*, *m1* alcoholic

alcólacht *f3* alcoholism

alfraits *f2* scoundrel, rogue, rascal **alfraits chríochnaithe** a right scoundrel, a confirmed rogue

alga *m4* alga

allabhair *f5* echo

allabhrach *adj* evocative

allagar *m1* 1. shout 2. loud talk, disputation **ag allagar** arguing

allaíre *f4* partial deafness

allas *m1* perspiration, sweat **ag bárcadh allais** sweating profusely

allasúil *adj* sweaty

allmhaire *f4* import **cáilíocht na n-allmhairí** quality of imports, **ionadú allmhairí** import substitution

allmhaireoir *m3* importer

allmhairigh *v* import

allmhairíocht *f3* importing **dleachtanna allmhairíochta** import duties

allmhairiú *m* importation

allta *adj* wild, primitive

alltacht *f3* 1. astonishment **chuir sé alltacht orm** he/it amazed me 2. wildness

allúrach *adj* foreign *m1* foreigner

almanag *m1* almanac

almóinn *f2* almond

almóir *m3* 1. niche 2. wall-cupboard

almsa *f* alms

aló *m4* aloe

alp *v* devour

alpach *adj* greedy, voracious

alpaire *m4* glutton, voracious eater

alpán *m1* chunk, lump

alsáiseach *m1* alsatian, German shepherd dog

alt *m1* 1. article, paragraph, section (*of act*) 2. hillock 3. knuckle 4. knot (*in timber*) 5. joint **as alt** out of joint 6. article (*grammar*)

altach *adj* 1. jointed, articulate 2. knotty 3. undulating

altaigh *v* **bia a altú** to say grace at mealtime

altán *m1* 1. ravine 2. hillock 3. streamlet

altóir *f3* altar

altram *m3* fosterage **tuismitheoirí altrama** foster-parents

altramaigh *v* foster **páiste a altramú** to foster a child

altranas *m1* nursing **teach altranais** nursing home

altú *m4* thanksgiving, grace at meals **altú roimh bhia** grace before meals, **altú tar éis bia** grace after meals

alúmanam *m1* aluminium **rothaí alúmanaim** aluminium wheels

am *m3* time **cén t-am é?** what time is it? **faoin am seo** by this time, **in am trátha** at the proper time, **ó am go chéile** from time to time, **tá sé in am agat é a dhéanamh** it is time for you to do it, **i ndiaidh an ama** after the event

amach *adv, adj* out **an bealach amach** the way out, **ó mo chroí amach** from the bottom of my heart, **amach anseo** later on, in the future, **bhí isteach is amach le deichniúr ann** there were approximately ten people there,

aidhm a bhaint amach to reach a goal

amadán *m1* fool **is mór an stumpa amadáin é** he is a proper fool

amadánta *adj* foolish

amadántacht *f3* foolishness, fooling

amadóir *m3* timekeeper, timer, timepiece

amaid *f2* foolish woman

amaideach *adj* foolish

amaideacht *f3* idiocy

amaidí *f4* nonsense, folly **níl ansin ach amaidí** that's only nonsense

amaitéarach *adj, m1* amateur

amanathar *adv, adj* the day after tomorrow

amárach *adv, adj* tomorrow

amarrán *m1* 1. misfortune 2. contention

amas *m1* 1. attempt 2. aim 3. attack **'ní cosaint go hamas'** attack is the best form of defence, **amas gan choinne** surprise attack, **amas marthanach** sustained attack, **fórsaí amais** attacking forces

amasóir *m3* attacker

ambaist(e) *interj* indeed, really **n'fheadar, ambaiste!** I don't really know

ambasadóir *m3* ambassador **ambasadóir na Fraince** the French ambassador

ambasáid *f2* embassy **ambasáid na Breataine** the British embassy

amchlár *m1* timetable

amh *adj* raw, uncooked

ámh *adv* however

amhábhar *m1* raw material

amhail *prep, conj* like, as **amhail agus** as if, **amhail duine ar meisce** like a drunk person

amháin *adj, adv, conj* one, only **uair amháin** one time, once, **ach amháin** except, **cailíní amháin** girls only

amhantar *m1* 1. windfall 2. chance **chuaigh sé san amhantar leis** he took a chance on it, he ventured it

amhantrach *adj* 1. lucky 2. risky, speculative

amhantraí *m4* speculator (*finance*)

amhantraíocht *f3* speculation (*finance*)

ámharach *adj* lucky, fortunate

ámharaí *f4* **ar ámharaí an domhain/ ar ámharaí an tsaoil** by the luckiest chance, by a stroke of luck

amharc *m1* 1. sight **chaill sé amharc na súl** he lost his sight 2. look **thug mé amharc géar uirthi** I gave her a sharp look 3. view **amharc tíre** landscape

amharclann *f2* theatre **amharclann na Péacóige** the Peacock theatre

amhas *m1* 1. mercenary **buíon amhas** band of mercenaries 2. hooligan, gangster

amhastrach *f2* barking (*of dog*)

amhiarann *m1* iron ore

amhlabhra *f4* inarticulateness

amhlachas *m1* 1. figure (*art*) 2. semblance

amhlaidh *adv* thus, so **is amhlaidh (mar) atá sé** the fact is, **tá sé amhlaidh liom** he is like myself, **dá mhéad é is amhlaidh is fearr é** the bigger the better

amhola *f4* crude oil

amhrán *m1* song **amhrán a rá** to sing a song, **Amhrán na bhFiann** Irish National Anthem

amhránaí *m4* singer

amhránaíocht *f3* singing **seisiún amhránaíochta** 'sing-song', singing session

amhras *m* 1. suspicion **bheith in amhras ar dhuine** to be suspicious about someone 2. doubt **gan amhras** without a doubt, undoubtedly, **sochar an amhrais** the benefit of the doubt

amhrasach *adj* 1. suspicious 2. doubtful

amhscarthanach *f2* twilight, daybreak

ámóg *f2* hammock

amóinia *f4* ammonia

amparán *m1* hamper

amparánaíocht *f3* disability, affliction **amparánaíocht a bheith ionat** to have a disability

ampla *m4* 1. covetousness, greed, voracity 2. great hunger

amplach *adj* 1. greedy 2. hungry

amplóir *m3* 1. glutton, greedy person 2. hungry person

amscaí *adj* 1. awkward 2. untidy

amú *adv* 1. astray **tá dul amú ort** you are mistaken 2. wasted, in vain **chuir sé amú é** he wasted it

amuigh *adj, adv, prep* out, outside, outer **amuigh faoin aer, amuigh faoin spéir** out in the open, **bí amuigh!** get out(side)! **an taobh amuigh** the outer side, the outside **taobh amuigh de sin** apart from that

an[1] *def art* the 1. **an fear** the man, **an domhan** the world, **an t-uisce** the water, **hata an fhir** the man's hat, **ar fud an domhain** throughout the world, **ag ól an uisce** drinking the water 2. **an bhean** the woman, **an oíche** the night, **an fhuinneog** the window, **hata na mná** the woman's hat, **ar feadh na hoíche** for the night, **ag dúnadh na fuinneoige** closing the window 3. **na capaill** the horses, **na heiseachtaí** the exceptions, **na fir / na mná** the men/the women, **i ndiaidh na gcapall** after the horses, **líon na n-eisceachtaí**, the amount of exceptions, **leithreas na bhfear / na mban** mens'/womens' toilets

an[2] *interrogative v part (always eclipses consonants)* **an dtógann tú siúcra?** do you take sugar? **an ólfaidh tú**

deoch? will you have a drink? **an maith leat í?** do you like her/it?

an³ see **is**

an-⁴ *prefix (always followed by hyphen)* **1.** great **bhí an-oíche againn** we had a great night **2.** very **an-bhreá** very nice

an-⁵ *prefix* **1.** over-, intense **2.** in-, un, not **andúchasach** non-native **3.** bad, unnatural **anchuma** bad, unnatural, appearance

anabaí *adj* immature, unripe **breith anabaí** premature birth

anabaíocht *f3* immaturity

anacair *adj* **1.** difficult **2.** uncomfortable **3.** uneven *f3* **1.** distress, difficulty **anacair leapa** bedsore **2.** discomfort **3.** unevenness

anachain *f2* **1.** harm **tá an anachain déanta** the harm is done **2.** calamity, mischance

anacrach *adj* distressful, difficult, distressed

anaemach *adj* anaemic

anaemacht *f3* anaemia

anagram *m1* anagram

anáil *f3* breath **bhí an anáil inti** she/it was still breathing

anáileadán *m1* breathalyser

anailís *f2* analysis

anailísí *m* analyst

anailísigh *v* analyse

anaithnid *adj* unknown, strange **file anaithnid** an unknown poet

analach *f2* analogy

análaigh *v* breathe

análaitheoir *m3* respirator

anall *adj, adv, prep* from beyond, hither **ag teacht anall ó Mheiriceá** coming over from America, **riamh anall** from time immemorial

anallód *adv* in olden/ancient times

análú *m4* respiration

anam *m3* **1.** soul **dar m'anam!** upon my soul! **2.** life **tá an-anam inti** sin she is full of life

anamchara *m5* **1.** confessor, spiritual adviser **2.** soul mate

anamúil *adj* spirited, lively

anamúlacht *f3* animation

anann *m1* pineapple

anas *m1* anus

anás *m1* **1.** awkward person **2.** poverty, distress, need

anásta *adj* **1.** clumsy **2.** distressed, needy

anatamaíocht *f3* anatomy

anbhá *m4* panic

anbhann *adj* weak

anbhuain *f2* unease, restlessness

ancaire *m4* anchor

anchaoi, in/ar anchaoi in a bad way

anchúinseach *adj* monstrous (*shape, behaviour, etc*)

anchuma *f4* unnatural, bad, appearance

anchumtha *adj* mis-shapen

andóch *adj* improbable

andóchas *m1* presumption

andóchasach *adj* presumptuous

andóigh *f2* improbability

andúchasach *adj* **1.** non-native **2.** exotic

andúil *f2* addiction, craving **andúil i ndrugaí** drug addiction

andúileach *m1* addict **andúileach drugaí** drug addict

andúilíocht *f3* addiction

aneas *adj, adv, prep* from the south **an ghaoth aneas** the south wind, **ag teacht aneas** coming from the south, coming north

anfa *m4* **1.** terror **2.** storm

angadh *m1* pus **rinne sé angadh** it festered

angaíoch *adj* purulent

angar *m1* distress, want **go bun an angair** to the bitter end

anghrách *adj* erotic

Anglacánach *adj, m1* Anglican

anglais *f2* milk and water **anglais tae** weak tea

anglait *f2* monkfish

angóra *m4* angora

aniar *adj, adv, prep* from the west **an ghaoth aniar** the west wind, **ag teacht aniar** coming from the west, coming east, **tháinig mé aniar aduaidh air** I caught him by surprise

aníos *adj, adv, prep* up **tháinig sí aníos an bóthar chugam** she came up the road to me

anlann *f2* sauce **anlann raidise fiáine** horseradish sauce

anlathach *adj* tyrannical; anarchical

anlathas *m1* tyranny; usurpation; anarchy

anluchtaigh *v* 1. overload 2. glut

ann¹ *adv* there **cé mhéad duine a bhí ann?** how many people were there? **níl ann ach (cluiche)** it's only (a game)

ann², in ann able to **an mbeidh tú in ann é a dhéanamh dom?** will you be able to do it for me?

annála *pl* annals **Annála Uladh** the Annals of Ulster

annálaí *m4* annalist

annamh *adj* seldom, rare, unusual **an rud is annamh is iontach** what's rare is wonderful

anó *m4* 1. distress, misery 2. discomfort

anocht *adj, adv* tonight

anoir *adj, adv, prep* from the east **an ghaoth anoir** the east wind, **ag teacht anoir** coming from the east, coming west

anóirthear *adj, adv* the day after tomorrow

anois *adv* now **anois beag, anois díreach, a tharla sé** it happened just now

anóiteach *adj* 1. miserable 2. uncomfortable

anonn *adj, adv, prep* over, to the other side **anonn agus anall** to and fro, **dul anonn go Sasana** to go over to England

anord *m1* chaos

anordúil *adj* chaotic

anraith *m4* soup **anraith glasraí le huachtar** cream of vegetable soup

anró *m4* 1. wretched, terrible, condition 2. hardship, distress

anróiteach *adj* 1. severe, inclement 2. distressing

ansa *adj* preferred, most beloved, dearest **an iníon is ansa liom** the daughter I love most

ansacht *f3* 1. affection, love 2. darling, loved one

anseo *adv* here **anseo is ansiúd** here and there

ansin *adv* 1. then **ansin féin** even then 2. there **thall ansin** over there

ansiúd *adv* there, yonder

ansmacht *m3* tyranny

ansmachtaigh *v* bully

anta(i)- *prefix* anti-

antaibheathach *adj, m1* antibiotic

antaiseipteach *adj* antiseptic

antaiseipteán *m1* antiseptic

Antartach, *m1* **an tAntartach** the Antarctic

Antartach *adj* Antarctic **an tAigéan Antartach** the Antarctic Ocean

antlás *m1* covetousness, greed

antlásach *adj* covetous, greedy

antoisceach *adj* extreme, *m1* extremist

antraicít *f2* anthracite

antraipeolaí *m4* anthropologist

antraipeolaíocht *f3* anthropology

antrapóideach *adj, m1* anthropoid

antrasc *m1* anthrax

antráth *m3* 1. unseasonable time, inopportune moment 2. late hour

antráthach *adj* untimely, late

anuas *adj, adv, prep* down **tháinig sí anuas** she came down, **le blianta beaga anuas** in recent years, **ná tarraing anuas an scéal sin** don't bring that matter up, **leag mé anuas ar an gcathaoir é** I laid it down on the chair

anuasal *adj* ignoble, low-born *m1* low-born person

anuraidh *adj, adv* last year

aodh *f4* inflammation

aoi *m4* guest, lodger

aoibh *f2* smile, pleasant aspect, pleasant expression

aoibheall *m1* gambolling **bhí na ba ag aoibheall** the cows were gadding

aoibhinn *adj* beautiful, delightful, blissful **tá an aimsir go haoibhinn** the weather is beautiful, **nach aoibhinn duit!** isn't it well for you!

aoibhiúil *adj* smiling, pleasant

aoibhneas *m1* delight, pleasure, bliss

aoileach *m1* manure, dung **aoileach leachtach** liquid manure

Aoine *f4* Friday **Dé hAoine** (on) Friday, **Aoine an Chéasta** Good Friday

aoir *f2* satire, lampoon

aoire *m4* 1. herdsman, shepherd 2. whip (*in parliament*) **an Príomh-Aoire** the Chief Whip 3. pastor

aoireacht *f3* herding

aoirigh *v* shepherd

aois *f2* 1. age **cén aois thú?** what age are you? **tá sí cúig bliana déag d'aois** she is fifteen years old, **tá aois na freagrachta coiriúla sroichte aige** he has reached the age of criminal responsibility, **ní thagann ciall roimh aois** sense comes with age 2. century **an**

seachtú haois déag the seventeenth century

aoiseachas *m1* age discrimination, agism

aoisghrúpa *m4* age group

aoisteorainn *f5* age-limit

aol *m1* lime *v* whitewash

aolchloch *f2* limestone

aolchoinneal *f2* stalagmite

aolchuisne *m4* stalactite

aoldath *m3* whitening, whitewash

aolmhar *adj* lime-white; containing lime

aon[1] *m1* 1. one person or thing; any **gach aon (duine)** everyone, **aon chailín amháin** one girl, **aon áit** anywhere, nowhere, **an bhfuil aon chiall agat?** have you any sense? **ní raibh aon am agam é a dhéanamh** I had no time to do it, **d'aon ghuth** unanimously, **d'aon turas, d'aon ghnó, d'aon aidhm** on purpose, deliberately, **mar aon le** in addition to 2. one; ace (in cards) **a haon** one, **a haon déag** eleven **ulmhir a haon** number one; **an t-aon muileata** the ace of diamonds

aon[2] *prefix* mono-, uni-, one **aonchéileachas** monogamy, **aonbheannach** unicorn

aonach *m1* fair, assembly

aonad *m1* unit **Aonad Dianchúraim** Intensive Care Unit (ICU)

aonar *m1* alone, lone person, individual **bhíomar inár n-aonar** we were on our own, alone, **duine aonair** single person, **tréithe aonair** individual characteristics

aonarach *adj* lone, solitary

aonarán *m1* solitary person

aonaránach *adj* solitary, alone

aonbheannach *m1* unicorn

aoncheallach *adj* unicellular

aonchéileachas *m1* monogamy

aonchineálach *adj* homogeneous

aonghnéasach *adj* of the same sex, unisexual

aonghnéitheach *adj* uniform, homogenous

aonraic *adj* alone, solitary

aonraigh *v* isolate

aonréad *m1* solo **aonréad pianó** piano solo

aonréadach *adj* solo

aonréadaí *m4* soloist

aonta *adj* unmarried, single

aontacht *f3* 1. union 2. unanimity 3. unity

Aontachtach *adj* Unionist

Aontachtaí *m4* Unionist

aontaigh *v* assent, agree; unite, combine **ní aontaím léi** I don't agree with her

aontaithe *adj* united **Stáit Aontaithe Mheiriceá** the United States of America

aontaitheach *adj* assenting, agreeing

aontaobhach *adj* unilateral **dí-armáil aontaobhach** unilateral disarmament

aontas *m1* union **an tAontas Eorpach (AE)** the European Union (EU)

aontíos *m1* living together, cohabitation

aontonach *adj* monotone; monotonous

aontumha *adj* celibate **ord aontumha** celibate order *f4* celibacy **móid aontumha** vow of celibacy

aonú *num adj* first **an t-aonú heisceacht** the first exception

aor *v* satirise

aorach *adj* satirical

aorthóir *m3* lampooner, satirist

aos *m3* people **aos óg na hÉireann** the young people of Ireland

aosacht *f3* adulthood

aosaigh *v* 1. age 2. come of age

aosánach *m1* youth, youngster, juvenile

aosmhar *adj* ageing **daonra aosmhar** ageing population

aosta *adj* old, aged

aothú *m4* crisis (*medical*)

ápa *m4* ape

apacailipsis *m4* apocalypse

apacailipteach *adj* apocalyptic

apacrafúil *adj* apocryphal

apaipléis *f2* apoplexy

apsaint *f2* absinth(e)

ar[1] *prep* (*pron forms* **orm, ort, air, uirthi, orainn, oraibh, orthu**) on, in, at **ní ormsa atá an locht** I am not to blame, **beidh ort teacht níos luaithe amárach** you'll have to come earlier tomorrow, **tá sé ar an scannán is fearr dá bhfaca mé riamh** it is the best film I've ever seen

ar[2] *defective v* says, said **ar sise** says, said, she

ar[3] *rel part* **an sruthán ar thit an madra isteach ann** the stream that the dog fell into *rel pron* **goideadh gach ar bhailigh sé** all that he collected was stolen

ar[4] *interrogative v part* **ar chaith tú an t-airgead?** did you spend the money? **ar mhaith leat deoch?** would you like a drink?

ar[5] see **is**

ár[1] *m1* slaughter; havoc

ár[2] *poss adj* our **ár n-anamchara** our soul mate, **ár mbaile** our home, **ár gcairde** our friends

ara *m4* temple (of head)

ára *f* kidney

árach *m1* 1. advantage 2. security 3. fetter

árachaigh *v* insure **gluaisteán a árachú** to insure a car

árachas *m1* insurance **árachas dóiteáin agus gada** fire and theft insurance, **rud a chur faoi árachas**

to insure something, **árachas gluaisteán** motor insurance, **árachas tríú páirtí** third party insurance, **árachas saoil** life insurance, life assurance, **Árachas Sláinte Saorálach (ASS)** Voluntary Health Insurance (VHI), **Árachas Sóisialach Pá-Choibhneasa** Pay-Related Social Insurance (PRSI)

árachóir *m3* insurer **árachóir gluaisteán** car insurer

arae *adj, conj* 1. because 2. however

aragail *f2* ledge

araí[1] *f* bridle **araíonacha** reins

araí[2] *f4* appearance

araicis *f2* meeting **chuaigh mé in araicis Phádraig** I went to meet Pádraig

araid *f2* chest, bin **araid seod, araid mhaoine** treasure-chest, **araid aeráilte** ventilated bin

araile *pron* **agus araile (srl)** et cetera (etc)

araíonacht *f3* (self-)restraint, control

aralt *m1* herald

araltach *adj* heraldic

araltas *m1* heraldry

arán *m1* bread **do chuid aráin a bheith ite** to be done for

arann *m1* feeling **níl aon arann i mo chosa agam** I have no feeling in my legs

araon *adv* both, together **sinn, muid, araon** us together, both of us

ararút *m1* arrowroot

áras *m1* 1. building, house, dwelling **Áras an Uachtaráin** Presidential Residence 2. household vessel

árasán *m1* flat, apartment **bloc árasán** block of flats

áraslann *f2* block of flats

arbhar *m1* corn **calóga arbhair** corn flakes

arcán *m1* piglet

ard[1] *adj* high, tall, loud **fear mór ard** big tall man, **farraigí arda** rough seas, **labhairt go hard** to speak loudly *m1* height, high part; hill **bhí sí in ard a réime ag an am** she was at the height, peak, of her career at the time, **ag béiceach in ard a chinn** shouting at the top of his voice

ard-[2] *prefix* 1. high, chief **ardmháistir** headmaster 2. noble 3. arch- **ardeaspag** archbishop

ardaigh *v* ascend; raise, increase **d'ardaigh sí an staighre** she ascended the stairs, **d'ardaigh sé leis é** he took it away with him, **ná hardaigh an ceol** don't raise the music, don't increase the volume

Ard-Aighne *m4* Attorney-General **Oifig an Ard-Aighne** Attorney-General's Office

ardaitheach *adj* ascending, ascendant

ardaitheoir *m3* 1. elevator, lift, hoist 2. lifter

ardán *m1* stage, stand, platform **bheith ar an ardán** to be on stage, **ardán taispeána** catwalk, **Ardán Uí Ógáin** the Hogan Stand, **ardán druileála** drilling platform, **ardán saothraithe ola agus gáis ar muir** off-shore oil and gas exploration platform

ardbhrú *m4* high pressure

ardchathair *f* metropolis

ardcheannas *m1* supremacy **Móid an Ardcheannais** Oath of Supremacy

ardchlár *m1* plateau

ardeaglais *f2* cathedral

ardeaspag *m1* archbishop

ardfhear *m1* sound man, excellent man **ardfhear!** good man yourself!

ardfheis *f2* national convention (*political*) **Ard-Fheis Fhianna Fáil** Fianna Fáil Ard-Fheis

ardintinneach *adj* 1. headstrong 2. high-spirited

ardmháistir *m4* headmaster

ardmháistreás *f3* headmistress

ardmhéara *m4* lord mayor **Ardmhéara Bhéal Feirste** Lord Mayor of Belfast

ardmhinicíocht *f3* very high frequency

ardnósach *adj* pompous, grand

ardteastas *m1* higher certificate, higher diploma **an tArdteastas (Oideachais)** Higher Diploma in Education

Ardteist(iméireacht) *f3* Leaving Certificate

ardtráthnóna *m4* mid-afternoon

ardú *m4* 1. elevation, increase **ardú pá** pay, salary, increase, **ardú céime** promotion 2. exaltation, excitement **ardú meanman** raising of spirits

aréir *adj, adv* last night

argóint *f2* argument

arís *adv* again

arm *m1* 1. army **Arm na Breataine** the British Army 2. arms; weapon, implement **mionairm** small arms, **arm uathoibreach** automatic weapon, **faoi iomlán airm** fully armed

armach *adj* armed **coinbhliocht armach** armed conflict, **meitheal armach** armed party

armadóir *m3* armourer; arms manufacturer **armadóir cathláin** battalion armourer

armadóireacht *f3* manufacture of arms **sáirsint armadóireachta** armourer sergeant

armáid *f2* armada **armáid na Spáinne** the Spanish armada

armáil *f3* armament *v* arm

armas *m1* shield; coat of arms

armchúirt *f2* court-martial **armchúirt a chur ar shaighdiúir** to court martial a soldier

armlann *f2* arsenal, magazine, armoury

armlón *m1* ammunition **armlón pollta armúir** armour-piercing ammunition

armóin *f2* harmony; harmonium

armónach *adj* harmonic

armónaí *m4* harmonist

armónaic *f2* harmonics (*music, geometry*)

armónaigh *v* harmonise

armtha *adj* armed **coinbhliocht armtha** armed conflict, **meitheal armtha** armed party

armthaisce *f4* arms dump, storehouse for ammunition/arms

armúr *m1* armour **piléar pollta armúir** armour piercing bullet

armúrtha *adj* armoured **carr armúrtha** armoured car

arna used with *v* **arna ithe dom** when I had eaten it, **arna fhoilsiú ag ...** published by ...

arócar *m1* monkey-puzzle (*tree*)

arracht *m3* 1. giant 2. spectre, monster 3. juggernaut

arrachtas *m1* strength, brawn

arraing *f2* sharp, stabbing pain, 'stitch' **in arraingeacha an bháis** in the throes of death

arsa *defective v* said, says **arsa mise** said I, says I

ársa *adj* aged; ancient, archaic

ársaíocht *f3* old age; antiquity; antiquarianism

ársaitheoir *m3* antiquarian

arsanaic *f2* arsenic

art *m1* stone **chomh marbh le hart** as dead as a stone, stone dead

Artach, an tArtach *m1* Arctic

Artach *adj* Arctic **an tAigéan Artach** the Arctic Ocean

artaire *m4* artery **artaire scamhógach** pulmonary artery, **artaire corónach** coronary artery

artaireach *adj* arterial **córas artaireach** arterial system

árthach *m1* 1. container **árthach fuail** chamber-pot 2. ship, vessel

artola *f4* petrol

arú *used with adv* **arú amárach** the day after tomorrow, **arú inné** the day before yesterday

arúil *adj* arable **talamh arúil** arable land

as 1. *prep* (*pron forms* **asam, asat, as, aisti, asainn, asaibh, astu**) out of, from **tá an duine sin as a mheabhair** that person is out of his mind, crazy, **chuir mé mo ghualainn as alt** I dislocated my shoulder, I put my shoulder out of joint 2. *adv* **éirigh as!** give it up! **as go brách léi** off she went **bheith go maith as** to be well off

asáitigh *v* dislodge

asal *m1* ass, donkey **A asail!** You ass! You fool!

asalaíocht *f3* asinine behaviour, stupid or stubborn behaviour

asaltaigh *v* dislocate **glúin, gualainn, a asaltú** to dislocate a knee, shoulder

asanálaigh *v* exhale

asarlaí *m4* 1. trickster, conjurer 2. sorcerer

asarlaíocht *f3* 1. conjuring tricks 2. sorcery

asbhaint *f2* deduction

asbheir *v* deduce **rud a asbheirt** to deduce something

ásc *m1* effort, step **ar an gcéad ásc** at the first effort/attempt, in the first place/instance

ascaill *f2* 1. avenue **Ascaill Chnoc Mhuirfean** Mount Merrion Avenue, **ascaill mhara** an arm of the sea 2. armpit **póca na hascaille** inside pocket of coat/jacket 3. recess

aschur *m1* output **aschur náisiúnta** national output

asclán *m1* 1. gusset 2. armful

asfalt *m1* asphalt

aslonnaigh *v* evacuate

aslonnú *m4* evacuation **aslonnú foirgnimh** evacuation of a building

asma *m4* asthma **taom asma** asthma attack

asmach *adj* asthmatic

aspairín *m4* aspirin

aspal *m1* apostle **an dá aspal déag** the twelve apostles

aspalacht *f3* apostolate; apostleship

aspalda *adj* apostolic

aspalóid *f2* absolution **aspalóid a fháil** to receive absolution

asparagas *m1* asparagus **anraith asparagais** asparagus soup

astaróideach *adj*, *m1* asteroid

astitim *f2* fall-out (*nuclear*)

astralaí *m4* astrologer

astralaíoch *adj* astrological

astralaíocht *f3* astrology

at *m1* swelling *v* swell; bloat **tá mo rúitíní ata** my ankles are bloated, swollen

atáirg *v* reproduce

atáirgeach *adj* reproductive

atáirgeadh *m* reproduction **atáirgeadh gnéasach** sexual reproduction, **atáirgeadh éighnéasach** asexual reproduction

atarlú *m* recurrence

ath- *prefix* 1. later, after **athchuardach** further search 2. old, ex-, counter- **athbhall** ex-member 3. re-, second **athaontaigh** reunite

áth *m3* 1. ford **Baile Átha Cliath** Dublin ('the settlement of the ford of the hurdles') 2. opening 3. spawning bed (*in river*)

athair[1] *m* 1. father **m'athair críonna, m'athair mór** my grandfather, **teach a hathair** her father's house 2. ancestor

athair[2] *f* creeper (*plants*) **athair lusa** ground-ivy

áthán *m1* anus

athaontaigh *v* reunite

athaontú *m* reunion

athartha *adj* paternal, ancestral **instinn athartha** paternal instinct

atharthacht *f3* paternity

áthas *m1* joy, happiness, gladness **bhí áthas uirthi an scéal a chloisteáil** she was happy to hear the news

áthasach *adj* joyful, happy, glad

athbheochan *f3* revival **athbheochan teanga** revival of a language, **an Athbheochan** the Renaissance

athbheoigh *v* revive, reanimate

athbhliain *f3* new year, coming year **athbhliain faoi shéan (agus faoi mhaise) duit!** happy new year!

athbhreithnigh *v* review, reconsider, revise

athbhreithniú *m* review, reconsideration, revision **athbhreithniú staire** revisionism

athbhrí *f4* 1. ambiguity 2. renewed strength, renewed vigour

athbhríoch *adj* 1. ambiguous 2. tonic, stimulating *m1* tonic **jin agus athbhríoch** gin and tonic

athbhuille *m4* 1. palpitation **athbhuille a bheith ar do chroí** to have palpitations 2. relapse **fuair sé athbhuille** he had a relapse (of sickness) 3. counterblow

athbhunú *m4* restoration, re-establishment

athchaint *f2* impudence; backbiting

athchairdeas *m1* reconciliation

athchaite *adj* 1. cast-off **éadaí athchaite** cast-off clothing 2. worn-out **tuairim athchaite** worn-out idea

athcheannaí *m4* second-hand dealer

athchluiche *m4* replay (of match, game)

athchogain *v* chew the cud (*of cow*), ruminate

athchogantach *adj, m1* ruminant

athchoilltiú *m* reafforestation

athchóirigh *v* re-arrange; renovate, restore **teach a athchóiriú** to renovate a house

athchóiritheoir *m3* restorer (*paintings, furniture, etc*)

athchóiriú *m4* 1. rearrangement, reform **athchóiriú dlí** law reform 2. renovation, restoration

athchomhair *v* recalculate, re-count **na figiúirí a athchomhaireamh** to recalculate the figures

athchomhaireamh *m1* recalculation, re-count **athchomhaireamh vótaí** re-count of votes

athchomhairle *f4* change of mind, reconsideration

athchraiceann *m1* thin covering, veneer

athchruthú *m4* re-creation **athchruthú (samhlaíoch) imeachtaí** (imaginative) reconstruction of events

athchuimhne *f4* reminiscence

athchuimhnitheach *adj* reminiscent

athchuir *v* 1. replace 2. replant 3. remand

athchum *v* 1. distort 2. reconstruct

athchuma *f4* 1. distortion 2. transformation

athchur *m1* 1. replacement 2. replanting 3. remand

athdhúchas *m1* atavism

athdhúchasch *adj* atavistic

athfhéachaint *f2* action replay

athfhéar *m1* aftergrass

athfhill *v* recur; refold

athfhillteach *adj* recurring, recurrent **stróghalar athfhillteach** repetitive strain injury

athfhreagra *m4* rejoinder, retort

athfhriotal *m1* quotation

athghabh *v* 1. recapture **athghabhadh an baile** the township was recaptured 2. recover **d'éirigh leis a chuid talún a athghabháil** he succeeded in recovering his land

athphlandaigh *f3* 1. recapture 2. recovery

athghairm *f2* 1. repeal 2. encore

athghlaoigh *v* recall

athghuthú *m4* dubbing

athiomrá *m4* 1. backbiting 2. slander

athlá *m* another day **curtha ar athlá** put off / postponed to another day / a later date

athlámh, ar athláimh *f2* second-hand **cheannaigh mé ar athláimh é** I bought it second-hand

athlasadh *m* inflammation

athleagan *m1* paraphrase, another version

athleáigh *v* refine (*metal*), remelt

athléim *f2* rebound

athlíon *v* refill

athluaigh *v* reiterate

athluaiteachas *m1* tautology

athmhagadh *m1* mimicry

athmhuintearas *m1* reconciliation

athnuachan *f3* 1. renewal 2. renovation 3. rejuvenation **obair athnuachana** renovation work

athnuaigh *v* renew, renovate, rejuvenate **ceadúnas tiomána a athnuachan** to renew a driving licence

athphlandaigh *v* transplant, replant

athphlandú *m4* transplantation

athrá *m4* repetition, reiteration **ní raibh ann ach athrá** it was only a repetition, a repeat of what was said before

athrach *m1* 1. change, transformation, alteration 2. alternative **chomh dócha lena athrach** as likely as not

athraigh *v* 1. move **d'athraíomar teach** we moved house 2. change, alter **d'athraigh sé a phort** he changed his story

athraitheach *adj* 1. movable 2. changeable 3. variant

athraon *v* refract

athraonadh *m* refraction

athróg *f2* variant, variable **athróga eacnamaíocha** economic variants, economic variables

athrú *m4* change, alteration

athrúchán *m1* variation

athscinn *v* recoil, spring back

athscinneadh *m* recoil

athscríobh *v* rewrite, copy, transcribe **stair a athscríobh** to rewrite history

athshondach *adj* resonant

athshondas *m1* resonance

athsmaoineamh *m1* afterthought **rinne mé athsmaoineamh air** I reconsidered it, I changed my mind about it

athuair *adv* again, a second time **ar tháinig sé (in) athuair?** did he come again?

atit *v* relapse

atitim *f2* 1. relapse 2. second fall

atitimeach *m* recidivist

Atlantach *adj* Atlantic **an tAigéan Atlantach** the Atlantic Ocean

Atlantach *m1* Atlantic **an tAtlantach** the Atlantic, **Eagraíocht Chonradh an Atlantaigh Thuaidh (ECAT)** North Atlantic Treaty Organisation (NATO)

atlas *m1* atlas

atmaisféar *m1* atmosphere **truailliú an atmaisféir** the pollution of the atmosphere, **ceol atmaisféir** mood music

atmaisféarach *adj* atmospheric

atóg *v* 1. rebuild 2. retake

atráth *m3* another time **cuireadh ar atráth é** it was adjourned

atreorú *m4* diversion **atreorú tráchta** diversion of traffic

atuirse *f4* 1. weariness 2. dejection

atuirseach *adj* 1. weary 2. dejected

aturnae *m4* solicitor

B

bá[1] *f4* sympathy, affection, liking **bá a bheith agat le rud, duine** to have a liking for something, a person

bá[2] *f4* bay **Bá an Daingin** Dingle Bay

bá[3] *m4* 1. quenching **tá bá tarta ann** it quenches your thirst, it has the quenching of thirst 2. drowning 3. inundation, immersion

babaí *m4* baby **baile lán de bhabaithe** village full of babies

babhdán *m1* 1. scarecrow 2. bogeyman

babhla *m4* bowl **babhla bainne** bowl of milk

babhláil *f3* bowling **ionad babhlála** bowling alley *v* bowl

babhlálaí *m4* bowler (*sport*)

babhta *m4* 1. time, turn **cúpla babhta** a couple of times, **is é do bhabhta é** it's your turn 2. bout, round, **babhta ólacháin** a drinking spree, **babhta dornálaíochta** a round of boxing, **babhta tobsmaointe** brain-storming

babhtáil *f3*, *v* 1. combat 2. swop, exchange, barter

bábhún *m1* 1. breakwater, bulwark 2. walled enclosure, bawn

bábóg *f2* doll **teach bábóige** doll's house

babún *m1* baboon

bac *m1* hindrance, impediment, balk; barrier **faoi bhac (meabhrach)** (mentally) handicapped, **bac (tine)** hob (of fire) *v* hinder, balk **ná bac leo** don't mind them, let them alone

bacach *adj* lame, halting **duine bacach** lame person, **Gearmáinis bhacach** broken, halting German *m1* beggar, lame person

bacadaíl *f3* limping

bácáil *v* 1. bake **ag bácáil císte** baking a cake 2. fire (*pottery*)

bacainn *f2* barrier, obstacle **bacainn trádála** trade barrier, **bacainn chustaim, bacainn taraifí** tariff barrier

bách *adj* affectionate

bachall *f2* 1. crosier 2. crook, staff **bhí siad go barra bachall ann** they were there in abundance 3. ringlet

bachallach *adj* 1. crooked 2. ringletted

bachlaigh *v* bud

bachlóg *f2* sprout, bud **bachlóg ascailleach** axillary bud, **bachlóga Bhruiséile** Brussels sprouts

bachlú *m* sprouting, budding

baclainn *f2* bent arm **fuair mé baclainn mhóna uaidh** I got an armful of turf from him, **bhí mná le páistí ina mbaclainn fáiscthe ann** there were women there holding children in their arms

bacstaí *m4* bread made of raw potatoes, boxty

bácús *m1* 1. bakehouse, bakery 2. pot-oven

bád *m1* boat **bád farantóireachta an Bhlascaoid Mhóir** the Great Blasket ferry-boat, **báid iomartha** rowing-boats, **bád beag seoil** small sailing-boat, **bád tarrthála Dhún Laoghaire** Dún Laoghaire lifeboat, **thóg sí an bád bán** she took the emigrant ship, she emigrated

badhbh *f2* 1. vulture 2. war-goddess

badmantan *m1* badminton **cluiche badmantain** game of badminton

bádóireacht *f3* boating

bagair *v* 1. threaten **bhí sé ag bagairt orm** he was threatening me 2. beckon **bhagair sí a méar orm** she beckoned to me with her finger

bagairt *f3* threat, menace

bagáiste *m4* luggage, baggage **giolla bagáiste** luggage porter, **leoraí bagáiste** baggage lorry

baghcat *m1* boycott **baghcat a dhéanamh ar rud** to boycott something

baghcatáil *v* boycott

bagrach *adj* threatening

bagún *m1* bacon **ceapaire bagúin, leitíse agus tráta** bacon, lettuce and tomato sandwich

baic *f2* nape **baic an mhuiníl** nape of the neck

báicéir *m3* baker

báicéireacht *f3* baking

baicle *f4* band of people, clique **baicle fear** group of men

baictéar *m1* bacterium **baictéir** bacteria

baidhtheáil *f3* swirl(ing) **baidhtheáil taoide** swirl of tide

báigh *v* 1. drown; soak **bádh triúr fear** three men were drowned, **bhí mé báite go craiceann / báite fliuch** I was soaked to the skin 2. sink **bád a bhá** to sink a boat

bail *f2* 1. condition, state **bail a chur ar rud** to put something in proper condition, to fix something, **beidh bail mhaith air** it will be in a good state 2. success, prosperity **bail ó Dhia air!** God bless him!

bailc *adj* stout, strong *f2* downpour (*of rain*)

baile *m4* 1. settlement, homestead **baile beag fearainn** small townland, **baile mór** town, **arán baile** home-made bread 2. home, **as baile** away from home, **ag baile, sa bhaile** at home, **ceardaíocht bhaile** home craftwork, **eacnamaíocht bhaile** home economics, **reoiteoir baile** home freezer, **leathanach baile** homepage (*internet*)

Baile Átha Cliath *m4* Dublin **muintir, pobal, Bhaile Átha Cliath** the people of Dublin

bailé *m4* ballet **ceol bailé** ballet music, **bailé ceoldráma** opera-ballet

baileach *adj* exact **sin é a dúirt sé go baileach** that's what he said exactly

bailéad *m1* ballad **seisiún bailéad** ballad session

bailí *adj* valid **ticéad bailí** valid ticket

bailigh *v* 1. gather, collect **ag bailiú eolais** collecting, gathering, information, **bhailigh na daoine le chéile ann** the people gathered, assembled, there 2. (*used with preps* le *and* de), **bailigh leat!** get lost! **táim bailithe de** I'm fed up with him/it

bailitheacht *f3* boredom, ennui

bailitheoir *m3* collector **bailitheoir cánach** tax collector

bailiú *m* collection

bailiúchán *m1* collection **bailiúchán dramhaíola** refuse collection

báille *m4* bailiff

Bailt, an Mhuir Bhailt the Baltic Sea

bain *v* 1. cut, dig **móin a bhaint** to cut turf 2. pick, reap **an fómhar a bhaint** to reap the harvest 3. win **cé a bhain? / who won?**

bain amach *v* 1. reach **aidhm a bhaint amach** to reach a goal 2. extract **fiacail a bhaint amach** to extract a tooth

bain anuas *v* dismantle, take down **fógra a bhaint anuas** to take down a sign

bain as *v* 1. extract, get from **ciall a bhaint as rud** to make sense of something 2. take from **bhain sé as mo lámh é** he took it from my hand 3. go, take off **bain as!** be off!

bain de *v* remove **bain díot do chóta** take off your coat

bain do *v* 1. happen to **bhain taisme dó** he met with an accident 2. touch **ní bhainim don deoch a thuilleadh** I don't touch drink any more

bain faoi *v* settle **bain fút sa chathaoir ansin** settle down on the chair there

bain le *v* 1. relate to, concern **ní bhaineann sé sin liom** that doesn't relate to me, that doesn't concern me 2. interfere with **deirtear gur fearr gan baint leo sin** it is said that it is better not to interfere with them

baincéir *m3* banker **baincéir imréitigh** clearing banker, **baincéir marsantach** merchant banker

baincéireacht *f3* banking **baincéireacht mharsantach** merchant banking, **córas baincéireachta** banking system

baineanda *adj* effeminate **duine baineanda** effeminate person

baineann *adj* 1. effeminate 2. female

báiní *f4* madness, fury **tá sí imithe le báiní** she is raging, she is in a fury

báinín *m4* 1. homespun material, cloth 2. white flannel jacket

baininscneach *adj* feminine (*grammar*) **ainmfhocal baininscneach** feminine noun

bainis *f2* wedding, wedding party, wedding reception **cáca, císte, bainise** wedding cake, **gúna bainise** wedding dress

bainisteoir *m3* manager **bainisteoir foirne** staff manager, **bainisteoir táirgeachta** production manager

bainisteoireacht *f3* managership, managing **gnó a bhainisteoireacht** to manage a business

bainistíocht *f3* management, thriftiness **bainistíocht airgeadais** finance management, **stiúrthóir bainistíochta** managing director

bainistiúil *adj* managerial **cur chuige bainistiúil** managerial approach

bainistreás *f3* manageress

bainne *m4* milk **bainne bearrtha, bainne caol** skim milk, 'light milk', **bainne milis** fresh milk, **bainne treisithe** fortified milk, 'supermilk'

báinseach *f2* lawn, green

bainseo *m4* banjo

baint *f2* 1. relevance **níl aon bhaint ag reiligiún leis** religion has nothing to do with it 2. connection **an mbíonn aon bhaint agat leo?** do you have anything to do with them?

bainteach (le) *adj* involved (in), relevant (to)

baintreach *f2* widow **baintreach mná** widow, **baintreach fir** widower

bairdéir *m3* warder **bairdéir príosúin** prison warder

báire *m4* 1. game of hurling 2. game, match, contest 3. goal **an-bháire é sin** that's a great goal 4. **cailín báire** tomboy, **buachaill báire** trickster, playboy

bairéad *m1* hat, beret

báireoir *m3* goalie, goal-keeper

bairille *m4* barrel **bairille beorach** barrel, keg, of beer, **ar bairille** on tap, **gunna dhá bhairille** double-barrelled gun, **gunna aonbhairille** single-barrelled gun

bairín *m4* cake, loaf **bairín breac** barm-brack

bairneach *m1* limpet

báirse *m4* barge

báirseach *f2* scold, virago

báisín *m4* basin **báisín taoide** tidal basin

baist *v* 1. name **long a bhaisteadh** to name a ship 2. baptise

báisteach *f2* rain **tá báisteach air** it's going to rain, **báisteach aigéadach** acid rain

baisteadh *m* baptism **Seán an t-ainm baiste atá orm** Seán is my Christian name

baistí *adj* baptismal **leanbh baistí** godchild, **athair baistí** godfather, **máthair bhaistí** godmother

báistiúil *adj* rainy **aimsir bháistiúil** rainy weather

báite *adj* soaked **fliuch báite** soaking wet, **Seán báite** watered whiskey

báiteach *adj* 1. pale **cuma bháiteach** pale appearance 2. watery

baithis *f2* crown (*of head*) **ó bhonn go baithis** from head to toe

baitín *m4* baton, little stick

baitsiléir *m3* bachelor **brídeog agus baitsiléir** bride and groom

bál *m1* ball, hooley

balastar *m1* banisters

balbh *adj* mute, dumb

balbhán *m1* dumb person

balcaire *m1* sturdy person **balcaire fir** sturdy man

balcais *f2* garment, rag **níl agam ach seanbhalcaisí** I have only old clothes, rags

balcánta *adj* stout, sturdily built

balcóin *f2* balcony

ball *m1* 1. member **ball saoil** life member 2. spot, patch **ball broinne** birthmark 3. part, article **baill ghiniúna** reproductive organs, genitals, **ball airtiléire** piece of artillery 4. **ar ball** later, not long ago

balla *m4* wall **balla cloiche** stone wall

ballach¹ *m1* wrasse (*fish*)

ballach² *adj* spotted **capall ballach** piebald horse, **fiabhras ballach** spotted fever

ballán *m1* teat **ballán ciche** nipple

ballasta *m4* ballast

ballchrith *f3* trembling **bhí mé ar ballchrith** I was trembling all over

ballóid *f2* ballot **bosca ballóide** ballot-box, **páipéar ballóide** ballot-paper

ballraíocht *f3* membership **cárta ballraíochta** membership card

ballstát *m1* member state

balsam *m1* balm, balsam

balscóid *f2* blotch; blister

bálseomra *m4* ballroom

balún *m1* balloon

bambú *m4* bamboo

ban- *prefix* female **banphríosúnach** female prisoner

bán¹ *adj* 1. white, fair **hata bán** white hat, **gruaig bhán** fair hair 2. blank **téip bhán** blank tape 3. **an bád bán** the emigrant ship *m1* 1. white 2. grassland **pocaire, preabaire, na mbánta** magpie

bán-² *prefix* pale, white **bánfholtach** white-haired, fair-haired

ban-ab *f3* abbess

bánaigh *v* 1. whiten, bleach 2. devastate **bhánaigh siad an áit** they devastated the place 3. evacuate, empty **bánaíodh an t-oileán** the island was evacuated

banaltra *f4* nurse **banaltra cheantair** district nurse

banaltracht *m3* nursing **riarachán banaltrachta** nursing administration

banana *m4* banana

banbh *m1* piglet

bánbhuí *adj* cream (*colour*)

banc *m1* bank **banc gluaisteach** mobile bank, **banc marsantach** merchant bank, **banc taisce** savings bank, **banc tráchtála** commercial bank, **Banc Ceannais na hÉireann** Central Bank of Ireland, **an Banc Domhanda** the World Bank

banchliamhain *m4* daughter-in-law

banda¹ *adj* feminine

banda² *m4* 1. belt **banda iompair** conveyor-belt 2. band **banda lámháltais** tolerance band, **banda rubair** rubber band

bándearg *adj* pink

bandia *m* goddess

banéigean *m1* rape **banéigean reachtúil** statutory rape

bang *m3* stroke (*swimming*) **níl oiread is bang aige** he can't even swim a stroke, **bang brollaigh** breast-stroke

banghiolla *m4* female servant

bánghlóthach *f2* blancmange

bánghnéitheach *adj* pale

banlámh *f2* 1. **an Bhanlámh,** Orion's Belt 2. cubit

banlaoch *m1* heroine

banmhaor *m1* stewardess

banna *m4* 1. bond, security **bannaí rialtais** government bonds 2. guarantee, bail **dul i mbannaí ar dhuine** to go bail for somebody, **ligeadh amach ar bannaí é** he was released on bail 3. **banna ceoil** band (*music*)

banoidhre *m4* heiress

banóstach *m1* hostess

banphrionsa *m4* princess **bainis an bhanphrionsa** the princess's wedding-feast

banrach *f2* enclosed field; paddock

banríon *f3* queen **Banríon Shasana** the Queen of England

bantiarna *f4* lady (*title*)

bantracht *f3* womenfolk

bánú *m* 1. dawning **bánú an lae** daybreak 2. depopulation **bánú na tuaithe** rural depopulation

banúil *adj* womanly, gentle, ladylike

baoi *m4* buoy

baois *f2* folly, silliness

baoisteach *m1* brothel

baoite *m4* bait

baol *m1* danger **tá sí i mbaol báis** she is in danger of dying, **beag an baol** not likely!

baolach *adj* dangerous **is baolach nach mbeidh mé ábalta teacht** I'm afraid I won't be able to come

baoth *adj* 1. vain 2. silly, foolish

bara *m4* barrow **bara rotha** wheelbarrow, **bara cruach** steel barrow

baracáid *f2* barricade **baracáid sráide** street barricade

baraiméadar *m1* barometer

barántas *m1* 1. warranty **barántas trí bliana** three-year warranty 2. warrant **barántas gabhála** arrest warrant

barántúil *adj* trustworthy

baratón *m1* baritone **aonréad baratóin** baritone solo, **eochair bharatóin** baritone clef

barbartha *adj* barbaric

barbarthacht *f3* barbarity

barbatúráit *f2* barbiturate **barbatúráití** barbiturates

bard *m1* bard **dánta na mbard** bardic poems

barda¹ *m4* garrison **trúpaí a chur ar barda** to garrison troops

barda² *m4* ward **barda ospidéil** hospital ward

bardach *m1* warden **bardach cathrach** city warden

bardal *m1* drake

bardas *m1* municipal authority, corporation **Bardas Bhaile Átha Cliath** Dublin Corporation, **tithe bardais** corporation houses

barócach *adj* baroque **ealaín bharócach** baroque art

barr¹ *m1* 1. top, peak, summit **i mbarr a réime** at the peak of his career, **barr an tsléibhe** summit, top of the mountain 2. tip **barr do mhéire** the tip of your finger 3. crop 4. superiority **thar barr** excellent 5. **de bharr** as a result of, due to, **dá bharr sin** consequently

barr² *m4* hindrance, bar

barrachód *m1* bar code

barraicín *m4* toe

barraíocht *f3* too much, excess **bhí barraíocht daoine ann** there were too many people there

barrchaolaigh *v* taper

barrchéim *f2* climax **barrchéim an dráma** the climax of the play

barrdhóigh *v* singe

barrdhóite *adj* singed

barriall *f2* bootlace, shoelace

barrloisc *v* singe

barrloiscthe *adj* singed

barróg *f2* hug, embrace **rug mé barróg air** I hugged him

barrshamhail *f3* ideal

barrthuisle *f4* stumble **bhain sé barrthuisle asat** he tripped you up

barrúil *adj* 1. funny **scéal barrúil** funny story 2. strange **duine barrúil** strange person

barúil *f3* opinion **is é mo bharúil go...** it's my opinion that..., **níl barúil ar bith agam** I have no idea

barún *m1* baron

barúntacht *f3* barony

bás *m1* death **ag fáil bháis** dying, **dath an bháis a bheith ort** to be the colour of death

básaigh *v* 1. die **bhásaigh sí** she died 2. execute, put to death **básaíodh triúr** three people were executed

basár *m1* bazaar

basc *v* 1. crush 2. injure, bash

Bascach *adj*, *m1* Basque **cailín Bascach** Basque girl, **na Bascaigh** the Basques, **Tír na mBascach** the Basque Country

bascaed *m1* basket

básmhar *adj* mortal

bastard *m1* bastard

bástcóta *m4* waistcoat

bastún *m1* lout, vulgar person

bású *m* killing, execution

basún *m1* bassoon

bata *m4* stick, baton **séirse bataí** baton charge, **bata croise** crutch, **tugadh bata is bóthar dom** I was dismissed, I got the sack

bataire *m4* battery **bataire airtléire** artillery battery, **bataire frith-aerárthach** anti-aircraft battery

batráil *f3* battering, bruising *v* batter

báúil *adj* sympathetic, partial **báúil le** sympathetic to, partial to

béabhar *m1* beaver

beacán *m1* mushroom

beach *f2* bee **beach ghabhair, chapaill,** wasp

beacht *adj* exact, correct, accurate **tá sé ráite go beacht agat** you've said it correctly

beachtaigh *v* 1. correct **bíonn sé de shíor do mo bheachtú** he constantly corrects me 2. **beachtaigh ar** to criticise

beadaí[1] *adj* 1. sweet-toothed 2. fastidious, fussy (*about food*) **billíní beadaí** dainties

beadaí[2] *m4* gourmet

béadán *m1* gossip **lucht béadáin** gossips

béadchaint *f2* slander **seachain ar eagla go ndéanfaidh tú béadchaint uirthi** mind in case you slander her

beag[1] *adj* (*comp* lú) small, little **cailín beag** small girl, **an buachaill is lú** the smallest boy, **is beag is fiú é** it is not worth much, **ní beag a bhfuil ráite** enough is said, **is é an rud is lú is gann é a d'fhéadfadh sé a rá** it's the least he could say, **anois beag** just now

beag[2] *m1* 1. few **is beag duine a labhraíonn leis** few people talk to him 2. little, small amount **ar a bheag** at least, **a bheag nó a mhór** more or less

beagán *adv* a little **beagán níos óige** a little younger *m1* small amount **mórán cainte ar bheagán cúise** much ado about nothing

beagmhaitheasach *adj* useless, worthless

beagmheastúil *adj* disrespectful, contemptuous **bheith beagmheastúil ar dhuine** to be contemptuous of someone

beagnach *adv* almost **bhí an áit beagnach lán** the place was nearly full

beaguchtach *m1* lack of courage **chuir sí beaguchtach air** she disheartened him

beaichte *f4* exactness, precision

beaignit *f2* bayonet **séirse beaignite** bayonet charge

beairic *f2* barracks

béal *m1* 1. mouth, opening **béal na habhann** the mouth of the river, **béal an ghoile** the pit of the stomach, **tinneas bhéal an ghoile** indigestion, **lán go béal** full to the brim, **tá sé i mbéal an phobail** everyone is talking about it/him 2. edge **béal na scine** the edge of the knife 3. muzzle **béal gunna** muzzle of a gun, **béalchlúdach** muzzle cover

Béal Feirste Belfast **muintir, pobal, Bhéal Feirste** the people of Belfast

bealach *m1* 1. way, road, route, method **ar bhealach** in a way, **Bealach na Bó Finne** the Milky Way, **an bhfuil eolas an bhealaigh, fios an bhealaigh, agat?** do you know the way? **bealach isteach** entrance, **mótarbhealach** motorway, **bealach iompair** transport route, **bealach trádála** trade route, **bealach oibre** method of work 2. sound **Bealach an Oileáin** the Blasket Sound

bealadh *m1* lubricant, grease **bealadh rubair** rubber lubricant

bealaigh *v* lubricate, grease

bealaithe *adj* lubricated, greased

béalaithris *f2* oral account

béalchnáimhseánaí *m4* complainer

béalchrábhadh *m1* hypocrisy

béalchráifeach *adj* sanctimonious

béaldath *m3* lipstick

béalghrá *m4* lip-service

béalmhír *f2* bit **béalmhír druileála** drill bit, **béalmhír uirlise** tool bit

béalóg *f2* 1. mouthpiece **béalóg chónúil** conical mouthpiece 2. muzzle

béaloideas *m1* folklore **an Roinn Bhéaloideasa** the Folklore Department

béaloscailte *adj* open-mouthed, wide open

béalscaoilte *adj* indiscreet

Bealtaine *f4* May **26 Bealtaine 1998** the 26th of May 1998, **idir dhá thine Bhealtaine** in a predicament, in a difficult situation

bean *f* woman **mo bhean (chéile)** my wife, **oifigeach mná** female officer, **mná na hÉireann** the women of Ireland, **bean léinn** academic, **beirt bhan** two women, **hata mná** a woman's hat, **leithreas na mban** the womens' toilets, **bean (Sheáin) Uí Dhuibhir** Mrs (Seán) Ó Duibhir

beangán *m1* 1. prong **píce trí bheangán** three-pronged fork 2. branch, shoot

beann[1] *f2* 1. antler, horn **púca na mbeann** the Devil 2. prong **píce trí bheann** three-pronged fork

beann[2] *f2* 1. heed, regard 2. dependence, **níl aon bheann agam air** I am independent of him

beannacht *f3* blessing, greeting **do bheannacht a chur chuig duine, a thabhairt do dhuine** to give someone your kind regards, **beannacht Dé lena n-anam** God rest their souls

beannaigh *v* bless, salute **níor bheannaigh sí dom** she didn't greet, salute, me

beannaithe *adj* holy **an Tír Bheannaithe** the Holy Land

beannú *m* 1. blessing **beannú air** God bless him 2. greeting **beannú a thabhairt do dhuine** to greet someone

beár *m1* bar **fear beáir** barman, **freastalaí beáir** bartender, lounge person

béar *m1* bear **béar donn** brown bear, cave bear, **béar dubh Himiléach, Meiriceánach** Himalayan, American, black bear, **béar bán** polar bear, **béar uisce** water bear

bearach *m1* young cow, heifer

bearbóir *m3* barber **siopa bearbóra** barber's shop

Béarla *m4* English language **ag Múineadh an Bhéarla mar Theanga Iasachta** Teaching English as a Foreign Language (TEFL)

Béarlachas *m1* Irish with an English construction, Anglicism

béarlagair *m4* jargon, cant, slang

Béarlóir *m3* English-speaker

bearna *f4* gap **an bhearna bhaoil** the breach, the gap of danger, **bearna ghiorria, bearna mhíl** hare-lip

bearnach *adj* gapped **cur síos bearnach** incomplete description, **Brian bearnach** hare

bearnaigh *v* 1. tap **bearnaigh an bairille** tap the barrel 2. breach, **bhearnaigh sé a chuid airgid ar fad** he used up all his money

bearr *v* shave, trim, clip, shear **tú féin a bhearradh** to shave yourself, **fál a bhearradh** to trim a hedge, **sciathán a bhearradh** to clip a wing, **caora a bhearradh** to shear a sheep

bearradh *m* clip, shave **bearradh gruaige** haircut, **bearradh caorach** cirrus cloud

beart[1] *m1* 1. parcel, bundle **oifig na mbeart** parcels office, **bailíonn brobh beart** many a little makes a large amount 2. deed, action **tá an beart déanta** the deed is done

beart[2] *m3* berth **tá an long i mbeart** the ship is berthed

beartaigh *v* 1. plan, propose, consider **tá scéim éigin beartaithe aige** he has devised, planned, some scheme 2. **beartaigh ar** decide upon 3. brandish **bheartaigh sí an claíomh** she brandished the sword

beartaíocht *f3* 1. planned course of action, scheming 2. transaction

beartán *m1* parcel

beartas *m1* set purpose, policy **beartas fioscach** fiscal policy, **beartas pleanála** planning policy

béas[1] *m3* habit, custom **is béas leis obair a dhéanamh istoíche** it is his custom to work at night, **béasa** manners, **níl aon bhéasa ag an teaghlach sin** that family has no manners

béas[2] *m3* beige

béasach *adj* well-mannered

beatha *f4* 1. food **beatha phríosúin** prison food 2. livelihood **cén tslí bheatha atá agat?** what is your livelihood? 3. life **Beatha Cholm Cille** the Life of Colm Cille, **beatha (do) dhuine a thoil** everybody has his own taste

beathaigh *v* feed, nourish **ainmhithe a bheathú** to feed animals, **plandaí a bheathú** to nourish plants

beathaisnéis *f2* biography

beathaisnéiseach *adj* biographical **saothar beathaisnéiseach** biographical work

beathaisnéisí *m4* biographer

beathaithe *adj* well-fed **fear beag beathaithe** plump little man

beathaitheach *adj* nourishing, fattening

beathra *m4* life (*living things*) **beathra éan** bird life, **beathra miocróbach** microbial life

beathú *m* feeding, nourishment **beathú leanaí** feeding of young children

beathúil *adj* nutritious

beathuisce *m4* whiskey

beathúlachas *m1* vitalism

béic *f2*, *v* scream, yell, shout **lig sé béic** he screamed, **bhéic mé orthu** I shouted at them

béicíl *f3* screaming, yelling

béile *m4* meal

Beilg *f2* **an Bheilg** Belgium, **muintir na Beilge** the people of Belgium

Beilgeach *adj*, *m1* Belgian

beilt *f2* belt **beilt tiomána** (driving) belt (*mechanical*)

béim *f2* 1. blow **fuair sí béim ghréine** she got sunstroke, **bhuail béim thinnis é** he suffered a blow of sickness 2. emphasis **chuir sé béim ar an gceist** he emphasised the question

beir *v* (see *irregular verbs*) 1. **beir ar** catch, **beir ar an bpeil** catch the football 2. take, bring **béarfaidh sé chugat é, uait é** he'll bring it to you, take it away from you 3. give birth to, lay **rug sí leanbh** she gave birth to a child, **ag breith uibheacha** laying eggs

beirigh *v* 1. bake **bheirigh sí císte duit** she baked a cake for you 2. boil **tá an t-uisce beirithe** the water has boiled

beirt *f2* two people, pair **beirt bhan** two women, **beirt bhuachaillí** two boys **beirt chailíní** two girls, **beirt fhear** two men, **beirt mhúinteoirí** two teachers, **an bheirt againn** both of us, the two of us

beith[1] *f2* being, entity

beith[2] *f2* birch tree

beithíoch *m1* 1. animal 2. beast **beithígh allta** wild beasts

beo *adj* alive, living **bhí an eangach beo le héisc** the net was alive with, full of, swarming with, fish, **gaineamh beo** quicksand, **an teanga bheo** the living language *m4* 1. life **níor tharla sé le mo bheo** it didn't happen in my

lifetime 2. living person, being **an beo** the living

beochan *f3* animation **beochan puipéad** puppet animation

beocht *f3* liveliness **cuir beocht éigin ann** put some life into it

beodhioscadh *m* vivisection

beoga *adj* 1. vivid **léirithe go beoga** expressed vividly 2. lively **caint bheoga** lively speech

beoigh *v* animate

beoir *f* beer **buidéal beorach** bottle of beer

beoite *adj* animated **scannán beoite** animated film

beola *pl* lips

beostoc *m1* livestock

bhuel *excl* well

bhur *poss adj* your **bhur gcara** your friend, **bhur n-ainmneacha** your names

bí *v* (see *irregular verbs*) be **bí go maith!** be good! **bheith bréan de rud** to be sick of something, **bhí mé sásta leis** I was happy with it, **cén fáth nach raibh tú ann?** why weren't you there? **beidh orm imeacht luath** I'll have to leave early, **an mbeadh go leor agat ansin?** would you have enough there?

bia *m* 1. food **bia mara** seafood, **bia ar fáil an lá ar fad** food served all day, **bia gunna mhóir** cannon-fodder, **nimhiú ó bhia** food poisoning, **leasú bia** food preservation, **stóráil bhia** food storage, **tástáil ar bhia** food test 2. substance **níor bhain mé aon bhia as an gcaint sin** I didn't make any sense out of what was said

biabhóg *f2* rhubarb **toirtín biabhóige** rhubarb tart

biachlár *m1* menu **biachlár lóin** lunch menu

bia-eolaí *m4* dietician

bialann *f2* canteen, restaurant

biashlabhra *m4* food chain

biatas *m1* beet, beetroot **biatas siúcra** sugar-beet

bib(e) *m4* bib

bicéips *f2* biceps **bicéips agus trichéips** biceps and triceps

bídeach *adj* tiny, very small **ceann beag bídeach** a tiny little one

bileog *f2* leaf **bileog eolais** leaflet, **bileoga páipéir** sheets of paper, **bileog shaothair** work sheet

bille *m4* bill **bille díola** bill of sale, **bille airgeadais** finance bill (*parliamentary*), **bille ó chomhalta príobháideach** private member's bill

billiún *m1* billion

binb *f2* venom, fury **tá binb sa chaint sin** there's venom in that speech

binbeach *adj* venomous, sharp **glór binbeach** sharp voice

bindealán *m1* bandage

binn¹ *f2* 1. gable **binn an tí** gable-end of house 2. peak **chuamar go binn an tsléibhe sin** we went to the peak of that mountain 3. cliff **thit siad le binn** they fell down a cliff

binn² *adj* melodious, sweet-sounding **ceol binn** sweet music

binneas *m1* sweetness, melodiousness

binse *m4* 1. bench **binse na nAirí** the front bench 2. tribunal **Binse Fiosraithe na Mairteola** the Beef Tribunal, **an Binse Fiosraithe um Íocaíochtaí do Pholaiteoirí** the Payments to Politicians Tribunal, **an Binse Achomhairc Fostaíochta** Employment Appeals Tribunal

Bíobla *m4* Bible

biocáire *m4* vicar

bíog *v* 1. start, stir **bhíog sé nuair a chuala sé é** he jumped (with fright) when he heard it 2. twitch **bíonn an meatán sin ag bíogadh**

de shíor that muscle constantly twitches *f2* chirp, squeak **ní raibh bíog as** there wasn't a squeak from him

bíogach *adj* 1. twitching, jumpy 2. chirpy

biogamacht *f3* bigamy

bíogúil *adj* lively, vivacious

biolar *m1* watercress, cress

biongó *m4* bingo **oíche bhiongó** bingo night

bior *m3* 1. point **chuir sé bior ar an mbata** he sharpened the stick 2. skewer, spit, spike **feoil a chur ar bior** to skewer, spit, meat 3. bit **bior sádrála (leictreach)** (electric) soldering bit

biorach *adj* pointed

bioraigh *v* sharpen **bata a bhiorú** to point a stick

biorán *m1* 1. pin **biorán hata** hairpin, **ag imirt biorán sop** casting lots 2. needle **bioráin chniotála** knitting needles

bioróir *m3* sharpener **scriosán agus bioróir** eraser and sharpener

bior-róst *v* spitroast

biotáille *f4* spirits **buidéal biotáille** bottle of spirits, **biotáille mheitileach** methylated spirit

bís *f2* 1. spiral 2. vice **bís láimhe** hand vice 3. **bheith ar bís le rud a dhéanamh** to be impatient to do something

biseach *m1* recovery, improvement **an bhfuil biseach uirthi fós?** is she better yet? **gach bliain bhisigh** each leap year

bísghreamán *m1* vice grip

bisigh *v* 1. increase 2. improve

bith *m3* 1. **ar bith** any, no (*with neg*) **an raibh duine ar bith ann?** was anybody there? **ní raibh duine ar bith ann** there was nobody there 2. existence, world **sa bhith** in the world

bithbheo *adj* eternal

bithcheimic *f2* biochemistry

bitheolaí *m4* biologist **bitheolaí muirí** marine biologist

bitheolaíoch *adj* biological **srianadh bitheolaíoch** biological control

bitheolaíocht *f3* biology **bítheolaíocht mhuirí** marine biology

bithghlas *adj* evergreen

bithiúnach *m1* 1. rascal, scoundrel 2. gangster

bithiúntas *m1* roguery, scoundrelism

bithmhais *f2* biomass

bith-theicneolaíocht *f3* biotechnology

biúró *m4* bureau **biúró ríomhaireachta** computer bureau, **an Biúró Eorpach do Theangacha Neamhfhorleathana** the European Bureau for Lesser-spoken Languages

bladar *m1* flattery, 'blather'

bladhaire *m4* flame, flare

bladhm *f3* flame, blaze *v* flame

bladhmann *m1* bragging, bombast

bladhmannach *adj* bombastic, boastful

bláfar *adj* 1. flowering, blooming 2. neat 3. proper

blagadach *adj* bald

blagadán *m1* baldy, bald person

blagaid *f2* bald head

blaincéad *m1* blanket

blais *v* taste **blais é, blais de** taste it

blaisínteacht *f3* sipping, nibbling **ag blaisínteacht ar do chuid bia** nibbling at your food

blaistigh *v* season, flavour **bia a bhlaistiú** to season food

blaosc *f2* 1. skull 2. shell **blaosc uibhe** eggshell

blár *m1* field, plain, open space **táim ar an mblár folamh** I'm down and out

blas *m1* 1. accent **tá blas na Fraince ar a cuid cainte** she speaks like a French person 2. taste, **tá blas ait air** it has a strange taste

blasta *adj* 1. well-spoken **dúirt sé go blasta é** he said it well 2. tasty **bia blasta** tasty food

blastán *m1* seasoning

bláth *m3* 1. bloom **bláth na hóige** bloom of youth 2. blossom, flower **fiche bliain faoi bhláth** twenty years a-blooming, **ceapach bláthanna** flowerbed

bláthach *f2* buttermilk

bláthadóir *m3* florist **siopa bláthadóra** florist's shop

bláthaigh *v* flower, blossom

bláthbhreac *adj* floral

bláthchuach *m4* flower vase

bláthfhleasc *f2* wreath

bláthola *f4* essential oil

bláthscaoileadh *m* menstruation

bleachtaire *m4* detective

bleachtaireacht *f3* detecting **úrscéal bleachtaireachta** detective novel

bleaistéir *m3* blaster **bleaistéir sráide** ghettoblaster

bleán *m1* milking, milk yield **bleán láimhe** hand milking, **bleán meaisíneach** machine milking

bleánlann *f2* milking parlour **bleánlann rothlach** rotary milking parlour

bleib *f2* bulb (*plant*)

bleid *f2* 1. wheedler, talkative person 2. **bhuail sé bleid orm** he accosted me

bléin *f2* groin

bléitse *m4* bleach

bliain *f* year **gach bliain bhisigh** each leap year, **dhá bhliain ó shin** two years ago, **trí, ceithre, cúig, sé, bliana** three, four, five, six, years, **seacht, ocht, naoi, deich, mbliana** seven, eight, nine, ten, years, **an bhliain seo caite, chugainn** last, next year, **Bliain úr faoi shéan (agus faoi mhaise) duit!** Happy

new year! **in aghaidh na bliana**
yearly, *per annum*

bliainiris *f2* annual, year-book

blianacht *f3* annuity

bliantóg *f2* annual (*plant*)

bliantúil *adj* yearly, annual

bligeard *m1* blackguard **bligeard
críochnaithe** proper blackguard

bligh *v* milk **ag bleán na bó** milking
the cow

bliosán *m1* artichoke (*plant*)

bloc *m1* block **bloc adhmaid** timber
block, wooden block, **bloc árasán
(cúig stór)** (five storey) block of
flats

blocáil *v* block

blogh *f3* fragment, small piece **rinne
sé bloghanna de** he made bits of it

blonag *f2* lard, fat, blubber **ná
baintear an t-ainm den bhlonag**
call a spade a spade, **blonag an
mhíl mhóir** whale blubber

blonagach *adj* fat, greasy, obese **feoil
róbhlonagach í sin** that meat is
too fat, **nach blonagach an ceann
é** what a fatty he is

blosc *m1* explosive sound, report
blosc gunna report of gun *v*
explode, crack

blúire *m4* morsel, bit, fragment

blús *m1* blouse

bó *f* cow **ag bleán na bó** milking the
cow, **na ba** the cows, **ag bleán na
mbó** milking the cows, **Bealach
na Bó Finne** the Milky Way, **galar
na bó buile** mad cow disease, BSE

bob *m4* trick, deception **buaileadh
bob orm** I was tricked

bobailín *m4* bob, tassel **scaoil amach
an bobailín!** let it loose! let it rip!

boc *m1* buck **na boic mhóra** the big
shots

bocáil *v* toss, bounce **ag bocáil
liathróide** bouncing a ball

bocaire *m4* small cake, muffin

bóchna *f4* ocean

bocht *adj* poor, sorry **an fear bocht**
the poor man, **is bocht an scéal é**
it's a sorry story, situation
m1 poor person

bochtaigh *v* impoverish

bochtaineacht *f3* poverty

bochtán *m1* poor person

bochtanas *m1* poverty

bocsaeir *m3* boxer (*dog*)

bod *m1* penis

bodach *m1* vulgar person, lout
bodaigh bheorach lager louts

bodhaire *f4* deafness **bodhaire Uí
Laoire** feigned deafness

bodhar *adj* 1. deaf 2. numb

bodhraigh *v* 1. bother, annoy **bíonn
an fear céanna de shíor do mo
bhodhrú** that same man is always
bothering me 2. deafen **táim
bodhraithe ag an gceol** the music
has deafened me 3. deaden
bodhróidh sé sin an phian duit
that will deaden, kill, the pain for
you

bodhrán[1] *m1* deaf person

bodhrán[2] *m1* hand drum

bodhránaí *m4* person who plays the
bodhrán

bodmhadra *m4* mongrel **tá dhá
bhodmhadra againn ag baile** we
have two mongrels at home

bodóg *f2* 1. heifer 2. sexy woman

bog *adj* soft, easy **lá bog** soft day, **tóg
(breá) bog é** take it easy
v 1. soften **tá an teas á bhogadh**
the heat is softening it 2. move,
loosen **bog sall beagán** move over
a little, **bogaigí libh** move on

bogach *m1* boggy ground

bogadh *m* 1. movement, stir **ní féidir
bogadh ná sá a bhaint as** nothing
can budge him, it, **tá bogadh ann**
he, it, is moving

bogadhmad *m1* softwood

bogás *m1* self-complacency, smugness

bogásach *adj* self-complacent

bogbháisteach *f2* soft rain, drizzle

bogearraí *pl* software **bogearraí córais** system software, **bogearraí feidhmiúcháin** applications software

bogfhiuchadh *m* simmering **tá sé ar bogfhiuchadh** it is simmering

bogha *m4* bow **bogha báistí, bogha ceatha, bogha síne** rainbow, **bogha is saighead** bow and arrow

boghdóir *m3* archer

boghdóireacht *f3* archery

bogoighear *m1* melting snow, sludge

bogshodar *m1* easy pace, trot **ar bogshodar** at an easy pace

bogtha *adj* merry (from drink)

bogthe *adj* lukewarm

boige *f4* softness

boigéis *f2* 1. easy-going attitude, outlook 2. gullibility

boigéiseach *adj* 1. easy-going 2. gullible

boilgearnach *f2* bubbling

boilgeog *f2* bubble

boilscitheach *adj* inflationary **éifeacht bhoilscitheach** inflationary effect, **géarchéim bhoilscitheach** inflationary crisis

boilsciú *m* inflation **boilsciú airgeadaíochta** inflation of the currency, **boilsciú athfhillteach** recurrent inflation

boilsciú-díbhoilsciú *m* inflation-deflation

bóín *f4* **bóín Dé, bóín samhraidh** ladybird

boinéad *m1* bonnet

boirbe *f4* abruptness, fierceness

boiseog *f2* 1. slap 2. ripple

bóitheach *m1* cowhouse

bóithreoireacht *f3* travelling around, vagrancy

bóithrín *m4* country lane

bólacht *f3* cattle, herd of cows

boladh *m1* smell **tá boladh breá uait** there is a lovely smell (*of perfume*) from you, **boladh bréan** horrible smell

bólaí *pl* **sna bólaí seo** in these parts, in this area

bolaigh *v* smell **bolaigh de seo** smell this

bolcán *m1* volcano **bolcán beo** active volcano, **bolcán marbh** extinct volcano, **bolcán suaimhneach** passive volcano, **bolcán suanach** dormant volcano

bolg *m1* belly, stomach, abdomen **nuair a bhíonn an bolg lán is maith leis na cnámha síneadh** when the stomach is full the body likes to rest, **cos ar bolg** oppression, **cos ar bolg a imirt ar chine** to oppress a race *v* 1. blister **tá an phéint sin ag bolgadh** that paint is blistering 2. bulge

bolgach *f2* smallpox **bolgach fhrancach** syphilis

bolgam *m1* mouthful **bolgam a ól** to drink a mouthful

bolgán *m1* 1. light-bulb 2. bubble

bolgchainteoir *m3* ventriloquist

bolgóid *f2* bubble

bolla *m1* bowl (*sport*) **cluiche bollaí** game of bowls

bollán *m1* boulder **bollán cloiche** boulder

bollóg *f2* loaf **bollóg aráin** loaf of bread

bológ *f2* bullock

bolscaire *m4* 1. announcer 2. propagandist

bolscaireacht *f3* 1. announcing 2. publicity, propaganda

bolta *m4* bolt **bolta clampála** clamping bolt, **bolta práis** brass bolt

boltáil *v* bolt

boltanach *adj* olfactory

bomaite *m4* minute **fan bomaite** wait a moment

bómán *m1* slow foolish person

bómánta *adj* slow, stupid

bómántacht *f3* stupidity

bóna *m4* 1. lapel 2. collar

bónas *m1* bonus

bonn[1] *m1* 1. sole **bonn bróige** sole of shoe 2. basc, foundation **bonn foirgnimh** foundation of building, **caithfimid tosú ó bhonn** we have to start from the beginning 3. tyre **boinn athmhúnlaithe** remoulds, **bonn aer-oibrithe** pneumatic tyre

bonn[2] *m1* coin, medal **bonn caoga pingin** fifty-pence piece, **an Bonn Míleata Calmachta** Military Medal for Gallantry, **bonn comhchruinn umha** circular bronze medal

bonnán *m1* 1. bittern (*bird*) **An Bonnán Buí** The Bittern (*song*) 2. horn, siren

bonneagar *m1* infrastructure

bonnóg *f2* scone

bonsach *f?* 1. twig 2. active young girl 3. javelin

bórach *adj* bandy-legged **duine beag bórach** small bandy-legged, bow-legged, person

borb *adj* 1. rough, coarse **deoch bhorb is ea an poitín** poitín is a harsh drink 2. rude, fierce **labhair sé go borb liom** he spoke to me rudely

bord *m1* 1. board **Bord Soláthair an Leictreachais (BSL)** Electricity Supply Board (ESB), **bord stiúrthóirí** board of directors 2. table **bord íseal** coffee table, **leag an bord** set the table, **tar amach ó ghabhal an bhoird** come out from under the table 3. deck **ná tit thar bord** don't fall overboard, **cé mhéad duine a bhí ar bord?** how many people were on board?

bordáil *v* board, go aboard **ag bordáil ar mheán lae** near midday

borgaire *m4* hamburger **borgaire agus sceallóga** burger and chips

borr *v* 1. increase, grow **tá na plandaí sin ag borradh leis an teas** those plants are growing fast with the heat 2. swell **tá an fharraige ag borradh** the sea is beginning to swell

borradh *m* 1. growth, boom, swell **borradh eacnamaíochta** economic boom, **borradh faoi thithíocht** housing boom, **tá borradh ann** there is a swell there (in the sea) 2. surge **borradh fuinnimh** surge of energy

borróg *f2* bun

borrtha *adj* 1. swollen 2. varicose **féith bhorrtha** varicose vein

borrúil *adj* 1. fast-growing **planda borrúil** fast-growing plant 2. enterprising **duine borrúil** enterprising person

bos *f2* 1. palm of hand **bualadh mór bos** a great round of applause, **ar iompú boise** immediately 2. blade of oar

bosadáil *f2* paddling

bosca *m4* box **bosca airgid** money box, **bosca bailiúcháin** collection box, **bosca ceoil** accordion, **bosca teileafóin** phone box

Bostún *m1* Boston

both *f3* hut, booth, kiosk

bothán *m1* hut

bóthar *m1* road **fuair sé an bóthar** he got the sack, **tá sé in am agam an bóthar a bhualadh** it is time for me to leave, hit the road

botún *m1* blunder, mess **tá an botún déanta** the mistake has been made

brabach *m1* profit, gain **rinne mé brabach ar an gcarr a dhíol mé** I made a profit on the car I sold

brablach *m1* 1. rabble 2. rubble

brabús *m1* 1. profit **brabús comhlán** gross profit, **brabús glan** net profit, **brabús fíorghlan** pure profit, **cuntas brabúis agus caillteanais** profit and loss account 2. advantage

brabúsach *adj* profitable, lucrative

brách, go brách for ever, never (*with neg*) **ní dhéanfaidh mé go brách arís é** I'll never do it again, **is fearr go déanach ná go brách** better late than never, **as go brách liom ar nós na gaoithe** off I went as fast as the wind

brachán *m1* porridge **babhla bracháin** bowl of porridge

bradach *adj* 1. thieving **is deacair claí a chur ar bhó bhradach** it is hard to keep a thieving cow within bounds, to check a rogue 2. stolen **bia bradach** stolen food

bradán *m1* salmon **bradán deataithe** smoked salmon, **bradán beatha** the essence of life

brádán *m1* drizzle **brádán báistí** drizzle of rain

braich *f2* malt

bráid *f* 1. neck **muince, bráisléad, brád** necklace, **branra brád** collar-bone 2. breast, bust 3. **chuaigh mé faoina bhráid** I went to meet him, **faoi bhráid na hollscoile** in preparation for the university, **dul thar bráid** to pass by

braighdeanach *m1* captive

braighdeanas *m1* captivity

braillín *f2* sheet **braillíní síoda** silk sheets

brainse *m4* branch

bráisléad *m1* bracelet **bráisléad óir** gold bracelet

braiteach *adj* perceptive **bheith braiteach ar rud** to be perceptive to, sensitive to, alert to, something

braiteoireacht *f3* hesitancy

braith *v* 1. feel, perceive **braithim go hainnis** I feel terrible, **bhraith mé**

nach raibh fáilte romham I felt I wasn't welcome 2. betray **bhraith siad mé** they betrayed me, they informed on me 3. (used with *preps* **ar** and **le**) **táim ag brath ort** I'm depending on you, **ag brath le duine** waiting for somebody

bráithreachas *m1* brotherhood **Bráithreachas Phoblacht na hÉireann** the Irish Republican Brotherhood (IRB)

Bráma *m4* Brahma

branar *m1* fallow land

branda[1] *m4* brand **branda siopa** shop brand

branda[2] *m4* brandy **gloine bhranda** glass of brandy

brandáil *v* brand **eallach a bhrandáil** to brand cattle

branra *m4* 1. support **bosa branra** crossed hands to carry something 2. gridiron 3. stand, tripod

braon *m1* drop **braon bainne** drop of milk, **braon báistí** drop of rain

Brasaíl *f2* **an Bhrasaíl** Brazil, **pobal na Brasaíle** the people of Brazil

Brasaíleach *adj*, *m1* Brazilian, **an pobal Brasaíleach** the Brazilian community, **cnó Brasaíleach** Brazil nut

brat *m1* 1. covering **brat péinte** layer of paint, **brat urláir** carpet 2. cloak **brat pósta** wedding gown 3. curtain (*theatre*)

bratach *f2* flag, banner **bratach na hÉireann** the Irish flag

bráth *m3* doomsday **lá an bhrátha** doomsday

brathadóir *m3* 1. informer 2. detector **brathadóir bréige** lie detector, **brathadóir leibhéil uisce** water-level detector

bráthair *m* 1. brother, friar 2. fellow member of society

bratlong *f2* flagship

bratóg *f2* rag

bratógach *adj* tattered, ragged

breá *adj* fine, excellent **bean bhreá** beautiful woman, **is breá liom é / í** I love him/her, **ba bhreá liom dul ann** I'd love to go there, **tóg breá bog é** take it nice and easy, **lá breá gréine** fine sunny day

breab *f2* bribe **thug sé breab di** he bribed her *v* bribe **bhreab sí é** she bribed him

breabaire *m4* briber

breabaireacht *f3* bribery

breac¹ *m1* 1. trout **chomh folláin le breac** as healthy as ever, having excellent health 2. fish

breac² *v* 1. speckle, spot 2. write down **rud a bhreacadh (síos)** to jot down something

breac³ *adj* speckled, spotted **bheith breac le rud** to be dotted with, rife with, something

breac-⁴ *prefix* 1. occasional **breacbháisteach** occasional rain 2. semi-, partly **breacoilte** semi-skilled

breacadh *m1* 1. clearing (*in weather*) 2. lightening **breacadh an lae** daybreak 3. writing

breacán *m1* plaid

breacbháisteach *f2* occasional rain

Breac-Ghaeltacht *f3* semi-Gaeltacht, part of the official Gaeltacht where both English and Irish are spoken

breacoilte *adj* semi-skilled **oibrithe breacoilte** semi-skilled workers

bréad *m1* braid

bréag¹ *f2* 1. lie **ar inis tú bréag dom?** did you tell me a lie? **brathadóir bréige** lie detector 2. **ainm bréige** pseudonym, false name, **fear bréige** scarecrow

bréag-² *prefix* pseudo-, false **bréagphóidiam** pseudopodium, **bréagthoradh** false fruit

bréagadóir *m3* liar, deceiver

bréagadóireacht *f3* deceit

bréagán *m1* toy

bréagéide *f4* costume, fancy dress **cóisir bhréagéide** fancy dress party

bréagfholt *m1* wig

bréagnaigh *v* refute, contradict **tá tú do do bhréagnú féin** you are contradicting yourself

bréagnaitheach *adj* contradictory

bréagríocht *m3* disguise **an-fhear bréagreachta é sin** he is a great man of disguise

breall *f2* 1. defect 2. **breall a bheith ort** to make a silly mistake, to make a fool of yourself 3. blubber lip **breall a chur ort féin** to sulk

breallán *m1* stupid man

breallóg *f2* stupid woman

brealsún *m1* stupid person

bréan *adj* foul, rotten **boladh bréan** foul smell, **táim bréan de** I'm tired of him/it

bréantas *m1* stench

Breatain *f2* **an Bhreatain (Mhór)** (Great) Britain, **an Bhreatain Bheag** Wales, **Corn na Breataine** Cornwall

breáthacht *f3* beauty, excellence

breathnaigh *v* 1. examine, observe 2. look **breathnaigh air sin look** at that

breathnóir *m3* observer

breathnóireacht *f3* observing, observation

Breatnach *adj* Welsh *m1* Welshperson **Breatnach mná** Welshwoman

Breatnais *f2* Welsh (*language*) **an pobal Breatnaise** the Welsh-speaking community

breicne *f4* freckle

breicneach *adj* freckled *f2* freckles

bréid *m4* 1. frieze 2. bandage 3. cloth, canvas

bréidín *m4* homespun cloth, tweed

bréige *f4* falseness

breis *f2* increase, addition **bhí breis agus trí mhíle duine ann** there was more than three thousand people there, **cuir breis leis** increase it, **breis ama** more time, **am breise** extra time, **roth breise** spare wheel, **cúpla lá breise** a couple of extra days

breischéim *f2* comparative degree (*grammar*)

breiseán *m1* additive

breisíocht *f3* increment

breith[1] *f2* decision, judgement **tugadh breith bháis dó** he was given the death sentence, **breith phearsanta ar fhiúntas** value judgement

breith[2] *f2* birth **lá breithe sona duit!** happy birthday (to you)! **breith anabaí** premature birth

breitheamh *m1* judge **breitheamh Ardchúirte** High Court judge

breithiúnas *m1* decision, judgement

breithlá *m* birthday **breithlá Mháire** Mary's birthday, **breithlá sona duit!** happy birthday!

breithmheas *m3* appraisal, assessment **breithmheas ar fheidhmiú** performance appraisal

breithnigh *v* adjudge **breithníodh an cás** the case was adjudicated upon

breochloch *f2* flint **páipéar breochloiche** flint paper

breoite *adj* sick **buaileadh breoite í** she was struck with an illness

breoiteacht *f3* sickness

breosla *m4* fuel

brí *f4* 1. meaning **cén bhrí atá leis sin?** what does that mean? 2. energy, strength **tá sé in ísle brí** he is feeling down, run down 3. **de bhrí go...** because..., **dá bhrí sin** for that reason, therefore

briathar *m1* 1. verb **an briathar saor** the autonomous verb 2. word

briathra díomhaoine idle words, **briathra móra** boastful words

briatharchath *m3* logomachy

briathartha *adj* verbal **ainm briathartha** verbal noun, **aidiacht bhriathartha** verbal adjective

bríce *m4* brick **bríce pollta** perforated brick

bríceadóir *m3* bricklayer

bricfeasta *m4* breakfast

bricín[1] *m4* minnow

bricín[2] *m4* freckle

brícín *m4* briquette **brícíní móna** peat briquettes

bricíneach *adj* freckled

brícléir *m3* bricklayer

brídeach *f2* bride

brídeog *f2* bride **brídeog agus baitsiléir** bride and groom

brilléis *f2* silly, foolish, talk **brilléis chainte** nonsensical talk

briocht *m3* 1. spell, charm 2. amulet

briogáid *f2* brigade **ceannasaí briogáide** brigade commander, **briogáid dóiteáin** fire-brigade

briogún *m1* skewer

bríomhar *adj* vigorous, strong

brionglóid *f2* dream

brionglóideach *adj* dreamy *f2* dreaming

brionnaigh *v* forge **airgead brionnaithe** counterfeit money, forged money

brionnú *m* forgery **brionnú breá** fine forgery

briosc *adj* 1. crisp 2. brittle

briosca *m4* biscuit

brioscán *m1* crisp **brioscáin (phrátaí)** (potato) crisps

briotach *adj* lisping **labhrann sé go briotach** he speaks with a lisp

Briotáin *f2* **an Bhriotáin** Brittany

Briotáinis *f2* Breton (*language*)

Briotanach *adj* British *m1* Briton

Briotánach *adj*, *m1* Breton

bris *f2* loss **bhí orm é a dhíol faoi bhris** I had to sell it at a loss *v* break **briseadh isteach sa bhanc aréir** the bank was broken into last night, **bíonn sé de shíor ag briseadh isteach orm** he constantly interrupts me, **ar bhris tú an seic?** did you cash the cheque? **briseadh as mo phost mé** I got the sack

briseadh *m* 1. change **an bhfuil briseadh bille fiche punt agat?** have you got change of a £20 note? 2. defeat **Briseadh na Bóinne** the Battle of the Boyne 3. break **an bhfuil aon bhriseadh san aimsir?** is there any change in the weather? 4. dismissal **briseadh as seilbh oifige** dismissal from holding office 5. **bristeacha (farraige)** (sea) breakers

briste *adj* broke, broken **táim briste** I'm broke, **tá Fraincis bhriste aige** he has broken French

bríste *m4* trousers

brístín *m4* pants

bró *f4* quern, millstone

brobh *m1* 1. blade **brobh féir** blade of grass 2. rush (*of marsh*) **bailíonn brobh beart** many a little makes a large amount

broc *m1* badger

brocach[1] *f2* badger's burrow

brocach[2] *adj* dirty **caint bhrocach** smutty talk

brocailí *m4* broccoli

brocaire *m4* terrier **brocaire Uí Mháil** Glen of Imaal terrier

brocais *f2* dirty place

brocamas *m1* dirt, rubbish

bród *m1* pride **beidh bród air asam** he will be proud of me

bródúil *adj* proud, arrogant

bróg *f2* shoe **bróga peile** football boots, **bróga reatha** runners, trainers

broghach *adj* dirty **an braon broghach** impure drink, spirits

broic (le) *v* tolerate, put up with **is deacair broic leis** it is difficult to put up with him

bróicéir *m3* broker **bróicéir árachais** insurance broker

bróicéireacht *f3* brokerage **táille bhróicéireachta** brokerage fee

broid[1] *f2* 1. urgency **bheith faoi bhroid oibre** to be under pressure of work 2. distress **broid bháis** distress from a death

broid[2] *v* 1. nudge **bhroid sé mé** he nudged me 2. goad

broidearnach *f2* pulsation, throbbing

broidiúil *adj* busy, pressed

bróidnéireacht *f3* embroidery

bróidnigh *v* embroider

broim *m3* fart **cé a lig, a scaoil, broim?** who farted? *v* fart **ag bromadh** farting

broincíteas *m1* bronchitis

broinn *f2* 1. womb **ball broinne** birthmark, **galar broinne** congenital disease 2. **broinn loinge** hold of ship

bróisiúr *m1* brochure

bróiste *m4* brooch

brollach *m1* 1. breast 2. prologue, foreword

bromach *m1* colt

bromaire *m4* farter

brón *m1* sorrow, sadness **tá brón orm** I'm sorry

brónach *adj* sad, sorrowful

bronn *v* bestow, confer, donate **cathain a bhronnfar an chéim ort?** when will you be conferred with your degree? **cé a bhronn an t-uaireadóir?** who donated the watch?

bronnadh *m* bestowal **bronnadh na céime** the conferring, **bronnadh na nduaiseanna** the awards ceremony

bronntanas *m1* gift, present

brosna *m4* kindling

brostaigh *v* hurry

brothall *m1* heat

brothallach *adj* hot **lá breá brothallach** fine hot day

brú *m4* 1. hostel **brú óige** youth hostel, **Slí an Bhrú** Newgrange 2. pressure, push **brú boilscíoch** inflatory pressure, **bruthaire brú** pressure cooker, **brú fola** blood pressure, **brú tráchta** traffic congestion, **tá siad faoi bhrú** they are under pressure, **brúchnaipe** push-button 3. bruise

bruach *m1* brink, edge **ar bhruach na habhann** on the riverbank, **an Bruach Thiar** the West Bank

bruachbhaile *m4* suburb

bruachsholas *m1* footlight

brúchnaipe *m4* push-button **meicníocht brúchnaipe** push-button mechanism, **rialú brúchnaipe** push-button control

brúcht *m3* 1. eruption, burst 2. belch *v* 1. erupt, burst 2. belch

brúchtadh *m* eruption **brúchtadh bolcánach** volcanic eruption

brúghrúpa *m4* pressure group

brúidiúil *adj* brutal, beastly

brúidiúlacht *f3* brutality, brutishness

brúigh *v* 1. press **brúigh an cnaipe** press the button 2. bruise **brúdh go dona é** he was badly bruised 3. crush, squash **bhrúigh sé mo mhéar** it crushed my finger 4. push **gluaisteán a bhrú** to push a car

bruíon *f2* 1. quarrel **ag lorg bruíne** looking for trouble 2. fairy dwelling **Bóthar na Bruíne** 'the road of the fairy dwelling', Boharnabreena

bruíonach *adj* quarrelsome

bruite *adj* boiled **glasraí bruite** boiled vegetables

brúite *adj* pressed, crushed, **prátaí brúite** mashed potatoes

bruith *v* 1. boil 2. burn 3. bake

brúitín *m4* mashed potatoes

bruitíneach *f2* measles **bruitíneach ghréine** freckles

brúlasc *f2* pressure switch

brúmhéadar *m1* pressure gauge

bruscar *m1* fragments, litter

brústocaireacht *f3* lobbying **brústocaireacht a dhéanamh** to lobby

bruth *m3* 1. heat 2. rash **bruth bruitíní** measles rash, **bruth rua** rust (*wheat, plants*), **bruth farraige** surf

bruthaire *m4* cooker **bruthaire brú** pressure cooker

bú *m4* hyacinth (*plant*)

bua *m4* 1. triumph, victory **bua a fháil ar dhuine** to triumph over somebody, **beir bua (agus beannacht)!** best wishes! 2. virtue **is mór an bua duit é sin** that is a great advantage for you 3. talent **tá bua na cainte acu** they have the gift of the gab

buabhall *m1* 1. bugle 2. buffalo **buabhall uisce** water buffalo

buacach *adj* 1. lofty 2. buoyant **táim go buacach** I'm in fine form

buacaire *m4* cock, tap **buacaire uisce** water cock

buach *adj* victorious **cath buach** victorious battle

buachaill *m3* boy, boyfriend **buachaillí bó** cowboys

buaf *f2* toad

buaic *f2* climax **buaic-am féachana** peak viewing-time

buaicphointe *m4* climax, highest point **buaicphointí an chluiche** highlights of the game

buaicuair *f2* peak-hour **trácht buaicuaire** peak-hour traffic

buaigh *v* 1. win **cé a bhuaigh?** who won? 2. **buaigh ar** defeat **níor**

bhuaigh sibh orainn fós you haven't beaten us yet

buail *v* 1. strike, hit **bhuail sé a cheann ina choinne** he struck his head against it 2. beat, defeat **buaileadh Corcaigh** Cork were beaten 3. strike repeatedly **ag bualadh arbhair** threshing corn, **ag bualadh sciathán** flapping wings 4. **buail le** meet, **buailim léi go minic** I meet her often 5. **buail isteach** drop in, **ní bhuaileann sé isteach chugam a thuilleadh** he doesn't drop into me any-more 6. mint (*money*)

buaile *f4* milking-place **ní raibh an dara suí sa bhuaile agam** I had no alternative

buaileam *m4* **buaileam sciath** ostentation, self-praise

buailte *adj* beaten

buailteoir *m3* beater, thresher **buailteoir painéil** panel-beater

buaine *f4* permanence **níl aon bhuaine ann** it's not permanent

buair *v* worry, distress **ná buair thú féin leis** don't trouble yourself with it

buaircín *m4* 1. toggle-pin 2. cone (*botany*)

buairt *f3* sorrow, worry **cén bhuairt atá air?** what ails him? **níl aon chúis bhuartha agat** you have no reason to worry

buaiteoir *m3* winner, victor

bualadh *m* striking, beating **bualadh bos** applause, clapping of hands, **buailtí croí** palpitations

bualtrach *f2* cow dung **bualtrach bó** cow dung, **ciaróg bhualtraí** scavenger-beetle

buama *m4* bomb **aerbhuama** air bomb, **buama eithneach** nuclear bomb, **buama loisceach** incendiary bomb, **buama moirtéara** mortar bomb, **buama tréanphléascach** high-explosive bomb

buamadhíonach *adj* bomb-proof

buamadóir *m3* bomber **buamadóir fadraoin** long-range bomber, **buamadóir scuibe** dive-bomber, **buamadóir troda** fighter-bomber

buamáil *v* bomb *f3* bombing **buamáil ard** high-level bombing, **buamáil íseal** low-level bombing

buan *adj* lasting, permanent **grá buan** enduring love, **rith buan** diarrhoea, **más buan mo chuimhne** if my memory serves me right

buan-[2] *prefix* lasting, permanent **buanuimhir** constant number

buanaí *m4* reaper

buanaigh *v* prolong, preserve **traidisiún a bhuanú** to preserve a tradition

buanfas *m1* durability

buanfasach *adj* durable

buannaíocht *f3* presumption, boldness

buanordú *m* standing order **buanordú bainc** bank standing order

buanseasmhach *adj* steadfast

buanseasmhacht *f3* perseverance

buantonn *f2* perm **buantonn a chur i do chuid gruaige** to put a perm in your hair

buartha *adj* troubled, worried **tá mé buartha** I'm sorry

buatais *f2* boot

búcla *m4* buckle

búcláil *v* buckle

Búda *m1* Buddha

Búdachas *m1* Buddhism

Búdaí *m4* Buddhist

Búdaíoch *adj* Buddhist

budragár *m1* budgerigar

buí[1] *adj, m4* yellow **Fear Buí** Orangeman

buí[2] *f4* thankfulness **a bhuí le Dia** thank God

buicéad *m1* bucket

buidéal *m1* bottle

buidéalaigh *v* bottle

buígh *v* tan **bhuígh an ghrian iad** the sun tanned them

buile *f4* madness **tá sé ar buile** he is furious, **galar na bó buile** mad cow disease, BSE

builín *m4* loaf

builitín *m4* bulletin

buille *m4* blow, stroke **tharraing sé buille orm** he threw a blow at me, **tabhair buille faoi thuairim** take a guess, **ar bhuille a haon** at one o'clock; on the stroke of one

buillean *m1* bullion

buime *f4* nurse

buinneach *f2* diarrhoea **go gcuire sé buinneach ort!** that it may give you diarrhoea (*curse*)

buinneán[1] *m1* 1. sapling 2. shoot (*of plant*)

buinneán[2] *m1* bunion

buíocán *m1* 1. yolk of egg 2. primrose

buíoch *adj* thankful, grateful **táim anbhuíoch díot as** I'm very grateful to you for it

buíochán *m1* jaundice **tá na buíocháin air** he has jaundice

buíochas *m1* thanks, gratitiude **ghabh sé buíochas liom** he expressed thanks to me, **buíochas le Dia!** thanks be to God!

buíon *f2* band, group **buíon cheoil** band (of musicians), **buíon fear** group of men

búir *f2, v* roar, bellow

búireach *f2* roaring, bellowing

buirg *f2* borough

buirgléir *m3* burglar

buirgléireacht *f3* burglary

búiríl *f3* bellowing

búisceáil *f3* 1. squelching (noise of water under foot) 2. noise of boat rocking on water

buiséad *m1* budget **buiséad reatha** current budget, **rialú buiséid** budgetary control

buiséadach *adj* budgetary

buiséadaigh *v* budget

buiséadú *m* budgeting

búiste *m4* 1. poultice 2. stuffing (*for chicken, turkey, etc*)

búistéir *m3* butcher **siopa búistéara** butcher's shop

buitléir *m3* butler

bulaí *m4* 1. **bulaí fir!** good man yourself! well done! 2. bully

bulc *m1* bulk

Bulgáir *f2* **an Bhulgáir** Bulgaria

Bulgáiris *f2* Bulgarian (*language*)

Bulgárach *adj, m1* Bulgarian

bulla[1] *m4* buoy **bulla feistithe** mooring-buoy

bulla[2] *m4* 1. bull (*papal*) 2. bull's eye

bullán *m1* bullock

bultúr *m1* vulture **bultúr ceannann** white-headed vulture

bumbóg *f2* bumblebee

bun[1] *m1* 1. base, bottom **bun an tsléibhe** the bottom of the mountain, **an é sin bun agus barr do scéil?** is that the whole of your story? 2. end **bun na leapa** the foot of the bed 3. (with *preps*) **rud a chur ar bun** to set up something, **faoi bhun** beneath, **i mbun** engaged in

bun-[2] *prefix* basic **bundath** primary colour

bunábhar *m1* 1. raw material 2. main outlines (*of literary text*) 3. rushes (*cinematography*)

bunachar *m1* foundation, base **bunachar sonraí** data-base

bunadh *m1* 1. stock **do bhunadh féin** your own kind 2. origin **de bhunadh Éireannach í sin** she is of Irish origin 3. gen as *adj* original, fundamental **an scéal bunaidh** the original story

bunaigh *v* found, establish **comhlacht a bhunú** to set up a company

bunaíoch *adj* primitive

bunaíocht *f3* establishment

bunáit *f2* base **bunáit chabhlaigh** naval base

bunáite *f4* majority **bunáite an phobail** the majority of the community

bunaitheoir *m3* founder

bunchóip *f2* original (*document*)

bunchúis *f2* 1. root cause 2. motive **bunchúis an dúnmharaithe** the motive for the murder

bundath *m3* primary colour **na bundathanna** the primary colours

bundúchasach *adj* aboriginal *m1* aborigine

bundún *m1* backside

buneolas *m1* elementary knowledge

bungaló *m4* bungalow **bungaló trí sheomra** three-bedroomed bungalow

bunóc *f2* infant

bunoideachas *m1* primary education

bunoscionn *adj* 1. upside-down 2. **bunoscionn le** contrary to

bunreacht *m3* constitution **Bunreacht na hÉireann** the Constitution of Ireland

bunreachtúil *adj* constitutional **cearta bunreachtúla** constitutional rights

bunscoil *f2* primary school

bunsmaoineamh *m1* original idea, main idea

buntáiste *m4* advantage

buntáisteach *adj* advantageous

buntús *m1* rudiments

bunú *m* foundation **bunú an stáit** the foundation of the state

bunúdar *m1* 1. root cause 2. primary authority

bunús *m1* 1. foundation 2. origin **Albanach ó bhunús** a Scotsman/ Scotswoman by origin 3. majority **tá bunús an airgid caite** most of the money is spent 4. basis **scéal gan bhunús** a story with no basis to it

bunúsach[1] *adj* basic, fundamental

bunúsach[2] *m1* fundamentalist (*in beliefs*)

burdach *adj* gossiping

burdún *m1* 1. gossip, tale 2. verse

burla *m4* bundle **burla airgid** bundle of money

burláil *v* bundle

bus *m4* bus **busanna friothála** feeder buses

busáras *m1* bus station

buta *m1* butt **buta féasóige** stubble, short beard

C

cá *interrogative adj, pron, adv* how, what, where **cá haois í?** what age is she? **cá fhad?** how long? **cá mhinice a thagann siad?** how often do they come? **cá mhéad a bhí air?** how much did it cost? **cá bhfuil tú?** where are you? **cá huair a tharla sé?** when did it happen?

cárb as di? where does she come from?

cab *m4* mouth, snout, muzzle

cába *m4* 1. collar 2. cape

cabaire *m4* chatterbox

cabaireacht *f3* chatting, chatter

cabáiste *m4* cabbage

cábán *m1* cabin

cabanta *adj* loquacious

cabhail *f5* body, trunk, hull or hold (*of ship*), body (*of garment*)

cabhair *f5* help **bean chabhrach** midwife

Cabhán *m1* **an Cabhán** Cavan

cabhlach *m1* navy, fleet (*of ships*) **cabhlach iascaigh** fishing fleet

cabhraigh *v* help, assist **níor chabhraigh aon duine leis** nobody helped him

cabhsa *m4* 1. causeway 2. lane, path

cábla *m4* cable **cábla cumhachta** power cable

cábóg *f2* ignoramus, clown, clodhopper

cábógach *adj* clownish, uncouth

cac *m3* excrement **cac asail, bó, caorach** donkey, cow, sheep, dung *v* excrete **faoi mar a chacfadh an t-asal é** as the donkey would excrete it (perfect!)

cáca *m4* cake

cacamas *m1* worthless thing **cacamas cainte** nonsense

cácas *m4* caucus

cách *m4* everyone

cachtas *m1* cactus

cad *interrogative pron* 1. what **cad chuige?** what for? why? **cad eile?** what else? 2. how **cad é mar tá tú?** how are you?

cadás *m1* cotton

cadhnaíocht *f3* **ar thús cadhnaíochta** leading the gang

cadhnra *m4* battery

cadóg *f2* haddock

cadráil *f3* chatter, gossip

cadránta *adj* obstinate, stubborn

cág *m1* jackdaw

caibheár *m1* caviar

caibidil *f2* 1. chapter 2. discussion, **cad tá faoi chaibidil?** what's being debated? what's under discussion?

caibinéad *m1* cabinet

caid *f2* 1. football 2. game of football

caidéal *m1* pump **caidéal rothair** bicycle pump

caidéalaigh *v* pump

caidéis *f2* inquisitiveness

caidéiseach *adj* inquisitive

cáidheach *adj* dirty, messy

caidhp *f2* cap, bonnet **caidhp an bháis** kibosh

caidhséar *m1* cutting, channel, gullet

caidreamh *m1* association, intercourse **Oifigeach Caidrimh Phoiblí (OCP)** Public Relations Officer (PRO)

caife *m4* 1. coffee 2. café

caiféin *f2* caffeine

caifirín *m4* head-scarf, cap worn by cook

caifitéire *m4* cafeteria

caighdeán *m1* 1. standard **an Caighdeán Oifigiúil** the Official Standard (*grammar, spelling*) 2. guage

caighdeánach *adj* standard

caighdeánaigh *v* standardise

cáil *f2* fame, quality, reputation **tá cáil an airgid orthu** they are reputed to be wealthy

cailc *f2* chalk

cailciam *m4* calcium

cáiligh *v* qualify

cailín *m4* girl, girlfriend **cailín aimsire** servant girl, **cailín báire** tomboy

cáilíocht *f3* 1. qualification **tá cáilíochtaí áirithe riachtanach** certain qualifications are necessary 2. quality

Cailíopsó *m4* Calypso

cailís *f2* chalice **cailís Ardach** the Ardagh chalice

cáilithe *adj* qualified

cáiliúil *adj* famous

caill *f2* 1. loss 2. níl caill air he/it is not bad *v* 1. lose chaill sí amharc na súl she lost her eyesight 2. miss chaill mé an cluiche dá bharr I missed the game because of it 3. die cailleadh go tobann é he died suddenly

caille *f4* veil

Caille, Lá Caille New Year's Day

cailleach *f2* hag cailleach feasa wise woman, fortune teller

cailleadh *m* loss cailleadh sú bleeding (*of trees*)

cailliúnaí *m4* loser

caillte *adj* lost, perished

caillteanas *m1* loss caillteanas iomlán total loss

caimiléir *m3* crook, cheat

caimiléireacht *f3* crookedness, dishonesty

caimín *m4* crook (*of shepherd*)

cáin *f5* 1. tax Cáin Bhreisluacha (CBL) Value Added Tax (VAT), liúntas saor ó cháin tax-free allowance 2. fine culreadh cain fiche punt orm I was fined twenty pounds *v* 1. fine 2. condemn, criticise bíonn siad de shíor á cháineadh they are always criticising him

cáinaisnéis *f2* budget, budgetary statement

cáineadh *m* condemnation

cainéal *m1* 1. channel 2. cinnamon

caingean *f2* 1. dispute 2. plea

cainneann *f2* leek

cainníocht *f3* quantity

caint *f2* talk, speech fear mór cainte a great man for talking

cainteach *adj* talkative

cáinteach *adj* fault-finding

cainteoir *m3* speaker, talker cainteoir breá a fine speaker, cainteoir dúchais native speaker

cáinteoir *m3* fault-finder

caintic *f2* canticle

cáipéis *f2* document mála cáipéisí brief-case

cáipéiseach *adj* documentary

caipín *m4* cap caipín sonais caul, caipín súile eyelid

caipiteal *m1* capital (*money*) caipiteal oibre working capital

caipĺtleachas *m1* capitalism

caipitlí *m4* capitalist

cairde *m4* 1. respite gan chairde at short notice, without respite 2. credit ar cairde on credit

cairdeagan *m1* cardigan

cairdeas *m1* friendship

cairdiach *adj* cardiac stad cairdiach cardiac arrest

cairdín *m4* accordion cairdín cnaipe button-accordion

cairdinéal *m1* cardinal

cairdíneoir *m3* accordionist

cairdiúil *adj* friendly

cairéad *m1* carrot

cairéal *m1* quarry (*stone*)

cáiréis *f2* carefulness

cáiréiseach *adj* careful

cairt[1] *f2* 1. cart 2. car

cairt[2] *f2* chart na cairteacha the charts (*music*)

cairtchlár *m1* cardboard

cairtfhostaigh *v* charter (*plane etc*) eitilt chairtfhostaithe chartered flight

cairtín *m4* go-kart

cáis *f2* cheese

Cáisc *f3* Easter Seachtain na Cásca Easter Week, Domhnach, Luan Cásca Easter Sunday, Monday, Éirí Amach na Cásca the Easter Rising

caiscín *m4* 1. wholemeal 2. brown bread

caiséad *m1* cassette

caiseal *m1* 1. stone fort 2. spinning-top

caisealta *adj* fortified, walled

caisearbhán *m1* dandelion

caisleán *m1* castle

caismír *f2* cashmere

caismirt *f2* 1. commotion 2. conflict

caite *adj* worn, spent, past, consumed **briste caite** worn-out trousers, **éadach caite** worn clothes, **seanchapall caite** spent old horse, **an mhí seo caite** last month, **tá an bia caite** the food is gone/consumed

caiteachas *m1* expenditure **caiteachas poiblí** public expenditure

caiteoir *m3* 1. spender **caiteoir airgid** money-spender 2. consumer **caiteoir dí** drinker 3. wearer

caith[1] *v* 1. spend **bíonn siad de shíor ag caitheamh airgid** they are always spending money 2. throw, fire **chaith mé amach é** I threw it/him out, **caitheadh urchair leo** shots were fired at them 3. consume **tá an bia caite** the food has been consumed, **an gcaitheann tú (tobac)?** do you smoke? 4. wear **culaith a chaitheamh** to wear a suit 5. **caith le** treat, **caitheann siad go maith liom** they treat me well

caith[2] *v* (*denoting necessity, obligation*) **caithfidh mé fágáil** I have to leave, **caithfear an obair a dhéanamh** the work has to be done

cáith *f2* chaff

cáitheadh *m* spray (*sea*) **cáitheadh sneachta** whirling snow

caitheamh *m1* 1. spending, using 2. wearing **briste gan chaitheamh** unused trousers 3. throwing **caitheamh na teisce** discus throwing 4. consuming, smoking **caitheamh gan toil** passive smoking

caithis *f2* 1. affection 2. attraction, charm

caithiseach *adj* 1. lovely, of good appearance 2. delicious

cáithne *m4* scrap, particle

cáithnín *m4* scrap, particle **cáithnín sneachta** hailstone, **bhí sé ag déanamh cáithnín dom** it was disturbing me

caithreachas *m1* puberty

caithréim *f2* triumph, fame

caithréimeach *adj* triumphant

Caitliceach *adj*, *m1* Catholic **an Eaglais Chaitliceach** the Catholic Church

Caitliceachas *m1* Catholicism

cál *m1* cabbage

caladh *m1* 1. port, harbour 2. landing-place, quay

calafort *m1* port, harbour

calaois *f2* 1. deceit, treachery, fraud **calaois a dhéanamh ar dhuine** to defraud someone 2. foul (*sport*)

calaoiseach *adj* deceitful, fraudulent

call *m4* 1. need, want **tá call agam leis** I am in need of it, **níl aon chall leis sin** there is no need for that 2. claim, right **níl call agam chuige** I have no claim to it

callaí *pl* wrappings, finery

callaire *m4* loudspeaker, speaker

callaistéinic *f2* calisthenics

callán *m1* noise, clamour, uproar **ag tógáil calláin** creating a disturbance

callánach *adj* noisy

calm *m1* calm, calms

calma *adj* brave, valiant

calmacht *f3* bravery

calóg *f2* flake **calóga arbhair** cornflakes

calra *m4* calorie

cálslá *m4* coleslaw

cam *adj* 1. bent, crooked 2. dishonest 3. distorted

camall *m1* camel

camán[1] *m1* 1. hurling stick **ní hé sin atá idir chamáin againn** that is not what we are discussing 2. quaver (*music*) **luachanna camáin** quaver values

camán[2] *m1* **camán meall, camán míonla** camomile

camas *m1* 1. cove 2. bend (*in river*)

camastaíl *f3* crooked dealing; dishonesty, fraud

cambheartaí *m4* racketeer

cambheartaíocht *f3* racketeering

camchosach *adj* bandy-legged

camhaoir *f2* twilight, day-break (*poetical*)

camóg *f2* 1. camogie stick 2. comma

camógaíocht *f3* camogie

campa *m4* camp **campa géibhinn** internment camp, **campa traenála** training camp

campáil *f3* camping **ionad campála, láithreán rampála** campsite *v* ramp

campálaí *m4* camper

camras *m1* sewage **díuscairt camrais** sewage disposal

can *v* 1. sing 2. speak **can leat** speak on

cána *m4* cane **cána siúcra** sugarcane

cánachas *m1* taxation **cánachas gluaisteán** motor taxation

canáil *f3* canal

canáraí *m4* canary

canbhás *m1* canvas

canbhasáil *f3* canvassing **ag canbhasáil ar son...** canvassing for...

canbhasálaí *m4* canvasser

cancrán *m1* ill-tempered person, crank

cangarú *m4* kangaroo

canna *m4* can **canna stáin** tin can, **tá sé (ag dul) ar na cannaí** he is (getting) drunk

cannabas *m1* cannabis

cannaigh *v* can

canóin *f3* canon **bia canóna** cannon fodder, **lámhach canóna** cannon fire

canónach *m1* canon (*clergy*)

canta[1] *m4* chunk **canta aráin** chunk of bread

canta[2] *adj* neat, pretty **cailín beag canta** pretty little girl

cantaireacht *f3* chanting

cantalach *adj* cranky, petulant

canú *m4* canoe

canúint *f3* 1. dialect **canúint na Mumhan, canúint Uladh, canúint Chonnacht,** the Munster, Ulster, Connaught dialects 2. accent

caoch *adj* 1. blind 2. blank **cartús caoch** blank cartridge *m1* blind creature, person *v* 1. blind, dazzle 2. wink **chaoch sé súil orm** he winked at me

caochadh *m* wink, winking

caochán *m1* 1. blind person, animal 2. mole (*animal*)

caochóg *f2* 1. blind person, animal 2. cubby-hole

caochspota *m4* blind spot

caoga *m* fifty

caogadú[1] *m4* fiftieth

caogadú[2] *adj* fiftieth **tháinig siad sa chaogadú háit,** they came in fiftieth position

caoi *f4* 1. way, manner **sin é an chaoi!** that's the way! **ar chaoi éigin** in some way, somehow 2. opportunity **caoi a fháil ar rud a dhéanamh** to find a way of doing something 3. condition **níl caoi mhaith orthu** they aren't in a good way, well off, **cén chaoi a**

bhfuil tú? how are you? **caoi a
chur ar rud** to repair something

caoin *adj* 1. smooth 2. gentle, mild,
refined *v* 1. lament 2. weep, cry
ag caoineadh crying

caoineadh *m* 1. weeping **glór
caointe** whimpering voice
2. lament **Caoineadh Airt Uí
Laoghaire** the Lament of Art
O'Leary 3. elegy

caointeach *adj* mournful, plaintive

caoireoil *f3* mutton **píóg caoireola**
mutton pie

caoithiúil *adj* opportune, convenient

caoithiúlacht *f3* opportuneness,
convenience

caol *adj* 1. narrow 2. thin, slender
m1 1. slender part **caol na coise,
an droma, na láimhe, na sróine**
ankle, small of the back, wrist,
bridge of the nose, **cuireadh
ceangal na gcúig gcaol uirthi** she
was bound hand and foot
2. narrow water

caolaigeanta *adj* narrow-minded

caolaigh *v* 1. narrow **caolaíonn sé
ag an mbarr** it narrows at the top
2. make/become thin 3. dilute **ag
caolú péinte** diluting paint
4. palatilise (*linguistics*)

caolas *m1* 1. strait **Caolas
Ghiobráltar** the Strait of Gibraltar
2. bottle-neck

caolchúiseach *adj* subtle

caolsráid *f2* alley

caomh *adj* gentle, noble

caomhnaigh *v* protect, guard,
conserve, preserve

caomhnóir *m3* 1. protector,
guardian 2. patron

caomhnú *m* protection, conservation

caonach *m1* moss **ní thagann
caonach ar chloch reatha** a
rolling stone gathers no moss

caor *f2* 1. berry **caor fíniúna** grape
2. glowing object **caor thine** fire-
ball, thunderbolt

caora *f* sheep **ag bearradh caorach**
shearing sheep, **bearradh
caorach** cirrus cloud

caorán *m1* 1. small piece of turf
2. bog

capall *m1* horse **capall céachta, rása**
plough-horse, racehorse, **capall na
hoibre an bia** one cannot work
without food

capsúl *m1* capsule

captaen *m1* captain

cár *m1* 1. grin, grimace **chuir sí cár
uirthi liom** she grinned at me
2. set of teeth

cara *m* friend **cara cleite / cara
pinn** pen-friend, **cara (as) Críost**
godparent, **A Chara** Dear
Sir/Madam, **Cairde na Cruinne**
Friends of the Earth

caracatúr *m1* caricature

carachtar *m1* character

caramal *m1* caramel

carat *m1* carat

carbad *m1* chariot

carbaihiodráit *f2* carbohydrate

carball *m1* palate

carbán *m1* carp

carbhán *m1* caravan **láithreán
carbhán** caravan site

carbhánlann *f2* caravanserai

carbhat *m1* cravat, tie

carbón *m1* carbon

carbradóir *m3* carburettor

carcair *f5* prison, jail

carghas *m1* 1. Lent **ag déanamh an
Charghais ar rud** abstaining from
something for Lent 2. self-denial
is carghas liom... I regret...

carn *m1* 1. heap, pile **carn aoiligh**
dunghill 2. cairn **carn cúirte**
horned cairn *v* heap (up), pile **ag
carnadh airgid** making loads of
money

carnabhal *m1* carnival

carnán *m1* small heap

carr *m1* car **carr sleamhnáin** sledge

carrach *adj* 1. rough-skinned, scabby 2. rocky

carraig *f2* rock

carráiste *m4* carriage

carrchlós *m1* car park **carrchlós ilstórach** multi-storeyed carpark

carria *m4* stag

carróstlann *f2* motel

cársánach *adj* wheezy

cársánacht *f3* wheeziness

cart *v* clear away **sneachta a chartadh** to clear away snow

cárt *m1* quart

cárta *m4* card **cártaí a imirt** to play cards, **cárta poist** postcard, **cárta aitheantais, ballraíochta, creidmheasa, muirir** identity, membership, credit, charge card

cartán *m1* carton **cartán bainne** carton of milk

carthanach *adj* charitable, kind

carthanacht *f3* charity

cartlann *f2* archives

cartlannaí *m4* archivist

cartún *m2* cartoon

cartús *m1* cartridge, cartouche **cartús caoch** blank cartridge

carúl *m1* carol

cas *v* 1. twist **chas sé a mhurnán** he twisted his ankle 2. turn **cas timpeall** turn around, **ar chas an taoide fós?** has the tide turned yet? 3. wind **uaireadóir a chasadh** to wind a watch 4. sing **amhrán a chasadh** to sing a song 5. **cas ar / le** meet

cás[1] *m1* 1. case, suite-case **cás cúirte** court case, **cuir i gcás** suppose 2. concern **níl cás ná náire orthu** they are quite unashamed

cás[2] *m1* 1. frame 2. cage

casacht *f3* cough

casachtach *f2* coughing **tá casachtach orm** I have a cough

casadh *m1* twist, turn **casadh súl** glance, **cuir ar casadh é** set it spinning

casaoid *f2* complaint, grievance **gnás casaoide** grievance procedure

casaoideach *adj* complaining

casaról *m1* casserole

caschlár *m1* turntable

casla *f4* small harbour

cásmhar *adj* 1. concerned 2. sympathetic

casóg *f2* coat, jacket

casta *adj* 1. twisted 2. complicated, intricate

castacht *f3* complexity, intricacy

castaire *m4* spanner **castaire incheartaithe** adjustable spanner

castán *m1* chestnut (*edible*)

casúr *m1* hammer

cat *m1* cat **ar mhaithe leis féin a dhéanann an cat crónán** a cat purrs for its own benefit

catach *adj* 1. curly(-haired) 2. twisted (*limb*) 3. dog-eared (*page*)

catalaíoch *adj* catalytic **tiontaire catalaíoch** catalytic converter *m1* catalyst

catalóg *f2* catalogue

catamarán *m1* catamaran

cath *m3* battle **láthair an chatha** the battle field, **Cath na Bóinne** the Battle of the Boyne

cathain *interrogative adv* when **cathain a bheidh siad anseo?** when will they be here? **cathain a fuair tú an léine sin?** when did you get that shirt?

cathair *f5* city **cathair Chorcaí** Cork city, **muintir na cathrach** the city people, **cathair ghríobháin** labyrinth

cathaoir *f5* 1. chair **cathaoir rothaí** wheelchair 2. throne **cathaoir ríoga** royal seat, throne

cathaoirleach *m1* chairperson

cathartha *adj* civic, civil **cogadh cathartha** civil war

cathéide *f4* 1. armour 2. battledress

cathlong *f2* battleship

cathróir *m3* citizen

cathróireacht *f3* citizenship

cathú *m4* 1. regret, sorrow **cathú a bheith ort faoi…** to be sorry about… 2. temptation **bhí an-chathú orm é a dhéanamh** I was very tempted to do it

cé¹ *interrogative pron* 1. who, whom **cé thú féin?** who are you? 2. what **cén t-am é?** what time is it? 3. which **cé acu is fearr leat?** which do you prefer? 4. **cé acu…nó…** whether…or… 5. **cé chomh fada a bhí an rang?** how long was the class?

cé² *conj* 1. although **cé gur/nach féidir liom é a dhéanamh** although I can/can't do it 2. **cé is moite (de)** except (for)

cé³ *f4* quay **an Ché Adhmaid** Wood Quay

ceacht *m3* lesson

céachta *m4* plough

ceachtar *pron* either, neither (*negative*) **ní raibh ceachtar acu ann** neither of them were there

cead *m3* 1. leave, permission **i gcead duit** with due respect to you 2. pass, permit **cead taistil** permit to travel

céad¹ *m1* 1. hundred **fuair mé céad punt uaithi** I got £100 from her, **bhí na céadta acu ann** there were hundreds of them there 2. century **an seachtú céad déag** the 17th century, **an fichiú céad** the 20th century, **go maire tú an céad** may you live to be 100

céad² *adj* 1. first **an chéad chluiche** the first game, **an chéad duine** the first person, **ainm an chéad fhir** the name of the first man,

muintir na chéad bhliana first years, the people of (the) first year, **na chéad daoine** the first people, **na chéad ghunnaí** the first guns 2. (with **eile**) next **an chéad uair eile** the next time

céad-³ *prefix* first **céadleifteanant** first lieutenant

ceadaigh *v* 1. allow, permit **cheadaigh siad dom é a dhéanamh** they allowed me to do it 2. consult **rud a cheadú le duine** to consult somebody about something

ceadaithe *adj* permitted, permissible

ceadaitheach *adj* permissive

ceadal *m1* recital (*music*) **clár ceadail** recital programme

Céadaoin *f4* Wednesday **Dé Céadaoin** (on) Wednesday, **Céadaoin an Bhraith** Spy Wednesday, **Céadaoin an Luaithrigh** Ash Wednesday

céadar *m1* 1. cheddar (*cheese*) 2. cedar

céadchabhair *f5* first aid **cóireáil chéadchabhrach** first aid treatment

céadchosach *m1* centipede **céadchosach cré** earth lover

céadfa *m4* 1. (bodily) sense **na cúig céadfaí** the five senses, **tá a chiall is a chéadfaí caillte aige** he has lost, has taken leave of, his senses 2. perception

céadfach *adj* 1. sensory 2. perceptive

ceadmhach *adj* permissible

céadú *adj* hundredth **an céadú teach** the hundredth house, **an céadú hurlár** the hundredth floor

ceadúnaigh *v* license

ceadúnaithe *adj* licensed

ceadúnas *m1* licence **ceadúnas tiomána** driving licence

ceaintín *m4* canteen

ceal *m4* 1. lack, want **ceal bia** lack of food, **de cheal eolais** for want of knowledge 2. extinction **rud a chur ar ceal** to abolish, cancel, something, **chuaigh siad ar ceal ón áit** they disappeared from the place

cealaigh *v* 1. cancel 2. do away with, remove

cealg *f2* sting, deceit, treachery *v* 1. sting, deceive, allure 2. lull to sleep

cealgach *adj* 1. treacherous 2. alluring

ceallach *adj* celled, cellular

ceallafán *m1* cellophane

cealú *m* cancellation

ceamara *m4* camera **cleachtadh ceamara** camera rehearsal

ceamthaifeadán *m1* camcorder

Ceanada *m4* Canada

Ceanadach *adj, m1* Canadian

ceangail *v* bind, tie **rud a cheangal de rud eile** to tie something to something else

ceangailte *adj* tied, bound, stuck fast

ceangal *m1* 1. binding, tie, connection, link **ceangal leabhair** binding of a book, **ní léir dom aon cheangal eatarthu** I don't see any connection/link between them 2. obligation **ceangal cairdis** bond of friendship

ceann[1] *m1* 1. head, roof **tinneas cinn** headache, **ceann comhairle** speaker, chairperson of Dáil Éireann, **ceann foirne** chief of staff, **ceann roinne** head of department, **ceann a chur ar theach** to roof a house, **teach ceann tuí** thatched house, **dul chun cinn** advance, progress 2. end, extremity **ceann cúrsa, ceann scríbe, a bhaint amach** to reach journey's end, **ag craoladh ó cheann ceann na tíre** broadcasting all around the country (i.e. from one end to the other), **Oíche Chinn Bhliana** New Year's Eve 3. one **ceann amháin,**

aon cheann amháin one, **dhá cheann** two (*of something*), **trí, ceithre, cúig, sé cinn** three, four, five, six (*of something*), **seacht, ocht, naoi, deich gcinn** seven, eight, nine, ten (*of something*), **ceann acu** one of them, **dhá phunt an ceann** £2 each, **ceann ar cheann** one by one

faoi cheann by, at the end of **faoi cheann bliana** after a year

dár gcionn ahead **an lá dár gcionn** the following day

go ceann 1. to the top/end of 2. for the duration of **go ceann seachtaine, tamaill eile** for another week, while

i gceann 1. at the end of **i gceann míosa** in a month's time 2. attending to **i gceann gnóthaí** attending business

os cionn 1. above **os cionn na dtithe** above the houses 2. more than **bhí os cionn míle duine ann** there was more than 1,000 people there 3. beyond

thar ceann on behalf of **ag labhairt thar ceann an chúisí** speaking on behalf of the accused

thar cionn excellent **bhí an cheolchoirm thar cionn** the concert was excellent

ceann-[2] *prefix* chief, main

céanna *adj* same **bhí tú ann an oíche chéanna** you were there the same night, **san am céanna** at the same time, nevertheless

ceannach *m1* purchase **ceannach earraí** the purchase of goods

ceannachán *m1* purchased item

ceannadhairt *f2* pillow

ceannaghaidh *f2* face **tá na ceannaithe céanna acu** they have the same features

ceannaí *m4* merchant **ceannaí onnmhairíochta** export merchant

ceannaigh *v* buy, purchase **earraí a cheannach** to purchase goods

ceannairc *f2* revolt, mutiny

ceannairceach *adj* rebellious, mutinous *m1* rebel

ceannaire *m4* leader

ceannaitheoir *m3* buyer, purchaser

ceannann *adj* **ceannann céanna** selfsame, **an bhean cheannann chéanna** the very same woman

ceannáras *m1* headquarters

ceannas *m1* 1. command, authority **dul i gceannas** to assume authority, **oifigeach ceannais** commanding officer, **post ceannais** command post 2. sovereignty

ceannasach *adj* 1. commanding 2. ruling 3. dominant (*music*)

ceannasaí *m4* 1. commander **an tArdcheannasaí** the Commander-in-Chief 2. controller

ceannasaíocht *f3* leadership, command **Ceannasaíocht an Deiscirt** the Southern Command

ceannbheart *m1* head-dress, headgear

ceannbhrat *m1* canopy

ceannchathair *f5* capital city, metropolis

ceanncheathrú *f5* headquarters **Ceanncheathrú an Airm** Army Headquaters

ceanndána *adj* headstrong, obstinate

ceannfort *m1* 1. commander 2. superintendent (*an Garda Síochána*) 3. commandant **céim cheannfoirt** the rank of commandant

ceannliath *adj* grey-haired

ceannlíne *f4* headline **ceannlínte na nuachta** news headlines

ceannlitir *f5* capital letter

ceannródaí *m4* 1. leader 2. pioneer

ceannteideal *m1* heading

ceanntréan *adj* headstrong, obstinate

ceansa *adj* gentle, meek, tame

ceansaigh *v* tame

ceant *m4* auction **cuireadh an teach ar ceant** the house was auctioned

ceantáil *f3* auction, auctioning *v* auction

ceantar *m1* district **ceantar faire** neighbourhood watch area

ceanúil *adj* loving, fond **tá sí ceanúil air** she is fond of him

ceap[1] *m1* 1. block, pad, stock (*of gun, tree, etc*) **ceap búistéara** chopping-block, **ceap oifigí** office block, **ceap tithe** block of houses, **ceap lainseála** launching pad 2. butt (*of joke, blame, etc*) **ceap magaidh a dhéanamh de dhuine** to make a laughing-stock of somebody, **ceap milleáin** scapegoat

ceap[2] *v* 1. think **cad a cheapann tú faoi sin?** what do you think about that? 2. appoint **ceapadh ina bainisteoir í** she was appointed as manager 3. compose, invent **ceol a cheapadh** to compose music, **ní mise a chum ná a cheap** it's not me who invented it 4. catch **an chaid a cheapadh** to catch the football

ceapach *f2* 1. bed **ceapach bláthanna** flowerbed 2. plot (*of land*)

ceapachán *m1* 1. appointment (*to position*) 2. (artistic) composition

ceapadh *m* 1. appointment **ceapadh rúnaí** appointment of a secretary 2. thought **ní raibh aon cheapadh agam go dtarlódh sé** I never thought it would happen

ceapaire *m4* sandwich **ceapaire bagúin, leitíse agus tráta** bacon, lettuce and tomato sandwich

cearc *f2* 1. hen **cearc fhrancach** turkey 2. **cearc cholgach** shuttlecock

cearchaill *f2* 1. log 2. crossbeam, girder

céard *interrogative pron* what **céard eile?** what else? **céard faoi?** what about it?

ceardaí *m4* tradesman, artisan, craftsman

ceardaíocht *f3* craftsmanship, craftwork, craft

ceardcholáiste *m4* technical college **Ceardcholáiste Réigiúnach Phort Láirge** Waterford Regional Technical College

ceardchumann *m1* trade union **an Ceardchumann Seirbhísí, Tionsclaíoch, Gairmiúil agus Teicniúil** the Services, Industrial, Professional and Technical Union (SIPTU)

ceardchumannachas *m1* trade unionism

ceardchumannaí *m4* trade unionist

ceardlann *f2* workshop

ceardscoil *f2* technical school

cearn *f3* corner **gach cearn den domhan** every corner of the world

cearnach *adj* 1. square **fréamh chearnach** square root, **ciliméadar cearnach** square kilometre 2. angular

cearnaigh *v* square

cearnamhán *m1* cockchafer

cearnóg *f2* square **Cearnóg Mhuinseo** Mountjoy Square

cearnógach *adj* square **gearradh cearnógach** square section

cearr *adj* wrong **cad tá cearr?** what's wrong?

cearrbhach *m1* gambler

cearrbhachas *m1* gambling

ceart *adj* right, proper *m1* right, justice, due **ceart go leor** all right, very well, **ceart agus éigeart** right and wrong, **chun a cheart a thabhairt dó** to give him his due, **cearta sibhialta** civil rights, **nach bhfuil an ceart agam?** amn't I right? **de cheart** by right, **bhí sé de cheart agam é a dhéanamh** I should have done it, **rud a chur ina cheart** to fix

something

ceárta *f4* forge

ceartaigh *v* correct, rectify, amend

ceartaiseach *adj* 1. insistent (on one's rights) 2. self-righteous

ceartas *m1* 1. just claims, rights 2. justice

ceartingearach *adj* plumb, vertical

ceartlár *m1* exact centre **i gceartlár na cathrach** in the centre of the city

ceartúchán *m1* correction

céas *v* 1. crucify 2. torment, torture

ceasacht *f3* grumble, complaining

céasadh *m* 1. crucifixion **Aoine an Chéasta** Good Friday 2. agony, torment, torture

céasla *m4* paddle

céaslaigh *v* paddle

céasta *adj* 1. crucified 2. tormented, tormenting

céatadán *m1* percentage

ceathair *m4* four **a ceathair** four, **a ceathair déag** fourteen, **an ceathair hart** the four of hearts (*cards*)

ceathairéad *m1* quartet **ceathairéad téadach** string quartet

Ceatharlach *m1* Carlow **Contae Cheatharlach** Co. Carlow

ceathracha *m5* forty **ceathracha bliain ó shin** forty years ago

ceathrar *m1* four **ceathrar múinteoirí** four teachers, **ceathrar fear** four men, **ceathrar ban** four women

ceathrú[1] *f5* 1. quarter **ceathrú uair an chloig ó shin** a quarter of an hour ago, **ceathrú tar éis, i ndiaidh, a dó** quarter past two, **ceathrú chun a deich** a quarter to ten 2. thigh **ceathrú uaineola** leg of lamb 3. stanza, quatrain **abair cúpla ceathrú d'amhrán dúinn** sing us a couple of verses of a song

ceathrú[2] *adj* fourth **fuair sí an ceathrú háit** she came fourth, **sin é an ceathrú carr dá chuid** that's his fourth car

ceil *v* conceal, hide

céile *m4* 1. spouse, mate **bean chéile** wife, **fear céile** husband, **céile comhraic** opponent in battle 2. **a chéile** each other, **bhí siad ag ithe a chéile** they were eating each other 3. **le chéile** together, **tiocfaidh siad le chéile** they will meet, they will agree 4. **as a chéile** one after another, **tá an teach sin ag titim as a chéile** that house is falling apart 5. **de réir a chéile** gradually, consistent, **de réir a chéile a thógtar na caisleáin** Rome wasn't built in a day 6. **trí chéile, trína chéile** confused, upset

céilí *m4* Irish dancing session

ceiliúir *v* 1. celebrate **ag ceiliúradh an dea-scéala** celebrating the good news 2. vanish, fade **tá an dath ag ceiliúradh** the colour is fading

ceiliúr *m1* 1. greeting **ceiliúr pósta a chur ar dhuine** to propose (marriage) to somebody 2. warble, song (*bird*)

ceiliúradh *m* celebration **ceiliúradh cuimhne** commemoration

céillí *adj* sensible

ceilt *f2* concealment **ceilt bróin** concealment of sorrow, **faoi cheilt** secretly

Ceilteach *adj* Celtic **Dámh an Léinn Cheiltigh** the Faculty of Celtic Studies *m1* Celt

Ceiltis *f2* Celtic (*language*)

céim *f2* 1. step **rud a dhéanamh céim ar chéim** to do something step by step 2. degree **naoi gcéim déag a bheidh an teocht is airde** the hottest will be seventeen degrees, **céim ollscoile** university degree 3. rank **ardú céime**

promotion, **ísliú céime** demotion 4. pass (*mountain*) **an Chéim** Stepaside

céimí *m4* graduate

ceimic *f2* chemistry

ceimiceach *adj* chemical **airm cheimiceacha** chemical weapons

ceimiceán *m1* chemical

ceimiceoir *m3* chemist

céimíocht *f3* rank, distinction

ceimiteiripe *f4* chemotherapy

céimiúil *adj* distinguished

céimseata *f5* geometry

ceint *m4* cent

ceinteagrád *m1* centigrade

ceinteagrádach *adj* centigrade **scála ceinteagrádach** centigrade scale

ceintiméadar *m1* centimetre

céir *f5* wax **músaem céarach** wax museum

ceird *f2* trade

ceirmeacht *f3* ceramics

ceirneoir *m3* disk jockey

ceirnín *m4* record (*gramophone*)

ceirt *f2* rag, cloth **ceirt chuimilte** duster

ceirtlín *m4* ball (*wool*)

ceirtlis *f2* cider

céislín *m4* tonsil

céislínteas *m1* tonsilitis

ceist *f2* 1. question, query **ceist ilroghnach** multiple choice (*question*) 2. point, issue **is éard atá i gceist anseo (ná)...** the issue here is...

ceistigh *v* question

ceistiú *m* questioning, interrogation

ceistiúchán *m1* questionnaire

ceithearnach *m1* 1. outlaw 2. pawn (*chess*) 3. foot-soldier

ceithre *adj* four **ceithre bhosca fholamha** four empty boxes

ceo[1] *m4* mist, haze, fog

ceo[2] *m4* **ní raibh aon cheo ann** there was nothing there

ceobhrán *m1* drizzle, mist

ceobhránach *adj* drizzly, misty

ceoch *adj* foggy, misty

ceol *m1* music **ceol a bhaint as rud** to enjoy something, **ceol atmaisféir** mood music, **mo cheol thú!** bravo!

ceoláras *m1* concert hall **an Ceoláras Náisiúnta** the National Concert Hall

ceolchoirm *f2* concert

ceoldráma *m4* opera

ceolfhoireann *f2* orchestra **ceolfhoireann shiansach** symphony orchestra

ceolmhar *adj* musical **blas ceolmhar** sweet, musical accent

ceoltóir *m3* musician

ceomhar *adj* foggy

cheana *adv* already, beforehand **tá sé feicthe agam cheana féin** I've seen it already

choíche *adv* ever, forever, never (*with negative*)

chomh *adv* as, so **chomh folláin le breac** as healthy as can be, **chomh haoibhinn** so delightful

chuig (*prep prons* = **chugam, chugat, chuige, chuici, chugainn, chugaibh, chucu**) *prep* to, toward(s) **chuaigh mé chuici** I went to(wards) her

chun (*prep prons* = **chugam, chugat, chuige, chuici, chugainn, chugaibh, chucu**) (+ *genitive*) *prep* 1. to, towards **cuireadh chun báis í** she was put to death 2. for **bheith ábalta chun oibre** to be able for work 3. in order to **chun an carr a cheannach** in order to buy the car

ciainíd *f2* cyanide

ciall *f2* sense, meaning **ní thagann ciall roimh aois** sense doesn't come before age, sense comes with age, **cur i gcéill** make-believe

ciallaigh *v* mean, signify

ciallmhar *adj* sensible, reasonable

cian[1] *f2* long time, distance **na cianta ó shin** a long time ago, **tír i gcéin** a country far away

cian[2] *m4* sadness **bhí cian orm** I was sad

cian-[3] *prefix* 1. long **cianchuimhne** long memory 2. distant **cianamharc** distant view

cianaosta *adj* primeval **san aimsir chianaosta** long long ago

cianghlao *m1* long-distance call

cianrialaithe *adj* remote-controlled

cianrialtán *m1* remote control, zapper

cianrialú *m* remote control

ciap *v* 1. annoy, harass 2. torment **táim ciaptha aici** she has me tormented

ciapadh *m* 1. harassment 2. torment

ciar *adj* dark, swarthy

ciardhuán *m1* black person

ciardhubh *adj* jet-black

ciaróg *f2* beetle **ciaróg dhubh** black-beetle, cockroach

Ciarraí *f4* Kerry

Ciarraíoch *m1* native of Kerry

ciarsúr *m1* handkerchief

cibé *pron* 1. whoever **cibé a bheidh ann** whoever will be there 2. whatever, whichever **cibé áit é** whatever, whichever place it is

cíbhí *m4* kiwi (*fruit*)

cic *m4* kick **cic saor** free kick

ciceáil *v* kick

ciclipéid *f2* encyclopedia

cigil *v* tickle

cigilt *f2* tickle, tickling

cigilteach *adj* ticklish, delicate **ceist chigilteach** delicate question

cigire *m4* inspector

cigireacht *f3* inspection

cíle *f4* keel

cileagram *m1* kilogramme

cileavata *m4* kilowatt

ciliméadar *m1* kilometre

cill *f2* 1. cell 2. church 3. churchyard

Cill Chainnigh *f2* Kilkenny

Cill Dara *f2* Kildare

Cill Mhantáin *f2* Wicklow

cillín *m4* cell (*prison*)

cime *m4* captive, prisoner

Cincís *f2* an Chincís Pentecost

cine *m4* race, tribe an cine daonna the human race

cineál *adv* somewhat cineál déanach somewhat late *m1* 1. kind, species de réir cineáil according to kind 2. class, sort cén cineál seafóide é sin? what sort of nonsense is that?

cineálta *adj* 1. kind fear cineálta a kind man 2. mild aimsir chineálta pleasant, mild weather

cineáltas *m1* kindness

cinedheighilt *f2* apartheid

cinéiteach *adj* kinetic

ciniceas *m1* cynicism

cinicí *m4* cynic

ciniciúil *adj* cynical

ciníoch *adj* racial, racist

ciníochaí *m4* racist

ciníochas *m1* racism

cinn *v* decide, determine cinneadh ar rud a dhéanamh to decide to do something

cinneadh *m1* determination, decision an bhfuil aon chinneadh déanta? has any decision been made? cinneadh tuairisce the findings of a report

cinniúint *f3* fate, chance, destiny

cinniúnach *adj* 1. fateful 2. fatal an buille cinniúnach the fatal blow

cinnte *adj* certain, definite, sure

cinnteacht *f3* certainty

cinnteoireacht *f3* decision-making

cinntigh *v* make certain, ensure

cinntitheach *adj* determinative *m1* determinant

cinntiú *m* confirmation

cinsire *m4* censor cinsire scannán film censor

cinsireacht *f3* censorship cinsireacht a dhéanamh ar leabhar to censor a book

cíoch *f2* breast bainne cíche breast milk

cíochbheart *m1* bra(ssiere)

cíocrach *adj* eager, greedy

cíocras *m1* eagerness, greed cíocras tobac, dí, a bheith ort to have a craving for tobacco, drink

ciombal *m1* cymbal ciombal ard-hata hi-hat cymbal

cion¹ *m3* 1. affection, love thug mé cion dó I became fond of him, ainm ceana pet name 2. influence, effect chuir sé i gcion é he drove it home (*of statement, blow, etc*)

cion² *m4* share rinne mé mo chion féin I did my own share

cion³ *m3* offence cion báis capital offence

ciondáil *f3* rationing ciordáil bia food rationing *v* ration

cionmhaireacht *f3* proportion, share

cionmhar *adj* proportional

cionroinn *v* allocate, apportion

cionroinnt *f2* allocation, apportionment cionroinnt dualgas allocation of duties

cionsiocair *f5* primary cause tusa is cionsiocair leis it is you who are the real cause of it

ciontach *adj* guilty ciontach i mí-iompar tromchúiseach guilty of serious misconduct *m1* offender

ciontacht *f3* guilt

ciontaí, is tusa is ciontaí you are to blame for it, **níl a ciontaí leis** she is not to blame for it

ciontaigh *v* 1. blame, accuse 2. convict

ciontóir *m3* offender

ciontú *m* conviction

cíor *f2* 1. comb, crest, set (*as of teeth*) 2. **cíor thuathail** confusion, **bhí an áit ina chíor thuathail acu** they had the place in a complete mess *v* 1. **comb do chuid gruaige a chíoradh** to comb your hair 2. examine minutely **ag cíoradh na ceiste** discussing the question minutely 3. **ag cíoradh a chéile** fighting, quarrelling

cíorach *adj* serrated **seafta cíorach** serrated shaft

cíoradh *m* 1. discussion 2. quarrelling 3. serration

ciorcad *m1* circuit **ciorcad digiteach** digital circuit, **ciorcad oscailte, iata** open, closed circuit

ciorcal *m1* circle **ciorcal lochtach** vicious circle

ciorclach *adj* circular

ciorclaigh *v* encircle, circle

ciorclán *m1* circular (*letter*)

cíorláil *v* comb, search

ciorraigh *v* 1. cut short 2. hack, maim, mutilate

ciorrú *m* 1. shortening, curtailment 2. mutilation 3. **ciorrú coil** incest

cíos *m3* rent, hire **ar cíos** hired, rented, let, **cíos dubh** extortion

ciotach *adj* 1. left-handed 2. awkward, clumsy

ciotóg *f2* 1. left hand 2. left-handed person, awkward person

ciotógach *adj* 1. left-handed 2. awkward

ciotrúnta *adj* 1. obstinate, obstreperous 2. clumsy

cipín *m4* 1. small stick **cipíní solais** matches 2. **bheith ar cipíní** to be on tenterhooks

Cipir *f2* **an Chipir** Cyprus

Cipireach *adj, m1* Cypriot

circeoil *f3* chicken (*meat*) **anraith circeola** chicken soup

círéib *f2* riot

círéibeach *adj* riotous **iompar círéibeach** riotous behaviour

círichleachtóir *m3* chiropractor

círíneach *adj* flushed (*of face*)

cis *f2* 1. basket, crate 2. restraint, handicap (*golf*)

ciseal *m* layer **ciseal (an) ózóin** the ozone layer

ciseán *m1* basket

cispheil *f2* basketball

ciste *m4* 1. fund **ciste sóisialta** social fund, **an Ciste Airgeadaíochta Eorpach (CIAE)** the European Monetary Fund (EMF), **ciste an stáit** treasury, state funds 2. treasure

císte *m4* cake

cisteóg *f2* casket

cisteoir *m3* treasurer

cistin *f2* kitchen

citeal *m1* kettle **cuir síos an citeal** put on the kettle

cith *m3* shower **ceathanna báistí** rain showers, **tuar ceatha** rainbow

cithfholcadh *m* shower **ag tógáil cithfholctha** taking a shower

cithréim *f2* maiming, deformity

citreas *m1* citrus **torthaí citris** citrus fruits

ciú *m4* queue

ciúb *m1* cube

ciúbach *adj* cubic

ciúbaigh *v* cube

ciúin *adj* quiet, calm, silent **fanaigí ciúin!** stay quiet! **farraige chiúin** calm sea, **an tAigéan Ciúin** the Pacific Ocean

ciumhais *f2* border, edge **ar chiumhais na mara** on the edge of the sea

ciúnaigh *v* quieten, calm **chiúnaigh siad** they quietened, they calmed down

ciúnas *m1* quietness, silence, calm(ness) **i gciúnas na hoíche** in the still of the night

ciúta *m4* 1. knack, 'know how' 2. clever remark 3. flourish (*of speech*)

clab *m1* open mouth

clabaire *m4* 1. noisy open-mouthed person, chatterer 2. clapperboard (*film-making*)

clabaireacht *f3* chattering

clábar *m1* mud

clabhstra *m4* cloister

clabhsúr *m1* closure, finish **cuirfimid clabhsúr ar an obair amárach** we'll bring the work to a close, we'll finish the work, tomorrow

cladach *m1* sea-shore, shore **iascaireacht chladaigh** rock-fishing

cladhaire *m4* 1. coward 2. ruffian, villain

cladhartha *adj* 1. cowardly, spineless 2. villainous

clag *v* 1. clatter 2. strike, pelt

clagarnach *f2* clatter(ing)

claí *m4* fence, wall, dyke **claí cloch** stone wall, **claí garraí** garden wall, **claí mór na réaltaí** the Milky Way

claibín *m4* lid **claibín buidéil** bottle-cap

claidhreacht *f3* 1. cowardice 2. villainy

claíomh *m1* sword

clairéad *m1* claret

cláiríneach *m1* cripple, handicapped person

Cláiríneach *m1* native of Clare

cláirnéid *f2* clarinet

cláirseach *f2* harp **cláirseach cheolchoirme** concert harp

cláirseoir *m3* harpist

clais *f2* 1. water channel, dyke, ditch 2. trench, furrow

claisceadal *m1* 1. group singing, choral singing 2. choir

clamhach *adj* mangy

clamhán *m1* 1. bald patch (*hair, land, etc*) 2. buzzard (*bird*)

clamhsán *m1* complaint

clamhsánach *adj* complaining, fault-finding

clampa *m4* clamp **clampa mearoscailte** quick-release clamp

clampáil *f3* clamping *v* clamp

clampar *m1* noisy quarrelling, commotion

clamprach *adj* quarrelsome, noisy, disorderly

clann *f2* 1. children, offspring **tá beirt chlainne orthu** they have two children, **tá triúr clainne ar Phól agus Síle** Pól and Síle have three children, **clann do chlainne** your grandchildren, **ag iompar clainne** pregnant, **bhí duine clainne aici** she had a child 2. race, descendants **clann Mhic Grianna** the Greenes

claochladán *m1* transformer

claochlaigh *v* 1. change (*for the worse*), deteriorate **tá a shláinte ag claochlú** his health is deteriorating 2. transform **teas na gréine á chlaochlú go fuinneamh** transforming the sun's heat to energy

claochlaitheach *adj* changing, variable

claochlú *m* 1. change 2. transformation, metamorphosis

claon[1] *adj* 1. inclined, sloping, slanting 2. perverse **beart claon** crooked act *m1* 1. incline, slope,

slant 2. inclination, tendency
v 1. incline, slope, slant, decline
chlaon sé a cheann he bowed his head

claon-[2] *prefix* 1. inclined, sloping
claonfhéachaint sidelong glance
2. crooked, evil, perverse
claonbheart crooked act
3. oblique, indirect **claoninsint**
indirect speech (*grammar*)

claonadh *m* 1. inclination, tendency, bias 2. perversion **claonadh na fírinne** perversion of the truth

claonchló *m4* negative (*photo*)

claonta *adj* partial, prejudiced

clapsholas *m1* twilight

Clár, an *m1* Clare **Contae an Chláir**
Co. Clare

clár *m1* 1. board **clár dubh**
blackboard, **clár na bhfógraí** the notice board, **clár táiplise**
draught-board, **clár toinne** surf-board 2. table (of contents), register **clár ama** timetable, **clár cinn** home page (*of worldwide web*), **clár an leabhair** the contents of the book, **clár comhardaithe** balance sheet
3. programme **clár imeachtaí**
programme of events, **clár teilifíse**
television programme 4. lid **clár corcáin** lid of pot 5. flat surface
clár éadain forehead 6. **os cionn cláir** laid out (*of dead person*), **faoi chlár** coffined

cláraigh *v* 1. enrol, register

cláraithe *adj* registered

cláraitheoir *m3* registrar

clárlann *f2* registry office

clárú *m* enrolment, registration

clasaiceach *adj* classic **ceol clasaiceach** classical music

clásal *m1* clause

claspa *m4* clasp

clástrafóibe *f4* claustrophobia

clé *adj, adv* left **ar thaobh na láimhe clé** on the left hand side,
cas ar clé turn left, **an eite chlé** the Left wing, **an Daonlathas Clé**
Democratic Left *f4* left hand side

cleacht *v* 1. perform habitually
2. practise 3. rehearse (*theatre*)

cleachta (le) *adj* used to

cleachtadh *m1* 1. habit 2. practice, experience **bheith as cleachtadh**
to be out of practice, **cleachtadh ginearálta ar mhíochaine** general medical practice 3. rehearsal
(*theatre*)

cleachtóir *m3* practitioner

cleamhnas *m1* marriage arrangement, match

cleas *m1* trick **cleas a imirt ar dhuine** to play a trick on somebody

cleasach *adj* playful, tricky, crafty

cleasaí *m4* trickster

cleasaíocht *f3* trickery

cleatar *m1* clatter

cleathóg *f2* stick, cue (*snooker*)

cléir *f2* clergy

cléireach *m1* clerk **cléireach oifige**
office clerk

cléireachas *m1* clerkship **oifigeach cléireachais** clerical officer

cléiriúil *adj* clerical

cleite *m4* 1. feather 2. quill **ainm cleite** pen-name, **cara cleite** penfriend

cléithín *m4* splint (*surgery*)

cliabh *m1* 1. basket 2. chest, bosom **cara cléibh** bosom friend

cliabhán *m1* cradle **tá Gaeilge ón gcliabhán aici** she has Irish from the cradle, she is a native Irish speaker

cliabhrach *m1* chest

cliamhain *m4* son-in-law

cliant *m1* client

cliantacht *f3* 1. clientship
2. clientele

cliarlathas *m1* hierarchy

cliath *f2* 1. hurdle **Baile Átha Cliath** Dublin ('the settlement of the ford of the hurdles) 2. darning

cliathán *m1* side, flank **cliatháin (amharclainne)** wings (of a theatre), **tháinig an bád le cliathán** the boat came alongside, **scáthán cliatháin** wing mirror

cliathánach *adj* sideways

cliathánaí *m4* winger (*sport*)

clibirt *f2* scrum(mage) (*sport*)

cling *f2, v* ring, tinkle

clingíní *pl* chimes

clinic *m4* clinic

cliniciúil *adj* clinical

cliobóg *f2* 1. filly 2. frisky person 3. **bhíomar ag caitheamh cliobóg** we were playing leapfrog

clis *v* 1. fail **chlis orm an scrúdú a fháil** I failed to get/pass the exam 2. jump, start up

cliseadh *m* 1. failure, collapse **cliseadh néaróg** nervous breakdown 2. jump **bhain sí cliseadh asam** she startled me

cliste *adj* clever, smart

clisteacht *f3* cleverness

cliúsaí *m4* flirt

cliúsaíocht *f3* flirting

cló *m4* 1. form, appearance **i gcló duine** in human form, **cló a chur ort féin** to smarten yourself up 2. print, type **cló gaelach** gaelic type, **i gcló, as cló** in print, out of print

clóbh *m1* clove

clóbhuail *v* print

clóca *m4* cloak

cloch *f2* 1. stone **cloch bhoinn** foundation stone, **balla cloiche** stone wall, **obair chloiche** stone work, **cloch dhuáin** kidney stone, **clocha duirlinge** cobble-stones, rounded shore-pebbles 2. **cloch (mheáchain)** stone (*weight*), **tá seacht gcloch déag meáchain aige** he is 18 stone in weight

clochán *m1* 1. stepping-stones, stony ground 2. **clochán (coirceogach)** beehive hut

clochaois *f2* **an Chlochaois** the Stone Age

clochar *m1* 1. convent 2. stone structure, stony place

clóchur *m* typesetting

clóchuradóir *m3* typesetter

clóchuradóireacht *f3* typesetting

clódóir *m3* printer

clódóireacht *f3* printing

clog *m1* 1. clock **clog aláraim** alarm clock, **uair an chloig** one hour (*by the clock*), **(trí) a chlog** (three) o'clock 2. bell **buail an clog** ring the bell 3. blister

clogad *m1* 1. helmet **clogad cruach** steel helmet, hard-hat, **clogad cosanta** crash helmet 2. head of cabbage

clogáil *f3* clocking **clogáil amach** clocking out, **clogáil isteach** clocking in

clogra *m4* set of bells, carillon

cloicheán *m1* prawn **cloicheáin Chuan Bhaile Átha Cliath** Dublin Bay prawns

cloigeann *m1* 1. skull 2. head

cloígh[1] *v* overcome, defeat, subdue

cloígh[2] *v* adhere, cling **cloígh le** adhere to, cling to, **má chloíonn tú leis an bplean** if you stick to the plan

clóigh *v* print

cloigín *m4* bell **cloigín dorais** door bell

cloigtheach *m5* belfry, round tower

clóire *m4* printer (*machine*)

clóirín *m4* chlorine

clois *v* (see *irregular verbs*) hear **ná clois a gcloisfidh tú** don't listen to everthing you hear

cloíte *adj* subdued, defeated, exhausted

clón *m1* clone

clónáil *f3* cloning

clórafluaracarbón (CFC) *m1* chloroflurocarbon (CFC) **CFCanna** CFCs

clós *m1* enclosure, yard **clós scoile** school yard

clóscríbhinn *f2* typescript

clóscríbhneoireacht *f3* typewriting, typing

clóscríobh *v* type

clóscríobhaí *m4* typist

clóscríobhán *m1* typewriter

clóscríofa *adj* typewritten

clostéip *f2* audiotape

clú *m4* reputation **tá clú agus cáil ar a bhflaithiúlacht** they are renowned for their generosity

cluain¹ *f3* flattery, persuasion, deception **chuir siad cluain air** they flattered him, they deceived him

cluain² *f3* meadow, pasture-land **Cluain Meala** Clonmel ('meadow/pasture of honey')

cluaisín *m4* tab, lobe, tag **cluaisín bróige** tag on shoe

cluanaire *m4* flatterer, deceiver

cluanaireacht *f3* flattery, deceitfulness

cluas *f2* 1. ear **an chluas bhodhar a thabhairt do dhuine** to turn a deaf ear to somebody, **cluas le héisteacht** attentive ear, **tá cluas do theangacha, do cheol, aici** she has an ear for languages, for music 2. handle **cluas cupáin** handle of cup

cluasán *m1* earphone, headphone **cuir ort na cluasáin** put on the earphones, headphones

club *m4* club **club óige** youth club, **clubanna oíche** night clubs

clubtheach *m* clubhouse

clúdach *m1* cover, covering **clúdach litreach** envelope, **clúdach dúnphoill** man-hole cover

clúdaigh *v* cover, wrap

cluiche *m4* game, match **cluiche cártaí** game of cards, **cluiche cairdeachais** friendly match, **cluiche craoibhe, sraithe** championship, league match, **cluiche leathcheannais** semi-final, **cluiche ceannais (na hÉireann)** (All-Ireland) final

clúid *f2* 1. corner, nook 2. cover(ing) **faoi chlúid** under cover, **clúid phéinte** covering of paint

clúidín *m4* baby's napkin, nappy

cluimhreach *f2* feathers

cluimhrigh *v* 1. pluck (*birds*) 2. preen **duine á chluimhriú féin** somebody sprucing himself up

clúiteach *adj* famous, well-known

clúmh *m1* 1. down, plumage, feathers 2. coat, fur (*of animal*) 3. hair (*on body*)

clúmhach *adj* 1. fluffy 2. feathery 3. hairy, furry *m1* fluff

clúmhill *v* slander, defame

clúmhilleadh *m* slander, defamation of character

clumhúil *adj* mildewed (*fruit*)

cluthar *adj* cosy, sheltered

clutharaigh *v* make warm, comfortable

cnag *m1* 1. knock, blow 2. crunch, crack *v* 1. knock, strike (down) **cnag ar an bhfuinneog** knock on the window 2. crack **cnó a chnagadh** to crack a nut

cnagadh *m* 1. striking, knocking 2. crunching, cracking

cnagaire *m4* 1. stricker, knocker 2. noggin **cnagaire fuisce** a noggin of whiskey 3. woodpecker

cnagaosta *adj* elderly

cnagarnach *f2* crackling noise, crunch

cnagbhruite *adj* parboiled, boiled until partly cooked

cnaígh *v* gnaw, corrode **miotal cnaíte** corroded metal

cnáimhseáil *f3* complaining, grumbling

cnáimhseálaí *f4* grumbler

cnaipe *m4* button

cnámh *f2* bone **cnámha an scéil** the main facts of the story, **cnámh droma** backbone, **cnámh an scadáin** herring-bone (pattern), **téann focal le gaoth ach téann buille le cnámh** actions speak louder than words

cnámhach *adj* bony

cnámharlach *m1* skeleton, bony animal

cnap *m1* 1. lump **cnap ime** lump of butter 2. heap **cnap airgid** heap of money, **bheith i do chnap codlata** to be fast asleep 3. mass **cnap báistí** downpour of rain

cnapach *adj* knotty, knobby, lumpy

cnapán *m1* lump **cnapán fola** blood clot

cnapánach *adj* lumpy, rough, rugged

cnapsac *m1* knapsack

cnapshiúcra *m4* lump sugar

cnapshuim *f2* lump sum

cneá *f4* wound, sore

cnead *f3* gasp, groan, grunt, pant *v* groan, pant

cneadaíl *f3* grunting, groaning

cneáigh *v* wound

cneámhaire *m4* 1. mean person, miser 2. rogue

cneas *m1* skin **éadach cnis** underwear, **sail chnis** dandruff

cneasaigh *v* heal

cneasaithe *adj* healed

cneasta *adj* 1. courteous 2. honest, sincere 3. mild **aimsir chneasta** mild weather

cneastacht *f3* 1. mildness, courteousness 2. sincerity

cniog *m4* blow, rap **thug sé cniog ar na hailt dom** he rapped me on the knuckles

cníopaire *f4* miser

cníopaireacht *f3* miserliness

cniotáil *f3* knitting *v* knit

cnó *m4* nut **cnó cócó** coconut

cnoc *m1* 1. hill **ar bharr an chnoic** at the top of the hill, **tá sí ag baint na gcnoc** she is attempting the impossible 2. **cnoc ailse** malignant tumour, **cnoc farraige** huge wave, **cnoc oighir** iceberg

cnocach *adj* hilly

cnocán *m1* hillock, mound

cnóire *m4* nutcracker

cnuasach *m1* collection **cnuasach gearrscéalta** collection of short stories

cnuasaigh *v* collect, gather, store

cnuasainm *m4* collective noun

cobhsaí *adj* stable

cobhsaigh *v* stabilise

cobhsaíocht *f3* stability

cobhsaitheoir *m3* stabiliser

cobhsú *m* stabilisation

coca *m4* cock **coca féir** hay-cock, **coca liathróide** ball-cock

cocáil *v* cock **chocáil sí an gunna** she cocked the gun

cócaire *m4* cook

cócaireacht *f3* cooking **ranganna cócaireachta** cookery classes

cócaireán *m1* cooker

cócaon *m1* cocaine

cochall *m1* 1. hood (*garment*) 2. cowl, mantle 3. **cochall an chroí** pericardium, protective wall of the heart

cócó *m4* cocoa **cnó cócó** coconut

cód *m1* code

codail *v* sleep **tá sé in am dul a chodladh** it's time to go to sleep

codán *m1* fraction

codarsnach *adj* contrary, opposite

codarsnacht *f3* contrast **i gcodarsnacht** in opposition

codladh *m3* sleep **an raibh tú i do chodladh?** were you asleep? **mála codlata** sleeping bag, **néal codlata** wink of sleep, **tá codladh grífín i mo lámh agam** I have pins and needles in my arm

codlaidín *m4* opium **síbín codlaidín** opium den

codlatach *adj* 1. sleepy 2. dormant

cófra *m4* press, trunk, chest

cogadh *m1* war **dul chun cogaidh le** to go to war with, **an Chéad Chogadh Domhanda** the First World War, **an Dara Cogadh Domhanda** the Second World War, **Cogadh na Saoirse** War of Independence, **cogadh cathartha** civil war

cogaíocht *f3* warfare **cogaíocht cheimiceach** chemical warfare

cogain *v* 1. chew **ag cogaint bia** chewing food 2. grind **bhí sé ag cogaint a chuid fiacla** he was grinding his teeth

cogaint *f3* chewing **guma coganta** chewing gum

cogar *m1* whisper **cogar (i leith chugam)!** (come here and) listen!

cogarnach *f2* whispering

cógas *m1* prepared medicine, medication

cógaslann *f2* pharmacy

coibhéiseach *adj* equivalent

coibhneas *m1* relationship, proportion **i gcoibhneas** in proportion

coibhneasta *adj* 1. comparative 2. relative (*grammar*) **an fhoirm choibhneasta** the relative form

coicís *f2* fortnight

coicíseán *m1* fortnightly (*magazine, periodical, etc*)

coicísiúil *adj* fortnightly

coigeartaigh *v* correct, adjust

coigeartú *m* correction, adjustment

coigil *v* 1. spare, economise, save 2. 'rake up' (*fire*)

coigilteach *adj* frugal, thrifty, economical

coigilteas *m1* sparingness, thrift

coigistigh *v* confiscate

coigistíocht *f3* confiscation

coigríoch *f2* foreign country **ar an gcoigríoch** abroad

coigríochach *adj* foreign, strange *m1* foreigner, stranger

coileach *m1* cock **coileach francach** turkey-cock

coileán *m1* puppy

coiléar *m1* collar **coiléar madra** dog collar

coiliceam *m1* colic

coilíneach *adj* colonial *m1* colonist

coilíneacht *f3* colony

cóilis *f2* cauliflower

coill[1] *f2* wood **lucht coille** wood-folk, outlaws

coill[2] *v* 1. castrate **asal a choilleadh** to castrate a donkey 2. violate **dlí a choilleadh** to violate a law

coillearnach *f2* woodland **coillearnach bhuaircíneach** coniferous woodland

coillteach *adj* wooded

coim *f2* 1. waist **thit sé go coim san uisce** he fell up to his waist in the water 2. cloak, cover **faoi choim na hoíche** under the cover of night

coimeád *m* 1. guard, protection **bheith ar do choimeád** to be on your guard, to be in hiding 2. detention, custody **duine a ghlacadh i gcoimeád** to take somebody into custody 3. maintenance *v* 1. keep, observe **an tsíocháin a choimeád** to keep the peace 2. guard **príosúnaigh a choimeád** to guard prisoners 3. hold, retain **coimeádtar uisce**

ann water is kept/held there
4. maintain **choiméad siad an gnó ag imeacht** they kept/maintained the business going 5. detain

cóiméad *m1* comet **cóiméad Halley** Halley's comet

coimeádach *adj, m1* conservative

coimeádaí *m4* keeper **coimeádaí páirce** groundsman

coiméide *f4* comedy (*theatre*)

cóimheá *f4* balance

coimhéad *m* 1. watch, guard **bheith ar do choimhéad** to be on your guard 2. observation *v* 1. watch over, guard 2. observe, keep observation 3. mind, attend to **do ghnó féin a choimhéad** to tend to, mind your own business

cóimheas *m3* 1. ratio **cóimheasa malairte** exchange ratios 2. comparison

coimheascar *m1* conflict, combat

cóimhéid *f2* equal amount, size

cóimhiotal *m1* alloy

coimhlint *f2* contest, rivalry, competition

coimhlinteach *adj* contesting, competitive

coimhthíoch *adj* 1. foreign, alien 2. strange 3. distant, shy, 4. exotic **deoch choimhthíoch** exotic drink *m1* foreigner, alien, stranger

coimirce *f4* guardianship, protection, patronage **faoi choimirce na roinne seo** under the aegis of this department

coimirceoir *m3* guardian, protector, patron

coimircí *m4* ward (*law*)

coimisinéir *m3* commissioner **an Coimisinéir Cosanta Sonraí** the Data Protection Commissioner

coimisiún *m1* commission **Coimisiún na Státseirbhíse** the Civil Service Commission

coimisiúnaigh *v* commission **obair a**

choimisiúnú do... to commission work to...

coimpléasc *m1* complex

coimrigh *v* sum up, summarise **ag coimriú ailt** summarising an article

coimrithe *adj* summarised

coinbhinsiún *m1* convention

coinbhinsiúnach *adj* conventional

coincheap *m3* concept

coincleach *f2* mildew, mould

coincréit *f2* concrete **bloc coincréite** concrete block, **coincréit threisithe** reinforced concrete

coincréiteach *adj* concrete

coincréitiú *m* concreting

cóineartaigh *v* strengthen, confirm (*by bishop*)

cóineartú *m* confirmation (*by bishop*)

coineascar *m1* twilight

coinfití *m4* confetti

coinicéar *m1* rabbit-warren

coinín *m1* rabbit

coinleach *m1* stubble

coinne *f4* 1. appointment, expectation (*to meet somebody*) **gan choinne** unexpectedly 2. (with *preps*), **faoi choinne** for, **i gcoinne** against, **cur i gcoinne** to oppose, **os coinne** in front of, opposite, **os a choinne sin, ina choinne sin** against that

coinneáil *f3* 1. keeping, maintaining, maintainance 2. detention **campa coinneála** detention camp 3. observance **coinneáil dlí** observance of law 4. retention

coinneal *f2* candle

coinneálach *adj* 1. supporting 2. retentive

coinnealbhá *m4* excommunication

coinnigh *v* 1. keep, maintain **coinníonn sí cuairteoirí ann** she keeps visitors there, **teach a**

choinneáil to maintain a house, **súil a choinneáil ar dhuine, rud** to keep an eye on somebody, something, **coinnigh ort!** carry on! **2.** retain, hold, withhold **coinnigh greim air** keep a hold of him/it, **coinníonn sé an t-uisce go maith** it retains the water well, **fianaise a choinneáil siar** to withhold evidence **3.** detain **coinníodh i bpríosún ar feadh seachtaine iad** they were detained for a week in prison **4.** observe **an dlí a choinneáil** to observe the law

coinníoll *m1* **1.** condition, stipulation, requirement **ar an gcoinníoll go...** on the condition that... **2.** honour

coinníollach *adj* conditional

coinnleoir *m3* candlestick **coinnleoir craobhach** chandelier

coinscríobh *v* conscript

coinscríofach *adj, m1* conscript

coinséartó *m4* concerto **coinséartó pianó** piano concerto

coinsias *m3* conscience

coinsiasach *adj* conscientious

coinsínigh *v* consign

coinsíniú *m* consignment

cointinn *f2* contention **chuaigh siad i gcointinn le chéile** they quarrelled, contended violently, with each other

cointinneach *adj* quarrelsome

coip *v* **1.** ferment, foam, froth **do chuid fola ag coipeadh** your blood boiling **2.** whip **ag coipeadh uachtair** whipping cream

cóip *f2* copy **cóip chúltaca** backup copy (*computers*)

cóipcheart *m1* copyright

coipeach *adj* foamy, frothy

coipeadh *m* fermentation, foam, froth **próiseas an choiptheh** the fermentation process

cóipeáil *f3* copying *v* copy

cóipleabhar *m1* copybook

coir *f2* crime, offence **níl coir ann** there is no harm in him

cóir *adj* proper, just **ba chóir di éisteacht leat** she should listen to you *f3* **1.** justice **cóir agus éagóir** justice and injustice **2.** due **ní bhfuair siad ach a gcóir** they only got their share, what was due to them **3.** proper means, equipment **cóir thaistil** means of transport **4.** proper condition **an bhfuil sé curtha i gcóir agat?** have you fixed it, put it in order? **5.** proper provision, accommodation **cóir leighis** medical treatment **6.** favourable wind **cóir shíne** favourable weather

coirce *m4* oats **Gort an Choirce** Gortahork ('the field of oats')

coirceog *f2* **1.** hive **coirceog bheach** beehive **2.** cone

coirdial *m1* cordial

coire *m4* **1.** cauldron **2.** boiler **coire gáis** gas boiler **3.** pit **4.** **coire guairneáin** whirlpool

Cóiré *f4* **an Chóiré Theas, Thuaidh** South, North Korea

cóireáil *f3* treatment **cóireáil chéadchabhrach** first-aid treatment, **cóireáil mhíochaine** medical treatment

coireál *m1* coral **scéir choiréil** coral reef

cóirigh *v* **1.** arrange, dress **leaba a chóiriú** to make a bed **2.** repair, mend, fix **chóirigh siad an díon dom** they fixed the roof for me

cóiriú *m* **1.** arrangement **fuair sí cóiriú nua gruaige** she got a new hair-style **2.** repair **tá an gluaisteán sin ó chóiriú** that car is beyond repair

coiriúil *adj* criminal

cóiriúil *adj* favourable

coirm *f2* **1.** feast, drinking-party **2.** ale **3.** **coirm cheoil** concert

coirnéad *m1* cornet (*music*)

coirnéal *m1* 1. corner 2. colonel

coirnín *m4* 1. curl (*of hair*) 2. bead

coirníneach *adj* 1. curled, curly (*of hair*) 2. beaded

coirpeach *m1* criminal

coirt *f2* 1. tree-bark 2. coating, scum

coisbheart *m1* footgear

coisc *v* 1. prevent, prohibit, obstruct 2. brake (*mechanical*)

coiscéim *f2* footstep, pace

coiscín *m4* condom

coisctheach *adj* preventive, restraining

coisí *m4* pedestrian, infantryman

coisíocht *f3* 1. travelling by foot 2. speed, pace **tá coisíocht faoi** he is going at a pace, with speed

cóisir *f2* (festive) party, feast, banquet

coisreacan *m1* 1. consecration 2. blessing

coisric *v* 1. consecrate **uisce coisricthe** holy water 2. bless

coiste *m4* 1. committee, board **coiste gnó** executive committee, **Coiste Idirnáisiúnta na gCluichí Oilimpeacha** International Olympic Committee 2. jury **coiste cróinéara** coroner's inquest

cóiste *m4* 1. coach, carriage 2. side-car

coiteann *adj* common **dlí coiteann** common law *m1* common people

coitianta *adj* ordinary, customary, common **nós coitianta** widespread custom

coitinne *f4* generality **i gcoitinne** in general

col *m1* 1. impediment to marriage, degree of blood relationship **ciorrú coil** incest, violation of impediment to marriage, **col ceathrair** first cousin, **col cúigir** first cousin once removed

2. incest 3. aversion, disliking **tá col aici leis an bhFraincis** she dislikes French

colainn *f2* 1. (living) body 2. flesh **ainmhianta na colainne** the lusts of the flesh

coláiste *m4* college **an Coláiste Ollscoile, Baile Átha Cliath** University College, Dublin

colaistéaról *m1* cholesterol

colbha *m4* kerb, edge, ledge, side **colbha bóthair** kerb, edge of road

colg *m1* rage, anger **tháinig colg uirthi** she became angry

colgach *adj* fierce, angry

colgán *m1* sword-fish

coll *m1* hazel **cnó coill** hazel-nut

collach *m1* boar

collaí *adj* sexual

colm¹ *m1* dove, pigeon

colm² *m1* scar

colmóir *m3* hake

colpa *m4* calf of leg

colscaradh *m* divorce

colún *m1* column, pillar

colúnaí *m4* columnist

colúnáid *f2* colonnade

colúr *m1* pigeon **colúr teachtaireachta** carrier-pigeon

comair *adj* 1. neat 2. brief, precise

comaoin *f2* favour, obligation **tá mé faoi chomaoin agat** I am in your debt

comaoineach *f4* communion **rinne mé mo chéad Chomaoineach anuraidh** I did my first Communion last year

comh- *prefix* 1. joint, common, co- **comhchoiste** joint committee 2. equal **comh-airde** equal height

comhábhar *m1* component part, ingredient

comhad *m1* file **comhad rialúcháin** controlling file

comhadbhainisteoir *m3* file manager

comhadchaibinéad *m1* filing-cabinet

comhadchosaint *f3* file protection

comhaimseartha *adj* contemporary

comhaimsir *f2* **i gcomhaimsir le...** contemporary with..., **lucht mo chomhaimsire** my contemporaries

comhainmneach *m1* namesake

comhainmneoir *m3* common denominator

comhair[1] *v* count, calculate

comhair[2] (with *preps*) **faoi chomhair, i gcomhair for, tá gach rud ullamh faoi chomhair, i gcomhair na hócáide** everything is ready for the occasion, **os comhair** in front of, opposite, **os comhair an tí** in front of the house

comh-aireacht *f3* cabinet (*government*)

comhaireamh *m1* counting, calculation

comhairle *f4* 1. advice **bheith ar chomhairle duine** to be influenced by someone, **táim idir dhá chomhairle faoi** I'm in two minds about it, **beimid i gcomhairle leis faoi** we'll be in consultation with him about it 2. council **comhairle contae** county council, **Ceann Comhairle** speaker, chairperson of Dáil Éireann, **an Chomhairle Ealaíon** the Arts Council, **Comhairle na hEorpa** Council of Europe

comhairleach *adj* consultative, advisory *m1* consultant **comhairleach bainistíochta** management consultant

comhairleoir *m3* 1. counsellor, adviser 2. councillor

comhairligh *v* advise

cómhaith *f2* equal in goodness

cómhalartach *adj* mutual, reciprocal

cómhalartaigh *v* reciprocate

comhalta *m4* member

comhaltacht *f3* fellowship

comhaltas *m1* membership

comhaois *f2* equal age **lucht bhur gcomhaoise** your contemporaries, **nach bhfuil tusa ar comhaois léi?** aren't you the same age as her?

comhaontas *m1* alliance **Comhaontas Idirnáisiúnta na gCumann Sacair** Federation of International Football Associations (FIFA)

comhaontú *m* agreement **an Comhaontú Angla-Éireannach** the Anglo-Irish Agreement

comhar *m1* co-operation **i gcomhar le** in co-operation with, **d'íoc/dhíol mé an comhar leis** I returned the favour to him, I repaid him

comharba *m4* successor

comharbas *m1* succession

comharchumann *m1* co-operative

comhardaigh *v* balance, adjust, equalise

comhardú *m* balance, equalisation **clár comhardaithe** balance sheet, **comhardú cuntas** balancing accounts

Cómhargadh *m1* **an Cómhargadh** the Common Market

comharsa *f5* neighbour **tithe na gcomharsan** the neighbours' houses, **comharsa bhéal dorais** next-door neighbour

comharsanacht *f3* neighbourhood, vicinity **ní raibh trioblóid sa chomharsanacht seo le fada** there hasn't been trouble in this neighbourhood, in the vicinity, for a long time

comharsanúil *adj* neighbourly

comhartha *m4* sign, signal, omen **comharthaí bóthair** roadsigns, **comhartha ceiste** question mark, **comhartha na croise** the sign of the cross, **comharthaí tinnis** signs of sickness, **is olc an comhartha é**

it's a bad omen, **comharthaí sóirt**
identifying marks, description,
comharthaí athfhriotail
quotation marks
comharthaigh *v* indicate, signify
comhbhá *f4* sympathy
comhbhrón *m1* sympathy,
condolence **(déanaim)**
comhbhrón leat my condolences
to you
comhbhrúigh *v* compress
comhbhrúiteoir *m3* compressor
comhbhrúiteoir aeir air
compressor
comhbhruith *f* concoction *v* concoct
comhbhuainteoir *m3* combine
harvester
comhchaidreamh *m1* association
comhchaint *f2* negotiation
comhchainteanna negotiations,
joint talks
comhcheangail *v* bind, join
together, combine
comhcheangal *m1* combination
comhcheilg *f2* conspiracy
comhchéim *f2* matching step
táimid ar comhchéim le chéile
we are on equal terms, on an
equal footing
comhcheol *m1* harmony (*music*)
comhchiallach *m1* synonym
comhchoiteann *adj* general,
communal
comhchosúil (le) *adj* similar (to)
comhchruinn *adj* spherical, perfectly
round
comhchruinnigh *v* gather together,
congregate
comhchuibhiú *m* harmonisation (*of
rules*)
comhchuid *f3* equal part,
component
comhchuntas *m1* joint account
comhdháil *f3* meeting, convention,
congress

comhdhéan *v* make up, constitute
comhdhéanamh *m1* structure,
composition
comhdhlúthaigh *v* 1. condense
2. press together, compact
comhdhlúthú *m* condensation
comhdhuille *m4* 1. counterfoil
2. stub **comhdhuille seic** cheque
stub
comhéadan *m1* interface
comhéadan caighdeánach
standard interface
comhfhiontar *m1* joint venture
comhfhios *m3* 1. consciousness
2. **gan fhios nó i gcomhfhios**
secretly or openly
comhfhiosach *adj* conscious
comhfhocal *m1* compound word
comhfhreagair *v* correspond
comhfhreagracht *f3*
correspondence
comhfhreagraí *m4* correspondent
comhfhreagraí spóirt sport
correspondent
comhfhreagras *m1* correspondence
(*letters*)
comhghairdeas *m1* congratulation
comhghairdeas (leat / libh)!
congratulations (to you)!
comhghaolmhaireacht *f3*
correlation
comhghaolmhar *adj* closely related,
interrelated
comhghleacaí *m4* colleague
comhghnás *m1* protocol, social
conventions
comhghnásach *adj* conventional
comhghuaillí *m4* ally
comhionann *adj* equivalent, identical
comhionannas *m1* equality
comhla *f4* 1. shutter **comhla
ceamara** camera shutter 2. door
leaf **comhla shleamhnáin** sliding
door, **comhla thógála** trap-door
3. valve **comhla croí** heart-valve,

comhla rialaithe control valve, **comhla shaorga** artificial valve

comhlachas *m1* association **comhlachas trádála** trade/trading association

comhlacht *m3* body, company, firm **comhlacht árachais** insurance company, **comhlacht fo-stáit/leath-stáit** semi-state body, **comhlacht teoranta** limited company, **Comhlacht Oideachais na hÉireann** the Educational Company of Ireland

comhlánaigh *v* complete, complement

comhlántach *adj* complementary

comhlann *m1* combat, contest

comhlathas *m1* commonwealth

comhlíon *v* fulfil, carry out, complete **chomhlíon siad a ngealltanas** they fulfilled their promise

comhluadar *m1* 1. company **comhluadar a choinneáil le duine** to keep somebody company 2. household, family **cén chaoi a bhfuil an comhluadar?** how's the family?

comhoibrí *m4* co-worker, workmate, co-operator

comhoibrigh (le) *v* co-operate, collaborate

comhoibritheach *adj* co-operative

comhoibriú *m* co-operation

comhoideachas *m1* co-education

comhoideachasúil *adj* co-educational

comhoiriúnach *adj* compatible, matching

comhoiriúnacht *f3* compatibility

comhordaigh *v* co-ordinate

comhordanáid *f2* co-ordinate **comhordanáidí polacha** polar co-ordinates

comhordanáidigh *v* co-ordinate (*maths*)

comhpháirt *f2* 1. component part **comhpháirt inathraithe** variable

component 2. **i gcomhpháirt le...** in partnership with...

comhpháirteach *adj* joint

comhpháirtí *m4* copartner, associate

comhphobal *m1* community an **Comhphobal Eorpach (CE)** the European Community (EC)

comhrá *m4* conversation **comhrá béil** gossip

comhrac *m1* contest, combat, fight **comhrac aonair** duel, **céile comhraic** opponent in battle

comhraic *v* encounter, fight

comhráiteach *adj* conversational

comhramh *m1* triumph, trophy

comhréir *f2* syntax, proportion **i gcomhréir le** proportional to

comhréireach *adj* syntactic(al), proportional

comhréiteach *m1* compromise, agreement

comhréitigh *v* compromise, agree

comhriachtain *f3* copulation, sexual intercourse

comhrialtas *m1* coalition government

comhscór *m1* equal score, draw **comhscór a bhí ann** it was a draw

comhshamhlaigh *v* assimilate

comhshamhlú *m* assimilation

comhshaolach *adj* contemporary

comhsheilbh *f2* joint possession

comhtharlaigh (le) *v* coincide (with)

comhtharlú *m* coincidence

comhtháthaigh *v* join together, merge, integrate

comhthéacs *m4* context

comhthionól *m1* 1. assembly 2. community (*religious*)

comhthíreach *m1* compatriot

comhtholgadh *m* concussion

comhthomhaiseach (le) *adj* commensurate (with)

comhthreomhar (le) *adj* parallel (to)

comóir *v* celebrate **bainis a chomóradh** to celebrate a wedding

comónta *adj* common

comóradh *m* celebration

comórtas *m1* 1. competition **comórtas amhránaíochta** singing competition 2. comparison **i gcomórtas le** in comparison with

compánach *m1* companion

compántas *m1* theatrical company

comparáid *f2* comparison

comparáideach *adj* comparative

compás *m1* compass, circumference

complacht *m3* company (*military*)

compord *m1* comfort

compordach *adj* comfortable

comrádaí *m4* comrade

comrádaíocht *f3* comradeship

común *m1* commune

conablach *m1* carcass, remains

conách *m1* success, betterment, wealth **a chonách sin ort!** may you reap your reward!, it serves you right!

cónaí *m* 1. dwelling, residence **áit chónaithe** place of abode, **tá cónaí orm i…** I live in… 2. peace, **dul faoi chónaí** to go to rest 3. **i gcónaí** always, still

cónaidhm *f2* federation **Cónaidhm na gComhlachas Trádála** Federation of Trade Associations

cónaigh *v* 1. dwell, reside **chónaigh a lán daoine ann** a lot of people lived there, **scoil chónaithe** boarding school 2. settle, rest **níor stad ná níor chónaigh siad gur shroich siad an baile** they neither stopped nor stayed until they reached home

conairt *f2* 1. pack of hounds 2. rabble

cónaisc *v* connect, merge, amalgamate **chónaisc an dá chomhlacht** the two companies amalgamated

cónaitheach *adj* 1. resident 2. constant

cónaitheoir *m3* resident

conamar *m1* fragments

conas *adv* how **conas atá tú?** how are you? **conas atá an misneach?** how's the form?

cónasc *m1* 1. connection, link 2. conjunction (*grammar*)

cónascach *adj* 1. connecting, linking, federal 2. conjunctive

cónascachas *m1* federalism

conchró *m4* kennel

conclúid *f2* conclusion

confach *adj* 1. furious 2. rabid

confadh *m1* 1. fury 2. rabies 3. **confadh fiacla** teething pains

cóngar *m1* 1. nearness, proximity 2. shortcut

cóngarach *adj* 1. near, convenient **tá sé cóngarach do Dhún Droma** it's near (to) Dundrum 2. concise (*of speech*)

conlaigh *v* gather

conláisteach *adj* convenient

conlán *m1* initiative **táim ar mo chonlán féin** I provide for myself, I'm independent, **rinne sé é ar a chonlán féin** he did it of his own accord, on his own initiative

Connachta *m5* Connaught **Cúige Connacht** (the province of) Connaught

Connachtach *adj* Connaught *m1* native of Connaught

cónacht *m3* equinox

cónra *f4* coffin

conradh *m3* treaty, league, contract **rinne mé conradh le…** I entered into an agreement with…, I made a contract with…, **obair chonartha**

contract work, **conradh síochána** peace treaty, **Conradh na Gaeilge** the Gaelic League, **Conradh na Róimhe** the Treaty of Rome

conraitheoir *m3* contractor

consal *m1* consul

consalacht *f3* consulate

consan *m1* consonant **is iad a, o, u na consain leathna** a, o, u are the broad consonants

consól *m1* console (*computer*) **consól ionaid sonraí** data station console

conspóid *f2* dispute, controversy

conspóideach *adj* argumentative, controversial

constábla *m4* constable

constáblacht *f3* constabulary **Constáblacht Ríoga Uladh, na hÉireann** Royal Ulster, Irish Constabulary

constaic *f2* obstacle, difficulty

contae *m4* county

contrabhanna *m4* contraband

contráilte *adj* 1. wrong **brí chontráilte** wrong meaning 2. contrary **fear contráilte** a contrary man

contrártha *adj* contrary, opposite **contrátha leis sin** contrary to that

contrárthacht *f3* contrast **i gcontrárthacht le rud** in contrast with something

contráth *m3* dusk

contúirt *f2* danger **i gcontúirt** in danger

contúirteach *adj* dangerous

cor *m1* 1. turn, twist, stir **cuireadh cor ann** it was twisted, **chuir siad cor san fhírinne** they distorted the truth, **níor chuir sé cor inniu fós** he hasn't stirred yet today, **cor cainte** turn of phrase, idiom, **in aon chor, ar chor ar bith** at all 2. haul (*of fish*) 3. reel (*dance*) **cor ceathrair** four-hand reel

cór¹ *m1* choir, chorus

cór² *m1* corps **an cór airtléire** the artillery corps, **an cór comharthaíochta** the signal corps, **an cór taidhleoireachta** the diplomatic corps

cora *f4* 1. weir 2. dam, crossing-place in river

coraintín *m4* quarantine **ainmhí ar coraintín** an animal in quarantine

córam *m1* quorum

Córán *m4* **an Córán** the Quran / Koran

córas *m1* system **córas díleáite** digestive system, **córas eolais bhainistíochta** management information system (MIS), **córas na gréine** the solar system, **córas ríomhaire** computer system, **an Córas Airgeadaíochta Eorpach (COAE)** European Monetary System (EMS), **an Córas Réaltrach** the Galactic System

córasach *adj* systematic

corc *m1* cork

Corcaigh *f2* Cork **cathair Chorcaí** Cork city

Corcaíoch *m1* native of Cork

corcairdhearg *adj, m1* crimson

corcairghorm *adj, m1* violet (*colour*)

corcán *m1* pot

corcra *adj* purple

corcsriú *m4* corkscrew

corda *m4* 1. cord, string 2. chord

corn¹ *m1* 1. horn **corn Francach** French horn 2. goblet **corn óil** drinking-horn 3. cup **Corn Mhic Cárthaigh** the McCarthy Cup

corn² *v* roll, coil

Corn³, an *m1* Cornwall **Corn na Breataine** Cornwall

corna *m4* coil, roll **cornaí féir** hay bales

Cornach *adj* Cornish

Cornais *f2* Cornish (*language*)

cornchlár *m1* sideboard

cornphíopa *m4* hornpipe

coróin *f5* crown **bhí Séarlas i gcoróin ag an am** Charles was wearing the crown, reigning at the time, **tháinig sé i gcoróin** he acceeded to the throne

coróineach *f2* carnation

corónaigh *v* crown **corónaíodh ina banríon í** she was crowned queen

corónú *m* coronation

corp *m1* 1. body **corp an leabhair** the body of the book 2. corpse **thángthas ar chorp ann** a corpse was found there

corpán *m1* corpse

corparáid *f2* corporation **cáin chorparáide** corporation tax, **corparáid ilnáisiúnta** multinational corporation

corparáideach *adj* corporate

corpartha *adj* physical, bodily, corporal **pléisiúr corpartha** bodily pleasure, **pionós corportha** corporal punishment

corpfhorbairt *f3* body building

corpoiliúint *m1* physical education

corr[1] *adj* odd, peculiar **níor theastaigh uaim a bheith corr** I didn't want to be the odd one

corr[2] *f2* 1. heron **corr bhán** stork 2. sand-eel **corr ghainimh** sand-eel

corr-[3] *prefix* odd-, occasional **na corruimhreacha** the odd numbers

corrabhuais *f2* 1. uneasiness 2. confusion

corrabhuaiseach *adj* 1. uneasy 2. confused

corrach *adj* unsteady, troubled, unsettled **bord corrach** an unsteady table, **saol corrach** a troubled life, **bheith corrach** to be uneasy, unsettled, troubled

corradh *m* addition **deichniúr agus corradh** more than ten, **corradh le, agus, ar...** more than...

corraí *m* stir, excitement, movement **tagann corraí air go minic** he get's stirred often, **ní féidir liom corraí a bhaint as** I can't budge him/it

corraigh *v* move, stir **ná corraigh chun feirge é** don't move him to anger

corraíl *f3* 1. stir, movement 2. excitement, thrill

corraithe *adj* excited

corraitheach *adj* 1. stirring, moving 2. exciting, thrilling

corrán *m1* 1. sickle 2. **corrán géill** jaw, lower jawbone 3. crescent **corrán gealaí** crescent moon

corrlach *m1* odds, odd amount

corrmhéar *f2* index finger

corrmhíol *m1* midge **corrmhíol uisce** water gnat

corróg *f2* hip

corrthónach *adj* restless, fidgety

corruair *adv* sometimes, occasionally

cortha *adj* tired, exhausted

corthacht *f3* tiredness, exhaustion

córúil *adj* choral

cos *f2* 1. foot, leg **cos duine, boird** leg of a person, table, **siúlaim de chois ar scoil gach maidin** I travel to school on foot every morning, **d'imigh sé leis ar cosa in airde** he left at a gallop, **bheith faoi chois** to be underfoot, oppressed, **cos ar bolg** oppression 2. handle, stem **cos scine** handle of knife, **cos píopa** stem of pipe 3. **cois na tine** beside the fire, **cois farraige** by the sea 4. **le cois** along with, in addition to, **ag siúl le cois a chéile** walking alongside each other, **lena chois sin** along with that, besides

cosain *v* 1. defend **tú féin a chosaint** to defend yourself 2. cost **cosnaíonn sé an t-uafás airgid** it costs too much money

cosaint *f3* defence 'ní cosaint go hamas' attack is the best form of defence, **fórsaí cosanta** defence forces, **cosaint cluas** earmuffs

cosán *m1* path(way), footpath, track

cosantach *adj* defensive, protective

cosantóir *m3* 1. defender, protector 2. defendant (*law*)

cosc *m1* prevention, prohibition **Cosc ar Thobac** Smoking Prohibited

coscair *v* 1. break up, shatter, disintegrate 2. slaughter, defeat 3. thaw

coscairt *f3* 1. breaking up, shattering, disintegration 2. defeat, slaughter 3. thaw

coscán *m1* brake **coscáin hiodrálacha** hydraulic brakes, **coscán láimhe** handbrake

coscrach *adj* 1. shattering, shocking 2. triumphant

coslia *m4* chiropodist

cosmhaisiú *m* pedicure

cosmhuintir *f2* proletariat, poor people

cosnochta *adj* barefooted

cósta *m4* coast

costas *m1* cost, expense **costas maireachtála** cost of living, **rud a cheannach ar a chostas** to buy something at cost

costasach *adj* costly, expensive

cosúil *adj* 1. like, resembling **tá siad cosúil le chéile** they are alike 2. **is cosúil go...** apparently, it appears that...

cosúlacht *f3* likeness, resemblance

cóta *m4* coat **cóta fionnaidh** fur coat, **cóta péinte** coat of paint

cothabháil *f3* maintenance *v* maintain

cothaigh *v* 1. feed, sustain **tá páistí le cothú acu** they have children to feed 2. harbour, promote **díoltas a chothú** to harbour revenge, **cothaíonn sé aighneas i gcónaí** he always aggravates an argument

cothroime *f4* evenness

cothrom *adj* 1. level, even, balanced 2. equal 3. fair *m1* 1. level, balance **ná cuir ó chothrom é** don't unbalance it, **i gcothrom le** level with, on a par with 2. equal amount 3. fair play, fairness **cothrom na Féinne a thabhairt do...** to give fair play to... 4. **cothrom an lae** on the corresponding day, date, **cothrom an lae seo ceithre bliana déag ó shin a rugadh mé** I was born 14 years ago today, today is my birthday

cothromaigh *v* equalise, even, level, balance

cothromaíocht *f3* equilibrium, evenness

cothrománach *adj* horizontal **suíomh cothrománach** horizontal position

cothú *m* 1. sustenance, nourishment 2. maintenance, promotion

cothúil *adj* nourishing

cotúil *adj* shy, bashful

crá *m4* 1. annoyance, torment 2. distress, **crá croí** overwhelming distress, sorrow

crág *f2* 1. claw, big hand 2. clutch (*mechanical*) **teip chráige** clutch failure

crágáil *v* 1. claw, handle roughly 2. walk awkwardly

craic *f2* 1. crack 2. chat

craiceann *m1* 1. skin **an craiceann a bhaint de na prátaí** to peel the potatoes 2. surface **craiceann bóthair** road surface

cráifeach *adj* pious, religious

cráifeacht *f3* piety

cráifisc *f2* crayfish

cráigh *v* annoy, torment **bíonn sé de shíor do mo chrá le ceisteanna** he is always tormenting me with questions

cráin *f5* sow **cráin mhuice** sow

cráinbheach *f2* queen bee

cráite *adj* troubled, tormented

crampa *m4* cramp

cranda *adj* stunted, decrepit

crandaí *m4* 1. hammock 2. **crandaí bogadaí** seesaw

crandaigh *v* become stunted, stunt

crangaid *f2* winch

crann *m1* 1. tree **crann toraidh** fruit tree 2. mast, pole **crann brataí** flag-pole, **crann loinge** mast of ship 3. handle 4. shaft **crann tógála** crane 5. lot, misfortune **chuireamar ar chrainn é** we cast lots for it, **ar do chrann atá sé** it's your turn, **bhí sé de chrann orthu...** they had the misfortune...

crannchur *m1* lottery, sweepstake **an Crannchur Náisiúnta** the National Lottery

crannóg *f2* 1. pulpit 2. lake dwelling, 'crannóg'

craobh *f2* 1. branch **craobhacha crainn** tree branches, **tá sé imithe le craobhacha** he has gone mad, **craobh den Chomhar Creidmheasa** a branch of the Credit Union 2. championship **cluiche craoibhe** championship match, **craobh an domhain** the championship of the world

craobhabhainn *f5* tributary (*river*)

craobhach *adj* 1. branched **coinnleoir craobhach** chandelier 2. flowing (*of hair, dress, etc*)

craobhchomórtas *m1* championship (*competition*)

craobhóg *f2* branchlet, twig

craobhscaoil *v* propagate, broadcast

craobhscaoileadh *m* propagation, broadcast

craobhtheach *m* daughter house

craoibhín *m4* 1. branchlet, twig 2. darling **an Craoibhín Aoibhinn** Douglas Hyde

craol *v* 1. announce 2. broadcast

craolachán *m1* broadcasting **cúntóir craolacháin** broadcasting assistant

craoladh *m* broadcast **craoladh seachtrach** outside broadcast (*television*)

craoltóir *m3* broadcaster

craos *m1* 1. throat, gullet 2. gluttony, greed

craosach *adj* 1. open-mouthed 2. gluttonous

craosaire *m4* glutton

craosfholc *v* gargle

crap *v* shrink, contract

crapadh *m* shrinkage, contraction

craplaigh *v* cripple

craptha *adj* crippled, cramped

cré[1] *f4* clay, earth **soitheach cré** earthen vessel, **tá sé ag dul i gcré** he is being buried

cré[2] *f4* creed **an Chré** the Creed

creach[1] *v* 1. plunder, loot 2. ruin 3. raid *f2* 1. plunder, prey **éan creiche** bird of prey 2. ruin **mo chreach nár éist mé leat** I regret that I didn't listen to you 3. raid **talamh creiche** land taken by force

creach[2] *v* brand (*cattle*), stain

creachadh *m* plunder, ruination

créacht *f3* wound, gash

créafóg *m2* clay, earth

creagach *adj* rocky, craggy, barren

créam *v* cremate

créamadh *m* cremation

créamotóiriam *m4* crematorium

creat *m3* frame, shape **creat loinge** framework of ship, **tá creat maith anois air** he/it is in good shape now

creatach *adj* weak, emaciated

creath *v* tremble **ag creathadh leis an bhfuacht** trembling with the cold

creathach *adj* 1. trembling, shaky 2. vibrating

creathán *m1* tremble, tremor, **creathán talún** earth, earthquake tremor

creathánach *adj* trembling

creathnaigh *v* tremble, take fright

creatlach *f2* framework, skeleton **creatlach foirgnimh** framework of building, **níl ansin ach creatlach an scéil** that's only the outline of the story

créatúr *m1* creature **fan leis an gcréatúr (bocht)!** wait for the poor thing!

cré-earra *m* article made of earth **cré-earraí** earthenware

creid *v* believe **creid mé / é nó ná creid** believe me/it or not

creideamh *m1* faith, belief, religion

creidiúint *f3* credit **tá an-chreidiúint ag dul duit** there is great credit due to you

creidiúnach *adj* creditable, respectable, reputable

creidiúnaí *m4* creditor

creidmheas *m3* credit **cárta creidmheasa** credit card, **an Comhar Creidmheasa** the Credit Union

creig *f2* crag, rock

creig-ghairdín *m4* rock garden, rockery

creim *v* 1. gnaw, nibble 2. erode, corrode

creimeadh *m* erosion

creimire *m4* rodent

cré-umha *m4* bronze

cré-umhaois *f2* **an Chré-Umhaois** the Bronze Age

crián *m1* crayon

criathar *m1* 1. sieve 2. quagmire

criathrach *m1* pitted bog

criathraigh *v* sieve, sift

críoch *f2* 1. boundary, limit **balla críche** boundary wall 2. region, territory **Críoch Lochlann**

Scandinavia 3. end, completion, purpose **rud a chur i gcrích** to complete, accomplish something

críoch-chomhartha *m4* landmark

críochfort *m1* terminal (*building*)

críochnaigh *v* finish, accomplish, compete **rud a chríochnú** to finish something

críochnaithe *adj* finished, accomplished, completed

críochnú *m* completion

críochnúil *adj* tidy, thorough

críochú *m* demarcation

criogar *m1* cricket (*insect*) **criogar féir** grasshopper

críonna *adj* 1. prudent, wise, shrewd 2. old **m'athair críonna** my grandfather, **do mháthair chríonna** your grandmother

críonnacht *f3* 1. wisdom, shrewdness 2. maturity

crios *m3* belt, zone **crios sábhála** seat belt, **crios iompair** conveyor-belt, **crios deighilte** buffer zone, **crios fiontraíochta** enterprise zone

Críost *m4* Christ

Críostaí *adj, m4* Christian

Críostaíocht *f3* Christianity

criostal *m1* crystal

Críostúil *adj* Christian

crith *m3* tremor, shake, tremble **crith talún** earthquake, **bhí mé ar crith le heagla** I was trembling with fear *v* tremble, quake

critheagla *f4* great fear, terror

critheaglach *adj* trembling with fear, terrified

crithlonraigh *v* shimmer

criticeoir *m3* critic

criticiúil *adj* critical

cró¹ *m4* 1. outhouse, shed, pen **cró cearc, muice** hen-house, pigsty, **cró folaigh** dug-out (*sport*) 2. hovel **ní fheicfear sa chró tí**

seo arís mé I will not be seen in this hole again **3.** bore (*gun, pipe*) **4.** eye (*needle*), socket **5.** aperture (*photography*) **6.** ring **cró sorcais** circus ring

cró² *m4* blood, gore

crobh *m1* hand, talons **crobh seod** handful of jewels (*archaic*)

croch *f2* **1.** cross, gallows **cuireadh chun na croiche é** he was sent to the gallows **2.** hanger *v* **1.** hang **2.** raise up **croch suas é!** strike up a/the song! **3.** lift, carry

crochadán *m1* **1.** hanger (*clothes, coat*) **2.** stand (*coat, hat*)

crochadh *m* hanging **bheith ar crochadh** to be hanging

crochadóir *m3* hangman

cróchar *m1* stretcher

crochóg *f2* (stocking) suspender, **crochóga** suspenders

crochta *adj* **1.** hanging **2.** raised, steep

cróga *adj* **1.** brave, heroic **2.** lively, hardy

crógacht *f3* bravery

crogall *m1* crocodile

croí *m4* heart, centre **cliseadh / teip croí** heart failure, **tá croí mór aici** she has a big heart, **croí an scéil** the heart of the matter, **croí na féile** the soul of generosity, **a chroí!** my dear!

croíbhriste *adj* broken-hearted

croílár *m1* exact centre

cróilí *adj* bed-ridden, disabled *m4* bed-ridden state, infirmity **i gcróilí an bháis** on the death-bed

croiméal *m1* moustache

cróimiam *m4* chromium

cróinéir *m3* coroner **coiste cróinéara** coroner's inquest

cróineolaíoch *adj* chronological

croinic *f2* chronicle

cróise *f4* crochet

croit *f2* croft

croith *v* **1.** shake **chroith sí a ceann** she shook her head, **chroitheamar lámha** we shook hands, **croitheadh chuig duine** to wave at somebody, **croith slán leo** wave them good-bye **2.** sprinkle, scatter **ag croitheadh uisce ar phlandaí** sprinkling plants with water

croitheadh *m* **1.** shake **croitheadh láimhe** handshake **2.** sprinkling, scattering

croíúil *adj* hearty, cheerful

crom *adj* stooped, bent, drooping *v* stoop, bend **chrom mé ar mo chuid oibre** I began to work

cróm *m1* chrome

cromán *m1* hip

crómasóm *m1* chromosome

cromleac *f2* cromlech

crompán *m1* **1.** creek, sea inlet **2.** knotty piece of wood

cromshlinneánach *adj* round-shouldered, stooped

crón *adj* dark brown, tan

cronaigh *v* miss **cronaím uaim go mór í** I miss her a lot

crónán *m1* hum(ming), drone, droning, purr(ing) **ar mhaithe leis féin a dhéanann an cat crónán** the cat purrs for its own benefit

cros *f2* **1.** cross **an Chros Dhearg** the Red Cross, **chomh siúráilte is atá cros ar asal** as sure as there is a cross on a donkey, as sure as can be **2.** prohibition **chuir sé cros in éadan an phlean** he prohibited the plan *v* hinder, forbid, prohibit **chros siad orm é a dhéanamh** they forbade me to do it

crosach *adj* crosswise, crossed

crosáil *v* cross **ba chóir seic a chrosáil i gcónaí** a cheque should always be crossed

crosaire *m4* crossroads, crossing

crosbhealach *m1* crossing, crossroad

crosbhóthar *m1* crossroad

croscheistigh *v* cross-examine

crosfhocal *m1* crossword

croslámhach *m1* crossfire

crosóg *f2* small cross

cros-síolraigh *v* crossbreed

crosta *adj* difficult, troublesome

crostagairt *f3* cross-reference

crotal *m1* rind, husk

crú *m4* horseshoe **nuair a thiocfaidh an crú ar an tairne** when it comes to the test

crua *adj* hard, difficult *m4* hard

cruach¹ *f2* 1. pile **cruach mhór airgid** big pile of money 2. stack **cruach fhéir** haystack *v* pile, stack

cruach² *f4* steel **cruach faobhair** sharpening steel, **cruach dhosmálta** stainless steel, **cruach tháite** welded steel

cruachás *m1* distress, difficulty, predicament **tá sé i gcruachás** he is in a difficulty, predicament

cruachóip *f2* hard copy

cruadhiosca *m4* hard disk

crua-earra *m4* piece of hardware **crua-earraí** hardware

cruaigh *v* harden

cruálach *adj* cruel

cruálacht *f3* 1. cruelty 2. meanness

cruan *m1*, *v* enamel

cruas *m1* 1. hardness 2. meanness

cruatan *m1* hardship

crúb *f2* 1. hoof **Fear na gCrúb** the Devil, the joker (*cards*) 2. claw

crúbáil *v* claw, paw

crúca *m4* crook, hook

crúcáil *v* hook, claw

cruib *f2* crib

cruicéad *m1* cricket (*sport*)

cruidín *m4* kingfisher

crúigh¹ *v* shoe (*a horse*)

crúigh² *v* milk **ag crú na mbó** milking the cows

cruimh *f2* maggot, grub

cruinn *adj* 1. accurate, exact 2. round 3. gathered, assembled

cruinne¹ *f4* roundness

cruinne² *f4* 1. universe 2. globe, orb **ar fud na cruinne** all over the globe, world

cruinneachán *m1* dome

cruinneas *m1* accuracy

cruinneog *f2* globe

cruinnigh *v* gather, collect, assemble **ag cruinniú airgid** collecting money, **chruinnigh an fhoireann le chéile ann** the team assembled there

cruinniú *m* gathering, meeting

crúiscín *m4* jug

cruit¹ *f2* hump **chuir sé cruit air féin** he hunched his shoulders, it (*cat*) arched its back

cruit² *f2* small harp

cruiteach *adj* hunchbacked

cruiteachán *m1* hunchback

cruithneacht *f3* wheat

cruitire *m4* harpist

crúóg *f2* urgent need **crúóg a bheith ort** to be pressed for time

crúógach *adj* pressing, busy

crúsca *m4* jug, jar

crústa *m4* 1. crust **an íosfaidh tú an crústa?** will you eat the heel, the crust? 2. blow **buaileadh crústa san aghaidh air** he got a blow in the face

cruth *m3* 1. shape, form, appearance **cuir cruth éigin ort féin** smarten yourself up 2. condition, state **cén cruth a bhí ar an teach?** what state was the house in?

cruthaigh *v* 1. prove **an féidir é a chruthú?** can it be proven? 2. create **ó cruthaíodh an saol** since the world was created 3. form

cruthaitheach *adj* creative

cruthaitheoir *m3* creator

cruthanta *adj* lifelike, exact **amadán cruthanta** a perfect idiot

cruthú *m* 1. creation 2. proof **an bhfuil aon chruthú agat leis?** have you any proof of it?

cruthúnas *m1* proof

cú *m4* greyhound, hound **cú dobhráin** otter, **Bord na gCon** Greyhound Racing Board

cuach[1] *m4* bowl, drinking-cup

cuach[2] *f2* 1. cuckoo 2. curl, tress (*hair*) 3. hug *v* 1. bundle, wrap 2. hug

cuaifeach *m1* gust (of wind), whirlwind

cuaille *m4* stake, pole, post **cuaillí báire** goalposts, **an cuaille tosaithe** the starting post

cuain *f2* 1. litter **bhí cuain coileán aréir aici** she had a litter of pups last night 2. pack **cuain gadaithe** band of thieves

cuairín *m4* circumflex

cuairt *f2* 1. visit **thug mé cuairt ar m'uncail aréir** I visited my uncle last night 2. round, circuit **tá sé chuairt sa rás seo** there are 6 laps in this race, **thug siad cuairt na hÉireann i gcurrach** the made a circuit of Ireland in a currach

cuairteoir *m3* visitor, tourist

cuallacht *f3* 1. company, fellowship 2. guild, corporation

cuan *m1* harbour

cuar *m1* curve, circle

cuarán *m1* sandal

cuarbhóthar *m1* circular road, ring road **an cuarbhóthar theas, thuaidh** the south, north circular road

cuardach *m1* search **barántas cuardaigh** search warrant

cuardaigh *v* search

cuartaíocht *f3* visiting

cuas *m1* 1. cove, creek 2. cavity 3. sinus

cuasach *adj* concave, hollow

cúb *f2* 1. (hen-)coop 2. bend *v* 1. bend 2. shrink, cower **chúb sé siar uaim** he cowered away from me

cúbláil *v* misappropriate, manipulate **airgead cúbláilte** misappropriated money, **bhí sé ag cúbláil na gcuntas** he was manipulating the accounts

cúcamar *m1* cucumber

cufa *m4* cuff

cuí *adj* appropriate, fitting

cuibheasach *adj* fair, middling **cuibheasach gan a bheith maíteach** just middling (without being boastful), **cuibheasach ard** fairly high, tall

cuibheoir *m1* adaptor (*electrical*)

cuibhiúil *adj* proper, seemly, decent

cuibhiúlacht *f3* seemliness, decency, decorum

cuibhreach *m1* fetter

cuibhreann *m1* 1. tilled field 2. mess (*soldiers*) **cuibhreann na n-oifigeach** the officers' mess

cuid *f3* part, portion **cuid acu** some of them, **an chuid is mó den phobal** the majority of the public, **mo chuid airgid** my money, **bhí cuid mhaith / mhór daoine ann** there were a lot of people there, **dán de do chuid féin** one of your own poems, **codanna cothroma** equal parts, **a chuid!** darling!

cuideachta *f4* 1. company **cé bhí i do chuideachta?** who was with you, in your company? **gluaisteán cuideachta** company car 2. fun, amusement **bhí an-chuideachta againn ann** we had great fun there

cuideachtúil *adj* sociable

cuidigh *v* help **ag cuidiú le m'athair** helping my father, **cuidím leis sin** I second that

cuiditheoir *m3* helper, seconder

cuidiú *m* assistance

cuidiúil *adj* helpful

cúig *m4* five **cúig chapall mhóra** five big horses, **cúig cinn** five (*of something*), **a cúig déag** fifteen

cúige *m4* province **Cúige Connacht** Connaught, **Cúige Laighean** Leinster, **Cúige Mumhan** Munster, **Cúige Uladh** Ulster

cúigeach *adj* provincial

cuigeann *f2* churn

cúigear *m1* five people **cúigear dochtúirí, múinteoirí** five doctors, teachers, **cúigear ban, fear** five women, men

cúigiú[1] *m4* fifth **trí chúigiú** three fifths

cúigiú[2] *adj* fifth **an cúigiú bliain** fifth year

cuil[1] *f2* fly, gnat **cuil ghorm** bluebottle

cuil[2] *f2* angry appearance **tháinig cuil troda air** he became aggressive

cúil *f5* corner, nook

cuileáil *v* 1. reject 2. put aside 3. embezzle

cuileann[1] *m1* holly

cuileann[2] *f2* fair lady

cuileog *f2* fly

cúilín *m4* point (*in Gaelic football, hurling*)

cuilithe *f4* 1. current, vortex 2. core

cuilithín *m4* ripple

cuilt *f2* quilt

cuimhin, is cuimhin liom... I remember..., **an cuimhin leat é?** do you remember it?

cuimhne *f4* memory **más buan mo chuimhne** if my memory serves me right, **cuimhní cinn** memoirs, recollections, **cuir i gcuimhne dom é** remind me of it

cuimhneachán *m1* 1. memorial, commemoration 2. souvenir, momento

cuimhneamh *m1* 1. recollection, thought 2. plan

cuimhnigh *v* 1. remember, consider **cuimhneoidh tú go deo uirthi** you'll always remember her, **cuimhnigh gur beag an taithí atá aige** consider that he has very little experience 2. remind **cuimhnigh dom é** remind me of it

cuimil *v* rub, stroke, wipe

cuimilt *f2* rubbing, stroking, wiping, friction

cuimilteoir *m3* wiper **cuimilteoirí gaothscátha** windscreen wipers

cuimleoir *m3* rubber

cuimse *f4* moderation, limit **chuaigh sé thar cuimse leis** he went too far with it, **as cuimse** extreme, exceeding

cuimsigh *v* include, comprehend, comprise

cuimsitheach *adj* inclusive, comprehensive

cuing *f2* 1. yoke **bheith faoi chuing** to be oppressed 2. obligation **cuing an phósta** bond of marriage, wedlock

cúinne *m4* corner, nook

cúinneach *m1* corner kick

cuinneog *f2* churn

cúinse *m4* purpose, condition, circumstance **ar an gcúinse go...** on condition that..., **ar aon chúinse** in any, under no circumstances

cuíosach = **cuibheasach**

cuir *v* 1. put, place **chuir sí síos an gunna** she put down the gun 2. bury **cuirfear amárach é** he'll be buried tomorrow 3. sow, plant **síol a chur** to plant seed 4. set, lay **cuirim airgead i leataobh gach seachtain** I set money aside every week 5. send **cuireadh an litir sa phost** the letter was sent in the post 6. **ag cur báistí / fearthainne** raining

cuir amach put out **cuireadh amach as a dteach iad** they were evicted from their house, **chuir sé amach a raibh ina bholg** he vomited all he had in his stomach

cuir ar put on/to, impose on **cuir ar vóta é** put it to a vote, **chuir an breitheamh fineáil orm** the judge imposed a fine on me, **cuirimse an locht ar Thomás** I blame Tomás

cuir as 1. put out of **cuireadh as an rang í** she was put out of the class 2. annoy **cur as do dhuine** to annoy, disturb somebody

cuir de accomplish, get done **an bhfuil an obair curtha díot agat?** have you finished the work?

cuir faoi 1. put under **cuir faoin mbord iad** put them under the table 2. settle down **chuir sé faoi i bPort Laoise** he settled in Port Laoise

cuir i put in **chuir pobal na hÉireann i gcumhacht é** the people of Ireland put him in power

cuir isteach 1. put in **cuir isteach d'ainm agus do sheoladh** fill in your name and address 2. annoy **cur isteach ar dhuine** to annoy, disturb, somebody

cuir síos 1. put down **cuir síos an peann** put down the pen 2. **cur síos ar rud** to describe something

cuir suas put up **is deacair cur suas leis** it's hard to put up with him/it

cuircín *m4* crest (*of bird*)

cuireadh *m1* invitation

cuireata *m4* knave, jack (*cards*)

cuirfiú *m4* curfew

cuirín *m4* currant

cúirséad *m1* courgette

cúirt *f2* court **cúirt leadóige** tennis court, **cúirt scuaise** squash court, **na Ceithre Cúirteanna** the Four Courts, **cúirt d'aosánaigh** juvenile court

cúirtéis *f2* 1. courtesy 2. salute (*military*) **thug siad an chúirtéis dá chéile** they exchanged salutes, **cúirtéis ghunna is fiche a scaoileadh** to fire a salute of 21 guns

cúirteoir *m3* courtier

cuirtín *m4* curtain

cúis *f2* 1. cause, reason **cúis ghearáin a bheith agat** to have cause for complaint 2. case, charge **cúis dlí** lawsuit 3. **an ndéanfaidh sé cúis?** will it do?

cúiseamh *m1* 1. accusation 2. charge, prosecution

cúisí *m4* accused person

cúisigh *v* 1. accuse 2. charge, prosecute

cúisín *m4* cushion

cúisitheoir *m3* prosecutor

cuisle *f4* pulse, vein **cuisle duine a bhrath, a fhéachaint** to feel somebody's pulse

cuisneoir *m3* refrigerator, fridge

cúiteach *adj* compensating

cúiteamh *m1* repayment, recompense, compensation

cúitigh *v* repay, compensate

cúl *m1* 1. back **ar chúl an tí** at the back of the house, **ag dul ar gcúl** going backwards, receding 2. reserve **cúl taca** reserve support, backing 3. goal, defender (*sport*)

cúlaí *m4* defender (*sport*)

cúlaigh *v* reverse, back, retreat **is deacair leoraí a chúlú** it is difficult to reverse a lorry

culaith *f2* suit, dress **culaith saighdiúra** soldier's uniform, **culaith ghleacaíochta** leotard

culaithirt *f2* gear, costume **culaithirt seanré** historical costume

cúlánta *adj* 1. shy, timid 2. backward **áit chúlánta** out-of-the-way place

cúlbhannaí *pl* collateral security

cúlbhrat *m1* backcurtain, backdrop (*theatre*)

cúlchaint *f2* backbiting, gossip

cúlchiste *m4* reserve **cúlchistí óir** gold reserves

cúlchnap *m1* float (*money*)

cúldoras *m1* backdoor

cúléisteacht *f3* eavesdropping **ná bí ag cúléisteacht leo** don't eavesdrop on them

cúlfhiacail *f2* backtooth, molar

cúlgharda *m4* rearguard

cúlhaiste *m4* hatchback

cúlpháirtí *m4* accessory (*to crime*)

cúlra *m4* background **torann cúlra** background noise

cúlráid *f2* secluded place **ar an gcúlráid** in seclusion

cúlráideach *adj* secluded (*place, thing, etc*), retiring (*of person*)

cúlsolas *m1* rearlight

cúlspás *m1* backspace

cúltaca *m4* 1. backup, standby **cóip chúltaca** backup copy, **córas cúltaca** standby system 2. reserve **trúpaí cúltaca** troops in reserve

cultas *m1* cult

cúltort *v* backfire

cultúr *m1* culture **cúrsaí cultúir** cultural affairs

cultúrtha *adj* cultured

cúlú *m* retreat **a gcúlú a chosc** to cut off/prevent their retreat

cum *v* 1. compose **ag cumadh filíochta** composing poetry 2. shape, form 3. devise **scéim a chumadh** to devise a scheme 4. invent **ní mise a chum ná a cheap** it wasn't me who invented it, **ag cumadh scéalta atá sé** he's only making up stories

cuma[1] *f4* 1. form, shape, appearance, state **tá cuma mhaith ar an mbád** the boat looks in a good state, in good shape, **tá an chuma sin air** it would appear so 2. **ar aon chuma, ar chuma ar bith** anyway, at any rate, **ar do chuma féin** like yourself

cuma[2] *f4* (with copula **is, ba** etc): **is cuma liom faoi...** I don't mind about..., I don't care about..., **nach cuma!** who cares! **bheith ar nós cuma liom** to be indifferent

cumadóir *m3* composer, inventor

cumadóireacht *f3* invention, composition

cumaisc *v* mix together, blend, combine

cumann *m1* 1. affection, love, relationship **bhris siad cumann le chéile** they broke up, they ended their relationship 2. society, club, association **Cumann Lúthchleas Gael (CLG)** the Gaelic Athletic Association (GAA), **cumann lucht tráchtála** chamber of commerce

cumannach *adj* communist

cumannachas *m1* communism

cumannaí *m4* communist

cumar *m1* 1. ravine 2. channel **cumar tráchta romhat** merging traffic ahead

cumarsáid *f2* communication **cúrsa cumarsáide** communications course

cumas *m1* ability, capability, power, capacity **tá an cumas ann** he has the capability, **déan de réir do chumais** do what you are capable of

cumasach *adj* able, capable, powerful, effective **scríbhneoir cumasach** an able writer

cumasc *m1* 1. mixture, blend 2. merger (*of companies*)

cumascóir *m3* blender

cumha *m4* loneliness, homesickness, grief **tá cumha air i ndiaidh an bhaile** he is homesick

cumhacht *f3* power, energy **cumhacht a bheith agat ar dhuine, rud** to have power, influence over somebody, something, **tháinig Fianna Fáil i gcumhacht** Fianna Fáil came into power

cumhachtach *adj* powerful

cumhartheiripe *f4* aromatherapy

cumhdach *m1* covering, protection, wrapper

cumhdaigh *v* protect, cover

cumhra *adj* fragrant, sweet-smelling

cumhracht *f3* fragrance, freshness, bouquet (*of wine*)

cumhrán *m1* scent, perfume

cumtha *adj* 1. invented **fianaise chumtha** fictitious evidence 2. comely, shapely **bean chumtha** comely woman

cúnamh *m1* help, aid **tabharfaidh mé cúnamh duit** I'll help you, **an Bord um Chúnamh Dlíthiúil** the Legal Aid Board, **rúnaí cúnta** assistant secretary

cúnant *m1* covenant

cúng *adj* narrow

cúngaigeanta *adj* narrow-minded

cúngaigh *v* narrow, restrict

cúngú *m* restriction

cunta *m4* count (*aristocrat*)

cúntach *adj* 1. helpful 2. auxiliary

cuntanós *m1* 1. countenance 2. civility

cuntaois *f2* countess **an Chuntaois Markievicz** the Countess Markievicz

cuntar[1] *m1* counter **cuntar oibre** worktop

cuntar[2] *m1* condition **gan chuntar** unconditionally, **ar an gcuntar go…** on the condition that…, provided that…

cuntas *m1* 1. account **cuntas bainc** bank account 2. count **déan cuntas air** make a count of it, **cuntas a choinneáil ar…** to keep a record of…

cuntasaíocht *f3* accounting, accountancy (*subject*)

cuntasóir *m3* accountant

cuntasóireacht *f3* accounting, accountancy (*profession*)

cúntóir *m3* assistant, helper

cuóta *m4* quota

cupán *m1* cup

cúpla *m4* 1. couple, few **cúpla bean, fear** a couple of women, men, **cúpla duine, rud** a few people, things 2. pair, twins **an Cúpla** Gemini

cúpón *m1* coupon

cur *m1* 1. sowing **an bhfuil an cur déanta?** has the sowing, tillage being done? 2. laying **cur tuí** thatching 3. burial 4. **cur amach** experience, **níl aon chur amach agam ar an obair seo** I have no experience/knowledge of this work 5. **cur thar maoil** overflow 6. **cur chun cinn** progress, advancement 7. **cur i gcás** supposition 8. **cur chun feidhme** application, **cur i ngníomh** implementation

cúr *m1* froth, foam

curach *f2* currach, coracle, canoe

curachóireacht *f3* canoeing

curaclam *m1* curriculum

curadh *m1* champion **curadh an domhain** world champion

curadhmhír *f2* prize

curaí *m4* curry

cúram *m1* 1. care, responsibility **tá sé faoina cúram** he/it is her responsibility, in her care 2. family **an bhfuil aon chúram air?** has he any children?

cúramach *adj* 1. careful 2. busy

curata *adj* heroic, brave

curfá *m4* chorus

curiarracht *f3* record (*sport*)

curra *m4* holster

cúrsa *m4* 1. course **cúrsa bliana, dhá bhliain, trí bliana** a year-long, 2 year, 3 year course, **ceann cúrsa** destination, end of journey, **cúrsa oiliúna** training course 2. affair, matter **cúrsaí gnó** business matters

cúrsáil *f3* 1. coursing **cúrsáil giorriacha** hare-coursing 2. cruise **bád cúrsála** cruise boat, **long chúrsála** cruiser *v* 1. course, chase 2. cruise

cúrsaíocht *f3* circulation, currency **cúrsaíocht airgeadra** currency circulation

cúrsóir *m3* 1. cruiser 2. cursor (*computer*)

cuspa *m4* model (*art*)

cuspóir *m3* aim, objective, purpose, object **bhí cuspóir folaithe aige** he had an ulterior motive

cuspóireach *m1* objective, accusative **an tuiseal cuspóireach** the accusative case

custaiméir *m3* customer

custam *m1* customs **Custam agus Mál** Customs and Excise

custard *m1* custard

cuthach *m1* frenzy, rage

cúthail *adj* 1. shy, bashful 2. modest, diffident

cúthaileacht *f3* 1. shyness 2. diffidence

D

dá¹ *conj* if **dá mba mise tusa rachainn abhaile** if I were you I'd go home, **dá bhfaighinn an seans** if I got the chance

dá² 1. = de + a of, from or off his/her/its/theirs **bhain sé an hata dá cheann** he took his hat off, **duine dá lucht aitheantais** one of his/her/their acquaintances 2. = do + a to or for his/her/its/theirs **tugann sí aire mhaith dá hathair** she looks after her father well, **ag saothrú airgid dá chlann** earning money for his family

dá³ 1. de + a of that which, of those who **chaill sé gach rud dá raibh aige** he lost everything he had 2. do + a to/for/on whom, which **an fear dá dtugann sí grá** the man whom she loves

dá⁴ = de + a however **dá fhad an lá tagann an oíche** however long the day is, night has to come, all good things come to an end, **dá mhéad é is amhlaidh is fearr é** the bigger the better

dá⁵ = dhá, **an dá chapall** the two horses

daba *m4* 1. dab 2. lump, blob **daba péinte** blob of paint 3. **mac an daba** third finger on right hand

dabhach *f2* vat, bath, tub **dabhach dhipeála** dipping tank (*for sheep etc*)

dabht *m4* doubt **gan dabht** without a doubt

dada *m4* anything, nothing **an bhfuil dada cloiste agat?** have you heard anything? **níl dada ann** there is nothing there

daibhir *adj* poor

daichead *m1* forty **tá sé sna daichidí** he is in his forties, **daichead bád** forty boats

daicheadú¹ *m4* fortieth **tá trí dhaicheadú de ann** there is three fortieths of it there

daicheadú² *adj* fortieth **tháinig siad sa daicheadú háit** they came in fortieth position

daid *m4* dad

daideo *m4* grand-dad **mamó agus daideo** granny and grand-dad

daidí *m4* daddy **Daidí na Nollag** Santa Claus

daigh *f2* 1. pain, pang, twinge **daigh chroí** heartburn, **daigh éada** pain or sting of jealousy 2. **daitheacha** rheumatism

dáigh *adj* stubborn, unreasoning

dáil *f3* 1. assembly, convention, parliament **Dáil Éireann** the Dáil, **i ndeireadh na dála** after all is said and done 2. meeting, encounter **chuaigh mé i ndáil Pheadair** I went to meet Peadar 3. circumstance, condition, matter **mo dhála féin** like myself, as in my own circumstances, **dála an scéil** by the way, **dálaí aeráide** climatic conditions *v* distribute, serve

dáilcheantar *m1* constituency

dáileadh *m* distribution **dáileadh daonra** distribution of population

dáileog *f2* dose **ródháileog** overdose

dáileoir *m3* 1. dispenser 2. distributor

dáilia *f4* dahlia

daille *f4* blindness

dáimh *f2* affection, fondness **tá dáimh agam leis** I am fond of him

daingean *adj* 1. strong, fortified, solid **baile daingean** fortified town 2. firm, steadfast **grá daingean** steadfast love *m1* stronghold, fortress, fort **an Daingean** Dingle

daingneán *m1* fixture

daingnigh *v* strengthen, fortify, secure, steady

daingnithe *adj* fortified **baile daingnithe** fortified town

daingniú *m* fortification

dainséar *m1* danger

dainséarach *adj* dangerous

dair *m5* oak **crann darach** oak tree

dáiríre *adj, adv* serious, earnest, in reality, in earnest **an bhfuil tú dáiríre?** are you serious? *m4* seriousness **tagann an magadh go leaba an dáiríre** what begins as a joke can become serious

dáiríreacht *f3* seriousness, earnestness

dairt *f2* 1. dart **cluiche dairteanna** a game of darts 2. clod, object to be thrown **dairteanna sneachta** snowballs

daite *adj* coloured, stained, dyed

dálach *m1* **bíonn sé ag obair Domhnach agus dálach** he works constantly, without a break

dalaí *m4* dolly

dalba *adj* bold, naughty

dall *adj* 1. blind, blinded 2. uninformed **tá sé dall air sin** he is in the dark about that, he is ignorant of that 3. dazed *m1* 1. blind person 2. uninformed, dull person *v* 1. blind 2. dazzle, daze 3. darken

dalladh *m* 1. blinding, dazzlement 2. lashings, plenty **dalladh airgid** plenty of money, **dalladh bia agus dí** lashings of food and drink 3. **ar dalladh** intensely

dallamullóg *m4* confusion, bluff, delusion, deception **chuir sé an dallamullóg orm** he fooled me

dallóg *f2* 1. blind **tarraing anuas na dallóga** pull down the blinds 2. blind creature **dallóg fhéir** dormouse

dalta *m4* pupil

damáiste *m4* damage

damanta *adj* 1. condemned, damned 2. wicked, terrible

damba *m4* dam

dambáil *v* dam

damh *m1* ox

dámh *f2* faculty (*university*) **Dámh na nEalaíon** the Faculty of Arts

damhán *m1* damhán alla spider

damhna *m4* matter, material

damhsa *m4* dance

damhsaigh *v* dance

damhsóir *m3* dancer

damnaigh *v* condemn, damn

damnaithe *adj* condemned, damned

damnú *m* condemnation, damnation damnú foirgnimh condemnation of a building, damnú ort! damn you!

dán *m1* 1. poem cnuasach dánta collection of poems 2. fate, destiny cad tá i ndán dúinn? what's in store, destined for us?

dána *adj* bold, daring is dána an mhaise uait é you have a cheek

dánacht *f3* boldness, presumption, nerve an bhfuil sé de dhánacht ann é a dhéanamh? has he got the nerve to do it?

Danar *m1* Dane (*Irish history*)

danartha *adj* cruel, barbarous

danarthacht *f3* cruelty, barbarity

dánlann *f2* art gallery an Dánlann Náisiúnta the National Gallery

Danmhairg, an *f2* Denmark

Danmhairgis *f2* Danish (*language*)

Danmhargach *adj* Danish *m1* Danish person

daoire *f4* costliness

daoirse *f4* slavery, oppression cuireadh i ndaoirse iad they were enslaved, oppressed

daol *m1* beetle

daonáireamh *m1* census of population

daonchairdiúil *adj* humanitarian

daonchumhacht *f3* manpower

daoniarsmalann *f2* folk museum

daonlathach *adj* democratic

daonlathaí *m4* democrat

daonlathas *m1* democracy an Daonlathas Clé Democratic Left

daonna *adj* 1. human an cine daonna the human race, víreas easpa imdhíonachta daonna (VEID) human immunodeficiency virus (HIV) 2. humane duine daonna humane person

daonnacht *f3* 1. humanity, human nature tá daonnacht ann he is humane, kind 2. menses tá mo dhaonnacht orm I'm having my period

daonnachtúil *adj* 1. humane 2. generous

daonnaí *m4* 1. human being 2. humanist

daonpháirc *f2* folk park

daonra *m4* population daonra aistreach shifting population, daonra faoi láthair existing population

daonscoil *f2* folk school

daor *adj* 1. costly, dear, expensive 2. severe d'íoc mé go daor as I paid for it dearly *m1* 1. slave 2. condemned person *v* 1. enslave 2. convict, condemn daoradh chun báis iad they were condemned to death

daorbhroid *f2* dire distress

daorchluiche *m4* baseball

daorghalar *m1* piles, haemorrhoids

daorsmacht *m3* oppression, slavery

daoscarshlua *m4* rabble, rank and file

dar¹ *prep* by dar an leabhar! upon my faith!

dar² dar le it seems, seemed, would seem tá deireadh leis, dar liom it seems to me that it's over

dar³ = de or do + ar (*indirect relative form of copula*) an duine dar mhiste é the person to whom it mattered, cé dar díobh í? from whom is she descended?

dár¹ 1. de + ár (*poss adj*) bheannaíomar dár n-athair we greeted our father 2. de + ár (*poss adj*) **duine dár gcairde** one of our friends

dár² 1. **de + ár** *(rel part)* **chaill sé gach pingin dár shaothraigh sé riamh** he lost every penny he ever earned 2. **do + ár** *(rel part)* **an pobal dár fhóin mé** the community that I served, **an fear dár thug mé grá** the man whom I loved

dár³ *prep* **(an tseachtain, an mhí, srl) dár gcionn** the following (week, month, etc)

dara *adj* second **an dara duais** the second prize, **an dára huair** the second time, **an dara lá déag de Mheán Fómhair** the twelfth (day) of September, **ní raibh an dara suí sa bhuaile agam** I didn't have another choice

dásacht *f3* daring, boldness

dásachtach *adj* 1. daring 2. furious

dáta *m4* date **dáta éaga** expiry date, **dáta díola is deireanaí** sell-by date

dátaigh *v* date

dath *m3* 1. colour, dye **tá dath an bháis uirthi** she is the colour of death 2. **a dhath** any(thing), nothing (*negative*) **ní dúirt sé a dhath** he didn't say anything

dathadóir *m3* painter, dyer

dathadóireacht *f3* painting, dyeing

dathaigh *v* paint, dye, colour

dathannach *adj* multicoloured, colourful

dathchaoch *adj* colour-blind

dathdhall *adj* colour-blind

dátheangach *adj* bilingual

dátheangachas *m1* bilingualism

dathú *m* colouring

dathúil *adj* handsome, good-looking, colourful

dathúlacht *f3* handsomeness, good looks

de (*prep prons* = **díom, díot, de, di, dínn, díbh, díobh**) *prep* (it becomes **d'** before **a, e, i, o, u** or **fh** + **a, e, i, o, u**) from, of, off **den chlann chéanna iad sin** they are from the same family, **cuid de theach** part of a house, **bhain mé an caipín d'fhear an tí** I took the hat off the man of the house, **a leithéid d'áit!** what a place!

dé¹ *f5* breath, puff **tá sé ar an dé deireadh** he is at his last gasp

dé-² *prefix* bi-, di-, two- **déghnéasach** hermaphrodite, bisexual, **décheannach** two-headed, two-ended

Dé³ Dé Luain, Dé Máirt, Dé Céadaoin, Déardaoin, Dé hAoine, Dé Sathairn, Dé Domhnaigh (on) Monday, Tuesday, Wednesday, Thursday, Friday, Saturday, Sunday

dea- *prefix* 1. good- **dea-theist** good report, repute 2. well- **dea-chruthach** well-shaped, handsome

deabhadh *m1* haste, hurry **cén deabhadh atá air?** what's his hurry?

deacair *adj* difficult *f5* difficulty, trouble

déach *adj* dual

dea-chlú *m4* good reputation, good name

dea-chroíoch *adj* good-natured, kind-hearted

deachtafón *m1* dictaphone

deachtaigh *v* 1. compose 2. instruct, direct 3. dictate **gléas deachtaithe** dictating machine

deachtóir *m3* dictator

deachtóireacht *f3* dictatorship

deachtú *m* 1. composition 2. dictation

deachúil *adj, f3* decimal

dea-chumtha *adj* well-shaped, shapely

deachúlach *adj* decimal

deacracht *f3* difficulty

déad *m1* 1. tooth 2. set of teeth **déad bréige** false teeth

déadach *adj* toothed, dental

déag *m* -teen (*in numerals*), tens, teens (*in plural*) **aon déag** eleven, **dó dhéag** twelve, **trí, ceathair, cúig, sé, seacht, ocht, naoi déag** thirteen, fourteen, fifteen, sixteen, seventeen, eighteen, nineteen, **níl sé / sí ach sna déaga** he/she is only in her teens, a teenager, **tharla sé sin i ndéaga na haoise seo** that happened in the second decade of this century

déagóir *m3* teenager

dealaigh *v* 1. separate **dealaigh na fir ó na mná** separate the men from the women 2. differentiate, distinguish **is deacair iad a dhealú ó chéile** it's difficult to differentiate between them 3. subtract **dealaigh ó** subtract from 4. **dealaigh le** depart

dealbh¹ *adj* poor, bare, destitute

dealbh² *f2* statue

dealbhóir *m3* sculptor

dealbhóireacht *f3* sculpture

dealbhú *m* sculpturing

dealg *f2* 1. thorn 2. brooch

dealrachán *m1* collar-bone

dealraigh *v* 1. appear, seem **dealraíonn sé go** it appears that 2. shine, illuminate

dealraitheach *adj* 1. **dealraitheach le** looking like 2. shining 3. apparent, probable, plausible

dealramh *m1* 1. resemblance, appearance **tá dealramh agat leis** you resemble him, **de réir dealraimh** apparently, **níl aon dealramh leis sin** that makes no sense, that's ridiculous 2. radiance, shine **dealramh gréine** sunshine

dealú *m* 1. separation 2. subtraction

dealús *m1* destitution

dealúsach *adj* destitute

deamhan *m1* demon **craosdeamhan** demon of gluttony (*Irish folklore*)

dea-mhéin *f2* goodwill, good wishes

dea-mhéineach *adj* well-wishing, benevolent

dea-mhúinte *adj* well-mannered

déan¹ *m1* dean **Déan na Tráchtála** the Dean of Commerce

déan² *v* (see *irregular verbs*) 1. make **dinnéar a dhéanamh** to make dinner, **déanfaidh sé oíche mhaith** it will make/be a good night, **nós a dhéanamh de rud** to make a habit of something 2. do **rinne sé dhá bhliain i bpríosún** he did/spent two years in prison, **foighne a dhéanamh** to have patience, **rinne siad go maith** they did well, **an ndearna tú an obair fós?** did you do the work yet? **rinne / ní dhearna** yes/no

déan ar make for **bhí sé ag déanamh ar a theach** he was making for his house, **tá sé ag déanamh ar a trí a chlog** it's nearly three o'clock

déan faoi go towards **rinne sé faoi mo dhéin** he made for me, **bhí siad ag déanamh gáire fúm** they were laughing at me

déan suas do, make up **carr a dhéanamh suas** to do up a car

déanach *adj* late **is fearr déanach ná ródhéanach, is fearr déanach ná go brách** better late than never

déanaí *f4* lateness **le déanaí** lately, **bí ann ar a hocht ar a dhéanaí** be there at eight at the latest

déanamh *m1* make, doing, making **tá siad den déanamh céanna** they are of the same make, **tá an obair sin gan déanamh fós** that work is undone still, **déanamh féir** haymaking

deannach *m1* dust

déanta *adj* 1. finished, complete 2. **déanta na fírinne** as a matter of fact, truthfully

déantóir *m3* maker, manufacturer

déantús *m1* make, manufacture **de dhéantús an duine** manmade

déantúsaíocht *f3* manufacturing

dear *v* draw, design

deara *m* 1. **thug mé faoi deara é** I noticed it 2. **mise faoi deara é** I am the cause of it

dearadh *m1* design, drawing **an Coláiste Náisiúnta Ealaíne agus Deartha** the National College of Art and Design

dearbhaigh *v* attest, declare, assure, confirm

dearbhán *m1* voucher

dearbhú *m* declaration, assurance, affirmation, confirmation

dearc *v* look, view

dearcadh *m1* 1. look 2. viewpoint, outlook

dearcán *m1* acorn

Déardaoin *m4* (on) Thursday

dearfa *adj* certain, sure

dearfach *adj* affirmative, positive

dearg¹ *adj* 1. red **rósanna dearga** red roses 2. lit, glowing **bhí sé dearg te** it was glowing red, red-hot 3. real **bíonn an t-ádh dearg leat i gcónaí** you always have great luck *m1* red *v* 1. redden 2. light, glow **toitín a dheargadh** to light a cigarette 3. blush **tá tú ag deargadh** you are blushing

dearg-² *prefix* 1. red **ar dearglasadh** red-hot, ablaze 2. real, intense **ar deargmheisce** blind drunk 3. utter **deargnáire** utter shame

deargiomaíocht *f3* cut-throat competition

dearmad *m1* mistake, forgetfulness **rinne mé dearmad air** I forgot it *v* forget, overlook **ná dearmad do mhála** don't forget your bag

dearmadach *adj* forgetful, absent-minded

dearna *f5* palm (*of hand*)

dearnáil *f3* darning *v* darn

dearóil *adj* 1. wretched, poor 2. chilly 3. frail, feeble

deartháir *m5* brother

dearthóir *m3* designer

deas¹, **ó dheas** southwards, **ag dul ó dheas** going south

deas² *adj* close, near **deas do bhaile** close to home

deas³ *adj* nice

deas⁴ *adj* right (*position*) **ar thaobh na láimhe deise, ar an taobh deas** on the right-hand side, **cos, lámh dheas** right leg, arm/hand

deasaigh *v* dress, prepare, arrange **deasaigh ort** dress yourself, **tá sé ag deasú an bhia** he is preparing the food, **troscán a dheasú** to arrange furniture

deasbhord *m1* starboard

deasc *f2* desk

deasca *m4* 1. dregs, sediment 2. yeast 3. **de dheasca … because of …**, in consequence of … 4. after-effects, ill-effects **tá deasca an fhliú orm fós** I still have the after effects of the flu

dea-scéal *m1* piece of good news

deasghnách *adj* ceremonial, formal

deasghnáth *m3* ritual, ceremony, formality

deaslabhartha *adj* well-spoken, eloquent

deaslabhra *f4* elocution **ceachtanna deaslabhra** elocution lessons

deaslámhach *adj* right-handed, dexterous, handy

deastógáil *f3* assumption (*of body to heaven*)

deatach *m1* smoke **bhí bús deataigh ann** there were clouds of smoke there

deataigh *v* smoke (*fish*) **bradán deataithe** smoked salmon

débhríoch *adj* ambiguous

débhríocht *f3* ambiguity

déchiallach *adj* equivocal, ambiguous

défhoghar *m1* diphthong

déghloiniú *m* double glazing

deic *f2* deck **deic caiséad** casette deck

deich *m4* ten **deich n-asal bheaga** ten small donkeys

deichiú[1] *m4* tenth **fuair mé an deichiú cuid de** I got a tenth (*part*) of it

deichiú[2] *adj* tenth **an deichiú hamhrán dá chuid** his tenth song

deichniúr *m1* 1. ten (*people*) **bhí deichniúr Meiriceánach ann** there was ten Americans there, **deichniúr rinceoirí** ten dancers 2. decade (*Rosary*)

deicibeil *f2* decibel

deifir *f2* hurry, haste **bhí an-deifir air** he was in a great hurry, **rinne mé faoi dheifir é** I did it in a hurry, **déan deifir!** hurry up!

deifreach *adj* hurried, hasty

deifrigh *v* hurry, hasten **caithfimid deifriú** we have to hurry

deighil *v* separate, divide, partition

deighilt *f2* separation, division, partition **deighilt tíre** partition of a country

deil *f2* 1. lathe 2. **ar deil** in good working order

deilbh *f2* figure, shape, appearance

deilbhíocht *f3* accidence (*grammar*)

déileáil *f3* dealing, trading **lucht déileála** dealers, traders, **déileáil thar lear** overseas trading *v* deal **ag déileáil i gcrua-earraí** dealing in hardware, **déileálfaidh mise leis** I'll deal with him/it

deilf *f2* dolphin

deilgneach *adj* thorny, barbed **sreang dheilgneach** barbed wire *f2* chicken-pox

deilín *m4* sing-song, rigmarole

deiliús *m1* sauciness, impudence

deiliúsach *adj* saucy, impudent

deimheas *m1* 1. shears 2. sharp tongue

deimhin *adj* sure, certain **go deimhin** really, indeed *f2* certainty **déan deimhin de** make sure of it

deimhneach *adj* 1. certain 2. positive

deimhneacht *f3* 1. certainty 2. positiveness

deimhnigh *v* certify, assure

deimhniú *m* certificate, assurance **deimhniú postála** certificate of posting/postage

deimhniúil *adj* affirmative

déin *m* **faoi dhéin** to meet, to fetch **téigh faoi dhéin Phóil** go to fetch Pól

déine *f4* vehemence, intensity, severity, hardness

deinim *m4* denim

déirc *f2* alms, charity

déirceach *adj* charitable *m1* charitable person

deireadh *m1* 1. end **deireadh ré** end of an era, **ó thús (go) deireadh** from beginning to end, **ag deireadh an lae** at the end of the day, **ag titim chun deiridh** lagging behind, **Deireadh Fómhair** October ('end of autumn') 2. last **faoi dheireadh, ar deireadh (thiar)** at (long) last 3. stern, back, rear **deireadh báid** stern of boat, **na rothaí deiridh** the back wheels, **deireadh an chairr** the rear of the car

deireanach *adj* 1. last, final, recent **an uair dheireanach** the last time, **an buille deireanach** the final blow, **an nuacht is deireanaí** the latest, most recent news 2. late **go deireanach** lately

deireanas *m1* lateness **ag dul chun deireanais** getting late, **le deireanas** recently

deirfiúr *f* sister

déirí *m4* dairy

déiríocht *f3* dairying

deirmitíteas *m1* dermatitis

deis *f2* 1. right hand, right-hand side **ar / faoi dheis** to the right, **ar dheis Dé go raibh sé** may he be at God's right hand 2. opportunity **tapaigh an deis** seize the opportunity, **má fhaighim an deis** if I get the chance/opportunity 3. proper condition **chuir sí deis ar an rothar** she repaired the bicycle 4. facility, means **deis snámha** swimming facility, **deis iompair** means of transport

deisbhéalach *adj* witty

deisbhéalaí *f4* repartee, wittiness

deisceabal *m1* disciple

deisceart *m1* south, southern part **Ceannasaíocht an Deiscirt** the Southern Command

deisceartach *adj* southern *m1* southerner

deiseal *adj, adv* right-hand, clockwise **iompaigh ar deiseal** turn right

deisigh *v* mend, repair

deisiú *m* repairing, repair

deismíneach *adj* refined

deismíneacht *f3* refinement, nicety **deismíneachtaí** niceties

déistin *f2* disgust **bhí déistin uirthi** she was disgusted

déistineach *adj* disgusting, distasteful

démhíosachán *m1* bimonthly (*magazine, report, etc*)

dénártha *adj* binary

deo, go deo for ever, always, never (*with negative*) **ní dhéanfaidh mé go deo arís é** I'll never do it again

deoch *f* drink **fear mór dí** a fierce drinker

dé-ocsaid *f2* dioxide **dé-ocsaíd charbóin** carbon dioxide

deoin *f2* will, accord, consent **rinne siad é dá ndeoin féin** they did it of their own free will

deoir *f2* 1. tear **bhain sé deoir asam** it/he made me cry 2. drop **deoir fola** drop of blood

deoirghás *m1* tear gas

deonach *adj* voluntary, willing

deonaigh *v* grant, consent

deontas *m1* grant **deontas rialtais** Government grant

deontóir *m3* donor **deontóir duáin** kidney donor

deonú *m* 1. grant, consent **deonú Dé** God's will 2. concession

deorach *adj* tearful

deoraí *m4* exile, wanderer

deoraíocht *f3* exile **bheith ar deoraíocht** to be in exile

deoranta *adj* strange, foreign

déshúileach *adj* binocular *m1* binocle **déshúiligh** binoculars

déthaobhach *adj* bilateral

déthoiseach *adj* two-dimensional

déthreo *adj* two-way

dhá *adj* two **dhá mhála fholmha** two empty bags, **an dá cheann is mó** the two biggest ones, **mo dhá chos** my legs

dháréag *m4* twelve people

dia, Dia *m* god, God **le cúnamh Dé** hopefully, with the help of God, **buíochas le Dia!** thanks be to God! **is dia beag acu é** he is their idol

diabhal *m1* devil

diabhalta *adj* mischievous

diabhlaí *adj* diabolical, devilish

diabhlaíocht *f3* devilish conduct, mischief

diaga *adj* divine, godly, pious, theological

diagacht *f3* divinity, divine nature, piety, theology

diagnóiseoir *m3* diagnostician

diaibéiteach *adj, m1* diabetic

diaidh 1. diaidh ar ndiaidh gradually **2. i ndiaidh** + *gen* after, **sos i ndiaidh oibre** a break after work, **tuirse i ndiaidh an lae** tiredness after the day, **cé atá i mo dhiaidh?** who is after me? **tháinig sé inár ndiaidh** he came after us, **céard a tharla ina dhiaidh sin?** what happened after that? **ina dhiaidh sin is uile** notwithstanding all that, **tá sé fiche i ndiaidh a haon** it's twenty past one

diail¹ *adj* excellent, wonderful, remarkable **go diail!** excellent!

diail² *f2* dial

diailigh *v* dial **ton diailithe** dialling-tone

dí-áirithe *adj* countless, innumerable

dialann *f2* diary

diallait *f2* saddle

diamant *m1* diamond

diamhair *adj* dark, secluded, mysterious, eerie

diamhasla *m4* blasphemy

diamhaslach *adj* blasphemous

diamhaslaigh *v* blaspheme

diamhracht *f3* darkness, mysteriousness

dian¹ *adj* severe, hard, intense

dian-² *prefix* hard, intense

dianchúram *m1* intensive care **aonad dianchúraim** intensive care unit (ICU)

dianchúrsa *m4* intensive course

dianmhachnamh *m1* deep thought, concentration

dianscaoil decompose

dí-armáil *f3* disarmament *v* disarm

dias *f2* 1. ear of corn 2. deuce (*tennis*)

diasraigh *v* glean

díbeartach *m1* outcast

díbheo *adj* lifeless, listless

díbhinn *f2* dividend

díbhirce *f4* eagerness, zeal

díbhirceach *adj* eager, zealous

díbhoilsciú *m* deflation (*money*) **díbhoilsciú airgeadra** currency deflation

díbholaíoch *m1* deodorant

díbholg *v* deflate (*balloon*)

díbir *v* banish, drive out, expel, banish

díbirt *f3* banishment, expulsion

díblí *adj* worn-out, dilapidated, decrepit

dícháiligh *v* disqualify

dícháilíocht *f3* disqualification

dícheall *m1* best endeavour **rinne siad a ndícheall** they did their best

dícheallach *adj* diligent, earnest

díchéillí *adj* senseless, foolish

díchóimeáil *f3* dismantling *v* dismantle

díchoimisiúnaigh *v* decommission

díchoimisiúnú *m* decommissioning **díchoimisiúnú airm** decommissioning of arms

díchreideamh *m1* unbelief, disbelief, lack of faith

díchuimhne *f4* forgetfulness, oblivion

dide *f4* nipple, teat (*infant's bottle*)

dídean *f2* shelter, sanctuary, refuge, asylum **easpa dídine** homelessness, **dídean a thabhairt do dhuine** to give shelter to somebody, to give someone asylum

dídeanaí *m4* refugee

difear *m1* difference

dífhabhtaigh *v* disinfect, debug

dífhabhtán *m1* disinfectant

dífhostaigh *v* dismiss (*from employment*), disemploy

dífhostaíocht *f3* unemployment **tréimhse dífhostaíochta** period of unemployment, **lucht dífhostaíochta** unemployed people, the unemployed

dífhostaithe *adj* unemployed **duine dífhostaithe** unemployed person

difríocht *f3* difference **ní dhéanann sé aon difríocht** it doesn't make any difference

difriúil *adj* different

diftéire *f4* diphtheria

dil *adj* dear, beloved **i ndilchuimhne** in loving memory, **do chara dil,** your dear friend

díláraigh *v* decentralise

díláraithe *adj* decentralised

dílárú *m* decentralisation

díle *f5* flood, deluge

díleá *m4* digestion

díleáigh *v* 1. digest **córas díleáite an duine** the human digestive system 2. dissolve

dílis *adj* 1. faithful, loyal **bí dílis don teanga, don chúis** be faithful to the language, to the cause 2. genuine, reliable **ór dílis** genuine gold 3. proper **ainm dílis** proper name, proper noun 4. dear **mo chailín beag dílis** my dear little girl

dílleachta *m4* orphan

dílleachtlann *f2* orphanage

dílse *f4* pledge, faithfulness, loyalty, allegiance **chuaigh siad i ndílse leis an gcúis** they pledged themselves to the cause

dílseacht *f3* loyalty, fidelity allegiance **mionn dílseachta** oath of allegiance

dílseoir *m3* loyalist

díluacháil *f3* devaluation *v* devalue

díluchtaigh *v* discharge, unload

dímheabhrach *adj* forgetful, oblivious

dímheas *m3* contempt, disrespect

dímheasúil *adj* contemptuous, disrespectful

dínáisiúnaigh *v* denationalise

ding[1] *f2, v* wedge

ding[2] *f2* dent **ding a chur i rud** to dent something

dinimiciúil *adj* dynamic

dinimít *f2* dynamite

dínit *f2* dignity

dinnéar *m1* dinner **am dinnéir** dinner-time

dinnireacht *f3* dysentery

dinnseanchas *m1* topography (*traditional*)

dintiúr *m1* indenture **dintiúir** credentials, **tá a dhintiúir anois aige** he is fully qualified now

díobháil *f3* 1. injury, harm, damage **ní haon díobháil é** it's no harm 2. loss, want **díobháil céille** lack of sense

díobhálach *adj* injurious, harmful

díocas *m1* eagerness

díocasach *adj* eager

díochlaon *v* decline (*grammar*)

díochlaonadh *m* declension **an chéad díochlaonadh** the first declension

díochra *adj* passionate, intense, fervent **go díochra** passionately, intensely

díog *f2* dyke, ditch

díogha *m4* the worst (of all), the dregs **rogha an dá dhíogha a bhí ann** it was a choice between two evils

díograis *f2* enthusiasm, zeal

díograiseach *adj* enthusiastic, zealous

díol *m3* 1. payment 2. sale **dáta díola is deireanaí** sell-by date 3. **díol trua** deserving of pity 4. sufficiency **díol ceathrair** enough for four *v* 1. pay **díolfaidh tú as** you'll pay for it 2. sell **ag díol is ag ceannach** buying and selling

díolachán *m1* sale **díolachán earraí** sale of work

díolaim *f3* compilation, collection **díolaim focal** collection of words

díolaíocht *f3* payment

díoltas *m1* vengeance, revenge **bhain sé díoltas amach** he exacted revenge

díoltasach *adj* vengeful, vindictive

díoltóir *m3* seller, dealer **díoltóir drugaí** drug dealer

díolúine *f4* exemption, immunity **díolúine ó cháin** exemption from tax

díomá *f4* disappointment **ná bíodh díomá ort** don't be disappointed

díomách *adj* disappointed

diomail *v* waste, squander

diomailt *f2* wasting, squandering, waste, extravagance

diomailteach *adj* wasteful, extravagant

diomaite, diomaite de apart from, other than, besides

díomhaoin *adj* idle, unused, unemployed

díomhaointeas *m1* idleness, vanity

díomua *m4* defeat

diomuch *adj* dissatisfied

díon *m1* 1. roof, covering 2. shelter *v* 1. roof, thatch 2. shelter, protect

díonach *adj* protective, impermeable **díonach ar uisce** proof against water

diongbháilte *adj* 1. worthy 2. firm, staunch **cara diongbháilte** staunch friend 3. positive, confirmed

diongbháilteacht *f3* 1. worthiness 2. firmness, staunchness 3. decisiveness, positiveness

díonteach *m* penthouse

dioplóma *m4* diploma **cúrsa dioplóma** diploma course

díorma *m4* band, troop, posse

díosal *m1* diesel

díosc *v* creak, grate, grind

diosca *m4* disk **diosca córais** system disk, **diosca crua / cruadhiosca** hard disk, **diosca flapach** floppy disk

díoscán *m1* squeak, creaking, grating, grinding

diosc-chomhad *m1* disk file

dioscó *m4* disco

dioscthiomáint *f3* disk drive

díospóireacht *f3* disputation, debate, discussion **comórtas díospóireachta** debating competition

díothú *m* extermination, destruction

dírbheathaisnéis *f2* autobiography

díreach *adj* 1. straight, direct **duine díreach** straight, honest person 2. *as adv* just, exact, exactly **anois díreach a d'imigh sé** he left just now, **go díreach!** exactly!

diréireach *adj* disproportionate

dírigh *v* 1. straighten 2. **dírigh ar** direct, aim **dhírigh sé an gunna orm** he aimed the gun at me, **díriú ar fhadhb** to focus on a problem

dís *f2* two persons, pair **dís fhear** two men

dísc *f2* dryness, barrenness, sterility **chuaigh an abhainn i ndísc** the river dried up

discéad *m1* diskette

díscigh *v* dry up, consume **tá an tobar díscithe** the well is dried up, **tá an bia díscithe** the food is consumed

disciplín *m4* discipline

discréid *f2* discretion

discréideach *adj* discreet

díscríobh *v* write off

díseart *m1* deserted place, retreat

díshalaigh *v* decontaminate

díshealbhaigh *v* evict, dispossess

díshealbhú *m* eviction, dispossession

díshioc *v* defrost

dísle *m4* die (*games*) **díslí** dice

díspeag *v* belittle, despise

díspeagadh *m* 1. scorn, belittlement **díspeagadh cúirte** contempt of court 2. diminutive (*grammar*)

dispeipse *f4* dyspepsia

díth *f2* 1. loss, deprivation **gan díth** without loss 2. want, lack, need **sin é atá de dhíth ort** that's what you need, **díth céille** silliness, foolishness

díthocsaigh *v* detoxify

díthreabhach *m1* hermit, recluse

diúg *v* 1. drain (*liquid*), drink to end **diúg siar é** knock it back 2. sponge **ná bí á dhiúgadh** don't sponge on him

diúgaire *m4* 1. drinker 2. sponger, leech

diúgaireacht *f3* 1. draining (*liquid*), drinking 2. sponging

diúilicín *m4* mussel

diúité *m4* duty **cé atá ar diúité anocht?** who is on duty tonight?

diúl *m1* sucking **tá sí á bhaint de dhiúl** she is weaning him (*of child*) *v* suck **diúlann sé a ordóg fós** he sucks his thumb still

diúlach *m1* lad, 'character' **cé hé an diúlach sin?** who's that lad?

diúltach *adj* 1. inclined to refuse or deny 2. negative **aischothú diúltach** negative feedback *m1* negative

diúltaigh *v* 1. refuse, deny **dhiúltaigh siad mé** they refused me 2. **diúltaigh do** reject, renounce **dhiúltaigh sé do bhia** he rejected food

diúltú *m* 1. refusal, denial 2. renunciation **diúltú coinsiasach** conscientious objection

diúracán *m1* missile **diúracán treoraithe, diúracán faoi threorú** guided missile, **diúracáin bhalaistíocha idir-ilchríochacha** intercontinental ballistic missiles

diurnaigh *v* 1. drain, swallow **dhiurnaigh sí a raibh sa ghloine** she drained all that was in the glass 2. embrace **dhiurnaigh sé go teann í** he embraced her tightly

diúscairt *f3* disposal **diúscairt fuíll** waste disposal, **diúscairt camrais** sewage disposal

dlaíóg *f2* wisp, lock (*of hair*) **chuir sé an dlaíóg mhullaigh ar an obair** he put the finishing touches to the work

dlaoi *f4* lock (*of hair*), wisp, tuft **an dlaoi mhullaigh a chur ar rud** to put the finishing touches to something

dleacht *f3* 1. due, lawful right, duty **dleachtanna custaim agus máil** customs and excise duty, **dleachtanna ceardchumainn** union dues 2. royalty **dleachtanna údair** author's royalties

dleathach *adj* lawful, legal

dlí *m4* law **dlíthe cosanta na timpeallachta** environmental protection laws

dlí-eolaí *m4* jurist

dligh *v* **dligh do** due to, entitled to **dlitear duit uaim (DDU)** I owe you (IOU)

dlíodóir *m3* lawyer

dlisteanach *adj* lawful, legitimate

dliteanas *m1* 1. lawful claim, right 2. liability **dliteanas teoranta** limited liability

dlíthairiscint *f3* legal tender

dlíthiúil *adj* legal, lawful, judicial **conradh dlíthiúil** legal, lawful contract, **fiosrúchán dlíthiúil** judicial enquiry

dlús *m1* 1. compactness, density 2. speed **cuireadh dlús leis an bpróiseas** the process was speeded up 3. abundance **tá dlús airgid acu** they have an abundance of money

dlúth *adj* 1. dense, compact, firm **ceo dlúth** dense fog, **ceangailte**

go dlúth tied firmly 2. close bhí siad dlúth dá/le chéile they were close together

dlúthbhaint *f2* close connection or association tá dlúthbhaint acu le chéile they have a close association/connection with each other

dlúthchaidreamh *m1* close intimacy

dlúthdhiosca *m4* compact disc (CD) dlúthdhiosca léImh amháin CD-ROM (compact disc - read only memory)

do[1] *poss adj* your (*singular*) do chóta your coat, d'ainm your name, d'fhear céile your husband

do[2] *v particle* d'imir mé, d'imrínn, d'imreoinn peil I played, I used to play, I would play

do[3] (*prep pruns* = dom, duit, dó, di, dúinn, daoibh, dóibh) *prep* to, for chuaigh sí don Iodáil, don Bheilg she went to Italy, to Belgium, bhuail mé le deirfiúr duit I met a sister of yours, thug sé bronntanas dom he gave me a present, bheannaigh siad dúinn they greeted us, bia agus deoch don chóisir food and drink for the party, ag teacht isteach dóibh as/when they were coming in

do-[4] *prefix* 1. impossible to, difficult to dodhéanta impossible to do 2. evil, ill doghníomh evil act

dóbair 1. *defective v* nearly, almost dóbair dom é a bhriseadh I nearly broke it, dóbair gur thit mé I nearly fell 2. *us noun* chuaigh sé go dtí an dóbair it was touch and go

dobharchú *m4* otter

dobhareach *m1* hippopotamus

do-bhithmhillte *adj* non-biodegradable

dobhréagnaithe *adj* undeniable, indisputable

dobhriathar *m1* adverb

dobhriste *adj* unbreakable

dobrón *m1* grief, sorrow

dobrónach *adj* grieving, afflicted *m1* grieving, afflicted person

dócha *adj* likely, probable is dócha go bhfeicfimid ann é we'll probably see him there, ní dócha é probably not, chomh dócha lena athrach / mhalairt as likely as not

dochar *m1* 1. harm cén dochar? what harm? ní dhéanfaidh sé dochar ar bith, aon dochar it won't do any harm 2. dochar díreach direct debit

dóchas *m1* hope, expectation táim i ndóchas go … I hope that …

dóchasach *adj* hopeful, confident

docheansaithe *adj* untameable, unmanageable

dochloíte *adj* invincible

dochrach *adj* harmful, hurtful

dochreidte *adj* incredible, unbelievable

docht *adj* tight, close, rigid, strict bhí greim docht daingean aige orm he had a strong grip on me

dochtaire *m3* hardliner

dochtúir *m3* doctor dochtúir ar fáil doctor on call, dochtúir teaghlaigh general practicioner

dochtúireacht *f3* 1. doctorate (*degree*) 2. doctoring gairm dochtúireachta profession of medicine

dóchúil *adj* likely

dóchúlacht *f3* probability, likelihood

dodhearmadta *adj* unforgettable

do-earráide *genitive* as *adj* infallible

dofheicthe *adj* invisible

doicheall *m1* inhospitality, reluctance níor dhruid doicheall a dhoras / theach riamh inhospitality never closed his door/house

doicheallach *adj* inhospitable, unwelcoming

doiciméad *m1* document

doiciméadach *adj* documentary

doiciméadaigh *v* document

doiciméadú *m* documentation

do-ídithe *adj* inexhaustible

dóigh¹ *f2* way, method, manner, condition, state **déan ar do dhóigh féin é** do it in your own way, **sin an dóigh atá acu** that's their manner, **chuir sé dóigh ar an rothar** he fixed the bicycle, **ar dóigh** excellent

dóigh² *f2* likely, probable **ní dóigh liom é** I don't think so

dóigh³ *v* burn

dóighiúil *adj* handsome

doiléir *adj* indistinct, obscure

doiléirigh *v* darken, obscure, blur

doiligh *adj* difficult **tá sé doiligh tú a thuigbheáil/thuiscint** it is difficult to understand you

doilíos *m1* sorrow, remorse, melancholy

doilíosach *adj* sorrowful, remorseful, melancholy

doimhneacht *f3* depth

doineann *f2* bad weather, storm

doinsiún *m1* dungeon

do-inste *adj* indescribable, untold

doire *m4* 1. oak-wood 2. wood

Doire *m4* Derry **Co. Dhoire** Co. Derry

doirseoir *m3* door-keeper, bouncer

doirt *v* 1. pour **dhoirt sí an tae amach** she poured the tea 2. spill **dhoirt sé uisce ar an urlár** he spilt water on the floor 3. shed, run (*of colour*) **ag doirteadh deor** shedding tears

doirteadh *m* pouring, spilling, spillage **doirteadh báistí** downpour of rain, **doirteadh ola** oil spillage

doirteal *m1* sink (*kitchen*)

do-ite *adj* inedible

dóite *adj* 1. burned, burnt 2. dry, withered 3. **dóite de rud** fed up of, tired of something

dóiteán *m1* conflagration, fire **briogáid dóiteáin** fire brigade, **fear dóiteáin** fire-fighter, **lucht múchta dóiteáin** fire-fighters

dol *m3* noose, snare

dól *m1* dole **ag tarraingt an dóil** getting the dole

dola *m4* 1. harm, loss 2. charge, imposition, toll **droichead dola** toll bridge

dolabhartha *adj* unutterable, unspeakable

dólás *m1* sorrow, anguish **dólás croí** deep affliction

dólásach *adj* sorrowful

doleigheasta *adj* incurable

doléite *adj* illegible

dollar *m1* dollar

dolúbtha *adj* inflexible, unyielding

domhain *adj* deep *f2* depth

domhainreoiteoir *m3* deep freezer

domhan *m1* world, earth **timpeall an domhain** around the world, **ar fud an domhain** all over the world

domhanda *adj* worldwide, global **an Dara Cogadh Domhanda** the Second World War

domhanfhad *m1* longitude

domhanleithead *m1* latitude

domhantarraingt *f* gravity (*of earth*)

domharaithe *adj* immortal

domharaitheacht *f3* immortality

domheanma *f5* despondency, low spirits

domheanmnach *adj* despondent, low-spirited

Domhnach *m1* Sunday **Dé Domhnaigh** (on) Sunday

domlas *m1* gall, bile, bitterness **mála an domlais** gall bladder, **domlas a bheith ionat** to be bitter

domlasta *adj* bitter, obnoxious

domplagán *m1* dumpling

dona *adj* 1. bad, wretched **tá sé go dona** he is seriously ill

2. unfortunate **an bhean dhona** the unfortunate woman

donacht *f3* badness, illness **dá dhonacht an bháisteach is measa an ghaoth** however bad the rain is the wind is worse, **bhí donacht uirthi** she was ill

donas *m1* **1.** misery, affliction **chuaigh sé chun donais ina dhiaidh sin** he got worse after that **2.** ill luck, misfortune

donn *adj* brown, brown-haired

donnbhuí *adj* yellowish brown

do-oibrithe *adj* unworkable

dó-ola *f4* fuel oil

doras *m1* door, doorway **thug sé an doras dom** he showed me the door, **sheas sé sa doras** he stood in the doorway, **doras feasa fiafraí** the way to knowledge is to question

dorcha *adj* dark, obscure

dorchacht *f3* darkness

dorchaigh *v* darken

dorchla *m4* corridor

dord *m1* **1.** hum(ming), buzz, drone **2.** bass **dord fuaimíoch** acoustic base *v* hum, buzz, drone

dordán *m1* buzz, hum(ming), drone **dordán a dhéanamh** to hum

dordfhocal *m1* buzz-word

dordghiotár *m1* bass guitar

dordghuth *m3* bass voice

dordvcidhil *f2* cello

doréitithe *adj* insoluble, irreconcilable

doriartha *adj* unruly, disobedient

dorn *m1* **1.** fist **2.** punch **3.** handle **dorn scuaibe** handle of brush

dornálaí *m4* boxer

dornálaíocht *f3* boxing **babhta dornálaíochta** a bout of sparring

dornán *m1* handful

dorú *m4* fishing line

dos *m1* **1.** tuft, bush **2.** drone (*in bagpipes*)

dosaen *m4* dozen

doshamhlaithe *adj* inconceivable, unimaginable

dosháraithe *adj* unbeatable, incomparable

dosheachanta *adj* unavoidable, inescapable

doshéanta *adj* undisputable, undeniable

doshrianta *adj* uncontrollable

dosmachtaithe *adj* ungovernable, uncontrollable

dóthain *f4* enough, sufficiency **tá mo dhóthain ite agam** I've had enough to eat

dothuigthe *adj* unintelligible

dóú *adj* second **an dóú teach ar dheis** the second house on the left, **fuair mé an dóú háit sa rás** I got second place in the race, **an dóú lá déag d'Iúil** the twelfth (day) of July

drabhlás *m1* debauchery, dissipation **chuaigh sé ar an drabhlás** he went on the tear

drabhlásach *adj* given to drinking, dissipated

drabhlásaí *m4* reckless, extravagant person

draein *f5* drain **córas draenacha** system of drains

draeinphíobán *m1* drainpipe

draenáil *f3* drainage **córas draenála faoi uisce** underwater drainage system *v* drain

dragan *m1* dragon

draid *f2* grin, mouth showing teeth

draighneán *m1* blackthorn

draíocht *m3* magic, enchantment, witchcraft **chuir sí draíocht orainn** she enchanted us

dram *m3* dram

dráma *m4* play, drama

drámadóir *m3* dramatist, playwright

drámaíocht *f3* dramatic art, drama

drámata *adj* dramatic

dramhaíl *f3* refuse **diúscairt dramhaíola** refuse disposal

drandal *m1* gum, gums

drann *v* 1. grin, snarl **bhí an madra ag drannadh linn** the dog was snarling at us 2. **drann le** touch, have to do with **ní dhrannfainn leis** I wouldn't touch him/it, I wouldn't have anything to do with him/it

drantaigh *v* 1. snarl, growl 2. threaten **bhí sé ag drantú liom le gunna** he was threatening me with a gun

draoi *m4* druid, wizard

draoib *f2* mire, mud

draoibeach *adj* muddy

drár *m1* drawer **drár(s)** underpants

dreach *m3* facial appearance, expression

dréacht *m3* part, portion, draft **dréacht bainc** bank draft, **dréacht dualgais** set piece (*of music*)

dréachtaigh *v* draft

dréachtóir *m3* draughtsman, draughtswoman

dream *m3* party of people, group

dreancaid *f2* flea

dreap *v* climb

dreapadóir *m3* climber

dreapadóireacht *f3* climbing **cumann dreapadóireachta** climbing club

dreas *m3* 1. bout, turn, spell **dreas cainte** a spell of talking, **dreas ceoil** a bit of music 2. round (*sport*)

dreasacht *f3* incentive

dréim *f2* 1. climb(ing), ascent 2. expecting, expectation 3. contending, contention 4. aspiration, striving *v* 1. climb, ascend 2. expect 3. contend, oppose 4. aspire to, strive after

dréimire *m4* ladder

dreoigh *v* wither, decay, decompose

dreoilín *m4* wren **Lá an Dreoilín** the Day of the Wren, St Stephen's Day, **dul ar an dreoilín** go around with the wren-boys, **dreoilín teaspaigh** grasshopper

dreoite *adj* withered, decayed, decomposed

dríodar *m1* dregs, sediment, slops **dríodar an bhairille** the dregs of the barrel

driog *v* distil

driogaire *m4* distiller

drioglann *f2* distillery

dris *f2* briar, bramble **dris chosáin** annoying obstruction

drithle *f4* spark, sparkle

drithleach *adj* sparkling, bright

drithleog *f2* small spark

drithligh *v* sparkle, glitter

droch- *prefix* bad, ill-, un-, poor, evil **droch-chaint** bad language, **drochghnóthach** up to no good, ill-employed, **drochbheartach** evil-doing

drochaimsir *f2* bad weather

drochamhras *m1* distrust, misgiving

drochbhéasach *adj* ill-mannered, rude

drochbhlas *m1* bad taste, distaste

droch-cháil *f2* bad reputation **tá droch-cháil air** he has a bad name

drochdhuine *m4* bad person, evil person

drochfhéachaint *f3* wicked, evil look

drochíde *f4* abuse **thug tú drochíde dó/air** you mistreated him, abused him

drochiompar *m1* bad behaviour

drochiontaoibh *f2* distrust

drochmheas *m3* contempt **tá drochmheas agam orthu** I despise them

drochmheasúil *adj* contemptuous, contemptible

drochmhisneach *adj* despondency, discouragement **chuir sé drochmhisneach orm** he/it disheartened me

drochmhúinte *adj* 1. ill-mannered, rude 2. vicious (*of animal*)

drochobair *f2* bad work, mischief **cén drochobair atá ar siúl agaibh?** what mischief are you up to?

drochscéal *m1* bad news

drochshaol *m1* hard life, hard times **an Drochshaol** the Famine

drochtheist *f2* ill repute **tá an drochtheist air** he is known to be bad

drochthuar *m1* bad omen

drochuair *f2* unfortunate occasion **ar an drochuair (duit)** unfortunately (for you)

drogall *m1* reluctance, unwillingness **bhí drogall air cabhrú liom** he was reluctant to help me

drogallach *adj* reluctant, unwilling

droichead *m1* bridge **droichead dola** toll-bridge

droim *m3* 1. back **cnámh droma** backbone 2. ridge **dromanna sléibhe** mountain ridges

droimneach *adj* curved, arched, undulating

droimnocht *adj* bareback **ag marcaíocht droimnocht ar chapall** riding a horse bareback

drólann *f2* colon, intestines

dromchla *m4* surface **dromchla réidh** flat surface

drong *f2* body of people, group **drong taistealaithe** group of travellers

dronn *f2* hump, bent back

dronnach *adj* humped, convex

dronuilleog *f2* rectangle

dronuilleogach *adj* rectangular

dronuillinn *f2* right angle

drualus *m3* mistletoe

drúcht *m3* dew

druga *m4* drug

drugáil *v* drug

druglann *f2* drugstore

druid[1] *v* 1. shut, close **druid an doras** shut the door 2. **druid le** move close to, approach **tá sé ag druidim le meán lae** it's approaching midday

druid[2] *f2* starling

druidte *adj* shut, closed

druil *f2* drill **druil dóiteáin** fire drill

druileáil *f3* drilling *v* drill

druilire *m4* drill **druilire cumhachta** power drill, **druilire leictreach** electric drill

drúis *f2* lust

drúisiúil *adj* lustful

druma *m4* drum **druma míleata** military drum

druncaeir *m3* drunk(ard) **paca druncaeirí** a pack of drunkards

drúthlann *f2* brothel

dtí, go dtí to, until **níor tháinig siad go dtí anois** they didn't come until now, **go dtí go mbeidh Éire saor** until Ireland is free

dua *m4* toil, difficulty **bhuaigh siad gan dua** they won without difficulty

duáilce *f4* 1. vice, defect, fault 2. unhappiness

duairc *adj* gloomy, dismal, joyless **is duine duairc é** he's a gloomy person

duairceas *m1* gloominess, joylessness

duais *f2* prize, reward **fuair mé an chéad duais sa chomórtas** I got the first prize in the competition

duaiseoir *m3* prizewinner

duaisiúil *adj* difficult, tedious

duaithnigh *v* camouflage **log mianach a dhuaithniú** to camouflage a minefield

duaithníocht *f3* camouflage
duaithníocht tanc tank camouflage

dual¹ *m1* 1. knot (*in wood*) 2. strand (*of rope*) 3. lock (*of hair*) 4. wisp, tuft

dual² *m1* natural, native, expected **is dual dóibh a bheith mar sin** it's their nature to be like that

dualgas *m1* duty, obligation **cé a bhí ar dualgas?** who was on duty?

duan *m1* poem

duán¹ *m1* hook **tá breac ar mo dhuán** I have a fish on my hook

duán² *m1* kidney **pianta sna duáin** kidney pains

duánaí *m4* angler

duanaire *m4* anthology of poetry

duántacht *f3* rod-fishing, angling **lucht duántachta** anglers

duartan *m1* torrential rain, downpour

dubáil *f3* dubbing (*process*)

dúbail *v* double

dúbailt *f2* double, duplication

dúbailte *adj* double(d)

dubh¹ *adj* black, dark **bhí an áit dubh le daoine** the place was swarming with people, **bhí an seomra dubh dorcha** the room was pitch-black *m1* black, blackness, darkness **chuireamar an dubh ina gheal air** we persuaded him black was white, we pulled the wool over his eyes

dubh-² *prefix* black, dark, intense **dubhoighear** black frost, **dubhaois** dark age, **dubhobair** hard work

dubhach *adj* gloomy, melancholy, mournful

dubhaigh *v* 1. blacken, darken 2. sadden

dubhfhocal *m1* conundrum, enigma

dú- *prefix* black, dark, intense **dúbheart** bad deed, **dúdhearg** dark red, **dúchrith** intense/violent trembling

dúch *m1* ink

dúchas *m1* 1. heritage **tá dúchas aige ann** he has a hereditary right to it 2. native place or country **an bhfillfidh tú ar do dhúchas?** will you return home/to where you belong? 3. native **is cainteoir dúchais (Gaeilge, Iodáilise, srl) é** he is a native (Irish, Italian, etc) speaker

dúchasach *adj* hereditary, inherent, native **Meiriceánach Dúchasach** Native American *m1* inhabitant, native **bundúchasach** aborigine

dúcheist *f2* puzzle, riddle

dúchroíoch *adj* blackhearted, joyless

Dúchrónach *m1* Black and Tan (*Irish history*)

dufair *m2* jungle

duga *m4* (ship) dock

dugaire *m4* docker

dúghorm *adj* dark blue, navy-blue

duibheagán *m1* abyss, deep, depths **poll duibheagáin** black hole, bottomless pit

duibheagánach *adj* deep

dúiche *f4* 1. native land/place **Dúiche Sheoigheach** Joyce Country 3. district, region **an Chúirt Dúiche** the District Court

dúil *f2* 1. desire, fondness, liking **an bhfuil dúil agat inti?** are you fond of her? 2. hope, expectation **tá dúil agam le litir sa phost inniu** I'm expecting a letter in the post today 3. **ag dúil le** looking forward to, expecting

dúil *f2* 1. element 2. being **an dúil bhocht** the poor thing

duileasc *m1* dulse

duilleog *f2* 1. leaf **duilleoga tae** tea-leaves 2. **duilleog bháite** water lily

duilleogach *adj* leafy

duillín *m4* docket **duillín lóisteála** lodgement docket

duilliúr *m1* foliage, leaves

duine *m4* 1. human being, humankind **cearta an duine** human rights 2. person **duine ait** strange person, **duine óg, fásta** young person, adult, **daoine uaisle** gentlemen, **caint na ndaoine** ordinary speech, **beatha (do) dhuine a thoil** everybody has his own taste, **aon duine, duine ar bith** anybody, nobody (*negative*), **duine éigin** somebody 3. one (*person*) **duine de na cailíní / múinteoirí** one of the girls/teachers

dúiseacht *f3* state of being awake **níl siad ina ndúiseacht fós** they are not awake yet

dúisigh *v* awake, wake up, start **dúisigh ar a hocht mé** wake me up at eight, **meaisín a dhúiseacht** to start a machine

dúisire *m4* starter (*car, motor, etc*)

dul *m3* 1. going, departure 2. way **dul ar aghaidh, dul chun cinn** progress, **dul ar gcúl** retreat, decline, **níl aon dul as aici** she has no way out of it 3. arrangement, style **tá dul na Gaeilge ar an abairt sin** that sentence has an Irish construction

dúlra *m4* nature **an dúlra** the elements

dúmhál *m1, v* blackmail

dumpáil *f3* dumping **dumpáil dramhaíola** dumping of rubbish/refuse *v* dump

dún¹ *v* 1. close, shut **fuinneog a dhúnadh** to close a window 2. secure, fasten **dún do chasóg** fasten your jacket

dún² *m1* fort, fortified place, fortress **Dún Chaoin** Dunquin

Dún, an *m1* Down **Co. an Dúin** Co. Down

Dun Eideann *m* Edinburgh

Dún na nGall *m* Donegal **Co. Dhún na nGall** Co. Donegal

dúnadh *m* 1. closing, fastening 2. stoppage, closure

dúnáras¹ *m1* 1. fortified dwelling 2. secured residence

dúnáras² *m1* reticence, reserve

dúnárasach *adj* reticent, reserved

dúnmharaigh *v* murder

dúnmharfóir *m3* murderer

dúnmharú *m* murder

dúnpholl *m1* man-hole **clúdach dúnphoill** man-hole cover

dúnorgain *f3* manslaughter

dúnta *adj* closed, shut, secured, fastened

dúr *adj* 1. stupid 2. dour, grim

dúradán *m1* 1. (black) speck 2. domino (*game*)

durdáil *v* coo

dúrud *m3* a great deal **an dúrud daoine** lots of people

dúshaothrú *m* exploitation **dúshaothrú acmhainní** exploitation of resources, **dúshaothrú oibrithe** exploitation of workers

dúshlán *m1* challenge, defiance **thug sé mo dhúshlán** he challenged me, he defied me

dúshlánach *adj* challenging, defiant

dúshraith *f2* foundation, base, basis

dusta *m4* dust

dustáil *v* dust

dúthracht *f3* 1. earnestness, devotion, diligence, zeal 2. good will

dúthrachtach *adj* earnest, zealous, diligent

E

é *pron* he, him, it **rachaimid ann gan é** we'll go there without him/it, **ní maith liom é** I don't like him/it

ea *pron* (with *copula*) **cara is ea é, nach ea?** he is a friend, isn't he? **is ea / ní hea** he is/he is not, **más ea** if so, even so

eabhar *m1* ivory

éabhlóid *f2* evolution

Eabhrac *m4* York **Nua-Eabhrac** New York

Eabhrach *adj, m1* Hebrew

Eabhrais *f2* Hebrew (*language*)

each *m1* steed, horse

each-chumhacht *f3* horsepower

eachma *f4* eczema

éacht *m3* exploit, feat, stunt, achievement **tá éacht déanta agat** you've made quite an achievement

éachtach *adj* wonderful, extraordinary

éachtóir *m3* stuntman

eachtra *f4* 1. adventure, expedition 2. event

eachtrach[1] *adj* adventurous, eventful

eachtrach[2] *adj* external **an tAire Gnóthaí Eachtracha** the Minister for Foreign Affairs

eachtraigh *v* narrate, tell (*story*)

eachtránaí *m4* adventurer

eachtrannach *adj* alien, foreign *m1* alien, foreigner

eachtrúil *adj* adventurous, eventful

eacnamaí *m4* economist

eacnamaíoch *adj* economical

eacnamaíocht *f3* economics, economy **eacnamaíocht fheidhmiúil** applied economics

Eacstais[1] *f2* **(E)** Ecstasy (*drug*)

eacstais[2] *f2* ecstasy

eacstaiseach *adj* ecstatic

éad *m3* jealousy, envy

éadach *m1* 1. cloth, material **éadaí glanta** cleaning cloths, **éadach dúbailte** double material 2. clothes, clothing **bain díot/cuir ort do chuid éadaigh** take off/put on your clothes, **éadaí cnis** lingerie, underwear, **éadach cosanta** protective clothing 3. sail **faoi iomlán éadaigh** under full sail

éadáil *f3* riches, wealth, gain, property, find

éadan *m1* 1. forehead, front, brow, effrontery, nerve 2. **in éadan** against, opposed to, **rinne sé in éadan mo thola é** he did it against my will

eadarlúid *f2* interlude

éadathach *adj* colourless

éadmhar *adj* jealous, envious

éadóchas *m1* despair

éadóchasach *adj* despairing, hopeless

éadoimhneacht *f3* shallowness

éadomhain *adj* shallow

eadra *m4* late morning **bhí codladh go headra agam** I had a sleep in, **chodail siad go headra** they slept in

eadráin *f3* arbitration, intervention in dispute **ag déanamh eadrána** mediating

eadránaí *m4* arbitrator, mediator

éadrócaireach *adj* merciless

éadroime *f4* lightness

éadrom *adj* light

éadromán *m1* balloon, float, bladder

éadruach *adj* pitiless

éag *m3* death **go héag** till death, for ever, never (*negative*) *v* die, expire

eagal, is eagal liom go bhfuil sibh ródhéanach I'm afraid you are too late, is eagal dom I am in danger

éagaoin *f2* lament, moan, complaint *v* lament, moan, complain

eagar *m1* arrangement, order an bhfuil gach rud in eagar? is everthing in order?

eagarfhocal *m1* editorial

eagarthóir *m3* editor

eagarthóireacht *f3* editing

eagla *f4* fear ná bíodh eagla ort / oraibh don't be afraid, tá eagla uirthi roimh ghadhair she is afraid of dogs ar eagla na heagla just in case

eaglach *adj* fearful, afraid

eaglais *f2* church, church building an Eaglais Chaitliceach the Catholic Church

eaglaiseach *m1* clergyman

eaglasta *adj* ecclesiastical

éagmais *f2* lack, absence beimid maith go leor in éagmais a gcabhrach we'll be alright without their help

eagna *f4* wisdom, learning Leabhar na hEagna the Book of Wisdom

éagobhsaí *adj* unstable

éagóir *f3* wrong, injustice rinne siad éagóir orm they did me wrong

éagoiteann *adj* uncommon, unusual

éagórach *adj* wrong(ful), unjust

éagothroime *f4* unevenness, imbalance, unfairness, inequality

éagothrom *adj* uneven, unfair

eagraí *m4* organiser

eagraigh *v* arrange, organise

eagraíocht *f3* organisation eagraíocht dheonach voluntary organisation

eagrán *m1* edition

eagras *m1* organisation

eagrú *m* organisation eagrú gnó business organisation

éagruth *m3* deformity, shapelessness

éagruthach *adj* deformed, shapeless

éagsúil *adj* varied, unlike, different tuairimí éagsúla various ideas

éagsúlacht *f3* variety, unlikeness

éagsúlaigh *v* vary, diversify

éagumas *m1* inability, incapacity, impotence

éagumasach *adj* unable, incapable, impotent

eala *f4* swan

éalaigh *v* 1. escape 2. elope

ealaín *f2* art, skill bheith ar an ealaín chéanna arís to be at the same carry-on again, Dámh na nEalaíon the Faculty of Arts

ealaíonta *adj* artistic, skilful

ealaíontóir *m3* artist ealaíontóir smididh make-up artist

éalaitheach *adj* fugitive, elusive *m1* fugitive, escapee

éalang *f2* defect, flaw, weakness faoi éalang handicapped

éalangach *adj* defective, flawed, debilitated, handicapped

eallach *m1* cattle

ealta *f4* flock of birds

éalú *m* 1. escape 2. elopement

éalúchas *m1* escapism

éan *m1* 1. bird 2. éan corr outsider, odd one out

éanadán *m1* bird-cage

Eanáir *m4* January

éaneolaí *m4* ornithologist

éaneolaíocht *f3* ornithology

eang *f3* notch, indentation

eangach *adj* notched, indented *f2* net(ting) (*fishing, sport, etc*)

eanglach *m1* numbness from cold, pins and needles

éanlaith *f2* birds, fowl éanlaith chlóis, éanlaith tí domestic fowl, poultry

éanlann *f2* aviary

earc *m1* lizard, reptile **earc luachra / sléibhe** newt

earcach *m1* recruit

earcaíocht *f3* recruitment **oifigeach earcaíochta** recruiting officer

earcaigh *v* recruit **saighdiúirí a earcú** to recruit soldiers

éarlais *f2* 1. deposit **an bhfuil éarlais curtha agat ann?** have you put a deposit on it? 2. token **éarlais leabhair** book token

éarlamh *m1* patron

earnáil *f3* sector, category **an earnáil phoiblí, phríobháideach** the public, private sector

earra *m4* article (*of goods*), ware **earraí malartacha** exchangeable goods, **earraí gloine** glassware

earrach *m1* spring (*season*)

earráid *f2* error, mistake

eas *m3* waterfall, swift current **ag snámh in aghaidh easa** swimming against the current, striving against the odds

easaontas *m1* disagreement, disunion

éasc *m1* flaw

éasca *adj* easy, quick, nimble

eascaine *f4* curse, swear-word

eascainigh *v* curse, swear **bíonn sí i gcónaí ag eascainí** she is always cursing

eascair *v* sprout, spring

eascairdiúil *adj* unfriendly

eascann *f2* eel **chomh sleamhain le bolg eascainne** as slippery as an eel's belly

easláinte *f4* ill-health

easláinteach *adj* sickly, invalid

easlán *adj* sickly, invalid *m1* sick person, invalid

easna *f4* rib

easnamh *m1* want, deficiency, shortage **níl aon rud in easnamh orthu** they lack nothing

easnamhach *adj* deficient

easóg *f2* stoat **tá cluas easóige aici** she has sharp ears

easonóir *f3* dishonour, insult

easpa[1] *f4* lack, want, deficiency, absence of **easpa dídine** homelessness, **easpa féinmhuiníne** lack of self-confidence, **siondróm easpa imdhíonachta faighte (SEIF)** acquired immunodeficiency syndrome (AIDS), **víreas easpa imdhíonachta daonna (VEID)** human immunodeficiency virus (HIV)

easpa[2] *f4* abscess

easpach *adj* incomplete, deficient, needy

easpag *m1* bishop

easpórtáil *f3* export, exportation **easpórtálacha** exports *v* export

easpórtálaí *m4* exporter

eastát *m1* estate **eastáit tithíochta** housing estates, **eastát tionsclaíoch** industrial estate

easumhal *adj* disobedient

easumhlaíocht *f3* disobedience

easurraim *f2* disrespect

easurramach *adj* disrespectful

eatramh *m1* interval, lull

eatramhach *adj* interim, intermittent

eibhear *m1* granite

éiceachóras *m1* ecosystem

éiceolaíoch *adj* ecological

éiceolaíocht *f3* ecology **tubaiste éiceolaíochta** ecological disaster

éide *f4* 1. clothes 2. dress, uniform **éide sheirbhíse** service uniform

eidhneán *m1* ivy

éifeacht *f3* effectiveness, meaning, force, significance **ní bhainim aon éifeacht as** I can't find the significance of it, I can't use it to good effect, **le héifeacht ó ...** with effect from ...

éifeachtach adj 1. effective 2. highly capable, efficient

éifeachtacht f3 efficiency

éigean m1 1. violence, force **éigean mná, banéigean** rape 2. **ar éigean** hardly, barely, scarcely **bheith beo ar éigean** to be barely alive 3. **is éigean do, go …** it is necessary for, to … **b'éigean dúinn siúl abhaile** we had to walk home

éigeandáil f3 emergency **cumhachtaí éigeandála** emergency powers

éigeantach adj compulsory

éigeart m1 injustice, wrong

éigiallta adj nonsensical, senseless, irrational

éigin adj some **lá éigin** some day, **uair éigin eile** some other time

éiginnte adj indefinite, uncertain, vague

éiginnteacht f3 uncertainty, vagueness

éigiontach adj innocent, not guilty

Éigipt, an f2 Egypt

éigneoir m3 violator **éigneoir mná, banéigneoir** rapist

éignigh v force, violate, rape

éigse f4 learning, poetry, literature **Éigse na Mí** cultural festival in Meath

eile adj, adv 1. other, another **mar a dúirt tú an lá eile** as you said the other day, **an mbeidh ceapaire eile agat?** will you have another sandwich? **sin scéal eile** that's another story 2. next, more **an chéad bhean eile** the next woman, **rud eile de** what's more 3. else **cad / céard eile?** what else? **cé eile?** who else?

éileamh m1 claim, demand **éileamh gan íoc** outstanding claim, **an bhfuil éileamh orthu?** are they in demand? **ar éileamh** on demand

eilifint f2 elephant

éiligh v claim, demand

eilimint f2 element

eilit f2 doe

éilitheach adj demanding

éilitheoir m3 1. claimant 2. plaintiff

Eilvéis, an f2 Switzerland

Eilvéiseach adj Swiss **cáis Eilvéiseach** Swiss cheese m1 Swiss

éineacht, in éineacht le … along with …, together with …

eipic f2 epic

eipidéim f2 epidemic

eipidéimeach adj epidemic

eipidéimeolaí m4 epidemiologist

eire m4 load, encumberance, burden

Éire f Ireland **in Éirinn** in Ireland, **dul go hÉirinn** to go to Ireland, **bratach na hÉireann** the Irish flag, **muintir/pobal na hÉireann** the people of Ireland, **Muir Éireann** the Irish Sea, **Éire réamh-Chríostaí, Éire roimh theacht na Críostaíochta** pre-Christian Ireland

eireaball m1 tail

Éireannach adj Irish m1 Irish person

éirí m4 rising, rise **éirí na gréine** sunrise, **Éirí Amach na Cásca** Easter Rising

éiric f2 retribution, compensation

eiriceach m1 heretic

eiriceacht f3 heresy

éirigh v 1. rise, get up **d'éirigh sí ina seasamh** she stood up 2. get, become **tá an lá ag éirí fuar** the day is getting cold

éirigh as give up, resign, retire **éirigh as sin!** give that up! **d'éirigh sé as a phost anuraidh** he resigned, retired from his job last year

éirigh idir, d'éirigh eadrainn we quarrelled, fell out

éirigh le succeed, do well **d'éirigh go maith leo sa scrúdú cainte**

they did well in the oral, **go n-éirí
an t-ádh / an bóthar leat** good
luck to you

éirim *f2* 1. intelligence, aptitude **tá
éirim aigne aici** she has
intelligence 2. substance **éirim an
scéil** the drift of the story

éirimiúil *adj* talented, intelligent

eirmín *m2* ermine

éis, d'éis, tar éis after **tar éis
tamaill** after a while, **tar éis an
tsaoil** after all, **tá sé fiche tar éis
a ceathair** it's twenty past four

eisceacht *f3* exception **rinne mé
eisceacht díobh** I made an
exception of them

eisceachtúil *adj* exceptional

eischeadúnas *m1* off-licence

eiscir *f5* esker, ridge of mounds

eisdíritheach *adj* extrovert

eisdíritheoir *m3* extrovert

eiseachadadh *m* extradition

eiseachaid *v* extradite

eiseachas *m1* existentialism

eiseamláir *f2* example, (exemplar)
model

eiseamláireach *adj* exemplary,
model

eisean *emphatic pron* he, himself
eisean a rinne an botún it was
he/himself who made the mistake

eisiach *adj* exclusive

eisigh *v* issue **ticéid arna n-eisiúint
ag Bus Éireann** tickets issued by
Bus Éireann

eisilteach *m1* effluent **umar eisiltigh**
effluent tank

eisimirce *f4* emigration

eisimirceach *m1* emigrant

eisiúint *f3* issue, release **eisiúint le
déanaí** recent release,
preaseisiúint press release

eisliún *m1* echelon

eispéireas *m1* experience

eisreachtaí *m4* proscribed person,
outlaw

eisreachtaigh *v* proscribe, outlaw

éist *v* 1. **éist (le)** listen (to) **éist leis
an bhfear sin** listen to that man
2. hear **éist mórán agus can
beagán** hear a lot and say little
3. be silent **éist do bhéal!** keep
quiet! shut up!

éisteacht *f3* hearing, listening **lucht
éisteachta** audience

éisteoir *m3* listener

eite *f4* 1. wing **an eite chlé/dheis**
the left/right wing 2. fin 3. quill

eiteach *m1* refusal **thug mé an
t-eiteach dóibh** I refused them

eiteog *f2* wing

éitheach *m1* lie, falsehood **mionn
éithigh** false oath, perjury

eithne *f4* kernel, nucleus

eithneach *adj* nuclear

eitic *f2* ethics

eiticiúil *adj* ethical

eitigh *v* refuse **d'eitigh siad mé
faoin gceadúnas** they refused me
the licence

eitil *v* fly

eitilt *f2* flying, flight

eitinn *f2* tuberculosis (TB)

eitleán *m1* (aero)plane **eitleán beag**
light aircraft

eitleog *f2* 1. short flight 2. kite
3. volley (*sport*)

eitleoir *m3* flyer, aviator

eitlíocht *f3* aviation

eitneolaí *m4* ethnologist

eitneolaíocht *f3* ethnology

eitpheil *f2* volleyball

eitre *f4* furrow, groove

eo *m* salmon **eo fis** salmon of
knowledge (*stories of the Fianna*)

eochair *f5* key **poll na heochrach**
the key-hole

eochairchlár *m1* keyboard

eochraí *f4* roe (*in fish*)

eolach *adj* knowledgeable *m1* well-informed person **is leor nod don eolach** a word to the wise is sufficient, 'a nod is as good as a wink'

eolaí *m4* 1. knowledgeable person 2. guide, guidebook, directory 3. scientist

eolaíoch *adj* scientific

eolaíocht *f3* science

eolaire *m4* directory

eolas *m1* knowledge, information **an bhfuil eolas agat ar an áit sin? do** you know that place? **cuireann sé daoine ar an eolas** he directs people, he sets people on the right road

Eoraip, an *f3* Europe **tíortha na hEorpa** the countries of Europe

eorna *f4* barley

Eorpach *adj, m1* European **an tAontas Eorpach** the European Union, **Feisire Eorpach** member of the European Parliament, MEP

cotanáis *f2* euthanasia

F

fabhal *f2* fable

fabhalscéal *m1* fable

fabhar *m1* favour **an ndéanfá fabhar dom?** could you do me a favour?

fabhcún *m1* falcon

fabhra *m4* eyelash

fabhrach *adj* favourable

fabht *m4* fault, defect

fabhtach *adj* faulty, unsound

fabraic *f2* fabric

facs *m4* fax

facsáil *v* fax

fad *m1* length (*time, distance, etc*), extent **fad an bhóthair** the length of the road, **fad is a bhí sí ann** while she was there, **fad is beo dom** as long as I am alive, **fad saoil duit!** long life to you! **deichniúr ar fad a bhí ann** there were ten people there altogether, **ar feadh i bhfad** for a long time, **i bhfad ó ...** far from ... **cá fhad?** how long?

fada *adj* long **le scéal fada a dhéanamh gairid** to make a long story short, **ní fhaca mé le fada í** I haven't seen her for a long time, **is fada liom uaim iad** I miss them a lot

fadaigh[1] *v* lengthen, prolong

fadaigh[2] *v* kindle

fadálach *adj* lingering, tedious

fadchainteach *adj* longwinded

fadcheirnín *m4* long-playing record (LP)

fadharcán *m1* 1. knot (*in wood*) 2. corn (*on foot*)

fadhb *f2* problem **fuascailt na faidhbe** the solution to the problem

fadó *adv* long ago

fadradharcach *adj* long-sighted

fadraon *m1* long-range **buamadóir fadraoin** long-range bomber

fadsaolach *adj* long-lived

fadtéarmach *adj* long-term

fadtréimhseach *adj* long-term

fág *v* leave **beidh sí ag fágáil amárach** she'll be leaving tomorrow

faí *f4* voice, cry, call **an fhaí chéasta** the passive voice (*grammar*)

fáibhile *m4* beech tree

faic *f4* nothing **ní bhfuair mé faic na fríde** I received nothing at all

faiche *f4* lawn, green, playing-field **faiche ghairdín** garden lawn, **Faiche Stiofáin** St Stephen's Green

faichill *f2* care, caution, watchfulness **níl faichill ar bith inti** she takes no precautions

faichilleach *adj* careful, cautious, wary

fáideog *f2* wick, taper

fáidh *m4* prophet, wise man **na Trí Fáithe** the Three Wise Men

fáidheadóireacht *f3* prophecy

fáidhiúil *adj* prophetic

faigh *v* (see *irregular verbs*) get **an bhfuair tú ceapaire?** did you get a sandwich? **fuair / ní bhfuair** I did/I didn't, **d'éirigh liom an scrúdú a fháil** I succeeded in getting the exam, **ní bhfaighidh tú aon eolas uaidh sin** you won't get any information from him, **gheofá airgead air sin** you would get money for that, **níl an post faighte aici** she hasn't got the job

faighin *f2* vagina

faighneog *f2* shell, pod

faighteoir *m3* receiver, recipient

fail *f2* hiccup **tá fail orm** I have the hiccups

fáilí *adj* stealthy **tháinig siad orm go fáilí** they sneaked up on me

faill *f2* opportunity, chance **uair na faille** the opportune moment

faillí *f4* neglect, delay **faillí a dhéanamh i rud** to neglect something

faillitheach *adj* negligent

fáilte *f4* welcome **chuir sí fáilte romhainn** she welcomed us, **fáilte romhat / romhaibh!** welcome! (*sing/pl*)

fáilteach *adj* welcoming

fáilteoir *m3* receptionist

fáiltigh *v* welcome, greet

fáiltiú *m* reception **oifig fháiltithe** reception office

fainic *f2* warning, caution *v* take care **fainic! beware!**

fáinleog *f2* swallow (*bird*)

fáinne *m4* ring, circle **fáinne cluaise, pósta** ear-ring, wedding ring, **méar an fháinne** (wedding-)ring finger, **rinne siad fáinne thart uirthi** they formed a circle around her

fair *v* 1. watch, guard, observe, expect **tá na gardaí ag faire orthu** the gardaí are watching them, **fair thú féin!** mind yourself! **táim ag faire ar thraein** I'm waiting for a train 2. wake **beidh an corp á fhaire ar feadh dhá lá** the corpse will be waked for two days

faire *f4* 1. watch **faire leictreonach** electronic surveillance, **fear faire** watchman, look-out, **post faire** look-out post (*military*) 2. wake

faireog *f2* gland **fiabhras na bhfaireog** glandular fever

faireogach *adj* glandular

fairsing *adj* 1. wide, extensive, spacious 2. plentiful

fairsinge *f4* 1. width, extent, spaciousness 2. plenty

fairsingigh *v* 1. widen, extend, broaden 2. become plentiful

fairsingiú *m* expansion, extension **fairsingiú uirbeach** urban expansion

fairtheoir *m3* watcher, sentry

fáisc *v* squeeze, press, wring **oráiste a fháscadh** to squeeze an orange, **d'fháisc mé é le mo chroí** I pressed him to my heart, **ag fáscadh éadaí** wringing clothes

fáiscín *m4* clip, fastener **fáiscín crogaill, gruaige, páipéir** crocodile, hair, paper clip

faisean *m1* fashion **tá an ceol sin as faisean** that music is out of fashion, **i bhfaisean, san fhaisean** in fashion

faiseanta *adj* fashionable, stylish

faisisteachas *m1* fascism

faisnéis *f2* information, intelligence **faisnéis mhargaíochta** marketing information, **clár faisnéise** documentary, **oifigeach faisnéise** intelligence officer, **de réir faisnéise** according to advice

faisnéiseach *adj* informative

fáistine *f4* prophecy

fáistineach *adj* 1. prophetic 2. future (*grammar*) **an aimsir fháistineach** the future tense *m1* 1. prophet 2. future tense

faiteach *adj* fearful, timid, shy

faiteadh *m1* blinking (*eyes*), striking (*arms, hands*) on each other **i bhfaiteadh na súl** in the blink of an eye, **tá sé ag déanamh faitidh** he is slapping himself across the body (*to keep warm*)

fáithim *f2* hem

faithne *m4* wart

faitíos *m1* 1. fear 2. timidity, shyness

fál[1] *m1* hedge, fence, barrier **ní fál go haer é** it is not an insurmountable barrier

Fál[2] *m1* **Fianna Fáil** Fianna Fáil ('the warriors of Ireland'), **fir, Inis, Críocha Fáil** the men, island, territories of Ireland

fálaigh *v* fence, enclose

fallaing *f2* cloak, loose gown **fallaing folctha** dressing-gown

fálródaí *m4* stroller, loiterer

fálróid *f3* sauntering, strolling

falsa *adj* false, lazy

falsaigh *v* falsify, forge

falsaitheoir *m3* falsifier, forger

falsóir *m3* lazy person

faltanas *m1* spitefulness, spite, grudge

fáltas *m1* 1. receipt, income, profit **fáltais** proceeds, **fáltais airgid** cash receipts 2. amount **fáltas pá** pay packet

fámaireacht *f3* strolling, sightseeing

fan *v* wait, stay, remain **cá bhfuil tú ag fanacht?** where are you lodging? **táim ag fanacht ag Pól** I'm staying at Pól's (house, place, etc), **fan nóiméad** wait a minute, **fan go fóill** hold on!

fan le wait for **bhí mé ag fanacht leis an mbus** I was waiting for the bus

fána *f4* slope, incline

fánach *adj* 1. occasional, seldom, scarce 2. wandering 3. aimless, futile

fánaí *m4* wanderer

fánaíocht *f3* wandering, straying aimlessly

fanaiceach *adj* fanatical *m1* fanatic

fanaiceacht *f3* fanaticism

fanaile *m4* vanilla

fánán *m1* 1. slope 2. ramp

fann *adj* weak, faint, feeble

fannchlúmh *m1* elderdown

fanntais *f2* swoon, faint, fainting-fit **thit sí i bhfanntais** she fainted

fantaiseach *adj* fantastic

fantaisíocht *f3* fantasy

faobhar *m1* sharp edge, edge **faobhar na scine** the blade of the knife, **faobhar na haille** the edge of the cliff, **fear faobhair** eager, determined man

faobhrach *adj* sharp(-edged), keen, eager

faobhraigh *v* sharpen, whet

faoi (*prep prons* = **fúm, fút, faoi, fúithi, fúinn, fúibh, fúthu**) 1. below, under **tá sé faoin gcathaoir** it's under the chair, **chuaigh sí faoi scian / obráid** she underwent an operation, **bheith faoi chomaoin ag duine** to be under an obligation to somebody, **is fútsa atá sé** it's up to you,

fágfaidh mé fútsa é a dhéanamh I'll leave it to you to do, **faoi mar** as if, as, **faoi mar a tharla** as it happened 2. around, about **faoin tuath** in the country, **tá sí buartha faoi** she is worried about him/it, **chuala mé go leor fúthu** I heard a lot about them, **faoi láthair** at the moment, **faoi dheireadh** at last

faoileán *m1* seagull

faoileoir *m3* glider

faoileoireacht *f3* gliding

faoiseamh *m1* relief, ease **ba mhór an faoiseamh dúinn é** it was a great relief to us

faoiste *m1* fudge

faoistin *f2* confession

faoitín *m4* whiting (*fish*)

faolchú *m4* wolf, wild dog

faon *adj* limp, languid

faonfhuascailt *f2* breakthrough

faopach *m* fix **san fhaopach** in a fix

fara (*prep prons* = **faram, farat, fairis, farae, farainn, faraibh, faru**) *prep* along with **cé a bhí farat?** who was along with you, in your company?

farantóireacht *f3* ferrying **bád farantóireachta** ferry

faraor *interj* alas!

fardal *m1* inventory

farraige *f4* sea **an fharraige mhór** the open sea, **cois farraige** by the sea, **breoiteacht fharraige, tinneas farraige** sea-sickness, **farraigí neamhnúicléacha** nuclear-free seas

fás *m1* growth **fás aon oíche** mushroom growth, sudden growth *v* grow **nuair a bhí mé ag fás aníos / suas** when I was growing up

fásach *m1* wilderness, waste, desert

fáscadh *m1* squeeze, press

fáslach *m1* upstart

fásra *m4* vegetation

fásta *adj* grown up **duine fásta** adult

fáth *m3* reason, cause, motive **cén fáth a raibh tú ann?** why were you there?

fathach *m1* giant

fáthanna *pl* edges **fáthanna mo bhéil** my lips

fáthchiallach *adj* figurative, allegorical

fáthmheas *m3* diagnosis *v* diagnose

fáthscéal *m1* parable, legend

feá¹ *f4* beech

feá² *m4* fathom

feabhas *m1* 1. improvement **cuir feabhas air** improve it, **tá sé / sí ag dul i bhfeabhas** he/she/it is getting better, improving 2. excellence **ar fheabhas (ar fad)** excellent (altogether)

Feabhra *f4* February

feabhsaigh *v* improve, get better

feabhsóir gruaige *n* hair conditioner

feac *v* bend

féach *v* 1. look, see **féachann sé sin go holc** that looks bad, **féach lastall / an taobh eile** see overleaf 2. try, test **féach mo chuisle** try my pulse, **d'fhéach sí na bróga uirthi** she tried the shoes on

féach ar watch, consider **d'fhéach sí idir an dá shúil orm** she looked at me straight in the eye

féach chuig look to, attend **féach chuige go mbeidh an obair críochnaithe amárach** see that the work is finished tomorrow

féach do have regard to **gan féachaint dó sin** without regard to him/that

féach le try (to), attempt **d'fhéach sé leis an gceacht a fhoghlaim** he tried to learn the lesson

féachadóir *m3* onlooker, observer

féachaint *f3* 1. look, watch **lucht féachana** audience, spectators 2. testing, trial **chuir siad féachaint orm** they tested me

feacht *m4* current (*of river, sea,* etc)

feachtas *m1* campaign **feachtas toghchánaíochta** election campaign

fead *f2* whistle **lig sí fead** she whistled

féad *v* 1. be able to **féadfaidh tú do rogha rud a dhéanamh** you can do whatever you want, **d'fhéadfá a rá** you could say 2. ought to **d'fhéadfá é a stopadh** you should have stopped him/it

feadaíl *f3* whistling

feadán *m1* tube, pipe, canal (*in body*) **feadán fallópach** fallopian tube

feadh *m3* 1. duration, extent **bhíomar ann feadh na hoíche** we were there for the night 2. **ar feadh** during, throughout **ar feadh tamaill fhada** for a long time, **bhí mé ann ar feadh bliana** I was there for a year

feadhain *f3* band, troop **ceann feadhna** leader

feadóg *f2* whistle **feadóg mhór** flute, **feadóg stáin** tin whistle

feag *f3* rush (*plant*)

feall *m1* treachery, deceit **d'imir tú feall orm** you deceived me *v* **feall ar** deceive, betray, fail **níor fheall sí orainn** she didn't let us down

feallmharaigh *v* assassinate

feallmharfóir *m3* assassin

feallmharú *m* assassination

fealltach *adj* treacherous

fealltóir *m3* traitor, deceiver

fealsamh *m1* philosopher

fealsúnach *adj* philosophical

fealsúnacht *f3* philosophy

feamainn *f2* seaweed

fean *m1* fan

feann *v* flay, skin, strip, plunder

feannóg *f2* scald-crow

feannta *adj* severe, sharp, impoverishing

fear *m1* man **fear dóiteáin, poist, sneachta** fireman, postman, snowman, **fear céile** husband, **fear léinn** academic, **fear siúil** tramp, itinerant, **fir fhichille** chessmen, **Fear na gCrúb** the Devil, **déanfaidh sé fear de** it will make a man of him

Fear Manach *m* Fermanagh **Co. Fhear Manach** Co. Fermanagh

féar *m1* grass, hay **baint an fhéir** the mowing of the grass (*céilí dance*)

féarach *m1* grazing, pasture **ar féarach** being grazed

féaráilte *adj* fair

fearann *m1* land, ground, territory **baile fearainn** townland, **an Fearann Fuar** Farranfore (*Kerry*)

fearas *m1* appliance, apparatus, equipment **fearas deisithe poill** puncture repair kit, **fearas oifige** office equipment

fearg *f2* anger **tá fearg orm** I am angry, **chuir tú fearg uirthi** you made her angry

fearga *adj* masculine, male, manly

feargach *adj* angry

fearthainn *f2* rain **ag cur fearthainne** raining

feartlaoi *f4* epitaph

fearúil *adj* manly, brave

fearúlacht *f3* manliness

feasach *adj* knowing **is feasach dom/mé** I am aware

feasachán *m1* bulletin **feasachán speisialta** special bulletin

feasacht *f3* awareness **feasacht chriticiúil** critical awareness

féasóg *f2* beard

féasógach *adj* bearded

feasta *adv* henceforth, in future, from now on, no more (*negative*) **beidh mé cúramach feasta** I'll be careful from now on, **ná déan feasta é** don't do it any more

féasta *m4* feast, banquet

feic *v* (see *irregular verbs*) 1. see an bhfaca tú an scannán sin? did you see that film? chonaic / ní fhaca I did/I didn't, fan go bhfeicfidh mé let me see 2. feictear dom go ... it appears to me that ...

feiceálach *adj* 1. conspicuous, prominent 2. showy

féichiúnaí *m4* debtor

féidearthacht *f3* feasibility, possibilty staidéar féidearthachta feasibility study

feidhm *f2* function, use feidhm bhainistíochta managerial function, déanfaidh sé sin feidhm dom that will serve my purpose, dlí a chur i bhfeidhm to enforce a law, chuir tú i bhfeidhm orm é you persuaded me of it

feidhmchúntach *adj* user-friendly (*computers*)

feidhmeannach *m1* official, executive, agent feidhmeannach ceardchumainn trade union official, príomhfheidhmeannach chief executive

feidhmigh *v* 1. exercise, enforce 2. function, operate

feidhmiú *m* 1. enforcement, application 2. performance, operation

feidhmiúchán *m1* executive function oifigeach feidhmiúcháin executive officer

feidhmiúil *adj* functional

féidir, is féidir it is possible, an féidir leat teacht inniu? can you come today, is féidir / ní féidir I can/I can't, b'fhéidir perhaps, b'fhéidir go mbeinn ann perhaps I will be there, ní bhíonn b'fhéidir láidir maybe is never sure

feighlí *m4* attendant, caretaker, watcher feighlí leanaí / páistí child-minder, baby-sitter

feil *v* suit ní fheileann na bróga sin duit those shoes don't suit you

féile *f4* 1. generosity, hospitality 2. feast day, festival Lá Fhéile Pádraig St Patrick's Day, oíche chinn féile eve of festival

féileacán *m1* butterfly féileacán oíche moth

feileastram *m1* wild iris (*plant*)

féilire *m4* calendar

feiliúnach *adj* suitable

feilt *f2* felt tá ceann feilte ar an mbothán sin that hut has a felt roof

féiltiúil *adj* 1. regular tagann sí ar cuairt go féiltiúil she comes on a visit regularly 2. festive

féimheach *m1* bankrupt

féimheacht *f3* bankruptcy dlí féimheachta bankruptcy law

féin[1] *pron* 1. -self mé féin, tú féin, é féin, í féin, sinn / muid féin, sibh féin, iad féin myself, yourself, himself, herself, ourselves, yourselves, themselves 2. own dar liom féin in my own opinion, bhur dteanga féin your (*pl*) own language 3. even mar sin féin even so

féin[2] *prefix* auto-, self- féinteagasc self-instruction

féinchosaint *f3* self-defence ranganna féinchosanta self-defence classes

féinfhostaithe *adj* self-employed

feiniméan *m1* phenomenon

féiníobairt *f3* self-sacrifice

féiniúlacht *f3* separate identity

féinmharú *m* suicide

féinmhuinín *f2* self-confidence

féinriail *f5* autonomy

féinrialaitheach *adj* self-governing, autonomous

féinseirbhís *f2* self-service stáisiún féinseirbhíse self-service station

féinsmacht *m3* self-control

féinspéis *f2* egotism

féinspéiseach *adj* egotistic

féinspéiseachas *m1* egotism

féinspéisí *m4* egotist

feirc *f2* 1. tilt, peak (*of cap, hat, etc*) 2. hilt (*of knife, etc*) 3. fringe

féirín *m4* present, gift

feirm *f2* farm **teach feirme** farmhouse

feirmeoir *m3* farmer **bean feirmeora** a farmer's wife

feirmeoireacht *f3* farming **feirmeoireacht éisc** fish-farming

feis *f2* assembly, festival **ardfheis** national convention

feisire *m4* MP **Feisire Eorpach** member of the European Parliament (MEP)

feisteas *m1* 1. dress, outfit, clothes **feisteas tráthnóna** evening wear, **seomra feistis** dressing-room 2. fitting(s), furnishings **daingneáin agus feisteas** fixtures and fittings, **feisteas lampa** lamp fitting

feisteoir *m3* fitter

feistigh *v* 1. arrange, fit, fix **píobán a fheistiú** to fit a pipe 2. dress, equip **d'fheistigh sí í féin** she dressed herself 3. secure, moor **bád a fheistiú** to moor a boat

feistiú *m* 1. fitting **feistithe tí** domestic fittings 2. fixing, arrangement, mooring

féith *f2* 1. vein **féith scarnhógach** pulmonary vein 2. natural bent, talent **tá féith an cheoil inti** she has a talent for music

feitheamh *m1* wait(ing), expectation **seomra feithimh** waiting-room

féitheog *f2* muscle, sinew

féitheogach *adj* muscular, sinewy

feitheoir *m3* supervisor

feitheoireacht *f3* supervision

feithicil *f2* vehicle

feithid *f2* insect

feithidicíd *f2* insecticide

feithidphailnithe *adj* insect-pollinated

féithiú *m* mainlining (*drug addiction*)

féithleann *m1* honeysuckle (*plant*)

féithleog *f2* climbing plant, vine

feochadán *m1* thistle

feoigh *v* wither, decay

feoil *f3* meat, flesh **ag ithe feola** eating meat, **feoil mhionaithe** mince, **feolta éagsúla** various meats

feoilséantach *adj* vegetarian **aiste bia fheoilséantaigh** vegetarian diet

feoilséantóir *m3* vegetarian

feolmhar *adj* fleshy, flabby

feothan *m1* (stiff) breeze **feothain ghaoithe** gusts of wind

fia *m4* deer **fia beannach** stag, **fia rua** red deer

fiabhras *m1* fever **fiabhras léana** hay-fever

fiabhrasach *adj* feverish

fiacail *f2* tooth **fiacail toraís** wisdom tooth, **tinneas fiacaile** tooth-ache, **fiacla bréige** false teeth, **sláinteachas fiacla** dental health, **briseadh a cuid fiacla sa timpiste** her teeth were broken in the accident, **dúirt sé faoina fhiacla é** he muttered it, **fiacla lainne** teeth of a blade

fiach[1] *m1* 1. debt **i bhfiacha** in debt, **táim i bhfiacha fiche punt dó** I owe him £20, **fiach gnó** business debt 2. price, cost **fiacha an chóta** the price of the coat 3. **chuir sé d'fhiacha orm (dul ann)** he forced me (to go there)

fiach[2] *m1* raven **chomh dubh leis an bhfiach** as black as a raven, **fiach mara** cormorant

fiach[3] *m1* hunt, chase **ar chuir siad an fiach ort?** did they chase you away? *v* hunt, chase **ag fiach i ndiaidh duine / ruda** chasing after somebody/something

fiachas *m1* 1. debt **fiachas náisiúnta** national debt 2. liability **fiachas teoranta** limited liability

fiachóir *m3* debtor

fiaclóir *m3* dentist **coinne fiaclóra** dentist appointment

fiaclóireacht *f3* dentistry **céim san fhiaclóireacht** a degree in dentistry

fiadhúlra *m4* wildlife

fiafheoil *f3* venison

fiafraí *m* enquiry, query

fiafraigh *v* ask, enquire **ná fiafraigh díomsa** don't ask me

fiagaí *m4* hunter

fiaile *f4* weed(s)

fiailnimh *f2* weed-killer

fiáin *adj* wild

fial *adj* generous

fianaise *f4* testimony, evidence **fianaise a thabhairt** to give evidence, testify, **ina fhianaise** in his presence, **fianaise ar cheannach** evidence of purchase

Fiann *f3* the 'Fianna', band of warriors **cothrom na Féinne a fháil / a thabhairt** to get/give fair play, **Coláiste na bhFiann** modern Irish-language summer college ('the College of the Fianna')

fiántas *m1* 1. wildness 2. wilderness

fiar *adj* 1. slanted, diagonal, oblique 2. bent *m1* 1. slant, veer **ar fiar** slanted, at an angle 2. twist, bend

fiarlán *m1* zigzag

fiarshúil *f2* squint(-eye)

fiarshúileach *adj* squint-eyed

fia-úll *m1* crab apple

fiche *m5* twenty **fiche duine / tarbh** twenty people/bulls, **tá sí sna fichidí** she is in her twenties, **ceol ó na fichidí** music from the twenties, **ceithre bliana is trí fichid d'aois** 64 years ('four years and three twenties') old

ficheall *f2* chess **ag imirt fichille** playing chess

fichiú[1] *m4* twentieth **trí fhichiú** three twentieths

fichiú[2] *adj* twentieth **an fichiú haois** the twentieth century

ficsean *m1* fiction

fidil *f2* fiddle

fidléir *m3* fiddler

fidléireacht *f3* fiddle-playing

fige *f4* fig

figh *v* weave, plait **tá siad fite fuaite ina chéile** they are interwoven

figiúr *m1* figure, number **tá mé go maith ag figiúirí** I am good with numbers

file *m4* poet

fileata *adj* poetic

filiméala *m4* nightingale

filíocht *f3* poetry **cnuasach filíochta** collection of poetry

fill *v* 1. return **ní fhillfidh sé go deo arís** he'll never return again 2. fold, bend, turn back **fill anseo** fold here, **d'fhill sí páipéar ar an mbronntanas** she wrapped the present

filléad *m1* fillet

filleadh *m1* fold, bend, return **ticéad fillte** return ticket, **filleadh beag** kilt

fillteán *m1* folder, wrapper

filltín *m4* wrinkle, fold, crease

fimíneach *adj* hypocritical *m1* hypocrite

fimíneacht *f3* hypocrisy

finéagar *m1* vinegar

fíneáil *f3* fine **ar gearradh fíneáil ort?** were you fined? *v* fine

fíneálta *adj* fine, smooth

finideach *adj* finite

Fínín *m4* Fenian

Fíníneachas *m1* Fenianism

finiúin *f3* 1. vine **caor fíniúna** grape 2. vineyard

finné *m4* witness

finscéal *m1* fable, legend, fiction

finscéalach *adj* fabled, fictional

finscéalaíocht *f3* fiction

fíocas *m1* piles, haemorrhoids

fíoch *m1* rage, feud

fíochán *m1* 1. tissue 2. web

fíochmhar *adj* furious, fierce, ferocious

fíodóir *m3* weaver

fíodóireacht *f3* weaving

fíogadán *m1* camomile **tae fíogadáin** camomile tea

fíoghual *m1* charcoal (*of wood*)

fíon *m3* wine **buidéal fíona** a bottle of wine

fíonchaor *f2* grape **triopall fíonchaor** bunch of grapes

fíonghort *m1* vineyard

Fionlainn *f2* **an Fhionlainn** Finland

Fionlainnis *f2* Finnish (*language*)

Fionlannach *adj* Finnish *m1* Finlander, Finn

fionn¹ *adj* 1. fair, blond **gruaig fhionn** fair/blond hair 2. bright, white

fionn² *m1* cataract (*eye*)

fionn³ *v* ascertain, discover

fionnachrith *m3* hair-raising fear **cuireann siad fionnachrith orm** they give me the goose pimples

fionnachtain *f3* 1. discovery 2. invention

fionnadh *m1* 1. hair 2. fur **cóta fionnaidh** fur coat

fionnuaire *f4* coolness, shelter (*from sun*)

fionnuar *adj* cool, refreshing

fionnuaraigh *v* cool, freshen

fionraí *f4* suspension, postponement **cuirfear ar fionraí thú** you will be suspended

fiontar *m1* venture, risk, enterprise

fiontraíocht *f3* enterprise **crios fiontraíochta** enterprise zone

fiontrach *adj* enterprising

fíor¹ *adj* true, real, genuine **fíor nó bréagach** true or false, **cara fíor** real/true friend, **is fíor duit** you are right *f2* truth

fíor² *f5* figure, shape, outline, sign **fíor na spéire** the horizon, **fíor na Croise** the sign of the Cross

fíor-³ *prefix* true, real, very, intense **fíorghrá** true love, **fíoreolas** real knowledge, **fíormhaith** very good, **fíorbhrú** intense pressure

fíoraigh *v* verify

fíoras *m1* fact **aimsiú fíoras** fact finding

fíorú *m* 1. verification 2. fulfilment

fíorúil *adj* virtual **réaltacht fhíorúil** virtual reality

fíoruisce *m4* fresh water, spring water

fios *m3* knowledge, information **níl a fhios agam** I don't know, **tabhair le fios dom roimh ré** let me know beforehand, **gan fhios** secretly, unknown, **fear feasa** wise man

fiosrach *adj* inquisitive

fiosracht *f3* inquisitiveness, curiosity

fiosraigh *v* inquire **ag fiosrú an scéil** inquiring about the matter

fiosrú *m* inquiry **binse fiosraithe** tribunal

fiosrúchán *m1* inquiry

firéad *m1* ferret

fireann *adj* male

fireannach *m1* male

fíric *f2* fact **aimsiú fíricí** fact finding

fírinne *f4* truth **ag insint na fírinne** telling the truth, **de dhéanta na fírinne** as a matter of fact

fírinneach *adj* truthful, genuine

firinscneach *adj* masculine (*grammar*)

firmimint *f2* firmament

fís[1] *f2* vision

fís-[2] *prefix* video- **fís-scannán** video film

físchaiséad *m1* video cassette

físcheamara *m4* video camera

físchomhdháil *f3* videoconferencing

fisic *f2* physics

fisiceach *adj* physical

fisiceoir *m3* physicist

fisiciúil *adj* physical

fisiteiripe *f4* physiotherapy

fisiteiripeach *m1* physiotherapist

fístaifeadán *m1* video(cassette) recorder

fístéacs *m4* videotext

fístéip *f2* video tape

fithis *f2* 1. passage 2. orbit

fithisigh *v* orbit

fiú 1. worth, price **an fiú é?** is it worth it? **is fiú go mór é** it's well worth it, **ní fiú faic é sin** he/it isn't worth a thing 2. even **níor tháinig siad chuig an gcóisir fiú** they didn't even come to the party, **d'imigh siad gan fiú slán a rá** they left without even saying goodbye

fiuch *v* boil **uisce fiuchta** boiling water

fiuchadh *m* boiling **ar fiuchadh** boiling

fiúntach *adj* worthy, respectable

fiúntas *m1* worth, merit

fiús *m1* fuse **fiús sábháilteachta** safety fuse

flainín *m4* flannel

flaith *m3* 1. prince, lord 2. lordship

flaitheas *m1* 1. dominion, sovereignty 2. **na Flaithis** heaven

flaithiúil *adj* generous

flaithiúlacht *f3* generosity

flannbhuí *adj* orange-colour **tá trí dhath ar bhratach na hÉireann:** uaine, bán agus flannbhuí there are three colours on the Irish flag: green, white and orange

flas *m3* floss **flas fiacla** dental floss, **flas candaí** candy-floss

fleá *f4* 1. feast, festive occasion 2. festival **fleá cheoil** music festival

fleáchas *m1* festivity

fleasc[1] *f2* 1. wand 2. wreath 3. (**thit sí) ar fhleasc a droma** (she fell) on the flat of her back

fleasc[2] *m3* flask **fleasc tae** a flask of tea

fleisc *f2* flex (*electrical*)

fleiscín *m4* hyphen

flichshneachta *m4* sleet

fliú *m4* influenza, flu

fliuch *adj* wet **fliuch báite / báite fliuch** soaking wet, drenched, **Seán báite** watered whisky *v* wet **an leaba a fhliuchadh** to wet the bed

fliúit *f2* flute

flocas *m1* flock of wool **flocas cadáis** cotton-wool

flúirse *f4* plenty, abundance **bhí flúirse bia ann** there was food in abundance there

flúirseach *adj* plentiful

fo- *prefix* under-, sub-, secondary, minor **fo-éadaí** underwear, **fochonraitheoir** sub-contractor, **focheist** minor question

fo-alt *m1* sub-section

fo-bhaile *m4* suburb

fobhealach *m1* underpass

fobhóthar *m1* secondary road

fo-bhrat *m1* undercoat (*painting*)

fobhríste *m4* underpants

focal *m1* word **tá cúpla focal Gearmáinise agam** I can speak a few words of German, **bíonn an duine sin de réir a fhocail** that person stands by his word, **i mbeagán focal** in a few words, **focal ar fhocal** word for word,

próiseáil focal, próiseálaí focal word processing, word processor

fócas *m1* focus **i bhfócas** in focus, **as fócas** out of focus

fochéimí *m4* undergraduate

fochla *m4* cavity, den, cave, grotto

fochma *m4* chilblain

fo-chomhfhios *m3* subconscious

fo-chomhfhiosach *adj* subconscious

fochuideachta *f4* subsidiary (company)

fochupán *m1* saucer **cupán agus fochupán** cup and saucer

foclóir *m3* dictionary, vocabulary

fód *m1* sod **fód móna** sod of turf, **seas an fód** stand your ground, **fód dúchais** native ground/place

fógair *v* proclaim, declare, advertise **poblacht a fhógair** to proclaim a republic, **d'fhógair sí an fhírinne** she declared the truth, **post a fhógairt** to advertise a position/job

fógairt *f3* proclamation, declaration, announcement

foghar *m1* sound

foghlaeir *m3* fowler

foghlaeireacht *f3* fowling

foghlaí *m4* plunderer, pirate, marauder

foghlaim *f3* learning *v* learn **foghlaimíonn sí tapa** she learns quickly

foghlaimeoir *m3* learner, trainee

foghlamtha *adj* learned

fo-ghnó *m4* sideline **rud a dhéanamh mar fho-ghnó** to do something as a sideline (business)

foghraíocht *f3* phonetics

fo-ghúna *m4* slip (*under dress*)

fógra *m4* notice, advertisement

fógraíocht *f3* advertising

fóibe *f4* phobia

foiche *f4* wasp

foighne *f4* patience **bíodh foighne agat / déan foighne** have patience

foighneach *adj* patient

fóill *adj* 1. quiet, gentle **fan go fóill** wait a while, **fóill! gently!** 2. **go fóill** yet, still **níor imigh siad go fóill** they haven't gone yet, **tá an carr sin agam go fóill** I still have that car

fóillíocht *f3* leisure, ease

foilseachán *m1* publication **Oifig Dhíolta Foilseachán Rialtais** Government Publications Sales Office

foilsigh *v* 1. publish **foilsithe ag an gComhlacht Oideachais** published by the Educational Company 2. reveal, disclose **foilsíodh an rún** the secret was disclosed

foilsitheoir *m3* publisher

foilsitheoireacht *f3* publishing **gnó foilsitheoireachta** publishing business

foilsiú *m* publishing, publication

fóin *v* suit, serve **ní thónann an lá sin dom** that day doesn't suit me

foinse *f4* source **foinsí cáipéiseacha** documentary sources

fóinteach *adj* useful, helpful, practical

fóir[1] *f5* edge, rim, border, boundary **ná téigh thar fóir leis** don't go too far with it

fóir[2] *v* 1. relieve, assist, help **fóir orainn!** help us! 2. **fóir do** suit, agree with **ní fhóireann an obair di** the work doesn't suit her

foirceann *m1* end, extremity, limit

fóirdheontas *m1* subsidy

foireann *f2* team, crew, staff **foireann sacair** soccer team, **foireann scannáin** film crew, **seomra foirne** staff room

foirfe *adj* perfect **go foirfe** perfectly, **an aimsir fhoirfe** the perfect tense (*grammar*)

foirfeacht *f3* perfection

foirfigh *v* perfect

foirgneamh *m1* building, structure **foirgneamh ilstórach** multistorey building

foirgneoir *m3* builder

foirgníocht *f3* building, construction **conradh foirgníochta** building contract

foirm *f2* form **foirm iarratais** application form

foirmigh *v* form, take shape

foirmiú *m* formation **foirmiú cladaigh** beach formation

foirmiúil *adj* formal

foirmle *f4* formula

foirnéis *f2* furnace

fóirsteanach *adj* fitting, suitable

folach *m1* hiding, covering **i bhfolach** in hiding, hidden

folachán *m1* 1. cache 2. hiding(-place)

folachánaí *m4* person in hiding, stowaway

folaigh *v* hide, cover (up)

folaíocht *f3* breeding, lineage **ainmhí folaíochta** thoroughbred, **madra folaíochta** pedigree dog

foláir, ní foláir ... it is necessary ..., **ní foláir dó** ... he must ..., **ní foláir léi** ... she feels it necessary ...

foláireamh *m1* warning, notice, injunction

folamh *adj* empty, vacant, blank **táim ar phócaí folmha** I have empty pockets, I'm broke

folc *v* bathe

folcadán *m1* bath-tub

folcadh *m* bath, wash **ag tógáil / ag glacadh folctha** having a bath, **folcadh béil** mouth-wash

foléim *f2* light jump, skip

foléine *f4* vest

folig *v* sublet

foligean *m1* subletting

folíne *f4* extension (*telephone*)

folláin *adj* sound, wholesome, healthy **chomh folláin le breac** as healthy as ever

folláine *f4* wholesomeness, soundness, healthiness

follasach *adj* obvious, clear, evident

folmhaigh *v* empty

folt *m1* hair (*of head*)

foltfholcadh *m* shampoo(ing)

foluain *f3* fluttering, flying, hovering **ní raibh an bhratach ar foluain ann** the flag was not flying there

folúil *adj* full-blooded, thoroughbred **capall folúil** a thoroughbred horse

folúntas *m1* vacancy

folús *m1* vacuum, emptiness, void

folúsghlanadh *m* vacuum-cleaning, hoovering

folúsghlantóir *m3* vacuum-cleaner, hoover

fómhar *m1* 1. autumn 2. harvest **ag baint an fhómhair** reaping the harvest

fo-mheaisínghunna *m4* sub-machine-gun

fomhuireán *m1* submarine

fón *m1* phone

fónamh *m1* 1. usefulness, benefit, service **bhí fónamh mór ann** it was most useful/beneficial, **bainfimid fónamh as** we will make good use of it 2. **ar fónamh** fit, excellent **níl sí ar fónamh** she is unwell

fondúireacht *f3* foundation **Fondúireacht an Bhlascaoid** the Blasket Foundation

fonn[1] *m1* inclination, desire, urge **tá fonn orm cabhrú leat** I am eager to help you, **bíonn fonn codlata ort i gcónaí** you always have the desire to sleep

fonn[2] *m1* tune, air, melody **ag gabháil fhoinn** singing

fonnmhar *adj* willing, eager **déanfaidh mé go fonnmhar é** I'll do it willingly

fonóid *f2* mockery, jeering **ná bí ag déanamh fonóide faoi** don't be ridiculing him

fonóideach *adj* mocking, jeering

fonóta *m4* footnote

fonsa *m4* hoop

fóntas *m1* utility

foráil *f3* provision (*in law, etc*) **forálacha achta** provisions of an act

forainm *m1* pronoun

foraois *f2* forest **foraois (theochriosach / thrópaiceach) bháistí** (tropical) rainforest, **foraois de dhéantús an duine** man-made forest

foraoiseacht *f3* forestry

foraoisiú *m* afforestation

foras *m1* institute **Foras Áiseanna Saothair (FÁS)** the Training and Employment Authority

forás *m1* development, progress

forásach *adj* developing, progressive

forbair *v* develop **táirge a fhorbairt** to develop a product

forbairt *f3* growth, development **forbairt chomhtháite na tuaithe** integrated rural development

forbhreathnú *m* overview

forbhríste *m4* overalls

forc *m1* fork

forchéimniú *m* progression

forchostas *m1* overhead (cost) **forchostais** overheads

fordhóite *adj* scorched, singed

foréigean *m1* violence, force

foréigneach *adj* violent, forcible

forghabh *v* take by force, seize, secure

forhalla *m4* foyer

forimeall *m1* rim, outer edge, periphery

forimeallach *adj* outer, peripheral

forleathadh *m* spread

forleathan *adj* widespread, extensive

forléine *f4* smock

forleitheadach / forleitheadúil *adj* widespread

forleithne *f4* extensiveness

forlíonadh *m1* supplement (*of newspaper etc*)

forluí *m* overlap

forluigh *v* overlap

forluiteach *adj* overlapping

formad *m1* envy **tá formad agam leat** I am envious of you

formáid *f2* format **formáid phriontála** print format

formáidigh *v* format **diosca a fhormáidiú** to format a disk

formhéadaigh *v* magnify

formhéadú *m* magnification

formhéadúchán *m1* magnification **gloine formhéadúcháin** magnifying glass

formhór *m1* majority, greater part **formhór (mór) na ndaoine** the majority of the people, **formhór (mór) an phobail** the majority of the community

formhuinigh *v* endorse

formhuiniú *m* endorsement

forneart *m1* force, violence

forógra *m4* announcement, proclamation **Forógra (na Cásca) 1916** the 1916 (Easter) Proclamation

forrán *m1* salute, accosting **forrán a chur ar dhuine** to salute/accost somebody

fórsa *m4* force **fórsaí amais** attacking forces, **Fórsa Cosanta Áitiúil FCA**

forscáth *m3* canopy

forsheomra *m4* lobby

forshuigh *v* superimpose

forshuíomh *m* superimposition

fórsúil *adj* forceful

fortún *m1* fortune, luck, chance

fós *adv* yet, still **níl a fhios agam fós** I don't know yet, **an bhfuil tú ag éisteacht fós?** are you still listening?

foscadh *m1* shelter, shade

foscúil *adj* 1. sheltered, shady 2. discreet

foshuiteach *adj*, *m1* subjunctive **an modh foshuiteach** the subjunctive mood (*grammar*)

fosta *adv* also **beidh Siobhán ann fosta** Siobhán will be there also

fostaí *m4* employee

fostaigh *v* 1. employ, hire **tá deichniúr fostaithe ann** there are ten people employed there 2. engage, catch

fostaíocht *f3* employment

fostóir *m3* employer, hirer **fostóir comhionannais deiseanna** equal opportunities employer

fostú *m* 1. employment, hiring **fostú bád** hiring of boats 2. entanglement **bhíomar i bhfostú ann** we were entangled in it

fótachóip *f2* photocopy

fótachóipeáil *f3* photocopying **meaisín fótachóipeála** photocopier

fótachóipire *m4* photocopier (*machine*)

fótagraf *m1* photograph

fótagrafach *adj* photographic

fótagrafaí *m4* photographer

fótaghrafaíocht *f3* photography

fótashamhail *f3* photofit

fotha *m4* feed (*printer*) **fotha aghaidh faoi / in airde** face down/up feed

fothaigh *v* feed (*printer*)

fothain *f3* shelter, shade

fothainiúil *adj* 1. sheltered, shady 2. discreet

fotháirge *m4* by-product

fotheideal *m1* sub-title

fothoghchán *m1* by-election

fothrach *m1* ruin

fothraig *v* bathe, dip, immerse

fothram *m1* noise, clamour, din

Frainc *f2* **an Fhrainc** France, **príomhchathair na Fraince** the capital city of France

frainceáil *f3* franking **meaisín frainceála** franking machine *v* frank

Fraincis *f2* French (*language*)

frainse *m4* fringe (*hair*)

fráma *m4* 1. frame 2. chassis

frámaigh *v* frame

Francach *adj* French *m1* French person

francach *m1* rat

fraoch[1] *m1* heather

fraoch[2] *m1* fury, ferocity, fierceness

fras *adj* copious, abundant *f2* shower

frása *m4* phrase

fraschanna *m4* watering-can

freagair *v* answer, respond

freagairt *f3* answer(ing), response

freagra *m4* answer

freagrach *adj* 1. answerable, responsible **bheith freagrach as …** to be responsible for … 2. responsive

freagracht *f3* responsibility **freagracht chomhpháirteach** joint responsibility

fréamh *f2* root

fréamhaí *m4* derivative (*grammar*)

fréamhaigh *v* 1. root (*plant, tree, etc*), settle 2. **fréamhaigh ó** spring from, descend from

freang *v* contort, twist

freanga *f4* dart of pain, contortion, twitch, spasm **freangaí tinnis** darts/twitches of pain

freasaitheoir *m3* reactor (*electrical*)

freastail *v* attend, serve **ag freastal ar dhuine** attending/serving a person

freastal *m1* attendance, service **lucht freastail** attendants

freastalaí *m4* waiter, attendant

freasúra *m* opposition

freasúrach *adj* opposing

freisin *adv* also

fríd *f2* flesh-worm, mite **faic na fríde** nothing at all

frídín *m4* germ

frioch *v* fry **bia a fhriochadh** to fry food

friochta *adj* fried

friochtán *m1* frying pan

friochtóg *f2* fritter

friotaíocht *f3* resistance (*electricity*) **tomhsaire friotaíochta** resistance gauge

friotal *m1* speech, expression

friotháil *f3* attending, service *v* attend, serve

friseáilte *adj* fresh

fritéis *f2* antithesis

frith- (**fri** before 't') *prefix* counter-, anti- **fritarraingt** counter-attraction, **frithreo** antifreeze

frithbheathach *m1* antibiotic

frithbhuaic *f2* anticlimax

frithbhualadh *m* repercussion

frithchaith *v* reflect (*light*)

frithchaiteoir *m3* reflector

frithchioclón *m1* anticyclone

frithchosúil *adj* paradoxical

frithchosúlacht *f3* paradox

fritheithneach *adj* anti-nuclear

frithgheallaí *m* underwriter (*insurance*)

frithghiniúint *f3* contraception

frithghiniúnach *adj, m1* contraceptive

frithghníomh *m1* counteraction, reaction

frithghníomhach *adj* reactionary

frithghníomhaí *m4* reactionary

frithionsaí *m4* counter-attack

frithnimh *f2* antidote

frithrá *m* contradiction

frithreo *m4* antifreeze

frithsheipteach *adj* antiseptic

frithsheipteán *m1* antiseptic

frithshóisialta *adj* anti-social

frithshuí *m* contrast

frithshuigh *v* set against, contrast

frog *m1* frog

frogaire *m4* frogman

fronsa *m4* amusing play, farce (*theatre*)

fruilcheannach *m1* hire-purchase

fruilcheannaigh *v* buy on hire-purchase **teilifíseán a fhruilcheannach** to buy a television on hire-purchase

fruiligh *v* hire

fruiliú *m* hiring, hire **fruiliú bád** boat hire

frustrachas *m1* frustration

fuacht *m3* cold **tá fuacht ann** it is cold

fuachtán *m1* chilblain

fuadach *m1* abduction, kidnapping

fuadaigh *v* abduct, kidnap, hijack

fuadaitheoir *m3* abductor, kidnapper, hijacker

fuadar *m1* hurry, rush, bustle **cén fuadar atá fút?** what's your rush?

fuadrach *adj* hurried, busy

fuadú *m1* abduction, kidnapping, hijacking

fuafar *adj* hateful

fuaidreamh *m1* batter (*food*)

fuaigh *v* sew, stitch

fuáil *f3* sewing, needlework

fuaim *f2* sound **éist le fuaim na habhann agus gheobhaidh tú breac** listen to the sound of the river and you'll catch a fish, **teicneoir fuaime** sound technician

fuaimbhac *m1* sound barrier

fuaimdhíonach *adj* soundproof

fuaimeolaíocht *f3* acoustics (*science*)

fuaimintiúil *adj* fundamental, substantial

fuaimíocht *f3* sound quality, acoustics

fuaimiúil *adj* acoustic **dord fuaimiúil** acoustic bass

fuaimnigh *v* sound, pronounce

fuaimniú *m* pronunciation

fuaimrian *m1* sound-track

fuaire *f4* coldness **ag dul i bhfuaire** getting colder

fual *m1* urine

fuar *adj* cold **bhí fuar agam dul ann** it was a waste of time my going there

fuaraigeanta *adj* cool-headed

fuaraigh *v* grow cold, chill **tá sé ag fuarú** it is getting cold

fuaraithe *adj* chilled

fuaraitheoir *m3* cooler

fuarán *m1* fountain, spring

fuarbholadh *m* musty, stale smell

fuarbhruite *adj* lukewarm, cold after cooking

fuarchroíoch *adj* cold-hearted, unfeeling, callous

fuarchúiseach *adj* 1. indifferent, unenthusiastic 2. imperturbable

fuarintinneach *adj* cool-headed

fuascail *v* 1. solve **fadhb a fhuascailt** to solve a problem 2. liberate, release 3. ransom, redeem

fuascailt *f2* 1. solution **an bhfuil fuascailt na faidhbe agat?** have you got the solution to the problem? 2. deliverance, release 3. ransom, redemption

fuascailteoir *m3* 1. liberator **an Fuascailteoir** the Liberator

(Daniel O'Connell) 2. ransomer, redeemer

fuath *m3* hatred, hate **thug sí fuath don Ghearmáinis ó thús** she took a dislike to German from the beginning, **tá fuath acu dó / air** they hate him, **is fuath liom an t-ábhar sin** I hate that subject

fuathaigh *v* hate

fud, ar fud all over, throughout **ar fud na tíre / an domhain** all over the country/the world

fuil *f3* blood **ag cur fola** bleeding, **bhí fuil lena béal / cluas / srón** her mouth/ear/nose was bleeding, **rith fola** haemorrhage

fuilaistriú *m* blood transfusion

fuileadán *m1* blood vessel

fuilghrúpa *m4* blood group

fuiliú *m* bleeding **fuiliú inmheánach** internal bleeding

fuílleach *m1* 1. surplus **beidh fuílleach ama againn** we'll have plenty of time 2. remainder, remains **fuílleach an airgid** the remainder of the money 3. remnants **ní bhfuaireamar ach an fuílleach** we got the leftovers

fuilteach *adj* bloody

fuin *v* 1. knead **ag fuineadh aráin** kneading bread, **crann fuinte** rolling-pin 2. knit together, mould

fuinneamh *m1* vigour, energy **tá fuinneamh sa bhuachaill sin** there's vigour/strength in that boy, **fuinneamh eithneach** nuclear energy

fuinneog *f2* window **ar leac na fuinneoige** on the window-sill, **fuinneoga dín** skylights

fuinniúil *adj* energetic, spirited

fuinseog *f2* ash **crann fuinseoige** ash tree

fuíoll *m1* 1. surplus **fuíoll na bhfuíoll** abundance of everything 2. waste **diúscairt fuíll** waste disposal

fuíollábhar *m1* waste (*material*)

fuip *f2* whip

fuipeáil *v* whip

fuireachas *m1* 1. anticipation
2. watchfulness

fuirseoir *m3* 1. fumbler, plodder
2. entertainer, comedian

fuirsigh *v* 1. fuss, rummage **ag fuirseadh anseo agus ansiúd** fussing about, rummaging here and there 2. harrow

fuisce *m4* whiskey

fuiseog *f2* lark

fuist! whisht! hush!

fulaing *v* suffer, endure, tolerate

fulaingt *f* suffering, endurance, tolerance

fulangach *adj* suffering, enduring, tolerant, patient

fungas *m1* fungus

furasta *adj* easy **níos fusa** easier, **is furasta é sin a rá** it's easy to say that

G

ga *m4* 1. ray, beam **ga gréine** ray of sun, **gathanna solais** beams of light, **gathanna ultraivialait** ultraviolet (UV) rays 2. radius **ga ciorcail** radius of circle 3. spear, dart **ga nimhe** poisoned dart 4. sting **cuirfidh mise mo gha iontu fós** I'll sting them yet, I'll make them suffer yet

gá *m4* need **níl gá leis an gcaint sin** that talk isn't needed, **is gá dom labhairt leat** I need to talk to you, **más gá** if necessary

gabh *v* 1. take, accept, catch, arrest, capture **seilbh ruda a ghabháil** to take possession of something, **gabh mo leithscéal!** sorry! excuse me! **gabhadh triúr gadaithe aréir** three thieves were arrested last night, **tá sí gafa acu** she has been captured by them 2. go **táim ag gabháil abhaile** I'm going home, **tá gach rud ag gabháil i gceart** everything is going well, **ag gabháil as faisean** going out of fashion 3. come **gabh i leith** come here, **ghabh sí aníos chugam agus dúirt ...** she came up to me and said ... 4. harness

ag gabháil capaill harnessing a horse 5. **ag gabháil fhoinn** singing

gábh *m1* peril, danger

gabha *m4* smith **gabha dubh**, **gabha óir** blacksmith, goldsmith

gabháil *f3* 1. taking, arrest, capture, seizure **gabháil seilbhe** possession taking, **tá tú faoi ghabháil** you're under arrest, **gabháil duine** arrest/capture of a person, **gabháil drugaí** seizure of drugs 2. armful **gabháil féir** armful of hay 3. **gabháil fhoinn** singing

gabhal *m1* 1. fork, junction **Gabhal Luimnigh** Limerick Junction 2. **bheith ar scaradh gabhail** to have your legs spread (apart)

gabháltas *m1* 1. capture, seizure 2. holding (*land, commercial, etc*), plot (*of land*)

gabhann *m1* pen, pound, dock (*law*) **bheith sa ghabhann** to be in the dock

gabhar *m1* goat **Baile na nGabhar** Goatstown, **an Gabhar** Capricorn

gabhdán *m1* holder, container

gabhlán *m1* martin (*bird*) **gabhlán binne** house-martin

gabhlóg *f2* fork, anything forked **gabhlóg thiúnta** tuning-fork

gach *adj* 1. each, every **i ngach áit** everywhere, **gach aon (duine), gach uile (dhuine)** every(body) 2. everything **d'ith mé gach a raibh ann** I ate everything that was there

gad *m1* 1. tough shoot used in binding, withe **tá an fear sin chomh righin le gad** that man is as tough/hardy as a withe 2. rope **tá sé faoi ghad aici** he is under her thumb, **an gad is gaire don scornach** the most urgent need

gadaí *m4* thief **goid ó ghadaí goid gan pheaca** a theft from a thief is a theft without sin

gadaíocht *f3* theft

gadhar *m1* dog

Gaeilge *f4* Irish (*language*) **Gaeilge Chonnacht, na Mumhan, Uladh** Connaught, Munster, Ulster Irish, **Gaeilge na hAlban** Scottish Gaelic

Gaeilgeoir *m3* Irish-speaker

Gaeilgeoireacht *f3* speaking Irish

Gael *m1* 1. Irish person 2. highlander (*Scotland*)

Gaelach *adj* Irish **stobhach Gaelach** Irish stew

Gaelscoil *f2* Irish (language) school

Gaeltacht *f3* Irish-speaking area **Raidió na Gaeltachta** a national radio station that serves the Gaeltacht

gág *f2* 1. fissure, crack 2. chap

gágach *adj* fissured, cracked, chapped

gaibhnigh *v* forge

gáifeach *adj* 1. dangerous, fierce 2. ostentatious, exaggerated

gaige *m4* fop, dandy

gailearaí *m4* gallery **gailearaí ealaíne** art gallery, **an Gailearaí Náisiúnta** the National Gallery

Gaillimh *f2* Galway **Co. na Gaillimhe Co. Galway**

Gaillmheach *m1* native of Galway

gailseach *f2* earwig

gaimbín *m4* 1. usury, interest **fear gaimbín** money-lender 2. morsel, bit **gaimbín tobac** a bit of tobacco

gainéad *m1* gannet (*bird*)

gaineamh *m1* sand

gaineamhchloch *f2* sandstone

gainmheach *adj* sandy

gainne[1] *m4* scale (*of fish*)

gainne[2] *f4* scantiness, scarcity

gáinneáil *f3* trafficking **gáinneáil drugaí** drug-trafficking

gáinneálaí *m4* trafficker

gair *v* 1. call, summon **sláinte a ghairm** to propose a toast, **gairim bhur sláinte** I bid you good health, **ghair siad orm** they summoned me, they called upon me 2. proclaim **gairmeadh banríon di** she was proclaimed queen

gáir[1] *f2* 1. shout, outcry **lig siad gáir mholta** they cheered 2. rumour, report

gáir[2] *v* laugh **bhíomar sna trithí ag gáire** we were in roars of laughter, **ná bí ag gáire faoin duine bocht** don't laugh at the poor thing

gairbhéal *m1* gravel **cosán gairbhéil** gravel path

gairbhseach *f2* roughage

gairdeas *m1* joy, rejoicing **ábhair gairdis is ea é** it is a cause for joy

gairdín *m4* garden **gairdín cúil, tosaigh** back, front garden

gáire *m4* laugh, laughter **bhain sé gáire asainn** he/it made us laugh, **bhuail taom / racht gáire mé** a fit of laughter came over me

gaireas *m1* apparatus, device, gadget **gaireas loisceach** incendiary device

gairid *adj* 1. short **níl ann ach achar gairid** it's only a short distance 2. near **tá tú gairid go maith dó** you are quite close to it 3. **le gairid** lately, recently

gairleog *f2* garlic **ionga gairleoige** clove of garlic

gairm *f2* 1. call, summons 2. profession, vocation **gairm bheatha** occupation

gairmeach *adj* vocative **an tuiseal gairmeach** the vocative case

gairmí *m4* professional

gairmiúil *adj* 1. professional **tiománaí gairmiúil** professional driver 2. vocational

gairmoideachas *m1* vocational education

gairmscoil *f2* vocational school

gairnis *f2* garnish

gairnisigh *v* garnish

gáirsiúil *adj* obscene, lewd

gáirsiúlacht *f3* obscenity, lewdness

gairtéar *m1* garter

gaisce *m4* 1. boasting, showing off **ag déanamh gaisce** boasting, showing off 2. valour, prowess **gníomh gaisce** act of valour

gaiscíoch *m1* champion, hero, warrior

gaisciúil *adj* valiant, heroic

gaisciúlacht *f3* valour, heroism

gaiste *m4* trap, snare

gal *f2* 1. vapour, steam **bád, inneall gaile** steam boat, steam engine 2. puff of smoke **ag ól gal** smoking, **gal soip** a short-lived thing 3. valour **gal agus gaisce** valour and prowess

gála *m4* 1. gale (*of wind*) **beidh sé ina ghála gaoithe anocht** it'll blow a gale tonight 2. gale (*of rent*) **is féidir é a íoc ina ghálaí** it can be payed in instalments

galach *adj* 1. steaming 2. valiant

galánta *adj* 1. fine, beautiful **pictiúr galánta** beautiful picture, **tá sin galánta** that's great 2. elegant, stylish **gléasann sí go galánta** she dresses elegantly 3. posh **blas galánta** posh accent

galar *m1* 1. disease, sickness **galar gnéas-tarchurtha** sexually transmitted disease, **galar tadhaill** contagious disease, **galar báis** terminal disease/sickness, **galar na bó buile** mad cow disease, BSE, **galar peiridhéadach** periodontal disease 2. affliction **galar dubhach** melancholy

galchorcán *m1* steamer (*of food etc*)

galf *m1* golf **cúrsa gailf** golf course

galfaire *m4* golfer

galfchúrsa *m4* golf course

galinneall *m1* steam engine

gall *m1* 1. foreigner 2. English person

gallán *m1* pillar-stone **gallán cloiche** stone pillar

gallchnó *m4* walnut

gallda *adj* 1. foreign 2. Anglicised

gallóglach *m1* gallowglass

gallsmacht *m3* foreign rule, English rule

galltacht *f3* **an Ghalltacht** English-speaking areas of Ireland / Scotland

gallúnach *f2* soap

gallúntraí *m4* soap opera

galrach *adj* diseased

galraigh *v* infect

galrú *m* infection

galtán *m1* steamer

galú *m* evaporation

galún *m1* gallon

gáma-gha *m4* gamma ray

gamal *m1* stupid person **nach ait an gamal é!** isn't he a strange one!

gamhain *m3* calf

gan *prep* without **gan mhoill** without delay, **caife gan chaiféin** decaffeinated coffee, **táim caillte gan é** I'm lost without him/it, **dúirt mé leo gan teacht** I told them not to come, **ná déan é gan chead** don't do it without permission, **i ngan fhios** in secret, unknown

gang *m3* gong

gangaid *f2* spite, bitterness

gangaideach *adj* spiteful, bitter

gann *adj* scarce, sparse **tá airgead gann faoi láthair** money is scarce at the moment, **ag éirí gann** getting sparse, **táimid gann i dtuairimí / ar thuairimí** we are short of ideas

gannchuid *f3* small portion, scarcity **tá siad ar an ngannchuid** they are in need

ganntanas *m1* want, scarcity, shortage **ganntanas a bheith ort** to be in want, **ganntanas airgid** shortage of money

gaofar *adj* windy

gaois *f2* wisdom, sagacity

gaol *m1* 1. relationship, kinship **tá gaol i bhfad amach agam léi** I have a distant relationship (*of blood*) with her, **bráithre gaoil** blood brothers, **tá gaol eatarthu** they are connected 2. relative, relation **mo ghaolta** my relations

gaolmhar *adj* related

gaosán *m1* nose

gaoth[1] *f2* wind **gaoth ghuairneáin** whirlwind, **bhain sé sin an ghaoth astu** that took the wind out of their sails, **fuair mé gaoth an fhocail go …** I got wind of the word that …, I heard a rumour that …, **tá gaoth orm** I'm full of wind

gaoth[2] *m1* sea-inlet, estuary

gaothaire *m4* 1. vent 2. ventilator

gaothraigh *v* fan

gaothscáth *m3* windscreen **cuimilteoirí gaothscátha** windscreen wipers

gar *adj* near **tá tú gar go maith dó** you are close enough to it *m1* 1. nearness **ní rachaidh mé i ngar don áit sin go deo arís** I'll never go near that place again 2. good turn, favour **an ndéanfá gar dom?** would you do me a favour? 3. use, benefit **níl gar i ngearán** there's no use complaining

garach *adj* obliging

garáiste *m4* garage

gar-amharc *m1* close-up (view)

garastún *m1* garrison

garbh *adj* rough, rugged, coarse **obair gharbh** rough work, **tírdhreach garbh** rugged landscape, **focal garbh** coarse/rude word, **tá an fharraige ag éirí garbh** the sea is becoming rough

garbhánach *m1* sea bream

garbhchríoch *f2* rough region **Garbhchríocha na hAlban** the Highlands of Scotland

garbhiascaireacht *f3* coarse angling

garchabhair *f5* first aid **cóireáil gharchabhrach** first aid treatment

garda *m4* guard **garda cósta** coastguard, **dualgas garda** guard duty, **garda onóra** guard of honour

gardáil *v* guard

garg *adj* rough, fierce, bitter, harsh **labhraíonn siad go garg** they speak roughly, **deoch gharg** harsh drink

gariníon *f2* granddaughter

garmhac *m1* grandson

garraí *m4* garden **Garraithe na Lus** the Botanic Gardens

garraíodóir *m3* gardener

garraíodóireacht *f3* gardening

garrán *m1* grove

garsún *m1* boy

garthimpeallacht *f3* immediate environment

gas *m1* stalk, sprig, stem **gas féir** blade of grass

gás *m1* gas **an Bord Gáis** the Gas Board

gásaigh *v* gas

gásmhéadar *m1* gas meter

gásoigheann *m1* gas oven

gasóg *f2* scout

gásphíopa *m4* gas pipe

gásphúicín *m4* gas mask

gasra *m4* group (*of people*), band (*of men, soldiers*)

gasta *adj* 1. quick **go gasta** quickly 2. clever

gastacht *f3* 1. quickness 2. cleverness

gastaireintríteas *m1* gastroenteritis

gastrach *adj* gastric

gasúr *m1* youth, boy, child **cén chaoi a bhfuil na gasúir?** how are the youngsters?

gátar *m1* want, necessity, distress **in am an ghátair** in time of need

gathach *adj* radial

gathaigh *v* radiate

gathaíocht *f3* radiation

gé *f4* goose **na Géanna Fiáine** the Wild Geese, **ní faide gob na gé ná gob an ghandail** what's good for the goose is good for the gander

geab *m4* chatter, gab **giob geab** chit-chat, **tá tú róthugtha don gheab** you're too fond of talking

geabach *adj* chatty, talkative

geábh *m3* quick trip/visit, short run

géag *f2* 1. limb, branch **géag craenach** crane jib 2. **géaga ginealaigh** family tree

géagán *m1* appendage

geáitse *m4* gesture **geáitsí** airs, **bíonn sí ag ligean geáitsí uirthi féin de shíor** she is always showing off

geáitsíocht *f3* showing off, gesturing

geal *adj* 1. white, bright, clear **craiceann geal** white skin, **soilse geala na cathrach** the bright lights of the city, **uiscí geala** clear waters, **fíon geal** white wine 2. happy, dear **ní bheidh sí rógheal linn** she won't be too happy with us, **cad é mar tá do ghrá geal?** how is your dear love? *v* 1. brighten, whiten **tá an lá ag gealadh** the day is brightening / dawning 2. make / become happy **ghealfadh sí do chroí** she / it would gladden your heart

gealacán *m1* 1. white (*of egg or eye*) 2. knee-cap

gealach *f2* moon **gealach lán** full moon, **gealacha lúpatair** the moons of Jupiter

gealbhan *m1* sparrow

gealgháireach *adj* cheerful, light-hearted

geall *m1* 1. promise, pledge, security **thug mé mo gheall** I gave my promise, I pledged my word, **tóg an carr ina gheall** take the car as security 2. wager, bet **geall a chur ar chapall** to put a bet on a horse, **cuirfidh mé geall leat** I'll bet you 3. **geall le** almost **tá an obair geall le bheith críochnaithe** the work is nearly finished 4. **mar gheall ar …, i ngeall ar …** because of, concerning *v* promise, pledge **gheall sé na hoirc is na hairc di** he promised her the world

gealladh *m* promise **tá gealladh fút mar scríbhneoir** you show promise as a writer

geallearbóir *m3* pawnbroker

geallghlacadóir *m3* bookmaker **siopa geallghlacadóra** bookmaker's shop, bookies

geallta *adj* pledged, promised, engaged (to be married)

gealltanas *m1* pledge, promise, undertaking (*legal*)

gealltóir *m3* punter, better

gealltóireacht *f3* betting

gealt *f2* crazy person, lunatic **tá sé i dteach gealt** he is in a lunatic asylum, madhouse

gealtacht *f3* insanity

geamaireacht *f3* pantomime

gean *m3* love, affection, liking **tá gean aici ort** she is fond of you

geancach *adj* snub-nosed

geanmnaíocht *f3* chastity **móid gheanmnaíochta** vow of chastity

geansaí *m4* gansey, jumper **geansaí spraoi** sweatshirt

geanúil *adj* 1. lovable 2. affectionate

géar *adj* sharp, steep, intense, sour **scian ghéar** sharp knife, **tá súil ghéar aici** she has a sharp eye, **fána ghéar** steep slope, **teas géar** intense heat, **bainne géar** sour milk *m1* sharp object

géaraigh *v* sharpen, quicken, intensify

gearán *m1* complaint **níl aon chúis ghearáin agat** you have no cause for complaint

géarchéim *f2* emergency, crisis **géarchéim éiceolaíoch** ecological crisis

géarchúis *f2* keenness, astuteness, shrewdness

géarchúiseach *adj* keen, astute, shrewd

géarleanúint *f3* persecution

Gearmáin *f2* **an Ghearmáin** Germany

Gearmáinis *f2* German (*language*)

Gearmánach *adj, m1* German

gearr *adj* short, near **cuntas gearr ar ...** short account of ..., **is gearr go mbeimid ann** it won't be long before we're there, **is giorra cabhair Dé ná an doras** God's help is always near *v* cut, shorten **ag gearradh an fhéir** cutting the grass, **gearrfaidh sé an turas** **dúinn** it will shorten the journey for us

gearradh *m* cut, cutting, slit

gearrán *m1* gelding

gearranáil *f3* shortness of breath **tá gearranáil orm** I'm short of breath

gearrcach *m1* nestling, fledgling

gearrchaile *m4* young girl

gearrchiorcad *m1, v* short-circuit

gearrfhógra *m4* short notice

gearrliosta *m4* shortlist

gearr-radharcach *adj* myopic, short-sighted

gearrscéal *m1* short story **cnuasach gearrscéalta** collection of short stories

gearrscríobh *m* shorthand

gearrshaolach *adj* short-lived, transitory

gearrthán *m1* clipping, cutting

géarshúileach *adj* observant, sharp-eyed

géarsmacht *f3* severe restraint, strict control

géarú *m* intensification, escalation **géarú ar chonspóid** escalation of dispute

géaruillinn *f2* acute angle

geata *m4* gate

geataire *m4* rush, taper **Pilib an gheataire** daddy-longlegs

geatóir *m3* gate-keeper

géibheann *m1* bondage, captivity, need, distress **campa géibhinn** internment camp, **i ngéibheann ruda** in need of something

géibheannach *m1* captive

geilignít *f2* gelignite

géill *v* submit, surrender, yield **is furasta géilleadh don chathú** it's easy to yield to temptation, **ní ghéillfeadh sé orlach** he wouldn't budge an inch, **géill slí** yield right of way

géilleadh *m* surrender, submission **géilleadh gan choinníoll** unconditional surrender

geilleagar *m1* economy **geilleagar dubh** black economy, **geilleagar an domhain** the world economy, **geilleagar saoriomaíochta / geilleagar margaidh neamhshrianta** free market economy

geilleagrach *adj* economic

géilliúil *adj* submissive, yielding

géillsine *f4* allegiance

géillsineach *m1* subject

géim[1] *f2* shout, bellow, lowing/mooing sound **géim bó** cry of cow *v* shout, bellow, low

géim[2] *m4* game (*bird or animal*)

geimheal *f2* chain, shackle, fetter **geimheal an mhill** ball and chain

geimhreadh *m1* winter **tús an gheimhridh** the start of winter

geimhriúil *adj* wintry

géimneach *f2* lowing of cattle, shouting, bellowing

géineolaí *f4* geneticist

géineolaíocht *f3* genetics

geir *f2* fat, grease

géire *f4* sharpness, shrewdness, sourness

geiréiniam *m1* geranium

geis *f2* 1. prohibition, taboo 2. spell **faoi gheasa** under a spell 3. binding restraint **chuir sí de gheasa orm dul ann** she placed a binding obligation on me to go there

geit *f2* start, sudden jump, shock **baineadh geit asainn** we got a fright

geiteach *adj* easily startled

geografach *adj* geographical

geografaí *m4* geographer

geografaíocht *f3* geography

geoifisic *f2* geophysics

geoifisiceoir *m3* geophysicist

geoiméadrach *adj* geometrical

geoiméadracht *f3* geometry

geolaí *m4* geologist

gealaíocht *f3* geology

geolbhach *m1* 1. jowl, jaw 2. gills (*of fish*)

giall[1] *m1* hostage **gabhadh triúr giall** three hostages were seized

giall[2] *m1* jaw

giar *m1* gear **ag athrú giaranna** changing gears

giarbhosca *m4* gear box

gibiris *f2* gibberish

gile *f4* whiteness, fairness, brightness **tá an ghile imithe as a súile** the brightness has gone from her eyes

gilitín *m4* guillotine

gin *f2* birth, foetus, offspring *v* give birth to, procreate, generate, produce

gineadóir *m3* generator

ginealach *m1* genealogy, pedigree

ginearál *m1* general

ginearálta *adj* general

gínéiceolaí *m4* gynaecologist

gínéiceolaíocht *f3* gynaecology

Ginéiv *f2* **an Ghinéiv** Geneva, **Coinbhinsiún na Ginéive** the Geneva Convention

ginideach *adj, m1* genitive **an ginideach / an tuiseal ginideach** the genetive case

giniúint *f3* birth, conception, reproduction, generation **baill ghiniúna** reproductive organs, **stáisiún giniúna** generating station

ginmhilleadh *m* abortion

giobal *m1* rag

gioblach *adj* ragged

Giobráltar *m4* Gibraltar

giodam *m1* liveliness, giddiness, friskiness

giodamach *adj* lively, giddy, frisky

giofóg *f2* gypsy

gíog *f2* squeak **ní raibh gíog astu** there wasn't a peep out of them *v* squeak

gíogaire *m4* bleeper

giolcach *f2* reed, cane

giolla *m4* servant, 'boy', attendant, caddie (*golf*)

giomcána *m4* gymkhana

giomnáisiam *m4* gymnasium

giorraigh *v* shorten **giorraíonn beirt bóthar** 'two (people) shorten a road'

giorraisc *adj* abrupt, curt

giorria *m4* hare

giorrú *m* abbreviation

giorrúchán *m1* abbreviation

giortach *adj* short, skimpy

giosta *m4* yeast

giota *m4* bit, piece **giota grinn** a bit of fun, **ag baint giota de** 'taking a piece off (the road)', going home

giotán *m1* bit (*computer*)

giotár *m1* guitar **ag seinm an ghiotáir** playing the guitar

gircín *m4* gherkin

girseach *f2* young girl

Giúdach *adj* Jewish *m1* Jew

Giúdachas *m1* Judaism

giúiré *m4* jury

giuirléid *f2* implement, tool **giuirléidí** personal belongings

giúis *f2* pine, fir **crann giúise** pine tree

giúistís *m4* magistrate, justice of the peace

giúmar *m1* humour **tá giúmar maith air** he's in good humour

giúróir *m3* juror

glac *v* take, accept **ghlac sí leis mar chúiteamh** she accepted it as repayment

glacadh *m* acceptance

glacadóir *m3* receiver

glacadóireacht *f3* receivership

glaine *f4* cleanness, purity

glaineacht *f3* cleanliness

glam *f2* howl, bark

glan *adj* clean, clear, net **aer glan** clean/fresh air, **brabús glan** clear/net profit *v* clean, clear **éadaí a ghlanadh** to clean clothes, **fiacha a ghlanadh** to clear debts

glanadh *m* clearance, cleaning, cleansing **glanadh eitneach** ethnic cleansing

glanbhearrtha *adj* clean-shaven

glanmhatamaitic *f2* pure mathematics

glanmheabhair *f5* **cuir de ghlanmheabhair é** learn it off by heart

glantach *adj* detergent, cleansing

glantóir *m3* cleaner

glao *m4* call, shout **glao inmheánach** internal call, **glao teileafóin** telephone call, **lig sí glao aisti** she shouted

glaoch *m1* call

glaoigh *v* call, shout

glaoire *m4* pager, bleeper

glas[1] *m1* lock **faoi ghlas** locked, **glais lámh** handcuffs

glas[2] *adj* green (*vegetation*), grey (*animals, eyes, clothes*), cold, chilly (*weather*) **chomh glas leis an bhféar** as green as the grass, **culaith ghlas** grey suit, **tá sé glas a dhóthain** it's cold enough *m1* green colour, grey colour

glasadóir *m3* locksmith

glasáil *v* lock **tá sé glasáilte isteach / amach** he's locked in/out

Glaschú *m4* Glasgow

glasra *m4* vegetable **siopa glasraí agus torthaí** fruit and vegetable shop

glé *adj* bright, glossy, vivid

gleacaí *m4* contender, gymnast, acrobat, wrestler

gleacaíocht *f3* contending, gymnastics, acrobatics, wrestling **halla gleacaíochta** gymnasium

gleann *m3* glen, valley **na Gleannta** Glenties (*Dún na nGall*)

gleanntán *m1* small glen **Gleanntán Glas Ghaoth Dobhair** 'the Green Little Glen of Gaoth Dobhair' (*song*)

gléas *m1* 1. instrument, device **gléas ceoil** musical instrument, **gléas facs** fax machine, **gléas scanála** scanner, **gléas cúléisteachta** eavesdropping/tapping device, 'bug' 2. facilities, accommodation **tá gléas oibre ann** there are working facilities there 3. **i ngléas** interlocked 4. gloss, glaze *v* 1. dress 2. equip 3. adjust

gléasadh *m* 1. attire 2. equipment

gléasta *adj* 1. dressed 2. equipped

gleic *f2* contest, struggle **dul i ngleic le ...** to engage with ...

gléigeal *adj* very bright, pure white

gléineach *adj* clear, distinct

gleo *m4* 1. strife, fight 2. noise

gleoite *adj* pretty, neat, lovely, charming **cailín gleoite í sin** she's a lovely girl

glic *adj* clever, cunning, crafty

gliceas *m1* cuteness, cleverness, ingenuity

gligín *m4* rattle (*for infant*)

glincín *m4* drop of spirits

glinn *adj* clear, sharp, distinct **cuimhne ghlinn** sharp memory

glinne *f4* distinctness, clarity

gliogar *m1* 1. rattle 2. silly talk

gliograch *adj* rattling

gliomach *m1* lobster **pota gliomaigh** lobster pot

gliondar *m1* joy

gliondrach *adj* joyful

glioscarnach *f2* sparkle, sparkling, glinting

gliú *m* glue

gliúáil *v* glue

gliúcaíocht *f3* peering

gloine *f4* glass **gloiní spectacles**, **gloiní cosanta** goggles, protective glasses, **gloine formhéadúcháin** magnifying glass, **gloine lámhshéidte** hand-blown glass

gloineadóir *m3* glazier

gloinigh *v* glaze (*glass*)

gloinithe *adj* glazed (*glass*)

gloiniú *m* glazing **gloiniú dúbailte** double glazing

glóir *f2* glory

glónraigh *v* glaze (*pottery*)

glónraithe *adj* glazed (*pottery*)

glór *m1* sound, voice

glórach *adj* noisy, loud

glórmhar *adj* glorious

glórphost *m1* voice mail

glóthach *f2* 1. jelly 2. gel

gluaireán *m1* complaining, whinging

gluais[1] *v* move

gluais[2] *f2* 1. explanatory note 2. glossary

gluaiseacht *f3* movement, motion **Gluaiseacht na hAthbheochana** the Revival Movement, **gluaiseacht ilchríochach** continental drift

gluaisrothaí *m4* motorcyclist

gluaisrothaíocht *f3* motorcycling

gluaisrothar *m1* motorbike

gluaisteach *adj* mobile **(teilea)fón gluaisteach, guthán gluaisteach** mobile (tele)phone

gluaisteán *m1* car **gluaisteán, guthán, gluaisteach cuideachta** company car

gluaisteánaí *m4* motorist

gluaisteánaíocht *f3* motoring

glúcós *m1* glucose

glúin *f2* 1. knee **ríomhaire glúine** lap top computer 2. generation 3. **bean ghlúine** midwife

glúinbhearna *f4* generation gap

glúinmhilleadh *m* kneecapping

gnách *adj* usual, common **is gnách leo a bheith anseo ar a naoi** they are usually here at nine

gnaíúil *adj* 1. kind, generous 2. beautiful

gnaoi *f4* 1. liking, affection 2. beauty

gnás *m1* practice, custom **gnás casaoide** grievance procedure

gnáth[1] *m1* common practice, custom **de ghnáth** usually

gnáth-[2] *prefix* usual, ordinary, common, routine **gnáthbhealach** usual way/route, **gnáthdhuine** ordinary person

gnáthaigh *v* practise, frequent

gnáthamh *m1* practice, routine

gnáthdhochtúir *m3* general practioner

gnáthóg *f2* haunt, lair, habitat

gné *f4* 1. kind, species 2. appearance, aspect

gnéas *m1* sex **an gnéas fireann / baineann** the male/female sex

gnéasach *adj* sexual

gnéasaíoch *adj* sexist

gnéaschiapadh *m* sexual harassment

gnéas-tarchurtha *adj* sexually transmitted **galar gnéas-tarchurtha** sexually transmitted disease

gníomh *m1* deed, action

gníomhach *adj* active, acting **uachtarán gníomhach** acting president

gníomhaí *m4* activist

gníomhaigh *v* act **gníomhú ar son duine** to act on behalf of somebody

gníomhaíocht *f3* activity

gníomhaire *m4* agent

gníomhaireacht *f3* agency **gníomhaireacht fostaíochta** employment agency

gníomhas *m1* deed (*law*)

gníomhú *m* action

gnó *m4* business, affair **tabhair aire do do ghnó féin** take care of your own business, **an tAire Gnóthaí Eachtracha** the Minister for Foreign Affairs

gnólacht *m3* business, firm

gnóthach *adj* busy

gnóthaigh *v* gain, win, earn, obtain

gnóthas *m1* business (concern), undertaking **gnóthas comhpháirteach** joint undertaking

gnúis *f3* face, countenance **nuair a imeoidh an luisne as do ghnúis** when the glow goes from your face

go[1], **go hard san aer** high in the sky, **tóg go bog é** take it easy, **go breá fine**, **go héasca** easily, **go hiontach** excellent, **go huile is go hiomlán** totally, entirely, **go tapa** quickly

go[2] *prep* to, till, until **troid go bás** to fight till death, **go dtí** to, until, **d'imigh sí go hAlbain, go Sasana, go dtí an Fhrainc, go dtí an Iodáil** she went to Scotland, England, France, Italy

go[3] *conj* (changes to **gur** in past tense of regular verbs) that **deir sé go mbíonn siad anseo ar a hocht gach lá** he says that they are here at eight every day, **b'fhéidir go dtabharfadh sé duit é** perhaps he will give it to you, **dúirt sí go bhfuair sí bronntanas uait** she said she got a present from you

go[4] *v particle* **go raibh maith agat** thank you, **go bhfága Dia agam thú!** may God keep you with me! thank you very much! **go maire tú an nuacht!** may you live to enjoy the news! congratulations!

gob *m1* 1. beak, snout 2. point (of land), projection *v* project **ag gobadh amach** sticking out

gobán[1] *m1* false teat **gobán súraic** soother

gobán[2] *m1* jack-of-all-trades **an Gobán Saor** legendary craftsman

gobharnóir *m3* governor

gogaide *m4* hunkers **bheith i do shuí ar do ghogaide** to be sitting on your hunkers

goid *f3* stealing, theft **goid ó ghadaí goid gan pheaca** a theft from a thief is a theft without sin *v* steal **ghoidfeadh sé an t-earra ón seangán** he would steal the shirt off your back

goil *v* weep, cry **ag gol** weeping, crying

goile *m4* 1. stomach **tinneas bhéal an ghoile** indigestion 2. appetite **tá a goile aici** she has a great appetite

góilín *m4* 1. small sea-inlet 2. gullet

goill *v* grieve, hurt **ghoill sé go mór uirthi** it upset her greatly

goilliúnach *adj* 1. sensitive, easily affected, touchy 2. painful

goimh *f2* venom, sting **bhí an ghoimh (dhearg) uirthi** she was in a (right) fury, **an ghoimh a bhaint as rud** to take the sting out of something

goimhiúil *adj* stinging, venomous

goin *f3* wound, hurt **gonta cogaidh** war wounds *v* wound, hurt

goineog *f2* 1. cutting/hurtful remark 2. stab, sting 3. **goineog nathrach** fang of serpent

goirín *m4* spot, pimple, lump

goiríneach *adj* pimply, spotty

goirt *adj* bitter, sour, salt(ed)

gol *m1* weeping, crying **bhris mo ghol orm** I burst into tears

gonta *adj* 1. wounded, hurt 2. terse, sharp (*in speech*)

gontacht *f3* sharpness, keenness (*in argument*), terseness

gor *m1* heat, incubation **cearc ar gor** clocking hen *v* heat, hatch, incubate

goradán *m1* incubator

goradh *m1* 1. heat(ing), warmth, warming **déan do ghoradh cois na tine** warm yourself by the fire 2. incubation, hatching

goraille *m4* gorilla

gorm *adj* 1. blue 2. **duine gorm** black person *m1* blue colour

gort *m1* field **tá an geimhreadh ar ghort an bhaile** the winter is coming

gorta *m4* famine, hunger **tá daoine ag fáil bháis den ghorta ann** people are dying from starvation there

gortach *adj* 1. stingy, mean 2. hungry

gortaigh *v* hurt, injure

gortaithe *adj* injured

gortú *m* injury, hurt

gotha *m4* gesture, appearance **gothaí a chur ort féin** to make gestures, to show off, **tá gotha na hainnise orthu** they look terrible

gothach *adj* posing

grá *m4* love **an bhfuil tú i ngrá léi?** are you in love with her? **grá a bheith agat do rud** to have love for something, **grá mo chroí** the love of my heart, **mo ghrá thú!** I love you! well done! **de ghrá an réitigh** for peace sake

grabhróg *f2* crumb

grád *m1* grade, class

grádaigh *v* grade, rate

gradam *m1* distinction, honour, award

gradamach *adj* esteemed

grádán *m1* gradient

grádú *m* grading, rating

graf *m1* graph, chart

grafach *adj* graphic

grafaic *f2* graphics

grafaíocht *f3* graphics

grág *f2* caw, squawk, croak, hoarse cry **grág a chur asat** to squawk

grágach *adj* cawing, croaking, hoarse

grágaíl *f3* squawking, cawing, cackling **ag déanamh grágaíola** cackling

grágán *m1* 1. bushy hair **féach an grágán gruaige air sin** look at the mop of hair on him 2. stump of tree 3. **chuaigh an deoch sa ghrágán aige** the drink went to his head

graí *f4* stud of horses

gráiciúil *adj* ugly

gráig *f2* hamlet, little village

gráigh *v* love

graiméar *m1* grammar (*book*)

gráin *f5* dislike, aversion, disgust **tá an ghráin (dhearg) agam air** I (really) hate him, **cuireann an chaint sin gráin orm** that talk disgusts me

grainc *f2* frown, scowl

gráiniúil *adj* hateful, horrible, ugly

gráinne *m4* grain **gráinne salainn** grain of salt

gráinneog *f2* hedgehog

gráinnín *m4* tiny particle, minute quantity **gráinnín salainn** pinch of salt

gráinseáil *v* nibble **ag gráinseáil** nibbling

graíre *m4* stud-horse

gram *m1* gram

gramadach *f2* grammar **nótaí gramadaí** grammar notes

gramadúil *adj* grammatical

gramaisc *f2* rabble, mob

grán *m1* 1. grain 2. shot **gunna gráin** shot-gun

gránach *adj, m1* cereal

gránáid *f2* grenade **gránáid bheo** live grenade, **gránáid loisceach** incendiary grenade

gránaigh *v* 1. scrape, graze 2. granulate

gránna *adj* ugly, horrid

gránnacht *f3* ugliness

gránphlúr *m1* cornflour

graosta *adj* obscene, lewd **caint ghraosta** obscene talk

graostacht *f3* obscenity, lewdness

gráscar *m1* struggle, scuffle

grásta *m4* grace

grástúil *adj* gracious

gráta *m4* grate

grátáil *f3* grating

gread *v* 1. beat, trounce **gread leat!** be off! 2. scorch, burn

greadadh *m* beating, trouncing

greadfach *f2* stinging pain

greadóg *f2* 1. slap, smack (*with hand*) 2. appetiser, apéritif

greadtóir *m3* whisk (*cooking utensil*)

Gréagach *adj, m1* Greek

greamachán *m1* 1. adhesive **greamachán gorm** blue tack 2. holdfast

greamaigh *v* 1. grip, affix, stick, fasten **greamú de rud** to stick/adhere to something 2. seize, obtain

greamaire *m4* pliers

greamaitheach *adj* adhesive, sticky

greamaitheoir *m3* sticker

greamán *m1* grip, clasp

grean[1] *v* engrave, carve

grean[2] *m1* coarse sand, gravel, grit

greanadóir *m3* engraver, carver

greanadóireacht *f3* engraving, carving

greann *m1* 1. fun, humour **tá acmhainn grinn / féith an ghrinn inti** she has a sense of humour, **fear grinn** joker, clown, **is doiligh**

greann a bhaint as it's difficult to find humour in it 2. fondness **thug sé greann di** he fell in love with her

greannmhar *adj* 1. comical, funny, humorous 2. odd

greanóir *m3* sander

greanpháipéar *m1* sandpaper **greanpháipéar a úsáid** to sandpaper

greanroiseadh *m* sandblasting

greanta *adj* 1. graven 2. shapely, well-finished

gréasaí *m4* shoemaker

gréasaíocht *f3* shoemaking

greasáil *f3* beating, trouncing

gréasán *m1* 1. web, tissue 2. network, tangle **gréasán domhanda** worldwide web, **tá sé ina ghréasán** it's in a tangle, **leathanach gréasáin** web-page, **láithreán gréasáin** website

greidimín *m4* beating

Gréig *f2* **an Ghréig** Greece

Gréigis *f2* Greek (*language*)

greille *f4* grill

greim *m3* 1. hold **bhí greim an fhir bháite agam air** I had a tight hold on him/it, **rug sí greim ar an sliotar** she caught (got a hold of) the sliotar 2. bite, bit **bainfidh an madra sin greim asat** that dog will bite you, **níor ith mé greim bia ó mhaidin** I didn't eat a bit of food since the morning 3. stitch **cuireadh seacht ngreim ina lámh** he was given seven stitches in the hand

greimlín *m4* adhesive plaster

grian[1] *f2* sun **ó éirí (na gréine) go luí na gréine** from sunrise to sunset, **amuigh faoin ngréin** out in the sun, **lus na gréine** sunflower

grian-[2] *prefix* solar **grianchóras** solar system

griancheallra *m4* solar battery

grianchloch *f2* quartz

grianchlog *m1* sundial

griandaite *adj* sun-tanned

griandath *m4* sun-tan

grianghraf *m1* photograph

grianghrafadóir *m3* photographer

grianghrafadóireacht *f3* photography

grianmhar *adj* sunny

grianspota *m4* sunspot

grianstad *m4* solstice **grianstad an gheimhridh, an tsamhraidh** winter, summer solstice

grinneall *m1* bottom (*of lake, sea, etc*)

grinnigh *v* examine closely, scrutinise

gríobhán *m1* **cathair ghríobháin** labyrinth, maze

griog *m3* irritating pain *v* 1. tantalise, tease, irritate 2. incite

gríos *m1* 1. hot ashes 2. skin-rash

gríosach *adj* glowing *f2* glowing embers, hot ashes

gríosaigh *v* incite, fire **duine a ghríosú chun troda** to incite somebody to fight, **ag gríosú na tine** stirring up the fire

gríosaitheach *adj* stirring, provocative *m1* stimulant

gríosc *v* grill **slisíní (bagúin) a ghríoscadh** to grill rashers

gríscín *m4* chop **gríscíní muiceola, uaineola** pork, lamb chops

gró *m4* crow-bar

grod *adj* sudden, short, abrupt

groí *adj* sturdy, vigorous **fear mór groí** a big, sturdy man

grósaeir *m3* grocer

grósaeireacht *f3* grocery

grua *f4* 1. cheek (*upper*) 2. brow, edge (*of road, drain, hill, etc*)

gruagach *adj* hairy *m1* 1. giant, ogre 2. warrior

gruagaire *m4* hairdresser

gruagaireacht *f3* hairdressing

gruaig *f2* hair **feabhsóir gruaige** hair-conditioner

gruaim *f2* gloom, ill-humour

gruama *adj* dejected, glum, gloomy

gruamacht *f3* gloominess

grúdaigh *v* brew

grúdaire *m4* brewer

grúdlann *f2* brewery

grúm *m1* groom (*wedding*)

grúmaeir *m3* groom (*horse*)

grúpa *m4* group

grúpárachas *m1* group insurance

guagach *adj* unsteady, frivolous, fickle

guailleáil *v* shoulder **féach ag guailleáil tríd an drong é** look at him shouldering his way through the crowd

guaim *f2* self-control/restraint **coinnigh guaim ort féin** restrain yourself

guairneán *m1* whirling movement, whirl **guairneáin** eddies, **gaoth ghuairneáin** whirlwind

guais *f2* danger, hazard **tá sí i nguais bháis** she is in danger of death, **guaiseacha** hazards

guaiseach *adj* dangerous

gual *m1* coal

gualach *m1* charcoal

gualainn *f2* shoulder **bhí an páiste in airde ar a ghuaillí aige** he had the child up on his shoulders

guí *f4* praying, prayer

guigh *v* pray

guma *m4* gum **guma coganta** chewing-gum

gúna *m4* dress, gown

gunna *m4* gun **gunna hilti / sádrála** hilti/soldering gun, **cúirtéis ghunnaí** gun salute, **gunna fadraoin** long-range gun, **púdar gunna** gunpowder

gunnadóir *m3* gunner

gunnán *m1* revolver

gur = past tense of **go** with regular verbs **dúirt mé leat gur chuir sé sa phost í** I told you he posted it, **chuala mé gur imigh sí an-luath** I heard she left very early

gura(b), gurb(h) see **is**

gus *m3* vigour, spirit

gustal *m1* wealth, resource

gustalach *adj* wealthy, resourceful

guta *m4* vowel

gúta *m4* gout

guth *m3* voice **labhair sé in ard a ghutha** he spoke at the top of his voice, **d'aon ghuth** unanimously

guthán *m1* telephone **glao(ch) gutháin** telephone call

H

haca *m4* hockey

haemaglóibin *f2* haemoglobin

haemaifiliach *adj, m1* haemophiliac

Hálg *f2* **an Háig** the Hague

haingear *m1* hangar **haingear eitleán** aeroplane hanger

hairicín *m4* hurricane

haiste *m4* hatch

halla *m4* hall **Halla na Cathrach** City Hall, **Halla na Saoirse** Liberty Hall

hanla *m4* handle

hart *m1* heart (*playing-cards*) **an t-aon hart** the ace of hearts

hata *m4* hat
héadónachas *m1* hedonism
hearóin *f2* heroin
héileacaptar *m1* helicopter
héileapad *m1* helipad
héileaport *m1* heliport
héiliam *m4* helium
heipitíteas *m1* hepatitis
heirméiteach *adj* hermetic(al)
heitrighnéasach *adj*, *m1*
  heterosexual
hidreachumhacht *f3* hydropower
hidreafóbach *adj* hydrophobic
hidreafóibe *f4* hydrophobia
hidreashaothrú *m* hydroculture
hidrigin *f2* hydrogen **hidrigin**
  leachtach liquid hydrogen
hidrileictreach *adj* hydro-electric
  cumhacht hidrileictreach hydro-
  electric power
hidrileictreachas *m1* hydro-
  electricity
hidriméadar *m1* hydrometer
hiéana *m4* hyena **hiéana breac**
  spotted hyena
hiodráitiú *m* hydration
hiodrálach *adj* hydraulic

hiodrálaic *f2* hydraulics
hiodrocsaíd *f2* hydroxide
Hiondúch *adj*, *m1* Hindu
Hiondúchas *m1* Hinduism
hiopnóiseach *adj*, *m1* hypnotic
  hiopnóisigh hypnotics
hiopnóiseachas *m1* hypnotism
hiopnóisí *m4* hypnotist
hiopnóisigh *v* hypnotise
hipitéis *f2* hypothesis
hipitéiseach *adj* hypothetical
histéire *f4* hysteria
histéireach *adj* hysterical
holagraf *m1* holograph
holagrafaíocht *f3* holography
holagram *m1* hologram
homaighnéasach *adj*, *m1*
  homosexual
hormón *m1* hormone
húda *m4* hood
húdú *m4* hoodoo
húm, ní dúirt sé húm ná hám he
  said not a word
huscaí *m4* husky (*dog*)
huth! huh! bhí sé ag cur huthanna
  agus hathanna as he was
  humming and hawing

I

i *prep* (*prep prons* = ionam, ionat, ann,
inti, ionainn, ionaibh, iontu) in
1. **in am** in time, **i mBaile Átha
Cliath** in Dublin, **i gcónaí** always, **i
nDún Droma** in Dundrum, **in
Éirinn** in Ireland, **i bhfolach**
hidden, **i nguais** in danger, **i
bponc** in a fix, **i Sasana** in
England, **i dtrioblóid** in trouble
2. **sa(n)** (= **i** + **an**), **sna** (= **i** + **na**)
sa bhaile at home, **sa charr** in the

car, **san fharraige** in the sea, **sa
Fhrainc** in France, **san Iodáil** in
Italy, **sna bailte móra** in the
towns, **sna seascaidí, seachtóidí,
hochtóidí, nóchaidí** in the sixties,
seventies, eighties, nineties
3. **níl aon dochar ann** there's no
harm in him/it, **an bhfuil suim
agat sa pheil?** are you interested
in football? **níl aon mhaith iontu**
there's no good in them, they are

no use **4. i gcaitheamh / i rith an lae** during the day, **in aisce** free, gratis

í *pron* she, it, her **cé hí sin?** who is she? **is breá an long í** it's a fine ship

iad *pron* they, them **is iad na daoine is deise ar domhan iad** they are the nicest people in the world, **gan, mar iad** without, like them

iaguar *m1* jaguar

iaidín *m4* iodine

iaigh *v* shut, close, enclose **ná hiaigh an doras** don't close the door, **d'iaigh sí sa litir é** she enclosed it in the letter

iairiglifí *pl* hieroglyphics

iall *f2* string, leash, lace, strap **iall gadhair / madra** dog leash, **coinnigh an madra ar éill** keep the dog on the leash, **iallacha bróg** shoelaces

iallach *m1* bond, tie **tá iallach orm dul ann** I have to go there, **chuir sé (d')iallach orm é a dhéanamh** he made me do it

ialtóg *f2* bat (*creature*)

iamh *m1* (en)closure **faoi iamh** enclosed

iamhchríoch *f2* enclave

ian *m1* ion

ianaigh *v* ionise

ianaisféar *m1* ionosphere

Iaráic, an *f2* Iraq

Iaráin, an *f2* Iran

iarann *m1* iron

iarchéim *f2* postgraduate degree

iarchéimí *m4* postgraduate

iardheisceart *m1* south-west

iarfhocal *m1* epilogue

iargúlta *adj* remote, backward, isolated

iargúltacht *f3* remoteness, inaccessibility

Iar-Indiach *adj*, *m1* West Indian

iarla *m4* earl **Teitheadh na nIarlaí** the Flight of the Earls

iarmhairt *f3* consequence, result **iarmhairt cheaptha teasa** greenhouse effect

iarmhar *m1* remainder, remnant, residue

iarmharach *adj* residual

iarmhéid *f2* balance **iarmhéid bainc** bank balance

Iarmhí *f4* **an Iarmhí** Westmeath, **Co. na hIarmhí** County Westmeath

iarmhír *f2* suffix

iarnáil *f3* ironing *v* iron

Iarnaois, an *f2* Iron Age

iarnóin *f3* afternoon, p.m.

iarnród *m1* railway, railroad **Iarnród Éireann** Irish Rail

iarr *v* ask, seek, request

iarracht *f3* attempt, effort **iarracht a dhéanamh** to make an effort

iarratas *m1* application **foirm iarratais** application form

iarratasóir *m3* applicant

iarrthóir *m3* candidate

iarsma *m4* **1.** relic, remnant **iarsmaí remains 2.** result, after-effect

iarsmalann *f2* museum

iarta *m4* hob

iarthar *m1* west **iarthar Bhéal Feirste** west Belfast

iartharach *adj* western

iarthuaisceart *m1* north-west **iarthuaisceart Dhún na nGall** north-west Donegal

iasacht *f3* loan **iasacht bhainc** bank loan

iasc *m1* fish **na hÉisc** the Fishes, Pisces, **ag ithe éisc** eating fish, **iasc órga** goldfish *v* fish **ag iascach** fishing

iascach *m1* fishing, fishery **baile beag iascaigh** fishing village,

Bord Iascaigh Mhara the Fishery Bord

iascaire *m4* fisherman

iascaireacht *f3* fishing

iata *adj* shut, closed, constipated **teilifís chiorcaid iata** closed circuit television

iatacht *f3* constipation

idé *f4* idea

íde *f4* abuse, plight **íde ar pháistí** child abuse, **íde na muc is na madraí a thabhairt do dhuine** to treat somebody badly, to give somebody terrible abuse, **tugadh íde béil dó** he was given a tongue-lashing, **is bocht an íde atá orthu** they are in a sorry plight

idéal *m1* ideal

idéalach *adj* ideal

idéalachas *m1* idealism

idéalaí *m4* idealist

idé-eolaíocht *f3* ideology

ídigh *v* 1. use (up), consume **tá an t-airgead ar fad ídithe** the money is all used up 2. destroy, abuse

idir *prep* (*prep prons* – **idir mé, idir tú, idir é, idir í, eadrainn, eadraibh, eatarthu**) between **idir mé féin, tú féin agus post an gheata** 'between myself and yourself', **céard atá eatarthu?** what's between them? what's the score? **cad atá idir lámha agat?** what's are you at? what are you engaged in? **idir chamáin** at issue, under discussion

idirbheart *m1* transaction, bargain

idirbheartaí *m4* negotiator

idirbheartaíocht *f3* negotiation

idirbhliain *f* transition year

idirchum *m4* intercom

idirdhealaigh *v* distinguish, differentiate, discriminate

idirdhealú *m* distinction, differentiation, discrimination

idirghabháil *f3* intervention, mediation

idirghabhálaí *m4* intermediary, mediator

idirghníomhach *adj* interactive **taispeántas idirghníomhach** interactive display

idirghníomhaire *m4* intermediary

idirghuí *f4* intercession

idirlinn *f2* intermission, pause, interlude, interval **san idirlinn** in the meantime

idirlíon *m1* internet

idirmhalartach *adj* interchangeable

idirmhalartú *m* interchange

idirmheánach *adj* intermediate, intermediary

idirnáisiúnta *adj* international **an Ciste Airgeadaíochta Idirnáisiúnta (CAI)** the International Monetary Fund (IMF)

idirstad *m4* colon (*punctuation*)

idirthréimhseach *adj* transitional

ídiú *m* consumption **ídiú peitril** consumption of petrol

ifreann *m1* Hell

ilbhliantóg *f2* perennial

ilbhliantúil *adj* perennial

ilchineálach *adj* multifarious, varied, mixed

ilchineálacht *f3* diversity **ilchineálacht timpeallachta** environmental diversity

ilchomórtas *m1* tournament

ilchreidmheach *adj* multidenominational **scoil ilchreidmheach** multidenominational school

ilchríoch *f2* continent **oileáin ilchríche** continental islands

ilchríochach *adj* continental **gluaiseacht ilchríochach** continental drift

ilchruthach *adj* many-shaped

ilchumasach *adj* versatile

ilchuspóireach *adj* general-purpose

ildánach *adj* versatile

ildathach *adj* multicoloured

ilearraí *pl* sundries

ilghnéitheach *adj* varied, diverse

ilghnéitheacht *f3* variety, diversity

ilmheánach *adj* multimedia

ilnáisiúnta *adj* multinational

ilstórach *adj* multi-storey **carrchlós ilstórach** multi-storey carpark *m1* skyscraper

ilstóras *m1* multistore

iltaobhach *adj* multilateral **trádáil iltaobhach** multilateral trade

iltaobhú *m* multilaterisation

iltoiseach *adj* multidimensional

iltréitheach *adj* of many traits/capabilities, versatile

ilúsáid *f2* multiple use

im *m* butter **blúire ime** knob of butter, **im piseanna talún** peanut butter

imbhualadh *m* collision

imdhíonach *adj* immune

imdhíonacht *f3* immunity **siondróm easpa imdhíonachta faighte (SEIF)** acquired immunodeficiency syndrome (AIDS), **víreas easpa imdhíonachta daonna (VEID)** human immunodeficiency virus (HIV)

imeacht *m3* 1. going, leaving, departure **imeacht gan teacht orthu!** let's hope they are gone for good 2. proceeding **imeachtaí** events

imeagla *f4* great fear, dread, terror

imeaglach *adj* fearful

imeall *m1* border, verge, edge

imeallach *adj* bordering upon, marginal

imeallbhord *m1* 1. shore, coastline 2. edge, verge, border

imeartas *m1* trickery, play **imeartas focal** pun, word-play

imeascadh *m* integration **imeascadh airgeadaíochta** monetary integration

imeasctha *adj* integrated

imghearradh *m* circumcision

imigéin, in **imigéin** far off, far away

imigéiniúil *adj* remote, far away

imigh *v* go **beidh sí ag imeacht amárach** she'll be going/leaving tomorrow, **tá sé imithe as a mheabhair** he has gone crazy, **d'imigh sé ann dhá uair inné** he went there twice yesterday

imir[1] *f2* tint, tinge **tá imir bhuí ann** there's a hint of yellow in it

imir[2] *v* play (*games*) **an imríonn tú cártaí?** do you play cards? **bhí Éire ag imirt leis an mBeilg** Ireland were playing against Belgium

imirce *f4* migration, emigration **imirce shéasúrach** seasonal migration

imirceach *adj* migratory **éan imirceach** migratory bird *m1* migrant, emigrant

imirceoir *m3* migrant, emigrant

imirt *f3* playing (*games*) **fiacha imeartha** playing/gambling debts

imleabhar *m1* volume, one of a series of books

imleacán *m1* navel **sreang imleacáin** umbilical cord

imlíne *f4* perimeter, circumference

imlínigh *v* outline

imlitir *f5* circular (*letter*)

imní *f4* anxiety, worry, concern **ní cúis imní é** it's not a cause for concern/worry, **ná bíodh imní ort!** don't worry!

imníoch *adj* anxious, concerned, worried

imoibreoir *m3* reactor **imoibreoir núicléach** nuclear reactor

imoibrigh *v* react

imoibríoch *adj* reactive

imoibriú *m* reaction **imoibriú slabhrúil** chain reaction

impí *f4* supplication, entreaty

impigh *v* beg, entreat

impire *m4* emperor

impireacht *f3* empire

impiriúil *adj* imperial

impiriúlachas *m1* imperialism

imprisean *m1* impression

impriseanachas *m1* impressionism

impriseanaí *m4* impressionist

impriseanaíoch *adj* impressionistic

imreas *m1* strife, contention

imreasach *adj* contentious

imreasc *m1* iris (*of eye*) **mac imrisc** pupil (*of eye*)

imreoir *m3* player

imshaol *m1* environment **limistéar imshaoil** environmental area

imshaolachas *m1* environmentalism

imshuí *m* siege

imshuigh *v* besiege

imshruthú *m* circulation (*of blood etc*)

imtharraingt *f* gravitation, gravity

imtheorannaí *m4* internee

imtheorannaigh *v* intern

imtheorannú *m* internment

imthosca *pl* circumstances **imthosca nárbh fhéidir a thuar** unforeseeable circumstances

inaistrithe *adj* transferable, translatable, movable

inathraithe *adj* changeable, variable

inbhear *m1* river mouth, estuary **an tInbhear Mór** Arklow ('the big river mouth')

inbhreathnaitheach *adj* introspective

incheartaithe *adj* adjustable **castaire incheartaithe** adjustable spanner

inchinn *f2* brain

inchurtha *adj* **inchurtha (le)** comparable (with), equal (to)

incrimint *f2* increment

incriminteach *adj* incremental

indéanta *adj* practicable, feasible

Ind-Eorpais *f2* Indo-European (*language*)

India, an *f4* India **na hIndiacha Thiar** the West Indies

Indiach *adj, m1* Indian **an tAigéan Indiach** the Indian Ocean

Indinéis, an *f2* Indonesia

indíreach *adj* indirect

indiúscartha *adj* disposable **tuáillí indiúscartha** disposable towels

infhaighte *adj* available

infhaighteacht *f3* availability

infheicthe *adj* visible

infheictheacht *f3* visibility

infheistigh *v* invest

infheistíocht *f3* investment **infheistíocht choigríche** foreign investment

infheistiú *m* investment

infhéitheach *adj* intravenous **instealladh infhéitheach** intravenous injection

infhillte *adj* foldable, collapsible **cathaoir infhillte** collapsible chair

infinideach *adj* infinite

infhuascailte *adj* redeemable

ingear *m1* perpendicular, vertical

ingearach *adj* perpendicular, vertical

ingearán *m1* helicopter

inghlactha *adj* admissible, acceptable

inghnóthaithe *adj* recoverable

inginiúil *adj* endogenous

Inid *f2* Shrovetide **Máirt na hInide** Pancake Tuesday, Shrove Tuesday

inimirce *f4* immigration

inimirceach *adj, m1* immigrant

iníoctha *adj* payable

iniompaithe *adj* reversible **seaicéad iniompaithe** reversible jacket

iniompartha *adj* portable **teilifíseán iniompartha** portable television

iníon *f2* daughter, miss **Iníon Uí Ghiollagáin** Miss Ní Ghiollagáin

iníor *m1* grazing

inis¹ *f2* island, isle **Inis Iocht** the Isle of Wight

inis² *v* tell **insíonn sé gach rud dá mháthair** he tells his mother everything, **ag insint éithigh** telling a lie

iniseal *m1* initial **d'inisealacha** your initials

inite *adj* edible

iniúch *v* inspect, scrutinise, audit

iniúchadh *m* inspection, scrutiny, audit

inlasta *adj* inflammable

inleigheasta *adj* curable

inmhalartaithe *adj* interchangeable

inmharthana *adj* able to survive, viable

inmhe, teacht in inmhe to mature, **an bhfuil siad in inmhe é a dhéanamh?** are they able to do it?

inmheánach *adj* internal **fuiliú inmheánach** internal bleeding

inmholta *adj* 1. advisable 2. commendable

inne *m4* bowel **inní** bowels

inné *adv* yesterday

inneach *m1* weft

innéacs *m4* index

innéacsaigh *v* index **leabhar a innéacsú** to index a book

inneall *m1* machine, engine

innealra *m4* machinery

innealta *adj* motorised

innealtóir *m3* engineer **innealtóir sibhialta, foirgníochta** civil, structural engineer

innealtóireacht *f3* engineering

innealtóireacht ghéiniteach genetic engineering

innilt *f2* grazing

in-nite *adj* washable

inniu *adv* today

inniúil *adj* capable, able, competent

inniúlacht *f3* competence, ability **tástáil inniúlachta** aptitude test

inoibrithe *adj* workable

inólta *adj* drinkable

inphrionta *m4* imprint (*publication*)

inscne *f4* gender

inscríbhinn *f2* inscription

inscríobh *v* inscribe

inse *m4* hinge

inséidte *adj* inflatable

inseolta *adj* navigable

insint *f2* relation, narration, version

insligh *v* insulate

inslitheoir *m3* insulator

inslin *f2* insulin

insliú *m* insulation

insocraithe *adj* adjustable **castaire insocraithe** adjustable spanner

inspéise *adj* interesting

inspioráid *f2* inspiration

insreabhadh *m* inflow **insreabhadh airgid** inflow of cash

insroichte *adj* attainable, accessible

insteall *v* inject

instealladh *m* injection **instealladh infhéitheach** intravenous injection

institiúid *f2* institute, institution **Institiúid Teicneolaíochta Bhaile Átha Cliath** Dublin Institute of Technology (DIT), **institiúid airgeadais** financial institution

intinn *f2* mind, intention, purpose **tá go leor ar a intinn aige** he has a lot on his mind, **an bhfuil sé ar intinn agat dul ann?** do you intend to go there? **táimid ar aon intinn le chéile** we are in agreement with each other

intíre *adj* home, domestic, interior, inland **olltáirgeacht intíre (OTI)** gross domestic product (GDP)

intleacht *f3* intellect, intelligence

intleachtach *adj, m1* intellectual

intuaslagtha *adj* soluble

intuigthe *adj* implied, intelligible, understandable

intuigtheacht *f3* intelligibility

íobair *v* sacrifice

íobairt *f3* sacrifice

íobartach *m1* victim (*of sacrifice*)

íoc *m3* 1. payment **gan íoc** unpaid 2. charge *v* pay **íocfaidh tú go daor as** you'll pay for it dearly, **fiacha a íoc** to pay debts, **íoc mar a thuillir (ÍMAT)** pay as you earn (PAYE)

íocaí *m4* payee

íocaíocht *f3* payment **íocaíocht roimh ré** payment in advance, **íocaíocht chúiteach** compensatory payment

íochtar *m1* lower part, bottom

íochtarach *adj* 1. lower **Sráid Uí Chonaill Íochtarach** Lower O'Connell Street 2. inferior

íochtarán *m1* inferior (*person*), subordinate

íochtaránach *adj* subordinate

íoclann *f2* dispensary

íocóir *m3* payer **íocóir cánach** taxpayer

íocshláinte *f4* healing balm

íocshláinteach *adj* remedial, refreshing

íoctha *adj* paid

Iodáil, an *f2* Italy

Iodáilis *f2* Italian (*language*)

Iodálach *adj, m1* Italian

íogair *adj* touchy, sensitive

íogaireacht *f3* touchiness, sensitivity

íógart *m1* yogurt

íol *m1* idol

iolar *m1* eagle **Sliabh an Iolair** Mount Eagle (*Dún Chaoin*)

iolra *m4* plural **an uimhir iolra** the plural

iolrach *adj* multiple **scléaróis iolrach** multiple sclerosis

iolrachas *m1* pluralism

iolraigh *v* multiply

iolrú *m* multiplication

iomad *m4* much, many **an iomad airgid, daoine** too much money, too many people

iomadúil *adj* numerous, infinite

iomadúlacht *f3* abundance

iomaí *adj* many, numerous **is iomaí duine a chonaic é** many people saw it

iomaíoch *adj* competitive

iomaíocht *f3* competition **iomaíocht shrianta** restricted competition, **saoriomaíocht** free competition, **geilleagar saoriomaíochta** free market economy

iomair *v* row **ag iomramh báid** rowing a boat

iomaire *m4* ridge

iomaitheoir *m3* competitor, contestant

iománaí *m4* hurler

iománaíocht *f3* hurling

iomann *m1* hymn

iomarbhá *m4* debate, controversy, dispute

iomarca *m4* excess, too much **bíonn an iomarca cainte aici sin** she talks too much

iomarcach *adj* excessive, redundant

iomarcaíocht *f3* redundancy **chaill sé a phost de bharr na hiomarcaíochta** he was made redundant

iomas *m1* intuition

iomasach *adj* intuitive

íomhá *f4* image

iomláine *f4* fullness, totality **sin é é ina iomláine** that's it in full

iomlaisc *v* wallow, roll about, flounder

iomlán *adj* whole, total, absolute

iompaigh *v* turn, upturn, invert

iompair *v* 1. carry **ag iompar clainne** carrying a baby, pregnant 2. transport 3. behave **ní iompraíonn sé féin go maith choíche** he never behaves himself

iompaitheach *m1* convert

iompar *m1* 1. transport, conveyance 2. conduct, behaviour **dea-iompar** good conduct/behaviour

iompú *m* turn

iomrá *m4* mention, rumour **níor chuala mé iomrá ar bith air** I never heard any mention of it

iomráiteach *adj* famous, much talked of, notorious

iomrall *m1* aberration, mistake

iomramh *m1* rowing **bád, rás iomartha** rowing boat, race

iomrascáil *f3* wrestling

iomrascálaí *m4* wrestler

iomróir *m3* oarsman, rower

íon *adj* pure

íonacht *f3* purity

ionad *m1* 1. place, location, position **ionad campála** camp(ing) site, 2. **in ionad** instead of, **in ionad m'athar** instead of my father

ionadaí *m4* substitute, representative

ionadaigh *v* 1. substitute 2. represent 3. position

ionadaíocht *f3* 1. substitution 2. representation **ionadaíocht chionmhar** proportional representation

ionadh *m1* surprise, wonder

ionanálach *m1* inhalant

ionanálaigh *v* inhale

ionanálú *m* inhalation

ionann *adj* same, identical **ionann is** almost

ionannaigh *v* identify, equate

ionannas *m1* sameness, uniformity, equality

ionas *adv* **ionas go ...** so that ...

ionathar *m1* entrails, bowels

ioncam *m1* income, revenue **cáin ioncaim** income tax, **ioncam measta** estimated income, **na Coimisinéirí Ioncaim** Revenue Commissioners

ionchas *m1* expectation, prospect

ionchollú *m* incarnation

ionchorpraigh *v* incorporate

ionchúiseamh *m1* prosecution **an Stiúrthóir Ionchúiseamh Poiblí** the Director of Public Prosecutions (DPP)

ionchúisigh *v* prosecute

ionchúisitheoir *m3* prosecutor

ionchur *m1* input

ionduchtóir *m3* inductor

iondúil *adj* usual **go hiondúil** usually

ionga *f5* 1. nail (*of finger, toe, thumb*), claw **ionga i bhfeoil** ingrowing toenail, **ingne iolair** eagle's claws 2. **ionga gairleoige** clove of garlic

ionlach *m1* lotion **ionlach iarbhearrtha** after-shave lotion

ionracas *m1* integrity, honesty

ionradh *m1* invasion

ionraic *adj* upright, honest, just

ionramháil *f3* attending, managing, handling, manipulation *v* manage, handle, manipulate

ionróir *m3* invader

ionsaí *m4* assault, attack

ionsaigh *v* attack

ionsaitheach *adj* aggressive, attacking, charging

ionsaitheoir *m3* aggressor, attacker

ionsar *prep* (*prep prons* = **ionsorm, ionsort, ionsair, ionsuirthi,**

ionsorainn, ionsoraibh, ionsorthu) to, towards

ionstraim *f2* instrument **ionstraim reachtúil** statutory instrument, **an Ionstraim Eorpach Aonair** the Single European Act

ionsú *m* absorption

ionsúigh *v* absorb

ionsúiteach *adj* absorbent

ionsúiteacht *f3* absorbency

iontach *adj* 1. wonderful, brilliant, unusual, surprising **an rud is annamh is iontach** what's rare is wonderful 2. very **iontach maith** very good

iontaise *f4* fossil

iontaisigh *v* fossilise

iontaisithe *adj* fossilised

iontaobhaí *m4* trustee

iontaobhas *m1* trust (*legal, commercial*)

iontaofa *adj* trustworthy

iontaoibh *f2* trust, confidence **an bhfuil iontaoibh agat astu?** do you trust them? do you have confidence in them?

iontas *m1* wonder, surprise **iontas na n-iontas** wonder of wonders, **chuir siad iontas orm** they surprised me

iontráil *f3* entry **iontráil ghiorraithe** abbreviated entry *v* enter

iontrálaí *m4* entrant

ionúin *adj* dear, beloved

iora *m4* squirrel **iora rua** red squirrel, **iora talún** chipmunk

Iordáin, an *f2* Jordan

íoróin *f2* irony

íorónta *adj* ironic

Iorua, an *f4* Norway

Ioruach *adj, m1* Norwegian

Ioruais *f2* Norwegian (*language*)

íos- *prefix* minimum, least **íosphá** minimum wage, **íosghníomhú** least action

Íosa *m4* Jesus

Íosánach *adj, m1* Jesuit

íoslach *m1* basement

Íoslainn, an *f2* Iceland

Ioslamach *adj* Islamic *m1* Islamist

Ioslamachas *m1* Islam

íosmhéid *f2* minimum amount

Iosrael *m4* Israel

Iosraelach *adj, m1* Israeli

íostachas *m1* minimalism

iostán *m1* cottage

íostas *m1* lodging, accommodation

iothlainn *f2* haggard

iris *f2* journal, gazette, magazine **iris choimriúcháin** abstract (*of magazine*)

iriseoir *m3* journalist

iriseoireacht *f3* journalism

irisleabhar *m1* magazine, journal

is[1] *copula* **is buachaill, cailín, bean, fear mé** I am a boy, girl, woman, man, **ní amadán é** he's not a fool, **an ainmhí é? is ea / ní hea** is it an animal? yes/no, **an maith leat mo charr? is maith / ní maith** do you like my car? yes/no, **ar mhaith leat pionta? ba mhaith / níor mhaith** would you like a pint? yes/no, **ba mhaith liom labhairt leat** I would like to talk to you, **an leatsa é? is liom / ní liom** do you own it? yes/no, **is fearr, is mó** best, largest, **is fearr liom tae ná caife** I prefer tea to coffee, **dúirt sé gurbh fhearr leis dul abhaile** he said he'd prefer to go home, **nach maith, nár mhaith léi dul ann?** doesn't, wouldn't she like to go there? **níorbh fhíor an ráiteas sin** that statement wasn't true, **gurab amhlaidh duit** the same to you, **measaim gurb í an fhírinne í** I think that it is the truth, **is cosúil nárbh é an fear céanna é** it seems that it wasn't the same man

is² *conj* and **dubh is bán** black and white

ise *emphatic pron* she, her **ise a bhí ann** it was she who was there, **seachas ise** apart from her

íseal *adj* low **rud a rá os íseal** to say something in a low voice, quietly

Ísiltír, an *f2* the Netherlands

ísligh *v* lower **ísligh an teas** lower the heat

ísliú *m* lowering, decline

ispín *m4* sausage **ispíní agus sceallóga prátaí** sausages and chips

isteach *adj, adv* in, into **dul, teacht, titim isteach** go, come, fall into, **isteach libh** in you (*pl*) go

istigh *adj, adv* in, inside, within **an raibh tú istigh ann?** were you in there? **fanann sé istigh i gcónaí** he always stays inside, **taobh istigh** indoors, within, **tá an t-am istigh** time up!

istoíche *adv* at/by night **istoíche amárach** tomorrow night

ith *v* (see *irregular verbs*) eat **ag ithe dinnéir** eating dinner

itheachán *m1* eating **teach itheacháin** restaurant, **seomra itheacháin** dining-room

ithir *f5* soil, earth **ithir bhocht, shaibhir** infertile, fertile soil

iubhaile *f4* jubilee

lúil *f4* July **mí lúil** July

iúl *m1* knowledge, attention **cuirfear in iúl duit é** you'll be informed of it, **cuir in iúl dom é** let me know about it

iúr *m1* yew **an tlúr** Newry, **Tír an lúir** Terenure

J

jab *m4* job

jabanailís *f2* job analysis

jableathán *m1* job sheet

jabshábháilteacht *f3* job security

jabthuairisc *f2* job description

jacaí *m4* jockey

jin *m4* gin **jín agus athbhríoch** gin and tonic

jíp *m4* jeep

jónaí an scrogaill *n* crane (*bird*)

júdó *m4* judo

juncaed *m1* junket

K

karaté *m4* karate

L

lá *m* day **i gcaitheamh / i rith an lae** during the day, **laethaenta m'óige, a n-óige** the days of my, their youth, **ceithre lá fhada** four long days, **an lá arna mhárach / an lá ina dhiaidh sin** the following day, **Lá Fhéile Vailintín** Saint Valentine's Day, **Lá Nollag** Christmas Day, **Lá Caille** New Year's Day, **lá an Luain / lá an bhrátha** doomsday, the day of Judgement

lábán *m1* 1. mire, mud, muck 2. milt

lábánach *adj* miry, muddy

labhair *v* speak, talk **labhraíonn sé an-mhall** he speaks very slowly, **bíonn an bheirt sin de shíor ag labhairt le chéile** those two are always talking to each other, **labhróidh mé leis amárach** I'll speak to him tomorrow, **níor labhair sí focal** she didn't utter a word

labhairt *f3* speaking, speech **ní bhfuair mé deis labhartha leis fós** I didn't get a chance to speak to him yet

labhandar *m1* lavender

labhras *m1* laurel **na Labhrais** the Laurels (*street name*)

lacáiste *m4* rebate, discount **lacáiste cánach** tax rebate, **cheannaigh mé an teilifíseán ar lacáiste** I bought the television at a discount

lách *adj* friendly, pleasant, affable **duine lách** friendly, pleasant person

lacha *f5* duck **ag ithe lachan** eating duck, **lachain fhiáine** wild ducks

ladar *m1* ladle

ladhar *f2* 1. space between fingers or toes 2. toe **an ladhar mhór** the big toe 3. fork **feicfidh tú ladhar sa bhóthar** you'll see a fork in the road

ladhróg *f2* 1. switch (*on rail track*) 2. forked stick

laethúil *adj* daily **tarlú laethúil** everyday occurrence

lag *adj* weak *m1* 1. weak person / animal 2. lowness **lag trá** low tide

lagaigh *v* weaken

lagar *m1* weakness

lágar *m1* lager

lagbhríoch *adj* weak

lagbhrú *m4* low pressure

laghad *m4* smallness, fewness **níl tuairim dá laghad agam** I haven't the faintest idea, **ar a laghad** at least

laghdaigh *v* diminish, decrease, lessen, reduce **laghdaigh méid an leathanaigh** decrease the size of the page, **an teas a laghdú** to reduce the heat

laghdú *m* reduction, decrease **laghdú daonra** population decrease

lagmhisneach *m1* low spirits **chuirfeadh sé lagmhisneach ort** it would dishearten you

lagú *m* weakening

láí *f4* spade, loy

láib *f2* mud, mire

lalbhe *f4* lava **sreabh laibhe** lava flow

laicear *m1* lacquer

Laidin, an *f2* Latin

Laidineach *adj, m1* Latin

láidir *adj* strong **is láidre Tomás ná Stiofán** Tomás is stronger than Stiofán, **an lámh láidir** the strong hand, **bhuaigh siad leis an lámh láidir** they won by force

láidreacht *f3* strength **tá an fhoireann sin ag dul i láidreacht** that team is getting stronger

láidrigh *v* strengthen

laige *f4* weakness

Laighin *m5* Leinster **Cúige Laighean** (the province of) Leinster

Laighneach *adj* Leinster *m1* native of Leinster

láimhdeachas *m1* handling, turnover **láimhdeachas gnó** handling of a business, **láimhdeachas stoic** stock turnover

láimhseáil *f3* handling, management *v* handle, manage **ag láimhseáil airgid** managing money

láimhsigh *v* handle, manipulate **gunna a láimhsiú** to handle a gun

laincis *f2* fetter, spancel

lainseáil *f3* launch **lainseáil leabhair** book launch *v* launch

laíon *m1* pulp, pith

láir *f5* mare **láracha breátha** fine mares, **Eireaball na Lárach Báine** the Milky Way

laiste *m4* latch

laistiar *adj, adv, prep* on the west side, behind **laistiar den Daingean atá sé** it's west of Dingle

laistigh *adj, adv, prep* inside, within **beidh mé ann laistigh d'uair an chloig** I'll be there within an hour

laistíos *adj, adv, prep* below

láithreach *adj* immediate, present **láithreach bonn** instantly, immediately

láithreán *m1* site **láithreán campála** campsite, **láithreán seandálaíochta, tochailte** archaeological, excavation site, **láithreán gréasáin** website

lamairne *m4* jetty

lámh *f2* hand, arm **mo dhá lámh** my hands, **lán na lámh** armful, **lámh chlé, dheas** left, right hand, **ar thaobh na láimhe clé, deise** on the left, right hand side, **lámh a chur i do bhás féin** to commit

suicide, **cad tá idir lámha agat?** what are you at? what are you engaged in? **ag obair as lámh a chéile** working together / in partnership, **an lámh láidir** the strong hand, **fuair siad an lámh in uachtar orainn** they got the upper hand of us, they defeated us, **láimh le** beside, close by, **in aice láimhe** close by, near at hand

lámhacán *m1* crawling

lámhach *m1* shooting **lámhach gunnaí** gunfire, **lón lámhaigh** ammunition *v* shoot **lámhachadh sa chos é** he was shot in the leg

lámhachóir *m3* shooter **lámhachóir fadraoin** long-range shooter, sniper

lamháil *f3* allowance *v* allow, permit

lámhainn *f2* glove

lámhchleasaí *m4* juggler

lámhchleasaíocht *f3* juggling

lámhchroitheadh *m* handshake

lámhdhaite *adj* hand-painted

lámhdhéanta *adj* handmade

lámhdhéantúsán *m1* artefact

lámhleabhar *m1* handbook, manual

lámh-mhaisiú *m* manicure, manicuring

lamhnán *m1* bladder

lámhoiliúint *f3* manual training

lámhrialú *m* manual control

lámhscríbhinn *f2* manuscript

lámhscríbhneoireacht *f3* handwriting

lámhscríofa *adj* handwritten

lampa *m4* lamp

lán *adj* full, complete **lán go barr / béal** full up, full to the brim *m1* full **lán glaice** handful, **lán tí de ghasúir** full house of children, **lán mara** high tide, **a lán bád** a lot of boats, **a lán páistí, daoine** a lot of children, people

lána *m4* lane

lánaimseartha *adj* full-time **post lánaimseartha** full-time position / job

lánfhostaíocht *f3* full employment

lann *f2* **1.** blade **lann rásúir** razor blade, **lann scine** blade of knife **2.** lamina **3.** scale (*of fish*)

lannach *adj* laminated **cárta, plaisteach lannach** laminated card, plastic

lannaigh *v* laminate, scale

lánroghnach *adj* discretionary **cistí lánroghnacha** discretionary funds

lansaigh *v* lance

lánseol, faoi lánseol in full swing, under full sail

lánsiúl, faoi lánsiúl at full speed

lánstad *m4* full stop

lánstaonaire *m4* teetotaller

lánsuim *f2* sum total

lántoilteanach *adj* fully willing, fully consenting

lántosaí *m4* full-forward (*sport*)

lánúin *f2* engaged or married couple **lánúin nuaphósta** newly-married couple

lao *m4* young calf

laoch *m1* hero, champion, warrior

laochas *m1* heroism, valour

laochra *m4* band of warriors

laochta *adj* heroic

laofa *adj* biased

laofacht *f3* bias **laofacht aoise** age discrimination, ageism

laofheoil *f3* veal

laoi *f4* poem, lay **laoithe na Féinne** the poems of the Fianna

Laoi, an *f4* the Lee (*river*)

Laois, an *f2* Laois **Co. Laoise** County Laois, **príosún Phort Laoise** Port Laoise prison

lapa *m4* paw

Laplainn, an *f2* Lapland

lár *m1* **1.** middle, centre **an mhéar láir** the middle finger, **i lár na**
hoíche in the middle of the night, **lár na cathrach** city centre, **lár na n-ochtóidí** the mid eighties **2.** ground, floor **thit sé ar lár** he fell to the ground **3. ar lár** omitted, missing **tá píosa ar lár** there's a piece missing, **ná fág ar lár é** don't omit it, **lúb ar lár** defect

laraing *f2* larynx

laraingíteas *m1* laryngitis

lárionad *m1* centre **lárionad léirithe, oidhreachta, siopadóireachta, spóirt** interpretative, heritage, shopping, sports centre, **an Lárionad Seirbhísí Airgid** the Financial Services Centre

lárlíne *f4* centre line, diameter

lárnach *adj* central **téamh lárnach** central heating

lárthosaí *m4* centre-forward (*sport*)

lárúchán *m1* centralisation

las *v* **1.** light **las an solas** put on the light **2.** blush **las a haghaidh** her face blushed **3.** swell **tá a glúine lasta amach ar fad** her knees are swollen badly

lása *m4* lace

lasadh *m* **1.** lighting **níl sé ar lasadh** it's not alight **2.** blush **lasadh náire** blush of shame

lasair *f5* flame, flash, blaze **lasair rabhaidh** (signal) flare, **bhí an teach ar bharr lasrach** the house was ablaze, **teilgeoir lasrach** flamethrower

lasairéan *m1* flamingo

lasán *m1* **1.** match **bosca lasán** box of matches **2.** flash, flame

lasánta *adj* fiery, flaming

lasc *f2* **1.** lash **fuair sí lasc fuipe ón timpiste** she got whiplash from the accident **2.** whip, switch **lasc adhainte** ignition switch *v* whip, flog, kick, lash

lascaine *f4* discount **thug sé ar lascaine dom é** he gave it to me at a discount

lasmuigh *adj, adv, prep* outside, outdoors **lasmuigh de sin** apart from that

lasta *m4* cargo, freight load

lastas *m1* shipment

lastoir *adj, adv, prep* on the east side **tá Órán Mór lastoir de Ghaillimh** Oranmore is east of Galway

lastóir *m3* shipper, freighter (*person*)

lastuaidh *adj, adv, prep* on the north side **tá Sráid Uí Chonaill lastuaidh den Life** O'Connell Street is on the north side of the Liffey

lastuas *adj, adv, prep* above, overhead **lastuas den doras** above the door

lathach *f2* mud, mire, slime **nuachtáin lathaí** gutter press

láthair *f5* 1. site, position, place, location **láthair tí** site of a house, **láthair gheografach** geographical location 2. presence **as láthair** absent, **i láthair** present, **i láthair na huaire** at the moment, **faoi láthair** at present

le *prep* (*prep prons* = **liom, leat, leis, léi, linn, libh, leo**) 1. with, for, to, against, by, as **tá sí ag siúl amach le Ciarán** she is going out with Ciarán, **ní fhaca mé le dhá bhliain í** I haven't seen her for two years, **ag caint / labhairt le duine** talking to somebody, **ag imirt le Corcaigh** playing against Cork, **taobh le taobh** side by side, **dán le Liam Ó Muirthile** a poem by Liam Ó Muirthile, **chomh milis le mil** as sweet as honey 2. **le linn** during, **le linn an tsamhraidh** during the summer 3. **cé leis an madra sin?** who owns that dog? **is liomsa é, ní liomsa é** it's mine, it's not mine

lé *f4* partiality, leaning **tá lé aige léi** he favours her/it

leá *m4* melting

leaba *f* bed **leaba luascáin** hammock, **bun na leapa** the bottom/foot of the bed, **leaba dhúbailte** double bed, **leapacha buinc** bunk beds

leabaigh *v* bed, set, embed

leabhair *adj* long, slender

leabhal *m1* libel

leabhar *m1* book **leabhar móréilimh** best-seller

leabharchoimeád *m* bookkeeping

leabharchoimeádaí *m4* bookkeeper

leabharlann *f2* library **leabharlann scannán** film library

leabharlannaí *m4* librarian

leabharmharc *m1* bookmark

leabhragán *m1* bookcase

leabhrán *m1* booklet

leac *f2* 1. flagstone, slab **ar leac na fuinneoige** on the window-sill 2. **leac oighir** sheet of ice

leacht[1] *m3* monument **leacht cuimhneacháin** memorial

leacht[2] *m3* liquid

léacht *f3* lecture

leachtach *adj* liquid **hidrigin leachtach** liquid hydrogen

leachtacht *f3* liquidity

leachtaigh *v* 1. liquefy, liquidise 2. liquidate

leachtaitheoir *m3* 1. liquifier, liquidizer 2. liquidator

léachtóir *m3* lecturer **léachtóir le stair** history lecturer

léachtóireacht *f3* lecturing, lectureship

leacú *m* slabbing

leadair *v* beat, thrash, hack

leadhb *f2* 1. clout, rag 2. strip **leadhb pháipéir** strip of paper

leadóg *f2* 1. slap **thug mé leadóg sa leiceann dó** I gave him a slap in the face 2. tennis **ag imirt leadóige** playing tennis, **leadóg bhoird** table tennis

leadrán *m1* slowness

leadránach *adj* tedious, slow

leadránacht *f3* tedium

leadránaí *m4* 1. loiterer, lingerer 2. bore

leafaos *m1* paste

leag *v* 1. knock down, fell **leagadh an foirgneamh** the building was knocked down, **crann a leagan to** fell a tree 2. set, laid **leag an bord** set the table, **leag sí ar an talamh é** she lay it on the ground

leagan *m1* 1. felling, knocking down 2. setting, laying 3. lowering 4. version **leagan cainte** turn of speech, expression 5. **leagan amach** lay-out, format, **leagan amach comhaid** file lay-out 6. **leagan as** lay-off (*employment*)

leaid *m4* lad **amuigh leis na leaideanna** out with the lads

leáigh *v* melt, thaw, liquefy

leaisteach *adj* elastic

leaisteachas *m1* elasticity

leaistic *f2* elastic

leamh *adj* 1. tasteless, insipid 2. uninteresting, dull

léamh *m1* reading **sin é mo léamhsa ar an scéal** that's my reading of the story, **léamh léarscáileanna** map-reading, **léamh profaí** proofreading

leamhan *m1* moth

leamhán *m1* elm (*tree*)

leamhas *m1* 1. tastelessness 2. sarcasm

leamhgháire *m4* sarcastic smile

leamhsháinn *f2* stalemate (*chess*)

leamhthuirse *f4* boredom

lean *v* follow, continue **mar a leanas** as follows, **ag leanúint den chomhrá** continuing the conversation

léan *m1* grief, affliction, anguish **léan ort!** bad cess to you! **mo léan!** alas!

léana *m4* meadow, lawn **fiabhras léana** hay-fever

leanbaí *adj* childlish, child-like

leanbaíocht *f3* childishness, childhood

leanbh *m1* child **aonad cúraim leanaí** child-care unit, **cé mhéad leanbh atá agaibh?** how many children have you? **ceathrar leanaí** four children

léanmhar *adj* sorrowful, grievous

leann *m3* ale, beer **leann úll** cider, **leann dubh** stout, **buidéal leanna dhuibh** a bottle of stout

léann *m1* learning, education **mac léinn** student, **ag déanamh léinn** studying, learning, **Dámh an Léinn Cheiltigh** the Faculty of Celtic Studies

leannán *m1* lover

léannta *adj* learned

leantóir *m3* 1. trailer 2. follower

leanúint *f3* following, continuation, pursuit **ar leanúint (ar lean)** continued (contd)

leanúnach *adj* 1. continuous 2. persistent

leanúnachas *m1* 1. continuity 2. faithfulness

leanúnaí *m4* follower

leáphointe *m4* melting-point

lear[1] *m1* sea, ocean **thar lear** overseas

lear[2] *m4* great amount, a lot **lear mór daoine** a lot of people

léaráid *f2* diagram, sketch, illustration **léarscáil staitistice** statistical diagram

léaráideach *adj* diagrammatic

léargas *m1* 1. insight, sight **thug sé an-léargas dom ar ...** he gave me a great insight into ..., **ó léargas** out of sight 2. visibility

léaró *m4* gleam, glimmer **léaró dóchais** a glimmer of hope

learóg *f2* larch (*tree*)

léarscáil *f2* map **léarscáil bhóithre** road map, **léarscáil an domhain** world map

leas[1] *m3* 1. welfare, benefit, use **leas sóisialta** social welfare, **sochair leasa shóisialaigh** social welfare benefits, **thug sí comhairle mo leasa dom** she gave me good advice, **níor bhain mé aon leas as** I never got any use/benefit from it 2. fertiliser, manure

leas-[2] *prefix* vice-, deputy, step- **leasphríomhoide gníomhach** acting vice-principal, **leasuachtarán** vice-president, **leaschlann** step-children

léas[1] *m3* lease **léas foirngníochta** building lease

léas[2] *m1* ray of light, radiance

leasachán *m1* fertiliser, manure

leasaigh *v* 1. amend, improve, reform **acht a leasú** to amend an act 2. preserve, cure, season **trátaí leasaithe** preserved tomatoes, **ag leasú bia** seasoning food 3. fertilise, manure (*land*)

léasaigh *v* lease

leasainm *m4* nickname

leasaithe *adj* 1. improved, amended 2. preserved, cured, seasoned 3. fertilised, manured

leasaitheach *adj* 1. improving, amending, reforming 2. preservative

léasar *m1* laser

léasarphrintéir *m3* laserprinter

leasathair *m5* stepfather

leasc *adj* lazy, reluctant, slow

leasdeartháir *m5* stepbrother

leasdeirfiúr *f5* stepsister

leasiníon *f2* stepdaughter

léaslíne *f4* horizon

leasmhac *m1* stepson

leasmháthair *f5* stepmother

léaspairt *f2* clever anecdote, witticism

leasú *m* 1. improvement, amendment, reform 2. fertiliser, manure

leasúchán *m1* amendment

leataobh *m1* 1. one side **ar leataobh na sráide** on one side of the street 2. **i leataobh** aside, **rud a chur i leataobh** to set something aside

leataobhach *adj* lopsided, one-sided, biased, partial

leath[1] *f2* 1. half **bhris sé ina dhá leath é** he broke it in half, **leath ama** half time, **d'imir sé sa dara leath (den chluiche)** he played in the second half (of the game), **níl ansin ach leath an scéil** that's only half the story, **(míle) go leith** (a mile) and a half 2. **ar / faoi leith** special, distinct, separate 3. **i leith** in the direction of, **gabh / tar i leith (chugam)** come here (to me), **ó shin i leith** since then 4. **rud a chur i leith duine** to accuse somebody of something

leath[2] *v* 1. spread 2. open wide 3. halve

leath-[3] *prefix* 1. half-, semi-, one of a pair **leathlá** half-day, **comhlacht leathstáit** semi-state body, **ar leathghlúin** on one knee 2. tilted, lopsided **ar leathcheann** tilted, slanted 3. partial

leathadh *m* spread, diffusion **leathadh aoiligh** manuring, **ar leathadh** wide open

leathan *adj* broad, wide, extensive **dearcadh níos leithne** a broader outlook

leathán *m1* sheet, sheeting **leathán aispeiste** asbestos sheeting

leathanach *m1* page, sheet **leathanach gréasáin** web-page, **leathanach baile** homepage (*internet*)

leathanaigeanta *adj* broad-minded

leathar *m1* leather

leathbhróg *f2* one shoe, one boot

leathchéad *m1* fifty

leathchiorcal *m1* semicircle

leathchluas *f2* one ear **tá an madra ar leathchluas** the dog has only one ear

leathchúlaí *m4* half-back (*sport*)

leathchúpla *m4* twin

leathdhosaen *m4* half dozen

leathdhuine *m4* half-wit

leathéan *m1* mate (*bird*)

leathfhocal *m1* hint **tuigeann fear léinn leathfhocal** an intelligent man understands a hint

leathghualainn *f2* one shoulder

leathlámh *f2* one arm/hand **tá sí ar leathláimh** she has only one arm/hand

leathlámhach *adj* 1. one-armed/one-handed 2. short of help

leathmharbh *adj* exhausted, half-dead

leathmheasartha *adj* poorish, indifferent

leathmhíle *m4* 1. half-mile **leathmhíle síos an bóthar** half a mile down the road 2. five hundred **leathmhíle bád** five hundred boats

leathnaigh *v* spread out, widen

leathnú *m* expansion, widening

leathóg *f2* plaice, flatfish

leathphionta *m4* half-pint **leathphionta beorach** half a pint of beer

leathphingin *f2* halfpenny **Droichead na Leathphingine** the Ha'penny Bridge

leathrann *m1* couplet

leathscoite *adj* semi-detached **teach leathscoite** semi-detached house

leathsféar *m1* hemisphere **an leathsféar thuaidh, theas** the northern, southern hemisphere

leathshúil *f2* one eye **tá sé ar leathshúil** he has only one eye

leathstad *m4* semi-colon

leath-thosaí *m4* half-forward (*sport*)

leath-thuairim *f2* vague idea

leathuair *f2* half-hour **tá sé leathuair tar éis a trí** it's half past three

leatrom *m1* affliction, oppression, injustice, inequality

leatromach *adj* oppressive, unjust, unfair

leibhéal *m1* level **leibhéal gníomhaíochta** level of activity

léibheann *m1* level space, terrace, platform, deck

leibide *f4* awkward, slovenly person, fool

leibideach *adj* slovenly, foolish

leiceann *m1* cheek

leicneach *f2* mumps

leictreach *adj* electrical

leictreachas *m1* electricity **Bord Soláthair an Leictreachais (BSL)** Electricity Supply Board (ESB)

leictreoir *m3* electrician

leictreon *m1* electron

leictreonach *adj* electronic

leictreonaic *f2* electronics **leictreonaic dhigiteach** digital electronics

leictrigh *v* electrify

leictriú *m* electrification

leid *f2* hint, clue, prompt

leifteanant *m1* lieutenant

léig *f2* decay, neglect **chuaigh sé i léig** it decayed/declined, it became neglected

léigear *m1* siege **Léigear Dhoire** the Siege of Derry

léigh *v* read **ag léamh leabhair** reading a book

leigheas *m1* remedy, cure, medicine **níl leigheas air** it can't be helped, there's no cure for it *v* cure, heal, remedy

léigiún *m1* legion **Léigiún Coigríochach na Fraince** the French Foreign Legion

léigiúnach *adj, m1* legionary

léim *f2* jump, bound, leap **Léim an Bhradáin** Leixlip ('the Leap of the Salmon') *v* jump, bound, leap

léimneach *adj* jumping, leaping, flickering *f2* jumping, leaping

léine *f4* shirt **léine oíche** nightdress

léir *adj* 1. entire, complete **go léir** entirely 2. clear, distinct **is léir (dom) go ...** it is clear (to me) that ...

léirbhreithniú *m* overview

léirigh *v* 1. explain, make clear, illustrate 2. produce (*a play, programme, etc*)

léiritheoir *m3* producer

léiriú *m* 1. clarification, illustration 2. production

léirléamh *m1* interpretation (*of map etc*)

léirmheas *m3* criticism, review

léirmheastóir *m3* critic

léirmheastóireacht *f3* criticism

léirmhíniú *m* interpretation **léirmhíniú sonraí** interpretation of data

léirscrios *m* devastation, destruction *v* devastate, destroy

léirsigh *v* demonstrate (*political*)

léirsitheoir *m3* demonstrator (*political*)

léirsiú *m* demonstration (*political*)

léirthuiscint *f* appreciation (*in understanding*)

leis¹ *f2* thigh **cnámh na leise** thighbone, femur

leis² *adv* also, either, too **bhí Cuán leis ann** Cuán was also there, **agus mise leis** and me too

leisce *f4* laziness, reluctance **giolla na leisce** idle person, lazybones, **bhí leisce orm labhairt leo** I was reluctant to talk to them

leisceoir *m3* lazy person

leisciúil *adj* lazy

leispiach *adj, m1* lesbian **an Cumann Homaighnéasach agus Leispiach** the Gay and Lesbian Society

leite *f* porridge **babhla leitean** bowl of porridge

leithcheal *m3* partiality, discrimination, exclusion

leithead *m1* width, breadth, expanse **dhá mhéadar ar leithead** two metres in width, **leithead talún** expanse of land

leitheadach *adj* 1. wide, broad, extensive 2. conceited

leithéid *f2* like, equal **a leithéid de raiméis** such nonsense, **ní bheidh ár leithéidí arís ann!** the likes of us will not be here again!

léitheoir *m3* reader

léitheoireacht *f3* reading **seomra léitheoireachta** reading-room

leithinis *f2* peninsula **Leithinis an Daingin** the Dingle Peninsula

leithleach *adj* 1. apart, peculiar, special, distinct 2. selfish

leithleachas *m1* 1. peculiarity 2. selfishness

leithlis *f2* isolation **barda leithlise** isolation ward (*in hospital*)

leithliseach *adj* isolated

leithlisigh *v* isolate

leithne *f4* breadth, broadness

leithreas *m1* toilet **leithreas na bhfear, na mban** the mens', womens' toilet

leithscéal *m1* excuse, apology **gabh mo leithscéal!** excuse me! sorry!

leithscéalach *adj* apologetic

leitís *f2* lettuce **ceapaire bagúin, leitíse agus tráta** bacon, lettuce and tomato sandwich

leochaileach *adj* frail, fragile, sensitive, delicate, tender

leochaileacht *f3* weakness, fragility, sensitiveness, delicacy, tenderness

leoga *interj* indeed, to be sure **beidh mé ann leoga** I'll be there indeed

leoicéime *f4* leukaemia **géarleoicéime** acute leukaemia

leoithne *f4* breeze **leoithne aniar** breeze from the west

leomh *v* 1. dare, presume 2. allow

leon¹ *m1* lion **an Leon** Leo

leon² *v* wound, sprain, hurt **tá a murnán leonta aici** she has sprained her ankle

leonadh *m* sprain, injury

leor *adj* 1. ample, sufficient **is leor sin** that's enough 2. **go leor** enough, **bhí go leor bia ann** there was enough food there, **ceart / maith go leor** all right

leoraí *m4* lorry

leorghníomh *m1* atonement, restitution, amends

lí *f4* hue, colour, complexion **lí bhuí** jaundice

lia¹ *m4* medical practitioner, physician **lia comhairleach** consultant, **lia ban** gynaecologist

lia² *m4* (pillar-)stone **lia oghaim** ogham stone

lia³ *adj* more numerous **ní lia tír ná nós** each country has its own customs

liamhán *m1* **liamhán gréine** basking shark

liamhás *m1* ham **sliseoga liamháis** slices of ham

lián *m1* 1. propellor 2. trowel

liath *adj* grey

liathróid *f2* ball **liathróidí sneachta** snowballs

Liatroim *m3* Leitrim **Co. Liatroma** Co. Leitrim

Libia, an *f4* Libya

licéar *m1* liqueur

Life, an *f4* the Liffey (*river*)

lig *v* 1. let, allow **níor lig mé dóibh dul amach** I didn't let them go out, **lig dó, di!** leave him, her alone! 2. release **ligeadh amach ar bannaí é** he was released on bail 3. let, hire **tá an siopa á ligean aici** she is letting the shop 4. **lig ar** let on, pretend, **lig ort nach bhfaca tú iad** let on you didn't see them

ligh *v* lick **ag lí an uachtair reoite** licking the ice-cream

lile *f4* lily

limistéar *m1* area, district, territory **limistéar cónaithe / uirbithe** residential / urbanised, **Limistéar Saorthrádála na hEorpa** European Free Trade Area

limistéarach *adj* areal

líne *f4* line **ar líne** on line, **líne amhairc** line of vision, **líne tháirgthe** production line

líneach *adj* linear

líneadach *m1* linen **brailliní líneadaigh** linen sheets

líneáil *f3* lining *v* line

línigh *v* line, rule, draw

líníocht *f3* drawing **líníocht mheicniúil / theicniúil** mechanical / technical drawing

línithe *adj* lined, ruled, drawn

línitheoir *m3* draughtsman/woman

linn¹ *f2* pool, pond **linn snámha** swimming-pool, **linn éisc** fish pond

linn² *f2* time, period **le linn** during, **le linn an chogaidh** during the war, **idir an dá linn** in the meantime

linntreog *f2* 1. small pool, puddle 2. pothole

Liobáin, an *f2* Lebanon

liobarnach *adj* 1. slovenly, tattered 2. hanging loose 3. clumsy

liobrálach *adj* liberal

liobrálachas *m1* liberalism

liobrálaí *m4* liberal

liocras *m1* liquorice

líofa *adj* 1. polished, fluent **tá Spáinnis líofa aici** she has fluent Spanish 2. sharpened **lann líofa** sharpened blade

líomanáid *f2* lemonade

líomh *v* 1. polish, smooth 2. sharpen, file

líomhain *f3* allegation *v* allege

líomhán *m1* file **líomhán láimhe** hand file

liomóg *f2* pinch, nip **bhain sé liomóg asam** he pinched me

líomóid *f2* lemon

líon¹ *m1* 1. full, requisite number **líon tí** household, **bhí líon mór daoine ann** there was a great number of people there 2. measure, fill *v* fill **gloine a líonadh** to fill a glass

líon² *m1* 1. flax 2. linen

líon³ *m1* net, web **idirlíon** internet, **líon damháin alla** cobweb

líon⁴ *adj* **líon lán** full to the brim

líonmhar *adj* numerous

lionn *m* (bodily) humour **lionn dubh** melancholy, depression

líonóil *f2* lino(leum)

líonra *m4* network **líonra ríomhairí** computer network, **líonra sonraí** data net(work)

líonrith *m4* excitement, palpitation, panic

líonrú *m* networking

lionsa *m4* lens **lionsaí tadhaill** contact lenses

liopa *m4* 1. lip 2. flap, tag, lobe

liopadaileap *m4* basking-shark

liopasta *adj* 1. untidy 2. clumsy, ungainly

lios *m3* ring-fort, fairy mound **Lios na gCearrbhach** Lisburn ('the Fort of the Gamblers')

liosta¹ *m4* list, inventory, catalogue **liosta poist** mailing list

liosta² *adj* slow, tedious, tiresome, persistent

liostaigh *v* list

liostáil *v* enlist **liostáil san arm** to enlist in the army

liotúirge *m4* liturgy

lipéad *m1* label **cuir lipéad air** label it

líreacán *m1* lollipop **líreacán reoite** ice-pop

liric *f2* lyric

liriceach *adj* lyrical

lítear *m1* litre **lítear bainne** a litre of milk

liteartha *adj* 1. literary, literate 2. literal

litearthacht *f3* literacy **neamhlitearthacht** illiteracy

litir *f5* letter **litir shlabhra** chain letter, **ag scríobh litreach** writing a letter, **litreacha** letters, lettering

litrigh *v* spell **d'ainm a litriú** to spell your name

litríocht *f3* literature

litriú *m* spelling, orthography

liúntas *m1* allowance **liúntas cíosa** rent allowance, **liúntas saor ó cháin** tax-free allowance

liús *m1* pike (*fish*)

lobh *v* rot, decay

lobhadh *m1* rot, decay

lobhar *m1* leper

lobhra *f4* leprosy

loc *m1* lock (*on canal*) *v* pen, enclose (*sheep, goats, etc*)

loca *m4* fold, pen (*sheep, goats, etc*)

loch *m3* lake, lough **loch fionnuisce** freshwater lake, **os cionn an locha** above the lake, **Loch Cuan** Strangford Lough (*Down*)

Loch Garman *m* Wexford

lochán *m1* pond

Lochlannach *adj, m1* Scandinavian, Viking

lóchrann *m1* torch, lamp, lantern

locht *m3* fault **ní ormsa atá an locht** it's not my fault

lochta *m4* loft

lochtach *adj* faulty, false **ciorcal lochtach** vicious circle

lochtaigh *v* fault, blame **bíonn siad de shíor do mo lochtú** they are always finding fault with me, they are always blaming me

lochtú *m* fault-finding

lód[1] *m1* load

lód[2] *m1* lode

lódáil *f3* load(ing) *v* load **an bhfuil an gunna lódáilte?** is the gun loaded?

lofa *adj* rotten

lofacht *f3* rottenness

log[1] *m1* 1. place 2. hollow **log súile** eye socket 3. log **log ionchuir** input log

log[2] *v* log **log ann** log in/on, **log as** log out/off

logainm *m4* place-name **Coimisiún na Logainmneacha** the Place-Names Commission

logall *m1* socket **logall fiacaile** tooth socket

loghadh *m* forgiveness, remission

loic *v* fail, flinch

loicéad *m1* locket

loiceadh *m* failure

loighciúil *adj* logical

loighic *f2* logic

loingeas *m1* shipping, fleet (of ships) **loingeas cogaidh, tráchtála** fleet of warships, merchant fleet

loingseoir *f3* navigator

loingseoireacht *f3* navigation, shipping **loingseoireacht thar chaolmhuir** cross-channel shipping

loinneog *f2* refrain, chorus

loinnir *f5* brightness, sheen, brilliance

loirgneán *m1* shin covering, shin guard

lóis *f2* lotion **lóis ghréine** sun lotion

loisc *v* burn, scorch, sting

loisceach *adj* incendiary **gaireas loisceach** incendiary device

lóiste *m4* lodge

lóisteáil *v* lodge **airgead, seic a lóisteáil** to lodge money, a cheque

lóistéir *m3* lodger

lóistín *m4* lodgings, accommodation

loit *v* spoil, injure, hurt, damage

loitiméir *m3* vandal, botcher

loitiméireacht *f3* destruction, vandalism

lom *adj* 1. bare, naked **an fhírinne lom** the naked truth 2. thin 3. close *v* shear, mow, lay bare

lomadh *m* shearing, baring, impoverishment

lomaire *m4* shearer, mower **lomaire faiche** lawnmower

lomán *m1* bare tree trunk, log

lómhar *adj* precious **cloch lómhar** precious stone

lomnocht *adj* bare, stark naked

lomra *m4* fleece **Lomra an Óir** the Golden Fleece (*legend*)

lon *m1* blackbird **lon dubh** blackbird

lón *m1* 1. food, rations, provisions **lón lámhaigh** ammunition 2. lunch(eon) **am lóin** lunchtime

lónadóir *m3* caterer

lónadóireacht *f3* catering **áiseanna, seirbhís lónadóireachta** catering facilities, service

Londain *f* London **Droichead Londan** London Bridge

long *f2* ship **saor loinge** shipwright, **long chogaidh, sheoil** warship, sailing ship

longadán *m1* rocking, swaying, unsteadiness

longbhriseadh *m* shipwreck

longbhriste *adj* shipwrecked

longcheárta *f4* shipyard

longchlós *m1* dockyard

longfort *m1* 1. camp 2. fort, stronghold

Longfort, an *m1* Longford **Co. an Longfoirt** Co. Longford

lonnaíocht *f3* settlement, occupation **lonnaíocht tuaithe, uirbeach** rural, urban settlement

lonnaigh *v* settle, occupy, frequent, haunt **lonnú in áit** to settle in a place

lonnaitheoir *m3* settler

lonrach *adj* shining, bright, luminous **péint lonrach** gloss paint

lonraigh *v* shine, illuminate

lorg *m1* mark, track, trace **lorg láimhe** handmark, handprint, **fuarthas lorg fola ann** a trace of blood was found, **ar lorg ...** in pursuit of ... *v* track, seek, look for **ag lorg eolais** seeking, looking for information

lorga *f4* 1. shin 2. stick, cudgel

lorgaire *m4* seeker, searcher, investigator, detective

lorgaireacht *f3* tracking, tracing, investigating

losaid *f2* 1. bread board 2. trough

losainn *f2* lozenge

loscadh *m* burning, scorching

loscann *m1* frog

lot *m1* hurt, harm, damage

lotnaid *f2* pest

Lú *m4* Louth **Co. Lú** Co. Louth

lua *m4* mention, reference (to)

luach *m3* value, worth, price, reward, recompense **luach malairte** exchange value, **luach na mbróg** the price of the shoes, **fuair tú luach do shaothair** you got your reward for work

luacháil *f3* valuation *v* value

luachálaí *m4* valuer

luachliosta *m4* price list

luachmhar *adj* valuable, precious

luachmhéadú *m* appreciation (*in value*)

luaidhe *f4* lead **peann luaidhe** pencil, **(peitreal) saor ó luaidhe** unleaded (petrol), **nimhiú ó luaidhe** lead poisoning

luaidreán *m1* 1. fluctuation, movement 2. rumour, gossip

luaigh *v* mention, announce **luaigh sí liom thú** she mentioned you to me

luaineach *adj* 1. nimble, agile 2. changeable, fluctuating

luaineacht *f3* fluctuation

luaith *f3* ashes

luaithe *f4* swiftness, quickness, earliness **a luaithe is féidir** as soon as (is) possible

luaithreach *m1* ashes

luaithreadán *m1* ashtray

luamh *m1* yacht

luamhaire *m4* yachtsman, pilot

luamhaireacht *f3* yachting, piloting, steering

luamhán *m1* lever **luamhán stiúrtha** joystick, control lever

luan *m1* loin (*food*)

Luan *m1* Monday **Dé Luain** (on) Monday, **(ó) Luan go hAoine** (from) Monday to Friday, **lá an Luain** Day of Judgement

luas *m1* speed, velocity **teorainn luais** speed limit

luasaire *m4* accelerator

luasbhád *m1* speedboat

luasc *v* swing, rock, oscillate

luascach *adj* swinging, rocking, oscillating

luascadán *m1* pendulum

luascadh *m* swing, oscillation

luascaire *m4* oscillator

luascán *m1* swing(ing), rocker, rocking **leaba luascáin** hammock

luascánach *adj* unsteady, rocking, swinging

luascdhoras *m1* swing door

luasghéaraigh *v* accelerate

luasghéarú *m* acceleration

luasmhéadar *m1* speedometer

luasmhoilligh *v* decelerate

luasmhoilliú *m* deceleration

luasraon *m1* speedway (*sport*)

luath *adj* 1. swift, fast 2. soon, early

luathaigh *v* hurry, hasten, accelerate

luathscríbhinn *f2* shorthand document

luathscríbhneoireacht *f3* stenography, shorthand writing

luathscríobhaí *m4* stenographer, shorthand writer

lúb *f2* 1. link, loop, noose, bend 2. stitch 3. craft, deceit *v* loop, bend, turn, twist

lúbach *adj* 1. looped 2. deceitful

lúbaireacht *f3* craftiness, double-dealing

lúbóg *f2* 1. loop 2. buttonhole

lúbra *m4* maze

luch *f2* mouse **luch chodlamáin** dormouse, **luch mhór / fhrancach** rat

lúcháir *f2* joy, delight, exultation **cuireann sí gliondar ar mo chroí** it/she delights my heart

lúcháireach *adj* elated, joyous

lucharachán *m1* pygmy, dwarf, elf

luchóg *f2* (little) mouse

lucht *m3* 1. (category or class of) people **an lucht oibre** the working class, the labour force, **lucht éisteachta, féachana** audience, spectators, **lucht siúil** the travelling people, **lucht**

múchta dóiteáin fire-fighters 2. cargo, load, capacity, content, charge (*battery*)

luchtaigh *v* load, charge (*battery*)

luchtaire *m4* charger (*battery*)

luchtaithe *adj* loaded, charged (*battery*)

Lucsamburg *m4* Luxembourg

lúfar *adj* active, agile, athletic

lug, thit an lug ar an lag aige he collapsed, he was completely perplexed

luí *m4* 1. lying down, setting, resting **luí (na) gréine** sunset, **am luí** bedtime, **tá siad ina luí** they are in bed 2. **rud a chur ina luí ar dhuine** to convince somebody of something, to impress something on somebody 3. tendency, inclination **tá luí aige leis an ól** he is fond of the drink 4. lie, slope

luibh *f2* herb **luibheanna leighis** healing herbs

luibheolaí *m4* botanist

luibheolaíoch *adj* botanical

luibheolaíocht *f3* botany

luibhiteoir *m3* herbivore

lúibín *m4* 1. bracket **idir lúibíní** between brackets 2. small hole, button-hole

lúide *prep* minus, less **a hocht lúide a trí** eight minus three

lúidín *m4* little finger, little toe

luifearnach *adj* weedy *m1* weeds

luigh *v* 1. lie **chuaigh sí a luí** she went to bed 2. **luí isteach ar an obair** to go to work in earnest

luimneach *m1* limerick (*verse*)

Luimneach *m1* Limerick **Co. Luimnigh** Co. Limerick, **Gabhal Luimnigh** Limerick Junction

luíochán *m1* lying down, lying in wait, ambush

luisne *f4* blush, sheen, glow

luisnigh *v* blush, glow

luisniúil *adj* blushing, flushed

lumbágó *m4* lumbago

lumpa *m4* lump

Lúnasa *m4* August

lus *m3* plant, herb **lus an chromchinn** daffodil, **Garraithe na Lus** the Botanic Gardens

lúth *m1* activity, vigorous movement

lúthchleas *m1* athletic exercise **lúthchleasa** athletics, **Cumann Lúthchleas Gael (CLG)** the Gaelic Athletic Association (GAA)

lúthchleasach *adj* athletic (*sport, exercise, etc*)

lúthchleasaí *m4* athlete

lúthchleasaíocht *f3* athletics

M

má[1] *conj* if **má bhíonn an t-ádh leat feicfidh tú ann iad** if you are lucky you'll see them there, **má thagann siad ar chor ar bith** if they come at all, **má dúirt sé leat é** if he told you so

má[2] *f4* plain

mac *m1* son **mac léinn** student, **mac tíre** wolf, **mac an mhí-áidh** (the) unfortunate fellow, **mac an daba** third finger on right hand, **Mac Uí Mhurchú** Mr Ó Murchú

Mac, Mac Dónaill Mac Donnell, **Corn Mhic Cárthaigh** the McCarthy Cup

macalla *m4* echo

macánta *adj* 1. honest 2. meek, gentle

macántacht *f3* 1. honesty 2. meekness, gentleness

macaomh *m1* young person, youth

macarón *m1* macaroni

macarónach *adj* macaronic

macasamhail *f3* 1. like, equal **níl a macasamhail le fáil** her equal/match is not to be found 2. copy, facsimile

máchail *f2* 1. defect, blemish **tá máchail ort** there's something wrong with you 2. harm, injury

machaire *m4* plain **Machaire Fíolta** Magherafelt (*Co. Down*)

machnaigh *v* think, reflect

machnamh *m1* thought, reflection, thinking **déan do mhachnamh air** think about it

machnamhach *adj* thoughtful, reflective

machnóir *m3* thinker

macnas *m1* 1. sportiveness, playfulness, friskiness 2. lust, wantonness

macnasach *adj* 1. sportive, playful, frisky 2. lustful

macra *m4* youths

madra *m4* dog **madra caorach** collie, sheep-dog, **madra daill** guide dog, **madra rua** fox, **madra uisce** otter, **íde na muc is na madraí a thabhairt do dhuine** to treat somebody badly, to give somebody terrible abuse

magadh *m1* joking, mocking, mockery **níl mé ach ag magadh** I'm only joking, **rinne siad ceap magaidh díot** they made a laughing-stock of you, **ag magadh atá tú!** you're not serious! **bhí siad ag magadh faoi** they were mocking / jeering him, **tagann an magadh**

go leaba a dáiríre what begins as a joke can become serious

magairle *m4* testicle

magairlín *m4* orchid

máguaird *adv* around, about **an ceantar / dúiche máguaird** the surrounding district / locality

magúil *adj* mocking, derisive

mahagaine *m4* mahogany

maicín¹ *m4* pet, spoilt child **tá sé ina mhaicín ag a mháthair** his mother has him spoilt

maicín² *m4* brawl, quarrel

maicréal *m1* mackerel **ag iascach maicréal** fishing for mackerel

maide *m4* stick, beam, piece of wood **maide siúil** walking-stick, **maidí rámha** oars, **maide gailf** golf club, **do mhaidí a ligean le sruth** to neglect things, to let things drift

maidhm *f2* 1. burst, break, crash, eruption **maidhm bháistí** cloudburst, **maidhm shneachta** avalanche, **maidhm thoinne** breaker (*wave*), **maidhmeanna tuile** flash floods, **maidhm sheicne** rupture 2. detonation, explosion *v* 1. burst, erupt 2. detonate

maidhmitheach *adj* detonating **aidhnín maidhmitheach** detonating fuse

maidhmitheoir *m3* detonator **maidhmitheoir leictreach** electric detonator

maidin *f2* morning **beidh mé ann ar maidin** I'll be there in the morning, **i rith na maidine** during the morning

maidir, maidir le as to, concerning, as regards

maígh *v* 1. declare, claim, state **mhaígh sí gur léi é** she declared / claimed she owned it 2. boast **bíonn sé de shíor ag maíomh as**

a shaibhreas he is always boasting about his wealth 3. begrudge

maighdean *f2* 1. maiden, virgin **an Mhaighdean** Virgo 2. **maighdean mhara** mermaid

maighdeanas *m1* virginity

maighdeanúil *adj* virginal

Maigh Eo *n* Mayo **Co. Mhaigh Eo** Co. Mayo

maighnéad *m1* magnet

maighnéadach *adj* magnetic

maighnéadaigh *v* magnetise

maighnéadas *m1* magnetism

maignéisiam *m4* magnesium

máilín *m4* small bag **máilín domlais** gall bladder

mailís *f2* 1. malice 2. malignancy

mailíseach *adj* 1. malicious 2. malignant

maille, maille le with, together with, along with

máilléad *m1* mallet

mailp *f2* maple **crann mailpe** maple tree

máindúlagar *m1* manic depression

máine *f4* mania

máineach *adj, m1* maniac

mainéar *m1* manor (house)

mainicín *m4* mannequin, model

mainicíneacht *f3* modelling

mainistir *f5* monastery, abbey **Amharclann na Mainistreach** the Abbey Theatre

máinlia *m4* surgeon **máinlia croí** heart surgeon

máinliach *adj* surgical **cóiriú máinliach** surgical dressing

máinliacht *f3* surgery (*profession*) **áit mháinliachta** surgery (*for consultation*)

máinneáil *f3* lingering, loitering

mainséar *m1* 1. manger 2. crib

maíomh *m1* 1. boast(ing) **tá cúis mhaíte acu** they have something to be proud of 2. assertion, statement

mair *v* live, last **ag maireachtáil ar an iascaireacht** living off the sea, **mhair an trioblóid deich mbliana** the trouble lasted ten years, **má mhairim** if I live, if I am alive, **go maire sibh an nuacht!** may you enjoy your news, congratulations! **go maire tú an céad** may you live to be a hundred, **Seán Ó Catháin, nach maireann** the late Seán Ó Catháin

maireachtáil *f3* living, livelihood **caighdeán / costas maireachtála** standard / cost of living

mairg *f2* sorrow, regret, woe **is mairg go ...** it's a pity that ..., **mo mhairg!** alas!

mairnéalach *m1* sailor, seaman

máirseáil *f3* 1. march(ing) 2. parade *v* 1. march 2. parade

máirseálaí *m4* marcher

Máirt *f4* Tuesday **Dé Máirt** (on) Tuesday, **Máirt na hInide** Shrove Tuesday, Pancake Tuesday

mairteoil *f3* beef **filléad mairteola** fillet of beef, **mairteoil stroganoff** beef stroganoff

mairtíneach *m1* crippled person

mairtíreach *m1* martyr

mairtíreacht *f3* martyrdom

maise *f4* beauty, adornment, becomingness **faoi mhaise** beautiful, flourishing, **Athbhliain faoi shéan agus faoi mhaise duit!** Happy New Year! **ba mhaith an mhaise duit é** it was becoming of you

maisigh *v* beautify, adorn

maisitheoir *m3* decorator, designer **maisitheoir istigh** interior decorator

maisiú *m* decoration, adornment

maisiúchán *m1* decoration, adornment **maisiúchán istigh** interior decorating, **maisiúcháin na Nollag** Christmas decorations

maisiúil *adj* handsome, beautiful, decorative

maisiúlacht *f3* comeliness, decorativeness

máisiún *m1* freemason

maistín *m4* 1. mastiff, fierce dog 2. bully

maistíneacht *f3* bullying behaviour

máistir *m4* 1. master **máistir ealaíne** master of arts, **na Ceithre Máistrí** the Four Masters 2. teacher

máistreacht *f3* 1. mastery, mastering 2. mastership **céim mháistreachta** master's degree

maistreadh *m1* churning

máistreás *f3* mistress (*school etc*)

maistrigh *v* churn

máistriúil *adj* masterful, bossy, authoritative

maiteach *adj* forgiving, forgiven

maíteach *adj* boastful

maith[1] *adj* good **táim go maith** I am well, **lá maith** good day, **maith an fear** good man, **chomh maith le ...** as well as ..., **is maith an rud é (go ndúirt tú liom é)** it's a good thing (that you told me), **an maith leat an aimsir? is maith / ní maith** do you like the weather? yes / no, **ar mhaith leat dul ag snámh? ba mhaith / níor mhaith** would you like to swim? yes / no, **más maith leat** if you like, **níos fearr, is fearr** better, best, **tá cuma níos fearr uirthi** she looks better, **is fearr súil le glas ná súil le huaigh** it's better to go to jail than to go to your grave

maith[2] *f2* 1. good **níl aon mhaith ann** he is no good, it is of no value, **tá sé ó mhaith anois** it is useless now, **gan mhaith** useless 2. **maithe agus móruaisle** gentry and nobility

maith[3] *v* forgive, remit, pardon **mhaith sí dom é** she forgave me it, **go maithe Dia duit é** may God forgive you

maithe *f4* goodness, good **ar mhaithe le ...** for the sake/good of ..., **ar mhaithe leis féin a dhéanann an cat crónán** a cat purrs for its own benefit

maitheamh *m1* pardon, forgiveness, remission

maitheas *f3* goodness, benefit, good **déanfaidh sé maitheas duit** it'll do you good

maithiúnas *m1* pardon, forgiveness

máithreachas *m1* motherhood, maternity **saoire mháithreachais** maternity leave, **ospidéal máithreachais** maternity hospital

máithreánach *adj, m1* matriculation

máithriúil *adj* motherly, mother-like

mál *m1* excise **Custam agus Mál** Customs and Excise

mala *f4* 1. eyebrow, brow **bhí muc ar gach mala aige** he was frowning darkly 2. slope, brow **Mala** Mallow

mála *m4* bag **mála taistil** travel bag, suitcase, **mála iompair** holdall, **mála lóin** haversack, **mála droma** rucksack, **mála codlata** sleeping bag, **mála cáipéisí** briefcase, **mála láimhe** handbag, **píb mhála** bagpipes

maláire *f4* malaria

malairt *f2* 1. change, exchange **luach malairte** exchange value, **malairt eachtrach** foreign exchange 2. alternative **tá sí ar mhalairt intinne / tuairime anois** she is of a different mind / opinion now

malartach *adj* 1. variable, changeable, fluctuating, changing 2. alternative

malartaigh *v* 1. exchange 2. change

malartán *m1* exchange (*office*) **malartán fostaíochta** employment exchange, **malartán eachtrach** foreign exchange

malartú *m* 1. exchange 2. change

mall *adj* 1. slow **is moille Colmán ná Tomás** Colmán is slower than Tomás 2. late **labhróidh mé leat faoi níos moille** I'll talk to you about it later

mallacht *f3* curse **mallacht Dé ort!** the curse of God on you!

mallaibh, ar na mallaibh lately, of late

mallaithe *adj* accursed, wicked, vicious **fear mallaithe** wicked man, **ainmhí mallaithe** vicious animal

mallaitheacht *f3* wickedness, viciousness

Mallarca *m4* Majorca

mallintinneach *adj* retarded, slow-witted

mallmhuir *f3* neap tide

malltriallach *adj* slow moving **trácht malltriallach** slow-moving traffic *m1* slow-moving person, slow-coach

malrach *m1* little boy, youngster

Málta *m4* Malta

mam *f2* mam (my)

mám[1] *f3* handful **mám dhusta** a handful of dust

mám[2] *m3* pass (*between mountains*) **Mám an Cheo** Maumakeogh (*Co. Mayo*)

mamach[1] *adj* mammary

mamach[2] *m1* mammal

mamaí *f4* mammy

mamat *m1* mammoth

mámh *m1* trump (*cards*)

mamó *f4* grandma **mamó agus daideo** granny and grand-dad

mana *m4* 1. omen, preomonition, sign 2. motto

manach *m1* monk **Baile na Manach** Monkstown

manachas *m1* monasticism

Manainn *f5* **Oileán Mhanann** Isle of Man

Manainnis *f2* Manx (*language*)

Manannach *adj* Manx *m1* Manx person

Manchain *f4* Manchester

mandáid *f2* mandate **mandáid dírdhochair** direct debit mandate

mandairín *m4* mandarin orange

mangaire *m4* pedlar, hawker, haggler **an Mangaire Súgach** the Merry Pedlar, **mangaire drugaí** drug-pusher

mangaireacht *f3* peddling, hawking, haggling **mangaireacht drugaí** drug-pushing

mangarae *m4* assorted ware, junk

manglam *m1* mixture, hotchpotch, cocktail (*drink*)

mangó *m4* mango

mánla *adj* gentle, pleasant

mánlacht *f3* gentleness, pleasantness

mant *m3* 1. gap in teeth **tá mant ann** he has a gap between his teeth 2. bite **mant a bhaint as rud** to take a bite of something 3. toothless gums

mantach *adj* gapped, gap-toothed

maoil *f2* 1. bald/bare top 2. hillock 3. **ag cur thar maoil** overflowing

maoildearg *f2* mulberry **faoi chrann maoildeirge** under a mulberry tree

maoile *f4* baldness, bareness

maoin *f2* property, wealth, means **maoin phearsanta** personal property

maoinigh *v* finance, endow **rud a mhaoiniú** to finance something

maoiniú *m* finance, financing

maoirseacht *f3* 1. stewardship 2. supervising **maoirseacht a dhéanamh ar rud** to supervise / oversee something, **post maoirseachta** supervisory position

maoirseoir *m3* supervisor

maoithneach *adj* emotional, sentimental

maoithneachas *m1* sentimentality

maol *adj* 1. bald, bare **duine maol** bald person 2. hornless **bó mhaol** hornless cow 3. blunt **claíomh maol** blunt sword 4. flat (*music*) **A maol** A flat

maolaigh *v* 1. become bald/bare 2. blunt **lann scine a mhaolú** to blunt the blade of a knife 3. decrease, modify **maolaíonn sé luas an bháid** it decreases the speed of the boat, **b'fhearr an ráiteas sin a mhaolú** it would be better to modify ('take the sting out of') that statement 4. lower **mhaolaigh sí a guth** she lowered her voice 5. **maolaigh ar** lessen, **ar mhaolaigh ar an bpian ó shin?** has the pain lessened since?

maolaire *m4* absorber (*of sound*), damper **maolaire innill** engine damper

maolán *m1* buffer (*computer*) **maoláin ionchuir is aschuir** input/output buffers

maolchluasach *adj* abashed, confused with shame, subdued

maolgháire *m4* suppressed laugh, chuckle

maolscríobach *adj* untidy, careless, slovenly

maolú *m* 1. alleviation, reduction, slackening 2. damping (*computer*)

maonáis *f2* mayonnaise

maor *m1* 1. steward 2. major **maor-ghinearál** major-general 3. warden **maor tráchta** traffic warden 4. prefect (*school*) 5. foreman **maor láithreáin** site foreman

maorga *adj* stately, dignified

maorgacht *f3* dignity, stateliness

maorlathach *adj* bureaucratic

maorlathaí *m4* bureaucrat

maorlathas *m1* bureaucracy

maorsháirsint *m4* sergeant-major

maos *m1* saturation **ar maos** steeping

maoth *adj* 1. moist 2. soft, tender

maothaigh *v* 1. moisten, soften 2. soak, steep

maothán *m1* earlobe

mapa¹ *m4* map

mapa² *m4* mop

mapáil¹ *v* map

mapáil² *v* mop

mar *adv, conj, prep* 1. like, as **mar shampla** for example, **mar an gcéanna** likewise, **mar sin féin** nevertheless, even so, **is mar a chéile iad** they are the same, identical 2. as, because **sin mar atá sé** that's how he/it is 3. **mar le** as regards 4. **mar dhea** indeed, no doubt

marachuan *m1* marijuana

Maracó *m4* Morocco

marana *f4* reflection, meditation **bheith ar do mharana** to be in contemplation

maranach *adj* thoughtful

marascal *m1* marshal

maratón *m1* marathon

marbh *adj* 1. dead **an Fear Marbh** the Dead Man (*one of the Blasket Islands*) 2. numb, spiritless 3. motionless **lochán marbh** stagnant pond 4. exhausted **marbh ag an obair** exhausted from the work 5. dull (*colour, sound, pain, etc*) *m1* dead person

marbhán *m1* corpse

marbhánta *adj* 1. lifeless 2. stagnant, dull 3. sultry

marbhghin *f2* still-born child

marbhlann *f2* morgue

marbhna *m4* elegy

marbhsháinn *f2* checkmate

marc *m1* mark **cuir marc le do rogha (freagra)** mark your choice (of answer)

marcach *m1* rider, horseman

marcaigh *v* ride **is fearr marcaíocht ar ghabhar ná coisíocht dá fheabhas** anything is better than walking

marcáil *v* mark

marcaíocht *f3* 1. riding 2. ride, lift **cé a thug marcaíocht duit?** who gave you a lift?

marcra *m4* cavalry

marcshlua *m4* 1. cavalcade 2. cavalry

marfach *adj* deadly, fatal, lethal **buille marfach** fatal blow

marfóir *m3* killer

margadh *m1* market, bargain **bíodh (sé) ina mhargadh** it's a deal, **margadh caorach, éisc** sheep, fish market, **margadh na míol** flea market, **margadh neamhshrianta** unrestricted / free market, **an margadh domhanda** the world market, **an margadh dubh** the black market

margadhluach *m3* market value

margadhphraghas *m1* market price

margaigh *v* market

margáil *f3* bargaining, negotiating

margaíocht *f3* 1. bargaining **lucht margaíochta** bargain-makers 2. marketing **margaíocht idirnáisiúnta** international marketing

margairín *m4* margarine

marglann *f2* mart

margú *m* marketing

marla *m4* modelling clay

marmaláid *f2* marmalade

marmar *m1* marble

maróg *f2* pudding **maróg Nollag** Christmas pudding

Mars *m3* Mars (*planet*)

marsantach *adj* mercantile, merchant **banc marsantach** merchant bank

Márta *m4* March **17 Márta 2000** 17 March 2000

marthain *f3* existence **ar marthain** alive

marthanach *adj* 1. lasting **amas marthanach** sustained attack 2. permanent

marthanóir *m3* survivor

marú *m* killing, slaughter

marún *m1* maroon colour

Marxach *adj, m1* Marxist

Marxachas *m1* Marxism

más *m1* thigh, buttock

másailéam *m1* mausoleum

masc *m1* mask

mascára *m4* mascara

masla *m4* insult

maslach *adj* 1. insulting, abusive 2. straining, taxing (*of work, journey, etc*)

maslaigh *v* 1. insult, abuse 2. strain

masmas *m1* nausea

masmasach *adj* nauseating

mata *m4* mat

máta *m4* mate (*of ship*)

matal *m1* 1. mantelpiece 2. mantle

matamaitic *f2* mathematics

matamaiticeoir *m3* mathematician

matamaiticiúil *adj* mathematical

matán *m1* muscle **matán cairdiach** cardiac muscle

máthair *f* mother **deartháir mo mháthar** my mother's brother, **máthair chéile** mother-in-law

máthairab *f3* abbess

máthartha *adj* maternal **instinn mháthartha** maternal instinct, **teanga mháthartha** mother tongue

mátrún *m1* matron

mé *pron* I, me **beidh mé ann** I will be there, **ní mé a bhí ag caint** it wasn't me who was talking, **bhuail sé mé** he hit me

meá *f4* balance, (weighing) scales **idir dhá cheann na meá** hanging in the balance, **an Mheá** the Scales, Libra

meabhair *f5* mind, memory, intelligence, meaning **tá siad as a meabhair** they are out of their mind, **an bhfuil aon mheabhair agat air?** have you any memory of it? **tá meabhair aige** he has intelligence, **bac meabhrach** mental handicap, **is é an mheabhair a bhain mise as go …** the meaning I got from it was that …

meabhairghalar *m1* mental illness

meabhlachas *m1* illusionism

meabhrach *adj* mindful, intelligent, conscious **duine meabhrach** an intelligent person

meabhraigh *v* memorise, remind, remember **meabhraigh dom é** remind me of it

meabhraíocht *f3* awareness intelligence

meabhrán *m1* memorandum

meacan *m1* (tuberous) root **meacan dearg** carrot, **meacan bán** parsnip

meáchan *m1* weight

méad, cé mhéad airgid atá agat? how much money have you? **cé mhéad duine a bhí ann?** how many people were there? **dá mhéad é** however great it may be, **dá mhéad é is amhlaidh is fearr é** the bigger the better, **ar a mhéad** at (the) most

méadaigh *v* increase

méadaitheach *adj* increasing

méadar *m1* meter, metre **méadar tacsaí** taximeter, **céad méadar** one hundred metres

meadaracht *f3* metre (*verse*), metrics

meadhrán *m1* dizziness, vertigo

meadhránach *adj* dizzy, vertiginous

méadrach *adj* metric

méadú *m* increase, enlargement

meafar *m1* metaphor

meafarach *adj* metaphorical

meáigh *v* 1. weigh, balance **tú féin a mheá** to weigh yourself 2. consider **tá sí ag meá na faidhbe** she is considering the problem

meaisín *m4* machine **meaisín díola** vending machine, **meaisín tacaíochta beatha** life support machine

meaisineoir *m3* machinist **meaisíneoir adhmaid** wood machinist

meaisínghunna *m4* machine-gun **fomheaisínghunna** sub-machine-gun

meaisínghunnadóir *m3* machine-gunner

meáite, bheith meáite ar rud a dhéanamh to be decided about doing something

mealbhacán *m1* wild carrot; melon

mealbhóg *f2* small bag, pouch

meall¹ *m1* 1. lump, mass, knob **meall ime** lump/knob of butter, **meall brád** Adam's apple 2. ball **meall súile** eyeball 3. **an meall mór ar deireadh** last but not least

meall² *v* 1. entice, coax 2. deceive, disappoint

meallacach *adj* charming, alluring

meallacacht *f3* charm, allure

mealladh *m* 1. enticement, allurement 2. deception, disappointment

mealltach *adj* 1. enticing, coaxing, seductive 2. deceptive, disappointing

mealltacht *f3* 1. allurement 2. deceptiveness

mealltóir *m3* 1. coaxer 2. deceiver

mealltóireacht *f3* 1. coaxing 2. deception

meamhlach *f2* miaowing

meamraiméis *f2* officialese

meamram *m1* memorandum

meán¹ *m1* 1. middle **meán lae** midday, **meán oíche** midnight, **Meán Fómhair** September 2. medium **na meáin (chumarsáide)** the (communications) media 3. average **ar (an) meán** on average

meán-² *prefix* mid(dle), intermediate, medium, average **meánséasúr** mid-season, **meánchúrsa** intermediate course, **meánmhéid** medium size, **meánchostas** average cost

meánach *adj* average, middle

meánaicme *f4* middle class

meánaicmeach *adj* middle-class

meánaois *f2* middle age **an Mheánaois** the Middle Ages

meánaoiseach *adj* mediaeval

meánaosta *adj* middle-aged

méanar *adj* happy **is méanar dó** it's well for him; lucky him!

meáncheannaí *m4* middleman

meánchiorcal *m1* equator

meánchrios *m3* equatorial region

meánchriosach *adj* equatorial

meancóg *f2* slip, mistake, blunder

meandar *m1* instant, second

meándearg *adj* medium red

méanfach *f2* yawn(ing) **bíonn sé de shíor ag méanfach / ag ligean meánfaí** he is always yawning

meangadh *m* smile **meangadh beag gáire** a little smile

meanma *f5* mind, morale, spirit **thugamar ardú meanman di** we raised her spirits, **tá meanma shiúil / taistil iontu** they have the urge / itch to travel

meánmheáchan *m1* middleweight **curadh meánmheáchain an domhain** middleweight champion of the world

Meánmhuir *f3* **an Mheánmhuir** the Mediterranean (sea)

meánmhuirí *adj* mediterranean

meanmnach *adj* spirited, courageous, lively

meann, an Mhuir Mheann the Irish Sea

meannán *m1* kid (*goat*)

meánoideachas *m1* secondary education

Meánoirthear, an *m1* the Middle East

meánscoil *f2* secondary school **daltaí meánscoile** secondary students

meantán *m1* tit (*bird*)

mear *adj* fast, quick, lively

méar *f2* 1. finger, toe **méara do chos** your toes, **an mhéar bheag, an mhéar láir, an mhéar thosaigh** the little finger, the middle finger, the index finger, **méar an fháinne** the ring-finger, **rud a chur ar an méar fhada** to put something 'on the long finger', to postpone something indefinitely 2. digit (*measuring*)

méara *m4* mayor **Ardmhéara Bhaile Átha Cliath** the Lord Mayor of Dublin

méaracán *m1* thimble

mearadh *m1* 1. insanity, madness 2. craving

mearaí *f4* frenzy, craziness, bewilderment **meascán mearaí** confusion (of mind), hallucination

mearaigh *v* confuse, derange

méaraigh *v* finger

mearbhall *m1* 1. (mental) confusion, bewilderment 2. dizziness

mearbhia *m4* fast food **siopa mearbhia** fast food shop

mearbhlach *adj* 1. confusing, bewildering 2. dizzy

mearcair *m4* mercury **Mearcair** Mercury (*planet*)

méarchlár *m1* keyboard

mearlámhach *m1* rapid fire (*of gun*)

méarlorg *m1* fingerprint

mearóg *f2* vegetable marrow

méaróg[1] *f2* pebble

méaróg[2] *f2* object shaped like a finger **méaróga éisc** fish fingers

mearoscailte *adj* quick-release **clampa mearoscailte** quick-release clamp

meas *m3* 1. estimation, opinion **cad é do mheas air?** what's your opinion of him/it? 2. esteem, respect **tá an-mheas agam ar Chathal** I have great respect for Cathal *v* think, estimate, value, judge **measaim go bhfuil dul amú uirthi** I think that she is mistaken, **gluaisteán a mheas** to value a car

measartha *adj* moderate, fairly **aimsir mheasartha** moderate weather, **bheith, déanamh go measartha** to be, do fairly well

measarthacht *f3* moderation

measc[1] *m4* 1. mix, confusion 2. midst **i measc** among, between, **as a measc** from among them

measc[2] *v* 1. mix (up) 2. stir

meascach *m1* half-breed, half-caste

meascán *m1* 1. mixture, muddle **meascán mearaí** confusion (of mind), hallucination 2. lump **meascán cáise** a lump of cheese

meascra *m4* miscellany, medley

measctha *adj* mixed, assorted

meascthóir *m3* mixer **meascthóir suiminte** cement mixer

meastachán *m1* estimate

meastóireacht *f3* evaluation
  meastóireacht oibre job evaluation

measúil *adj* esteemed, respected, respectful

measúlacht *f3* esteem, respectability

measúnacht *f3* assessment

measúnaigh *v* assess

measúnóir *m3* assessor

measúnú *m* assessment

meata *adj* 1. cowardly **duine meata** a cowardly person 2. sickly

meatach *adj* 1. perishable, declining, decadent, decaying **earraí meatacha** perishable goods 2. cowardly

meatachán *m1* 1. weakling 2. coward

meatacht *f3* 1. decay, decline 2. cowardice

meath *m3* 1. decay, decadence, decline 2. failure, degeneration *v* 1. decay, decline 2. fail, degenerate 3. waste

meathbhruith *f2* simmer **ar meathbhruith** simmering

meathlú *m* recession, slump **meathlú geilleagrach / eacnamaíochta** economic recession

meicneoir *m3* mechanic

meicnic *f2* mechanics

meicnigh *v* mechanise

meicníocht *f3* mechanism **meicníocht bhrúchnaipe** push-button mechanism

meicnithe *adj* mechanised

meicniúil *adj* mechanical **líníocht mheicniúil** mechanical drawing

Meicsiceach *adj, m1* Mexican

Meicsiceo *m4* Mexico **Murascaill Mheicsiceo** the Gulf of Mexico

méid¹ *m4* amount, quantity **chaill sí an méid sin airgid** she lost that amount of, so much money, **sa mhéid go …** in so far as …

méid² *f2* size **tá siad ag dul i méid** they are getting bigger

meidhir *f2* joy, delight

meidhreach *adj* merry, frisky

meigeall *m1* goat's beard, goatee

meigeallach *f2* bleating of goats

meil *v* 1. grind, wear away 2. pass/kill the time, waste **ag meilt ama** killing time, **mheill sé an lá orainn** he/it wasted the day on us

méileach *f2* bleating of sheep

meilt *f2* 1. grinding, crushing 2. wasting

meilteoir *m3* grinder

meiningíteas *m1* meningitis

meirbh *adj* 1. sultry, close (*weather*) 2. languid

meirbhe *f4* 1. sultriness 2. languor

meirdreach *f2* prostitute

meireang *m4* meringue

meirg *f2* rust

meirgdhíonach *adj* rust-proof

meirge *m4* flag, banner, standard **meirge an uachtaráin** the presidential standard

meirgeach *adj* rusty

meirgigh *v* rust

meirgire *m4* standard-bearer, ensign (*military rank*)

meirgiú *m* rusting

Meiriceá *m4* America **Meiriceá Thuaidh, Theas** North, South America, **Meiriceá Láir** Central America, **Stáit Aontaithe Mheiriceá** United States of America

Meiriceánach *adj, m1* American

meirleach *m1* malefactor, thief, outlaw

meisce *f4* drunkenness, intoxication **bhí siad ar meisce** they were drunk

meisceoir *m3* drunkard

meisciúil *adj* intoxicating

méiseáil *f3* messing

méiseálaí *m4* messer

Meisias *m4* Messiah

meitéar *m1* meteor

meitéareolaíocht *f3* meteorology

méith *adj* 1. fat **feoil mhéith** fat meat 2. rich, fertile (*land*)

meitheal *f2* working party, work-group

Meitheamh *m1* June

meitifisic *f2* metaphysics

meon *m1* mind, mood, temperament **an seanmheon** the old mode of thought

mí[1] *f* month **ar feadh míosa** for a month, **mí na meala** honeymoon, **míonna an tsamhraidh** the summer months

mí-[2] *prefix* ill-, un-, bad, evil, dis-, mis- **míchinniúnach** ill-fated, **mímhuinteartha** unfriendly, **míbhainistí** bad management, **míbheart** evil deed/plan, **mí-aigeanta** dispirited, **mírialú** misgovernment, misrule

Mí[3] *f4* **an Mhí** Meath, **Co. na Mí** Co. Meath

mí-ádh *m1* bad luck, misfortune **a leithéid de mhí-ádh!** what bad luck!

mí-ádhúil *adj* unlucky

mí-áisiúil *adj* inconvenient

mí-ámharach *adj* unfortunate

mian *f2* wish, desire **ba mhian liom labhairt leat faoi arís** I would like to talk to you about it again

mianach *m1* 1. material, quality, substance **tá an mianach ceart iontu** they have the right quality / stuff in them 2. mine **mianach óir** goldmine 3. mine (*warfare*) **mianach talún** landmine

mianadóir *m3* miner

mianadóireacht *f3* mining

mianaigh *v* desire, long for

mianra *m4* mineral

mianrach *adj* mineral **uisce mianrach** mineral water

mias *f2* dish

míbhéas *m3* bad habit or practice

míbhéasach *adj* ill-mannered, rude

míbhuíoch *adj* ungrateful

míbhuntáiste *m4* disadvantage

míbhuntáisteach *adj* disadvantageous

mícháil *f2* ill fame, ill repute

mícháiliúil *adj* ill-famed, infamous

míchairdeas *m1* unfriendliness

míchairdiúil *adj* unfriendly

mícharthanach *adj* uncharitable

míchéadfa *f4* crankiness, peevishness, ill humour

míchéadfach *adj* cranky, peevish, bad-tempered

mícheart *adj* wrong, incorrect

míchiall *f2* 1. craziness, folly **tá siad ar míchiall** they are crazy 2. misinterpretation **ná bain míchiall as** don't misinterpret it

míchineálta *adj* unkind

míchlú *m4* ill repute **cuireadh míchlú orthu** they were defamed

míchompord *m1* discomfort

míchompordach *adj* uncomfortable

míchothrom *adj* uneven, rough, unbalanced

míchumas *m1* 1. incapability, inability 2. disability

míchumasach *adj* 1. incapable 2. disabled

míchumtha *adj* deformed

míchúramach *adj* careless

micrea- *prefix* micro- **micreacnamaíocht** micro-economics, **micreagraf** micrograph

micreafón *m1* microphone

micreascannán *m1* microfilm

micreascóp *m1* microscope

micreascópach *adj* microscopic

micreathonnach *adj* microwave **oigheann micreathonnach** microwave oven

micri- *prefix* micro- **micribhitheolaíocht** microbiology

micrishlis *f2* microchip

mídhaonna *adj* inhuman

mídhealraitheach *adj* unlikely

mídhílis *adj* disloyal, unfaithful

mídhílseacht *f3* disloyalty, unfaithfulness

mídhleathach *adj* illegal

mídhlisteanach *adj* 1. illegitimate 2. disloyal

mí-éifeacht *f3* inefficiency

mífheiliúnach *adj* unsuitable

mífhoighne *f4* impatience

mífhoighneach *adj* impatient

mífholláin *adj* unwholesome, unhealthy

mífhortún *m1* misfortune

mífhortúnach *adj* unfortunate

mígréin *f2* migraine

mí-iompar *m1* misconduct **mí-iompar tromchúiseach** serious misconduct

mí-ionracas *m1* dishonesty

mí-ionraic *adj* dishonest

mil *f3* honey **lá meala** beautiful day, **mi na meala** honeymoon

milaois *f2* millennium **an tríú mílaois** the third millennium

míle *m4* 1. thousand, great amount **míle bliain ó shin** a thousand years ago, **bhí na mílte duine ann** there were thousands of people there 2. mile **tá sé cúpla míle siar an bóthar** it is a couple of miles back the road

míleáiste *m4* mileage

míleata *adj* military **seirbhís mhíleata** military service

míleatach *adj, m1* militant

milis *adj* sweet

milíste *m4* militia

milítheach *adj* pale, sickly looking

míliú *m4* thousandth **an míliú huair** the thousandth time

mill *v* spoil, ruin, destroy **tá an leanbh millte acu** they have spoiled the child, **mhill siad an lá orainn** they ruined the day on us

milleadh *m* ruination, destruction

milleagram *m1* milligram

milleán *m1* blame **cuireadh an milleán ormsa** I was blamed (for it)

milliméadar *m1* millimetre

milliún *m1* million **trí mhilliún duine** three million people

milliúnaí *m4* millionaire

millteach *adj* 1. destructive 2. enormous **bád mór millteach** an enormous boat

millteanach *adj* 1. terrible, horrible **bhí am millteanach acu ann** they had a terrible time there 2. extreme, enormous **tá sé millteanach casta** it is extremely complicated

milseacht *f3* sweetness

milseán *m1* sweet

milseog *f2* dessert

milseogra *m4* confectionery

milsigh *v* sweeten

mím *f2, v* mime

mímhacánta *adj* dishonest

mímhacántacht *f3* dishonesty

mímheas *m3* direspect, disrepute

mímhodhúil *adj* 1. disrespectful 2. immodest

mímhorálta *adj* immoral

mímhoráltacht *f3* immorality

mímhúineadh *m* rudeness

mímhuinín *f2* distrust, lack of confidence

mímhuiníneach *adj* distrustful

mímhúinte *adj* rude, unmannerly

min *f2* meal **min sáibh** sawdust, **min choirce** oatmeal

mín *adj* 1. gentle, calm (*of person, manner, etc*), tame (*of animal*) 2. fine, smooth, delicate (*of thing, touch, etc*)

mínádúrtha *adj* unnatural

mínáire *f4* shamelessness, immodesty

mínáireach *adj* shameless, immodest

míne *f4* fineness, smoothness

minc *f2* mink

míneas *m1* minus (sign)

minic *adj* often, frequent **is minic a tharla sé mar sin** it often happened like that, **cé chomh minic?** how often? **go minic** often, frequently, **níos minice, is minice** more often, most often

minicíocht *f3* frequency **ardmhinicíocht** very high frequency (VHF)

mínigh *v* 1. explain 2. smooth

ministir *m4* minister (*of church*)

ministreacht *f3* ministry

mínitheach *adj* explanatory

míniú *m* explanation

míniúchán *m1* explanation

míntír *f2* mainland

míntíreachas *m1* reclamation of land **talamh a tugadh chun míntíreachais** reclaimed land

míochaine *f4* medicine **cleachtadh ginearálta ar mhíochaine** general medical practice

miocrób *m1* microbe

miodóg *f2* dagger

míofar *adj* ugly, ungainly

mí-oiriúnach *adj* unsuitable

mí-oiriúnacht *f3* unsuitability

míol *m1* 1. animal, insect, beast **míol mór** whale 2. louse **míolta (cnis)** lice

míolach *adj* lice-infected, lousy

míolra *m4* vermin

míoltóg *f2* midge

mion[1] *adj* 1. minute, detailed **tuairisc mhion** detailed report / account 2. small **clocha miona** small stones 3. fine, powdered

mion-[2] *prefix* 1. minute, small, minor, petty **mionchloch** small stone, pebble, **mionghoid** petty theft 2. mini-, micro- **mionmharatón** mini-marathon

mionaigh *v* mince, powder, break into small pieces

mionairgead *m1* petty cash, small change

mionbhruar *m1* small scraps, crumbs

mionbhus *m4* minibus

mionchruinn *adj* detailed

mionchúiseach *adj* meticulous, over-particular

mionchuntas *m1* detailed account

miondealú *m* analysis **miondealú ar an gcaiteachas** breakdown of expenditure

miondíol *m3, v* retail

miondíoltóir *m3* retailer

mionéadach *m1* haberdashery

mioneolas *m1* detailed information / knowledge

mionfheoil *f3* mincemeat

mionfhile *m4* minor poet

mionghadaí *m4* petty thief

miongháire *m4* smile

mionghalf *m1* mini-golf

mionghearr *v* mince, shred, cut fine

mionghléas *m1* minor key (*music*)

mionlach *m1* minority

mionn *m3* oath **mionn éithigh** false oath, perjury

mionnaigh *v* swear **coiste a mhionnú** to swear in a jury

mionnscríbhinn *f2* affidavit

mionoifigeach *f1* petty officer

mí-onóir *f3* dishonour

mí-onórach *adj* dishonourable

mionpháirt *f2* small part **bhí mionpháirt aici sa dráma** she had a small part in the play

mionphointe *m4* small point, detail

mionra *m4* mincemeat

mionrud *m3* minor thing, trifle

mionsamhail *f3* miniature / small-scale model

mionscála *m4* small scale **ar mhionscála** on a minor scale

mionsciorta *m4* mini-skirt

mionscrúdaigh *v* examine / scrutinise in detail

mionsonra *m4* minor detail

miontas *m1* mint

miontóir *m3* mincer

miontuairisc *f2* detailed account **miontuairiscí (cruinnithe)** minutes (of a meeting)

mionúr *adj* minor **an fhoireann mhionúr** the minor team

mí-ordú *m4* disorder

míorúilt *f2* miracle

míorúilteach *adj* miraculous

míosachán *m1* monthly (*journal, magazine, etc*)

mioscais *f2* spite, hatred, malice, mischief

mioscaiseach *adj* spiteful, malicious, mischievous

míosta *adj* menstrual **fuil mhíosta** menstruation

míostraigh *v* menstruate

míostrú *m* menstruation

míosúil *adj* monthly

miosúr *m1* measure, measurement

miotal *m1* 1. metal **miotal trom** heavy metal 2. mettle **tá miotal sa chine sin** that race / those people are hardy

miotalach *adj* 1. metallic 2. mettlesome, hardy

miotalóir *f3* metalworker

miotalóireacht *f3* metalwork

miotas *m1* myth

miotasach *adj* mythical

miotaseolaíocht *f3* mythology

miotóg[1] *f2* pinch **bhí siad ag baint miotóg as** they were pinching him

miotóg[2] *f2* glove, mitten

mír *f2* 1. portion, share, bit **míreanna beaga eolais** little bits of information 2. section, paragraph **an chéad mhír, an dara mír** the first, second section, **míreanna mearaí** jigsaw puzzle

mire *f4* 1. rapidity, quickness 2. frenzy, madness **tá sí ar mire** she is mad / in a frenzy

míréasún *m1* unreason

míréasúnta *adj* unreasonable

míréasúntacht *f3* unreasonableness

mírialta *adj* 1. irregular 2. unruly

mírialtacht *f3* irregularity, disorder, unruliness

mirlín *m4* marble (*toy*) **ag imirt mirlíní** playing marbles

mise *emphatic pron* I, me **dá mba mise tusa** if I were you, **mise a bhí ann** it was I who was there, **ní bhuailfeadh sé mise** he wouldn't hit me

misean *m1* mission

míshásamh *m1* dissatisfaction, displeasure

míshásta *adj* dissatisfied, displeased

míshástacht *f3* dissatisfaction

míshásúil *adj* unsatisfactory

míshibhialta *adj* uncivil, rude

míshlacht *m3* untidiness

míshlachtmhar *adj* untidy, botched

míshocair *adj* restless, uneasy, unstable

míshona *adj* unhappy

míshonas *m1* unhappiness

míshuaimhneach *adj* uneasy, restless

míshuaimhneas *m1* unease, restlessness

misinéir *m3* missioner, missionary

misneach *m1* 1. courage **misneach a thabhairt do dhuine** to give somebody courage, to encourage somebody 2. spirit **conas tá an misneach?** how's the spirit / form?

misnigh *v* encourage

misniúil *adj* courageous

miste *adj* **an miste leat ...?** do you mind ...? **ní miste liom** I do not mind, **ní miste a rá go ...** it is no harm to say that ...

misteach *adj*, *m1* mystic

mistéir *f2* mystery

mistéireach *adj* mysterious

mistíc *f2* mystique

místuaim *f2* 1. clumsiness 2. thoughtlessness

místuama *adj* 1. clumsy 2. thoughtless

míthaitneamh *m1* displeasure, dislike

míthaitneamhach *adj* unpleasant, disagreeable

míthapa *adj* unready *m4* 1. unreadiness 2. mischance, mishap

mithid *adj* due time **is mithid duit (imeacht)** it is time for you (to go), **más mall is mithid** better late than never

míthráthúil *adj* inopportune, untimely

míthrócaireach *adj* pitiless, merciless

míthuiscint *f3* misunderstanding

miúil *f2* mule

mí-úsáid *f2* abuse, misuse **mí-úsáid (ghnéis) ar pháistí** child (sexual) abuse

mí-úsáideoir *m3* abuser **mí-úsáideoir drugaí go hinfhéitheach** intravenous drug abuser

mo *poss adj* my **m'uncail** my uncle, **mo chara** my friend, **m'fheadóg stáin** my tin whistle, **is é mo thuairim go ...** it is my opinion that ...

mó *adj* **an mó duine a bhí ann?** how many people were there? **ní mó ná sásta a bhí mé** I wasn't too happy, **is mó seans eile a gheobhaidh tú** you'll get many more chances

moch *adj* early **go moch ar maidin** early in the morning

modartha *adj* murky, dark, overcast, morose

modh *m3* 1. method, procedure **modhanna gnó, teagaisc** business, instruction methods, **modhanna oifige** office procedures 2. manner, mode **ar an modh seo** in this manner / way 3. mood (*grammar*) **an modh coinníollach** the conditional mood

Modhach *adj*, *m1* Methodist

modheolaíocht *f3* methodology

modhnaigh *v* modulate, modify

modhúil *adj* gracious, mannerly, modest

modúlach *adj* modular

mogall *m1* 1. mesh 2. **mogall súile** eyeball

mogallach *adj* 1. meshed 2. having prominent eyes

moghlaeir *m3* boulder

móid *f2* vow **móid gheanmnaíochta** vow of chastity

móide *comp* more, plus **ní móide go ...** it is not likely that ..., **daichead móide a sé déag** forty plus sixteen

móidigh *v* vow

moiglí *adj* tender, soft, placid, easy

móihéar *m1* mohair

moileasc *m1* mollusc

móilín *m4* molecule

moill *f2* delay, stop **cuireadh moill orm** I was delayed, **cad é an mhoill atá ort?** what's to stop you?

moilleadóireacht *f3* delaying

moilligh *v* delay

moillitheach *adj* delaying

moilliú *m* delay

móiminteam *m1* momentum

móin *f3* 1. turf, peat **móin a bhaint** to cut turf 2. moor

móinéar *m1* meadow

moing *f2* 1. mane **moing an chapaill** the horse's mane 2. swamp

móinteán *m1* bogland, moor

móiréis *f2* haughtiness

móiréiseach *adj* haughty, 'stuck up'

moirfín *m4* morphine

moirt *f2* dregs, sediment

moirtéal *m1* mortar

móitíf *f2* motif

mol *v* 1. praise, commend **mol an óige agus tiocfaidh sí** praise the youth and they will respond 2. recommend, advise **molaim duit gan é a dhéanamh** I advise you not to do it 3. propose **scéim a mholadh** to propose a scheme

moladh *m* 1. praise, compliment **thug sé an-mholadh di** he praised her immensely, **gáir mholta** cheer, shout of praise 2. recommendation, proposal **moltaí an choiste** the committee's recommendations

moltach *adj* complimentary

moltóir *m3* 1. umpire, adjudicator 2. referee 3. nominator, proposer

moltóireacht *f3* umpiring, adjudication

mómhar *adj* graceful, dignified

monabhar *m1* murmur(ing)

monagamach *adj* monogamous

monogamaí *m4* monogamist

monogamas *m1* monogamy

monailt *f2* monolith

monailiteach *adj* monolithic

monaíocht *f3* coinage

monaplacht *f3* monopoly

monarc *m4* monarch

monarcacht *f3* monarchy

monarcaí *m4* monarchist

monarcha *f* factory, plant **monarcha phróiseála** processing plant

monatóir *m3* monitor

monatóireacht *f3* monitoring **monatóireacht a dhéanamh ar rud** to monitor something

moncaí *m4* monkey

monsún *m1* monsoon **dúichí na monsún** the monsoon lands

monsúnach *adj* monsoon **foraois mhonsúnach** monsoon forest

monuar! *interj* alas!

mór[1] *adj* 1. big, great, extensive **tá croí mór aige** he has a big heart, **braithim uaim go mór í** I miss her greatly, **go mór mór** especially, **níos mó** bigger, more, **is mó** biggest, most, **fuair Pól an duais ba mhó** Pól got the biggest prize, **is í Síle is mó a bhí ag caint** it was mostly Síle who was talking 2. important, notable **tá lá mór roimhe amárach** he has a big / important day ahead of him, **bean mhór le rá** a notable woman 3. friendly **an bhfuil tú mór léi?** are you a friend of hers? 4. **ní mór …** it is necessary …, **ní mór duit an obair a dhéanamh** you have to do the work

mór[2] *m* 1. much, many 2. friendliness

mór[3] *v* 1. magnify, extol, increase **ag móradh a mhaoine** increasing his wealth 2. celebrate **ag móradh na Samhna** celebrating Hallowe'en 3. **móradh as rud** to boast about something mór-⁴ *prefix* big, main, major, great-, grand- **mórshrónach** big-nosed, **mórthráchtas** major thesis, **mórmhisneach** great courage

móráil *f3* pride, vanity **tá an mhóráil inti** she is vain

mórálach *adj* proud, vain **bheith mórálach as rud** to be proud of something

morálta *adj* moral

móráltacht *f3* morality

móramh *m1* majority

mórán *m1* many, much **mórán daltaí, tuismitheoirí** many pupils, teachers, **mórán oibre, ama** much work, time, **níl mórán céille / meabhrach aici** she hasn't much sense

mórchóir, **ar an mórchóir** on a large scale

mórchuid *f3* large amount / number **an mhórchuid den bhliain** most of the year, **mórchuid an phobail** the majority of the community

mórchúis *f2* self-importance, pride

mórchúiseach *adj* self-important, proud

mórdhíol *m3* wholesale, wholesaling **trádstóras mórdhíola** wholesale warehouse

mórdhíoltóir *m3* wholesaler **mórdhíoltóir íoc is iompair** cash-and-carry wholesaler

mórfhoclach *adj* boastful, high-sounding

mórfhoclacht *f3* boastfulness

mórga *adj* exalted, great, majestic

mórgacht *f3* greatness, majesty

morgáiste *m4* mortgage **morgáiste dearlaice** endowment mortgage

morgáistigh *v* mortgage

mórleabhar *m1* ledger

Mormannach *adj, m1* Mormon

mórphianó *m4* grand piano

mór-roinn *f2* continent **ar an Mór-Roinn** on the Continent (of Europe)

mórscála *m4* large scale **ar mhórscála** on a large scale

mórsheisear *m1* seven people

mórshiúl *m1* procession

mórtas *m1* pride

mórtasach *adj* proud, boastful

mórthaibhseach *adj* spectacular

mórthimpeall *adv, prep* all round **thaisteal siad mórthimpeall an domhain** they travelled all round the world

mórthír *f2* mainland **ar an mórthír** on the mainland

móruaisle *pl* nobility **maithe agus móruaisle** gentry and nobility

mósáic *f2* mosaic

Moscó *m4* Moscow

Moslamach *adj, m1* Muslim

móta *m4* moat

mótar¹ *m1* 1. motor **bád mótair** motor boat, **mótar dúisithe** starter motor 2. motor car

mótar-² *prefix* motorised, motor- **mótarghluaiste** motor-driven

mótarbhád *m1* motorboat

mótarbhealach *m1* motorway

mothaigh *v* 1. feel **ní mhothaím rómhaith** I don't feel too well 2. sense **mothóidh tú ar an gcaint nach bhfuil fáilte romhat** you will sense from the talk that you are not welcome 3. hear **ar mhothaigh tú a dhath?** did you hear anything?

mothaitheach *adj* perceptive

mothálach *adj* sensitive, responsive

mothall *m1* mop of hair

mothallach *adj* shaggy, hairy, bushy (*of hair*)

mothú *m* feeling, perception

mothúchán *m1* feeling, emotion

mothúchánach *adj* emotional

muc *f2* pig **muc ghuine** guinea pig, **muc mhara** porpoise, **cráin mhuice** sow, **bhí muc ar gach mala aige** he was frowning darkly, **íde na muc is na madraí a thabhairt do dhuine** to treat somebody badly, to give somebody terrible abuse, **ar mhuin na muice** 'on the pig's back', in luck

múcas *m1* mucus

múch¹ *f2* fumes **ag déanamh múiche** emitting fumes

múch² *v* 1. quench, extinguish, turn / switch off **is é an tae an deoch is fearr le tart a mhúchadh** tea is the best drink to quench thirst, **múch an solas** switch off the light 2. smother **tá sí múchta ag slaghdán** she is stuffed up with a cold

múchadh *m* 1. quenching **lucht múchta dóiteáin** firefighters 2. smothering, suffocation 3. asthma **tá an múchadh ag cur uirthi** she is suffering from asthma

múchta *adj* 1. quenched, extinguished, turned / switched off 2. smothered

múchtóir *m3* extinguisher **múchtóir dóiteáin** fire-extinguisher

muga *m4* mug

muiceoil *f3* pork **gríscíní muiceola** pork chops

muid *pron* we, us **agus muid ag feitheamh leat** and we waiting for you, **muid féin** ourselves

muidne *emphatic pron* we, us **muidne a bhí ann** it was us who were there

muileann *f2* mill **muileann gaoithe** windmill, **Baile an Mhuilinn** Milltown

muileata *m4* diamond (*cards*) **an t-aon muileata** the ace of diamonds

muilleáil *f3* milling *v* mill

muilleoir *m3* miller

muilleoireacht *f3* milling

Muimhneach *adj* Munster *m1* native of Munster

muin *f2* back **ar mhuin na muice** 'on the pig's back', in luck, **ar muin capaill** on horseback

múin *v* teach

muince *f4* necklace

muinchille *f4* sleeve

Muineachán *m1* Monaghan **Co. Mhuineacháin** Co. Monaghan

múineadh *m* 1. teaching, instruction **múineadh eolaíochta, teangacha** the teaching of science, languages 2. good behaviour **bíodh múineadh éigin ort** have some manners 3. moral (of a story)

muineál *m1* neck **chomh cinnte is atá ceann ar do mhuineál** as sure as you are alive

muinín *f2* 1. confidence, trust **níl muinín ar bith agam astu** I don't trust them at all, I have no confidence at all in them 2. dependence **dul i muinín duine, ruda** to depend, rely on somebody, something

muiníneach *adj* 1. trusting, confident 2. dependable, reliable

múinte *adj* polite, mannerly

muintearas *m1* 1. friendship **rinne siad muintearas le chéile** they made friends with each other 2. relationship, kinship **an bhfuil muintearas agat di?** are you related to her?

muinteartha *adj* 1. friendly **tá sí an-mhuinteartha** she is very friendly 2. related **daoine muinteartha** relations

múinteoir *m3* teacher **múinteoir bitheolaíochta** biology teacher

múinteoireacht *f3* teaching

muintir *f2* 1. people, folk **muintir na háite** the local people 2. family, parents **mo mhuintir** my family, **teach mo mhuintire** my parents' house **3. muintir Chearnaigh** the Ó Cearnaighs, **muintir Dhrisceoil** the Ó Drisceoils

muir *f3* sea **ar muir** at sea, **ar muir agus ar tír** on sea and land, **thar muir** beyond / over the sea, **chuamar ann de mhuir** we went there by sea, **truailliú na mara** marine pollution, **dlí na mara** maritime law, **maighdean mhara** mermaid, **éin mhara** sea-birds, **iascach mara** sea-fishing, **Bord Iascaigh Mhara** the Fishery Board, **an Mhuir Bhailt** the Baltic Sea, **Muir Éireann, an Mhuir Mheann** the Irish Sea, **Oileáin Mhuir nIocht** the Channel Islands

Muire *f4* Mary (*Bible*)

muirear *m1* **1.** responsibility, burden **ba mhór an muirear uirthi é** it was a great burden on her **2.** charge **muirear seasta** fixed charge **3.** family **an bhfuil muirear air?** has he a family (to support)?

muirghalar *m1* sea-sickness

muirí *adj, m4* marine, maritime

muirín[1] *f2* family **fear muirín** family man

muirín[2] *m4* scallop

múirín *m4* mould, compost **múirín potaithe** potting compost

muirneach *adj* affectionate, loving, caressing

muirnigh *v* fondle, caress

muirnín *m4* sweetheart, darling

muirshaothrú *m* mariculture

muirthéacht *f3* revolution

múisc *f2* vomit, feeling of nausea / disgust

múisciúil *adj* **1.** nauseous **2.** dank (*weather*)

múisiam *m4* **1.** upset, feeling of sickness / nausea **2.** drowsiness, heaviness

muisiriún *m1* mushroom

muislín *m4* muslin

mullach *m1* top, summit **mullach an tsléibhe** the mountain top / summit, **mullach do chinn** the top / crown of your head, **thit siad i mullach a chéile** they fell on top of one another, **cad a dhéanfaimid nuair a bheidh an geimhreadh sa mhullach orainn?** what will we do when winter is upon us?

mullard *m1* bollard

Mumhain *f5* Munster **Cúige Mumhan** (the province of) Munster

mún *m1* urine *v* urinate

mungail *v* **1.** chew **2.** mumble

múnla *m4* mould(ing), form, shape

múnlach *m1* liquid manure

múnlaigh *v* mould, form, shape

múnláil *f3* moulding

múnlú *m* moulding, shaping

múr *m1* **1.** wall, fortification, rampart **2.** abundance **chuir sí na múrtha fáilte romham** she gave me an overwhelming welcome

mura, murar, murab, murabh *conj* if not, unless **mura bhfuil dearmad orm** unless I am mistaken, **murar chaith tú an t-airgead cá bhfuil sé?** if you didn't spend the money where is it? **murab ionann is an fear eile** unlike the other man, **murab é an ceann sin é** if it isn't that one

murach *conj* if not, only **ní bhfaighinn é murach tusa** I wouldn't have got it only for you, **bheimis sa bhaile anois murach an mhoill** we'd be at home now only for the delay, **bheinn caillte anois murach gur chabhraigh tú liom** I'd be lost now had you not helped me

múrail *f3* showers **beidh múrail san iarthar** there will be showers in the west

murascaill *f2* gulf **Cogadh na Murascaille** the Gulf War, **Murascaill Mheicsiceo** the Gulf of Mexico

murlach *m1* lagoon

murlán *m1* knob **murlán an dorais** the doorknob

murlas(c) *m1* mackerel

múrmhaisiú *m* mural **múrmhaisithe** murals

murnán *m1* ankle

mursanta *adj* domineering, tyrannous

mursantacht *f3* domination, tyranny

murúch *f2* mermaid

mús *m1* moose

músaem *m1* museum

múscail *v* awake, wake up, rouse **múscail as a codladh í** wake her from her sleep

múscailt *f2* awakening, rousing

múscailte *adj* awake

múscán *m1* mould (*fungus*)

músclóir *f3* activator

múslaí *m4* muesli

mustar *m1* 1. muster, assembly 2. ostentation, arrogance **mustar a dhéanamh** to show arrogance

mustard *m1* mustard

mustrach *adj* ostentatious, pompous, arrogant

N

na the 1. (*pl of def art* **an**) **na cailíní** the girls, **na trioblóidí** the troubles, **na hainmhithe** the animals, **na húlla** the apples, **leithreas na mban, na bhfear** the womens', mens' toilets 2. (*f gen sing of def art* **an**) **ar fud na cruinne** throughout the world, **i rith na hoíche** during the night, **cóta na mná** the woman's coat, **muintir na hÉireann** the people of Ireland

ná¹ *neg v part* 1. *used with imperative* (do) not **ná bíodh aon eagla ort, oraibh** don't be afraid, **ná hól é** don't drink it, **ná smaoinigh air** don't think of him/it 2. *used with pres subjunctive of* **bí**, **ná raibh maith agat(sa)** no thanks to you, **sláinte chugat is cabhair, agus dealbh go deo ná rabhair** (= **raibh tú**) health and help to you, and may you never be destitute

ná² *conj* nor, or **níl bean ná páiste aige** he has neither wife nor child

ná³ *conj* than **is óige Seán ná Séamas** Seán is younger than Séamas, **is fearr an tsláinte ná na táinte** health is better than wealth, **níos fearr, níos mó ná ...** better, bigger than ...

ná⁴ *conj* but **cad a bheadh romham ná tarbh?** what should I find there but a bull?

ná⁵ *conj* (with *copula*) **is é a dúirt sí ná ...** what she said was ...

nach¹ *neg v part* 1. **nach bhfaca tú Máire?** did you not see Máire? **nach bhfuil sí dochreidte?** isn't she/it unbelievable? 2. **an té nach bhfuil láidir ní foláir dó a bheith glic** he who is not strong has to be clever, **sin é an cineál duine nach maith liom** that's the type of person I don't like

nach² *conj* that (*negative*) **dúirt sé nach raibh sé ann** he said he wasn't there, **ceapaim nach n-aithníonn sí mé** I think she doesn't recognise me, **b'fhéidir**

nach mbeadh aon dochar ann perhaps there will be no harm in him/it, **mar nach raibh mé ag smaoineamh i gceart** because I wasn't thinking properly

nach beag, nach mór *adv* almost

nádúr *m1* nature **ó nádúr** by nature, **tá nádúr inti** she has a kind nature

nádúrachas *m1* naturalism

nádúraí *m4* naturalist

nádúrtha *adj* natural, good-natured **acmhainní nádúrtha** natural resources

nádúrthacht *f3* naturalness, good-nature

naí *m4* infant

naíchóiste *m4* pram

náid *f2* nothing, nought, zero

naimhdeach *adj* hostile

naimhdeas *m1* enmity, spite, hostility

naíonacht *f3* infancy

naíonán *m1* infant **naíonán nuabheirthe** newborn infant

naíonlann *f2* nursery, crèche **naíonlann lae** crèche

naíonra *m4* kindergarten (school)

naipcín *m4* napkin

nairciseas *m1* narcissus

naircisíocht *f3* narcissism

náire *f4* shame, shyness, modesty **tá náire orm** I am ashamed, **mo náire thú!** shame on you! **ní ligfeadh an náire dom labhairt leo** I'd be ashamed to talk to them

náireach *adj* shameful, coy, modest

náirigh *v* shame

naíscoil *f2* nursery school, play-school, play-group

náisiún *m1* nation **na Náisiúin Aontaithe** the United Nations

náisiúnach *m1* national

náisiúnachas *m1* nationalism

náisiúnaí *m4* nationalist

náisiúnaigh *v* nationalise

náisiúnaíoch *adj* nationalistic

náisiúnta *adj* national **olltáirgeacht náisiúnta (OTN)** gross national product (GNP)

náisiúntacht *f3* nationality

Naitseachas *m1* Nazism

Naitsí *m4* Nazi

Naitsíoch *adj* Nazi

namhaid *m* enemy **fórsaí an namhad** enemy forces, **naimhde** enemies, **namhaid an phobail** public enemy

naofa *adj* holy

naofacht *f3* holiness

naoi *adj* nine **naoi gcarr dhearga** nine red cars, **naoi n-úll mhilse** nine sweet apples

naomh *m1* saint **Naomh Pádraig** Saint Patrick

naomhluan *m1* halo

naomhóg *f2* currach

naonúr *m1* nine people **naonúr cailíní, buachaillí, scoláirí** nine girls, boys, scholars, **naonúr fear, ban** nine men, women

naoscach *f2* snipe

naoscaire *m4* sniper (*shooting*)

naoscaireacht *f3* sniping

naoú¹ *m4* ninth **ocht naoú de** eight ninths of it

naoú² *adj* ninth **an naoú haois / céad** the ninth century, **an naoú lá déag de Lúnasa** the nineteenth (day) of August

naprún *m1* apron

nár¹ *neg v* part 1. who(m), which (*negative*) **bean nár phós riamh** a woman who never married, **cé mhéad duine nár tháinig?** how many people did not come? 2. **nár thug mé duit é?** did I not give it to you? 3. **nár fheice tú Dia!** may you never see God! blast you!

nár², **nárbh** see **is**

nasc *m1* tie, bond, link **nasc cábla** cable link *v* tie, bind, connect

nath *m3* adage **nath cainte** idiom, figure of speech

nathair *f5* snake **nathair shligreach** rattlesnake, **nathracha nimhe** poisonous snakes

nathán *m1* aphorism, adage

neach *m4* person, being **neacha daonna** human beings

neacht *f3* niece

neachtlann *f2* laundry

nead *f2* nest **nead éin** bird's nest, **nead damháin alla** spider's web

neadaigh *v* nest, nestle

neafais *f2* triviality, matter of little concern

neafaiseach *adj* trivial, unsubstantial

néal *m1* 1. cloud **néal doininne** storm-cloud 2. nap **ní raibh néal codlata aréir agam** I didn't get a wink of sleep last night

néaltach *adj* cloudy

neamart *m1* negligence, carelessness, neglect

neamartach *adj* negligent, neglectful

neamh¹ *f2* heaven

neamh-² *prefix* non-, un-, in- *suffix* less **neamh-inathnuaite** non-renewable, **neamhbháúil** unsympathetic, **neamh-aistreach** intransitive, **neamh-aireach** careless

neamhábalta *adj* incapable, unable

neamhábhartha *adj* immaterial, irrelevant

neamhaí *adj* heavenly, celestial

neamhaibí *adj* unripe, immature

neamhaiceanta *adj* unaccented

neamhaird *f2* disregard, inattention **thug siad neamhaird ar mo chomhairle** they disregarded my advice

neamhaireachtálach *adj* unconscious

neamhbhailí *adj* invalid

neamhbhailigh *v* invalidate

neamhbhalbh *adj* quick, unhesitating (*in speech*)

neamhbheo *adj* lifeless, dead, inanimate, still **ábhar neamhbheo** still life (*art*)

neamhbhlasta *adj* tasteless

neamhbhrabúsach *adj* non-profitable

neamhbhuan *adj* impermanent, temporary

neamhbhuartha *adj* untroubled, carefree

neamhbhuíoch *adj* ungrateful

neamhbhuíochas *m1* ingratitude

neamhchaifeach *adj* frugal, thrifty

neamhcháillthe *adj* unqualified

neamhchinnte *adj* uncertain

neamhchionmhar *adj* non-contributory

neamhchiontach *adj* not guilty, innocent

neamhchlaon *adj* impartial

neamhchlaontacht *f3* impartiality

neamhchodladh *m3* insomnia, sleeplessness

neamhchoinneálacht *f3* incontinence

neamhchoinníollach *adj* unconditional

neamhchóir *adj* unjust

neamhchoitianta *adj* unusual, uncommon

neamh-chomhoiriúnacht *f3* incompatibility

neamhchostasach *adj* inexpensive

neamhchosúil *adj* dissimilar, unlike

neamhchothrom *adj* uneven, unbalanced, unjust, unfair

neamhchríochnaithe *adj* incomplete, unfinished

neamhchúis *f2* lack of concern

neamhchúiseach *adj* indifferent, unconcerned

neamhchúram *m1* carelessness, neglect

neamhchúramach *adj* careless, negligent

neamhdhíobhálach *adj* harmless (**earra atá**) **neamhdhíobhálach don timpeallacht** environmentally friendly (product)

neamhdhóchúil *adj* unlikely

neamhdhuine *m4* nobody, nonentity

neamheaglach *adj* unafraid, fearless

neamhéifeacht *f3* inefficiency, incompetence

neamhéifeachtach *adj* inefficient, incompetent

neamheolach *adj* ignorant

neamheolas *m1* ignorance

neamhfhabhrach *adj* unfavourable

neamhfhaiteach *adj* fearless

neamhfheiceálach *adj* unnoticeable, inconspicuous

neamhfhicsean *m1* non-fiction

neamhfhiúntach *adj* unworthy

neamhfhoirfe *adj* incomplete, imperfect

neamhfhoirmiúil *adj* informal

neamhfhóirsteanach *adj* unsuitable

neamhfhonn *m1* unwillingness, reluctance

neamhfhonnmhar *adj* reluctant

neamhfhorbartha *adj* undeveloped

neamhfhreagrach *adj* not answerable

neamhghéilliúil *adj* insubordinate, unsubmissive, uncompromising

neamhghlan *adj* unclean, impure

neamhghnách *adj* unusual, uncommon

neamhghníomhach *adj* inactive, passive

neamh-inaistrithe *adj* non-negotiable, not negotiable (*cheque*)

neamhiomlán *adj* incomplete

neamhionann *adj* unequal, unlike

neamhionannas *m1* inequality

neamhláithreach *adj* absent

neamhláithreacht *f3* absence, absenteeism

neamhláithrí *m4* absentee

neamhlochtach *adj* blameless, faultless

neamh-mheisciúil *adj* non-alcoholic **beoir, deoch neamh-mheisciúil** non-alcoholic beer, drink

neamh-mhuinteartha *adj* unfriendly

neamhnáireach *adj* shameless

neamhní *m4* nothing, nil **ar neamhní** null, void

neamhoifigiúil *adj* unofficial

neamhoilte *adj* untrained, inexperienced

neamhoiriúnach *adj* unsuitable

neamhómósach *adj* disrespectful

neamhorgánach *adj* inorganic

neamhphearsanta *adj* impersonal

neamhpholaitiúil *adj* non-political

neamhphósta *adj* unmarried

neamh-ranníocach *adj* non-contributory

neamhréir *f2* inconsistency

neamhréireach *adj* inconsistent

neamhrialta *adj* irregular

neamhscagach *adj* impermeable

neamhscrupallach *adj* unscrupulous

neamhshaolta *adj* unworldly, unearthly

neamhsheasmhach *adj* unstable, inconsistent

neamhshocair *adj* restless, uneasy, unsteady

neamhshochrach *adj* unprofitable

neamhshocracht *f3* unrest, uneasiness, unsteadiness

neamhshrianta *adj* unrestricted **geilleagar margaidh neamhshrianta** free market economy

neamhshuim *f2* disregard, disinterest, indifference

neamhshuimiúil *adj* insignificant

neamhshúiteach *adj* non-absorbent

neamhshuntasach *adj* unnoticeable, inconspicuous

neamhspéis *f2* disinterest, indifference

neamhspéisiúil *adj* uninteresting, uninterested

neamhspleách *adj* independent

neamhspleáchas *m1* independence

neamhthábhacht *f3* unimportance

neamhthábhachtach *adj* unimportant

neamhthairbheach *adj* useless, unprofitable

neamhtharraingteach *adj* unattractive

neamhtheoranta *adj* unlimited **fiachas neamhtheoranta** unlimited liability

neamhthoilteanach *adj* reluctant, unwilling

neamhthorthúil *adj* infertile, unprofitable

neamhthrócaireach *adj* merciless, ruthless

neamhthruaillithe *adj* unspoiled, uncorrupted

neamhthuairimeach *adj* casual

neamhthuilleamaíocht *f3* self-sufficiency

neamhthuisceanach *adj* thoughtless, inconsiderate, uncomprehending

neamhthuiscint *f3* thoughtlessness, incomprehension

neamhúdaraithe *adj* unauthorised

neamhurchóideach *adj* harmless, inoffensive

neantóg *f2* nettle

néarchóras *m1* nervous system

néaróg *f2* nerve **cliseadh néaróg** nervous breakdown

néaróis *f2* neurosis

néaróiseach *adj* neurotic

néarólaíocht *f3* neurology

neart *m1* 1. strength, power, force **tá siad ag dul i neart** they are growing strong, becoming powerful 2. sufficient amount, plenty **tá neart ama againn** we have plenty of time 3. **níl neart air** it can't be helped, **níl neart agam air** I can't do anything about it

neartaigh *v* strengthen

neartmhar *adj* strong, powerful, forceful

neas- *prefix* approximate, close-, near-

neascóid *f2* boil (*on skin*)

neasghaol *m1* next of kin

neasluach *m3* approximate value

neasraon *m1* close range

néata *adj* neat

neirbhís *f2* nervousness

neirbhíseach *adj* nervous

neodrach *adj* neutral, neuter

neodracht *f3* neutrality

neodraigh *v* neutralise, neuter

neon *m1* neon **feadán neoin** neon tube, **soilse neoin** neon lights

ní[1] *m4* thing, something, nothing (*negative*) **an bhfuil aon ní le rá agat?** have you anything to say? **díolann sé nithe éagsúla** he sells various things, **ní nach ionadh** no wonder

ní[2] *f4* washing, cleansing

ní[3] *neg v part* **ní raibh mé ann** I was not there, **ní théann siad ann a thuilleadh** they don't go there any more, **ní dheachaigh siad abhaile fós** they didn't go home yet, **ní bhfaighidh tú pingin uaim** you won't get a penny from me

ní[4] *pres neg of copula* **ní amadán / óinseach mé** I'm not a fool, **an ainmhí é?** **ní hea** is it an animal? no, **ní maith liom an duine sin** I don't like that person, **nach maith leat tae?** **ní maith** do you not like tea? no (see **is**)

ní[5], **ní mé** I wonder

Ní[6], **Nuala Ní Shúilleabháin** Nuala O'Sullivan, **Lís Ní Chatháin** Lís Kane

nia *m4* nephew

nialas *m1* zero

niamh *f2* brightness, lustre, brilliance

niamhrach *adj* bright, lustrous

Nic/Nig, Eithne Nic Grianna Eithne Greene, **Méabh Nig Uidhir** Méabh Maguire

nicil *f2* nickel

nicitín *m4* nicotine

nigh *v* wash **na soithí a ní** to wash the dishes

nimh *f2* poison, venom **nimh francach** rat poison, **tá nimh san fheoil agam di** I hate her venomously

nimheanta *adj* venomous, spiteful

nimhigh *v* poison

nimhíoc *f2* antidote

nimhiú *m* poisoning **nimhiú ó luaidhe** lead poisoning

nimhiúil *adj* poisonous

nimhneach *adj* 1. painful, hurtful 2. touchy, over-sensitive, spiteful

níochán *m1* washing, laundry **meaisín níocháin** washing machine

níolón *m1* nylon

níor[1] *neg v part* **níor aithin tú mé** you didn't recognise me, **níor chuala mé thú** I didn't hear you, **níor tugadh tada di** she wasn't given anything, **níor casadh aon duine orm** I didn't meet anybody

níor[2] *past and cond neg of copula* **níor**

chluiche maith é it wasn't a good game, **níor mhaith liom a bheith ina áit** I wouldn't like to be in his position, **ar mhaith leat deoch?** **níor mhaith** would you like a drink? no (see **is**)

níorbh see **is**

níos *adv* 1. more **tá sé ag éirí níos fearr** it/he is getting better, **bhí níos mó, níos lú daoine ann i mbliana** there were more, fewer people there this year, **tá Proinsias níos airde ná mé** Proinsias is taller than me 2. (in past tense and conditional mood **níos** becomes **ní ba**) **bheadh saol ní ba shona againn** we'd have a happier life, **níor fhan sí ní b'fhaide** she didn't wait any longer

niteoir *m3* washer (*person*)

nithiúil *adj* concrete, real, actual

nítrigin *f2* nitrogen

niúmóine *m4* pneumonia

nó *conj* or **a trí nó a ceathair de bháid** four or five boats

nócha[1] *m5* ninety **sna nóchaidí** in the nineties

nócha[2] *adj* ninety **tá sí os cionn nócha bliain d'aois** she's over ninety years old

nóchadú[1] *m4* ninetieth

nóchadú[2] *adj* ninetieth

nocht *adj* naked, bare, revealed **téann siad ag snámh ann nocht** they go swimming naked there *m1* naked person, nude (*art*) *v* 1. bare, uncover, reveal **rún a nochtadh** to reveal a secret 2. appear **nocht an taibhse** the ghost appeared

nochtach *m1* naked person, nudist

nochtacht *f3* nudity

nochtadh *m* 1. exposure **nochtadh mígheanasach** indecent exposure 2. disclosure **nochtadh faisnéise rúnda** disclosure of secret information

nod *m1* 1. hint **ná tabhair aon nod dó** don't give him any hint 2. abbreviation

nódaigh *v* graft, transplant (*surgery, horticulture, etc*)

nódú *m* graft, transplant **nódú craicinn** skin graft

nóiméad *m1* minute, moment **beidh mé leat i gceann nóiméid** I'll be with you in a minute, moment

nóin *f3* 1. noon **roimh nóin** before noon, a.m., **um nóin** at noon 2. afternoon **bíonn sí ann ar maidin agus ar nóin** she is there morning and evening

nóinín *m4* daisy

nóisean *m1* 1. notion, idea **níl nóisean agam** I haven't a notion, an idea 2. fancy **tá nóisean aige di** he fancies her

noitmig *f2* nutmeg

Nollaig *f* 1. Christmas **maisiúcháin / rudaí na Nollag** Christmas decorations, **Oíche Nollag** Christmas Eve, **Lá Nollag** Christmas Day, **Nollaig faoi shéan agus faoi mhaise duit / daoibh! / Nollaig Shona (duit / daoibh)!** Happy Christmas! **Nollaig Bheag / Nollaig na mBan** Little Christmas 2. December **mí na Nollag** December, **31 Nollaig 1999** 31 December 1999

normálta *adj* normal

normáltacht *f3* normality

Normannach *adj, m1* Norman

nós *m1* 1. custom, habit **bhíodh sé de nós agam dul ann** I had a habit of going there, **nósanna imeachta** procedures, **nósanna itheacháin níos sláintiúla** healthier eating habits 2. **ar nós ...** like ..., in the manner of ..., **ar aon nós** anyway

nósmhar *adj* 1. formal, polite 2. customary, usual

nósúil *adj* particular, fashionable

nósúlacht *f3* particularity, mannerism

nóta *m4* note

nótáil *v* note

nótáilte *adj* notable **amhránaí nótáilte ba ea Máire Áine** Máire Áine was a notable singer

nótaire *m4* notary

nua[1] *adj* new, recent, modern **fear nua is ea anois é** he's a new man now, **an bealach is nua** the most recent way *m4* new thing **an sean agus an nua** the old and the new, **rud a thosú as an nua** to start something afresh

nua-[2] *prefix* new(ly)-, modern, recent **nuaphósta** newly-wed, **nua-stair** modern history

nua-aimseartha *adj* modern

nua-aoiseach *adj* modern

nuabheirthe *adj* newborn **naíonán, leanbh nuabheirthe** newborn infant, child

nuachar *m1* spouse

nuachóirigh *v* modernise

nuachóiriú *m* modernisation

nuacht *f3* news

nuachtán *m1* newspaper **na nuachtáin** the press, **nuachtáin lathaí** gutter press

nuachtánaí *m4* newsagent

nuachtlitir *f5* newsletter

nuachtpháipéar *m1* newsprint

Nua-Eabhrac *m4* New York

Nua-Ghaeilge *f4* Modern Irish **Roinn na Nua-Ghaeilge** the Department of Modern Irish

nuair *conj* when, since **nuair a fhillfidh sí abhaile** when she returns home, **d'imigh mé nuair nach raibh sé ann** I left since he wasn't there

nuanósach *adj* new-fashioned

Nua-Shéalainn, an *f2* New Zealand

nuatheanga *m4* modern language

núicléach *adj* nuclear

núicléas *m1* nucleus

nuige, go nuige until, as far as, **go nuige seo** up to now, hitherto

nuinteas *m1* nuncio (*papal*)

núíosach *m1* novice, beginner, newcomer

núis *f2* nuisance **bhí sé ag déanamh núise dó féin** he was making a nuisance of himself

O

ó¹ 1. *prep* (*prep prons* = **uaim, uait, uaidh, uaithi, uainn, uaibh, uathu**) from **ó thús (go) deireadh** from start to finish, **ó áit go háit** from place to place, **ó Chorcaigh go Béal Feirste** from Cork to Belfast, **an airíonn / mbraitheann tú uait í?** do you miss her? **céard tá (ag teastáil) uathu?** what do they want? **ná creid focal uaidh** don't believe a word from him, **saor ó ...** free of ..., **saor ó chaiféin, saor ó cháin, saor ó dhleacht, saor ó luaidhe** decaffeinated, tax-free, duty-free, unleaded **2.** *conj* since, after **ó d'imigh sí go dtí an Astráil** since she went to Australia, **ó tharla go raibh dearmad orm** since I happened to be mistaken, **ós againn a bhí an ceart** since we were in the right

ó², Dónall Ó Conaíle Dónall Connelly, **Seán Ó Tuathail** Seán O'Toole, **máthair Sheáin Uí Thuathail** Seán O'Toole's mother, **Mac, Bean, Iníon Uí Mhurchú** Mr, Mrs, Miss Ó Murchú, **Ráth Ó gCormaic** Rathgormuck (Port Laoise), **Uíbh Ráthach** Iveragh

ó³, ó dheas, ó thuaidh southwards, northwards

ob *v* refuse

obadh *m* refusal, rejection

obair *f2* work, labour **obair allamuigh, obair bhaile, obair láimhe, obair pháipéir, obair thógála** fieldwork, homework, handiwork, paperwork, construction work, **ag obair** working, at work, **lucht oibre** working class, labour (force), **Páirtí an Lucht Oibre** the Labour Party, **tá neart oibre ann** there's plenty of work there, **oibreacha uisce** waterworks, **Oifig na nOibreacha Poiblí** Office of Public Works

óbó *m4* oboe

obrádlann *f2* operating-theatre

obráid *f2* operation **dul faoi obráid** to go for an operation

ócáid *f2* occasion

ócáideach *adj* occasional, casual **obair ócáideach** casual work

ochón *excl* alas!

ocht¹ *m4* eight **a hocht déag** eighteen

ocht² *adj* eight **ocht dtuáille ghorma** eight blue towels, **na hocht n-asal bheaga** the eight small donkeys

ócht *f3* virginity

ochtagán *m1* octagon

ochtagánach *adj* octagonal

ochtapas *m1* octopus

ochtar *m1* eight people **ochtar cailíní, dochtúirí, fear, bean** eight girls, doctors, men, women

ochtó¹ *m5* eighty **ceol na n-ochtóidí** eighties music

ochtó² *adj* eighty **táimid ochtó míle ó Dhoire** we are eighty miles from Derry

ochtódú¹ *m4* eightieth **trí ochtódú** three eightieths

ochtódú² *adj* eightieth **an t-ochtódú buachaill, an t-ochtódú huair** the eightieth boy, the eightieth time, place

ochtú¹ *m4* eighth **seacht n-ochtú de rud** seven eighths of something

ochtú² *adj* eighth **an t-ochtú lá, an t-ochtú huair** the eighth day, the eighth time, place

ocrach *adj* hungry

ocras *m1* hunger **an bhfuil ocras ort?** are you hungry?

ocsaigin *f2* oxygen

ofráil *f3* offering *v* offer

óg *adj* young **cailín óg** young girl *m1* young (*person*) **beirt óga** two young ones

óganach *m1* young man, youth

ógbhean *f5* young woman

ógchiontóir *m3* juvenile delinquent

ógh *f2* virgin

ogham *m1* ogham **cloch oghaim** ogham stone, **aibítir oghaim** ogham alphabet

óglach *m1* volunteer (*military*) **Óglaigh na hÉireann** the Irish Volunteers

oibiachtúil *adj* objective

oibleagáid *f2* obligation **tá tú faoi oibleagáid di** you are under an obligation to her

oibreoir *m3* operator

oibrí *m4* worker, labourer **oibrí oilte, neamhoilte** skilled, unskilled worker

oibrigh *v* work, operate

oibríochtúil *adj* operational

oibriú *m* operation

oibriúchán *m1* operation **córas oibriúcháin** operating system (*computer*)

oíche *f4* night, eve **i rith na hoíche** during the night, **bíonn oícheanta ceoil acu ann** they have nights of music there, **Oíche Chinn Bliana** New Year's Eve, **Oíche Shamhna** Hallowe'en, **Oíche Nollag** Christmas Eve

oíchí *adj* nocturnal

oide *m4* teacher, tutor

oideachas *m1* education

oideas *m1* 1. teaching, instruction 2. prescription (*medicine*), recipe (*cookery*) **oideas dochtúra** doctor's prescription

oidhre *m4* heir

oidhreacht *f3* 1. inheritance, heritage **láthair / lárionad oidhreachta** heritage centre 2. legacy

oidhreachtúil *adj* hereditary

oifig *f2* office **oifig (an) phoist** post office

oifigeach *m1* officer **oifigeach rialúcháin ar talamh** ground control officer, **oifigeach cléireachais** clerical officer

oifigiúil *adj* official **tuairisc oifigiúil** official report

óige *f4* youth **brú, club óige** youth hostel, club, **is trua nach bhfanann an óige** it's a pity that youth doesn't last

úigeanta *adj* youthful

oigheann *m1* oven **oigheann micreathonnach** microwave oven

oighear *m1* ice

oighearaois *f2* ice-age

oigheareolaíocht *f3* glaciology

oighearshruth *m3* glacier

oighreach *adj* glacial

oighreata *adj* icy, frozen

oighreatacht *f3* iciness

oighrigh *v* ice, congeal, glaciate

oighriú *m* glaciation

oil *v* teach, train, foster, rear

oileán *m1* island **Oileán an Ghuail** Coalisland

oileánach *adj* insular *m1* islander **an tOileánach** the Islandman (*book*)

oileánrach *m1* archipelago

Oilimpeach *adj* Olympic **na Cluichí Oilimpeacha** the Olympic Games

oilithreach *m1* pilgrim

oilithreacht *f3* pilgrimage

oiliúint *f3* 1. training **oiliúint i gcuideachta** (in-)company training, **oiliúint foirne** staff training, **an rannóg oiliúna** the training section 2. rearing **is treise duchas ná oiliúint** nature is stronger than nurture

oiliúnú *m* training, coaching

oilte *adj* trained, skilled

oilteacht *f3* training, skill

oineach *m1* generosity, honour **rúnaí oinigh** honorary secretary

óinmhid *f2* simpleton, fool

oinniún *m1* onion

óinseach *f2* fool (*female*)

oir *v* fit, suit **ní oireann sé duit** it doesn't suit you

óir *conj* because, for **óir tharla sé go tobann** because / for it happened suddenly

oirdheisceart *m1* south-east

oireachtas *m1* assembly **an tOireachtas** the Legislature, **Oireachtas na Gaeilge** annual Irish-language festival run by Conradh na Gaeilge

oiread *m4* amount **oiread na fríde** the tiniest bit, **bhí a dhá oiread (daoine) ann anuraidh** there were twice as many (people) there last year, **ach oiread** either, **ní rachaidh mé féin ach oiread** I won't go either

oirirc *adj* illustrious, renowned

oiriúint *f3* suitability **cuir in oiriúint dóibh é** make it suitable / fitting for them, **oiriúintí** fittings, accessories

oiriúnach *adj* suitable, fitting

oiriúnacht *f3* suitability

oiriúnaigh *v* adapt, make suitable, fit

oirmhinneach *adj* reverend *m1* reverence

oirnigh *v* ordain

oirniú *m* ordination, inauguration

oirthear *m1* east **Bord Sláinte an Oirthir** the Eastern Health Board, **san Oirthear** in the Orient

oirthearach *adj* eastern, oriental **teanga oirthearach** oriental language

oirthuaisceart *m1* north-east

oiseoil *f3* venison

oisín *m4* 1. fawn 2. **Oisín** the son of Fionn Mac Cumhaill

oisre *m4* oyster

ól *m1* drink **teach óil** public house, **bheith tugtha don ól** to be fond of the drink *v* drink **níor ól mé ó shin** I haven't taken a drink since

ola *f4* oil **ola olóige** olive oil, **ola bhealaithe** lubricating oil, **an ola dhéanach** last rites

olach *adj* oily

ólachán *m1* drinking **babhta ólacháin** a drinking spree

olacheantar *m1* oilfield

olagón *m1* wailing, lament

olann *f5* wool **olann chadáis** cotton wool, **éadach olla** woollen cloth

olc *adj* bad, wicked, evil **tá Marcas go holc** Marcas is terribly ill, **níos measa, is measa** worse, worst, **is measa tusa ná iadsan** you are worse, more wicked than them, **is olc an ghaoth nach séideann do dhuine éigin** it's an ill wind that blows nobody good *m1* evil, wickedness, spite, anger **ná cuir olc orm** don't annoy me, don't make me angry

olcas *m1* badness, wickedness, evil **dá olcas é an áit seo is measa an áit eile** however bad this place is the other place is worse, **tá cúrsaí ag**

dul in olcas de réir a chéile bit by bit things are getting worse

oll- *prefix* great, vast, huge, gross **ollstailc** general strike, **olliompar** mass transportation, **ollinfheistíocht** gross investment

Ollainn, an *f2* Holland

ollamh *m1* professor **ollamh le stair** professor of history

Ollannach *adj* Dutch *m1* native of Holland

olldord *m1* double bass

ollghairdeas *m1* jubilation

ollmhaitheas *m3* wealth, luxury

ollmhargadh *m1* supermarket

ollmheáin, na **hollmheáin chumarsáide** the mass media

ollmhór *adj* enormous, huge

ollphéist *f2* monster, serpent

ollphuball *m1* marquee

ollscartaire *m4* bulldozer

ollscoil *f2* university **an Coláiste Ollscoile, Baile Átha Cliath** University College, Dublin, **mac léinn ollscoile** university student

ollscolaíocht *f3* university education

olltáirgeacht *f3* gross production **olltáirgeacht intíre, náisiúnta (OTI, OTN)** gross domestic, national product (GDP, GNP)

olltáirgeadh *m* mass production

olltáirgeolr *m3* mass producer

olltoghchán *m1* general election

ollúnacht *f3* professorship

ológ *f2* olive **ola olóige** olive oil, **crannológ** olive tree

óltach *adj* drunk

óltóir *m3* drinker

olúil *adj* oily

ómós *m1* respect, homage **in ómós do ...** in honour of ...

ómósach *adj* respectful

ómra *m4* amber

ómrach *adj* amber

onnmhaire *f4* export

onnmhaireoir *m3* exporter

onnmhairigh *v* export

onnmhairiú *m* exporting

onóir *f3* honour **bhain sí céim onóracha amach** she got an honours degree

onórach *adj* 1. honorable **duine onórach** honorable person 2. honorary **post onórach** honorary position

onóraigh *v* honour

optach *adj* optic

optaic *f2* optics

optúil *adj* optical

ór *m1* gold **fáinne óir** gold ring, **ní fhágfainn an áit ar ór na cruinne** I wouldn't leave the place for all the money in the world, **ní dhéanfainn ar ór ná ar airgead é** I wouldn't do it for any amount of money

óráid *f2* oration, speech, address

óráidí *m4* orator

óráidíocht *f3* speech-making

oráiste *m4* orange (*fruit*) **deoch oráistí** orange drink

Oráisteach *m1* Orangeman

Oráisteachas *m1* Orangeism

órcheardaí *m4* goldsmith

ord[1] *m1* 1. order, arrangement, procedure **cuir in ord aibítre iad** put them in alphabetical order 2. religious community **ord crábhaidh** religious order

ord[2] *m1* sledgehammer

ordaigh *v* order, prescribe **díreach mar a d'ordaigh an dochtúir** exactly what the doctor ordered, prescribed

ordaitheach *m1* imperative (*grammar*)

ordanás *m1* ordnance **an tSuirbhéireacht Ordanáis** the Ordnance Survey

órdhonn *adj* auburn

ordóg *f2* thumb **ordóg do choise** your big toe, **tá sí faoin ordóg aige** she is under his thumb

ordú *m* ordering, order, command **ordú cúirte, poist** court, postal order, **rudaí a choinneáil in ordú** to keep things in order

ordúil *adj* orderly, neat

órga *adj* golden

orgán *m1* organ **orgáin an ghutha** the vocal organs, **orgáin atáirgthe fireann, baineann** male, female reproductive organs, **orgán béil** mouth organ

orgánach *adj* organic *m1* organism

orlach *m1* inch **tomhais ina orlaí é** measure it in inches

ornáid *f2* ornament

ornáideach *adj* ornamental

ornáideachas *m1* ornamentation

ornáidigh *v* ornament

órnite *adj* gilded, gilt

órphlátáil *f3* gold-plating

órphlátáilte *adj* gold-plated **bráisléad órphlátáilte** gold-plated bracelet

órshúlach *m1* golden syrup

ortadocsach *adj, m1* orthodox

ortaipéideach *adj* orthopaedic **leaba ortaipéideach** orthopaedic bed

ortha *f4* spell, charm **Ortha na Seirce** the Love Spell

os *prep* above, over **os ard** aloud, **os cionn** over, above, **os comhair** in front of, opposite

ósais *f2* oasis

oscail *v* open **ní osclaíonn an siopa sin go dtí a deich a chlog** that shop doesn't open until ten o'clock

oscailt *f2* opening **oscailt súl a bhí ann** it was an eye-opener

oscailte *adj* open

oscailteacht *f3* 1. openness 2. exposure

osclóir *m3* opener **osclóir buidéal** bottle-opener

osna *f4* sigh **lig sí osna** she sighed

osnádúrtha *adj* supernatural

osnaíl *f3* sighing

ospidéal *m1* hospital **ospidéal máithreachais** maternity hospital

ospís *f2* hospice

osréalach *adj* surrealist

osréalachas *m1* surrealism

ósta *m4* 1. hospitality, lodging 2. **(teach) ósta** inn, public house

óstach *m1* host

óstaíocht *f3* hospitality, lodging

Ostair, an *f2* Austria

óstán *m1* hotel

Ostarach *adj, m1* Austrian

osteilgeoir *m3* overhead projector

óstlann *f2* hotel

óstóir *m3* hotelier, publican

ostrais *f2* ostrich

othar *m1* invalid, patient

otharcharr *m1* ambulance

otharlann *f2* infirmary, hospital

othras *m1* 1. sickness 2. ulcer

ózón *m1* ozone **ciseal an ózóin** the ozone layer

P

pá *m4* pay, wage(s) **pá íosta** minimum wage(s), **pá seachtaine, míosa** weekly, monthly wage

pábháil *f3* paving **cloch / leac phábhála** paving stone *v* pave **gairdín pábháilte** paved garden

paca *m4* pack **paca bligeard** a pack of blackguards, **paca cártaí** pack of cards

pacáil *f3* packing *v* pack

pacáiste *m4* package **pacáiste pá** pay packet

págánach *m1* pagan

págánacht *f3* paganism

págánta *adj* pagan

paicéad *m1* packet

paidir *f2* prayer **rinne sé paidir chapaill de** he dragged the story out

paidreoireacht *f3* praying

paidrín *m4* 1. rosary 2. rosary beads **is é an chloch is mó, is lú ar mo phaidrín é** it is my greatest, least concern

Páil *f2* **an Pháil** the Pale

pailin *f2* pollen

pailléad *m1* pallet

pailliún *m1* pavilion

pailm *f2* palm (tree)

paimfléad *m1* pamphlet

paincréas *m1* pancreas

paindiachas *m1* pantheism

painéal *m1* panel **painéal ionstraimí** instrument panel

painéaladh *m* panelling

páipéar *m1* paper **páipéar balla, páipéar carbóin, páipéar leithris, páipéar nuachta, páipéar rianúcháin, páipéar súite** wallpaper, carbon paper, toilet paper, newspaper, tracing paper, blotting paper, **beart páipéir** bundle of paper, **siopa páipéir** stationer's shop, **páipéar bán, uaine** white, green paper (*politics*)

páipéarachas *m1* stationery

páirc *f2* field, park **páirc imeartha** playing-field, **Páirc an Fhionnuisce** Phoenix Park

páirceáil *f3* parking **ált pháirceála** parking space / place *v* park

páircíneach *adj* checquered (*cloth*)

pairifín *m4* paraffin

pairilis *f2* paralysis

pairilíseach *adj* paralytic

páirt[1] *f2* 1. part, portion **sna páirteanna seo** in these parts 2. role **páirt neamhghníomhach** passive role 3. **i bpáirt le … in** partnership with …

páirt-[2] *prefix* partial, part- **páirtéiclips** partial eclipse

páirtaimscartha *adj* part time

páirteach *adj* partaking, sharing, participating

páirteachas *m1* participation

páirteagal *m1* particle (*grammar*)

páirtghlacadh *m* role-playing

páirtí *m4* partner, party **páirtí leasmhar** interested party, **an Páirtí Daonlathach (PDanna)**, Progressive Democrats (PDs)

páirtíneach *m1* partisan

páirtíocht *f3* partnership, involvement **tá siad i bpáirtíocht le chéile** they are in partnership together, **páirtíocht rialtais** government involvement

páirtiú *m* sharing **páirtiú in obair, páirtiú i mbrabús** job sharing, profit sharing

páis *f2* suffering, passion **Seachtain na Páise** Holy Week

paisean *m1* passion

paiseanta *adj* passionate

páiseog *f2* passion fruit

paisinéir *m3* passenger

paiste *m4* patch **paiste tiúbdheisithe** tube repair patch, **obair phaistí** patchwork, **paiste a chur ar bhríste** to patch trousers

páiste *m4* child **feighle páistí** childminder, babysitter

paisteáil *f3* patching *v* patch

paistéar *v* pasteurise **bainne paistéartha** pasteurised milk

páistiúil *adj* childish

páistiúlacht *f3* childishness

paiteanta *adj* patent, clear, definite, correct

paiteolaí *m4* pathologist

paiteolaíoch *adj* pathological

paiteolaíocht *f3* pathology **an roinn paiteolaíochta** the pathology department

paitinn *f2* patent **cearta paitinne** patent rights

Palaistín *f2* **an Phalaistín** Palestine

Palaistíneach *adj, m1* Palestinian

pálás *m1* palace

pána *m4* pane **pána gloine, fuinneoige** glass, window pane

Pan-Cheilteach *adj* Pan-Celtic **an Fhéile Phan-Cheilteach** the Pan-Celtic Festival

pancóg *f2* pancake

panda *m4* panda

pantar *m1* panther

pápa *m4* pope

pápach *adj* papal

pápacht *f3* papacy

pár *m1* parchment **ar phár** on paper, recorded, **peann agus pár** pen and paper

parabal *m1* parable

paradacsa *m4* paradox

paradacsúil *adj* paradoxical

paragraf *m1* paragraph

paráid *f2* parade

parailéal *m1* parallel **tá siad i bparailéal le chéile** they are parallel with each other

parailéalach *adj* parallel

paraimíleatach *adj, m1* paramilitary

paraisít *f2* parasite

paraisiút *m1* parachute

paramhíochaineoir *m3* paramedic

paranóia *f4* paranoia

paranóiach *adj* paranoiac

Páras *m4* Paris

parasól *m1* parasol, umbrella

pardún *m1* pardon **gabhaim pardún!** pardon me!

parlaimint *f2* parliament **Parlaimint na hEorpa** the European Parliament

parlaiminteach *adj* parliamentary

parlús *m1* parlour

paróiste *m4* parish

paróisteach *adj* parochial *m1* parishioner

párolla *m4* payroll

parthas *m1* paradise **Gairdín Pharthais** the Garden of Eden

parúl *m1* parole **ar parúl** on parole

pas *m4* 1. pass **d'éirigh léi pas a fháil sa scrúdú** she succeeded in getting a pass in the exam 2. passport, permit **pas bordála** boarding pass 3. bout, spell, bit **pas rince** bout of dancing, **pas déanach** a little bit late, latish

pasáil *v* pass (*exam, ball, etc*)

pasáiste *m4* passage, corridor

pasfhocal *m1* password

pasta *m4* pasta

páthairiscint *f3* pay offer

patraisc *f2* partridge

patról *m1* patrol **bheith ar patról** to be on patrol

patrún *m1* pattern, design

pátrún *m1* patron

pátrúnacht *f3* patronage

patuaire *f4* indifference

patuar *adj* lukewarm, non-enthusiastic

pé *adj, conj, pron* 1. whoever, whatever, whichever **pé hiad féin** whoever they are, **pé am a oireann duit** whatever time suits you, **pé áit a bhfuair tú é** wherever you got it, **pé acu den bheirt againn a bhuaigh** whichever of the two of us won, **pé acu Tomás nó Ruth a dúirt é** whether it was Tomás or Ruth who said it, **pé scéal é** anyhow 2. whether **pé olc maith leis é** whether he likes it or not

péac *v* germinate, sprout

peaca *m4* sin **peaca an tsinsir** original sin, **peaca marfach** mortal sin

peacach *adj* sinful *m1* sinner

péacach *adj* 1. pointed, peaked **caipín péacach** peaked cap 2. showy, colourful

peacaigh *v* sin

péacán *m1* sprout, bud, shoot

péacóg *f2* peacock **Amharclann na Péacóige** the Peacock Theatre

péacógach *adj* vain

peacúil *adj* sinful

peann *m1* pen **peann luaidhe** pencil, **peann albhsithe** highlighter, **cara pinn** pen friend

peannaid *f2* pain, torment, punishment

peannaideach *adj* penal, painful

péarla *m4* pearl **bráisléad péarlaí** pearl bracelet

pearóid *f2* parrot

pearsa *f5* person, character (*in story etc*)

pearsanaigh *v* impersonate

pearsanra *m4* personnel **an rannóg pearsanra** the personnel department

pearsanta *adj* personal, personable

pearsantacht *f3* personality

pearsantú *m* personification

pearsanú *m* impersonation

peasghadaí *m4* pickpocket

peata *m3* pet **peata lae** 'pet' day, **is í peata an mhúinteora í** she is the teacher's pet

péatar *m1* pewter

péidiatraic *f2* paediatrics

péidifile *m4* paedophile

péidifilia *m* paedophilia

peidléir *m3* pedlar

peidléireacht *f3* peddling

peil *f2* football **cluiche peile** game of football, **ag imirt peile** playing football, **foireann peile** football team, **peil ghaelach** gaelic football

peilbheas *m1* pelvis

peileacán *m1* pelican

peileadóir *m3* footballer

péindlí *m4* penal law **na Péindlíthe** the Penal Laws

peinicillin *f2* penicillin

péint *f2* paint **brat péinte** coat of paint, **péint lonrach** gloss paint

peinteagán *m1* pentagon

peinteatlán *m1* pentathlon

péinteáil *f3* painting *v* paint

péintéir *m3* painter

péintéireacht *f3* painting (*art*)

péintrollóir *m3* paint roller

péire *m4* pair **níl agam ach péire** I've only two, a pair, **nach deas an péire iad** don't they make a nice pair, couple

peireascóp *m1* periscope

peiriméadar *m1* perimeter

péirse *f4* perch

Peirse *f4* **an Pheirse** Persia, **Murascaill na Peirse** the Persian Gulf

Peirseach *adj, m1* Persian

peirsil *f2* parsley **peirsil agus tím** parsley and thyme

peirspictíocht *f3* perspective (*drawing*)

péist *f2* 1. worm **péist talún** earthworm, **casadh na péiste** the worm turning 2. serpent, reptile **péist mhara** sea-serpent

peitreal *m1* petrol

peitriliam *m4* petroleum

péitseog *f2* peach (*fruit*)

piachán *m1* hoarseness

piachánach *adj* hoarse

pian *f2* pain **tá pian orm, táim i bpian** I'm in pain

pianbhreith *f2* sentence **cuireadh pianbhreith (bháis) orthu ar maidin** they were sentenced (to death) this morning

pianmhar *adj* painful

pianmhúchán *m1* painkiller

pianó *m4* piano

pianóchairdín *m4* piano-accordion

pianódóir *m3* pianist

piardán *m1* prawn

piardóg *f2* crayfish

piasún *m1* pheasant

píb *f2* pipe (*musical*) **ag seinm ar na píoba** playing the pipes, **píb uilleann** uilleann pipes, **píb mhála** bagpipes

píblíne *f4* pipeline **píblíne gháis nádúrtha** natural gas pipeline

pic *f2* pitch

píce *m4* 1. fork **píce féir** hayfork, **píce trí bheann** three-pronged fork 2. peak (*of cap, sail, etc*) **Síle an phíce** earwig

picéad *m1* picket **picéad glan amach** all-out picket

picéadaigh *v* picket

picéadú *m* picketing

píchairt *f2* pie chart

picil *f2, v* 1. pickle 2. dip (*food*)

picilte *adj* pickled

picnic *f2* picnic

pictiúr *m1* picture, painting **dul chuig na pictiúir** to go to the pictures, **pictiúr a tharraingt** to draw, take a picture

pictiúrlann *f2* cinema, picture-house

pictiúrtha *adj* picturesque

pigmí *m4* pygmy

piléar *m1* 1. bullet **piléar pollta armúir** armour-piercing bullet, **piléar a scaoileadh le duine, rud** to fire a bullet at somebody, something 2. pillar

píléaráid *f2* pie diagram

piléardhíonach *adj* bullet-proof **veist philéardhíonach** bullet-proof vest

piliúr *m1* pillow **cogar an philiúir** pillow-talk

pillín *m4* pad **pillíní coscáin** brake pads

pingin *f2* penny **dhá phingin** two pence, **trí, ceithre, cúig, sé pingine** three, four, five, six pence, **seacht, ocht, naoi, deich bpingine** seven, eight, nine, ten pence, **luach do phingine a fháil** to get your money's worth, **pinginí beaga airgid** small sums of money

pinsean *m1* pension **pinsean seanaoise** old-age pension

pinsinéir *m3* pensioner **pinsinéir seanaoise** old-age pensioner, OAP

píobaire *m4* piper

píobaireacht *f3* 1. piping 2. (uilleann, bag) pipe music

píobán *m1* 1. pipe, windpipe, tube **píobán fuíollábhair** waste pipe, **fliuch do phíobán leis** wet your whistle with it (*said of drink*), **píobán garbh** trachea, **píobán sceite** exhaust pipe 2. throat, neck **rug mé greim píobáin air** I grabbed him by the throat 3. hose **píobán dóiteáin** fire-hose

píobar *m1* pepper

pioc[1] *m4* jot, bit **níl mé pioc buartha** I'm not a bit worried, **tá sí gach uile phioc chomh maith leatsa** she is every bit as good as you

pioc[2] *v* 1. pick, choose **pioctar duine as gach míle** one person in every thousand is picked 2. pluck **cearc a phiocadh** to pluck a chicken

piocadh *m4* picking, pick

piochán *m1* pore (*of skin*)

piocóid *f2* pickaxe

pioctha *adj* spruce, neat **pioctha bearrtha** spick and span

piocúil *adj* 1. tidy, neat 2. smart, quick

pióg *f2* pie **pióg an aoire** shepherd's pie, **pióg úll** apple pie, **pióg mhuiceola** pork pie

piollaire *m4* 1. pill 2. pellet

píolón *m1* pylon

píolóta *m4* pilot

píolótach *adj* pilot **clár píolótach** pilot programme

píolótaigh *v* pilot **eitleán a phíolótú** to pilot a plane

piongain *f2* penguin

pionna *m4* peg, pin **pionna éadaigh, pionna pubaill** clothes-peg, tent-peg, **plocóid trí phionna** three pin plug

pionós *m1* punishment, penalty **cuireadh pionós báis air** he got the death penalty

pionósaigh *v* punish, penalise

pionsóir *f3* fencer, swordsman

pionsóireacht *f3* fencing (*sport*)

pionsúirín *m4* tweezers

pionsúr *m1* pincers

pionta *m4* pint **pionta pórtair** a pint of porter

píopa *m4* pipe **píopa a chaitheamh** to smoke a pipe, **píopaí uisce** water-pipes

piorra *m4* pear **crann piorraí** pear tree

píosa *m4* piece **píosa cáca / císte** piece of cake, **rinne sé píosaí de** he broke it into pieces, **píosa óir** gold piece

píosáil *v* patch, piece together

píosáilte *adj* patched, pieced together

piostal *m1* pistol

Piréiní, na *pl* the Pyrenees

pirimid *f2* pyramid

pis *f2* pea **piseanna talún** peanuts

piscín *m4* kitten

piseán *m1* pea

piseánach *m1* lentils, peas, pulse

piseog *f2* 1. superstition, pishogue 2. charm, spell **piseog a dhéanamh** to cast a spell

piseogach *adj* superstitious

piteogach *adj* effeminate

pitseámaí *pl* pyjamas

piúratánach *adj* puritanical *m1* puritan

piúratánachas *m1* puritanism

pizza *m4* pizza

plá *f4* 1. plague **plá mhíoltóg a** plague of midges 2. pest (*of person*)

plab *m4* slam, bang **dhún mé an doras de phlab** I slammed the door *v* slam, bang **plabadh an doras** the door was slammed

plaic *f2* bite **bhain mé plaic as an úll** I took a bite of the apple

pláigh *v* 1. plague 2. pester

pláinéad *m1* planet **pláinéid dhomhanda** terrestrial planets

pláinéadach *adj* planetary **timthriall pláinéadach** planetary cycle

plaisteach *adj* plastic **mála plaisteach** plastic bag *m1* plastic **plaisteach lannach** laminated plastic

pláistéir *m3* plasterer

plait *f2* bald head, bald patch

pláitín *f4* knee-cap

plámás *m1* flattery

plámásach *adj* flattering

plána *m4* plane (*carpentry*)

plánáil *v* plane

planda *m4* plant

plandaigh *v* plant

plandáil *f3* plantation **Plandáil na Mumhan, Plandáil Uladh** the Plantation of Munster, the Plantation of Ulster

plandlann *f2* nursery (*botanic*)

plandúil *adj* vegetal, plant-like

plás *m1* 1. level place, lawn, plot 2. place **Plás Mhic Liam** Fitzwilliam Place

plásaíocht *f3* flattery

plásánta *adj* smooth **caint phlásánta** smooth talk

plásóg *f2* lawn, green (*golf*)

plástar *m1* plaster **plástar Pháras** plaster of Paris

plástarchlár *m1* plasterboard

plástráil *f3* plastering *v* plaster

plástrálaí *m4* plasterer

pláta *m4* plate **pláta armúir** armour plate

plátáilte *adj* armoured **carr plátáilte, long phlátáilte** armoured car, armoured ship

platanam *m1* platinum

plé *m4* 1. disputation, discussion **an mbeidh aon phlé ar an ábhar?** will there be any discussion on the matter? 2. dealings **ní raibh plé agam leo ó shin** I haven't had any dealings with them since

pléadáil *f3* 1. plea 2. disputation *v* 1. plead 2. dispute

plean *m4* plan **plean forbartha** development plan, **plean deartha** design plan

pleanáil *f3* planning **pleanáil straitéiseach** strategic planning, **pleanáil clainne** family planning *v* plan **rud a phleanáil** to plan something

pleanálaí *m4* planner

pléaráca *m4* uproar, revelry

pléasc *f2* explosion, bang, burst **ollphléasc** 'big bang', **de phléasc** suddenly, like a shot *v* explode, burst **phléasc an buama ar a trí ar maidin** the bomb exploded at three in the morning

pléascach *adj* explosive **ábhar tréanphléascach** highly explosive material

pléascadh *m4* explosion

pléascán *m1* explosive, blast, bomb **tréanphléascáin** high explosives

pléascóg *f2* cracker **pléascóga Nollag** Christmas crackers

pléata *m4* pleat

pléatáil *v* pleat

pleidhce *m4* simpleton, fool **a phleidhce!** you fool!

pleidhcíocht *f3* acting foolishly, fooling **ná bí ag pleidhcíocht** don't be messing

pleidhciúil *adj* stupid, foolish

pléigh *v* 1. discuss, debate **an cheist a phlé** to discuss the question 2. plead, dispute 3. **pléigh le** deal with

pléisiúr *m1* pleasure

pléisiúrtha *adj* entertaining, enjoyable, pleasant

plimp *f2* sudden crash, bang **de phlimp** instantaneously, **plimpeanna toirní** thunderclaps

plocóid *f2* plug **plocóid trí phionna** three pin plug

plód *m1* crowd

plódaigh *v* fill up, crowd, throng

plódaithe *adj* crowded

plódcheantar *m1* slum (*district*)

plódteach *m* slum

plódú *m* crush, jam, overcrowding **plódú tráchta** traffic jam

plota *m4* plot

pluais *f2* cave, den

pluc *f2* cheek

plucamas *m1* mumps

plúch *v* 1. suffocate, smother **plúchadh sa teas muid** we were suffocated in the heat 2. fall heavily (*snow*) **tá sé ag plúchadh sneachta** it is snowing heavily

plúchadh *m* 1. suffocation 2. asthma **tá plúchadh uirthi** she suffers from asthma 3. heavy downfall **plúchadh sneachta** heavy fall of snow

plúchtach *adj* suffocating, stuffy, stifling

pluda *m4* slush, mud

pludach *adj* slushy, muddy

pludgharda *m4* mudguard

pluga *m4* plug

pluid *f2* blanket

pluiméir *m3* plumber

pluiméireacht *f3* plumbing

plúirín *m4* 1. little flower **plúiríní sneachta** snowdrops 2. pretty girl

pluma *m4* plum **crann plumaí** plum tree

plúr *m1* 1. flour **plúr éiritheach** self-raising flour 2. flower **plúr na maighdean** the choicest of maidens

plus *m4* plus (sign) **a seacht déag plus a naoi** seventeen plus nine

Plútó *m4* Pluto

pobal *m1* people, community, population **os comhair an phobail** in public, **fear an phobail** ombudsman, **namhaid an phobail** public enemy, **pobal tuaithe** rural community, **pobal uirbeach** urban population / community, **pobal oibre / saothair** working population, **tá sé i mbéal an phobail** everyone is talking about it / him, **teach pobail** church, chapel

pobalbhreith *f2* 1. plebiscite 2. opinion poll

pobalfheasacht *f3* community awareness

pobalscoil *f2* community school **Pobalscoil Chábán tSíle** Cabinteely Community School

poblacht *f3* republic **gluaiseacht na poblachta** the republican movement

poblachtach *adj, m1* republican

poblachtachas *m1* republicanism

poc *m1* 1. buck, he-goat **poc gabhair** billy-goat 2. blow, puck (*in hurling, boxing, etc*) **poc saor** free puck

póca *m4* pocket **bheith ar phócaí folmha** to be penniless / broke, **(teilea)fón póca, guthán póca** mobile (tele)phone

pócar *m1* poker (*cards*)

pocléimneach *f2* frolicking

póg *f2* kiss *v* kiss **chaith sé póg chugam** he blew a kiss at me

poibleog *f2* poplar

poiblí *adj* public **oifigeach caidrimh phoiblí (OCP)** public relations officer (PRO)

poibligh *v* make public, publicise

poiblíocht *f3* publicity

póillín *m4* policeman, policewoman **na póilíní** the police

póilínigh *v* police

poimp *f2* pomp

poimpéis *f2* pomposity

poimpéiseach *adj* pompous

pointe *m4* point **ar an bpointe (boise)** immediately, instantly, **pointe cumhachta** power point, **pointe dáilte** distribution point,

pointe fiuchta, leáite boiling, melting point, **pointe eolais** point of information (*debating*), **pointe tagartha** reference point, **pointe trasnaithe** point of intersection, **pointe deachúil** decimal point, **nócha a naoi pointe a naoi faoin gcéad** ninety nine point nine per cent

pointeáilte *adj* 1. exact, punctual 2. particular, fussy

pointeáilteacht *f3* 1. exactness, punctuality 2. particularity, fussiness

poipín *m4* poppy

poirceallán *m1* porcelain **soithí poircealláin** china

póirín *m4* small round stone, small potato **póirín cloiche** pebble

póirse *m4* porch

póirseáil *f3* rummaging, searching

póirseálaí *m4* rummager, searcher

póit *f2* 1. excessive drinking 2. hangover **leigheas na póite** the cure of a hangover

poitigéir *m3* chemist

poitín *m4* poteen

póitseáil *f3* poaching

póitseálaí *m4* poacher

pol *m1* pole **an pol theas, an pol thuaidh** the south pole, the north pole

polach *adj* polar

polagán *m1* polygon

polaimiailíteas *m1* polio(myelitis)

Polainn *f2* **an Pholainn** Poland

Polainnis *f2* Polish (*language*)

polaiteoir *m3* politician

polaitíocht *f3* politics

polaitiúil *adj* political

Polannach *adj* Polish *m1* Pole

polaraigh *v* polarise **polaraithe** polarised

polarú *m* polarisation

polasaí *m4* policy **polasaí árachais** insurance policy, **polasaí an Rialtais** Government policy

poll *m1* 1. hole, pit **rud a chur i bpoll** to hide something, **poll eochrach** keyhole, **poll guail** coalpit 2. puncture **fearas deisithe poill** puncture repair kit 3. sea **chuaigh an bád go tóin poill** the boat sank *v* 1. hole, perforate, pierce 2. puncture **bonn a pholladh** to puncture a tyre

polla *m4* pole, post

polladh *m* piercing, perforation **piléar pollta armúir** armour-piercing bullet

polláire *m4* nostril

pollóg *f2* pollock (*fish*)

polltach *adj* piercing, stabbing **pian pholltach** stabbing pain

póló *m4* polo **cluiche póló uisce** game of water polo

pomagránait *f2* pomegranate

pónaí *m4* 1. pony 2. ponytail (*in hair*)

pónaire *f4* bean

ponc *m1* 1. point, dot, full stop 2. detail, point **ponc dlí** point of law 3. difficulty, 'fix' **táimid i bponc** we're in a fix

poncaíocht *f3* punctuation

Poncánach *adj*, *m1* Yank, American

poncúil *adj* precise, exact, punctual

poncúlacht *f3* punctuality

popcheol *m1* pop music

pór *m1* breed, seed **tá pór Gearmánach inti** she has German blood in her, **na pórtha a bhaint as rud** to extract the seeds from something

póraigh *v* breed, propagate

pornagrafaíocht *f3* pornography

port[1] *m1* 1. tune **bíonn an port céanna acu i gcónaí** they never change their tune, **tá do phort seinnte anois** you're done for now 2. jig

port² *m1* harbour, port **port na bpaisinéirí** passenger terminal, **Port an Dúnáin** Portadown (*Co. Armagh*), **an Port Thoir** East Wall (*Dublin*)

portach *m1* bog

Portaingéalach *adj, m1* Portuguese

Portaingéil *f2* **an Phortaingéil** Portugal

Portaingéilis *f2* Portuguese (*language*)

portaireacht *f3* humming, lilting

portán *m1* crab **an Portán** Cancer

pórtar *m1* porter **pionta pórtair** a pint of porter

pórtfhion *m3* port (*wine*)

pórtheastas *m1* pedigree

Port Láirge *m* Waterford **Co. Phort Láirge** Co. Waterford

portráid *f2* portrait

pórú *m* breeding

pós *v* marry

pósadh *m* marriage, wedding **bheith ag / ar pósadh** to be at a wedding

pósae *m4* posy

post *m1* 1. post **an Post** the postal service, **saorphost** freepost, **liosta poist** mailing list, **oifig (an) phoist** (the) post office, **fear an phoist** the postman, **post de mhuir is de thalamh** overseas surface mail 2. job, position, post **tá an-phost aici** she has a great job, **post maoirseachta** supervisory position, **post faire** look-out post (*military*)

pósta *adj* married **bean phósta** a married woman

póstaer *m1* poster

postáil *v* post (*letter, parcel, etc*)

postas *m1* postage **postas íoctha** postage paid

postmharc *m1* postmark

postroinnt *f2* job sharing

postúil *adj* self-important

pota *m4* pot **pota caife, tae** pot of coffee, tea

potaire *m4* potter

pótaire *m4* tippler, drunkard

potaireacht *f3* pottery

pótaireacht *f3* habitual drinking, drunkenness

potrálaí *m4* 1. potterer 2. quack

praghas *m1* price **praghsanna stocmhargaidh** stock market prices

praghaschoimhlint *f2* price war

praghasliosta *m* price list

práinn *f2* urgency, hurry, rush

práinneach *adj* urgent, pressing

praiseach *f2* 1. porridge 2. mess **rinne siad praiseach de** they made a 'dog's dinner' of it

praiticiúil *adj* practical

praiticiúlacht *f3* practicality

pram *m4* pram

pramsáil *f3* prancing, frolicking *v* prance, frolic

pras *adj* quick, prompt **rud a dhéanamh go pras** to do something promptly

prás *m1* brass **banna práis** brass band

prásóg *f2* marzipan

práta *m4* potato **an craiceann a bhaint de phráta** to peel a potato, **prátaí brúite, rósta** mashed, roast potatoes

preab *f2* 1. start, bound **bhain tú preab asam** you startled me 2. throb **tá sí i ndeireadh na preibe** she is at her last gasp 3. bounce **preab dhúbailte** double bounce (*basketball*) *v* 1. jump, spring 2. throb **tá a chroí ag preabadh** his heart is palpitating 3. bounce **liathróid a phreabadh** to bounce a ball

preabchlár *m1* springboard

préachán *m1* crow

préachta *adj* freezing **táim préachta leis an bhfuacht** I'm freezing cold

preas *m3* press

preasagallamh *m1* press conference

preasáil *v* press

preaseisiúint *f3* press release

préimh *f2* premium **préimh árachais** insurance premium

Preispitéireach *adj, m1* Presbyterian

priacal *m1* risk, peril **bagáiste ar phriacal an úinéara** baggage at owner's risk

priaclach *adj* risky, perilous

pribhléid *f2* privilege

printéir *m3* printer (*device*) **printéir léasair** laser printer

printéireacht *f3* printing

printíseach *m1* apprentice

printíseacht *f3* apprenticeship

príobháideach *adj* private

príobháideacht *f3* privacy

príobháidiú *m* privatisation

prioc *v* prick, sting, goad, prod **phrioc an bheach é** the bee stung him, **cad a phrioc tú é a dhéanamh?** what got into you to do it?

priocadh *m* prick, sting, prod **priocadh beiche** bee-sting

príomh- *prefix* chief, prime, principal, main, **príomh-bhreitheamh** chief justice, **príomhthalamh** prime land, **an príomhoide** the principal, **an príomhrud** the main thing, **an phríomhchúis** the primary cause

príomha *adj* primary, prime

príomh-aire *m4* prime minister **príomh-aire na Breataine** the prime minister of Britain

príomhalt *m1* leading article, editorial

príomhamhránaí *m4* lead singer

príomhbhóthar *m1* main road

príomhchathair *f5* capital city

príomhchúirt *f2* **an Phríomh-Chúirt Choiriúil** the Central Criminal Court

príomhghiotáraí lead guitarist

príomhlíne *f4* main line (*railway*)

príomhlíonra *f4* mains (*electricity*)

príomhpháirt *f2* lead (*in play, film, etc*)

príomhshráid *f2* main street

prionsa *m4* prince

prionsabal *m1* principle

prionta *m4* print

priontáil *f3* printing *v* print

prios *m4* press **prios aerála** hot-press

príosún *m1* prison, jail **gearradh príosún saoil uirthi** she was given a life sentence, **Príosún Chill Mhaighneann** Kilmainham Gaol

príosúnach *m1* prisoner, inmate **príosúnach cogaidh** prisoner of war

príosúnacht *f3* imprisonment

príosúnaigh *v* imprison

próca *m4* crock, pot, jar, urn **próca óir** crock of gold, **próca bia** food jar

prochóg *f2* 1. hovel 2. hole, cave, den

profa *m4* proof (*publishing*) **léamh profaí** proofreading

prognóis *f2* prognosis

proifisiúnta *adj* professional

proifisiúntacht *f3* professionalism

proinn *f2* meal, buffet

proinnteach *m* canteen

Proinsiasach *adj, m1* Franciscan

próiseáil *f3* processing **próiseáil focal** word processing, **próiseáil éisc** fish processing *v* process **sonraí a phróiseáil** to process data

próiseálaí *m4* processor **próiseálaí focal** word processor

próiseas *m1* process **próiseas foghlama** learning process, **próiseas síochána** peace process

próitéin *f2* protein

promanád *m1* promenade

promh *v* prove, test

promhadán *m1* test tube **leanbh promhadáin** test-tube baby

promhadh *m1* 1. proof, test 2. probation **tá sé ar promhadh** he is on probation

prompa *m4* rump

prós *m1* prose **cnuasach próis** a collection of prose

prótacal *m1* protocol

Protastúnach *adj*, *m1* Protestant

Protastúnachas *m1* Protestantism

prúna *m4* prune

puball *m1* tent **ollphuball** marquee

púca *m4* ghost, hobgoblin, 'pooka' **púca na n-adharc** public enemy, bugbear

púdal *m1* poodle

púdar *m1* powder **púdar bácála** baking powder, **púdar gunna** gunpowder, **púdar níocháin** washing powder, **chomh cinnte is atá púdar i nDoire** as sure as there's powder in Derry, as sure as ever

púic *f2* 1. covering over the eyes, blindfold 2. cover **púic tae tea cosy** 3. frown, scowl

púlcín *m4* 1. covering over the eyes, blindfold, blinkers 2. frown, scowl

puilpid *f2* pulpit

puimcín *m4* pumpkin

puinn *m* not much **níl puinn céille aige** he has no sense, **ní raibh puinn aithne againn ar a chéile** we didn't know each other at all

puins *m4* punch (*hot drink*)

puipéad *m1* puppet

puisín *m4* 1. pussy cat 2. lip **chuir sí puisín uirthi féin** she pouted, sulked

puiteach *m1* mud

puití *m4* putty

púitse *m4* pouch

púl *m4* pool **ag imirt púil** playing pool

pulc *v* stuff, pack tightly, cram, crowd

pulsár *m1* pulsar

pumpáil *f3* pumping *v* pump

punann *f2* 1. sheaf 2. portfolio

punc-rac *m4* punk rock

punt *m1* pound **milliún punt** a million pounds, **punt meáchain** pound in weight

punta *m4* punt (*boat*)

purgadóir *f3* purgatory

purgóid *f2* purgative, laxative, purge **purgóid na manach** rhubarb

púróg *f2* pebble **púróg chloiche** pebble

pus *m1* snout (*of animal*), protruding mouth (*of person*), pout **bhí pus air** he was sulky, **éirigh as nó brisfidh mé do phus** give it up or I'll break your mouth

pusach *adj* 1. in a huff, pouting 2. whimpering

pusachán *m1* whiner, pouter, sulky person

puslach *m1* muzzle

puth *f2* puff, whiff

putóg *f2* 1. pudding **putóg bhán, dhubh** white, black pudding 2. intestine, gut

Q

quinín *m4* quinine

R

rábach *adj* 1. lavish, reckless
2. dashing 3. profuse, plentiful
4. **go rábach** easily

rabairne *m4* extravagance **rabairne
a bheith ionat** to be an
extravagant person

rabairneach *adj* extravagant

rabhadh *m1* warning, caution
tugadh rabhadh dó faoi he was
warned, cautioned about it, **gléas
rabhaidh** warning device

rabharta *m4* 1. overflow, flood,
torrent **rabharta cainte** flood of
speech, **beidh rabharta ar bhia
agus deoch ann** there will be a
great supply of food and drink
there 2. spring tide

rabhchán *m1* warning signal, beacon

rabhlóg *f2* tongue-twister

raca *m4* rack **raca irisí** magazine
rack, **raca silte** draining board

ráca *m4* rake (*gardening*)

racáil *v* rack

rácáil *v* rake

racán *m1* row, brawl, rumpus, racket,
uproar, turmoil

ráchairt *f2* (great) demand

rachmas *m1* wealth, prosperity

rachmasach *adj* wealthy, prosperous

rachmasaí *m4* wealthy person

racht *m3* emotion, fit, outburst
racht feirge, gáire fit of anger,
laughter

rachta *m4* 1. rafter 2. beam

rachtúil *adj* emotional

rada(i)- *prefix* radio- **radaiteiripe**
radiotherapy

radacach *adj, m1* radical

radachur *m1* (radioactive) fall-out

radadh *m1* showering **tugadh
radadh cloch dóibh** they were
showered / pelted with stones

radagrafaíocht *f3* radiography

radaighníomhach *adj* radioactive

radaighníomhaíocht *f3* radioactivity

radaíocht *f3* radiation

radaitheoir *m3* radiator

radar *m1* radar

radar-rialaithe *adj* radar-controlled

radharc *m1* 1. sight, view, vision
chaill sé radharc na súl he lost
his eyesight, **níl radharc uirthi** she
/ it is nowhere to be seen,
radharc tíre scenery 2. scene (*in
play*)

radharcach *adj* visual, optical

radharceolaí *m4* optician

radharceolaíocht *f3* optics

radharcra *m4* scenery (*stage*)

radúil *adj* radial

rafar *adj* prosperous, thriving

ráfla *m4* report, rumour

rafta *m4* raft

ragairne *m4* dissipation, revelry
chuaigh siad ar ragairne they
went on the 'tear'

ragobair *f2* overtime

ráib *f2* 1. sprint, dash **d'fhág siad de ráib** they left in a dash   2. rape (*crop*)

raibí *m4* rabbi

raic *f2* 1. wreck, wreckage **bád raice** wreck, **adhmad raice** driftwood 2. riot, racket, uproar **thóg sé raic** he started a row

raicéad *m1* racket **raicéad leadóige** tennis racket

raidhfil *m4* rifle

raidhse *f4* abundance, profusion **bhí raidhse bia ann** there was plenty of food there

raidhsiúil *adj* plentiful, abundant

raidió *m4* radio **stáisiún raidió, teilifíse** radio, television station

raidis *f2* radish **anlann raidise fiáine** horse-radish sauce

ráig *f2* sudden rush, bout **ráigeanna báistí** sudden showers, **ráig óil** bout of drinking

ráille *m4* rail, railing

raiméis *f2* nonsense

rainse *m4* ranch

ráiteas *m1* statement

ráithe *f4* season (*of three months*), quarter **sa chéad ráithe den bhliain** in the first quarter of the year

ráithiúil *adj* quarterly

raithneach *f2* fern, bracken

ramallae *m4* slime

rámh *m3* oar **maidí rámha** oars

rámhaigh *v* row **ag rámhaíocht** rowing

rámhaille *f4* raving, delirium

rámhailleach *adj* raving, ranting, delirious

rámhainn *f2* spade

rámhaíocht *f3* rowing **bád rámhaíochta** rowing boat

ramhar *adj* fat, thick **is raimhre Micheál ná Peadar** Micheál is

fatter than Peadar, **tá tú ramhar sa cheann** you are thick-headed

ramhraigh *v* fatten

rang *m3* 1. class **rang a sé** sixth class (*in school*) 2. rank

rangabháil *f3* particle

rangaigh *v* classify, arrange in order, sort

rangú *m* classification

rann *m1* verse, quatrain

ranníocaíoch *adj* contributory

ranníocaíocht *f3* contribution (*payment*)

rannóg *f2* section, department **an rannóg pearsanra** the personnel department

rannpháirteach *adj* participating, partaking

rannpháirteachas *m1* participation

rannpháirtí *m4* 1. participator 2. subscriber

ransaigh *v* ransack, search, rummage

raon *m1* 1. range **as raon** out of range, **cearca, uibheacha saor raoin** free-range hens, eggs 2. trail, track **raon rothar** cycle track (*on road*)

raonchulaith *f2* tracksuit

rás *m3* race **rás sealaíochta** relay race, **rásaí ó phointe go pointe** point-to-point races

rásaíocht *f3* racing **carr rásaíochta** racing-car

ráschúrsa *m4* racecourse

rásúr *m1* razor **lann rásúir** razor blade

ráta *m4* rate **ráta malairte** exchange rate

rath *m3* luck, success, prosperity **rath Dé ort!** God prosper you! **chuir tú ó rath é** you rendered it useless, she ruined it, **ní bhíonn an rath ach mar a mbíonn an smacht** there can be no success without discipline

ráth¹ *m3* 1. rath, ring-fort 2. drift **ráth sneachta** snowdrift 3. shoal **ráth éisc** a shoal of fish

ráth² *m3* guarantee

rathaigh *v* succeed, prosper, thrive **go rathaí an Rí na Gaeil** God prosper the Gaels!

ráthaigh *v* guarantee

ráthaíocht *f3* guarantee **faoi ráthaíocht** guaranteed

ráthóir *m3* guarantor

rathúil *adj* 1. lucky, fortunate 2. prosperous, successful

rathúnas *m1* 1. prosperity, success 2. abundance

re, gach re ... every second ..., **gach re bean, fear, duine** every second woman, man, person

ré *f4* 1. moon **lán na ré** the full moon 2. period, time, age, era **an Ré Órga** the Golden Age, **roimh ré** beforehand, in advance, **le mo ré** as long as I live, **deireadh ré** end of an era

réab *v* tear, rip up, shatter, burst, violate

réabhlóid *f2* revolution **Réabhlóid na Fraince** the French Revolution

réabhlóideach *adj* revolutionary

réabhlóidí *m4* revolutionary

reacaire *m4* 1. vendor, seller 2. narrator

reacht *m3* statute, decree, law **leabhar reachtanna** statute book

reachtaigh *v* legislate, decree

reáchtáil *f3* running *v* run **gnóthas a reáchtáil** to run a business

reachtaíocht *f3* legislation

reachtaire *m4* administrator, steward

reachtas *m1* administration, stewardship

reachtúil *adj* statutory **banéigean reachtúil** statutory rape

réadach *adj* real **eastát réadach** real estate

réadaigh *v* realise, make real

réadán *m1* woodworm

réadlann *f2* observatory **réadlann réalteolaíoch** astronomical observatory

réadú *m* realisation **réadú sócmhainní** realisation of assets

réadúil *adj* realistic, real

réal *v* develop (*film*)

réalachas *m1* realism

réaladh *m* 1. development, processing (*of film*) 2. manifestation

réalaí *m4* realist

réalaíoch *adj* realistic

réalta *f4* star **réalta reatha** falling / shooting star, **réalta eolais** guiding star, **réalta scannán** film star

réaltach *adj* starry

réaltacht *f3* 1. clearness, clarity 2. reality **réaltacht fhíorúil** virtual reality

réaltbhraisle *f4* cluster (*of stars*)

réaltbhuíon *f2* constellation

réalteolaíocht *f3* astronomy

réaltfhisic *f2* astrophysics

réaltóg *f2* small star

réaltra *m4* galaxy

réama *m4* rheum, phlegm, catarrh

réamatacht *f3* rheumatism

réamh- *prefix* pre-, afore-, previous, prior **réamhshocraithe** pre-arranged, **réamhráite** aforesaid

réamhaisnéis *f2* forecast **réamhaisnéis na haimsire** the weather forecast

réamhaiste *m4* introduction (*book*)

réamhcheol *m1* 1. overture 2. rave music

réamhdhéanta *adj* ready-made, prefabricated

réamhfhocal *m1* preposition **réamhfhocal simplí, comhshuite** simple, compound preposition

réamhíoc *v* prepay

réamhíocaíocht *f3* prepayment

réamhíoctha *adj* prepaid

réamhrá *m4* preface, introduction

réamhthaispeántas *m1* preview

réamhtheachtaí *m4* predecessor, forerunner

réasún *m1* reason, sense **luíonn sé le réasún go ...** it stands to reason that ...

réasúnach *adj* rational

réasúnachas *m1* rationalism

réasúnaigh *v* rationalise, reason

réasúnaíocht *f3* reasoning, rationale

réasúnta *adj* reasonable, middling, moderate

réasúntacht *f3* reasonableness

reathaí *m4* runner

réchúiseach *adj* 1. easy-going, placid 2. indifferent

reibiliún *m1* rebellion

reibiliúnach *adj* rebellious

reibiliúnacht *f3* rebelliousness

reic *m3* sale **reic clabhsúir** closing down sale *v* sell

réidh *adj* 1. easy **tóg go réidh é** take it easy 2. ready, finished **an bhfuil tú réidh fós?** are you ready / finished yet? 3. level, smooth **talamh réidh** level ground

réidhe *f4* levelness, smoothness

Reifirméisean, an *m1* the Reformation

reifreann *m1* referendum

réigiún *m1* region **réigiúin uathrialacha** autonomous regions, **réigiún talmhaíochta** agricultural region

réigiúnach *adj* regional **ceardcholáiste réigiúnach, coláiste teicniúil réigiúnach (CTR)** regional technical college (RTC)

reilig *f2* graveyard, cemetery, burial ground **bóthar na reilige** the graveyard road

reiligiún *m1* religion

reiligiúnach *adj* religious

réiltín *m4* 1. starlet **réiltín scannán** film star 2. asterisk

réim *f2* 1. regime, sway **tháinig Páirtí an Lucht Oibre i réim** the Labour Party came to power 2. course, career **tá siad i mbarr a réime** they are at their peak 3. range, field **réim radhairc** field of vision 4. course **réim (chothrom) bia** (balanced) diet

réimeas *m1* reign, authority

réimír *f2* prefix (*grammar*)

réimnigh *v* conjugate

réimniú *m* conjugation (*grammar*)

réimse *m4* range, field **réimse eolais** range of knowledge

Réin, an *f2* the Rhine

réinfhla *m4* reindeer

reiptíl *f2* reptile

réir *f2* wish, will, command **de réir ...** according to ..., **de réir a chéile** gradually, consistent, **de réir dealraimh** apparently, **faoi réir ...** subject to ...

réise *f4* span **réise sciathán** wing-span

reisimint *f2* regiment

réiteach *m1* 1. solution, resolution of difficulty **réiteach na faidhbe / ceiste** the solution to the problem 2. clearance, preparation **réiteach slí** clearance / clearing of way, **an bhfuil an réiteach déanta?** has the preparation been done?

réiteoir *m3* referee (*sport*), umpire

reithe *m4* ram **an Reithe** the Ram, Aries

réitigh *v* 1. settle, solve **fadhb a réiteach** to solve a problem 2. clear, level **do scornach a réiteach** to clear one's throat 3. disentangle, unravel 4. **réitigh le** agree with, get on with **ní réitíonn sé liom** it does not agree with me, **ní réitíonn siad (le chéile)** they don't get on (with each other)

reitine *f4* retina

reitric *f2* rhetoric

reitriciúil *adj* rhetorical

reo *m4* frost, freezing

reoán *m1* icing

reoánta *adj* iced

reoigh *v* freeze **líreacán reoite** ice-pop

reoite *adj* frozen

reoiteoir *m3* freezer

reophointe *m4* freezing-point

ré-uimhir *f5* even number

rí[1] *m4* 1. king **ríthe an domhain** the kings / monarchies of the world 2. **rí rua** chaffinch

rí-[2] *prefix* 1. royal **ríshliocht** royal race 2. exceedingly, extremely, very **rímhaith** exceedingly good, very well, **rí-olc** extremely bad

riabhach *adj* 1. striped, brindled, streaked 2. gloomy, dismal **aimsir riabhach** dismal weather

riachtanach *adj* necessary, essential, vital

riachtanas *m1* need, necessity **riachtanais chontrártha** conflicting needs

riail *f5* rule **rialacha an bhóthair** the rules of the road

rialaigh *v* rule, govern, reign, regulate

rialóir *m3* ruler (*tool*)

rialta *adj* regular **go rialta** regularly, **bean rialta** nun, **briathra rialta** regular verbs

rialtacht *f3* regularity

rialtán *m1* 1. regulator **rialtán fuaime** sound regulator 2. control **rialtáin tiomána** driving controls

rialtas *m1* government **rialtas áitiúil** local government

rialtóir *m3* ruler (*person*)

rialú *m* regulation, rule, control

riamh *adv* ever, never (*negative*), always **níos mó ná riamh** more than ever, **ní fhaca mé riamh é / í** I never saw it, **bhí an laigeacht sin riamh ann** he always had that weakness

rian *m1* trace, track, sign, stain, mark **fuarthas rian óil ina chuid fola** traces of drink were found in his blood, **rian coise** footprint, **tá a rian uirthi** she looks it

rianaigh *v* track, trace

rianóir *m3* marker (*pen*)

rianpháipéar *m1* tracing-paper

rianphiléar *m1* tracer bullet

rianúchán *m1* tracing **páipéar rianúcháin** tracing-paper

riar *m4* 1. managing, administration 2. provision *v* 1. manage, administer 2. provide **riar ar ...** to provide for ... 3. serve 4. allot, distribute

riarachán *m1* administration

riaráiste *m4* arrears

riarthóir *m3* administrator

riasc *m1* marsh, wetland

ribe *m4* 1. hair (*single*) **níor fágadh ribe gruaige air** he was left bald 2. blade **ribe féir** blade of grass 3. **ribe róibéis** shrimp

ribeach *adj* hairy

ribín *m4* ribbon, tape, streamer

ríchathaoir *f5* throne

rídhamhna *m4* royal heir

ridire *m4* knight

ridireacht *f3* knighthood, chivalry

ridiriúil *adj* knightly, chivalrous

rige *m4* rig **rige ola** oil rig

righin *adj* 1. tough, stiff 2. slow

righneas *m1* 1. toughness, tenacity 2. slowness

rigín *m4* 1. rigging 2. ribbing (*knitting*)

ríl *f2* reel (*dance*)

rilif *f2* relief

rím *f2* rhyme

ríméad *m1* delight, joy

ríméadach *adj* delighted, overjoyed

rinc¹ *f2* rink

rinc² *v* dance

rince *m4* dance, dancing **rince seit** set dance

rinceoir *m3* dancer

rinn¹ *f2* 1. point, tip 2. headland, cape **Rinn an Dóchais** the Cape of Good Hope 3. apex

rinn² *m3* planet, star

rinse *m4* wrench

riocht *m3* 1. shape, form **as riocht** out of shape / place 2. condition, state **sa riocht sin** in that state / condition

riocht *f3* kingdom, realm

ríog *f2* spasm, impulse **tagann sé ina ríoga orm** I get it in spasms

ríoga *adj* royal, regal

ríomh *v* 1. count, compute, calculate 2. narrate

ríomhaire *m4* computer **ríomhaire glúine** lap top computer

ríomhaireacht *f3* information technology, computer science

ríomhchlár *m1* computer program

ríomhchláraigh *v* program (*computer*)

ríomhchláraitheoir *m3* computer programmer

ríomheolaíocht *f3* computer science

ríomhghrafaic *f2* computer graphics

ríomhphost *m1* e-mail

ríon *f3* queen

rírá *m4* confusion, clamour, uproar **bhí rírá agus ruaille buaille ann** there was a terrible commotion there

rís *f2* rice **rís fhriochta** fried rice

rísín *m4* raisin

rite *adj* tense, stretched, distended **téad rite** taut rope

riteoga *pl* tights

rith *m3* 1. run, running **rith fola** haemorrhage, **rith cainte** flow of speech, **bróga reatha** runners, trainers 2. **i rith** during, **i rith na seachtaine** during the week *v* run **tá a rás rite** his / her / their race is run

rithim *f2* rhythm

ró- *prefix* too, very, most, over- **róbheag** too small, **ró-óg** too young, **ródhócha** very / most likely, **ródhaonra** overpopulation

róba *m4* robe

robáil *f4* robbing, robbery **robáil bainc** bank robbery *v* rob

robálaí *m4* robber

róbaitic *f3* robotics

róbat *m1* robot

roc *m1, v* wrinkle

rocach *adj* wrinkled, creased

rochtain *f3* access

ród *m1* 1. road 2. anchorage **téad róid** mooring-rope

ródháileog *f2* overdose **ródháileog drugaí** overdose of drugs

rógaire *m4* rogue

rógaireacht *f3* roguery

rogha *f4* 1. choice, selection **do rogha ceoil** your choice of music, **togha gach bia agus rogha gach dí** the choicest of food and drink 2. option, alternative **níl an dara rogha agam** I have no other option

roghnach *adj* optional

roghnaigh *v* select, choose

roghnú *m* selection, choice

ró-iascaireacht *f3* overfishing

roicéad *m1* rocket

roimh *prep* (*prep prons* = romham, romhat, roimhe, roimpi, romhainn, romhaibh, rompu)

before **dúirt mé leat roimhe sin
é** I said it to you before that, **bhí
siad ann romhainn** they were
there before us, **roimh i bhfad**
before long, **roimh ré** in advance,
roimh Chríost before Christ (BC)

Róimh, an *f2* Rome

roimhe *adv* before **ní fhaca mé
riamh roimhe é** I never saw him
/ it before

Róin, an *f2* the Rhone

roinn *f2* 1. portion, share **fuair tú do
roinn** you got your share
2. department **ranna Rialtais**
Government departments, **an
roinn taismeach** the casualty
department *v* 1. share, divide
roinn ina chodanna é divide it
into parts 2. distribute, deal

roinnt *f2* 1. division **roinnt tíre**
partitioning of a country, **gan
roinnt** undivided 2. some **roinnt
airgid, daoine, oibre** some money,
people, work, **roinnt mhaith (...)**
a good deal (of ...)

rois¹ *f2* 1. volley **scaoileadh rois
urchar os cionn na huaighe** a
volley of shots was fired over the
grave 2. blast **rois toirní** blast of
thunder, thunderclap

rois² *v* tear, rip, unravel

roiseadh *m* 1. tear, rip 2. spate
roiseadh cainte spate of talk

roisín *m4* resin

ról *m1* role

rólghlacadh *m* role-playing

roll *v* roll

rolla *m4* 1. roll **rollaí leithris** toilet
rolls 2. register **an bhfuil tú ar an
rolla fós?** have you enrolled yet?

rollaigh *v* enrol

rollóg *f2* roll **rollóg aráin** bread roll

rollóir *m3* roller

rollú *m* enrolment

Rómáin, an *f2* Romania

Rómáinis *f2* Romanian (*language*)

Rómánach *adj, m1* Romanian

rómánsach *adj* romantic

rómánsaí *m4* romantic

rómánsaíocht *f3* romance

rómhair *v* dig, till

Rómhánach *adj, m1* Roman

rón *m1* seal **smugairle róin** jellyfish

ronna *m4* dribble, slobber

ronnach *m1* mackerel

rop *v* 1. stab, thrust **ropadh le scian
é** he was stabbed with a knife
2. dash **rop mé amach an doras**
I dashed out the door

rópa *m4* rope **dréimire rópa** rope
ladder

ropadh *m* 1. stab, thrust 2. dash

ros¹ *m1* headland

ros² *m1* flax-seed, linseed **ola rois**
linseed oil

rós *m1* rose

rósach *adj* rosy

rosán *m1* thicket, shrubbery

rosc¹ *m1* rhetorical address or poem
rosc catha battle hymn, war-cry

rosc² *m1* eye

rosca *m4* rusk

Ros Comáin *m* Roscommon **Co. Ros
Comáin** Co. Roscommon

rósóg *f2* rose-tree, rose-bush

róst *v* roast

rósta *adj* roasted *m4* roast

rostram *m1* rostrum

rosualt *m1* walrus

róta *m4* rota

roth *m3* wheel **cathaoir rothaí**
wheelchair, **roth breise** spare
wheel

rotha *m4* ray (*fish*)

rothaí *m4* cyclist

rothaíocht *f3* cycling

rothar *m1* bicycle **raon rothar** cycle
track (*on road*)

rótharraingt *f2* overdraft
  rótharraingt bhainc bank overdraft

rothlach *adj* rotatory, rotating, revolving **doras rothlach** revolving door

rothlaigh *v* rotate

rothlú *m* rotation

rua *adj* red(-haired), reddish-brown, foxy **bean rua** red-haired woman, **an Mhuir Rua** the Red Sea, **níl pingin rua fágtha agam** I haven't a penny left

ruacan *m1* cockle

ruaig *f2* chase **chuir tú an ruaig orthu** you chased them away, you got rid of them *v* chase (away)

ruaille, ruaille buaille commotion, ruction

ruainne *m4* fragment, scrap, shred **níl ruainne den fhírinne ann** there's not a shred of truth in it, **ruainne tobac** a small piece of tobacco

ruathar *m1* rush, charge, attack

rubar *m1* rubber

rud *m3* thing, object **an bhfuair tú aon rud ann?** **cúpla rud** did you get anything there? a couple of things

rufa *m4* frill

rufach *adj* frilled

ruga *m4* rug

rugbaí *m4* rugby

rúibín *m4* ruby

rúibíneach *adj* ruby

rúid *f2* short run, sprint

rúidbhealach *m1* runway

ruifíneach *m1* ruffian

rúiléid *f2* roulette **rúiléid Rúiseach** Russian roulette

rúipí *m4* rupee

Rúis, an *f2* Russia

Rúiseach *adj, m1* Russian

Rúisis *f2* Russian (*language*)

rúitín *m4* ankle

rum *m4* rum

rún *m1* 1. secret **faoi rún** in secret 2. intent **tá rún agam dul ann I** intend to go there 3. motion (*debate*) 4. **a rún** my darling

rúnaí *m4* secretary **rúnaí stáit** secretary of state

rúnaíocht *f3* secretariat

rúnda *adj* 1. secret, confidential 2. mysterious

rúndacht *f3* secrecy

rúndiamhair *adj* mysterious *f2* mystery

runga *m4* rung (*ladder*)

rúnmhar *adj* secretive

rúnscríbhinn *f2* secret writing, cipher

rúnseirbhís *f2* secret service

Rúraíocht *f3* Ulster epic cycle

rúta *m4* root

ruthag *m1* run, sprint

S

sa, san = **i** + **an** in the, **sa charr** in the car, **sa tslí** in the way, **san fhómhar** in (the) autumn, **san uisce** in the water

sá *m4* thrust, stab, push

sabaitéir *m3* saboteur

sabaitéireacht *f3* sabotage

sábh *m1* saw (*carpentry*)

sábhadóireacht *f3* sawing

sábháil *f3* saving, sparing, protecting, rescue *v* save, protect, rescue

sábháilte *adj* safe

sábháilteacht *f3* safety **cigire sábháilteachta** safety inspector, **an tÚdarás Sláinte agus Sábháilteachta** the Health and Safety Authority

sabhaircín *m4* primrose

sábhálach *adj* sparing, economical

sabhdán *m1* sultan

sabhdánach *m1* sultana

sabóid *f2* sabbath

sabóideach *adj* sabbatical

sacar *m1* soccer **cluiche sacair** soccer match

sách *adj, adv* 1. satisfied, full 2. enough **sách ard** high enough, fairly high

sacraimint *f2* sacrament

sacsafón *m1* saxophone

sádach *adj* sadistic *m1* sadist

sádar *m1* solder

sádráil *f3* soldering *v* solder

sagart *m1* priest

sagartacht *f3* priesthood

saghas *m1* sort, kind, type, variety **saghsanna difriúla bia** different kinds of food

Sahára, an *m4* the Sahara

saibhir *adj* rich, wealthy, fertile **daoine saibhre** wealthy people, **talamh saibhir** fertile land *m4* rich person

saibhreas *m1* riches, wealth

saibhrigh *v* enrich

saifír *f2* sapphire

sáigh *v* thrust, stab, push

saighdiúir *m3* soldier

saighdiúireacht *f3* soldiering

saighead *f2* arrow **bogha is saighead** bow and arrow

saighid *v* egg on, incite, provoke

saighneáil *v* sign

Saighneáin, na *pl* the Northern Lights

sail *f2* dirt **sail chnis** dandruff, **sail chluaise** ear-wax, **sail liath** blue mould

sáil *f2* heel (*of foot*) **sáil bróige** heel of shoe

sailchuach *f2* violet (*flower*)

sáile *m4* sea-water, sea **dul thar sáile** to go abroad

saileach *f2* willow **crann sailí** willow-tree

sailéad *m1* salad

saill *f2* 1. fat, fat meat 2. salted meat

sailleach *adj* fatty

sáimhín *m4* quiet, easy mood **bheith ar do sháimhín só** to be perfectly content

sain- *prefix* special, specific, particular **sainfheidhm** special function, **sainleigheas** specific cure

saincheaptha *adj* custom-built

sainchomhartha *m4* characteristic

sainchreideamh *m1* denomination

saineolaí *m4* specialist, expert **saineolaí cothúcháin** nutritionist

saineolas *m1* special knowledge, expertise

sainiúil *adj* specific

sainleas *m3* special interest **grúpaí sainleasa** special-interest groups

sainmharc *m1* hallmark

sainmhíniú *m* definition

sáinn *f2* trap, 'corner', fix **tá mé i sáinn** I'm in a fix, **sáinn!** check! (*chess*)

sáinnigh *v* trap, corner

sainordaitheach *adj* mandatory **pionós sainordaitheach** mandatory sentence

saint *f2* greed

saintréith *f2* characteristic, distinctive quality

saíocht *f3* learning, wisdom

sairdín *m4* sardine

sáirsint *m4* sergeant

sais *f2* sash

sáiste *m4* sage (*herb*)

sáith *f2* fill, enough, sufficiency **tá mo sháith (ite) agam** I have (eaten) my fill, **tá sáith ceathrair ann** there is enough for four there

saithe *f4* swarm **saithe beach** swarm of bees

salach *adj* dirty

salachar *m1* dirt

salaigh *v* dirty

salann *m1* salt **salann folctha** bath salts

sall *adv* over, across **dul sall go Sasana** to go over to England

salm *m1* psalm

salón *m1* salon **salón gruaige** hair salon

salún *m1* saloon (*car*)

sámh *adj* easy, tranquil **codladh sámh!** sleep well!

samhail *f3* 1. likeness, simile 2. model 3. ghost, phantom

samhailchomhartha *m4* symbol

samhailteach *adj* imaginary

Samhain *f3* November **mí na Samhna** November, **Oíche Shamhna** Hallowe'en

samhlaigh *v* imagine

samhlaíoch *adj* imaginative

samhlaíocht *f3* imagination

samhlaoid *f2* illustration, image **samhlaoidí** imagery

samhnas *m1* nausea

samhnasach *adj* disgusting

samhradh *m1* summer **i rith an tsamhraidh** during the summer

samhrata *adj* summer-like

sampla *m4* example, sample **mar shampla** for example, **sampla a thógáil de rud** to sample something

samplach *adj* exemplary, model, typical

San *m* Saint (*canonised*) **San Nioclás** Santa Claus

sanasaíocht *f3* etymology

sann *v* assign

sannadh *m* assignment

santach *adj* greedy

santacht *f3* greediness

santaigh *v* covet, desire

saobhghrá *m4* infatuation

saoi *m4* wise man, expert **ní bhíonn saoi gan locht** even Homer nods, nobody's perfect

saoire *f4* holiday **saoire láneagraithe** package holiday

saoirse *f4* freedom, liberty **na Saoirsí** the Liberties

saoirseacht *f3* craftsmanship **saoirseacht (chloiche)** masonry

saoiste *m4* boss, ganger, foreman

saoithiúil *adj* cultured, learned, wise

saol *m1* life, world **i rith a saoil** during her life, **cúrsaí an tsaoil** worldly affairs, **tá a fhios ag an saol is a mháthair anois** the whole world knows now

saolta *adj* worldly

saonta *adj* naive, gullible

saontacht *f3* naivety

saor[1] *adj* free, easy, cheap, exempt **saor in aisce** free of charge, **saor ó chaiféin** decaffeinated, **saor ó cháin** tax-free, **saor ó dhleacht** duty-free, (**peitreal**) **saor ó luaidhe** unleaded (petrol), **cearca, uibheacha saor-raoin** free-range hens, eggs *v* save, free, liberate, acquit, release **tír a shaoradh** to free a country

saor[2] *m1* craftsman **saor cloiche** stonemason, **saor loinge** shipwright

saor-[3] *prefix* free, freelance **saormheas** free estimate, **saoririseoir** freelance journalist

saoradh *m* acquittal, liberation

saoráid *f3* facility

saoráideach *adj* easy

saoránach *m1* citizen

saoránacht *f3* citizenship

saoránaíocht *m1* civics

saorchic *f2* free kick

saorchumasc *m1* promiscuity

saorfhón *m1* freefone

saorga *adj* artificial **comhla, cos shaorga** artificial valve, leg

saoriomaíocht *f3* free competition **geilleagar saoriomaíochta** free-market economy

saorphost *m1* freepost

saorstát *m1* free state

saorthrádáil *f3* free trade

saorthuras *m1* excursion

saothar *m1* labour, work **saothar in aisce** labour in vain, **líon saothair** work force, **clár saothair** bibliography, **tá saothar orm** I'm out of breath (from hard work)

saotharlann *f2* laboratory

saothraí *m4* worker, labourer

saothraigh *v* 1. labour, toil 2. work, cultivate, till **ag saothrú na talún** working the land 3. earn **tá sé ag saothrú a bheatha as** he's earning his living from it

saothrú *m* 1. cultivation 2. earnings

sár[1] *m1* tsar

sár-[2] *prefix* super, excellent **sárchluiche** an excellent game

sáraigh *v* 1. outdo, surpass, overcome **ní féidir é a shárú** it/he can't be beaten, **deacracht a shárú** to surmount a difficulty 2. violate, infringe

sáraíocht *f3* arguing, disputation

sárchéim *f2* superlative degree (*grammar*)

sármhaith *adj* excellent

sárú *m* 1. surpassing, overcoming **níl a shárú ann** it can't be beaten 2. violation, infringement

sás *m1* 1. contrivance, device 2. trap **sás luiche** mouse-trap

sásaigh *v* satisfy, please

sásamh *m1* satisfaction

Sasana *m4* England

Sasanach *adj* English *m1* English person

sásar *m1* saucer

sáspan *m1* saucepan

sásta *adj* satisfied, content

sástacht *f3* satisfaction

sásúil *adj* satisfactory

satail *v* tread, trample

satailít *f2* satellite **satailít teileachumarsáide** telecommunications satellite

Satarn *m1* Saturn

Sathairn *m1* Saturday **Dé Sathairn** (on) Saturday

scabhat *m1* narrow passage, alley, gap

scabhta *m4* scout

scadán *m1* herring

scafaire *m4* spirited, strapping fellow

scafall *m1* scaffold

scafalra *m4* scaffolding

scafánta *adj* 1. spirited, strapping 2. speedy, fit

scáfar *adj* 1. bashful, shy, timid 2. dreadful, frightful

scag *v* 1. filter, strain 2. refine

scagadh *m* filtering

scagaire *m4* filter, strainer

scaif *f2* scarf

scáil *f2* 1. shadow, reflection **faoi scáil na hoíche** under the shadows/dark of the night, **scáil na gréine** the sun's reflection 2. shade **sa scáil** in the shade

scáileán *m1* screen

scáinte *adj* scanty, scarce

scaip *v* scatter, spread, squander, disperse **cé atá ag scaipeadh ráflaí fúm?** who's spreading rumours about me? **do chuid airgid a scaipeadh** to squander one's money, **scaip an ceo** the fog lifted

scaipeadh *m* dispersion, dissemination

scaipthe *adj* 1. scattered, dispersed 2. confused

scair *f2* share

scaird *f2* squirt, jet *v* squirt, spout, splash

scairdeitleán *m1* jet plane

scairdtuirse *f4* jet lag

scairp *f2* scorpion **an Scairp** Scorpio

scairshealbhóir *m3* shareholder

scairt *f2* shout, summons, call *v* 1. shout, call out, yell 2. burst out **scairt sí amach ag gáire** she burst into laughter

scairteadh *f2* 1. shouting 2. burst **scairteadh gáire** burst of laughter

scaitheamh *m1* short space of time, while **ar feadh scaithimh** for a while, **scaití** at times

scal *f2* burst, flash **scal ghréine** sunburst *v* burst out

scála *m4* scale

scall *v* 1. scald, poach (*egg*) 2. scold

scallta *adj* miserable

scalltán *m1* fledgling, nestling

scamall *m1* cloud

scamallach *adj* cloudy

scamh *v* peel, strip

scamhard *m1* nutrition, nourishment

scamhardach *adj* nutritious, nourishing

scamhóg *f2* lung **ailse (na) scamhóg** lung cancer

scan *m4* scan

scanadh *m* scanning **scanadh míochaine** medical scanning, **scanadh ultrafhuaime** ultrasound scanning

scanáil *f3* scanning **gléas scanála** scanner

scannal *m1* scandal

scannalach *adj* scandalous, disgraceful

scannán *m1* film **scannán cumhdaithe** cling film, **scannán mór-eachtraíochta** blockbuster, **scannán mór-ratha** box-office hit, **scannán uafáis** horror film

scannánaigh *v* film

scannánú *m* filming, shooting **scannánú faoi uisce** underwater shooting, **scannánú ón aer** aerial shooting

scanóir *f3* scanner **scanóir barrachód** bar-code scanner

scanradh *m1* fright, terror **chuir sé scanradh orm** it frightened me, **is mór an scanradh é** it is most amazing

scanraigh *v* frighten, scare, become frightened

scanraithe *adj* frightened

scanrú *m* scare

scanrúil *adj* terrifying, frightening

scaoil *v* release, discharge, loosen **scaoileadh urchair leo** shots were fired at them

scaoileadh *m* release, discharge, firing (*of shot, missile, etc*)

scaoilte *adj* loose

scaoilteacht *f3* 1. looseness, laxity 2. diarrhoea

scaoll *m1* panic, fright

scaollmhar *adj* panicky

scaoth *f2* swarm **scaoth beach** swarm of bees

scar *v* separate, part **scaradh le duine** to part company with somebody

scaradh *m* separation, parting

scarlóideach *adj* scarlet

scartha *adj* separate(d), divorced

scata *m4* crowd

scáta *m4* skate scátaí rothacha roller-skates

scátáil *f3* skating *v* skate

scátálaí *m4* skater

scáth *m3* 1. shade, shadow, shelter, cover scáth báistí, scáth fearthainne umbrella, faoi scáth na hoíche under the cover of night 2. fright cuireann siad scáth orm they frighten me 3. bashfulness

scáthach *adj* sheltered, shady

scáthaigh *v* shade, cover, protect, screen

scáthán *m1* mirror

scáthchruth *m3* silhouette

scáthlán *m1* screen, visor scáthlán gréine sun visor

scáthlínithe *adj* shaded (*graphic art*)

sceabha *m4* slant, skew ar sceabha askew, slantwise

sceach *f2* thorn bush, briar sceach gheal hawthorn

sceadamán *m1* throat, windpipe

scéal *m1* story, tale scéalta taibhsí ghost stories, inis scéal grinn (dúinn) tell (us) a funny story

scéala *m4* news, tidings

scéalaí *m4* storyteller

scéalaíocht *f3* storytelling

sceallóg *f2* chip, slice sceallóga (prátaí) chips

scealp *f2* splinter *v* splinter, chip

sceamhaíl *f3* barking, yelping

sceanra *m4* cutlery

sceartán *m1* tick (*blood-sucking*)

sceideal *m1* schedule

scéilín *m4* anecdote

scéim *f2* scheme scéim phíolótach pilot scheme

scéiméir *m3* schemer

scéiméireacht *f3* scheming

scéimh *f2* 1. appearance 2. beauty

sceimhle *m4* terror, panic

sceimhlitheoir *m3* terrorist

sceimhlitheoireacht *f3* terrorism

scéin *f2* fright, terror

scéiniúil *adj* frightening, frightened-looking

scéinséir *m3* thriller (*book, film*)

sceipteach *m1* sceptic

sceipteachas *m1* scepticism

sceiptiúil *adj* sceptical

sceir *f2* reef sceir bhacainneach, choiréil barrier, coral reef

sceirdiúil *adj* bleak

sceith *f2* 1. overflow, discharge, exhaust 2. spawn sceith fhroig frog spawn 3. vomit sceith fola blood-vomit *v* 1. overflow, discharge 2. spawn 3. vomit, spew 4. divulge sceith sé orainn he informed on us

sceitheadh *m* discharge, exhaust píobán sceite exhaust pipe

sceithire *m4* informer, telltale

sceithireacht *f3* informing

sceitimíneach *adj* excited, rapturous

sceitimíní *pl* excitement, raptures

sceitse *m4* sketch

sceitseáil *v* sketch

scí *m4* ski

sciáil *f3* skiing *v* ski

sciálaí *m4* skier

sciamhach *adj* beautiful, elegant

sciamhacht *f3* beauty, elegance

scian *f2* knife lann scine blade of knife, sceana feola carving knives, dul faoi scian (dochtúra) to have an operation

sciar *m4* share, portion

sciath *f2* shield

sciathán *m1* 1. wing, extension sciatháin eitleáin the wings of an aeroplane, sciathán foirgnimh the wing of a building 2. arm 3. sciathán leathair bat (*mammal*)

scidil *f2* skittle cluiche scidilí skittles (*game*)

scigaithris *f2* parody, funny imitation

scigdhráma *m4* farce

scige *f4* tittering, jeering

scigire *m3* mocker, jeerer

scigireacht *f3* mockery

scigiúil *adj* derisive

scigmhagadh *m1* derision, jeering

scigmhagúil *adj* derisive

scigphictiúr *m1* caricature

scil *f2* skill **scileanna aireachtála** perceptual skills, **scileanna cumarsáide** communication skills

sciliúil *adj* skilful

scilling *f2* shilling

scimeáil *v* skim

scinn *v* 1. dart off, escape 2. spring, fly up

sclob *v* snatch, grab, swipe **sciob mé as a lámh é** I swiped it from his / her hand

scioból *m1* barn

sciobtha *adj* fast

scioll *v* scold

sciomair *v* scour, cleanse, scrub

sciorr *v* slip, slide, skid

sciorrach *adj* slippery

sciorradh *m* slip, slide, skid **sciorradh focail** slip of the tongue, **sciorradh Freudach** Freudian slip

sciorta *m4* skirt

sciortáil *v* skirt

sciotach *adj* skimpy, short

sciotaíl *f3* giggling, tittering **ag sciotaíl gháire** giggling, tittering

scipéad *m1* cash register, till

scíth *f2* rest, relaxation **lig do scíth** take a rest, relax

sciuird *f2* rush, dash **sciuird a thabhairt ar áit** to pay a flying visit to a place

sciúirse *m4* scourge, affliction

sciúr *v* scrub, scour

sciurd *v* dash, rush

sciúrsáil *f3* scourging

sclábhaí *m4* 1. labourer 2. slave

sclábhaíocht *f3* 1. labouring 2. slavery

scláta *m4* slate

scléaróis *f2* sclerosis **scléaróis iolrach** multiple sclerosis

scléip *f2* fun, sport, hilarity

scliúchas *m1* rumpus

scóig *f2, v* throttle

scoil *f2* school **scoil mheasctha** mixed school

scoilt *f2* 1. split, rift **bhí scoilt sa ghluaiseacht** there was a split in the movement 2. crack, slit **tá scoilt sa ghloine seo** there's a crack in this glass *v* split

scoilteach *f2* acute pain **scoilteacha** rheumatics

scóip *f2* scope

scóipiúil *adj* wide, spacious

scoir *v* cease, desist, retire **scoir sé den obair** he retired from work

scolaíocht *f3* schooling

scoláire *m4* scholar

scoláireacht *f3* scholarship **ghnóthaigh sí scoláireacht** she won a scholarship

scolártha *adj* scholarly

scolb *m1* 1. splinter 2. 'scollop', stick used in thatching

sconna *m4* water-spout, tap

sconsa *m4* fence

scor *m1* termination, retirement **mar fhocal scoir** to conclude, **aois scoir** retirement age

scór *m1* twenty, score **tá sé dhá bhliain is ceithre scór** he is eighty two ('two years and four twenties'), **bhí na scórtha daoine ann** there were scores of people there, **tá siad ar comhscór** they are level (*sport*)

scornach *f2* throat

scoth *f3* choice **scoth na mban, na bhfear** the best of women, men, **scoth lae, oibre** great day, work, **den chéad scoth** of the best quality

scothbhruite *adj* soft-boiled, medium **ubh scothbhruite** soft-boiled egg, **feoil scothbhruite** medium-cooked meat

scothóg *f2* 1. flower 2. tassel

scothúil *adj* beautiful, choice

scragall *m1* foil **scragall alúmanaim** aluminium foil

scraith *f2* covering, coating

scréach *f2* screech *v* screech, shriek

scread *f3* scream *v* scream, bawl, shout

screamh *f2* scum

scríbhinn *f2* writing, (written) document

scríbhneoir *m3* writer

scríbhneoireacht *f3* handwriting **scríbhneoireacht chruthaitheach** creative writing

scrín *f2* shrine

scríob *f2* 1. scratch, scrape **scríob den teanga a thabhairt do dhuine** to give somebody verbal abuse 2. spell **scríob oibre, scríob reatha** a spell of work, a short run *v* scratch, scrape

scríobach *adj* 1. scraping 2. abrasive

scríobadh *m* scratch, scrapings

scríobh *m3* writing **tá scríobh breá aige** he has fine handwriting *v* write

scrios *m* destruction *v* 1. delete, rub out 2. ruin, destroy

scriosach *adj* ruinous, destructive

scriosán *m1* eraser, rubber

script *f2* script

scriú *m4* screw

scriúáil *v* screw

scriúire *m4* screwdriver

scrogall *m1* long thin neck, bottleneck **Jónaí an Scrogaill** heron

scrolla *m4* scroll

scrúdaigh *v* examine

scrúdaitheoir *m3* examiner **scrúdaitheoir seachtrach** external examiner

scrúdú *m* examination **scrúdú cainte** oral exam, **scrúdú dochtúra** medical examination

scrupall *m1* scruple

scrupallach *adj* scrupulous

scuab *f2* brush **scuab gruaige** hairbrush *v* brush, sweep

scuad *m1* squad **scuad lámhaigh** firing squad

scuadrún *m1* squadron

scuaine *f4* queue

scuais *f2* squash (*sport*)

scuib *f2* lunge, descent to attack **buamadóir scuibe** dive-bomber

scúnc *m1* skunk

scúp *m1* scoop

scútar *m1* scooter

sé[1] *pron* he, it **bhuail sé mé** he hit me, **tá sé ite** it is eaten

sé[2] *m4* six **sé mhadra bheaga** six small dogs, **a sé déag** sixteen

sea, 'sea = is ea, see ea

seabhac *m1* hawk

seabhdar *m1* chowder **seabhdar breallach** clam chowder

séabra *m4* zebra

seacál *m1* jackal

seach, faoi seach in turn, respectively

Seacaibíteach *adj, m1* Jacobite

Seacaibíteachas *m1* Jacobitism

seachadadh *m* 1. delivery **íoc ar sheachadadh (í.a.s.)** cash on delivery (c.o.d.) 2. tip **seachadtaí láimhe** tips

seachaid *v* 1. deliver 2. pass (*football*)

seachain *v* 1. avoid, evade **duine a sheachaint** to avoid somebody

2. take care **seachain thú féin!** mind yourself!

seachaint *f3* avoidance, evasion

seachantach *adj* elusive, evasive, wary

seachas *prep* besides, compared with

seachmall *m1* illusion, aberration

seachphósta *adj* extra-marital

seachrán *m1* 1. straying 2. derangement 3. error

seachránach *adj* 1. straying 2. deranged 3. wrong

seachránaí *m4* wanderer, vagrant

seacht *m4* seven **seacht dtuáille bhána** seven white towels, **a seacht déag** seventeen

seachtain *f2* week **sna seachtainí romhainn** in the weeks ahead, **dhá sheachtain** two weeks, **trí, ceithre, cúig, sé, seacht, ocht, naoi, deich seachtaine** three, four, five, six, seven, eight, nine, ten weeks

seachtainiúil *adj* weekly

seachtanán *m1* weekly (*magazine, journal, etc*)

seachtar *m1* seven people **seachtar imreoirí** seven players

seachtó *m* seventy **ceol na seachtóidí** seventies music

seachtódú¹ *m4* seventieth **naoi seachtódú de rud** nine seventieths of something

seachtódú² *adj* seventieth **an seachtódú bliain** the seventieth year

seachtrach *adj* external, outside **scrúdaitheoir seachtrach** external examiner, **craoladh seachtrach** outside broadcast (*television*)

seachtú¹ *m4* seventh **sé sheachtú de** six sevenths of it

seachtú² *adj* seventh **an seachtú lá déag** the seventeenth (day)

seacláid *f2* chocolate

séad *m3* valuable object **séad fine** heirloom

séadaire *m4* pacemaker

séadchomhartha *m4* monument

seadóg *f2* grapefruit

seafóid *f2* nonsense

seafóideadh *adj* nonsensical, ridiculous

seafta *m4* shaft

seagal *m1* rye

seaicéad *m1* jacket **seaicéad fálaithe** lagging jacket, **seaicéad tarrthála** life jacket

seaimpéin *m4* champagne

seaimpín *m4* champion **seaimpín an domhain** the world champion

seal *m3* 1. turn **ní hé mo sheal é** it's not my turn 2. while, spell, period, shift (*of work*) **chaith sí seal ag taisteal timpeall na hEorpa** she spent a while travelling around Europe, **níl sa saol seo ach seal** nothing lasts for ever

seál *m1* shawl

séala *m4* 1. seal (*on letter*) 2. **ar shéala ...** about to ...

sealadach *adj* temporary, provisional **post sealadach** temporary position, **na Sealadaigh** the Provisionals

séalaigh *v* seal

sealaíocht *f3* alternation, rotation, relay **déanfaimid sealaíocht air / leis** we'll take it in turns, **rás sealaíochta** relay race

sealán *m1* 1. (hangman's) noose 2. washer, ring

sealbhach *adj, m1* possessive

sealbhaigh *v* possess

sealbhaíocht *f3* tenure, possession

sealbhóir *m3* occupier, holder

sealgaire *m4* hunter

sealgaireacht *f3* hunting

sealobair *f2* shift work

Sealtainn *f4* the Shetlands

sealúchas *m1* possession, property

seamair *f2* clover **tá an tseamair Mhuire aici** she has the four-leaved shamrock, she is very lucky

seamhan *m1* semen

seamlas *m1* shambles, slaughterhouse

seampú *m4* shampoo

seamróg *f2* shamrock **seamróg na gceithre gcluas a bheith agat** to have the four-leaved shamrock, to be very lucky, **ag fliuchadh na seamróige** drinking

sean¹ *adj* old **is sine Deirdre ná Clíona** Deirdre is older than Clíona *m4* 1. ancestor, senior 2. old **an sean agus an nua** the old and the new

sean-² *prefix* old **sa sean-am** in olden times, **seancharr** old car

séan *v* deny

seanad *m1* senate

séanadh *m* denial

seanadóir *m3* senator

seanaimseartha *adj* old-fashioned

seanaois *f2* old age **pinsean, pinsinéir seanaoise** old-age pension, pensioner

seanársa *adj* primitive

seanathair *m5* grandfather

seanchailleach *f2* old woman

seanchaí *m4* storyteller

seanchaíocht *f3* storytelling

seanchaite *adj* worn-out

seanchas *m1* 1. lore, storytelling 2. gossip

seanda *adj* old, antique, ancient

seandacht *f3* antiquity **seandachtaí** antiques

seandaí *m4* shandy

seandálaí *m4* archaeologist

seandálaíocht *f3* archaeology **láithreán seandálaíochta** archaeological site

seanduine *m4* old person

seaneolaí *m4* gerontologist

seaneolaíocht *f3* gerontology

seanfhaiseanta *adj* old-fashioned

seanfhear *m1* old man

seanfhocal *m1* proverb

seanfhondúir *m3* old-timer, veteran

seang *adj* slim, slender

seangán *m1* ant **nead seangán** ant-hill, **ghoidfeadh sé an t-earra ón seangán** he'd steal the shirt off your back

seanléim *f2* **bheith ar do sheanléim** to be your old self

seanmháthair *f5* grandmother

seanmóir *f3* sermon

seanmóireacht *f3* preaching

seanóir *m3* old person, elder

sean-nós *m1* 1. old custom 2. traditional unaccompanied singing

seans *adv* possibly **seans go mbeidh mé ann** perhaps I'll be there *m4* chance **dul sa seans** to run/take a risk, **téigh sa seans** risk it, **de sheans a tharla sé** it happened by chance

séans *m4* seance

seansaighdiúir *m3* veteran

seansailéir *m3* chancellor

seantán *m1* shed, shack

Sean-Tiomna *m4* Old Testament

Seapáin *f2* **an tSeapáin** Japan

Seapáinis *f2* Japanese (*language*)

Seapánach *adj, m1* Japanese

séarachas *m1* sewerage

searbh *adj* bitter, sour **bíonn an fhírinne searbh** the truth hurts

searbhaigh *v* embitter, sour

searbhas *m1* sarcasm, bitterness

searbhasach *adj* sarcastic, bitter

searbhónta *m4* servant

searc *f2* love **céadsearc mo chroí** my (heart's) first love

searg *v* shrivel

seargán *m1* mummy

searmanas *m1* ceremony

searr *v* stretch **tú féin a shearradh** to stretch yourself

searrach *m1* foal **brat searraigh** caul

searradh *m* stretching

seas *v* stand **deoch a sheasamh** to stand a drink, **caithfidh tú an fód a sheasamh** you have to stand your ground, **ní féidir liom é a sheasamh níos mó** I can't stand him/it any more

seasamh *m1* stand(ing) **tá mé i mo sheasamh ó mhaidin** I'm standing since morning, **níl seasamh agam léi** I can't put up with her

seasc *adj* barren, dry, unfruitful

seasca *m5* sixty **sna seascaidí** in the sixties

seascadú[1] *m4* sixtieth **aon seascadú do rud** one sixtieth of something

seascadú[2] *adj* sixtieth **scaoileadh saor (ó phríosún) é in aois a sheascadú bliain** he was released (from prison) in his sixtieth year

seascair *adj* comfortable, cosy, snug

seascann *m1* marsh, bog, swamp

seasmhach *adj* steadfast, consistent

seasmhacht *f3* constancy, consistency, durability

seasta *adj*, standing, fixed **ús seasta** fixed interest

seastán *m1* stand

séasúr *m1* season

séasúrach *adj* seasonal, seasonable

seat *m4* shot **seatanna scannáin** film shots, **seat ón aer** aerial shot

seatnaí *m4* chutney

seic *m4* cheque

Seic *f2* Czech **Poblacht na Seice** the Czech Republic

Seiceach *adj, m1* Czech

seiceáil *f3* check(ing) **seiceáil siar** checking back *v* check **rud a sheiceáil** to check something

seicheamh *m1* sequence

seicin *f4* membrane **maidhm sheicne** rupture

Seicis *f2* Czech (*language*)

seicleabhar *m1* chequebook

seict *f2* sect

seicteach *adj* sectarian

seicteachas *m1* sectarianism

séid *v* blow, inflate **adharc a shéideadh** to beep a horn, **fiús a shéideadh** to blow a fuse, **balún a shéideadh** to inflate a balloon

séideadh *m* blowing, draught, blast, inflation

séideán *m1* 1. gust 2. pant (*from exertion*) **bhí séideán orm tar éis na siúlóide** I was panting after the walk

séideog *f2* puff **séideog ghaoithe** puff of wind

SEIF (siondróm easpa imdhíonachta faighte) AIDS, **SEIF iomlán** full-blown AIDS

seift *f2* device, plan

seiftigh *v* devise, improvise

seiftiú *m* improvisation

seiftiúil *adj* resourceful, ingenious

seilbh *f2* possession **teacht i seilbh ruda** to come into possession of something

seile *f4* spit, saliva

seilf *f2* shelf

seilg *f2* hunt *v* hunt, prey on

seilide *m4* snail

séimeantach *adj* semantic

séimeantaic *f2* semantics

séimh *adj* mild, gentle, pleasant

séimhigh *v* become mild, mellow

séimhiú *m* lenition (**h** *after consonant*)

seimineár *m1* seminar

seinm *f3* playing (*music*)

seinn *v* play (*music*)

seinnteoir *m3* player **seinnteoir dlúthdhioscaí** compact disc player

séipéal *m1* chapel

séiplíneach *m1* chaplain, curate

seipteach *adj* septic **umar seipteach** septic tank

seirbhís *f2* service **seirbhís eolais / faisnéise** information service

seirbhíseach *m1* servant

seirbil *f2* gerbil

seiris *f2* sherry

séirse *m4* charge **séirse bataí / smachtíní** baton charge

seisean *emphatic pron* he **ní raibh seisean ann fiú** even he wasn't there

seisear *m1* six people **seisear amhránaithe** six singers

seisiún *m1* session **seisiún ceoil is amhránaíochta** session of music and song

seit *m4* set **rince seit** set dance

seithe *f4* skin, hide

seitreach *f2* neighing

seo *adj, adv, demonstrative pron* this, these **an ceann seo** this one, **na deochanna seo** these drinks, **faoi seo** by now, **as seo amach** from now on, **seo leat** come on, **seo linn, leo** here we, they go, **seo duit** here, take this

seó *m4* show **seó bóthair** road show, **seó cainte** talk show

seobhaineach *adj, m1* chauvinist

seobhaineachas *m1* chauvinism

seodóir *m3* jeweller

seodra *m4* jewellery

seoid *f2* jewel, precious thing **seoid is ea í** she's a jewel

seoigh *adj* wonderful **táimid ag déanamh go seoigh** we're doing great

seoinín *m4* shoneen

Seoirseach *adj* Georgian **foirgneamh Seoirseach** a Georgian building

seoithín *m4* whispering sound **seoithín seó** lullaby

seol¹ *m1* 1. sail **bád seoil** sailing boat 2. course, direction, flow 3. loom

seol² *v* 1. sail 2. launch, guide **leabhar a sheoladh** to launch a book, **cé atá do bhur seoladh?** who is guiding you (*pl*)? **ba a sheoladh** to drive cattle 3. send **litir a sheoladh** to send a letter

seol³ *m1* **i luí seoil** in childbirth

seoladh *m* 1. sailing 2. guidance, direction **ar sheoladh an mhúinteora** at the guidance of the teacher 3. launch **seoladh leabhair** book launch 4. address **leabhar seoltaí** address book

seoltóir *m3* 1. sailor 2. conductor (*electrical*) 3. sender (*of letter, money, etc*)

seoltóireacht *f3* sailing **seoltóireacht toinne** surfing

seomra *m4* room **seomra folctha, suí** bathroom, sitting-room

séú¹ *m4* sixth **cúig shéú de** five sixths of it

séú² *adj* sixth **an séú bliain** sixth year

sféar *m1* sphere

sí¹ *pron* she, it **dúirt sí liom é** she said it to me, **sular bhuail sí an talamh** before it hit the ground

sí² *m4* 1. fairy mound **bean sí** banshee, **an slua sí** the fairy host 2. magic, enchanting **ceol sí** enchanting music

sia *adj* longer, further **an t-oileán is sia siar in Éirinn** the most westerly island in Ireland

siabhrán *m1* mental confusion, delusion **siabhrán mórgachta** delusion of grandeur

siad *pron* they **chaith siad an t-airgead ar fad** they spent all the money, **tagann siad uair sa bhliain** they come once a year

siamsa *m4* amusement, entertainment **Siamsa Tíre** National Folk Theatre

siansa *m4* symphony, melody

siansach *adj* symphonic, melodious

siar *adj, adv, prep* 1. westwards **téigh siar go Carna agus feicfidh tú é** go west to Carna and you'll see it 2. back **suigh siar sa chathaoir** sit back in the chair, **tharla sé sin i bhfad siar** that happened long ago, **ól / caith siar é** knock it back (*of drink*), **ag siúl siar is aniar** walking back and forth

sibh *pron* you (*pl*) **an bhfuil sibh go maith?** are you well? **tabharfar ar cuairt go dtí an tArd-Mhúsaem sibh** you will be brought on a visit to the National Museum, **nach sibh atá cliste?** aren't you clever?

sibhialta *adj* civil

sibhialtach *adj, m1* civilian

sibhialtacht *f3* civilisation, civility **sibhialtacht na Gréige is na Róimhe** Greek and Roman civilisation

sibhse *emphatic pron* you (*pl*) **sibhse a bheidh thíos leis** it'll be you who will pay for it

síbín *m4* shebeen

síc *m4* sheik

síceach *adj* psychic

síceolaí *m4* psychologist

síceolaíoch *adj* psychological

síceolaíocht *f3* psychology

síciatrach *adj* psychiatric

síciatracht *f3* psychiatry

síciatraí *m4* psychiatrist

Sicil *f2* **an tSicil** Sicily

Sicileach *adj, m1* Sicilian

sicín *m4* chicken

sifilis *f2* syphilis

sil *v* drip, drain, shed **tá uisce ag sileadh (anuas) ón tsíleáil** there is water dripping (down) from the ceiling, **rud a shileadh** to drain something, **ag sileadh deor** shedding tears, weeping

síl *v* think **ní shílim é** I don't think so

Síle *f1* **an tSíle** Chile

sileadh *m1* drip, drain, discharge **raca silte** draining board, **sileadh cluaise** ear discharge

síleáil *f3* ceiling

siléar *m1* cellar

siléig *f2* neglect **rinne mé siléig ann** I neglected it

siléigeach *adj* neglectful

silín *m4* cherry

silteach *adj* dripping, fluid

siméadrach *adj* symmetrical

siméadracht *f3* symmetry

simléar *m1* chimney

simpeansaí *m4* chimpanzee

simpleoir *f3* simpleton

simplí *adj* simple

simplíocht *f3* simplicity

sin *adj, adv, demonstrative pron* that, **those an scannán sin** that film, **na pobail sin** those communities, **go dtí sin** until then, **mar sin** like that, thus, **agus mar sin de** and so on, **cúpla lá ó shin** a couple of days ago, **ní raibh mé ag caint léi ó shin** I haven't been talking to her since

Sín *f2* **an tSín** China

sín *v* 1. stretch **nuair a bhíonn an bolg lán is maith leis na cnámha síneadh** when the stomach is full the bones like to rest 2. extend, point **méid ruda a shíneadh** to extend the size of something, **ná**

sín do mhéar chugamsa arís
don't point your finger at me again

sin-seanathair *m5* great-grandfather

sin-seanmháthair *f5* great-grandmother

sinc *f2* zinc

sindeacáit *f2* syndicate

sine *f4* nipple, teat

sineach *adj* mammilary *f2* mammal

Síneach *adj, m1* Chinese

síneadh *m1* stretching, extension **síntí láimhe** tips, **síneadh fada** accent on vowel, **síneadh ama (i mbeár)** extension (in a bar)

singil *adj* single

sínigh *v* sign

Sínis *f2* Chinese (*language*)

síniú *m* autograph, signature

sinn *pron* we, us **agus sinn ag feitheamh leat** and we waiting for you, **sinn féin** ourselves

sinne *emphatic pron* we, us **sinne a bhí ann** it was us who were there

sinsear *m1* 1. ancestor 2. senior **na sinsir, foireann na sinsear** the seniors (*team*)

sinséar *m1* ginger

sinsearach *adj* 1. ancestral 2. senior *m1* 1. ancestor 2. senior

sinsearacht *f3* 1. ancestry 2. seniority

sinseartha *adj* ancestral

sínte *adj* extended, outstretched

sínteán *m1* stretcher

sintéis *f2* synthesis

sintéiseach *adj* synthetic **snáithíní sintéiseacha** synthetic fibres

síntiús *m1* subscription

síntiúsóir *m3* subscriber

síob *f2* ride, lift **ní bhfaighidh tú síob uaimse** you won't get a lift from me

síobadh *m* blow, drift **rugadh air sa síobadh sneachta** he was caught in the blizzard

síobhas *m1* chive

síobshiúil *v* hitch-hike

síobshiúlóir *m3* hitch-hiker

sioc *m3* frost *v* freeze

siocair *f5* cause **siocair bháis** cause of death, **as siocair...** on account of...

siocaire *m4* chicory

siocán *m1* frost, frosty weather

síocanailís *f2* psychoanalysis

síocanailísí *m4* psychoanalyst

síocháin *f3* peace **próiseas síochána** peace process

síochánta *adj* peaceful, passive

sioc-obacht *f3* frost-resistance

sioctha *adj* frosted

siocúil *adj* frosty

síoda *m4* silk **cuir síoda ar ghabhar agus is gabhar i gcónaí é** you can't make a silk purse out of a sow's ear

síodúil *adj* 1. silky, smooth 2. courteous

sióg *f2* fairy

siogairlín *m4* pendant

síol *m1* seed, sperm, semen

siolla *m4* syllable

siollabas *m1* syllabus

síolraigh *v* 1. breed, reproduce 2. **síolraigh ó** descend from

siombail *f2* symbol

siombalach *adj* symbolic

siombalachas *adj* symbolism

siombalaigh *v* symbolise

síon *f2* bad weather **lá idir dhá shíon** pet day, **bogha síne** rainbow

sionad *m1* synod

sionagóg *f2* synagogue

Sionainn *f2* **an tSionainn** the Shannon

siondróm *m1* syndrome **siondróm easpa imdhíonachta faighte (SEIF)** acquired immunodeficiency syndrome (AIDS)

sionnach *m1* fox **Carraig an tSionnaigh** Foxrock

siopa *m4* shop **siopa ilranna** department store, **siopaí sraithe** chain stores

siopadóir *m3* shopkeeper

siopadóireacht *f3* shopping **lárionad siopadóireachta** shopping centre

síor *adj* eternal **de shíor** constantly

sioráf *m1* giraffe

síoraí *adj* eternal, continual

síoraíocht *f3* eternity

siorc *m3* shark

síorghlas *adj* evergreen

síoróip *f2* syrup

síos *adj, adv, prep* down(wards) **chuaigh sí síos faoin tír** she went down the country

siosarnach *f2* hissing, rustling, whispering

siosma *m4* schism

siosúr *m1* scissors

siosúrtha *adj* scissors-like, sharp (*tongue*)

síota *m4* cheetah

síothlaigh *v* 1. strain, drain 2. die, pass away

síothlán *m1* strainer, colander

sip *m4* zip

sipdhúntóir *m3* zip

sirriam *m4* sheriff

síscéal *m1* fairy-tale

sise *emphatic pron* she, her **bhí sise ann romhainn** she was there before us, **ní fhéadfainn é a dhéanamh gan sise** I wouldn't be able to do it without her

siséal *m1* chisel

siúcra *m4* sugar

siúd *demonstrative pron* that, those **seo is siúd** this and that, **ná habair siúd** don't say that, **a leithéidí siúd** the likes of them

siúicrín *m4* saccharine

siúil *v* 1. walk **chuaigh sé ag siúl ann** he went there walking 2. **siúl amach le duine** to go out with somebody, to date somebody

siúinéir *m3* joiner, carpenter

siúinéireacht *f3* joinery, carpentry

siúl *m1* walk **ar siúl** in progress, going on, **faoi shiúl** in motion, **sa siúl** on the move, **de shiúl na gcos** on foot

siúlóid *f2* walk

siúlóir *f3* walker

siúlscéalaí *m4* walkie-talkie

siúntaigh *v* joint

siúr *f* sister **an tSiúr Treasa** Sister Treasa

siúráilte *adj* certain **chomh siúráilte is atá cros ar asal** as sure as ever

slabhra *m4* chain

slabhrúil *adj* chain **imoibriú slabhrúil** chain reaction

slacán *m1* bat (*sport*)

slacht *m3* neatness, good appearance, finish **slacht a chur ar rud** to put something in order

slachtmhar *adj* neat, in good condition, finished

slad *m3* plunder, loot

sladmhargadh *m1* bargain, low price

slaghdán *m1* cold **tá slaghdán uirthi** she has a cold

sláinte *f4* health, toast **cad é mar atá an tsláinte?** how's the health?

sláinteachas *m1* hygiene

sláintíoch *adj* sanitary **súitín sláintíoch** sanitary towel, tampon

sláintíocht *f3* sanitation

sláintiúil *adj* healthy

slán *adj* 1. safe, sound **slán sábháilte** safe and sound, **ná déan talamh slan de go ...** don't take it for granted that ... 2. entire, whole **tá an trí scór slán aici** she is full sixty years old *m1* 1. healthy person 2. health, farewell **d'fhágamar slán aici** we bade her goodbye, **slán go fóill!** so long!

slánaigh *v* 1. redeem, save **d'anam a shlánú** to save your soul 2. complete, reach (*a certain age*) **tá ocht mbliana déag slánaithe aige** he has turned eighteen

slánaíocht *f3* guarantee, indemnity **polasaí slánaíochta** indemnity policy

slánaitheoir *m3* saviour

slánchéillí *adj* sane

slánchiall *f2* sanity

slándáil *f3* security **garda slándála** security guard

slánlann *f2* sanitorium

slánú *m* 1. salvation 2. completion

slánuimhir *f5* whole number

slaparnach *f2* splashing

slat *f2* 1. rod **slat iascaigh / iascaireachta** fishing rod, **slat draíochta** (magic) wand, **slat tomhais** measuring-rod, criterion 2. yard **tá sé cúpla céad slat suas an bóthar** it's a couple of hundred yards up the road

sleá *f4* spear, javelin

sleabhac *m1* slouch, droop **tá sleabhac air** he walks with a slouch *v* droop

sléacht *v* bow down, kneel

sleamhain *adj* smooth, slippery

sleamhnaigh *v* slip, slide

sleamhnán *m1* slide **carr sleamhnáin** toboggan

sleamhnú *m* slip, slide

sléibhteoir *m3* mountaineer

sléibhteoireacht *f3* mountaineering

sléibhtiúil *adj* mountainous

slí *f4* way, space, method **tá tú sa tslí orm** you are in my way, **an bhfuil dóthain slí sa charr dó?** is there enough space in the car for him/it? **slí bheatha** livelihood

sliabh *m* mountain

sliabhraon *m1* mountain range

Sligeach *m1* Sligo **Co. Shligigh** Co. Sligo

slim *adj* slender, slim, sleek, smooth

slinn *f2* slate, tile **ceann slinne** slate roof

slinneán *m1* shoulder blade

slinneánach *adj* broad-shouldered

slíoc *v* stroke, pat, pet

sliocht *m3* 1. descendants, offspring 2. extract (*from literature*)

sliochtach *m1* descendant

slíoctha *adj* sleek

sliogán *m1* shell

slios *m3* 1. side, slice 2. inclination

sliotán *m1* slot

sliotar *m1* sliotar, hurling ball

slipéar *m1* slipper

slis *f2* chip, sliver, slice

sliseog *f2* small chip, sliver, thin slice

slisín *m4* rasher

sloc *m1* pit, shaft (*of mine*)

slog *m1* gulp, swig, swallow **níor ól mé ach cúpla slog** I only had a couple of swigs *v* gulp, swallow **slog siar é** knock it back, **b'fhearr liom go slogfadh an talamh mé ná a bheith ann** I'd prefer the earth to swallow me up than to be there

slógadh *m1* 1. rally 2. **Slógadh** Irish-language youth festival

sloinne *m4* surname

slua *m4* host, crowd, multitude, throng **an slua sí** the fairy host, **bhí na sluaite ann** there was a great crowd there

sluaisteáil *v* 1. shovel 2. gather a lot **tá sí ag sluaisteáil airgid ann** she's making loads of money there

sluasaid *f2* shovel

sluma *m4* slum

smacht *m3* control, discipline **ní bhíonn an rath ach mar a**

mbíonn an smacht there can be no success without discipline

smachtaigh *v* control, discipline

smachtbhanna *m4* sanction smachtbhannaí eacnamaíocha economic sanctions

smachtín *m4* baton, club séirse smachtíní baton charge

smachtú *m* rule, control

smailc *f2* 1. snack, bite 2. pull smailc a bhaint as toitín to take a pull of a cigarette *v* 1. gobble (*food*) 2. puff (*a cigarette, pipe, etc*)

smál *m1* stain, blemish gan smál flawless, immaculate

smaoineamh *m1* thought, thinking, idea

smaoinigh *v* think, consider, reflect

smaointeach *adj* thoughtful, pensive

smaointeoir *m3* thinker

smeach *m3* 1. snap, flick (*of fingers*), smack (*of lips*) 2. sob *v* snap, flick, click

smear *v* smear, smudge

sméar *f2* berry sméara dubha blackberries

smearadh *m1* 1. cream smearadh gréine, oíche sun, night cream 2. smear, smudge 3. spread (*butter, paste, etc*)

sméid *v* wink, nod, beckon

smid *f2* 1. word, syllable ná habair smid don't say a word 2. breath ní raibh smid ghaoithe ann there wasn't a breath of wind

smideadh *m1* make-up (*cosmetic*)

smidiríní *pl* smithereens tá sé ina smidiríní it's in bits, it's shattered

smig *f2* chin

smior *m3* marrow

smiot *v* hit, smash, break into fragments

smólach *m1* thrush

smolchaite *adj* partly worn, threadbare

smúdáil *v* iron ag smúdáil éadaí ironing clothes

smuga *m4* mucus, snot

smugairle *m4* spit smugairle róin jellyfish, smugairle an tseoil Portuguese man-of-war

smuigleáil *v* smuggle

smuigléir *m3* smuggler

smuigléireacht *f3* smuggling

smúit *f2* 1. dust, smoke, mist 2. gloom

smúitiúil *adj* 1. smoky, misty 2. gloomy

smúr *v* sniff

smúrthacht *f3* sniffing, nosing, snooping

smut *m1* 1. snout smut madra dog's snout 2. huff, pout tá smut air liom he's in a huff with me 2. portion chaitheamar smut den lá ann we spent some of the day there

snag¹ *m3* 1. hiccup tá snag orm I have the hiccups 2. lull tá snag san aimsir there's a lull in the weather 3. catch in breath, sob

snag² *m3* snag breac magpie

snagcheol *m1* jazz

snaidhm *f2* knot, plot scaoileadh na snaidhme the unravelling of the plot *v* 1. knot, join, tie 2. knit (*bone, wound, etc*)

snáithe *m4* thread

snáithín *m4* fibre snáithín cothaitheach dietary fibre, snáithíní sintéiseacha synthetic fibres, gloine snáithíní fibreglass

snámh *m3* swim linn snámha swimming pool *v* 1. swim, float (*of boat*) 2. crawl leanbh ag snámh thart a child crawling about

snámhóir *m3* swimmer

snaoisín *m4* snuff

snas *m3* polish, finish snas a chur ar rud to polish/finish something

snasán *m1* polish **snasán bróg** shoe polish

snasta *adj* polished, elegant, refined, glossy, finished

snáth *m3* thread, yarn

snáthaid *f2* 1. needle 2. hand of watch or clock, pointer

snáthaidpholladh *m* acupuncture

sneachta *m4* snow **ráth sneachta** snow drift

sneachtúil *adj* snowy

sní *f4* flow **sní uisce** flow of water

snigh *v* flow, pour, crawl (*as snail*)

sníomh *m3* spinning, weaving *v* spin, weave

snoigh *v* 1. sculpture, carve 2. waste away

snoíodóir *m3* sculptor

snoíodóireacht *f3* sculpture, carving

snoite *adj* 1. shaped, smoothed 2. wasted away, worn down

snua *m4* complexion, appearance

snúcar *m1* snooker

so- *prefix* easy to **so-athraithe** easy to change

só *m4* ease, luxury

só-árasán *m1* luxury flat/apartment

sobal *m1* froth, suds, lather

so-bhlasta *adj* palatable, tasty

sobhogtha *adj* movable

sobhriste *adj* easily broken, fragile

sobhuailte *adj* easy to beat

sóbráilte *adj* sober

soc *m1* 1. snout, muzzle 2. nozzle

socair *adj* quiet, settled, calm, steady **fan socair!** stay quiet! settle! **tá lámha socra aici** she has steady hands

sochaí *f4* society

sochar *m1* 1. benefit **sochair leasa shóisialaigh** social welfare benefits, **sochar an amhrais** the benefit of the doubt 2. credit

socheolaíocht *f3* sociology

sochorraithe *adj* excitable

sochrach *adj* beneficial, profitable

sochraid *f2* funeral

sochreidte *adj* credible

sócmhainn *f2* asset **réadú sócmhainní** realisation of assets

sócmhainneach *adj* solvent

sócmhainneacht *f3* solvency

socracht *f3* rest, ease, quietness

socraigh *v* settle, arrange

socraithe *adj* settled, arranged, fixed

socrú *m* settlement, arrangement

sócúlach *adj* easy, comfortable

sócúlacht *f3* ease, comfort

sodar *m1* trot, trotting **ag sodar i ndiaidh na n-uasal** sucking up to the gentry

só-earra *m4* luxury good

sofaisticiúil *adj* sophisticated

sofheicthe *adj* visible, obvious

soghluaiste *adj* mobile

soghonta *adj* vulnerable

soibealta *adj* cheeky, impudent

soibealtacht *f3* cheek, impudence

soicéad *m1* socket **soicéad balla** wall socket

soicind *f2* second **fan soicind** wait a second

sóid *f2* soda **uisce sóide** soda-water

soighe *m4* soya

soilbhir *adj* cheerful, pleasant

soilbhreas *m1* cheerfulness

soiléir *adj* obvious, plain, clear

soiléireacht *f3* obviousness, clarity

soiléirigh *v* clarify

soiléiriú *m* clarification

soilire *m4* celery

soilsigh *v* 1. shine, illuminate 2. enlighten

soilsiú *m* illumination, enlightenment

soineann *f2* good weather

soineanta *adj* innocent, naive

soineantacht *f3* innocence, naivety

sóinseáil *f3, v* change

soir *adj, adv, prep* eastwards **ag dul soir go Béal na mBláth** going east to Béal na mBláth, **soir ón teach** to the east of the house

soirbhíoch *m1* optimist

soirbhíochas *m1* optimism

soiscéal *m1* gospel

soiscéalach *adj* evangelical

soiscéalaí *m4* evangelist, preacher

sóisear *m1* junior **na sóisir, foireann na sóisear** the juniors (*team*)

sóisearach *adj* junior

sóisialach *adj* 1. socialist 2. social **sochair leasa shóisialaigh** social welfare benefits

sóisialachas *m1* socialism

sóisialaí *m4* socialist

sóisialta *adj* social **leas sóisialta** social welfare

soith *f2* bitch (*animal*)

soitheach *m1* vessel, ship, dish **soitheach cogaidh** warship, **ag ní (na) soithí** washing (the) dishes

sól *m1* sole (*fish*) **sól sleamhain** lemon sole

solad *m1* solid

soladach *adj* solid

soláimhsithe *adj* manageable

sólann *f2* leisure centre

solaoid *f2* example

solas *m1* light **múch an solas, na soilse** turn off the light, the lights, **le solas an lae** by daylight, **rud a thabhairt chun solais** to bring something to light

sólás *m1* solace, comfort

sólásaigh *v* comfort, console

solasmhar *adj* bright

soláthair *v* procure, supply **seirbhís a sholáthar do dhuine** to provide a service for somebody

soláthar *m1* provision, supply **soláthairtí** provisions, supplies, **éileamh agus soláthar** demand and supply

soláthraí *m4* provider, supplier

soléite *adj* readable, legible

sollúnta *adj* solemn

solúbtha *adj* flexible

son, ar son for the sake of, **ar son na cúise** for the cause, **ar mo shon féin** for my own sake

sona *adj* happy, fortunate, lucky

sonas *m1* happiness, prosperity

sonra *m4* detail **sonraí data**, **bunachar sonraí** database, **próiseáil sonraí** data processing, **an tAcht um Chosaint Sonraí** the Data Protection Act

sonrach *adj* particular, specific

sonraigh *v* 1. specify, state 2. distinguish, perceive

sonraíoch *adj* peculiar, noticeable, remarkable, striking

sonraíocht *f3* specification, peculiarity **tógtha de réir sonraíochta** built to specification

sonrasc *m1* invoice

sonrú *m* specification, detail

sop *m1* wisp, (drinking-)straw **am soip** bed-time

soprán *m1* soprano

sorcas *m1* circus

sorcóir *m3* cylinder **sorcóir gáis** gas cylinder

sorn *m1* furnace

sornóg *f2* stove

sórt *m1* kind, sort **cén sórt raiméise é sin?** what kind of nonsense is that?

sórtáil *v* sort

sos *m3* cessation, rest, pause, intermission **sos comhraic** ceasefire, **sos cogaidh** truce, **sos caife, tae** coffee, tea break

sotalach *adj* arrogant

sothuigthe *adj* easily understood, comprehensible

sóúil *adj* comfortable

spá *m4* spa

spád *f2* spade

spadánta *adj* slow, sluggish

spadhar *m1* fit, notion **bhuail spadhar mé** I got a notion

spadhrúil *adj* mentally unbalanced, moody

spág *f2* big, clumsy foot

spaga *m4* purse

spágach *adj* clumsy (*with feet*)

spágáil *v* trudge, walk clumsily

spailpín *m4* migratory labourer, 'spalpeen'

spailpínteacht *f3* working as a 'spalpeen'

Spáinn, an *f2* Spain

Spáinneach *adj* Spanish *m1* Spaniard

spáinnéar *f2* spaniel

Spáinnis *f2* Spanish (*language*)

spaisteoireacht *f3* strolling, rambling

spallta *adj* parched, dried up **tá mé spallta leis an tart** I'm parched with the thirst

spáráil *v* spare, save **an mbeadh aon ní le spáráil agat?** would you have anything to spare?

sparán *m1* purse **sparán na caillí mairbhe** egg case (*of squid*), mermaid's purse

sparánaí *m4* treasurer, bursar

spártha *adj* spare

spás *m1* space

spásáil *f3* spacing *v* space

spásaire *m4* 1. astronaut 2. someone who is 'spaced', spacer

spásárthach *m1* spacecraft

speach *f2* 1. kick **speach asail, chapaill** donkey's, horse's kick, **speach ghunna** kick of a gun 2. **speach ghearáin** flick, snap of fingers

spéaclaí *pl* glasses **an gcaitheann sí spéaclaí?** does she wear glasses?

speal *f2* scythe

speiceas *m1* species

speictream *m1* spectrum

spéir *f2* sky **fíor na spéire** the horizon

spéirbhean *f5* beautiful woman (*in poetry*)

spéireata *m4* spade (*cards*)

spéirling *f2* thunderstorm

speirm *f2* sperm

spéis *f2* 1. interest **is beag spéis atá agam san ábhar** I have little interest in the matter/subject 2. affection **thug sé spéis di** he became fond of her

speisialta *adj* special

speisialtacht *f3* speciality

speisialtóir *m3* specialist

speisialtóireacht *f3* specialisation

spéisiúil *adj* interesting

spiaire *m4* spy

spiaireacht *f3* spying

spíce *m4* spike

spideog *f2* 1. robin 2. drop from nose

spíon *v* 1. comb, tease out 2. exhaust, wear out

spionáiste *m4* spinach

spíonán *m1* gooseberry

spionnadh *m1* vigour, force

spíonta *adj* worn-out, exhausted

spior spear, spior spear a dhéanamh de rud to dismiss something, to make nothing of something

spiorad *m1* spirit

spioradálta *adj* spiritual

spíosra *m4* spice

spíosrach *adj* spicy

splanc *f2* flash **splancacha agus toirneach** thunder and lightning, **splanc thintrí** flash of lightning *v* flash, flame

spleách *adj* dependent

spléach *v* glance **spléach sí air** she glanced at it

spléachadh *m1* glimpse, glance **ní bhfuair mé spléachadh orthu** I couldn't get a glimpse of them

spleáchas *m1* dependence

spléach-chárta *m4* flashcard

spleodar *m1* glee, cheerfulness, exuberance

spleodrach *adj* gleeful, cheerful, exuberant, boisterous

spóca *m4* spoke

spoch *v* 1. annoy, tease **bíonn siad de shíor ag spochadh aisti** they are always teasing her 2. geld, castrate

spól *m1* spool

spóla *m4* joint (*meat*)

spontáineach *adj* spontaneous

spontáineacht *f3* spontaneity

spor *m1* spur

spórt *m1* sport, fun **lárionad spóirt** sports centre

spórtúil *adj* sportive, sporty, amusing

spota *m4* spot

spotsolas *m1* spotlight

sprae *m4* spray

spraeáil *v* spray

spraíúil *adj* playful

spraoi *m4* fun, play **geansaí spraoi** sweat shirt

spraoithiománaí *m4* joyrider

spré *f4* dowry **is fearr bean ná spré** a (good) woman is better than a dowry

spréach *f2, v* spark

spréachphlocóid *f2* spark plug

spreag *v* 1. encourage, inspire, urge 2. stimulate

spreagadh *m* 1. encouragement, inspiration, incentive 2. stimulus

spreagthach *adj* stimulating *m1* stimulant

spreagúil *adj* encouraging, inspiring, stimulating

spréigh *v* spread, scatter, disperse

spréire *m4* spreader, sprinkler

sprid *f2* 1. spirit, ghost 2. courage, spirit

spridiúil *adj* spirited

sprioc *f2* target, objective, goal **súil sprice** bull's eye

spriocdháta *m4* deadline

sprioclá *m* deadline

sprionga *m4* spring (*metal*)

sprionlaithe *adj* miserly, mean

sprionlaitheacht *f3* miserliness, stinginess

sprionlóir *m3* miser

sprochaille *f4* 1. gill 2. loose skin **tá sprochaillí faoi na súile aici** she has bags under her eyes

sprús *m1* spruce

spuaic *f2* 1. welt, blister 2. spire, steeple

spúinse *m4* sponge

spúinseach *adj* spongy

spúinseáil *v* sponge

spúnóg *f2* spoon

srac *v* 1. tear 2. drag

sracfhéachaint *f2* glance

sráid *f2* street **Sráid an Mhuilinn** Millstreet

sráldbhaile *m4* village an **Sráidbhaile** Stradbally ('the village')

sralth *f2* 1. row, series **sraith tithe** row of houses, **comórtas sraithe** league (*competition*) 2. layer

sraithadhmad *m1* plywood

sraithchomórtas *m1* league (*competition*)

sraitheog *f2* sequence **sraitheog moillithe** slow-motion sequence

sraithscéal *m1* serial

srann *f2* snore, snort **bhí sí ina srann chodlata** she was fast asleep *v* snore, snort **ag srannadh** snoring

sraoth *m3* snecze **sraoth a ligean** to sneeze

srapnal *m1* shrapnel

sreabh *f2* flow, current **sreabh laibhe** lava flow

sreabhann *m1* chiffon

sreang *f2* wire, string **sreang mhearbhia** fast food chain, **sreang imleacáin** umbilical cord, **sreang dheilgneach** barbed wire

sreangach *adj* stringy, stringed, (*of eye*) bloodshot

sreangra *m4* wiring

sreangscéal *m1* telegram, wire

sreangscuab *f2* wire brush

sreangshiopaí *pl* chain stores **comhlacht sreangshiopaí mearbhia** fast food chain

sreangú *m* wiring

srian *m1* 1. rein 2. bridle 3. restraint **srian a chur ort féin** to restrain yourself *v* restrain, curb **tú féin a shrianadh** to restrain yourself

srianta *adj* restrained, restricted

sroich *v* reach, attain, arrive at

sról *m1* satin

srón *f2* nose **poll sróine** nostril

srónáil *f3* nasalisation **ag srónáil** talking through the nose

srónbheannach *m1* rhinoceros

sruth *m3* stream

sruthaigh *v* stream, flow

sruthán *m1* stream

sruthlaigh *v* rinse, flush **éadaí a shruthlú** to rinse clothes, **an leithreas a shruthlú** to flush the toilet

sruthlam *m1* turbulence

sruthlamach *adj* turbulent

stábla *m4* stable **stáblaí** stables, mews

stad *m4* stop, halt, impedement **stad an bhus** (the) bus stop, **tá stad cainte aige** he has a speech impediment *v* stop, halt

stádas *m1* status

stadláithreán *m1* halting-site

staduaireadóir *m3* stopwatch

staic *f2* 1. stake, post 2. stubborn person **staic áiféise, staic mhagaidh** laughing-stock

staid *f2* 1. state, condition 2. stadium 3. furlong

staidéar *m1* study **ag déanamh staidéir** studying

staidéarach *adj* studious, sensible, steady

staidreamh *m1* statistics

staighre *m4* stairs **staighre beo** escalator

stail *f2* stallion

stailc *f2* strike

stailceoir *m3* striker

stair *f2* history **athbhreithniú staire** revisionism

stairiúil *adj* historic(al)

stáirse *m4* starch

stáiseanóir *m3* stationer

stáiseanóireacht *f3* stationery

stáisiún *m1* station **stáisiún cumhachta, dóiteáin, peitril, traenach** power, fire, petrol, train station, **stáisiún na nGardaí** Garda station

staitistic *f2* statistic

staitistiúil *adj* statistical

stáitse *m4* stage

stáitsigh *v* stage

stálaithe *adj* stale

stampa *m4* stamp

stampáil *v* stamp

stán[1] *m1* tin

stán[2] *v* stare

stánadh *m* stare **cad é an stánadh a bhí aige orm?** why was he staring at me?

stánaithe *adj* tinned **bia stánaithe** tinned food

stánosclóir *m3* tin-opener

staon *v* desist, stop, cease **staonadh ó rud** to abstain from something

staonadh *m* abstention, cessation

staonaire *m4* teetotaller

stápla *m4* staple

stápláil *v* staple

stáplóir *m3* stapler

staraí *m4* historian

starrfhiacail *f2* prominent tooth, tusk, fang

stát *m1* state (*political*) **ballstát** member-state, **na Stáit Aontaithe** the United States

statach *adj* static

státaire *m4* statesman, stateswoman

státrúnaí *m4* secretary of state

státseirbhís *f2* civil service

státseirbhíseach *m1* civil servant

státúil *adj* stately, dignified

steall *f2* squirt, splash *v* splash, pour

stealladh *m1* downpour **ag stealladh báistí** pouring rain

steallaire *m4* syringe

steanc *m4, v* splash, squirt

stéig *f2* 1. steak 2. intestine

steiréafón *m1* stereo **córas steiréafóin** stereo system

steiréafónach *adj* stereo

steiréisheinnteoir *m3* stereo player **steiréisheinnteoir caiséad** stereo cassette player

stiall *f2* 1. strip, piece of something 2. slap, stroke **stiall den teanga a thabhairt do dhuine** to give somebody verbal abuse

stil *f2* still (*for distilling whiskey, poitín, etc*)

stíl *f2* style, fashion

stiléir *m3* distiller

stiléireacht *f3* distilling, making poitín

stiogma *m4* stigma

stionsal *m1* stencil

stíoróip *f2* stirrup

stiúgtha *adj* parched, famished, starving **tá mé stiúgtha leis an ocras, leis an tart** I am starving, parched

stiúideo *m4* studio

stiúir *f5* 1. steering apparatus, rudder, helm 2. control **faoi stiúir** under control *v* 1. steer, guide 2. control, direct

stiúradh *m* 1. steering 2. guidance, supervision

stiúrthóir *m3* director **an Stiúrthóir Ionchúiseamh Poiblí** Director of Public Prosecutions (DPP)

stobh *v* stew

stobhach *m1* stew **stobhach gaelach** Irish stew

stoc *m1* 1. stock 2. trumpet

stoca *m4* stocking, sock

stócach *m1* young man

stocaireacht *f3* campaigning

stocáireamh *m1* stocktaking

stocbhróicéir *m3* stockbroker

stocmhalartán *m1* stock exchange

stocmhargadh *m1* stock market **praghsanna stocmhargaidh** stockmarket prices, **stocmhargaí an domhain** the world's stockmarkets

stocphota *m4* stockpot

stoda *m4* stud (*on clothing*)

Stoidiaca, an *m4* the Zodiac

stoirm *f2* storm

stoirmeach *adj* stormy

stoith *v* pluck, extract **fiacail a stoitheadh** to extract a tooth

stól *m1* stool

stolpach *adj* stodgy, constipating (*of food*)

stop *m4, v* stop

stopallán *m1* stopper, plug

stór[1] *m1* store, treasure **stór ilranna** department store, **a stór** darling

stór² *m1* storey **foirgneamh deich stór** ten-storey building

stóráil *f3* storage *v* store

stóras *m1* storeroom, storehouse

stórchiste *m4* thesaurus **stórchiste focal** thesauras

strae *m4* wandering, straying **ar strae** astray

stráice *m4* strip **aerstráice** airstrip

strainc *f2* grimace

strainséartha *adj* strange

strainséir *m3* stranger

straitéis *f2* strategy

straitéiseach *adj* strategic **pleanáil straitéiseach** strategic planning

strataisféar *m1* stratosphere

streachail *v* 1. struggle 2. drag

streachailt *f3* struggle

streachlánach *adj* trailing, straggling

striapach *f2* prostitute

striapachas *m1* prostitution

stríoc *f2* stripe, streak, stroke *v* 1. strike 2. yield

stró *m4* stress, difficulty **gan stró** without difficulty, easily

stróc *m4* stroke (*medical*)

stróghalar *m1* injury from exertion, strain injury **stróghalar athfhillteach** repetitive strain injury

stróic *f2* 1. tear 2. stroke (*of work, stick, etc*) *v* tear

stróiceadh *m* tear

stroighin *f2* cement

stroighnigh *v* cement

struchtúr *m1* structure **struchtúir trasteorann** cross-border structures

struchtúrach *adj* structural

strus *m1* strain, stress

stua *m4* arch, arc

stuacach *adj* 1. peaked 2. obstinate, sulky

stuaic *f2* 1. spire, peak 2. sulk **tá stuaic air** he's in a huff

stuáil *f3* stuffing, padding *v* stuff, pad

stuaim *f2* 1. prudence, self-control 2. skill, initiative **rud a dhéanamh as do stuaim féin** to do something on your own initiative

stuama *adj* 1. prudent, sensible 2. skilful

stuara *m4* arcade

stuif *m4* stuff, material

stumpa *m4* stump **stumpa amadáin** a stump of a fool, a terrible fool

sú¹ *m4* 1. juice **sú oráistí, trátaí, torthaí** orange, tomato, fruit juice 2. soup **sú circe** chicken soup 3. sap, energy **an sú a bhaint as rud** to take the sap/good out of something

sú² *f4* berry **sútha talún** strawberries, **sútha craobh** raspberries

sú³ *m4* suction

suáilce *f4* 1. virtue 2. joy

suáilceach *adj* 1. virtuous 2. joyful, pleasant

suaimhneach *adj* tranquil, quiet, peaceful

suaimhneas *m1* tranquillity, rest, peace

suaimhneasán *m1* tranquilliser, sedative

suaimhnigh *v* pacify, calm

suaimhnitheach *adj* pacifying, relaxing

suairc *adj* pleasant, agreeable

suaite *adj* confused, disturbed, upset

suaith *v* 1. mix **suimint a shuaitheadh** to mix cement 2. massage 3. confuse, disturb

suaitheadh *m* mix, confusion, disturbance

suaitheantas *m1* emblem, badge

Sualainn *f2* **an tSualainn** Sweden

Sualainnis *f2* Swedish (*language*)

Sualannach *adj* Swedish *m1* Swede

suan *m1* slumber, rest, sleep **chuirfeadh sé chun suain thú** it/he would put you to sleep

suanán *m1* tranquilliser, sedative

suanlios *m3* dormitory

suanmhar *adj* sleepy

suansiúl *m1* sleep-walking

suansiúlaí *m4* sleep-walker

suantraí *f4* lullaby

suarach *adj* trivial, petty, mean

suarachas *m1* triviality, pettiness, meanness

suas *adj, adv, prep* up **ag dul suas an staighre** going up the stairs, **tá sé cúpla míle suas an bóthar** it's a couple of miles up the road, **ar tháinig tú suas leo?** did you catch up with them?

suathaire *m3* masseur

suathaireacht *f3* massage

subh *f2* jam **subh oráiste** marmalade

subhach *adj* merry, cheerful

subhachas *m1* mirth, cheerfulness

substaint *f2* substance

substaintiúil *adj* substantial

súgach *adj* tipsy, merry

súgradh *m* playing, fun

suí *m1* sitting, out of bed **seomra suí** sitting-room, **laethanta suí na Dála** Dáil sitting days, **tá sí ina suí óna sé a chlog** she is up since six o'clock, **fan i do shuí** stay seated

suibiachtúil *adj* subjective

súiche *m4* soot

suigh *v* sit **suigh síos, suas** sit down, up

súigh *v* suck, soak up, absorb **páipéar súite** blotting-paper

súil *f2* 1. eye **caipín súile** eyelid, **súil sprice** bull's eye, **buaileadh i lár na súile mé** I was hit right in the eye, **ba bheag nár chaill tú radharc na súl** you nearly lost your eyesight 2. hope, expectation **beidh mé ag súil leat amárach** I'll be expecting you tomorrow, **tá súil agam** I hope so

súilaithne *f4* **tá súilaithne agam ort** I know you to see

súilfhéachaint *f3* glance

súilín *m4* bubble

súilíneach *adj* bubbly

suim *f2* 1. sum, amount **an tsuim iomlán** the full amount, total 2. interest **níl aon suim agam san fhisic** I've no interest in physics

suimigh *v* add

súimín *m4* sip

suimint *f2* cement **suimint a shuaitheadh** to mix cement

suimiúil *adj* interesting

suíochán *m1* seat

suíomh *m1* site, position, location, situation

suipéar *m1* supper

suirbhé *m4* survey

suirbhéir *m3* surveyor

suirbhéireacht *f3* survey **an tSuirbhéireacht Ordanáis** the Ordnance Survey

suirí *f4* courting

suiríoch *m1* suitor, wooer

suite *adj* 1. situated 2. stocky

súiteach *adj* absorbent

suiteáil *f3* installation **suiteáil gáis** gas installation

súiteoir *m3* 1. sucker 2. squatter

súitín *m4* small absorbent pad **súitín sláintíoch** sanitary towel, tampon

sula *conj* before **sular tháinig siad** before they came, **sula gcaillfear thú** before you die

súlach *m1* juice, sap, gravy

sult *m1* enjoyment, pleasure **bhain mé sult as** I enjoyed it

sultmhar *adj* enjoyable, pleasant

súmaire *m4* 1. sucker, leech, scrounger 2. quagmire **súmaire gainimh** quicksand

súmaireacht *f3* sucking, scrounging

súmhar *adj* juicy, succulent

súmóg *f2* sip

suntas *m1* notice, attention **níor thug mé suntas dó** I didn't notice him/it

suntasach *adj* distinctive, noticeable

súp *m1* soup **bain súp as!** enjoy (it)!

súrac *m1* suction **gobán súraic** soother

súraic *v* suck

súsa *m4* blanket, rug

suth *m3* embryo, foetus

svaeid¹ *f2* swede (*turnip*)

svaeid² *f2* suede

svaistce *f4* swastika

T

tábhacht *f3* importance, significance

tábhachtach *adj* important

tabhair *v* (see *irregular verbs*) give, take, bring

tabhair amach give out, bring out **bíonn sé i gcónaí ag tabhairt amach** he is always giving out

tabhair chuig bring to **tabharfaidh mé chugat amárach é** I'll bring it to you tomorrow

tabhair do give to **má thugann sí seans dúinn** if she gives us a chance

tabhair faoi 1. undertake, attempt **tabharfaimid faoi arís amárach** we'll attempt it again tomorrow 2. attack **thug an madra fúm** the dog attacked me

tabhair le take along **tabhair leat é** take it with you

tabhair suas 1. give up **tá sé tugtha suas agam** I've given it up 2. abdicate

tábhairne *m4* public house, pub **teach tábhairne** pub

tábhairneoir *m3* publican

tabhall *m1* sling **crann tabhaill** catapult

tabhartas *m1* gift, donation

tabharthach *adj, m1* dative (*grammar*)

tábla *m4* table

tablóideach *adj* tabloid **nuachtán tablóideach** tabloid newspaper

taca *m4* 1. support, prop 2. (point of) time **um an dtaca seo anuraidh** about this time last year 3. **i dtaca le ...** as regards ...

tacaí *m4* supporter

tacaigh *v* support, hold up **beidh mé ag tacú leat** I will be supporting you, backing you

tacaíocht *f3* support, guarantee, back-up **meaisín tacaíochta beatha** life support machine, **lucht tacaíochta** supporters

tacair *adj* artificial, 'false', makeshift **leathar tacair** imitation leather

tacar *m1* collection, gleaning, set (*mathematics*)

tachrán *m1* child

tacht *v* choke, strangle

tachtaire *m3* choke (*car*)

tacóid *f2* tack (*nail*) **tacóid ordúige** drawing-pin

tacsaí *m4* taxi

tadhall *m1* touch, contact **galar tadhaill** contagious disease, **lionsaí tadhaill** contact lenses

Tadhg,Tadhg an dá thaobh two-faced person, **Tadhg an mhargaidh** the man in the street, **Tadhg Ó Rudaí** Mr So-and-So

tadhlaí *m4* tangent

tae *m4* tea

taephota *m4* teapot

taespúnóg *f2* teaspoon

tafann *m1* barking

tagair *v* 1. refer **níor thagair sé duit** he didn't refer to you 2. mention **ní thagróidh mé leo é** I won't mention it to them

tagairt *f3* reference, mention **leabhar tagartha** reference book, **téarmaí tagartha** terms of reference

taghdach *adj* prone to fits of anger

taibhreamh *m1* dream **tháinig sí i dtaibhreamh chugam** it/she came to me in a dream

taibhrigh *v* dream **taibhríodh rud aisteach dom aréir** I dreamt something strange last night

taibhse *f4* ghost, phantom **taibhse an chnádáin** the bogey man

taibhseach *adj* spectacular, showy, flamboyant

taibhsigh *v* appear, seem, loom

táibléad *m1* tablet

taidhleoir *m3* diplomat

taidhleoireacht *f3* diplomacy

taifead *m1* record *v* tape, record

taifeadadh *m* recording

taifeadán *m1* recorder

taifí *m4* toffee

taighde *m4* research **obair thaighde** research work

táille *f4* fee, charge, fare **táille íosta** minimum fee/charge, **táillí coláiste** college fees, **táille isteach / iontrála** entrance fee, **táille bus** bus fare

táillefón *m1* pay phone

táilliúir *m3* tailor

táilliúireacht *f3* tailoring

tailm *f2* thump, bang

táin *f3* herd, cattle-drive, cattle-raid **Táin Bó Chuaille (an Táin)** the Cattle-Raid of Cooley

táinrith *m3* stampede

tainséirín *m4* tangerine

taipéis *f2* tapestry

táiplis *f2* draughts (*game*) **táiplis bheag** draughts, **táiplis mhór** backgammon

táir *adj* base, vile, mean

tairbhe *f4* benefit, use, profit **rachaidh sé chun tairbhe duit** it will benefit you, **gan tairbhe** useless, **de thairbhe ...** on account of ..., because of ...

tairbheach *adj* beneficial, useful, profitable

tairg *v* offer, propose, bid

táirg *v* produce

táirge *m4* product, produce **táirge deiridh** final/finished product, **táirgí talmhaíochta** agricultural produce

táirgeacht *f3* production, output

táirgeadh *m* production

tairgeoir *m3* bidder

táirgeoir *m3* producer

táirgiúil *adj* productive

táirgiúlacht *f3* productivity

tairiscint *f3* offer, proposal, bid(ding)

tairne *m4* nail (*metal*)

tairneáil *v* nail

tairngir *v* prophesy, predict

tairngreacht *f3* prophecy, prediction

tairseach *f2* threshold

tais *adj* 1. damp, moist, humid 2. gentle

taisc *v* 1. store **rud a thaisceadh** to hoard something (away) 2. deposit, lodge **airgead a thaisceadh sa bhanc** to deposit money in the bank

taisce *f4* 1. store, hoard, treasure **tóraíocht taisce** treasure hunt 2. lodgement, deposit

taisceadán *m1* safe, locker

taiscéal *v* examine, explore, reconnoitre

taiscéalaí *m4* explorer, prospector **taiscéalaí na gealaí** lunar probe

taiscéalaíocht *f3* exploration, reconnaissance

taiscumar *m1* reservoir

taise *m* 1. moistness, dampness 2. gentleness, compassion

taiséadach *m1* shroud

taisire *m4* humidifier

taisiúil *adj* compassionate

taisleach *m1* moisture, damp

taisme *f4* accident, mishap **de thaisme** by chance

taismeach *adj* accidental, tragic *m1* casualty **roinn taismeach** casualty department

taispeáin *v* show, display, exhibit

taispeáint *f3* show, display, exhibition **ar taispeáint** on show

taispeánadh *m* revelation, apparition

taispeántach *adj* demonstrative

taispeántas *m1* show, exhibition

taisteal *m1* travel(ling) **an Lucht Taistil** the Travelling Community

taistealaí *m4* traveller

taistil *v* travel

táite *adj* welded

taithí *f3* experience, practice **taithí láimhe** practical experience

taithigh *v* 1. experience, practise 2. frequent

taithíoch *adj* familiar, accustomed **taithíoch ar ...** familiar with ..., accustomed to ...

taitin *v* 1. please **taitníonn sí leis** he likes her/it 2. shine **tá an ghrian ag taitneamh** the sun is shining

taitneamh *m1* 1. liking **thug mé taitneamh dó** I took a liking to him/it 2. pleasure **bhain mé taitneamh as** I enjoyed it 3. shine, brightness

taitneamhach *adj* 1. likeable 2. pleasing, appealing 3. shining

tál *m1* yield

talamh *m & f* land, ground, earth **os cionn talún, os cionn talaimh** above land/ground, **faoi thalamh** underground, **uisce faoi thalamh** conspiracy, **crith talún** earthquake, **péist talún** earthworm, **urlár na talún** (the) ground floor, **ná déan talamh slán de** don't take it for granted

talamhiata *adj* land-locked

talcam *m1* talcum **púdar talcaim** talcum powder

tallanach *adj* 1. talented 2. impulsive

tallann *f2* 1. talent **tá tallann aici** she has talent 2. impulse **bhuail tallann feirge í** she got a sudden fit of anger

talmhaigh *v* 1. earth (*electricity*) 2. dig in

talmhaíocht *f3* agriculture **réigiún talmhaíochta** agricultural region

talmhaithe *adj* earthed

talmhú *m* earthing (*electricity*)

tamall *m1* space of time or distance, while **tar éis / i ndiaidh tamaill** after a while, **ar feadh tamaill** for a while, **ní bheidh sí anseo go ceann tamaill eile** she won't be here for another while, **tá tú tamall maith uaidh** you are some distance from it

támh *f2* sleep, trance **támh chodlata** nap, **tá sé i dtámh éigin** he is in some sort of trance

támhnéal *m1* trance, swoon **cuireadh i dtámhnéal mé** I was put in a trance

támhshuan *m1* narcosis

támhshuanach *adj* narcotic

tanaí *adj* 1. thin, diluted **fear tanaí** a thin man, **tae tanaí** weak tea 2. shallow **talamh tanaí** shallow ground

tanaigh *v* thin, dilute **ní mór an phéint sin a thanú** that paint has to be thinned/diluted

tánaiste *m4* deputy head of government

tánaisteach *adj* secondary

tanc *m4* tank (*military*) **gunnaí, airm in aghaidh tanc** anti-tank guns, weapons

tancaer *m1* tanker **tancaer ola** oil-tanker

tanú *m* attenuation, dilution

taobh *m1* side, flank **ar thaobh na láimhe clé, deise** on the left-hand, right-hand side, **taobh istigh, taobh amuigh** inside, outside, **taobh tíre** countryside, **i dtaobh** concerning, **i dtaobh le ...** depending upon ..., **cad ina thaobh?** why?

taobhach *adj* partial, biased

taobhaigh *v* 1. side **taobhú le duine** to side with somebody 2. approach, draw near **ag taobhú leis an teach dúinn** as we were approaching the house

taobhaitheoir *m3* sympathiser, supporter

taobhlíne *f4* sideline

taobhmhaor *m1* linesman

taobhroinn *f2* aisle

taobhshráid *f2* side street

taoide *f4* tide **taoide thrá** ebb tide, **taoide thuile** flood tide

taoiseach *m1* 1. leader, chief 2. head of government **Roinn an Taoisigh** Department of the Taoiseach

taom *m3* fit, seizure **bhuail taom gáire, feirge mé** a fit of laughter, anger came over me, **taom croí** heart attack

taomach *adj* 1. fitful 2. capricious, moody

taos *m1* 1. paste **taos fiacla** toothpaste 2. dough

taosc *v* bail out **bád a thaoscadh** to bail out a boat

taoscadh *m* bailing

taoschnó *m4* doughnut

taosrán *m1* pastry

tapa *adj* quick *m4* quickness

tapaigh *v* quicken **tapaigh an deis** seize the opportunity

tapúlacht *f3* quickness, speediness

tar *v* (see *irregular verbs*) come **an bhfuil an post tagtha fós?** has the post come yet? **tháinig tú isteach déanach aréir** you came in late last night, **tiocfaidh do lá** your day will come, **dúirt sí liom gan teacht** she told me not to come, **an dtagann tú anseo go minic?** do you come here often?

tar aníos come up **ag teacht aníos an bóthar** coming up the road

tar anuas come down **tar anuas as sin** come down out of there

taraif *f2* tariff

tarbh *m1* bull **tarbh róin** male seal, bull-seal, **an Tarbh** Taurus

tarbhealach *m1* viaduct

tarbhghadhar *m1* bulldog

tarcaisne *f4* insult, contempt, scorn

tarcaisneach *adj* contemptuous, insulting, offensive

tarcaisnigh *v* insult, belittle

tarchuir *v* transmit **galar gnéastarchurtha** sexually transmitted disease

tarchur *m1* transmission **teip tarchuir** transmission breakdown

tarchuradóir *m3* transmitter

targaid *f2* target

tarlaigh *v* happen, occur

tarlú *m* 1. happening, occurrence 2. haulage **tarlú bóthair** road haulage

tarnocht *adj* stark naked

tarra *m4* tar

tarracóir *m3* tractor

tarraiceán *m1* drawer

tarraing *v* pull, tug, draw, attract **fiacail a tharraingt** to pull a tooth, **pictiúr a tharraingt** to draw a picture, **tarraingíonn sé na sluaite** it attracts the crowds

tarraing ar approach **tá sé ag tarraingt ar a deich a chlog** it's nearly ten o'clock

tarraingt *f* pull, traction (*medical*), tug, draw, attraction **tá sí ar tarraingt** she is on traction, **tarraingt téide** tug of war, **tá tarraingt ann** it/he is attractive

tarraingteach *adj* attractive

tarrtháil *f3* rescue, salvage **bád tarrthála** life-boat *v* save, rescue

tarrthálaí *m4* rescuer

tarscaoil *v* waive **do chearta a tharscaoileadh** to waive your rights

tart *m3* thirst **an bhfuil tart ort?** are you thirsty?

tartar *m1* tartar

tartmhar *adj* thirsty

tasc *m1* task, assignment

tásc *m1* indication **ní raibh tásc ná tuairisc air** there was no sign of it/him

táscach *m1* indicative

táscaire *m4* indicator

tascfhórsa *m4* task force

tástáil *f3* trial, test, examination **tástáil inniúlachta** aptitude test, **tástáil éirime** intelligence testing, **tástáil tiomána** driving test *v* test, try, taste

tástálaí *m3* tester **tástálaí béaldatha** lipstick tester

tátal *m1* prognosis, deduction **sin é an tátal a bhain mé as** that's the conclusion I drew from it

tathag *m1* strength, substance, solidity, body

táthaigh *v* weld

táthaire *m4* welder

tatú *m4* tattoo

tatúáil *v* tattoo

tatúch *adj* tattooed

T-chearnóg *f2* T-square

te *adj* warm, hot **bíonn an aimsir níos teo sa deisceart de ghnáth** the weather in the south is usually warmer, **deoch the** hot drink

té *pron* whoever, the one who **an té nach bhfuil láidir ní foláir dó a bheith glic** he who is not strong would need to be clever

téac *f2* teak

teach *m* house **fear, bean an tí** the man, woman of the house, **Tithe an Oireachtais** the Houses of the Oireachtas, **teach gloine, teach solais** greenhouse, lighthouse, **teach itheacháin** restaurant, **teach ósta** inn, public house, **teach altranais** nursing home, **teach téarnaimh** convalescent home, **teach an asail** toilet, **n.b.** *the dative singular form* **tigh** *is used adverbially:* **thíos tigh Phádraig** down at Pádraig's house

teachín *m4* cottage

teacht *m3* 1. arrival, approach 2. **teacht aniar** stamina, **tá teacht i láthair aici** she has presence, **níl aon teacht isteach agam** I have no income

teachta *m4* deputy **Teachta Dála** TD

téacht *v* clot, coagulate

téachtadh *m* clotting **téachtadh fola** blood clot

teachtaire *m4* messenger, courier

teachtaireacht *f3* message, errand

téachtán *m1* clot

téacs *m4* text

téacsleabhar *m1* textbook

téad *f2* rope, string, cord **téad rite** tight-rope, **téada an ghutha** (the) vocal cords, vocal folds

téadchleasaí *m4* tight-rope walker

téadléimneach *f2* skipping

téagar *m1* thickness, bulk, body

téagartha *adj* bulky, substantial, stout

teagasc *m1* teaching, instruction, tuition **rang teagaisc** tutorial *v* instruct, teach

teagascóir *m3* instructor, tutor

teaghlach *m1* family, household **dochtúir teaghlaigh** general practitioner

teaglaim *f3* collection, compilation **teaglaim dánta** a collection of poems

teagmhaigh *v* 1. happen 2. **teagmhaigh do** touch, meet

teagmháil *f3* contact, communication **ní raibh teagmháil agam léi ó shin** I haven't had contact with her since

teagmhas *m1* contingency, happening, incident

teagmhasach *adj* contingent, incidental, additional

teallach *m1* hearth, fireplace

téama *m4* theme

téamh *m1* heating **téamh aeráide** global warming, warming of climate, **téamh lárnach** central heating

teampall *m1* temple, church **Baile an Teampaill** Churchtown

teanchair *f2* 1. pliers, pincers **teanchair bísghreama** vice grip 2. tongs

teanga *f4* tongue, language **tá teanga ghéar aige** he has a sharp tongue, **teanga dhúchais** native language

teangeolaí *m4* linguist

teangeolaíocht *f3* linguistics

teanglann *f2* language laboratory

teann *adj* 1. firm, strong 2. tight, taut 3. bold, forceful *m3* force, strength *v* 1. tighten, make firm 2. squeeze

teannadh *m1* squeeze, tightening, stress **teannadh cnis** face-lift

teannaire *m* bicycle pump

teannas *m1* tightness, tautness, tension, strain

teannta *m4* 1. support, prop 2. **i dteannta** along with, in a fix

teanntaigh *v* 1. support, prop 2. put in a fix, corner

teanntán *m1* 1. clamp 2. brace

teanntás *m1* audacity, boldness

teanntásach *adj* audacious, bold

teanór *m1* tenor

tearc *adj* scarce, few

téarma *m4* term **téarmaí tagartha** terms of reference

téarmaíocht *f3* terminology **an Coiste Téarmaíochta** the Irish Terminology Committee

tearmann *m1* asylum, reservation, sanctuary **tearmann na Meiriceánach Dúchasach** Native American reservation, **tearmann éan** bird sanctuary

téarnaigh *v* 1. convalesce, recover 2. survive

téarnamh *m1* convalescence, recovery **teach téarnaimh** convalescent home

teas *m3* heat, warmth

teasaí *adj* hot, hot-tempered, fiery

teasc *v* chop off, amputate

teascadh *m* amputation

teascán *m1* segment

teasdíonach *adj* heatproof

teastaigh *v* be wanted/needed **cad a theastaíonn uathu?** what do they want? **bhí sé ag teastáil go géar** it was badly needed

teastas *m1* certificate **an Teastas Sóisearach** the Junior Certificate, **teastas breithe** birth certificate

teibí *adj* abstract

teibíocht *f3* abstraction

téic *f2* take (*film*) **téic eile** retake

teicneoir *m3* technician **teicneoir fuaime** sound technician

teicneolaíoch *adj* technological

teicneolaíocht *f3* technology **teicneolaíocht (an) eolais** information technology

teicníc *f2* technique

teicníocht *f3* technique

teicniúil *adj* technical **líníocht theicniúil** technical drawing, **coláiste teicniúil réigiúnach (CTR)** regional technical college (RTC)

teicniúlacht *f3* technicality

teideal *m1* title, claim, right **bheith i dteideal ruda** to be entitled to something

teifeach *adj, m1* fugitive

téigh[1] *v* (see *irregular verbs*) **go an ndeachaigh tú go dtí an cheolchoirm?** did you go to the concert? **chuaigh, ní dheachaigh** yes, no, **tá sí dulta abhaile** she has gone home, **dúirt sé liom dul amach** he told me to go out, **téann sí go Gaillimh go minic** she goes to Galway often, **ní rachaidh mé ann go deo arís** I won't go there ever again, **go dté tú slán** farewell

téigh[2] *v* warm, heat **téifidh sé sin thú** that'll warm you (up), **rud a théamh** to heat something

teile *f4* lime (*fruit*)

teiléacs *m4* telex

teileachumarsáid *f2* telecommunications **satailít teileachumarsáide** telecommunications satellite

teileafón *m1* telephone **teileafón gluaisteach / póca** mobile (tele)phone, **uimhir theileafóin** telephone number

teileafónaí *m4* telephonist

teileagraf *m1* telegraph

teileagram *m1* telegram

teileascóp *m1* telescope

teilg *v* 1. throw, cast, fling 2. condemn, convict

teilgcheárta *f4* foundry

teilgean *m1* cast(ing), projection

teilgeoir *m3* 1. projector 2. **teilgeoir lasrach** flamethrower

teilifís *f2* television **teilifís chábla** cable television, **teilifís chiorcaid iata** closed-circuit television

teilifiseán *m1* television (*set*)

teilifisigh *v* televise

teilitéacs *m4* teletext

teimhligh *v* darken, shade, tarnish

teip *f2* failure, breakdown **teip tarchuir** transmission breakdown, **gan teip** without fail *v* fail **theip orm sa scrúdú** I failed the exam, **ná teip orm** don't let me down

téip *f2* tape

téipthaifeadadh *m* tape recording

téipthaifeadán *m1* tape recorder

teiripe *f4* therapy **teiripe urlabhra** speech therapy

teiripí *m4* therapist **teiripí urlabhra** speech therapist

teirmeach *adj* thermal

teirmeastat *m1* thermostat

teirmiméadar *m1* thermometer

teist *f2* 1. reputation **tá drochtheist air** he has a bad reputation 2. testimony, recommendation 3. test

teistiméireacht *f3* testimony, certificate, reference

teiteanas *m1* lockjaw, tetanus

teith *v* flee, abscond

teitheadh *m1* flight, retreat, escape **Teitheadh na nIarlaí** the Flight of the Earls, **dul ar do theitheadh** to go on the run

téitheoir *m3* heater **téitheoir gáis, leictreach** gas, electric heater

Teochrios, an *m3* the Tropics

teochriosach *adj* tropical **foraois theochriosach bháistí** tropical rain-forest

teocht *f3* temperature

teoiric *f2* theory

teoiriciúil *adj* theoretical

teoirim *f2* theorem

teolaí *adj* snug, comfortable

teorainn *f* border, limit, boundary **teorainn luais** speed limit, **teorainneacha cathrach** city boundaries

teoranta *adj* limited

teorantach *adj* limiting **tosca teorantacha** limiting factors, **teorantach le** bordering on

thall *adj, adv, prep* over, beyond **chaith sí an chuid eile dá saol thall san India** she spent the rest of her life in India, **thall is abhus** here and there, **féach thall** see overleaf

thar *prep* (*prep prons* = **tharam, tharat, thairis, thairsti, tharainn, tharaibh, tharstu**) over, across, by, beyond, more than **thar lear** abroad, **shiúil sé tharam** he walked by me, **thar barr, thar cionn** excellent, **thar aon ní eile** more than anything, **thairis sin** moreover

thart *adv, prep* 1. about, round **feicfidh mé thart ar a ceathair thú** I'll see you about four, **tá sí thart anseo áit éigin** she/it is around here somewhere 2. past, by **an tseachtain seo a chuaigh thart** last week, **tá an cluiche thart** the game is over

theas *adj, adv* south, in the south **an taobh theas** the south side, **Meiriceá Theas** South America

thiar *adj, adv* 1. west, in the west **thiar i Maigh Eo** west in Mayo 2. back, behind **d'fhág mé thiar**

sa teach é I left it back in the house, **taobh thiar (den chathaoir)** behind (the chair)

thíos *adj, adv* down, below **tá siad thíos (an) staighre** they are downstairs, **féach thíos** see below, **is tusa a bheidh thíos leis** it's you who'll be sorry, it's you who'll have to pay

thoir *adj, adv* east, in the east **thoir i gCill Dara** east in Kildare

thuaidh *adv, adj* in the north, north **an Chóiré Thuaidh** North Korea, **an Mol Thuaidh** the North Pole

thuas *adv, adj* up, above **níl sé thuas (an) staighre** it's not upstairs, **an mbeidh mé thuas leis?** will I gain by it?

tí[1] *f4* **ar tí** on the point of, about to, **ar tí imeacht** about to go

tí[2] *m4* tee

tiachóg *f2* small bag, satchel, wallet

tiarna *m4* lord **tiarna talún** landlord

tiarnas *m1* lordship

tiarnúil *adj* domineering

tic *m4* tick **cuir tic sa bhosca cuí** tick the appropriate box

ticéad *m1* ticket **ticéad aerthaistil** airline ticket

tíl *f2* tile

tím *f2* thyme **peirsil agus tím** parsley and thyme

timire *m4* 1. organiser 2. messenger

timireacht *f3* doing odd jobs, running errands

timpeall[1] *m1* circuit, round

timpeall[2] *prep* about, around, approximately **taisteal timpeall na hÉireann, na hEorpa** to travel around Ireland, Europe, **d'fhágamar timpeall (ar) a hocht a chlog** we left about eight o'clock, **timpeall le dhá mhíle ar fhad** approximately two miles long

timpeallach *adj* circuitous, roundabout

timpeallacht *f3* environment, surroundings

timpeallaigh *v* encircle, surround

timpeallán *m1* roundabout

timpeallghearr *v* circumcise

timpeallghearradh *m* circumcision

timpiste *f4* accident, mishap

timpisteach *adj* accidental

timthriall *m3* cycle **timthriall pláinéadach** planetary cycle

timthriallach *adj* cyclic, recurring

tincéir *m3* tinker

tine *f4* fire **cois na tine** beside the fire, **tinte cnámh** bonfires, **idir dhá thine Bhealtaine** in a predicament, in a difficult situation

tinn *adj* 1. sick **tá sé tinn le seachtain anuas** he has been sick for a week now 2. sore **an bhfuil sé tinn?** is it sore?

tinneas *m1* sickness, pain **tinneas cinn** headache, **tinneas muice** feigned sickness

tinreamh *m1* attendance

tinsil *m4* tinsel

tinteán *m1* hearth

tintreach *f2* lightning

Tiobraid Árann *f* Tipperary

tíogar *m1* tiger

tíolaic *v* bestow, dedicate

tiomáin *v* drive

tiomáint *f3* drive, driving **tástáil tiomána** driving test, **níl tiomáint agam** I can't drive

tiománaí *m4* driver

tiomántán *m1* propellant

tiomna *m4* testament, will

tiomnaigh *v* 1. will, bequeath 2. dedicate **thiomnaigh sé an leabhar dá mháthair** he dedicated the book to his mother

tiomnú *m* 1. bequeathal 2. dedication

tiompán *m1* tympanum

tiomsaigh *v* collect, gather, accumulate

tionchar *m1* effect, influence **bhí tionchar aige orm** he/it had an effect on me, he/it influenced me

tionlaic *v* escort, accompany

tionlacan *m1* escort, accompaniment **gan tionlacan** unaccompanied

tionóil *v* assemble, convene, muster

tionóisc *f2* accident

tionóisceach *adj* accidental

tionól *m1* 1. assembly, gathering 2. community (*religious*)

tionónta *m4* tenant

tionóntacht *f3* tenancy

tionóntán *m1* tenement

tionscadal *m1* project

tionscain *v* begin, initiate

tionscal *m1* industry **tionscal seirbhíse** service industry

tionscantach *adj* 1. initial 2. having initiative, enterprising

tionsclach *adj* industrious

tionsclaí *m4* industrialist

tionsclaigh *v* industrialise

tionsclaíoch *adj* industrial

tionsclaíocht *f3* industrialisation

tionscnamh *m1* 1. initiative 2. promotion

tionscnóir *m3* 1. initiator 2. promoter

tiontaigh *v* turn, translate

tiontaire *m4* converter **tiontaire catalaíoch** catalytic converter

tiontú *m* turning, turn

tíoránach *m1* tyrant

tíoránta *adj* tyrannical

tíorántacht *f3* tyranny

tíos *m1* 1. housekeeping 2. thrift

tíosach *adj* economical, thrifty

tipiciúil *adj* typical

tír *f2* country, land **tíortha na Meánmhara** (the) Mediterranean countries, **tír dhúchais** native country, **faoin tír** in the country, ceol tíre folk music, **ar tír mór** on the mainland, **ar tír is ar muir** on land and at sea

tírdhreach *m3* landscape

tíreolaíocht *f3* geography

tírghrá patriotism

tírghrách *adj* patriotic

tírghráthóir *m3* patriot

tirim *adj* dry **airgead tirim** cash

tirimghlan *v* dry-clean

tirimghlanadh *m* dry-cleaning

tirimghlantóir *m3* dry-cleaner

tíriúil *adj* homely

Tír Chonaill *f* Donegal

Tír Eoghain *f* Tyrone

tit *v* fall **thit sé as mo lámh** it fell out of my hand, I dropped it

tithíocht *f3* housing

titim *f2* falling, fall

tiúb *f2* tube

tiúbdheisiú *m* tube repair **paiste tiúbdheisithe** tube repair patch

tiubh *adj* thick **níos tibhe, is tibhe** thicker, thickest

tiubhaigh *v* thicken **tá an t-anlann ag tiúchan** the sauce is thickening

tiúilip *f2* tulip

tiúin *f2* tune **níl sé i dtiúin** it's not in tune *v* tune

tiúnadh *m* tuning

tiúnóir *m3* tuner

tiús *m1* thickness

tláith *adj* 1. mild, tender 2. weak

T-léine *f4* T-shirt

tlú *m4* tongs

tnúth *m3* 1. longing, expectation 2. envy *v* 1. desire, long for **ag tnúth leis an Nollaig** longing for Christmas 2. envy

tnúthánach *adj* expectant, eager for

tobac *m4* tobacco

tobacadóir *m3* tobacconist

tobán *m1* tub

tobann *adj* sudden **go tobann** suddenly, unexpectedly

tobar *m1* well

tobhach *m1* levy

tobthitim *f2* slump, crash (*financial*)

tóch *v* dig

tochail *v* dig, excavate

tochailt *f2* digging, excavation **láithreán tochailte** excavation site

tochais *v* scratch

tochas *m1* itching, itch

tochasach *adj* itchy

tochrais *v* wind

tocht[1] *m3* 1. emotional catch **bhí tocht orm** I couldn't speak with emotion 2. stoppage (*medical*)

tocht[2] *m3* mattress

tochtmhar *adj* deeply emotional

tocsain *f2* toxin

tocsaineach *adj* toxic **ábhar tocsaineach** toxic material

todhchaí *f4* future

todhchaíoch *adj* futuristic

todóg *f2* cigar

tofa *adj* choice **duine tofa** outstanding person

tóg *v* take (up), build, raise, lift, rear **teach a thógáil** to build a house, **raic a thógáil** to cause a row, **tógadh thall in Albain iad** they were reared/brought up over in Scotland

tóg ar 1. blame **ná tóg ormsa é** don't blame it on me 2. undertake **rud a thógáil ort féin** to undertake to do something, **tógfaidh sé lá orm** it will take me a day

tógáil *f3* taking, building, raising, lifting, rearing, upbringing

tógálach *adj* 1. infectious, catching **galar tógálach** infectious disease 2. touchy

tógálachas *m1* constructivism

tógálaí *m4* builder

togh *v* 1. choose 2. elect

togha *m4* choice **togha mná!** good woman! **togha fir!** good man!

toghadh *m* selection, choice

toghair *v* invoke, summon

toghairm *f2* summons

toghchán *m1* election

toghchánaíocht *f2* electioneering

toghthóir *m3* elector, constituent

togra *m4* proposal

tógtha *adj* 1. excited **bhí sí antógtha leis** she was very excited by it 2. built **tógtha de réir sonraíochta** built to specification

toicí *m4* tycoon (*business*)

toil *f3* wish, will, desire **más é do thoil é, le do thoil** please

toiligh *v* consent, agree

toill *v* fit, find room (in)

toilleadh *m* capacity

toilteanach *adj* willing, voluntary

toilteanas *m1* willingness

tóin *f3* bottom, backside **tóin na mara** the bottom of the sea, **chuaigh an bád go tóin poill** the boat sank

tointeáil *f3* shuttle movement **tá seirbhís tointeála acu chuig an áit** they have a shuttle service to the place

tointeálaí *m4* shuttle

tóir *f3* pursuit, chase **tá siad sa tóir ort** they are in pursuit of you, **tá tóir ar an leabhar** the book is in demand

toirbhir *v* present, deliver, dedicate

toirbhirt *f3* presentation, delivery, dedication

tóireadóir *m3* probe

tóirfhocal *m* in-word

toirmeasc *m1* prohibition

toirneach *f2* thunder **splancacha agus toirneach** thunder and lightning

toirniúil *adj* thundery

toirpéad *m1* torpedo **bád toirpéid** torpedo boat

tóirse *m4* torch

tóir-rud *m3* in-thing

tóirsholas *m1* searchlight

toirt *f2* 1. volume, bulk, mass 2. **ar an toirt** on the spot, immediately

toirtín *m4* scone, cake, tart

toirtís *f2* tortoise

toirtiúil *adj* bulky

toisc *f2* 1. circumstance, condition, factor **tosca teorantacha** limiting factors 2. because **toisc na ndaoine sin** because of those people

toise *m4* measurement

toit *f2* smoke

toitcheo *m4* smog

toitín *m4* cigarette

tolg[1] *v* 1. attack 2. catch **galar, slaghdán a tholgadh** to catch a disease, cold

tolg[2] *m1* sofa

tolglann *f2* lounge bar **tolglann imeachta** departure lounge

toll *v* bore, pierce **poll a tholladh** to bore a hole

tollán *m1* tunnel

tolltach *adj* penetrating, piercing

tom *m1* bush, shrub, tuft

tomhais *v* 1. measure **rud a thomhas** to measure something 2. guess **tomhais céard a tharla** guess what happened

tomhaltóir *m3* consumer **treoiruimhir praghsanna do thomhaltóirí** consumer price index

tomhas *m1* 1. measure, measurement 2. riddle, guess

tomhsaire *m4* gauge **tomhsaire doimhneachta** depth gauge

ton *m1* tone

tonn *f2* wave **clár toinne** surf-board, **seoltóireacht toinne** surfing

tonna *m4* ton

tonnadóir *m3* funnel

tonnchrith *m3* vibration *v* vibrate

tonnfhad *m1* wavelength

tonnúil *adj* wavy, undulating

tonóir *m3* toner **tonóir éadain** facial toner

tor *m1* bush, shrub **lá faoin tor** an idle day, **tor aitinn** furze bush

toradh *m1* fruit, result **sú torthaí** fruit juice, **torthaí scrúduithe** examination results, **ní bheidh de thoradh air ach …** it will only result in …

tórai *m4* 1. pursuer 2. bandit 3. **na Tóraithe** the Tories

tóraigh *v* pursue

tóraíocht *f3* pursuit, search **tóraíocht taisce** treasure hunt

torann *m1* noise **torann cúlra** background noise

torbán *m1* tadpole

torc *m1* 1. boar 2. torque (*Celtic art*)

torcán *m1* 1. young boar 2. **torcán craobhach** porcupine

tormán *m1* noise

tormánach *adj* noisy

tornádó *m4* tornado

tornapa *m4* turnip

torrach *adj* pregnant

tórramh *m1* 1. wake 2. funeral

torthóir *m3* seller of fruit

torthúil *adj* fertile, fruitful

tosach *m1* start, beginning, front **cliathán, suíochán, tuairteoir tosaigh** front wing, seat, bumper, **an mhéar thosaigh** the index finger, **i dtosach** at first, **cé atá chun tosaigh?** who is ahead? who is in the lead?

tosaí *m4* forward (*sport*)

tosaigh *v* begin, start

tosaíocht *f3* priority, precedence, preference **de réir tosaíochta** according to priority

tosaitheoir *m3* beginner

toscaire *m4* delegate, deputy

toscaireacht *f3* delegation

tost *m3* silence **fan i do thost! fanaigí in bhur dtost!** stay quiet! *v* become silent, silence

tósta *m4* toast

tostach *adj* silent, taciturn

tóstaer *m1* toaster

tóstáil *v* toast

tóstal *m1* 1. pageant 2. muster, assembly

tosú *m* beginning, start

trá¹ *m4* 1. ebb 2. decline, recession

trá² *f4* strand, beach **ní féidir leat an dá thrá a fhreastal** you can't have it both ways

trach *m4* trough

trácht *m3* 1. mention **gan trácht ar …** not to mention … 2. traffic **trácht buaicuaire** peak-hour traffic, **plódú tráchta** traffic jam *v* mention, comment (on)

tráchtáil *f3* commerce, trade **an Bord Tráchtála** Irish Export Board

tráchtaire *m4* commentator

tráchtaireacht *f3* commentary

tráchtas *m1* thesis, dissertation

tráchtearra *m4* commodity

trádáil *f3* trading, trade **trádáil taobh istigh** insider trading, **trádáil isteach** trade-in *v* trade **rud a thrádáil isteach le haghaidh ruda eile** to trade something in for something else

trádálaí *m4* trader **trádálaí aonair** sole trader

trádbhac *m1* embargo (*trade*)

trádmharc *m1* trade-mark

trádstóras *m1* warehouse **trádstóras mórdhíola** wholesale warehouse

traein *f* train **ar an traein** by train, **stáisiún traenach** train station

traenáil *f3* training, coaching *v* train, coach

traenáilte *adj* trained, coached

traenálaí *m4* trainer, coach

tragóid *f2* tragedy

tragóideach *adj* tragic

traidhfil *f2* 1. trifle (*desert*) 2. small amount **traidhfil bheag oibre** a small bit of work

tráidire *m4* tray

traidisiún *m1* tradition **traidisiún béil** oral tradition

traidisiúnta *adj* traditional

traigéide *f4* tragedy (*stage*)

tráigh *v* 1. ebb 2. subside, decline, dry up

traipisí *pl* personal belongings, scrap **tá sé caite i dtraipisí agam** I have discarded it

trálaer *m1* trawler

tralaí *m4* trolley

tram *m4* tram

trampailín *m4* trampoline

tranglam *m1* confusion, clutter, disorder

traoch *v* exhaust, wear out

traochta *adj* exhausted, worn out

trasatlantach *adj* transatlantic

trasghearradh *m* cross-section

trasna *adj, adv, prep* across **trasna an chlóis** across the yard

trasnaigh *v* 1. cross 2. interrupt

trasnaíocht *f3* 1. contradiction 2. interference

trasnán *m1* diagonal, crossbar

trasnú *m* 1. contradiction 2. intersection

trasraitheoir *m3* transistor

trasrian *m1* crossing **trasrian coisithe** pedestrian crossing

trastomhas *m1* diameter

tráta *m4* tomato **sú trátaí** tomato juice

tráth *m3* 1. time, period **focal i dtráth** a word in time, **tráth na gceist** quiz, question time 2. once

sin mar a bhí tráth that's how it was once

tráthnóna *m4* afternoon, evening

tráthrialta, go tráthrialta punctually, regularly

tráthúil *adj* opportune, punctual, timely

treabh *v* plough **ag treabhadh ar aghaidh** working away

treabhsar *m1* trousers

tréad *m3* herd, flock

tréadaí *m4* shepherd

tréadúil *adj* gregarious

trealamh *m1* equipment, gear **trealamh oifige** office equipment

treallús *m1* enterprise, industriousness, self-assertion

treallúsach *adj* enterprising, industrious, assertive

trealmhaigh *v* equip

trealmhaithe *adj* equipped

tréan *adj* strong, powerful **bhí siad ann go tréan** they were there in good numbers

tréanphléascach *adj* highly explosive **ábhar tréanphléascach** highly explosive material

tréanphléascán *m1* high explosive

tréas *m3* treason

tréasach *adj* treasonable

treascair *v* overthrow, knock down

treascairt *f3* overthrow

treascrach *adj* overpowering

tréaslaigh *v* congratulate **tréaslaím d'ardú céime leat** I congratulate you on your promotion

treaspás *m1* trespass **lucht treaspáis** trespassers

tréatúir *m3* traitor

tréatúireacht *f3* treachery, treason

trédhearcach *adj* transparent

trédhearcacht *f3* transparency

treibh *f2* tribe

tréidlia *m4* veterinary surgeon

tréidliacht *f3* veterinary medicine

tréig *v* 1. abandon, desert 2. fade

tréimhse *f4* period (*of time*)

tréimhseachán *m1* periodical

tréimhsiúil *adj* periodic

treis, i dtreis in power, at issue, in conflict

treisigh *v* 1. strengthen, fortify, reinforce **bainne treisithe** fortified milk, 'supermilk' 2. **treisigh le** support

tréith *f2* trait, characteristic, quality

tréitheach *adj* 1. talented, gifted 2. characteristic

treo *m4* 1. direction, way, approach 2. **i dtreo** towards, **shiúil sé i dtreo na fuinneoige** he walked towards the window, **i dtreo is go ... so that ...**

treocht *f3* trend

treodóireacht *f3* orienteering

treoir *f5* guidance, direction, instruction **treoracha** directions, instructions

treoirlíne *f4* guideline

treoirscéim *f2* pilot scheme

treoiruimhir *f5* index (number) **treoiruimhir praghsanna do thomhaltóirí** consumer price index

treoraí *m4* guide

treoraigh *v* guide, direct

trí[1] three **trí mhíle bád** three thousand boats, **trí dhuine dhéag** thirteen people

trí[2] *prep* (*prep prons* = **tríom, tríot, tríd, tríthi, trínn, tríbh, tríothu**) through **dul trí Mhuineachán** to go through Monaghan, **tríd an bhfuinneog** through the window, **tríd is tríd** by and large

triacla *m4* treacle

triail *f5* trial, test, experiment *v* try, test

trialach *adj* experimental

triall *m3* 1. attempt 2. journey **cá bhfuil do thriall?** where are you going? *v* 1. attempt 2. travel

triantán *m1* triangle

triantánach *adj* triangular

triarach *adj* triple

tríchosach *adj* three-legged *m1* tripod

trídhathach *adj, m1* tricolour

trilseán *m1* tress, plait

trinse *m4* trench **cogaíocht trinse** trench warfare

trioblóid *f2* trouble

trioblóideach *adj* troublesome

tríocha *m* thirty **tá sí sna tríochaidí** she's in her thirties

tríochadú[1] *m4* thirtieth **tríochadú de rud** a thirtieth of something

tríochadú[2] *adj* thirtieth **an tríochadú huair** the thirtieth time

triomach *m1* drying, drought

triomadóir *m3* dryer

triomaigh *v* dry

Tríonóid *f2* trinity **Coláiste na Tríonóide** Trinity College

triopall *m1* bunch, cluster **triopall fíonchaor** bunch of grapes

triopallach *adj* 1. bunched, clustered 2. tidy

trírín *m4* triplet

trírothach *m1* tricycle

tríthoiseach *adj* three-dimensional

tríú[1] *m4* third **seacht dtríú déag de rud** seven thirteenths of something

tríú[2] *adj* third **níor ith mé ach an tríú cuid de** I only ate the third of it

triuch *m3* whooping cough

triuf *m4* club (*cards*) **an naoi triuf** the nine of clubs

triúr *m1* three people **triúr amadán / óinseach** three fools

triús *m1* trousers **triús marcaíochta** jodhpurs, riding trousers

trócaire *f4* mercy, compassion **go ndéana Dia trócaire uirthi** may God have mercy on her

trócaireach *adj* merciful, compassionate

trodaí *m4* fighter, quarrelsome person

troid *f3, v* fight, quarrel

troigh *f2* foot **cúig troithe ar airde** five feet tall

troisc *v* fast

troitheán *m1* pedal

trom *adj* heavy *m1* weight

tromaíocht *f3* blaming, harsh criticism

tromán *m1* weight

trombóis *f2* thrombosis

trombón *m1* trombone

tromchroíoch *adj* heavy-hearted

tromchúis *f2* importance, gravity

tromchúiseach *adj* important, grave **mí-iompar tromchúiseach** serious misconduct

tromlach *m1* majority

tromluí *m4* nightmare

trom-mheáchan *m1* heavyweight

trópaic *f2* tropic **na Trópaicí** the Tropics

trópaiceach *adj* tropical **foraois thrópaiceach bháistí** tropical rainforest

trosc *m1* cod

troscadh *m* fasting

troscán *m1* furniture

trua *adj* 1. pitiable **is trua nár labhair tú liom** it's a pity you didn't talk to me, **is trua liom do chás** I'm sorry for your trouble 2. lean (*meat*) *f4* 1. pity **is mór an trua é** it's a terrible pity 2. wretch

truaill *f2* scabbard, sheath

truailligh *v* pollute

truaillithe *adj* polluted

truailliú *m* pollution

truamhéalach *adj* pitiful, pathetic

trucail *f2* truck, trolley **trucail altach** articulated truck

truflais *f2* rubbish, garbage

truicear *m1* trigger

truinnín *m4* tuna

trumpa *m4* trumpet **trumpa béil** Jew's harp

trumpadóir *m3* trumpet player

trunc *m3* trunk

trup *m4* tramp, noise

trúpa *m4* troop **trúpaí airm** army troops

tú, thú *pron* you **tú féin atá ann!** it's yourself! **an bhfuil tú ag dul abhaile fós?** are you going home yet? **ní aithneoidh sí thú** she won't recognise you

tua *f4* axe, hatchet

tuáille *m4* towel **tuáille sláintíochta** sanitary towel

tuailm *f2* spring (*metal*)

tuaiplis *f2* blunder

tuaiplisiúil *adj* blundering

tuairim *f2* 1. opinion, idea **níl tuairim dá laghad agam** I haven't a clue, **tabhair buille faoi thuairim** have a guess 2. tuairim (is) about, **beimid ann tuairim is a seacht** we'll be there about seven

tuairisc *f2* 1. report **tuairisc bhliantúil** annual report 2. information, account **bhí Seán ag cur do thuairisce** Seán was asking for you, **ní raibh tásc ná tuairisc air** there was no sign of it/him

tuairisceoir *m3* reporter

tuairiscigh *v* report

tuairisciú *m* coverage

tualrt *f2* thud, crash

tuairteáil *v* thump, bump

tuairteoir *m3* bumper (*car*) **tuairteoir tosaigh** front bumper

tuaisceart *m1* north

tuaisceartach *adj* northern *m1* northerner

tuama *m4* tomb, tombstone

tuar[1] *m1* omen, foreboding **tháinig an tuar faoin tairngreacht** the prophecy was fulfilled, **tuar ceatha** rainbow *v* forebode, predict **thuar sé go ...** he predicted that ...

tuar[2] *v* bleach

tuarascáll *f3* report

tuarascálaí *m4* reporter

tuarastal *m1* salary

tuaslagán *m1* solution

tuaslagóir *m3* solvent

tuaslaig *v* dissolve

tuata *adj* lay *m4* lay person

tuath *f2* country, countryside **pobal tuaithe** rural community, **faoin tuath** in the country

tuathal *adv* anti-clockwise, wrong side/direction **an taobh tuathail amach** inside out *m1* blunder **bhí an áit ina chíor thuathail acu** they had the place in a complete mess

tuathalach *adj* blundering, tactless

tuathánach *m1* peasant

tubaiste *f4* disaster, calamity

tubaisteach *adj* disastrous, calamitous

tuga *m4* tug (*boat*)

tugtha *adj* 1. exhausted 2. **tugtha do** prone to, fond of, **tá sé róthugtha don ól** he is too fond of the drink

tuí *f4* 1. straw 2. thatch **teach ceann tuí** thatched house

tuig *v* understand **is deacair í a thuiscint** it's difficult to understand her, **tuigim duit** I sympathise with you

tuil *v* flood, overflow

tuile *f4* flood, current **taoide thuile** incoming tide, flood tide

tuill *v* earn, merit, deserve **tá sé tuillte agat** you deserve it, **rud a thuilleamh** to earn something

tuilleadh *m1* addition, more **an mbeidh tuilleadh agat?** will you have more? **gan a thuilleadh moille** without further delay

tuilleamaí *m4* dependence **i dtuilleamaí duine, ruda** depending on somebody, something

tuilleamh *m1* earnings

tuilsolas *m1* floodlight

Tuirc, an *f2* Turkey

Tuircis *f2* Turkish (*language*)

túirín *m4* turret

tuirling *v* alight, dismount, descend, land

tuirlingt *f2* descent, landing

tuirne *m4* spinning-wheel

tuirpintín *m4* turpentine

tuirse *f4* fatigue, tiredness

tuirseach *adj* fatigued, tired, weary **tá mé tinn tuirseach de** I'm sick and tired of him/it

tuirsigh *v* tire, become tired

tuirsiúil *adj* tiresome, tiring

túis *f2* incense

tuisceanach *adj* understanding, thoughtful

tuiscint *f3* understanding, thoughtfulness

tuiseal *m1* case (*grammar*) **an tuiseal ginideach** the genitive case

tuisle *m4* stumble, trip **baineadh tuisle asam** I (was) tripped

tuisligh *v* stumble, trip

tuismeá *f4* horoscope

tuismitheoir *m3* parent

tulach *m1* mound, hillock

tum *v* dive, dip, immerse, plunge

tumadh *m* dive, dip, immersion, plunge

tumadóir *m3* diver

tumadóireacht *f3* diving

tumtha *adj* submerged

tumthéitheoir *m3* immersion heater

tur *adj* dry, arid **freagra tur** dry, short answer

túr *m1* tower

turas *m1* 1. journey, trip, tour 2. occasion, time **déan i gceart é an turas seo** do it correctly on this occasion, **d'aon turas** on purpose

turasóir *m3* tourist

turasóireacht *f3* tourism **tionscal na turasóireachta** the tourist industry

Turcach *adj* Turkish *m1* Turk

turcaí *m4* turkey

turcaid *f2* turquoise

turgnamh *m1* experiment

turraing *f2* 1. shock, impact 2. stumble

turtar *m1* turtle

tús *m1* beginning, start **ó thús deireadh** from start to finish, **ar dtús** at first

tusa *emphatic pron* you **an tusa a bhí ann?** was it you who was there?

tútach *adj* 1. clumsy, awkward 2. rude

U

uabhar *m1* pride, arrogance

uacht *f3* will, testament **d'fhág sí a carr le huacht agam** she left me her car in her will

uachtaigh *v* will, bequeath

uachtar *m1* 1. top, upper part **fuair sé an lámh in uachtar orm** he got the upper hand of me 2. cream **uachtar reoite** ice-cream, **uachtar súl** eye cream

uachtarach *adj* 1. upper 2. superior

uachtarán *m1* president, superior **Uachtarán na hÉireann** the President of Ireland

uachtaránacht *f3* presidency

uachtarúil *adj* creamy

uafar *adj* horrible, dreadful

uafás *m1* 1. terror, horror **scannán uafáis** horror film 2. astonishment **chuirfeadh sé uafás ort** it would astonish you 3. vast amount **tá an t-uafás airgid acu** they have loads of money, **bhí an t-uafás gardaí ann** there was a huge crowd of gardaí there

uafásach *adj* 1. terrible, horrible, awful 2. astonishing, vast

uaibhreach *adj* 1. proud, arrogant 2. luxuriant

uaigh *f2* grave

uaigneach *adj* lonely, eerie, spooky, solitary

uaigneas *m1* loneliness, solitude

uaillbhreas *m3* exclamation

uaillmhian *f2* ambition

uaillmhianach *adj* ambitious

uaim *f3* 1. seam 2. alliteration

uaimh *f2* cave **an Uaimh** Navan ('the Cave')

uain *f2* 1. occasion, time **nuair a gheobhaidh tú uain chuige** when you get time for it 2. spell, turn **is é d'uain é** it's your turn 3. weather **tá an uain go haoibhinn** the weather is beautiful

uainchlár *m1* roster, rota

uaine *adj* green *f4* green, greenness

uaincoil *f3* lamb (*meat*)

uainíocht *f3* alternation, rotation **déanfaimid uainíocht air / leis** we'll take it in turns

uainobair *f2* shiftwork

uair *f2* 1. hour **cúpla uair an chloig** a couple of hours 2. occasion, time **cúpla uair** a couple of times, **bhí mé ann uair (amháin)** I was there once, **uair sa tseachtain** once a week, **tarlaíonn sé sin uaireanta** that happens occasionaly, sometimes, **dhá uair** twice, **trí, ceithre, cúig, sé huaire** three, four, five, six times, **seacht, ocht, naoi, deich n-uaire** seven, eight, nine, ten times, **an chéad uair eile** the next time, **i láthair na huaire** at the moment, **ar ala na huaire** on the spur of the moment

uaireadóir *m3* watch

uaisleacht *f3* nobility

ualach *m1* load, burden

ualaigh *v* load, burden, encumber

uamhan *m1* fear, dread **uamhan clóis** claustrophobia

uan *m1* lamb

uas- *prefix* maximum **uasphraghas** maximum price

uasaicme *f4* upper class

uasaicmeach *adj* upper-class

uasal *adj* noble, eminent, precious **a dhaoine uaisle** ladies and gentlemen, **ní íseal ná uasal ach thíos seal thuas seal** everybody has their ups and downs in life *m1* gentleman, noble **an tUasal Ó Cinnéide** Mr Ó Cinnéide

uaschamóg *f2* apostrophe

uaslathaí *m4* aristocrat

uaslathas *m1* aristocracy

uasmhéid *f2* maximum

uath- *prefix* auto-

uatha *adj, m4* singular (*grammar*)

uathoibríoch *adj* automatic

uathoibriú *m* automation

uathrialach *adj* autonomous **réigiúin uathrialacha** autonomous regions

uathscamhóg *f2* aqualung

uathúil *adj* unique

uathúlacht *f3* uniqueness

ubh *f2* egg **uibheacha Cásca** Easter eggs, **ubh faoi mhaonáis** egg mayonnaise, **ubh scallta, scrofa** poached, scrambled egg

ubhagán *m1* ovary

ubhchruth *m3* oval

ubhchruthach *adj* egg-shaped, oval

ubhchupán *m1* egg-cup

ubhsceitheadh *m* ovulation

ubhthoradh *m1* aubergine

U-chasadh *m* U-turn

U-chruthach *adj* U-shaped

ucht *m3* 1. bosom, breast, chest 2. lap 3. **as ucht …** for the sake of …, **as ucht Dé** for God's sake

uchtach *m1* encouragement, hope, bravery, courage **thug tú uchtach dom** you encouraged me, you gave me courage

uchtaigh *v* adopt

uchtóg *f2* armful

úd¹ *adj* that, yon, yonder **an t-amadán úd** that fool

úd² *m1* try (*rugby*)

údar *m1* 1. author 2. authority **ráiteas gan údar** an unreliable statement 3. reason, cause **níl údar ar bith agam tabhairt suas** I've no reason to give up

údarach *adj* authentic

údaraigh *v* authorise

údaraithe *adj* authorised **duine údaraithe** authorised person

údarás *m1* authority **na húdaráis áitiúla** the local authorities, **Údarás na Gaeltachta** the Gaeltacht Authority

údarásach *adj* authoritative

údarú *m* authorisation

ugach *m1* encouragement, courage

uibheagán *m1* omelette

Uíbh Fhailí *n* Offaly

uige *f4* web, tissue, gauze

uigeacht *f3* texture

uile *adj* all, every, whole **gach uile** (= **chuile**) **dhuine** everybody, **d'ith sé an císte uile** he ate the whole cake, **go huile (is go hiomlán)** totally

uilechoiteann *adj* universal

uilechumhachtach *adj* all-powerful, almighty

uilefhóinteach *adj* all-purpose

uileghabhálach *adj* comprehensive

uileláithreach *adj* ever-present, ubiquitous

uileloscadh *m* holocaust

uilíoch *adj* universal

uiliteoir *m3* omnivore

uilleach *adj* angular

uillinn *f2* 1. angle **ar uillinn céad fiche céim** at an angle of one hundred and twenty degrees 2. elbow **píb uilleann** uilleann pipes 3. bend (*in road*)

úim *f3* harness

uimhir *f5* number **uimhir ghutháin / theileafóin** telephone number, **uimhir chláraithe** registration number

uimhirphláta *m4* number-plate

uimhrigh *v* number

uimhríocht *f3* arithmetic

uimhriúil *adj* digital, numerical

úinéir *m3* owner

úinéireacht *f3* ownership

úir *f2* soil, earth

uirbeach *adj* urban

úire *f4* freshness

uireasa *f4* want, lack, deficiency **déanfaimid é dá uireasa** we'll do it without it

uireasach *adj* wanting, lacking, deficient

uiríseal *adj* 1. humble, lowly 2. base

uirísligh *v* 1. humble 2. humiliate

uirísliú *m* humiliation

uirlis *f2* tool, instrument **uirlis cheoil** musical instrument

uisce *m4* water **uisce beatha** whiskey, **uisce faoi thalamh** conspiracy, **scannánú faoi uisce** underwater shooting

Uisceadóir *m3* **an tUisceadóir** Aquarius

uiscedhath *m3* watercolour

uiscedhíonach *adj* waterproof

uiscerian *m1* aqueduct

uiscigh *v* irrigate, water

uisciú *m* irrigation

uisciúil *adj* watery

uisinn *f2* temple (*of the head*)

ulchabhán *m1* owl

Ulaidh *f5* Ulster **Cúige Uladh** (the province of) Ulster

úll *m1* apple **úll na scornaí** Adam's apple, **úll na haithne** the forbidden fruit

ullamh *adj* ready, prepared, finished, willing

ullmhaigh *v* prepare, ready, fix

ullmhú *m* preparation

ullmhúchán *m1* preparation

úllord *m1* orchard

ultrafhuaim *f2* ultrasound **scanadh ultrafhuaime** ultrasound scanning

um *prep* (*prep prons* = **umam, umat, uime, uimpi, umainn, umaibh, umpu**) about, around, concerning **um Nollaig** at Christmas, **um an dtaca seo** by this time, **um thráthnóna** in the afternoon

umar *m1* 1. trough 2. tank **umar peitril, seipteach** petrol, septic tank, **umar stórála ola** oil storage tank 3. font **umar baiste** baptismal font

umha *m4* bronze

umhal *adj* humble, obedient, submissive

umhlaigh *v* 1. submit 2. bow, kneel 3. humble

umhlaíocht *f3* humility, obedience, submission

umhlú *m* 1. submission 2. genuflection

uncail *m4* uncle

únfairt *f2* wallowing, rolling movement

ungadh *m* ointment

unsa *m4* ounce

úr *adj* fresh, new

urchar *m1* shot **urchair ghunna** gunshots

urchóid *f2* 1. malice, harm 2. malignancy

urchóideach *adj* 1. harmful 2. malignant

urghabh *v* seize (*legal*)

urgharda *m4* vanguard

urghránna *adj* ghastly, hideous

urlabhra *f4* speech **teiripe urlabhra** speech therapy

urlabhraí *m4* spokesperson

urlacan *m1* vomit **urlacan folamh** retching

urlaic *v* vomit

urlámhas *m1* control

urlár *m1* floor **urlár na talún** (the) ground floor

urnaí *f4* prayer, praying

úrnua *adj* brand-new

urra *m4* 1. guarantor 2. sponsor

urraigh *v* 1. go surety for 2. sponsor **urraithe ag ...** sponsored by ...

urraim *f2* respect

urraíocht *f3* sponsorship

urramach *adj* respectful *m1* reverend person

urrúnta *adj* robust, strong

urrús *m1* security, guarantee

úrscéal *m1* novel **úrscéal bleachtaireachta** detective novel

úrscéalaí *m4* novelist

urthrá *f4* foreshore

urú *m* eclipse (*of sun, moon, etc*), eclipsis (*grammar*)

ús *m1* interest **ús seasta** fixed interest, **ráta úis** interest rate

úsáid *f2* use **in úsáid** in use *v* use

úsáideach *adj* useful

úsáideoir *m3* user

úsáidí *f4* usefulness

usc *m1* grease, fat *v* ooze

úscach *adj* greasy, fatty, oily

úscra *m4* essence

útamáil *f3* fumbling

útaras *m1* uterus

úth *m3* udder

V

vacsaín *m4* vaccine

vacsaínigh *v* vaccinate

vadca *m4* vodka

vaidhtéir *m3* best man

vaigín *m4* wagon

vailintín *m4* valentine **cárta Lá Fhéile Vailintín** valentine card, **Lá Fhéile Vailintín** St Valentine's Day

válsa *m4* waltz

válsáil *v* waltz

vardrús *m1* wardrobe

vása *m4* vase

vástáil *v* waste

vástchóta *m4* waistcoat

vata *m4* watt

Vatacáin, an *f2* the Vatican

veain *f4* van
vearnais *f2* varnish
véarsa *m4* verse
véarsaíocht *f3* verse (*in general*)
veasailín *m4* vaseline
veidhleadóir *m3* violinist
veidhlín *m4* violin
veigeatóir *m3* vegetarian
veigeatóireachas *m1* vegetarianism
veilbhit *f2* velvet
veist *f2* vest, waistcoat **veist philéardhíonach** bullet-proof vest
Vín, an *f4* Vienna
vinil *f2* vinyl
vióla *f4* viola
víosa *f4* visa **cárta víosa** visa card

víreas *m1* virus **víreas easpa imdhíonachta daonna (VEID)** human immunodeficiency virus (HIV)
vitimín *m4* vitamin
Vítneam *m4* Vietnam **Cogadh Vítneam** the Vietnam War
Vítneamach *adj, m1* Vietnamese
Vítneamais *f2* Vietnamese (*language*)
volta *m4* volt
voltas *m1* voltage
voltmhéadar *m1* voltmeter
vóta *m4* vote **vóta réitigh** casting vote
vótáil *f3* voting *v* vote
vótálaí *m4* voter

X

X-chrómasóm *m1* X-chromosome
x-gha *m4* X-ray (*ray*)

x-ghathú *m* X-ray (*photo*) **x-ghathú cíche** mammography

Y

Y-chrómasóm *m1* Y-chromosome

Y-chruthach *adj* Y-shaped

Z

zó-eolaíocht *f3* zoology

zú *m4* zoo

Countries, Cities, Rivers, etc of the World

Aden, Áidin.
Admirality Islands, Oileáin na hAimiréalachta.
Adriatic (Sea), (An Mhuir) Aidriad.
Aegean (Sea), (An Mhuir) Aeigéach.
Afghanistan, An Afganastáin.
Africa, An Afraic.
Alaska, Alasca.
Albania, An Albáin.
Aleutian Islands, Oileáin Ailiúit.
Alexandria, Cathair Alastair.
Algeria, An Ailgéir.
Algiers, Cathair an hAilgéire.
Alps (The), Na hAlpa.
Alsace, An Alsáis.
Amazon, An Amasóin.
America, Meiriceá.
Amsterdam, Amstardam.
Andes (The), Na hAindéis.
Andorra, Andóra.
Angola, Angóla.
Antarctic, An tAntartach, **Antarctic Ocean** an tAigéan Antartach
Antarctica, An Antartaice.
Antilles, Na hAintillí, Oileáin Aintillí.
Antwerp, Antuairp.
Appalachian Mountains, Na Sléibhte Apaláiseacha.
Appenines, Na hAipiníní
Arabia, An Araib.
Arctic, An tArtach, **Arctic Ocean,** an tAigéan Artach.
Argentina, An Airgintín.
Armenia, An Airméin.
Ascension Island, Oileán na Deascabhála.
Asia Minor, An Áise Bheag.
Asia, An Áise.
Astrak(h)an, An Astracáin.
Athens, An Aithin, Cathair na hAithne.
Atlantic, An tAtlantach, **Atlantic Ocean,** an tAigéan Atlantach.
Atlas Mountains, Sléibhte Atlais.
Australasia, An Astraláise.
Australia, An Astráil.
Austria, An Ostair.
Azores (The), Na hAsóir.
Azov, (Sea of), An Mhuir Mheoid.

Babylon, An Bhablóin.
Babylonia, An Bhablóinia.
Bahamas (The), Na Bahámaí.

Bahrein, Bairéin.
Balearic Islands (The), Na hOileáin Bhailéaracha.
Balearic Sea, An Mhuir Bhailéarach.
Balkan Peninsula, An Leithinis Bhalcánach.
Balkan States, Na Stáit Bhalcánacha.
Balkans, Na Balcáin.
Baltic Sea (The), An Mhuir Bhailt.
Baluchistan, An Bhalúchastáin.
Bangla Desh, An Bhainglaidéis.
Barbados, Barbadós.
Barbary, An Bharbair.
Belarus, An Bhealarúis.
Belfast, Béal Feirste.
Belgium, An Bheilg.
Belgrade, Béalgrád.
Bengal, Beangál.
Benin, Bcinin.
Bering Straits, Caolas Bheiring.
Berlin, Beirlín.
Bermuda, Beirmiúda.
Bermudas (The), Na Beirmiúdaí.
Berne, Beirn.
Bethlehem, An Bheithil.
Bhutan, An Bhútáin.
Biafra, Biafra.
Biscay (Bay of), Bá na Bioscáine.
Black Sea, An Mhuir Dhubh.
Bolivia, An Bholaiv.
Borneo, Boirneo.
Bosnia, An Bhoisnia.
Bosnia-Herzegovina, An Bhoisnia-Heirseagaivéin
Bosp(h)orus, An Bhosparais.
Boston, Bostún.
Botswana, An Bhotsuáin.
Brazil, An Bhrasaíl.
Bristol, Briostó.
Britain, An Bhreatain.
British Commonwealth, An Comhlathas Briotanach.
Brittany, An Bhriotáin.
Brussels, An Bhruiséil.
Bucharest, Búcairist.
Budapest, Búdaipeist.
Bulgaria, An Bhulgáir.
Burgundy, An Bhurgúin.
Burma, Burma.
Burundi, An Bhurúin.
Byelorussia, An Bhílearúis.
Byzantium, An Bhiosáint.

Cairo, Caireo.
Calcutta, Calcúta.
Cambodia, An Chambóid.
Cameroons (The), Na Camarúin.
Canada, Ceanada.
Canary Islands (The), Na hOileáin Chanáracha.
Cape Colony, Coilíneacht na Rinne.
Cape Horn, Rinn an Choirn.
Cape of Good Hope, Rinn an Dóchais.
Caribbean Sea, An Mhuir Chairib.
Carpathian Mountains, Sléibhte Cairp.
Carthage, An Chartaig.
Caspian Sea, An Mhuir Chaisp.
Castile, An Chaistíl.
Catalonia, An Chatalóin.
Caucasus Mountains, Sléibhte Cugais.
Celebes, An Cheilibéis.
Celtic Sea, An Mhuir Cheilteach.
Central African Republic, Poblacht na hAfraice Láir.
Chad, Sead.
Channel Islands, Oileáin Mhuir nIocht.
Chechnia, An tSeisnia.
Chile, An tSíle.
China, An tSín.
Columbia, An Cholóim.
Comoro Islands, Oileáin Chomóra.
Congó, An Congó.
Copenhagen, Cóbanhávan.
Corinth, An Choraint.
Cork, Corcaigh; Cork City, Cathair Chorcaí.
Cornwall, Corn na Breataine.
Corsica, An Chorsaic.
Costa Rica, Cósta Ríce.
Crete, An Chréit.
Crimea, An Chrimé.
Croatia, An Chróit.
Cuba, Cúba.
Cyprus, An Chipir.
Czech Republic (The), Poblacht na Seice.

Dagestan, An Dagastáin.
Dalmatia, An Dalmáit.
Damascus, An Damaisc.
Danube, An Danóib.
Dardanelles, An Dardainéil.
Dead Sea, An Mhuir Mharbh.
Delhi, Deilí.
Democratic Republic of Congo, Poblacht Dhaonlathach an Chongó.

Denmark, An Danmhairg.
Derry, Doire; Derry City, Cathair Dhoire.
Dnieper, An Dnípir.
Dniester, An Dnísir.
Dominican Republic, An Phoblacht Dhoiminiceach.
Dublin, Baile Átha Cliath.

East Indies, Na hIndiacha Thoir.
East Timor, Tíomór Thoir.
Ebro, An Eabró.
Ecuador, Eacuadór.
Edinburgh, Dun Eideann.
Egypt, An Éigipt.
El Salvador, An tSalvadóir.
Elbe, An Eilbe.
England, Sasana.
English Channel, An Mhuir nIocht.
Equatorial Guinea, An Ghuine Mheánchriosach.
Estonia, An Eastóin.
Ethiopia, An Aetóip.
Euphrates, An Eofrait.
Europe, An Eoraip.

Falkland Islands, Oileáin Fháclainne.
Faroe Islands, Oileáin Fharó, Na Scigirí.
Fiji Islands, Oileáin Fhidsí.
Finland, An Fhionlainn.
Flanders, Flóndras.
Florence, Flórans.
France, An Fhrainc.
Friesland, An Fhreaslainn.

Gabon, An Ghabúin.
Galillee (Sea of), Muir na Gailíle.
Galway, An Ghaillimh; Galway City, Cathair na Gaillimhe.
Gambia, An Ghaimbia.
Ganges, An Ghainséis.
Gaul, An Ghaill.
Geneva, An Ghinéiv.
Georgia, An tSeoirsia.
Germany, An Ghearmáin.
Ghana, Gána.
Gibraltar, Giobráltar.
Glasgow, Glaschú.
Great Britain, An Bhreatain Mhór.
Greece, An Ghréig.
Greenland, An Ghraonlainn.
Guadeloupe (and Dependencies), Guadalúip (agus a Spleáchríocha).
Guam, Gúam.
Guatemala, Guatamala.
Guernsey, Geansaí.

Guinea Bissau, Guine Bhissau.
Guinea, An Ghuine.
Gulf of Mexico, Murascaill
Mheicsiceo.
Guyana, An Ghuáin.

Hague (The), An Háig.
Haïti, Háití.
Havana, Havána.
Hawaii, Haváí.
Hebrides, Inse Ghall.
Helsinki, Heilsincí.
Himalayas (The), Na Himiléithe.
Holland, An Ollainn.
Holy Land, An Talamh Naofa, an Tír
Bheannaithe.
Honduras, Hondúras.
Hong Kong, Hong Cong.
Hungary, An Ungáir.

Iberia, An Ibéir.
Iceland, An Íoslainn.
India, An India.
Indian Ocean (The), An tAigéan
Indiach.
Indies (The East, West), Na
hIndiacha (Thoir, Thiar).
Indo-China, An Ind-Sín.
Indonesia, An Indinéis.
Indus, An Iondúis.
Iran, An Iaráin.
Iraq, An Iaráic.
Irish Sea (The), An Mhuir Mheann,
Muir Éireann.
Isle of Man, Oilcán Mhanann.
Isle of Wight, Inis Iocht.
Israel, Iosrael.
Istanbul, Iostanbúl.
Italy, An Iodáil.
Ivory Coast, An Cósta Eabhair.

Jamaica, Iamáice.
Japan, An tSeapáin.
Java, Iáva.
Jericho, Iarachó.
Jersey, Geirsí.
Jerusalem, Iarúsailéim.
Johannesburg, Ióhanasburg.
Jordan, An Iordáin.
Jutland, An Iútlainn.

Kampuchea, An Champúis.
Karelia, An Chairéil.
Kashmir, An Chaismír.
Kenya, An Chéinia.
Korea, An Chóiré.
Kosovo, An Chosaiv.

Kurdistan, An Chordastáin.
Kuwait, An Chuáit.

Labrador, Labradar.
Laos, Laos.
Lapland, An Laplainn.
Latin America, Meiriceá Laidineach.
Latvia, An Laitvia.
Lebanon, An Liobáin.
Leeward Islands (The), Oileáin na
Fothana.
Lesotho, Leosóta.
Levant (The), An Leiveaint.
Lewis Island, Leódhas.
Liberia, An Libéir.
Libya, An Libia.
Liechtenstein, Lichtinstéin.
Limerick, Luimneach; Limerick City,
Cathair Luimnigh.
Lisbon, Liospóin.
Lithuania, An Liotuáin.
Liverpool, Learpholl.
Lombardy, An Lombaird.
London, Londain.
Lorraine, An Lorráin.
Louvain, Lováin.
Low Countries (The), Na Tíortha
faoi Thoinn.
Luxembourg, Lucsamburg.

Macedonia, An Mhacadóin.
Madagascar, Madagascar.
Maderia, Maidéara.
Madrid, Maidrid.
Majorca, Mallarca.
Malagasy Republic, An Phoblacht
Mhalagásach.
Malawi, An Mhaláiv.
Malay Peninsula, Leithinis Mhalae.
Malaysia, An Mhalaeisia.
Maldive Islands (The), Oileáin
Mhaildíve, Na hOileáin Mhaildíve.
Mali, Mailí
Malta, Malta.
Manchester, Manchain.
Manchuria, An Mhanchúir.
Manila, Mainile.
Mauritania, An Mháratáin.
Mauritius, Oileán Mhuirís.
Mecca, Meice.
Mediterranean (Sea), An
Mheánmhuir.
Mesopotamia, An Mheaspatáim.
Mexico, Meicsiceo.
Minorca, Mionarca.
Moldova, An Mholdóiv.
Molucca Islands (The), Na Molacaí.

Monaco, Monacó.
Mongolia, An Mhongóil.
Montenegro, Montainéagró.
Montserrat, Montsarat.
Morocco, Maracó.
Moscow, Moscó.
Mozambique, Mósaimbíc.
Muscat, Muscat.

Namibia, An Namaib.
Natal, Natal.
Naura, Nárú.
Nazareth, Nasaireit.
Nepal, Neipeal.
Netherlands (The), An Ísiltír.
New Delhi, Deilí Nua.
New Guinea, An Nua-Ghuine.
New York, Nua-Eabhrac.
New Zealand, An Nua-Shéalainn.
Newfoundland, Talamh an Éisc.
Nicaragua, Nicearagua.
Niger, An Nígir.
Nigeria, An Nigéir.
Nile, An Níl.
Normandy, An Normainn.
North Channel (The), Sruth na
    Maoile.
North Ossetia, An Oiséit Thuaidh.
North Sea (The), An Mhuir
    Thuaidh.
Norway, An Iorua.
Novia Scotia, Albain Nua.
Nyasaland, An Niasalainn.

Oceania, An Aigéine.
Oman, Oman.
Orinoco, An Oranócó.
Orkneys (The), Inse Orc.
Oslo, Osló.
Ossetia, An Oiséit.
Ostend, Ostainn.

Pacific (Ocean), An tAigéan Ciúin.
Pakistan, An Phacastáin.
Palestine, An Phalaistín.
Panama, Panama.
Papua, Papua.
Paraguay, Paragua.
Paris, Páras.
Patagonia, An Phatagóin.
Peking, Péicing.
Persian Gulf (The), Murascaill na
    Peirse.
Peru, Peiriú.
Philippines (The), Na Filipíneacha.
Phoenicia, An Fhéiníc.
Po, An Phó.

Poland, An Pholainn.
Polynesia, An Pholainéis.
Pontian Sea, An Phontmhuir.
Portugal, An Phortaingéil.
Prague, Prág.
Principality of Monaco, Prionsacht
    Mhónacó.
Prussia, An Phrúis.
Puerto Rico, Portó Ríce.
Punjab, An Phuinseaib.
Pyrenees (The), Na Piréiní.

Qatar, Catar.

Red Sea (The), An Mhuir Rua.
Republic of Ireland, Poblacht na
    hÉireann.
Rhine, An Réin.
Rhineland (The), Dúiche na Réine.
Rhodes, Ródas.
Rhodesia, An Róidéis.
Rhone, An Róin.
Riviera (The), An Rivéara.
Rocky Mountains (The), Na Sléibhte
    Creagacha.
Rome, An Róimh.
Rumania, An Rómáin.
Russia, An Rúis.
Russian Federation, Cónaidhm na
    Rúise.
Rwanda, Ruanda.

Sahara (The), An Sahára.
Saint George's Channel, Muir
    Bhreatan.
Saint Helena, San Héilin.
Samaria, An tSamáir.
Samaria, An tSamáir.
Samoa, Samó.
San Marino, San Mairíne.
Sardinia, An tSairdín.
Sargasso Sea (The), An Mhuir
    Shargasach.
Saudi Arabia, An Araib Shádach.
Scandinavia, Críoch Lochlann.
Scheldt, An Sceilt.
Scilly Islands (The), Na Scillí.
Scotland, Albain.
Scottish Highlands (The),
    Garbhchríocha na hAlban.
Seine, An tSéin.
Senegal, An tSeineagáil.
Serbia, An tSeirbia.
Shannon (The), An tSionainn.
Shetland, Sealtainn.
Siberia, An tSibéir.
Sicily, An tSicil.

Sierra Leone, Siarra Leon.
Singapore, Singeapór.
Slovenia, An tSlóivéin.
Somalia, An tSomáil.
South Africa, An Afraic Theas.
Spain, An Spáinn.
Sri Lanka, Srí Lanca.
Stockholm, Stócólm.
Sudan, An tSúdáin.
Suez, Suais.
Swaziland, An tSuasalainn.
Sweden, An tSualainn.
Switzerland, An Eilvéis.
Syria, An tSiria.

Tahiti, Taihítí.
Taiwan, An Téaváin.
Tajikistan, An Taidsíceastáin.
Tanzania, An Tansáin.
Tartary, An Tartair.
Tasmania, An Tasmáin.
Thailand, An Téalainn.
Thames, An Tamais.
Tiber, An Tibir.
Tibet, An Tibéid.
Tigris, An Tígris.
Timor, Tíomór.
Tobago, Tobága.
Togo, Tóga.
Tokyo, Tóiceo.
Tonga, Tonga.
Trinidad, Oileán na Tríonóide;
   Trinidad and Tobago, Oileán na
   Tríonóide agus Tobága.
Tripoli, Tripili.
Troy, Traí.
Tunis, Túinis.
Tunisia, An Túinéis.
Turkestan, An Turcastáin.
Turkey, An Tuirc.
Tuscany, An Tuscáin.
Tyrol, An Tioróil.
Tyrrhenian Sea, Muir Thoirian.

Udmurt, An Udmairt.
Uganda, Uganda.

Ukraine, An Úcráin.
United Arab Emirates, Aontas na
   nÉimíríochtaí Arabacha.
United Kinglom, An Ríocht
   Aontaithe.
United States of America (USA),
   Stáit Aontaithe Mheiriceá (SAM).
Ural (The River), An Úrail.
Ural Mountains (The), Sléibhte na
   hÚraile.
Uruguay, Uragua.
Uzbekistan, An Úisbéiceastáin.

Vatican City State, Stát Chathair na
   Vatacáine.
Venezuela, Veiniséala.
Venice, An Veinéis.
Vienna, Vín.
Viet-Nam, Vítneam.
Vojvodina, An Vóvaidín.
Volga, An Volga.
Volta River (The), An Volta.
Voltaic Republic, Poblacht na Volta.

Wales, An Bhreatain Bheag.
Warsaw, Vársá.
Western Samoa, Samó Thiar.
West Indies, Na hIndiacha Thiar.
Wight, The Isle of, Inis Iocht.
Windward Islands (The), Oileáin na
   Gaoithe.

Yakut (Yakutsk), An Iacúit (Iacútsc).
Yellow Sea (The), An Mhuir Bhuí.
Yemen, Éimín.
York, Eabhrac.
Yugoslavia, An Iúgslaiv.

Zaire, An tSáír.
Zambesi, An tSaimbéis.
Zambia, An tSaimbia.
Zanzibar, Sainsibeár.
Zealand, An tSéalainn.
Zimbabwe, An tSiombáib.
Zululand, An tSúlúlainn.

Provinces, Counties, and Major Towns of Ireland

Connaught, Cúige Connacht.
Co. Galway, Co. na Gaillimhe.
  Ballinasloe, Béal Átha na
    Sluaighe.
  Galway, Gaillimh.
  Loughrea, Baile Locha Riach.
  Tuam, Tuaim.
Co. Leitrim, Co. Liatroma.
  Ballinamore, Béal an Átha
    Móir.
  Carrick-on-Shannon, Cora
    Droma Rúisc.
  Manorhamilton, Cluainín.
Co. Mayo, Co. Mhaigh Eo.
  Ballina, Béal an Átha.
  Castlebar, Caisleán an
    Bharraigh.
  Westport, Cathair na Mart.
Co. Roscommon, Co. Ros Comáin.
  Ballaghaderreen, Bealach an
    Doirín.
  Boyle, Mainistir na Búille.
  Roscommon, Ros Comáin.
Co. Sligo, Co. Shligigh.
  Ballymote, Baile an Mhóta.
  Sligo, Sligeach.
  Tobercurry, Tobar an Choire.

Leinster, Cúige Laighean.
Co. Carlow, Co. Cheatharlach.
  Carlow, Ceatharlach.
  Leighlinbridge, Leithghlinn an
    Droichid.
  Muine Bheag (Bagenalstown),
    Muine Bheag.
  Tullow, An Tulach.
Co. Dublin, Co. Bhaile Átha
  Cliath.
  Balbriggan, Baile Brigín.
  Dublin, Baile Átha Cliath.
  Dún Laoghaire, Dún
    Laoghaire.
  Howth, Binn Éadair.
Co. Kildare, Co. Chill Dara.
  Naas, An Nás.
  Athy, Baile Átha Í.
  Maynooth, Maigh Nuad.
  Kildare, Cill Dara.
  Newbridge, Droichead Nua.
  Kilcullen, Cill Chuillinn.
Co. Kilkenny, Co. Chill Chainnigh.
  Callan, Callainn.

  Castlecomer, Caisleán an
    Chomair.
  Kilkenny, Cill Chainnigh.
Co. Laois, Co. Laoise.
  Abbeyleix, Mainistir Laoise.
  Mountmellick, Móinteach
    Mílic.
  Port Laoise, Port Laoise.
  Portarlington, Cúil an
    tSúdaire.
Co. Longford, Co. an Longfoirt.
  Edgeworthstown, Meathas
    Troim.
  Granard, Gránard.
  Lanesborough, Béal Átha Liag.
  Longford, An Longfort.
Co. Louth, Co. Lú.
  Ardee, Baile Átha Fhirdhia.
  Carlingford, Cairlinn.
  Drogheda, Droichead Átha.
  Dundalk, Dún Dealgan.
  Dunleer, Dún Léire.
Co. Meath, Co. na Mí.
  Athboy, Baile Átha Buí.
  Kells, Ceanannas.
  Navan, An Uaimh.
  Oldcastle, An Seanchaisleán.
  Trim, Baile Átha Troim.
Co. Offaly, Co. Uíbh Failí.
  Banagher, Beannchar.
  Birr, Biorra.
  Edenderry, Éadan Doire.
  Tullamore, Tulach Mhór.
Co. Westmeath, Co. na hIarmhí.
  Athlone, Baile Átha Luain.
  Kilbeggan, Cill Bheagáin.
  Moate, An Móta.
  Mullingar, An Muileann
    gCearr.
Co. Wexford, Co. Loch Garman.
  Enniscorthy, Inis Córthaidh
  New Ross, Ros Mhic Thriúin.
  Wexford, Loch Garman.
Co. Wicklow, Co. Chill Mhantáin.
  Arklow, An tInbhear Mór.
  Bray, Bré.
  Glen of the Downs, Gleann Dá
    Ghrua.
  Greystones, Na Clocha Liatha.
  Wicklow, Cill Mhantáin.

Munster, Cúige Mumhan.
  Co. Clare, Co. an Chláir.
    Ennis, Inis.
    Kilkee, Cill Chaoi.
    Killaloe, Cill Dalua.
    Kilrush, Cill Rois.
  Co. Cork, Co. Chorcaí.
    Bandon, Droichead na
      Bandan.
    Cobh, An Cóbh.
    Cork, Corcaigh.
    Fermoy, Mainistir Fhear Maí.
    Mallow, Mala.
  Co. Kerry, Co. Chiarraí.
    Dingle, An Daingean.
    Killarney, Cill Airne.
    Listowel, Lios Tuathail.
    Tralee, Trá Lí.
  Co. Limerick, Co. Luimnigh.
    Abbeyfeale, Mainistir na Féile.
    Limerick, Luimneach.
    Newcastle, An Caisleán Nua.
    Rathkeale, Ráth Caola.
  Co. Tipperary, Co. Thiobraid
    Árann.
    Clonmel, Cluain Meala.
    Nenagh, An tAonach.
    Thurles, Durlas.
    Tipperary, Tiobraid Árann.
  Co. Waterford, Co. Phort Láirge.
    Cappoquin, Ceapach Choinn.
    Dungarvan, Dún Garbhán.
    Lismore, Lios Mór.
    Waterford, Port Láirge.

Ulster, Cúige Uladh
  Co. Antrim, Co. Aontroma.
    Belfast, Béal Feirste.
    Carrickfergus, Carraig
      Fhearghais.
    Lisburn, Lios na gCearrbhach.
  Co. Armagh, Co. Ard Mhacha.
    Armagh, Ard Mhacha.

    Crosmaglen, Crois Mhic
      Lionnáin.
    Lurgan, An Lorgain.
    Portadown, Port an Dúnáin.
  Co. Cavan, Co. an Chabháin.
    Ballyjamesduff, Baile
      Shéamais Dhuibh.
    Belturbet, Béal Tairbirt.
    Cavan, An Cabhán.
    Cootehill, Muinchille.
  Co. Derry, Co. Dhoire.
    Coleraine, Cúil Raithin.
    Derry, Doire.
    Limavady, Léim an Mhadaidh.
    Portstewart, Port Stíobhaird.
  Co. Donegal, Co. Dhún na nGall,
    Tír Chonaill
    Ballyshannon, Béal Átha
      Seanaidh.
    Donegal, Dún na nGall.
    Letterkenny, Leitir Ceanainn.
    Lifford, Leifear.
  Co. Down, Co. an Dúin.
    Banbridge, Droichead na
      Banna.
    Bangor, Beannchar.
    Downpatrick, Dún Pádraig.
    Newry, An tIúr.
  Co. Fermanagh, Co. Fhear
    Manach.
    Beleek, Béal Leice.
    Enniskillen, Inis Ceithleann.
    Lisnaskea, Lios na Scéithe.
  Co. Monaghan, Co. Mhuineacháin.
    Carrickmacross, Carraig
      Mhachaire Rois.
    Clones, Cluain Eois.
    Monaghan, Muineachán.
  Co. Tyrone, Co. Thír Eoghain.
    Dungannon, Dún Geanainn.
    Greystone, An Chloch Liath.
    Omagh, An Ómaigh.
    Strabane, An Srath Bán.

Table of Declensions

(Article, Noun, Adjective)

The plural form of a noun is *Strong* when the plural form for all cases is the same: nithe, nósanna.
The plural form of a noun is *Weak* if the plural ends in a consonant or is formed by adding *a* to the nom. sg.: báid, ulla.

1st Decl. nouns (m1). *All Mas. and end in a broad consonant. Gen. sg. formed by attenuation of final consonant.*

		sg.	pl.
N. & A.	:	an capall bán	na capaill bhána
Gen.	:	an chapaill bháin	na gcapall bán
Dat.	:	ar an gcapall bán	ar na capaill bhána
Voc.	:	a chapaill bháin	a chapaill bhána

Similarly:
bád, bord, buidéal, clog, casúr, fear, focal, leabhar, poll, port, punt, sagart, scamall, séipéal, sparán, *etc*

		sg.	pl.
N. & A.	:	an bacach ciallmhar	na bacaigh chiallmhara
Gen.	:	an bhacaigh chiallmhair	na mbacach ciallmhar
Dat.	:	ar an mbacach ciallmhar	ar na bacaigh chiallmhara
Voc.	:	a bhacaigh chiallmhair	a bhacacha ciallmhara

Similarly:
coileach, cléireach, fathach, oifigeach, sionnach, *etc*
also beithíoch, gaiscíoch, *etc, with pl. and gen. sg. ending* -igh.

		sg.	pl.
		an t-úll beag	na húlla beaga
		an úill bhig	na n-úll beag
		ar an úll beag	ar na húlla beaga
		a úill bhig	a úlla beaga

Similarly:
cág, ceart, cleas, gob, cuas, nod, *etc*

		sg.	pl.
		an seol maisiúil	na seolta maisiúla
		an tseoil mhaisiúil	na seolta maisiúla
		ar an seol maisiúil	ar na seolta maisiúla
		a sheoil mhaisiúil	a sheolta maisiúla

Similarly:
ceol, gaol, néal, saol, scéal, síol, stól, braon, cuan, dán, dún, líon, srian, *etc*

Nouns ending in -ch with strong plurals in -í: bealach, cladach, mullach, soitheach, orlach, *etc*
Nouns with strong plurals in -anna: bás, carr, gléas, luas, marc, nós, saghas, spás, *etc*
Nouns with strong pl. in -e after syncopation: bóthar (bóithre), solas (soilse), doras (doirse), *etc*
Other nouns with strong plurals: aonach (aontaí), cúram (cúraimí), tobar (toibreacha), muileann (muilte), smaoineamh (smaointe), breitheamh (breithiúna), ollamh (ollúna), briathar (briathra).

2nd Decl. nouns (f2). *All Fem. (except im, sliabh, teach) and end in a consonant. Gen. sg. formed by adding -e after attenuation (if necessary) or by changing final -(e)ach to -í (-aí).*

	sg.	pl.
N. & A. :	an tslat mhór	na slata móra
Gen. :	na slaite móire	na slat mór
Dat. :	ar an tslat mhór	ar na slata móra
Voc. :	a shlat mhór	a shlata móra

Similarly:
beach, bos, bróg, bréag, casóg, cearc, cloch, cluas, cos, féasóg, fuinneog, long, méar, scuab, speal, *etc*

	sg.	pl.
N. & A. :	an ghealach ard	na gealacha arda
Gen. :	na gealaí airde	na ngealach ard
Dat. :	ar an ngealach ard	ar na gealacha arda
Voc. :	a ghealach ard	a ghealacha arda

Similarly:
báisteach, baintreach, cailleach, cláirseach, girseach, óinseach, scornach, toirneach, *etc*

A few nouns (dúil, glún, súil) add -e for the nom. pl. (dúile, glúine, súile) and end in broad consonant in gen. pl. (dúl, glún, súl).

Nouns with strong plurals in:

-eanna : áit, aois, céim, ceist, cóir, cuairt, cúis, duais, feis, páirc, scoil, sráid, stailc, *etc*
-í : aisling, earráid, feoirling, liathróid, oifig, pingin, scilling, seachtain, *etc*
-(e)acha : carraig, ceirt, cistin, cracbh, feirm, iníon, maidin, nead, paidir (paidreacha), ubh (uibheacha), *etc*
-ta : buíon, líon, mian, pian, -onn.
-tha : (with broadening) gáir (gártha), spéir (spéartha), tír (tíortha).

The nouns im, sliabh, teach are Mas. (gen. sg. ime, sléibhe, tí; pl. –, sléibhte, tithe).

3rd Decl. nouns (m3 & f3). *Mas. and Fem. All end in broad or slender consonant. Gen. sg. formed by adding -a to Nom. sg. (broadened, if necessary). Most have strong plurals.*

	sg.	pl.
N. & A. :	an bádóir fearúil	na bádóirí fearúla
Gen. :	an bhádóra fhearúil	na mbádóirí fearúla
Dat. :	ag an mbádóir fearúil	ag na bádóirí fearúla
Voc. :	a bhádóir fhearúil	a bhádóirí fearúla

Similarly:
cáinteoir, moltóir, búistéir, siúinéir, dochtúir, buachaill, saighdiúir, tincéir, *etc*

	sg.	pl.
N. & A. :	an ríocht fhairsing	na ríochtaí fairsinge
Gen. :	na ríochta fairsinge	na ríochtaí fairsinge
Dat. :	sa ríocht fhairsing	sna ríochtaí fairsinge
Voc. :	a ríocht fhairsing	a ríochtaí fairsinge

Similarly:
beannacht, cáilíocht, gluaiseacht, filíocht, iasacht, impireacht, mallacht, cumhacht, *etc*

Mas. nouns with strong plurals in -anna:
acht, am, bláth, ceacht, cíos, cuid (codanna), dath, guth, loch, rang, sos, tráth, stad, *etc and the following which are broadened to form the*
Gen. sg.: cuid-coda, droim-droma, fuil-fola, *etc*

Fem. nouns ending in -áint, -úint, -irt, with strong plurals:

	gen. sg.		*pl.*			*Similarly,*	
tiomáint,	"	tiomána,	"	tiomántí		taispeáint, iomáint;	
canúint,	"	canúna,	"	canúintí.		cinniúint, eisiúint, oiliúint;	
bagairt,	"	bagartha,	"	bagairtí.		tagairt, buairt.	

Various other nouns.

Mas.	*gen. sg.*		*pl.*			*Fem.*	*gen. sg.*		*pl.*		
anam,	"	anama	"	anamacha		bliain,	"	bliana	"	blianta	
flaith	"	flatha	"	flatha		feoil	"	feola	"	feolta	
gleann	"	gleanna	"	gleanna		móin	"	móna	"	móinte	
fios	"	feasa				síocháin	"	síochána			
síoc	"	seaca				troid	"	troda	"	troideanna	

4th Decl. nouns (m4 & f4). *All have strong plurals. Most are Mas. All cases have the same form each in the sg. and in the pl. Most end in a vowel except diminutives in -ín and some Mas. nouns ending in a consonant.*

	sg.	*pl.*		*sg.*	*pl.*
N. & A.:	an coinín óg	na coiníní óga		an balla íseal	na ballaí ísle
Gen. :	an choinín óig	na gcoiníní óga		an bhalla ísil	na mballaí ísle
Dat. :	ag an gcoinín óg	ag na coiníní óga		ag an mballa íseal	ag na ballaí ísle
Voc. :	a choinín óig	a choiníní óga		a bhalla ísil	a bhallaí ísle

Similarly:
báisín, cailín, caipín, crúiscín, dreoilín, féirín, nóinín, sicín, toitín, *etc*

Similarly:
bata, bóna, cárta, hata, halla, lapa, mála, nóta, pionta, píopa, siopa, tiarna, *etc*

Nouns ending in -e and -(a)ire are declined like balla:
béile, bríste, ciste, cnaipe, cóiste, fáinne, file; aire, iascaire, dréimire, rógaire, *etc*
Nouns ending in -í, -(a)í, -(ao)í with strong plurals in -the:
ainmhí, ceannaí, cleasaí, Críostaí, dlí, gadaí, ní, oibrí, rí, daoi, saoi, *etc*
Nouns with strong plurals in -nna:
trá, ceo, cnó, cú, tlú, fleá, fogha, rogha, tua, *etc, and some words of foreign origin:* bus, club, pas, seic, tram.

5th Decl. nouns (m5 & f5). *Most are Fem. and end in a slender consonant (-in, -ir, -il) or a broad vowel. The Gen. sg. ends in a broad consonant. All nouns have strong plurals.*

	sg.	pl.	sg.	pl.
N. & A.	an chathair ghlan	na cathracha glana	an traein mhór	na traenacha móra
Gen.	na cathrach glaine	na gcathracha glana	na traenach móire	na dtraenacha móra
Dat.	sa chathair ghlan	sna cathracha glana	ag an traein mhór	ag na traenacha móra
Voc.	a chathair ghlan	a chathracha glana	a thraein mhóir	a thraenacha móra

Similarly:
beoir, cabhair, cathaoir, coróin, eochair, itir, lasair, meabhair, riail, triail, uimhir, *etc*

Similarly:
céimseata, ionga, monarcha, pearsa, ceathrú, lacha (*pl.* lachain).

The nouns fiche, tríocha, caoga, seasca, seachtó, ochtó, nócha *are Mas.*
gen. sg. fichead, tríochad, caogad, seascad, seachtód, ochtód, nóchad.
pl. fichidí, tríochaidí, caogaidí, seascaidí, seachtóidí, ochtóidí, nóchaidí.

Nouns ending in -ir, -in(n) *which have plurals in* -eacha:
athair, aithreacha; deartháir, deartháireacha; máthair, máithreacha; abhainn, aibhneacha; teorainn, teorainneacha, *etc*; bráthair *has pl.* bráithre.

Some Irregular Nouns

Nom. sg.	gen. sg.	pl.	Nom. sg.	gen. sg.	pl.
cara	carad	cairde	namhaid	namhad	naimhde
deoch	dí	deochanna	Nollaig	Nollag	Nollaigí
deirfiúr	deirféar	deirfiúracha	olann	olla	"
Dia	Dé	déithe	siúr	siúrach	siúracha
leaba	leapa	leapacha	teach	tí	tithe
			talamh	{ talún / talaimh }	tailte

	Nom. sg.	gen. sg.	nom. pl.	gen. pl.
	bean	mná	mná	ban
and	caora	caorach	caoirigh	caorach

Table of Regular Verbs

Regular verbs are divided into two main classes according to the form of the verb in the 3rd per. future tense: if that form ends in -fidh, -faidh, the verb belongs to the First Conjugation; if it ends in -óidh, -eoidh, it belongs to the Second Conjugation. The Stem of a verb is its form in the 2nd per. sg., Imperative Mood.

1st Conjugation
(a) Verbs with stems of one syllable. (b) Verbs with stems of more than one syllable and ending in -áil.
   (a) glan, clean; glanaim, I clean; v.n. glanadh; v.adj. glanta.

Pres. (Indic.)	Past (Indic.)	Hab.Past (Indic.)	Fut. (Indic.)	Cond. Mood	Pres. Subj.*	Impr. Mood
glanaim	ghlan mé	ghlanainn	glanfaidh mé	ghlanfainn	glana mé	glanaim
glanann tú	ghlan tú	ghlantá	glanfaidh tú	ghlanfá	glana tú	glan
glanann sé	ghlan sé	ghlanadh sé	glanfaidh sé	ghlanfadh sé	glana sé	glanadh sé
glanaim·d	ghlanamar	ghlanaimis	glanfaimid	ghlanfaimis	glanaimid	glanaimis
glanann sibh	ghlan sibh	ghlanadh sibh	glanfaidh sibh	ghlanfadh sibh	glana sibh	glanaigi
glanann siad	ghlan siad	ghlanaidis	glanfaidh siad	ghlanfaidis	glana siad	glanaidis

Aut. glantar...glanadh...ghlantaí...glanfar...ghlanfaí...glantar...glantar

Similarly:
báigh, baist, buail, bronn, caill, can, cas, ceap, cnag, lig, líon, ól, scaip, scaoil, scríobh, scuab, sín, etc

Verbs with stems of one syllable ending in: -igh: dóigh, léigh.
dóigh, burn; dóim, I burn; v.n. dó: v. adj. dóite.

Pres. (Indic.)	Past (Indic.)	Hab. Past (Indic.)	Fut. (Indic.)	Cond. Mood	Pres. Subj.*	Impr. Mood
dóim	dhóigh mé	dhóinn	dófaidh mé	dhófainn	dó mé	dóim
dónn tú	dhóigh tú	dhóiteá	dófaidh tú	dhófá	dó tú	dóigh
dónn sé	dhóigh sé	dhódh sé	dófaidh sé	dhófadh sé	dó sé	dódh sé
dóimid	dhómar	dhóimis	dófaimid	dhófaimis d	dóimid	dóimis
dónn sibh	dhóigh sibh	dhódh sibh	dófaidh sibh	dhófadh sibh	dó sibh	dóigí
dónn siad	dhóigh siad	dhóidís	dófaidh siad	dhófaidís	dó siad	dóidís

Aut. dóitear...dódh...dhóití...dófar...dhófaí...dóitear...dóitear

Similarly:
báigh, brúigh, cráigh, glaoigh, guígh, léigh, luigh, nigh, sáig 1, suigh, etc

(b)
sábháil, save; v.n. sábháil; v. adj. sábháilte.

Pres. (Indic.)	Past (Indic.)	Hab. Past (Indic.)	Fut. (Indic.)	Cond. Mood	Pres. Subj.*	Impr. Mood
sábhálaim	shábháil mé	shábhálainn	sábhálfaidh mé	shábhálfainn	sábhála mé	sábhálaim
sábhálann tú	shábháil tú	shábháilteá	sábhálfaidh tú	shábhálfá	sábhála tú	sábháil
sábhálann sé	shábháil sé	shábháladh sé	sábhálfaidh sé	shábhálfadh sé	sábhála sé	sábháladh sé
sábhálaimid	shábhálamar	shábhálaimis	sábhálfaimid	shábhálfaimis	sábhálaimid	sábhálaimis
sábhálann sibh	shábháil sibh	shábháladh sibh	sábhálfaidh sibh	shábhálfadh sibh	sábhála sibh	sábhálaigí
sábhálann siad	shábháil siad	shábhálaidís	sábhálfaidh siad	shábhálfaidís	sábhála siad	sábhálaidís

Aut. sábháiltear...sábháladh...shábháiltí...sábháiltear...shábhálfar...shábháilfaí...sábháiltear...sábháiltear

Similarly:
bácáil, cardáil, cniotáil, marcáil, ofráil, robáil, spáráil, tástáil, etc

2nd Conjugation

(a) Verbs of two syllables or more ending in -igh or -aigh; (b) Syncopated Verbs.
a) bailigh, gather; bailím, I gather; v.n. bailiú; v. adj. bailithe.

Pres. (Indic.)	Past (Indic.)	Hab. Past (Indic.)	Fut. (Indic.)	Cond. Mood	Pres. Subj.*	Impr. Mood
bailím	bhailigh mé	bhailínn	baileoidh mé	bhaileoinn	bailí mé	bailím
bailíonn tú	bhailigh tú	bhailíteá	baileoidh tú	bhaileofá	bailí tú	bailigh
bailíonn sé	bhailigh sé	bhailíodh sé	baileoidh sé	bhaileodh sé	bailí sé	bailíodh sé
bailímid	bhailíomar	bhailímis	baileoimid	bhaileoimis	bailímid	bailímis
bailíonn sibh	bhailigh sibh	bhailíodh sibh	baileoidh sibh	bhaileodh sibh	bailí sibh	bailígí
bailíonn siad	bhailigh siad	bhailídís	baileoidh siad	bhaileoidís	bailí siad	bailídís

Aut. bailítear...bailíodh...bhailítí...bhaileofaí...baileofar...bailítear...bailítear

*There is also the Past Subjunctive. It is not included in the Table as it always has the same form as the Habitual Past (without initial aspiration).

Similarly:
ceannaigh, cónaigh, clúdaigh, corraigh, cumhnigh, dúisigh, éirigh, fiafraigh, imigh, réitigh, scrúdaigh, socraigh, smaoinigh, teastaigh, tosaigh, *etc*

(b) *Syncopated Verbs, .i. verbs of more than one syllable ending in -il, -in, -ir, -is.*
cosain, *protect, cost;* cosnaím, *I protect; v.n.* cosaint; *v.adj.* cosanta.

Pres. (Indic.)	Past (Indic.)	Hab. Past (Indic.)	Fut. (Indic.)	Cond. Mood	Pres. Subj.*	Impr. Mood
cosnaím	chosain mé	chosnaínn	cosnóidh mé	chosnóinn	cosnaí mé	cosnaím
cosnaíonn tú	chosain tú	chosnaíteá	cosnóidh tú	chosnófá	cosnaí tú	cosain
cosnaíonn sé	chosain sé	chosnaíodh sé	cosnóidh sé	chosnódh sé	cosnaí sé	cosnaíodh sé
cosnaímid	chosnaíomar	chosnaímis	cosnóimid	chosnóimis	cosnaímid	cosnaímis
cosnaíonn sibh	chosain sibh	chosnaíodh sibh	cosnóidh sibh	chosnódh sibh	cosnaí sibh	cosnaígí
cosnaíonn siad	chosain siad	chosnaídís	cosnóidh siad	chosnóidís	cosnaí siad	cosnaídís

Aut. cosnaítear...cosnaíodh...chosnaítí...cosnófar...chosnófaí...cosnaítear...cosnaítear

Similarly:
aithin, bagair, ceangail, codail, díbir, fógair, eitil, freagair, iompair, imir, inis, labhair, múscail, oscail, taitin.

Verbs of more than one syllable which are not syncopated:
foghlaim, foghlaimím; freastail, freastalaím; fulaing, fulaingím; tarraing, tarraingím; taisteal, taistealaím; lorg, lorgaím.

*There is also the Past Subjunctive. It is not included in the Table as it always has the same form as the Habitual Past (without initial aspiration).

I-regular Verbs

Irregular verbs do not keep the same stem throughout their conjugation. Some have special Dependent forms which are used after the following verbal particles: an, cá, dá, go, mura, nach, ní, sula, a (= all).

1. **abair**, *say*; deirim, *I say*; *v.n.* rá; *v.adj.* ráite.
   Indic. Pres. deirim, *etc* : *Past* dúirt mé, *etc* : *H. Past* deirinn, *etc* : *Future* déarfaidh mé, *etc*
   (*Aut.* deirtear) : (*Aut.* dúradh): (*Aut.* deirtí) (*Aut.* déarfar).
   Cond. Mood déarfainn, *etc* : *Pres. Subj.* deire mé, *etc* : *Impr. M.* abraím, *etc*
   (*Aut.* déarfaí) : (*Aut.* deirtear) : (*Aut.* abairtear).

2. **beir**, *catch or bring*; beirim, *I catch, bring*; *v.n.* breith; *v.adj.* beirthe.
   Regular in *Pres., H. Past, Pres. Subj. and Imperative*: beirim, bheirinn, beire mé, beirim.
   Past rug mé, *etc*: *Future* béarfaidh mé, *etc*: *Cond. Mood* bhéarfainn, *etc*
   (*Aut.* rugadh) : (*Aut.* béarfar) : (*Aut.* bhéarfaí).

3. **clois** *and* **cluin**, *hear*; cloisim, cluinim, *I hear*; *v.n.* cloisteáil, cluinstin; *v. adj.* cloiste, cluinte.
   Both are conjugated regularly except in the *Past (Indic.) which has the same form for both verbs.*
   Past (Indic.): chuala mé, – tú, – sé, chualamar, chuala sibh, – siad. *Aut.* chualathas.

4. **déan**, *do*; déanaim, *I do*; *v.n.* déanamh; *v. adj.* déanta.
   Conjugated regularly except in Past (Indic.).
   Past (Indic.) : rinne mé (tú, sé), rinneamar, rinne sibh (siad). *Aut.* Rinneadh.
   or dhein mé (tú, sé), dheineamar, dhein sibh (siad) *Aut.* deineadh.
   Dependent form : dearna mé (tú, sé), dearnamar, dearna sibh (siad). *Aut.* dearnadh.

5. **faigh**, *get*; faighim, *I get*; *v.n.* fáil; *v. adj.* faighte.
   Regular except in the Past, Future and Conditional.
   Past: fuair mé (tú, sé), fuaireamar fuair sibh (siad). *Aut.* fuarthas.
   Future: gheobhaidh mé (tú, sé), gheobhairnid, gheobhaidh sibh (siad), *Aut.* gheofar.
   Cond. Mood: gheobhainn, gheofá, gheobhadh sé, gheobhaimis, gheobhadh sibh, gheobhaidís. *Aut.* gheofaí.
   The Future and Conditional have Dependent forms which are regular:

   Fut. Dep.: (ní, go, *etc*) bhfaighidh mé (tú, sé), *etc Aut.* (ní, go, *etc*) bhfaighfear.
   Cond. Dep.: (ní, go, *etc*) bhfaighinn, bhfaighfeá, *etc Aut.* (ní, go, *etc*) bhfaighfí.

6. feic *see;* feicim (chím), *I see; v.n.* feiceáil; *v. adj.* feicthe.
   Regular except in Past (Independent and Dependent forms).
   Past (Indep.): chonaic mé (tú, sé), chonaiceamar, chonaic sibh (siad). *Aut.* chonacthas.
   Past (Dep.): (ní) fhaca mé (tú, sé), fhacamar, fhaca sibh (siad). *Aut.* ní fhacthas.
   Note: This verb has the following alternative forms:-
   Pres. Indic. (Ind. only): chím, chíonn tú (sé), chímid, chíonn sibh (siad). *Aut.* chítear.
   Fut. Indic. (Ind. only): chífidh mé (tú, sé), chífimid, chífidh sibh (siad). *Aut.* chífear.

7. ith, *eat;* ithim, *I eat; v.n.* ithe; *v. adj.* ite.
   Regular except in Future and Cond. Mood
   Future: íosfaidh mé (tú, sé), íosfaimid, íosfaidh sibh (siad). *Aut.* íosfar.
   Cond. Mood: d'íosfainn, d'íosfá, d'íosfadh sé, d'íosfaimis, d'íosfadh sibh, d'íosfaidís. *Aut.* d'íosfaí.

8. tabhair, *give;* tugaim, *I give; v.n.* tabhairt; *v. adj.* tugtha.
   Regular in Future (tabharfaidh mé, *etc*) *and Cond. Mood* (thabharfainn, *etc*) *with* tabhair *as stem.*
   All other forms have tug *as stem:-*
   Pres. tugaim, *etc: Past* thug mé, *etc: H. Past* thugainn, *etc: Pres. Subj.* tuga mé, *etc*
   Imperative tugaim, *etc* (*but* tabhair *in 2nd per. sg.*).

9. tar *come;* tagaim, *I come; v.n.* teacht; *v. adj.* tagtha.
   The pres. H. Past, Pres. Subj. and Imper. are conjugated regularly with tag *as stem.*
   Pres: tagaim, *etc: H. Past* thagainn, *etc: Pres. Subj:* taga mé, *etc: Imper.* tagaim, *etc* (*but tar in 2nd sg.*)
   Past: tháinig mé (tú, sé), thángamar, tháinig sibh (siad). *Aut.* thángthas.
   Future: tiocfaidh mé (tú, sé), tiocfaimid, tiocfaidh sibh (siad). *Aut.* tiocfar.
   Cond. Mood: thiocfainn, thiocfá, thiocfadh sé, thiocfaimis, thiocfadh sibh, thiocfaidís. *Aut.* thiocfar.

10. téigh, *go;* téim, *I go; v.n.* dul; *v. adj.* dulta.
    The pres. (téim, *etc.*), *H. Past* (théinn, *etc*), *Pres. Subj.* (té mé, *etc*) *and Imper.* (téim) *are regular.*
    Past (Indep.): chuaigh mé (tú, sé), chuamar, chuaigh sibh (siad). *Aut.* chuathas.
    Past (Dep.): deachaigh mé (tú, sé), deachamar, deachaigh sibh (siad). *Aut.* deachthas.
    Future: rachaidh mé (tú, sé), rachaimid, rachaidh sibh (siad). *Aut.* rachfar.
    Cond.: rachainn, rachfá, rachfá, rachadh sé, rachaimis, rachadh sibh, rachaidís. *Aut.* rachfaí.

11. **bí**, *be.* táim (tá mé), *I am; v.n.* bheith.

Present

(Positive)	(Negative)*	(Dependent)
táim (tá mé)	nílim (níl mé)	(go...) bhfuilim (ᴛᴇ)
tá tú	níl tú	" bhfuil tú
tá sé	níl sé	" bhfuil sé
táimid	nílimid	" bhfuilimid
tá sibh	níl sibh	" bhfuil sibh
tá siad	níl siad	" bhfuil siad

Aut. táthar... / níltear ... / " bhfuiltear...

Past

(Positive)	(Dependent)
bhí mé	(go...) raibh mé
" tú	" " tú
" sé	" " sé
bhíomar	" rabhamar
bhí sibh	" raibh sibh
bhí siad	" " siad

bhíothas... / "rabhthas...

Hab. Past

bhínn
bhíteá
bhíodh sé
bhímis
bhíodh sibh
bhídís

bhítí...

Future

beidh mé
beidh tú
beidh sé
beimid
beidh sibh
" siad

Aut. beifear

Conditional

bheinn
bheifeá
bheadh sé
bheimis
bheadh sibh
bheidís

Aut. bheifí...

Pres. Subj.

raibh mé
raibh tú
raibh sé
rabhamar
raibh sibh
" siad

rabhthar...

Past Subj.

beinn
beifeá
beadh sé
beimis
beadh sibh
beidís

beifí...

Imperative

bím
bí
bíodh sé
bímis
bígí
bídís

bitear...

Defective Verbs

A Defective verb is one which has not all the usual verbal forms.

1. *is,* the Copula, is irregular. It is also defective as it has no Imperative or Autonomous forms, no verbal noun or verbal adjective.

Present and Future	Past and Conditional
In Principal Sentences: is *(affirmative)*, ní *(negative)*	In Principal Sentences: ba, b' *(affirmative)*, níor, níorbh *(neg.)*
In Interogative Sentences: an " , nach "	In Interogative Sentences: ar, arbh " , nár, nárbh "
In Dependent Sentences: gur(b) " , nach "	In Dependent Sentences: gur, gurbh " , nár, nárbh "
Relative forms: –	Relative forms: –
(i) direct: is " , nach "	(i) direct: ba, ab " , nár, nárbh "
(ii) indirect: ar(b) " , nach "	(ii) indirect: ar; arbh, nár, nárbh

Pres. Subj. gura, gurab *(positive)*: nára, nárabh *(negative)*.

2.   ar (arsa), *said.*
     It is used only in the Past Indicative.
     ar *is used only before* seisean, sise, siadsan.
     arsa *is used with any subject:* arsa Máire, an fear, mise, sinne.

3.   dar, *seems (appears), has only this one form.*
     It is usually followed by the preposition le.
     Tá sé briste, dar liom. Dar liom go bhfuil sé briste.

4.   dóbair, *nearly, almost (happened).*
     Used only in the Past Indicative.
     dóbair dom é a bhriseadh: dóbair go dtitfinn.

Declension of most common Verbal Nouns

(i) The gen. singular of verbal nouns is similar in form to their verbal adjectives in the case of verbal nouns
  (a) ending in -eadh, -adh (masculine):
  (caoineadh) caointe; (casadh) casta; (moladh) molta.
  (b) ending in a vowel (masculine):
  (ceartú) ceartaithe; (míniú) mínithe; (ionsaí) ionsaithe.
  (c) ending in -ilt, -int, -irt (feminine):
  (oscailt) oscailte; (cogaint) coganta; (bagairt) bagartha.

(ii) Many verbal nouns form their gen. singular as common nouns.
  1st declension (masculine) ending in broad consonant:
  (ceangal) ceangail; (machnamh) machnaimh; (ól) óil; (gearán) gearáin.
  2nd declension (feminine) by adding -e:
  (baint) bainte; (aithris) aithrise; (fóirithint) fóirithinte.
  3rd declension (feminine) ending in -áil, -ail, -úint, -int, -cht:
  (admháil) admhála; (feadaíl) feadaíola; (iomáint) iomána; (leanúint) leanúna; (marcaíocht) marcaíochta.

The plural forms of verbal nouns are used as ordinary common nouns and the main groups are formed as follows:
  (i) the endings -adh, -eadh become -taí, -tí:
  (moladh) moltaí; (casadh) castaí (baisteadh) baistí.
  (ii) the endings -ú, -iú become -uithe, -ithe:
  (scrúdú) scrúduithe; (ceartú) ceartuithe; (míniú) mínithe.
  (iii) the ending -cht has -aí added to it:
  (imeacht) imeachtaí, (tóraíocht) tóraíochtaí.
  (iv) the endings -it, -nt, -rt have -í added:
  (eitilt) eitiltí; (tairiscint) tairscintí (bagairt) bagairtí.
  (v) the endings -áil, -ail, have the final l broadened and -acha added:
  (admháil) admhálacha; (tarrtháil) tarrthálacha; (bradaíl) bradaíolacha.

Table of Prepositional Pronouns

agam	agat	aige	aici	againn	agaibh	acu
asam	asat	as	aisti	asainn	asaibh	astu
chugam	chugat	chuige	chuici	chugainn	chugaibh	chucu
díom	díot	de	di	dínn	díbh	díobh
dom	duit	dó	di	dúinn	daoibh	dóibh
faram	farat	fairis	fairsti	farainn	faraibh	farstu
fúm	fút	faoi	fúithi	fúinn	fúibh	fúthu
				eadrainn	eadraibh	eatarthu
ionam	ionat	ann	inti	ionainn	ionaibh	iontu
liom	leat	leis	léi	linn	libh	leo
orm	ort	air	uirthi	orainn	oraibh	orthu
romham	romhat	roimhe	roimpi	romhainn	romhaibh	rompu
tharam	tharat	thairis	thairsti	tharainn	tharaibh	tharstu
tríom	tríot	tríd	tríthi	trínn	tríbh	tríothu
uaim	uait	uaidh	uaithi	uainn	uaibh	uathu
umam	umat	uime	uimpi	umainn	umaibh	umpu

A

abandon *v* tréig

abandoned *adj* tréigthe

abbess *n* máthairab

abbey *n* mainistir **the Abbey Theatre** Amhraclann na Mainistreach

abbot *n* ab

abbreviate *v* giorraigh

abbreviated *adj* giorraithe **abbreviated entry** iontráil ghiorraithe

abbreviation *n* giorrúchán, nod

abdicate *v* tabhair suas

abdomen *n* bolg

abduct *v* fuadaigh

abduction *n* fuadach

abductor *n* fuadaitheoir

aberration *n* seachmall

ability *n* ábaltacht, inniúlacht, cumas

ablaze *adj* ar bharr lasrach

able *adj* ábalta, cumasach, inniúil **to be able to do something** a bheith in ann rud a dhéanamh

abnormal *adj* mínormálta, neamhghnách

abode *n* áitreabh

abolish *v* cuir ar ceal

abortion *n* ginmhilleadh

about *adv, prep* máguaird, thart, tuairim is, um **about to do something** ar tí rud a dhéanamh

above *prep* os, os cionn, thar, thuas, lastuas

abrasive *adj* scríobach

abroad *adv* thar lear, thar sáile, ar an gcoigríoch

abrogate *v* aisghair

abrogation *n* aisghairm

abrupt *adj* giorraisc, grod

abscess *n* easpa

abscond *v* éalaigh, teith

absence *n* éagmais, easpa, neamhláithreacht

absent *adj* as láthair, neamhláithreach

absentee *n* neamhláithrí

absent-minded *adj* dearmadach

absolutely *adj* lánchinnte

absolution *n* aspalóid **to receive absolution** aspalóid a fháil

absorb *v* súigh, ionsúigh

absorbency *n* ionsúiteacht

absorbent *adj* súiteach **absorbent cotton** olann chadáis shúiteach

absorption *n* ionsú

abstain from *v* staon ó

abstract *adj* teibí *n* achomaireacht, (*of magazine*) iris choimriúcháin

abstraction *n* (**art**) teibíocht

absurd *adj* áiféiseach

abundance *n* flúirse, iomadúlacht, raidhse, rathúnas **in abundance** go barra bachall

abundant *adj* raidhsiúil, fras

abuse[1] *n* íde, mí-úsáid **to give somebody terrible abuse** íde na muc is na madraí a thabhairt do dhuine, **child (sexual) abuse** mí-úsáid (ghnéis) ar pháistí

abuse[2] *v* maslaigh

abusive *adj* maslach

abyss *n* duibheagán

academic *adj* acadúil, fear léinn, bean léinn

academy *n* acadamh

accelerate *v* luasghéaraigh, luathaigh

acceleration *n* luasghéarú

accelerator *n* luasaire
accent *n* aiceann, blas, canúint
  accent on vowel síneadh fada
accept *v* glac (le)
acceptable *adj* inghlactha
acceptance *n* glacadh
accepted *adj* aitheanta
access *n* rochtain **access time** am rochtana
accessible *adj* insroichte, **(of person)** sochaideartha
accessories *pl* oiriúintí
accessory (to crime) *n* cúlpháirtí
accidence *n* deilbhíocht **(grammar)**
accident *n* taisme, timpiste, tionóisc
accidental *adj* taismeach, timpisteach, tionóisceach
acclamation *n* gáir mholta
acclimatisation *n* clíomúchán
acclimatise *v* clíomaigh
accommodation *n* cóir, iostas, lóistín
accompaniment *n* tionlacan
accompany *v* tionlaic
accomplice *n* comhchoirí
accomplish *v* críochnaigh
accomplished *adj* críochnaithe
according to *prep* dar le, de réir
accordion *n* cairdín
accost *n* cuir caint ar, buail bleid ar
account *n* cuntas, tuairisc **savings account** cuntas taisce, **current account** cuntas reatha, **on account of** de thairbhe, **to give an account of something** tuairisc a thabhairt ar rud
accountancy *n* **(profession)** cuntasóireacht, **(study of)** cuntasaíocht
accountant *n* cuntasóir
accumulate *v* tiomsaigh
accuracy *n* cruinneas
accurate *adj* cruinn, beacht
accusation *n* cúiseamh

accusative *adj, n* cuspóireach **(grammar)**
accuse *v* ciontaigh, cúisigh
accused person *n* cúisí
accustomed (to) *adj* taithíoch (ar)
ace *n* aon **ace of hearts** an t-aon hart, **ace of diamonds** an t-aon muileata
achieve *v* cuir i gcrích
achievement *n* éacht
acid *adj* aigéadach *n* aigéad **acid rain** báisteach aigéadach
acidification *n* aigéadú
acidity *n* aigéadacht
acknowledge *v* admhaigh, aithin
acknowledgement *n* admháil
acorn *n* dearcán
acoustic *adj* fuaimiúil
acoustics *n* fuaimeolaíocht, **(of building)** fuaimíocht
acquaint *v* rud a chur in iúl do, aithne a chur ar
acquaintance *n* aitheantas, aithne **acquaintances** lucht aitheantais
acquire *v* faigh
acquisitive *adj* santach
acquit *v* saor
acquittal *n* saoradh
acre *n* acra
acrobat *n* gleacaí
acrobatics *n* gleacaíocht
across *adj* anall, anonn, thar, trasna
act *n* gníomh *v* gníomhaigh, **(in play)** aicteáil
acting *n* aisteoireacht
acting principal *n* príomhoide sealadach
action *n* gníomh, gníomhú, **(film)** aicsean **actions speak louder than words** téann focal le gaoth ach téann buille le cnámh
action replay *n* athfhéachaint
activate *v* gníomhachtaigh

activator *n* músclóir

active *adj* gníomhach

activist *n* gníomhaí

activity *n* gníomhaíocht

actor *n* aisteoir

acupuncture *n* snáthaidpholladh

acute *adj* géar **acute angle** géaruilinn

adage *n* nath, nathán

adamant *adj* daingean

Adam's apple *n* úll na scornaí, meall brád

adapt *v* oiriúnaigh

adaptor *n* (electrical) cuibheoir

add *v* suimigh

addict *n* andúileach **drug addict** andúileach drugaí

addiction *n* andúil, andúilíocht **drug addiction** andúil i ndrugaí, andúilíocht drugaí

addictive *adj* andúileach **to be addicted to drink** bheith tugtha don ól

addition *n* tuilleadh, suimiú

additional *adj* breise

additive *n* breiseán

address[1] *n* (speech) óráid, aitheasc

address[2] *n* (of letter) seoladh *v* seol

adenoids *pl* adanóidí

adequate *adj* sásúil

adhere *v* greamaigh (do), cloígh (le) **to adhere to something** greamú do rud

adhesive *adj* greamaitheach *n* greamachán

adjective *n* aidiacht

adjourn *v* cuir ar atráth **to adjourn something** rud a chur ar atráth

adjudicate *v* moltóireacht a dhéanamh

adjust *v* coigeartaigh, gléas

adjustment *n* coigeartú

administer *v* riar

administration *n* reachtas, riar, riarachán

administrator *n* riarthóir, reachtaire

admirable *adj* fónta

admiral *n* aimiréal

admiration *n* ardmheas

admire *v* ardmheas a bheith agat ar

admissible *adj* inghlactha

admission *n* admháil

admit *v* admhaigh

adolescence *adj* inmheach

adolescent *n* ógánach

adopt *v* uchtaigh

adore *v* adhair

adorn *v* maisigh

adornment *n* maise, maisiú, maisiúchán

adrenalin *n* aidréanailín

adrift *adj* ag imeacht le sruth

adult *n* duine fásta

adultery *n* adhaltranas

adulthood *n* aosacht

advance[1] *n* (of progress) dul chun cinn, (of money, payment) réamhíocaíocht, airleacan **in advance** roimh ré

advance[2] *v* cuir chun cinn

advancement *n* réamhshocrú

advantage *n* buntáiste, árach, bua

advantageous *adj* buntáisteach

Advent *n* Aidbhint

adventure *n* eachtra

adventurer *n* eachtránaí

adverb *n* dobhriathar

adversary *n* céile comhraic

advertise *v* fógair

advertisement *n* fógra

advertising *n* fógraíocht

advice *n* comhairle

advisable *adj* inmholta

advise *v* comhairligh

advocate *n* abhcóide

aerial *adj* aerga, *n* aeróg

aerial shot (of film) *n* seat ón aer

aerial shooting (of film) *n* scannánú ón aer

aerobics *n* aclaíocht aeróbach

aerodrome *n* aeradróm

aeronautics *n* aerloingseoireacht

aeroplane *n* eitleán

aerosol *n* aerasól

aerospace *n* aerspás

aesthetic *adj* aeistéitiúil

afar *adv* i gcéin

affable *adj* mánla, lách

affairs *pl* cúrsaí **current affairs** cúrsaí reatha

affect *v* goill ar

affection *n* cion, gean, spéis

affectionate *adj* geanúil, muirneach, bách

affidavit *n* mionnscríbhinn

affiliate *v* comhcheangail le

affirm *v* deimhnigh

affirmation *n* dearbhú

affirmative *adj* dearfach, deimhniúil

affix *v* greamaigh

afflict *v* goill ar

afflicted *adj* dobrónach

affliction *n* galar, sciúirse, amparánaíocht

affluent *adj* toiciúil

afford, **I can't afford (to buy it)** níl sé d'acmhainn agam (é a cheannach)

afforestation *n* coillteoireacht, foraoisiú

affront *v* maslaigh, tarcaisnigh

afloat *adv* ar snámh

afoot *adv* ar bun

afraid *adj* eaglach **I'm afraid of dogs** tá eagla orm roimh mhadraí

afresh *adj* as an nua

Africa *n* an Afraic

African *adj*, *n* Afracach

after *adv* tar éis, i ndiaidh **after all** tar éis an tsaoil

aftergrowth *n* athbharr

afternoon *n* iarnóin, nóin, tráthnóna **in the afternoon** um thráthnóna

after-shave lotion *n* ionlach iarbhearrtha

afterthought *n* athsmaoineamh

afterwards *adj* ina dhiaidh sin

again *adv* arís, athuair

against *prep* in aghaidh, i gcoinne

age[1] *n* aois **she is a year old** tá sí bliain d'aois, **the Golden Age** an Ré Órga

age[2] *v* aosaigh

aged *adj* aosta, ársa

age discrimination *n* laofacht aoise

age group *n* aoisghrúpa

age-limit *n* aoisteorainn, teorainn aoise **age of criminal responsibility** aois na freagrachta coiriúla, **age structure** struchtúr aoise

ageism *n* laofacht aoise

agency *n* gníomhaireacht **travel agency** gníomhaireacht taistil

agenda *n* clár oibre

agent *n* feidhmeannach, gníomhaire

aggravate *v* géaraigh, méadaigh

aggregate *n* comhiomlán

aggression *n* ionsaí

aggressive *adj* ionsaitheach

aggressor *n* ionsaitheoir

agile *adj* aclaí, lúfar

agitate *v* corraigh

agitated *adj* tógtha, corraithe

agitation *n* corraí

ago *adj* ó shin, fadó

agony *n* céasadh

agrarian *adj* talúntais

agree *v* aontaigh, réitigh, toiligh

agreeable *adj* suáilceach

agreement *n* margadh, conradh, socrú, aontú, comhaontú, comhréiteach

agriculture *n* talmhaíocht

agricultural produce *n* táirgí talmhaíochta

ah *excl* á

ahead *adv* chun cinn, chun tosaigh

aid *n* cúnamh **the Legal Aid Board** an Bord um Chúnamh Dlíthiúil

AIDS *n* SEIF (siondróm easpa imdhíonachta faighte)

ail *v* **what ails her?** cad tá uirthi?

aim[1] *n* aidhm, amas, aimsiú

aim[2] *v* aimsigh

air *n* aer

airbase *n* aerionad

air-conditioned *adj* aeroiriúnaithe

air-conditioning *n* aeroiriúnú

aircraft *n* aerárthach

air force *n* aerfhórsa

airing *n* aeráil

air letter *n* aerlitir

airline *n* aerlíne

airline ticket *n* ticéad aerthaistil

airliner *n* aerlínéar

airlock *n* aerbhac

airmail *n* aerphost

airport *n* aerfort **Cork, Dublin, Shannon Airport** Aerfort Chorcaí, Bhaile Átha Cliath, na Sionainne

air raid *n* aer-ruathar

airtight *adj* aerdhíonach

airy *adj* aerach

aisle *n* taobhroinn

alacrity *n* éascaíocht

alarm *n* aláram, rabhadh

alarm clock *n* clog aláraim

alas *interj* faraor, monuar, mo léan!

albatross *n* albatras

album *n* albam

alcohol *n* alcól

alcoholic *adj*, *n* alcólach

alcoholism *n* alcólachas

alder *n* fearnóg

ale *n* leann

alert *adj* airdeallach

alertness *n* airdeall

alga *n* alga

algebra *n* ailgéabar

alias *n* ainm bréige

alibi *n* ailibí

alien *adj*, *n* coimhthíoch, eachtrannach

allenate *v* duine a chur in aghaidh duine eile **they became alienated** thug siad cúl dá chéile

alight *v* tuirling

align *v* ailínigh

alike *adv* mar an gcéanna

alimentary canal *n* conair an bhia

alimony *n* ailiúnas

alive *adj* ar marthain, beo

alkaline *adj* alcaileach

all *adj*, *adv*, *pron* go léir, ar fad, iomlán **at all costs** ar ais nó ar éigean

allegation *n* líomhain

allege *v* líomhain

allegiance *n* dílse, dílseacht

allegory *n* fáthscéal

allergic *adj* ailléirgeach

allergy *n* ailléirge

alleviate *v* maolaigh

alleviation *n* maolú

alley *n* scabhat

alliance *n* comhaontas

Allied Forces *pl* Fórsaí na gComhghuaillithe

alligator *n* ailigéadar

alliteration *n* uaim

allocate *v* cionroinn

allocation *n* cionroinnt

allot *v* riar, roinn

allotment *n* áirithe, roinnt

allow *v* lamháil, leomh, lig

allowance *n* lamháil, liúntas **tax free allowance** liúntas saor ó cháin

all powerful *adj* uilechumhachtach

all purpose *adj* uilefhóntach

all round *adv, prep* mórthimpeall

allure *n* cealg, meallacacht *v* meall

alluvium *n* glár

ally *n* comhghuaillí

almanac *n* almanag

almighty *adj* uilechumhachtach

almond *n* almóinn

almost *adv* beagnach, nach beag, nach mór

alms *n* déirc

aloe *n* aló

alone *adj* aonraic, aonaránach **I am alone** tá mé i m'aonar

along with *adv* maille le

alphabet *n* aibítir **in alphabetical order** in ord aibítire

Alpine *adj* Alpach

already *adv* cheana (féin)

alright *adj* ceart go leor, maith go leor

alsatian *n* alsáiseach

also *adv* freisin, fosta, leis

altar *n* altóir

alter *v* athraigh

alteration *n* athrach, athrú

alternate *adj* gach re

alternation *n* sealaíocht, uainíocht

alternative *n* athrach, malairt, rogha **I had no alternative** ní raibh an dara suí sa bhuaile agam

although *conj* cé go

altitude *n* airde

altogether *adj* go hiomlán, ar fad

aluminium *n* alúmanam

aluminium foil *n* scragall alúmanaim

always *adv* go deo, i gcónaí, riamh

a.m. *adv* ar maidin, r.n.

amalgamate *v* cónaisc

amateur *adj, n* amaitéarach

amaze *v* alltacht a chur ar

amazement *n* iontas, alltacht

ambassador *n* ambasadóir

amber *adj* ómrach *n* ómra

ambidextrous *adj* comhdheas

ambiguity *n* athbhrí, débhríocht

ambiguous *adj* débhríoch, déchiallach, athbhríoch

ambition *n* uaillmhian

ambitious *adj* uaillmhianach

ambulance *n* otharcharr

ambush *n* luíochán

amend *v* ceartaigh, leasaigh

amending *adj* leasaitheach

amendment *n* leasú, leasúchán

amends *pl* leorghníomh

America *n* Meiriceá

American *adj, n* Meiriceánach

amethyst *n* aimitis

amiable *adj* geanúil, lách

amicable *adj* carthannach, cairdiúil

ammonia *n* amóinia

ammunition *n* armlón **armour-piercing ammunition** armlón pollta armúir

amnesia *n* aimnéise

amnesty *n* pardún ginearálta

among *prep* i measc

amoral *adj* dímhorálta

amorous *adj* grámhar

amorphous *adj* éagruthach

amount *n* méid, oiread

amp *n* aimpéar

amphibian *n* débheathach

ample *adj* leor

amplifier *n* aimplitheoir

amplify *v* aimpligh

amputate *v* teasc

amputation *n* teascadh

amuse *v* siamsa a dhéanamh do, taitneamh a thabhairt do

amusement *n* siamsa

amusing *adj* spórtúil, greannmhar, barrúil

anaemia *n* anaemacht

anaemic *adj* anaemach

anaesthetic *adj, n* ainéistéiseach

anaesthetist *n* ainéistéisí

anagram *n* anagram

analogous *adj* ar aon dul le

analogy *n* analach, cosúlacht

analyse *v* anailísigh

analysis *n* anailís

analyst *n* anailísí

analytical *adj* anailíseach

anarchical *adj* anlathach, ainrialta

anarchist *n* ainrialaí

anarchy *n* ainriail, anlathas

anatomy *n* anatamaíocht

ancestor *n* sean, sinscar, sinsearach, athair

ancestral *adj* sinseartha, sinsearach athartha

ancestry *n* sinsearacht

anchor *n* ancaire **to weigh anchor** an t-ancaire a thógáil

anchorage *n* ancaireacht

anchored *adj* ar ancaire

anchovy *n* ainseabhaí

ancient *n* ársa, seanda

and *conj* agus, is

anecdote *n* scéilín

angel *n* aingeal

anger *n* colg, fearg

angina *n* aingíne

angle *n* cúinne, uilinn **angle of one hundred and twenty degrees** ar uillinn céad fiche céim

angler *n* duánaí

anglers *pl* lucht duántachta

Anglican *adj, n* Anglacánach

anglicisation *n* galldú

anglicised *adj* gallda

anglicism *n* béarlachas

angling *n* duántacht

Anglo-Irish *adj* Angla-Éireannach **the Anglo-Irish Agreement** an Comhaontú Angla-Éireannach

angora *n* angóra

angry *adj* colgach, feargach **I am angry** tá fearg orm

anguish *n* crá, léan

angular *adj* cearnach, uilleach

animal *n* ainmhí, míol

animate *v* beoigh

animated *adj* anamaithe, beoite **animated film** scannán beoite

animation *n* anamúlacht, beochan

animosity *n* naimhdeas

ankle *n* caol na coise, murnán, rúitín

annals *pl* annála **the Annals of Ulster** Annála Uladh

annalist *n* annálaí

annihilate *v* díothaigh

annihilation *n* díothú

anniversary *n* cothrom an lae **the anniversary of their marraige** cothrom an lae a pósadh iad

announce *v* craol, fógair

announcement *n* fógairt

announcer *n* bolscaire

annoy *v* ciap, cuir isteach ar, cuir as do

annual *adj* bliantúil *n* **(of book)** bliainiris, **(of plant)** bliantóg

annuity *n* blianacht

annul *v* neamhnigh, cuir ar neamhní, cuir ar ceal

annulment *n* cur ar ceal, neamhnú

anomaly *n* aimhrialtacht

anomalous *adj* aimhrialta

anonymous *adj* gan ainm

another *adj, pron* eile

answer *n* freagra, freagairt *v* freagair

answerable *adj* freagrach

ant *n* seangán

antagonism *n* eascairdeas

Antarctic *adj, n* Antartach

antelope *n* antalóp

antenna *n* aintéine

anthem *n* aintiún **national anthem** amhrán náisiúnta

ant-hill *n* nead seangán

anthology *n* duanaire

anthracite *n* antraicít

anthrax *n* antrasc

anthropoid *adj* antrapóideach

anthropology *n* antraipeolaíocht

anti- *prefix* anta-, frith-

anti-aircraft battery *n* bataire frith-aerárthach

antibiotic *n* antaibheathach, frithbheathach

anticipate *v* bheith ag súil le

anticipation *n* fuireachas, súil

anticlimax *n* frithbhuaic

anticlockwise *adj, adv* tuathal

antidote *n* **(for poison)** frithnimh, nimhíoc

antifreeze *n* frithreo

antinuclear *adj* fritheithneach, frithnúicléach

antiquarian *adj* seanda *n* ársaitheoir

antique *adj* seanda

antiques *pl* seandachtaí

antiquity *n* seandacht

anti-Semitic *adj* frith-Ghiúdach

antiseptic *adj* antaiseipteach, frithsheipteach *n* frithsheipteán, antaiseipteán

antisocial *adj* frithshóisialta

antithesis *n* fritéis

anti-tank guns / weapons *pl* gunnaí/airm in aghaidh tanc

Antrim *n* Aontroim **Co. Antrim** Co. Aontroma

anus *n* anas, áthán

anxiety *n* imní

anxious *adj* imníoch **she is anxious** tá imní uirthi

anybody *n, pron* duine ar bith, aon duine

anyhow *adv* pé scéal é, ar aon chuma, ar chaoi ar bith

anything *n, pron* dada, tada, rud ar bith, aon ní

anyway *adv* ar aon chor, ar aon chaoi, ar chaoi ar bith

anywhere *adv* aon áit, áit ar bith

apart *adj* leithleach *adv* i leataobh, ó chéile **apart from the fact that ...** gan trácht ar ...

apartment *n* árasán

apartheid *n* cinedheighilt

apathetic *adj* fuarchúiseach

apathy *n* fuarchúis

ape *n* ápa

apéritif *n* greadóg

aperture *n* poll, **(in photography)** cró

apex *n* rinn, barr

aphorism *n* nath

apologise *v* leithscéal a ghabháil (le)

apocalypse *n* apacailipsis

apocalyptic *adj* apacailipteach

apocryphal *adj* apacrafúil

apology *n* leithscéal

apoplexy *n* apaipléis

apostle *n* aspal **the Twelve Apostles** an Dá Aspal Déag

apostleship *n* aspalacht

apostolate *n* aspalacht

apostolic *adj* aspalda

apostrophe *n* uaschamóg

apothecary *n* poitigéir

appal *v* scanraigh, cuir uafás ar

apparatus *n* fearas, gaireas

apparent *adj* dealraitheach

apparently *adv* de réir cosúlachta, de réir dealraimh

apparition *n* taispeánadh

appeal *v* achomharc

appealing *adj* taitneamhach

appear *v* dealraigh, nocht it
appears that... dealraíonn sé
go..., the ghost appeared nocht
an taibhse

appearance *n* cló, cruth, cuma,
dealramh, deilbh, gotha, scéimh

appease *v* ceansaigh

appendicitis *n* aipindicíteas

appendix[1] *n* (of book) aguisín

appendix[2] *n* (anatomy) aipindic

appetite *n* goile

appetiser *n* greadóg

appetising *adj* blasta

applaud *v* mol os ard

applause *n* bualadh bos

apple *n* úll

appliance *n* fearas

applicant *n* iarratasóir

application *n* iarratas

application form *n* foirm iarratais

applications software *n* bogearraí
feidhmiúcháin

applied *adj* feidhmeach

apply *v* cuir isteach ar

appoint *v* ceap

appointment *n* ceapachán, ceapadh,
(meeting) coinne

apportion *v* cionroinn

appreciation *n* (in value)
luachmhéadú, (understanding)
léirthuiscint

apprehend *v* gabh

apprehension *n* gabháil, tuiscint,
eagla

apprehensive *adj* eaglach

apprentice *n* printíseach

approach *n* teacht *v* druid,
taobhaigh le, tarraing ar

approachable *adj* (of person)
sochaideartha

appropriate *adj* cuí, oiriúnach
feiliúnach *v* leithghabh

approval *n* ceadú

approve *v* aontaigh (le)

approximately *adv* timpeall, isteach
is amach le

apricot *n* aibreog

April *n* Aibreán

April Fools' Day *n* Lá na nAmadán

apron *n* naprún

apt *adj* tráthúil, fóirsteanach

aptitude *n* éirim

aptitude test *n* tástáil inniúlachta

aqualung *n* uathscamhóg

aquarium *n* uisceadán

Aquarius *n* Iompróir an Uisce, an
tUisceadóir

aqueduct *n* uiscerian

Arab *n* Arabach

Arabian *adj* Arabach

Arabic *adj* Arabach *n* (language) an
Araibis

arable *adj* arúil

arbitration *n* eadráin

arbitrator *n* eadránaí

arc *n* stua

arcade *n* stuara

arch *n* áirse, stua

archaeologist *n* seandálaí

archaeology *n* seandálaíocht

archaic *adj* ársa

archbishop *n* ardeaspag

archipelago *n* oileánrach

architect *n* ailtire

architecture *n* ailtireacht

archives *pl* cartlann

archivist *n* cartlannaí

archway *n* áirse

Arctic *adj, n* Artach

ardent *adj* díocasach, díograiseach

ardour *n* díograis

arduous *adj* dian

area *n* réimse, limistéar

arena *n* airéine

arguable *adj* inargóinte

argue *v* áitigh he argued that...
d'áitigh sé go...

arguer *n* áititheoir

arguing *n* áiteoireacht, sáraíocht

argument *n* argóint, agall, aighneas,
conspóid, sáraíocht

argumentation *n* áiteoireacht

argumentative *adj* aighneasach

aria *n* áiria

arid *adj* tur

arise *v* éirigh

aristocracy *n* uaslathas

aristocrat *n* uaslathaí

arithmetic *n* uimhríocht

ark *n* áirc

arm[1] *v* armáil

arm[2] *n* lámh, sciathán

armada *n* armáid the Spanish
Armada Armáid na Spáinne

Armagh *n* Ard Mhacha

armament *n* armáil

armchair *n* cathaoir uilleann/
uilleach

armed *adj* armach, armtha fully
armed faoi iomlán airm, armed
conflict coinbhliocht armach/
armtha

armful *n* asclán, uchtóg armful of
turf baclainn mhóna, she was
carrying the child in her arms
bhí an leanbh ina/ar a baclainn
aici

armistice *n* sos cogaidh

armour *n* armúr, cathéide

armoured *adj* armúrtha, plátáilte
armoured car carr armúrtha /
plátáilte

armourer *n* armadóir

**armour-piercing bullet,
ammunition** *n* piléar, armlón
pollta armúir

armoury *n* armlann

armpit *n* ascaill

arms *pl* arm small arms mionairm,
arms manufacturer armadóir

arms dump *n* armthaisce

army *n* arm

aroma *n* dea-bholadh

aromatherapy *n* cumhartheiripe

arrange *v* cóirigh, deasaigh,
eagraigh, feistigh, socraigh

arranged *adj* socraithe properly
arranged in ord is in eagar

arrangement *n* cóiriú, socrú, eagar

array *n* cóiriú, ordú

arrears *pl* riaráiste

arrest *n* gabháil *v* gabh

arrival *n* teacht

arrive *v* sroich

arrogance *n* uabhar

arrogant *adj* sotalach, uaibhreach

arrow *n* saighead bow and arrow
bogha is saighead

arrowroot *n* ararút

arsenal *n* armlann

arsenic *n* arsanaic

arson *n* coirloscadh

art *n* ealaín the National College
of Art and Design an Coláiste
Náisiúnta Ealaíne agus Deartha

artefact *n* lámhdhéantúsán, déantán

arterial *adj* artaireach

artery *n* artaire

artesian *adj* airtéiseach

arthritis *n* airtríteas

article *n* airteagal, alt

articulate *adj* deaslabhartha, altach

articulated lorry *n* leoraí altach

artificial *adj* saorga, tacair artificial
value comhla shaorga

artillery *n* airtlére

artisan *n* ccardaí

artist *n* ealaíontóir

artistic *adj* ealaíonta

as *adv* chomh, mar, amhail

as likely as not chomh dócha lena athrach

as regards maidir le

as sure as can be chomh cinnte is atá ceann ar do mhuineál, chomh siúráilte is atá cros ar asal, chomh cinnte is atá púdar i nDoire

asbestos *n* aispeist

ascend *v* ardaigh, téigh suas

ascendancy *n* ceannas, cinsealacht

ascent *n* bealach suas

ascendant *adj* ardaitheach *n* uachtar, sinsear

ascending *adj* ardaitheach

ascertain *n* fionn

ascetic *adj* aiséitiúil *n* aiséiteach

aseptic *adj, n* aiseipteach

ash (tree) *n* fuinseog

ashes *pl* luaith **hot ashes** gríosach

ashamed *adj* náireach

ashore *adv* i dtír

ashtray *n* luaithreadán

Asia *n* an Áise

Asia Minor *n* an Áise Bheag

Asian *adj, n* Áiseach

ask *v* **(for information)** fiafraigh, **(for service, thing, etc)** iarr **ask him how he is** fiafraigh de conas tá sé, **to ask somebody for help** cabhair a iarraidh ar dhuine

askew *adv* ar sceabha

asleep *adj* **she is asleep** tá sí ina codladh, **to be fast asleep** bhcith i do shrann chodlata

asparagus *n* lus súgach, asparagas

aspect *n* aghaidh, gné

aspersions *pl* **to cast aspersions on somebody** drochmheas a chaitheamh ar dhuine, míchlú a chur ar dhuine

asphalt *n* asfalt

asphyxia *n* lánmhúchadh, plúchadh

asphyxiate *v* múch, plúch

aspirate *v* análaigh

aspiration after something *n* tóir ar rud

ass *n* asal

assail *v* ionsaigh, tabhair faoi

assailant *n* ionsaitheoir

assassin *n* feallmharfóir

assassinate *v* feallmharaigh

assassination *n* feallmharú

assault *n* ionsaí

assemble *v* cruinnigh, tionóil

assembled *adj* cruinn

assembly *n* comhthionól, mustar, tionól, tóstal

assent *n* aontú, toiliú

assenting *adj* aontaitheach, toiliúil

assert *v* dearbhaigh

assertive *adj* treallúsach

assess *v* meas, measúnaigh

assessment[1] *n* **(financial)** measúnú

assessment[2] *n* breithmheas, measúnacht

assessor *n* measúnóir

asset *n* sócmhainn **realisation of assets** réadú sócmhainní

assiduous *adj* dúthrachtach

assign *v* sann, dáil (ar)

assignment *n* sannadh, tasc

assimilate *v* comhshamhlaigh

assist *v* cabhraigh, cuidigh

assistance *n* cuidiú, cabhair, cúnamh

assistant *n* cúntóir

associate *n* comhpháirtí

association[1] *n* cumann, comhchaidreamh, comhlachas

association[2], **in association with …** i bpáirt le …

assorted *adj* measctha

assume *v* **(responsibility)** gabh, **(idea)** cuir i gcás

assumption *n* **(responsibility)** glacadh, gabháil, **(idea)** cur i gcás

assurance n dearbhú, deimhniú

assure v dearbhaigh, deimhnigh

asterisk n réiltín

asteroid adj, n astaróideach

asthma n asma, múchadh, plúchadh

asthma attack n taom asma

astonishment n alltacht, uafás **to astonish somebody** alltacht/uafás a chur ar dhuine

astound v uafás a chur ar

astray adv amú, ar strae, ar seachrán

astride (on) adj ar scaradh gabhail (ar)

astrologer n astralaí

astrological adj astralaíoch

astrology n astralaíocht

astronaut n spásaire

astronomy n réalteolaíocht

astute adj fadcheannach, géarchúiseach

astuteness n géarchúis

asylum n dídean, tearmann **to seek asylum** dídean a lorg

asymmetrical adj neamhshiméadrach

at prep um, ar, ag **at Christmas** um Nollaig, **at eleven o' clock** ar a haon déag a chlog, **at Dáithí's house** ag teach Dháithí

atavism n athdhúchas

atavistic adj athdhúchasach

atheism n aindiachas

atheist n aindiachaí

athlete n lúthchleasaí

athletic adj lúfar, lúthchleasach **athletic exercise** lúthchleas

athletics pl lúthchleasa, lúthchleasaíocht

Atlantic adj, n Atlantach **the Atlantic Ocean** an tAigeán Atlantach

atlas n atlas

atmosphere n aerbhrat, atmaisféar

atmospheric adj atmaisféarach

atmospheric pressure n brú aeir

atom n adamh

atomic adj adamhach **atomic bomb** buama adamhach, **atomic energy** fuinneamh adamhach

atrocious adj uafásach, millteanach

atrocity n ainghníomh

attach (to) v ceangail (do), greamaigh (do)

attack n ionsaí, amas v ionsaigh, tolg **attack is the best form of defence** ní cosaint go hamas, **sustained attack** amas/ionsaí marthanach

attacker n ionsaitheoir, amasóir

attain v sroich, bain amach

attempt[1] n iarracht, amas, triall **at the first attempt** ar an gcéad ásc

attempt[2] v tabhair faoi

attend v freastail (ar)

attendance n freastal, tinreamh

attendant n freastalaí, giolla

attention n aird, aire, iúl, suntas

attentive adj aireach

attenuate v caolaigh

attenuation n tanú

attest v dearbhaigh

attested adj dearfa

attic n áiléar

attire n gléasadh

attitude n meon

attorney n aturnae

Attorney-General n Ard-Aighne

attract v tarraing, meall

attraction n caithis, tarraingt

attractive adj tarraingteach

attractiveness n tarraingteacht

attribute n cáilíocht, bua

aubergine n ubhthoradh

auburn adj órdhonn

auction n ceant v ceantáil **to auction a house** teach a chur ar ceant

audacious adj teanntásach

audacity n teanntás

audible adj inchloiste

audience n lucht éisteachta, lucht féachana

audio- prefix clos-

audiotape n clostéip

audiovisual adj closamhairc
  audiovisual aid áis chlosamhairc

audit n iniúchadh v iniúch

Audit Bureau of Circulation (ABC) n an Biúró Iniúchta Scaipthe

audition n triail

auditorium n halla éisteachta

augment v méadaigh

August n Lúnasa

aunt n aintín

Australia n an Astráil

Australian adj, n Astrálach

Austria n an Ostair

Austrian adj, n Ostarach

authentic adj údarach

authenticity n údaracht

author n údar

authorisation n údarú

authorise v údaraigh

authorised adj údaraithe **authorised person** duine údaraithe

authoritarian adj údárasach

authoritative adj údarásach

authority n ceannas, údar, údarás
  the local authorities na húdaráis áitiúla, **the Gaeltacht Authority** Údarás na Gaeltachta

autism n ainfhéinspéis

auto- prefix uath-

autobiography n dírbheathaisnéis

autograph n síniú

automate v uathoibrigh

automatic adj uathoibríoch

automatic gun / weapon n gunna / arm uathoibreach

automation n uathoibriú

autonomous féinrialaitheach, uathrialach **autonomous regions** réigiúin uathrialacha

autonomy n féinriail

autopsy n corpdhioscadh

autumn n fómhar

auxiliary adj cúntach

avail of v leas a bhaint as **of no avail** gan éifeacht

availability n infhaighteacht

available adj infhaighte, ar fáil

avalanche n maidhm sheachta

avarice n saint, cíocras

avenge v díoltas a imirt, éiric a bhaint amach

avenue n ascaill

average adj meánach n meán prefix meán-

aversion n col

aviary n éanlann

aviation n eitlíocht

avid adj cíocrach

avoid v seachain

avoidance n seachaint

awake[1] v dúisigh, múscail

awake[2] adj múscailte **are you awake?** an bhfuil tú i do dhúiseacht?

awakening n dúiseacht, múscailt

award n gradam

aware adj feasach **I am aware** is feasach dom

awareness n meabhrafacht

away adj ar shiúl **right away** láithreach bonn, **far away** i bhfad ó bhaile, i bhfad ar shiúl

awe n eagla, uafás

awful adj uafásach, millteanach

awkward adj amscaí, ciotach

awning n scáthbhrat

axe n tua

axis n ais

axle n fearsaid, aiseal

B

babble *n* cabaireacht, crónán

babbling *n* píobaireacht

baboon *n* babún

baby *n* babaí

babysitter *n* feighlí páistí/leanaí

bachelor *n* baitsiléir

back[1] *n* cúl, deireadh, droim, muin **the back of the house** cúl an tí, **back seat** suíochán deiridh, **backbone** cnámh droma, **on the pig's back** ar mhuin na muice

back[2] *adv* ar ais, ar gcúl, siar

back[3] *v* cúlaigh, tacaigh le

back answer *n* aisfhreagra

backbencher *n* cúlbhinseoir

backbiting *n* athiomrá, cúlchaint

backbone *n* cnámh droma

backdrop *n* cúlbhrat

backfire *n* cúltortadh *v* cúltort

backgammon *n* táiplis mhór

background *n* cúlra **background noise** torann cúlra

backlash *n* frithradadh

backlog *n* riaráiste

backside *n* tóin

backspace *n* cúlspás

back-up *n* tacaíocht, cúltaca **back-up copy** cóip chúltaca

backward *adj* cúlánta

backwards *adv* siar, ar gcúl

bacon *n* bagún

bacon, lettuce and tomato sandwich (BLT) *n* ceapaire bagúin, leitíse agus tráta

bad[1] *adj* olc, dona **however bad they are** dá dhonacht iad, **however bad it is** dá olcas é, **to be in a bad way** bheith go holc, bheith i ndroch-chaoi

bad[2] *prefix* an-, mí- **bad luck** mí-ádh **bad appearance** anchuma

bad-tempered *adj* míchéadfach

badger *n* broc

badly *adj* go dona, go holc

badminton *n* badmantan

baffle *v* mearaigh, cuir amú

badge *n* suaitheantas

badness *n* donacht, olcas

bag *n* mála **bags under the eyes** sprochaillí faoi na súile

baggy skin *n* sprochaille

bagpipe *n* píb mhála, na píoba

bail *n* banna **they were released on bail** ligeadh amach ar bannaí iad

bail out *v* taosc

bailing *n* taoscadh

bake *v* bácáil

bakehouse *n* bácús

baker *n* báicéir

bakery *n* bácús

baking *n* bácáil

balance[1] *n* cóimheá, cothrom, comhardú, meá **balance sheet** clár comhardaithe, **hanging in the balance** idir dhá cheann na meá

balance[2] *n* cothromaigh, meáigh

balanced diet *n* réim chothrom bia, aiste chothrom bia

balcony *n* balcóin

bald *adj* maol **bald patch** plait

bale *n* corna **hay bales** cornaí féir

ball[1] *n* liathróid, meall **hurling ball** sliotar, **eyeball** meall súile

ball[2] *n* (of wool) ceirtlín

ball and chain *n* geimheal an mhill

ballerina *n* rinceoir bailé

ballet *n* bailé

ballistics *n* balaistíocht

balloon *n* éadromán, balún

ballot *n* ballóid

ballot-box *n* bosca ballóide

ball-point pen *n* peann gránbhiorach

balm *n* íocshláinte

Baltic Sea *n* an Mhuir Bhailt

ban *n* cosc, toirmeasc **to ban something** cosc a chur ar

banana *n* banana

band *n* banda, **(of people)** feadhain, **(of music)** banna ceoil

bandage *n* bindealán

bandit *n* tóraí

bandy-legged *adj* camchosach

bang *n* plimp, pléasc, plab, tailm *v* pléasc **'big bang'** ollphléasc

banish *v* díbir

banishment *n* díbirt

banister *n* balastar

bank *n* banc, bruach **bank of river** bruach abhann, **mobile bank** banc gluaisteach, **commercial bank** banc tráchtála, **Central Bank of Ireland** Banc Ceannais na hÉireann, **the World Bank** an Banc Domhanda

bank balance *n* iarmhéid bainc

banker *n* baincéir

banking *n* baincéireacht

bank loan *n* iasacht bhainc

banknote *n* nóta bainc

bankrupt *n* féimheach

bankruptcy *n* féimheacht

banner *n* meirge

banquet *n* cóisir

banshee *n* bean sí

banter *n* nathaíocht

baptism *n* baisteadh

baptismal *adj* baistí **baptismal font** umar baiste

baptise *v* baist

bar[1] *n* barra **chocolate bar** barra seacláide

bar[2] *n* **(of public house)** beár

barbarian *adj, n* barbarach

barbarity *n* danarthacht

barbecue *n* fulacht, bearbaiciú

barbed *adj* deilgneach **barbed wire** sreang dheilgneach

barber *n* barbóir

bar code *n* barrchód

bar-code scanner *n* scanóir barrachód

bard *n* bard

bare *adj* lom, maol, nocht

bareback *adj* droimnocht

barefaced lie *n* bréag chruthanta

barefooted *adj* cosnochta

barely *adv* ar éigean

bargain *n* margadh, sladmhargadh

bargaining *n* margáil

barge *n* báirse

baritone *n* baratón

bark[1] *n* **(of tree)** coirt

bark[2] *n* **(of dog)** glam

barking *n* amhastrach, sceamhail, tafann

barley *n* eorna

barman *n* fear beáir

barn *n* scioból

barnacle *n* giúrann

barometer *n* baraiméadar

barracks *n* beairic

barrel *n* baraille

barren *adj* aimrid, seasc

barrenness *n* dísc

barricade *n* baracáid

barrier *n* bac, bacainn

barrier reef *n* sceir bhacainneach

barrister *n* abhcóide

barrow *n* bara

bartender *n* freastalaí beáir

barter *n, v* babhtáil

base[1] *n* dúshraith, bonn, bunáit **naval base** bunáit chabhlaigh

base[2] *adj* táir, uiríseal

baseball *n* (game) daorchluiche
baseball bat *n* slacán
basement *n* íoslach
bash *v* basc
bashful *adj* cotúil, cúthail
basic *adj* bunúsach
basilica *n* baisleac
basin *n* báisín **river basin** abhantrach
basis *n* dúshraith, bonn
bask *v* grianaíocht a dhéanamh, bolg le gréin a dhéanamh
basket *n* cis, ciseán
basketball *n* cispheil
basking shark *n* liopadaileap, liamhán gréine
Basque *adj*, *n* Bascach **a Basque girl** cailín Bascach, **the Basque Country** Tír na mBascach
bass *n* dord **bass guitar** dordghiotár, **(of voice)** dordghuth
bassoon *n* basún
bat[1] *n* (creature) ialtóg, sciathán leathair
bat[2] *n* (sports equipment) slacán
batch *n* scata, lucht
bath *n* folcadh **to have a bath** folcadh a ghlacadh, a thógáil
bath salts *pl* salann folctha
bathe *v* folc, fothraig
bathroom *n* seomra folctha
bath-tub *n* folcadán
baton *n* bata, baitín, smachtín
baton charge *n* séirse bataí / smachtíní
batter *n* fuaidreamh
battery *n* cadhnra, ceallra
battle *n* cath **the Battle of the Boyne** Cath/Briseadh na Bóinne
battlements *pl* forbhalla
battleship *n* cathlong
bawn *n* bábhún
bay *n* bá **Bantry Bay** Bá Bheanntraí

bazaar *n* basár
be *v* 1. *copula* is **he is an expert** is saineolaí é, **she was a good teacher** ba mhúinteoir maith í 2. *v* bí **we are tired** táimid tuirseach, **to be tall** bheith ard
beach *n* trá
beacon *n* rabhchán
bead *n* coirnín
beak *n* gob
beam *n* (of light) ga, (of wood) maide, rachta
bean *n* pónaire
bear *n* béar **polar bear** béar bán
bearable *adj* sofhulaingthe
beard *n* féasóg
beast *n* beithíoch
beat *v* buail, buaigh ar, gread **to beat somebody** duine a bhualadh, **Down beat Dublin** bhuaigh an Dún ar Bhaile Átha Cliath
beating *n* bualadh, greadadh, greasáil, greidimín
beautiful *adj* álainn, sciamhach
beauty *n* áilleacht, gnaoi, maise, sciamhacht, scéimh
beaver *n* béabhar
because *conj* mar, arae, óir
because of *prep* de thairbhe, de bharr **(positive)**, de dheasca **(negative)**
beckon *v* sméid
become *v* éirigh **he became afraid** d'éirigh sé faiteach, tháinig eagla air
become silent *v* tost
bed *n* leaba
bedclothes *pl* éadach leapa
bed-ridden *adj* cróilí
bedroom *n* seomra leapa
bedsore *n* anacair leapa
bed-time *n* am soip, am luí
bee *n* beach

beech *n* feá **beech tree** fáibhile

beef *n* mairteoil

beehive *n* coirceog

beep *v* séid **to beep a horn** adharc a shéideadh

beer *n* beoir, leann

bee-sting *n* priocadh beiche

beet *n* biatas

beetle *n* ciaróg, daol

beetroot *n* meacan biatais

befitting *adj* oiriúnach, cuí

before *adv* roimhe *conj* sula *prep* roimh

beforehand *adv* cheana

befriend *v* éirigh cairdiúil le, caradaigh

beg *v* impigh **begging** ag iarraidh déirce

beggar *n* bacach

begin *v* tosaigh, tionscain

beginner *n* tosaitheoir

beginning *n* tosach, tosú, tús

begrudge *v* maígh

beguile *v* meall

behalf, on behalf ar son, thar ceann

behave *v* iompair

behaviour *n* iompar **good behaviour** dea-iompar

behind *adv* laistiar, (taobh) thiar

beholden *adj* faoi chomaoin, i dtuilleamaí

being *n* (person) neach **human being** neach daonna

beige *n* béas

belated *n* mall, deireanach, déanach

Belfast *n* Béal Feirste **West Belfast** Iarthar Bhéal Feirste

belfry *n* cloigtheach

belief *n* creideamh **it is my belief that ...** is é mo thuairim go ...

believe *v* creid **believe it or not** creid nó ná creid

belittle *v* díspeag

belittlement *n* díspeagadh

bell *n* clog, cloigín

bellow *n*, *v* búir

belong *v* **it belongs to me** is liomsa é

belongings *pl* giuirléidí

beloved *adj* dil, ionúin

below *adv* faoi, laistíos, thíos

belt *n* crios, bcilt **seat belt** crios sábhála, **Orion's Belt** an Bhanlámh

bench *n* binse

bend[1] *n* lúb, cúb, cor, **(in road)** uillinn

bend[2] *v* lúb, cúb, crom, fill, feac

beneath *prep* faoi

benefactor *n* pátrún

beneficial *adj* sochrach, tairbhiúil, tairbheach, fóinteach

beneficiary *n* tairbhí

benefit *n* gar, leas, maitheas, sochar, tairbhe **social welfare benefits** sochair leasa shóisialta, **the benefit of the doubt** sochar an amhrais, **for your own benefit** ar mhaithe leat féin

benevolent *adj* dea-mhéineach

benign *adj* caoin

bent *adj* cam

bequeath *v* tiomnaigh, uachtaigh

berry *n* caor, sméar, sú

berth *n* leaba loinge *v* calaigh

beseech *v* impigh

beset *v* ionsaigh

beside *adv* láimh le, in aice, le hais

besides *adv* diomaite de, seachas

besiege *v* imshuigh, cuir faoi léigear

best *adj* is fearr *n* scoth **at best** ar a fheabhas

best man *n* vaidhtéir

best seller *n* leabhar móréilimh

best wishes! *excl* beir bua (agus beannacht)!

bestow *v* dáil, bronn, tíolaic

bet *n*, *v* geall

betray *v* feall (ar)

betrothal *n* cleamhnas

better *adj* níos fearr *v* feabhsaigh

between *prep* idir

beverage *n* deoch

beware! *excl* fainic! seachain!

bewilder *v* mearaigh

bewildering *adj* mearbhlach

bewilderment *n* mearaí, mearbhall

beyond *adv* thall *prep* thar, taobh thall de

bias *n* claonadh

biased *adj* taobhach, claonta

bible *n* bíobla

bibliography *n* clár saothair, leabharliosta

bicentenary *n* comóradh dhá chéad bliain

biceps *n* bícéips **biceps and triceps** bícéips agus trícéips

bicycle *n* rothar

bid *n* tairiscint *v* tairg

bidder *n* tairgeoir

bidding *n* tairiscint

biennial *adj* débhliantúil *n* débhliantóg

bier *n* cróchar

big *adj* mór **bigger** níos mó, **biggest** is mó, **the bigger the better** dá mhéad é is amhlaidh is fearr é

bigamy *n* biogamacht, déchéileachas

bigot *n* biogóid

bike *n* rothar

bikini *n* bicíní

bilateral *adj* déthaobhach

bilingual *adj* dátheangach

bilingualism *n* dátheangachas

bill *n* bille

bill-board *n* clár fógraíochta

billet *n* billéad

billion *n* billiún

billow *n* brúcht farraige

bimonthly *adv* gach dara mí *n* **(of journal)** démhíosachán

bin *n* araid, gabhdán

binary *adj* dénártha

bind *v* ceangail **he was bound hand and foot** cuireadh ceangal na gcúig gcaol air

binding *adj* ceangailteach *n* ceangal

binge *n* ragús óil, babhta meisce

bingo *n* biongó

binoculars *pl* déshúiligh

biochemist *n* bithchemiceoir

biochemistry *n* bithcheimic

biography *n* beathaisnéis

biologist *n* bitheolaí

biology *n* bitheolaíocht

biomass *n* bithmhais

biotechnology *n* bith-theicneolaíocht

birch tree *n* beith

bird *n* éan

bird life *n* beathra éan

birth *n* gin, giniúint, breith

birth certificate *n* teastas breithe, teastas beireatais

birthday *n* lá breithe **Happy Birthday!** Lá Breithe Sona duit!

birthmark *n* ball broinne

bishop *n* easpag

bit[1] *n* giota, mír, pioc, blúire, greim **computer bit** giotán, **little bits of information** míreanna beaga eolais, **I'm not a bit worried** níl mé pioc buartha, **a bit of fun** giota grinn, **a bit of food** greim bia

bit[2] *n* béalmhír **drill bit** béalmhír druileála, **tool bit** béalmhír uirlise

bitch *n* **(animal)** soith

bite *n* plaic, greim **to take a bite of an apple** plaic/greim a bhaint as úll

bitter *adj* goirt, searbh

bittern *n* bonnán (buí)

bitterness n domlas, searbhas, seirbhe

black adj dubh, (of skin) gorm

Black and Tan n Dúchrónach (Irish history)

blackberry n sméar (dubh)

blackbird n lon (dubh)

blackboard n clár dubh

blacken v dubhaigh

blackguard n bligeard

black-haired n dubh, ciardhubh

black hole n poll dubh

blackmail n, v dúmhál

black market n margadh dubh

Black Sea n an Mhuir Dhubh

blacksmith n gabha (dubh)

blackthorn n draighneán

blade n lann, ribe **blade of knife** lann scine, **blade of grass** ribe féir

blame n milleán v ciontaigh **he is to blame** eisean is ciontaí, **don't blame her** ná tóg uirthi é

blameless adj gan locht

blaming n (act of) tromaíocht

bland adj leamh

blank adj caoch **blank cartridge** cartús caoch

blanket n pluid, súsa, blaincéad

blaspheme v diamhaslaigh

blasphemous adj diamhaslach

blasphemy n diamhasla

blast n pléascán, rois **blast of thunder** rois toirní

blast you! excl nár fheice tú Dia!

blaze n lasair, bladhm

blazer n bléasar

bleach n tuarthóir v tuar

bleak adj sceirdiúil, gruama

bleary adj geamhchaoch, sramach

bleating n (of goats) meigeallach (of sheep) méileach

bleed v cuir fuil **her nose was bleeding** bhí fuil lena srón

bleeding n fuiliú **internal bleeding** fuiliú inmheánach

bleeper n gíogaire

blemish n smál, máchail, mill

blend n cumasc v cumaisc

blender n cumascóir

bless v beannaigh, coisric **to bless yourself** tú féin a choisreacan

blessed adj coisricthe

blessing n beannacht, coisreacan

blind[1] adj caoch, dall v dallraigh

blind[2] n dallóg **Venetian blind** dallóg Veinéiseach

blinded adj dall

blindfold n púic, púicín

blind spot n caochspota

blink v caoch (na súile)

bliss n aoibhneas, sonas

blissful adj aoibhinn, sona

blister n spuaic, clog

blizzard n síobadh sneachta

bloat v at

bloated adj ata

blob n daba **blob of paint** daba péinte

block[1] n bloc, ceap **office block** ceap oifigí, **block of flats** áraslann, bloc árasán

block[2] v stop

blockade n imshuí

blockbuster n scannán mór-eachtraíochta

blond adj fionn

blood n fuil, cró

blood clot n cnapán fola

blood group n fuilghrúpa

bloodshed n doirteadh fola

bloodshot adj sreangach

bloodthirstiness n cíocras fola

blood transfusion n fuilaistriú

blood vessel n fuileadán

bloody adj fuilteach **Bloody Sunday** Domhnach na Fola

blossom *n* bláth

blot *n* smál *v* cuir smál ar

blotch *n* smál *v* cuir smál ar

blotting-paper *n* páipéar súite

blouse *n* blús

blow[1] *n* buille, cnag, cniog, síobadh

blow[2] *v* séid **to blow a fuse** fiús a shéideadh

blowpipe *n* séideadán

blubber *n* blonag

blue *n* gorm

bluebottle *n* cuil ghorm

blues *pl* gruaim, **(music)** na gormacha

blue tack *n* greamachán gorm

bluff *n* cur i gcéill

blunder *n* meancóg, tuaiplis, tuathal

blunderer *n* tuathalán

blundering *adj* tuaiplisiúil, tuathalach

blunt *adj* maol, **(of person)** giorraisc **blunt knife** scian mhaol

blur *v* doiléirigh

blush *n* lasadh, luisne *v* dearg, las

blushing *adj* luisniúil

boar *n* collach, torc

board *n* clár, bord **notice board** clár fógraí, **the Electricity Supply Board (ESB)** Bord Soláthair an Leictreachais (BSL)

boarder *n* lóistéir

boarding pass *n* pas bordála

boarding-house *n* teach lóistín

boarding-school *n* scoil chónaithe

boast *n* maíomh *v* maígh

boastful *adj* maíteach

boat *n* bád

bodily *adj* corpartha

body[1] *n* cabhail, colainn, corp

body[2] *n* **(substance)** tathag, téagar

body building *n* corpfhorbairt

bodyguard *n* garda cosanta

bog *n* caorán, portach, seascann

bogeyman *n* babhdán, taibhse an chnádáin

boil[1] *v* fiuch, beirigh, bruith

boil[2] *n* neascóid

boiler *n* coire **gas boiler** coire gáis

boisterous *adj* spleodrach

bold *adj* dalba, dána, teann, teanntásach

boldness *n* dánacht, teanntás

bollard *n* mullard

bolt *n* bolta *v* boltáil **brassbolt** bolta práis

bomb *n* pléascán, buama *v* buamáil **nuclear bomb** buama eithneach, **incendiary bomb** buama loisceach, **mortar bomb** buama moirtéara, **high-explosive bomb** buama tréanphléascach

bombastic *adj* mórfhoclach

bomber *n* buamadóir **long-range bomber** buamadóir fadraoin, **dive-bomber** buamadóir scuibe, **fighter-bomber** buamadóir troda

bombing *n* buamáil **high-level bombing** buamáil ard, **low-level bombing** buamáil íseal

bomb-proof *adj* buamadhíonach

bond *n* ceangal, nasc *v* ceangail, nasc

bondage *n* braighdeanas

bone *n* cnámh *v* díchnámhaigh

bonfire *n* tine chnámh

bonnet *n* boinéad

bonus *n* bónas

bony *adj* cnámhach

book[1] *n* leabhar

book[2] *v* **to book something** rud a chur in áirithe/áirithint

bookcase *n* leabhragán

booking *n* áirithint

bookkeeper *n* leabharchoimeádaí

bookkeeping *n* leabharchoimeád

book launch *n* seoladh leabhair

booklet *n* leabhrán

bookmaker *n* **(turf accountant)** geallghlacadóir

bookmark *n* leabharmharc

book token *n* éarlais leabhair

boom *n* **(of trade)** borradh (trádála)

boost *n* treisiú *v* treisigh

boosting *n* treisiú

boot *n* buatais

booth *n* both

border *n* teorainn, ciumhais, imeall, imeallbhord

bore[1] *n* leadránaí

bore[2] *v* toll **to bore a hole** poll a tholladh

boring *adj* leadránach

borrow *v* faigh ar iasacht

bosom *n* cliabh, ucht **bosom friend** cara cléibh

boss *n* saoiste

bossy *adj* tiarnúil

botanist *n* luibheolaí

Botanic Gardens *pl* Garraithe na Lus

botanical *adj* luibheolaíoch

botany *n* luibheolaíocht

both *adj, pron* araon **both of us** sinn araon

bother *n* stró *v* buair

bottle *n* buidéal *v* buidéalaigh

bottle-opener *n* osclóir buidéil

bottleneck *n* caolas, scrogall

bottom *n* bun, tóin, íochtar, **(of sea)** grinneall

bottomless pit *n* poll duibheagáin

bough *n* craobh

boulder *n* moghlaeir

bounce *n, v* preab **double bounce** preab dhúbailte

boundary *n* críoch, fóir, teorainn **boundary wall** balla críche, **city boundaries** teorainneacha cathrach

bounty *n* fóirdheontas

bouquet *n* **(of wine)** cumhracht, **(of flowers)** crobhaing

bout *n* babhta

boutique *n* búitíc

bovine *adj* buaibheach

bow[1] *n* bogha **bow and arrow** bogha agus saighead

bow[2] *v* umhlaigh **bow down** sléacht

bowels *pl* inní, ionathar

bowl *n* babhla, cuach *v* babhláil

bowler *n* babhlálaí

bowling *n* babhláil

bowling alley *n* ionad babhlála

box *n* bosca *v* cuir i mbosca

boxer *n* dornálaí

boxing *n* dornálaíocht

box-office *n* oifig ticéad

box-office hit *n* scannán mór-ratha

boxty *n* bacstaí

boy *n* buachaill, garsún, gasúr, giolla

bra(ssiere) *n* cíochbheart

brace *n* teanntán

bracelet *n* bráisléad

bracken *n* raithneach

bracket *n* lúibín

brag *v* maígh

braggart *n* buaileam sciath

Brahma *n* Bráma

brain *n* inchinn

brain haemorrhage *n* rith fola san inchinn

brains *pl* **he has brains** tá meabhair aige

brain-storming *n* babhta tobsmaointe

brainwave *n* smaoineamh intleachtach

brainy *adj* meabhrach, intleachtach

braise *v* galstobh

brake *n* coscán **to put the brakes on** na coscáin a theannadh

bramble *n* dris

branch[1] *n* craobh, géag, brainse

branch[2] *v* craobhaigh

brand *n* branda *v* brandáil, creach

brandish *v* beartaigh **he brandished the sword** bheartaigh sé an claíomh

brand-new *adj* úrnua

brandy *n* branda

brass *n* prás

bravado *n* gaisciúlacht

brave *adj* cróga, calma *v* aghaidh a thabhairt go dána ar

bravery *n* calmacht, crógacht

brawn *n* arrachtas

brazen *adj* prásach, dínáireach

bread *n* arán

breadth *n* leithead, leithne

break *v* bris

breakable *adj* sobhriste

breakdown *n* cliseadh, teip **nervous breakdown** cliseadh néarógach, **breakdown of expenditure** miondealú ar an gcaiteachas, **transmission breakdown** teip tarchuir

breaker *n* **(wave)** maidhm thoinne

breakers *pl* **(along the shore)** bristeacha (le taobh an chladaigh)

breakfast *n* bricfeasta

breakthrough *n* **(in negotiations)** faonfhuascailt

breakwater *n* babhún

breast *n* cíoch, ucht, brollach

breast-stroke *n* **(swimming)** bang brollaigh

breath *n* anáil, dé, smid **breath of wind** smid ghaoithe, dé ghaoithe, **out of breath** as anáil, **to draw a breath** anáil a tharraingt, **under one's breath** faoi d'anáil

breathe *v* análaigh

breathalyser *n* anáileadán

breed *n* pór *v* póraigh, síolraigh

breeding *n* folaíocht

breeze *n* feothan, leoithne

brevity *n* achomaireacht

brew *v* grúdaigh, **(of tea)** tarraing

brewer *n* grúdaire

brewery *n* grúdlann

briar *n* dris, sceach

bribe *n* breab *v* ceannaigh, breab

brick *n* bríce

bricklayer *n* bríceadóir

bride *n* brídeach **bride and groom** brídeog agus baitsiléir

bridegroom *n* grúm, baitsiléir

bridesmaid *n* cailín coimhdeachta

bridge *n* droichead *v* **to bridge the gap** an bhearna a líonadh, athmhuintearas a dhéanamh

bridle *n* araí, srian

brief *adj* gearr, gonta, achomair *v* achoimre a thabhairt

briefcase *n* mála cáipéisí

brigade *n* briogáid **fire brigade** briogáid dóiteáin

bright *adj* fionn, geal, glé, lonrach, solasmhar

brighten *v* geal

brightness *n* gile, loinnir, taitneamh

brilliant *adj* lonrach, iontach

brilliance *n* loinnir, niamh

brim *n* **(of glass)** béal (gloine), **(of hat)** duilleog (hata) *v* líon go béal/barr **full to the brim** lán go béal/barr

brimstone *n* ruibhchloch

brine *n* sáile

bring *v* tabhair chuig

brink *n* bruach

Britain *n* an Bhreatain

brittle *adj* briosc

broad *adj* leathan, leitheadach

broadcast[1] *v* craobhscaoil, craol

broadcast[2] *n* craobhscaoileadh, craoladh **outside broadcast** craoladh seachtrach

broadcaster *n* craoltóir

broadcasting *n* craolachán

broadcasting assistant *n* cúntóir craolacháin

broaden *v* fairsingigh

broadminded *adj* leathanaigeanta

broccoli *n* brocailí

brochure *n* bróisiúr

broil *v* gríosc

broke *adj* I'm broke níl pingin rua agam

broken *adj* briste

broken-hearted *adj* croíbhriste

broker *n* bróicéir

bronze *n* cré-umha, umha

Bronze Age *n* an Chré-Umhaois

brooch *n* dealg

brood *n* ál

brook *n* sruthán

broom *n* scuab

broth *n* anraith

brothel *n* baoisteach, drúthlann, teach striapachais

brother *n* deartháir

brother-in-law *n* deartháir céile

brow *n* éadan, grua, mala

brown *adj* donn *v* donnaigh

browse *v* iníor

bruise *n* brú *v* brúigh

brush *n, v* scuab

brutal *adj* brúidiúil

brutality *n* brúidiúlacht

brute *n* brúid

bubble *n* bolgán, súilín

buck *n* poc

bucket *n* buicéad

buckskin *n* craiceann fia

bud[1] *n* bachlóg

bud[2] *v* bachlaigh

budding *n* bachlú

budget *n* cáinaisnéis, buiséad *v* buiséadaigh

budgie (budgerigar) *n* budragár

buffalo *n* buabhall

buffer *n* maolán **input / output buffers** maoláin ionchuir is aschuir

buffer zone crios deighilte

bug[1] *n* fríd

bug[2] *n* **(tapping)** gléas cúléisteachta

bugle *n* buabhall

build *v* tóg **to build a house** teach a thógáil

builder *n* foirgneoir, tógálaí

building *n* áras, foirgneamh, tógáil

built (to specification) *adj* tógtha (de réir sconraíochta)

bulk *n* téagar, toirt

bulky *adj* téagartha, toirtiúil

bull *n* tarbh

bulldog *n* tarbhghadhar

bulldozer *n* ollscartaire

bullet *n* piléar **to fire a bullet** piléar a scaoileadh

bullet-proof *adj* piléardhíonach

bulletin *n* **(news)** ráiteas nuachta, builitín

bullock *n* bullán

bull's eye *n* súil sprice, bulla

bully *n* maistín *v* ansmachtaigh

bullying *n* maistíneacht

bulwark *n* bábhún

bumble bee *n* bumbóg

bump *n* tuairt *v* tuairteáil

bumper *n* **(of car)** tuairtceoir

bumpy *adj* míchothrom

bunch *n* triopall **bunch of grapes** triopall fíonchaor

bunched *adj* triopallach

bundle *n, v* cuach

bungalow *n* bungaló

bunk beds *pl* leapacha buinc

bunker *n* **(in golf)** abar

buoy *n* baoi, bulla

buoyant *adj* **(of thing)** snámhach

burden *n* eire, muirear, ualach *v* ualaigh

bureau *n* biúró

bureaucracy *n* maorlathas

bureaucrat *n* maorlathaí

bureaucratic *adj* maorlathach

burglar *n* gadaí, buirgléir
burglary *n* buirgléireacht
burial *n* adhlacadh, cur
burn *n* dó *v* dóigh, loisc
burned *adj* dóite
burning *n* loscadh, dó
burrow *n* (of rabbit) poll (coinín), (of badger) brocach (broic) *v* poll a dhéanamh
bursar *n* sparánaí
burst *n* maidhm, pléasc, scal sunburst scal ghréine
burst out *v* scal
bury *v* adhlaic, cuir
bus *n* bus the bus stop stad an bhus
bus fare *n* táille bus
bush *n* dos, tom, tor furzebush tor aitinn
bushy *adj* (of hair) mothallach
business *n* cúram, gnó, gnólacht mind your own business tabhair aire do do ghnó féin
business organisation *n* eagrú gnó
bustle *n* fuadar
bustling *adj* fuadrach
busy *adj* cruógach, fuadrach, gnóthach
but *conj* ach, ná what should I find there but a bull cad a bheadh romham ná tarbh
butt *n* bun, (of gun) bota *v* to butt into a conversation do theanga a shá i gcomhrá

butcher *n* búistéir
butler *n* buitléir
butter *n* im peanut butter im píseanna talún
butterfly *n* féileacán
buttermilk *n* bláthach
buttock *n* más
button *n* cnaipe *v* cnaipí ruda a dhúnadh
buttonhole *n* lúbóg
buy *v* ceannaigh
buyer *n* ceannaitheoir
buzz *n* dord, dordán
buzzard *n* (bird) clamhán
buzz-word *n* dordfhocal
by *prep* thar, dar, faoi by Christmas faoi Nollaig
by and large tríd is tríd
by chance de thaisme
by-election *n* fothoghchán
by God! *excl* dar Dia!
by means (of) trí mheán
by night istoíche
bypass *n* (of road) seachród *v* seachain
by-product *n* fotháirge, seachtháirge
by-road *n* fobhóthar
bystander *n* féachadóir bystanders lucht féachana
by train ar an traein
by this time next year faoin am seo arís

C

cab *n* tacsaí
cabbage *n* cál, cabáiste
cabin *n* cábán
cabinet[1] *n* caibinéad filing cabinet caibinéad comhad, display cabinet caibinéad taispeántais

cabinet[2] *n* (of government) comhaireacht, shadow cabinet comhaireacht fhreasúra
cable *n* cábla
cable car *n* carr cábla
cable link *n* nasc cábla

cable television n teilifís chábla

cache n folachán

cackle n grág (circe)

cackling n grágaíl to cackle grágaíl a dhéanamh

cactus n cachtas

caddie n giolla

cadet n dalta

cadging n diúgaireacht

café n caife

cafeteria n caifitéire

cage n cás bird-cage éanadán

cairn n carn horned cairn carn cúirte

cajoler n plámásaí

cajolery n plámás

cajoling adj plámásach

cake n cáca, císte, toirtín

calamitous adj anacrach, tubaisteach

calamity n anachain, tubaiste

calcium n cailciam

calculate v áirigh, ríomh

calculation n comhaireamh

calculator n áireamhán programmable calculator áireamhán in-ríomhchláraithe

calculus n calcalas

calendar n féilire

calf¹ n (of leg) colpa

calf² n (animal) gamhain, lao

calibre n (of person) mianach, (of gun) cailibre

calisthenics pl callaistéinic

call¹ n glao, glaoch, gairm

call² v gair, glaoigh

calligraphy n peannaireacht

callous adj fuarchroíoch

calm adj ciúin, socair, suaimhneach n suaimhneas, ciúnas v ciúnaigh, suaimhnigh

calm down! excl tóg (go) bog é! déan go réidh!

calorie n calra

Calypso n Cailíopsó

camcorder n ceamthaifeadán

camel n camall

camera n ceamara

camera crew n criú ceamara

camera operator n ceamradóir

camogie n camógaíocht camogie stick camóg

camomile n fíogadán, camán meall / míonla camomile tea tae fíogadáin

camouflage n ceileatram, duaithníocht v duaithnigh

camp n campa, longfort v campáil holiday camp campa saoire, concentration camp sluachampa géibhinn, internment camp campa géibhinn

campsite n ionad campála, láithreán campála

campaign n feachtas

campaigning n stocaireacht

camper n campálaí

camphor n camfar

can n canna v cannaigh petrol can canna peitril

Canada n Ceanada

Canadian adj, n Ceanadach

canal n canáil

canary n canáraí

Canary Islands pl na hOileáin Chanáracha

cancel v cuir ar ceal, cealaigh

cancellation n cealú

cancer n ailse breast cancer ailse chíche, lung cancer ailse (na) scamhóg

Cancer n an Portán

cancerous adj ailseach

candidate n iarrthóir

candle n coinneal

candlestick n coinnleoir

candy n candaí candy-floss flas candaí

cane *n* cána **sugarcane** cána siúcra

canine *n* **(tooth)** géarán

canister *n* ceanastar

cannabis *n* cannabas

cannibal *adj, n* canablach

canoe *n* canú, curach

canoeing *n* curachóireacht

canon *n* canóin, gunna mór

cannon-fodder *n* bia canóna, bia gunna mhóir

canopy *n* ceannbhrat, forscáth

cantankerous *adj* cantalach

canteen *n* ceaintín, proinnteach, bialann

canter *n* bogshodar

canticle *n* caintic

canvas *n* anairt, canbhás

canvass (for) *v* canbhasáil (ar son)

canyon *n* cainneon

cap *n* caidhp, caipín, claibín **swimming cap** caipín snámha, **bottle-cap** claibín buidéil

capability *n* cumas

capable *adj* cumasach, inniúil

capacity *n* acmhainn, cumas, lucht, toilleadh

cape *n* ceann tíre, rinn, cába

Cape of Good Hope *n* Rinn an Dóchais

capillary *n* ribeadán

capital[1] *n* **(letter)** ceannlitir

capital[2] *n* **(money)** caipiteal

capital city *n* príomhchathair

capital punishment *n* pionós báis

capitalism *n* caipitleachas

capitalist *n* caipitlí

capitulate *v* géill (ar choinníollacha)

capricious *n* taomach

Capricorn *n* an Gabhar

capsize *v* iompaigh béal faoi

capsule *n* capsúl

captain *n* captaen

caption *n* ceannteideal, ceann-scríbhinn

captivate *v* meall

captive *n* cime, géibheannach

captivity *n* géibheann

capture *v* gabh

car *n* gluaisteán, carr **cable car** carr cábla, **car park** carrchlós, **company car** gluaisteán cuideachta

carafe *n* caraf

caramel *n* caramal

carat *n* carat **nine carat gold** ór naoi gcarat

caravan *n* carbhán

caravanserai *n* carbhánlann

caravan site *n* láithreán carbhán

carbohydrate *n* carbaihíodráit

carbon *n* carbón

carboniferous *adj* carbónmhar

carburettor *n* carbradóir

carcass *n* conablach

card *n* cárta **bank card** cárta bainc, **cash card** cárta airgid, **cheque card** cárta seic, **credit card** cárta creidmheasa, **identity card** cárta aitheantais,

cardboard *n* cairtchlár

cardiac *adj* cairdiach

cardiac arrest *n* stad cairdiach

Cardiff *n* Caerdydd

cardigan *n* cairdeagan

cardinal *n* cairdinéal

cardiographer *n* cairdeagrafaí

care[1] *n* aire, cúram, faichill **intensive care unit (ICU)** aonad dianchúraim

care[2] *v* **I don't care** is cuma liom, ní chuireann sé aon tinneas orm

career *n* réim, gairm bheatha

carefree *adj* aerach

careful *adj* cúramach, cáiréiseach

carefulness *n* cáiréis

careless *adj* míchúramach, neamhchúramach

carelessness *n* neamhchúram

caress *v* muirnigh

caressing *adj* muirneach

caretaker *n* airíoch, feighlí

cargo *n* lucht

Caribbean *adj* Cairibeach the Caribbean Sea an Mhuir Chairib

caricature *n* caracatúr, scigphictiúr

Carlow *n* Ceatharlach Co. Carlow Co. Cheatharlach

carnage *n* ár, coscairt

carnal *adj* collaí carnal knowledge fios collaí

carnation *n* coróineach

carnival *n* carnabhal

carnivorous *adj* feoiliteach

carnivore *n* feoiliteoir

carol *n* carúl, duan Nollag

carouse *v* ragairne a dhéanamh

carp *n* carbán

carpenter *n* siúinéir

carpentry *n* siúinéireacht

carpet *n* cairpéad, brat urláir

carriage *n* carráiste, cóiste

carrot *n* cairéad, meacan dearg

carry *v* croch, iompair, tabhair le

cart *n* cairt

cartilage *n* loingeán

cartography *n* cartagrafaíocht

carton *n* cartán

cartoon *n* cartún

cartridge *n* cartús blank cartridge cartús caoch

carve *v* snoigh, grean, (meat) gearr carving snoíodóireacht

carvery *n* spólann

cascade *n* eas

case *n* cás, cúis, (grammar) tuiseal

case history *n* saintuairisc

cash *n* airgead, airgead tirim *v* to cash a cheque seic a dhéanamh

cash on delivery (c.o.d.) íoc ar sheachadadh (í.a.s.)

cashier *n* airgeadóir

cashmere *n* caismír

cash register *n* scipéad

casing *n* cásáil

casket *n* cisteog

casserole *n* casaról casserole (of smoked haddock) casaról (de chadóg dheataithe)

cassette *n* caiséad

cassette recorder *n* taifeadán caiséad

cast[1] *v* caith, teilg to cast a vote vóta a chaitheamh

cast[2] *n* teilgean, (of actors) foireann aisteoirí

castanet *n* castainéad

casting vote *n* vóta réitigh

castle *n* caisleán

cast-off *adj* athchaite

castor oil *n* ola ricne

castrate *v* spoch, coill

casual *adj* ócáideach, neamhthuairimeach

casualty *n* taismeach the casualty (emergency) department an roinn taismeach

cat *n* cat

catacomb *n* catacóm

catalogue *n* catalóg

catalyst *n* catalaíoch

catalytic *adj* catalaíoch

catalytic converter *n* tiontaire catalaíoch

catamaran *n* catamarán

catapult *n* crann tabhaill

cataract *n* (of eye) fionn, (of river) eas

catarrh *n* réama

catastrophe *n* tubaiste

catch v tolg, ceap **to catch hold of somebody** greim a bhreith ar dhuine, **to catch a disease / cold** galar/slaghdán a tholgadh, **to catch up with somebody** teacht suas le duine, **to catch the ball** an liathróid a cheapadh

catching adj tógálach

catchphrase n leathfhocal

category n earnáil, rang

cater (for) v soláthair (do)

caterer n lónadóir

catering n lónadóireacht

caterpillar n cruimh chabáiste

cathedral n ardeaglais

Catholic adj, n Caitliceach

Catholicism n Caitliceachas

cattle n bólacht, airnéis, eallach

cattle-drive n táin

cattle-raid n táin **the Cattle-Raid of Cooley** Táin Bó Cuaille (an Táin)

catwalk n ardán taispeána

caucus n cácas

caul n brat searraigh, caipín sonais

cauldron n coire

cauliflower n cóilis

cause n cionsiocair, cúis, fáth, siocair, údar **cause for complaint** cúis ghearáin, **cause of death** siocair bháis

causeway n cabhsa

caustic adj, n loiscneach

cauterise v poncloisc

caution n faichill, fainic

cautious adj faichilleach

cavalcade n marcshlua

cavalry n marcra, marcshlua

Cavan n an Cabhán **Co. Cavan** Co. an Chabháin

cave n fochla, pluais, uaimh

caviare n caibheár

cavity n cuas, fochla

CD n dlúthdhiosca

CD-ROM (compact disc – read only memory) n dlúthdhiosca léimh amháin

cease v scoir, staon

cease-fire n sos comhraic

cedar n céadar

ceiling n síleáil

celebrate v ceiliúir, comóir, mór

celebration n comóradh, ceiliúradh **centenary celebration** comóradh / ceiliúradh céad bliain

celebrity n duine mór le rá

celery n soilire

celibacy n aontumha

celibate adj aontumha

cell n (in prison) cillín, (in body) cill **red, white blood cells** cealla dearga, bána (na) fola

cellar n siléar

cello n dordveidhil

cellophane n ceallafán

cellular adj ceallach

celluloid n ceallalóid

cellulose n ceallalós

Celt n Ceilteach

Celtic adj Ceilteach n (language) Ceiltis

cement n stroighin, suimint v straighnigh **to mix cement** suimint a shuaitheadh

cemetery n reilig

censor n cinsire

censorship n cinsireacht

censure n cáineadh, lochtú v cáin, lochtaigh

census n (of population) daonáireamh

cent n ceint

centenary n (comóradh) céad bliain

centimetre n ceintiméadar

centipede n céadchosach

central adj lárnach

Central America n Meiriceá Láir

Central Bank of Ireland n Banc Ceannais na hÉireann

centralisation n lárúchán

centralise v láraigh

central heating n téamh lárnach

centre n lár, lárionad the city centre lár na cathrach, interpretive, heritage, shopping, sports centre lárionad léirithe, oidhreachta, siopadóireachta, spóirt

centre-forward n lárthosaí

century n céad, aois the twentieth century an fichiú haois

ceramic adj criaga

ceramics n criadóireacht

cereal adj, n gránach

cerebral adj ceirbreach

ceremonial adj deasghnách

ceremony n deasghnáth, searmanas

certain[1] adj, n áirithe a certain amount méid áirithe

certain[2] adj cinnte, dearfa, deimhin, deimhneach, siúráilte make certain cinntigh

certainly adv go cinnte, siúráilte

certainty n cinnteacht, deimhneacht

certificate n deimhniú, teastas, teistiméireacht the Junior Certificate an Teastas Sóisearach, birth certificate teastas breithe, teastas beireatais

certify v deimhnigh

cessation n staonadh

CFC(s) n CFC(anna)

chaffinch n rí rua

chain adj slabhrúil n slabhra

chain letter n litir shlabhra

chain reaction n imoibriú slabhrúil

chain stores pl sreangshiopaí

chair n cathaoir

chairperson n cathaoirleach

chalet n sealla

chalice n cailís

chalk n cailc

challenge n dúshlán to challenge somebody dúshlán a thabhairt do dhuine

challenger n fear/bean dúshláin

challenging adj dúshlánach

chamber n seomra

chamber of commerce n cumann lucht tráchtála

champagne n seaimpéin

champion n curadh, scaimpín world champion seaimpín/curadh an domhain

championship n craobh, (competition) craobhchomórtas championship match cluiche craoibhe

chance n amhantar, áiméar, faill, cinniúint, seans to take a chance dul san amhantar, dul sa seans, by chance de thaisme

chancellor n seansailéir

chandelier n coinnleoir craobhach

change[1] n athrach, athrú, malairt, claochlú, malartú v athraigh, malartaigh, claochlaigh change of climate athrach aeráide, to change direction treo a athrú, she has changed a lot tá athrú mór uirthi, change of mind athchomhairle

change[2] n (money) sóinseáil

changeable adj athraitheach, luaineach, malartach

changeling n síofra, iarlais

changing adj malartach

channel n caidhséar, clais, (television) cainéal

chant(ing) n cantaireacht

chaos n anord

chaotic adj anordúil

chap n gág

chapel n séipéal Chapelizod Séipéal Iosóid

chaplain n séiplíneach

chapped *adj* gágach

chapter *n* caibidil

character[1] *n* nádúr, tréith

character[2] *n* **(of keyboard, computer, etc)** carachtar

characterise *v* tréithigh

characteristic *adj* tréitheach *n* saintréith, sainchomhartha **characteristic curve** sainchuar

charcoal *n* fioghual, gualach

charge[1] *n* **(expense)** dola, muirear, táille *v* gearr (ar)

charge[2] *n* **(law)** cúis, cúiseamh *v* cúisigh

charge[3] *v* **(battery)** luchtaigh

charge[4] *n* **(fast movement)** séirse **baton charge** séirse bataí/ smachtíní

chariot *n* carbad

charitable *adj* carthanach, déirceach

charity *n* carthanacht, déirc, **(of group, society)** cumann carthannachta

charm[1] *n* **(characteristic)** caithis, **(of spell)** ortha, piseog

charm[2] *v* cuir faoi dhraíocht, tabhair aoibhneas do

charming *adj* aoibhinn, gleoite

chart *n* graf, cairt **the charts (music)** na cairteacha

charter *v* **(plane etc)** cairtfhostaigh **chartered flight** eitilt chairtfhostaithe

chase[1] *n* fiach, tóir, ruaig **to chase** an ruaig a chur ar

chase[2] *v* fiach, ruaig **to chase somebody** dul sa tóir ar dhuine

chaser *n* ruagaire

chasm *n* duibheagán

chassis *n* fráma

chaste *n* geanmnaí

chastity *n* geanmnaíocht **vow of chastity** móid gheanmnaíochta

chastise *v* smachtaigh

chattels *n* airnéis

chatter *n* geab, cabaireacht *v* cabaireacht a dhéanamh

chatterbox *n* cabaire

chatting *n* cabaireacht

chatty *adj* geabach

chauvinism *n* seobhaineachas

chauvinist *n* bodlathach, seobhaineach

cheap *adj* saor

cheat *n* caimiléir *v* caimiléireacht a dhéanamh ar

check[1] *v* seiceáil

check![2] *excl* **(chess)** sáinn!

checked *adj* **(cloth)** páircíneach

checkmate *n* marbhsháinn

check out *v* seiceáil amach

cheddar *n* céadar

cheek[1] *n* grua, pluc, leiceann

cheek[2] *n* soibealtacht

cheekbone *n* cnámh grua

cheeky *adj* soibealta

cheerful *adj* aigeanta, soilbhir, gealgháireach, subhach, súgrach, spleodrach

cheerfulness *n* croíúlacht, soilbhreas, spleodar, subhachas

cheers! *excl* sláinte!

cheese *n* cáis

cheeseburger *n* cáisbhorgaire

cheetah *n* síota

chemical *adj* ceimiceach *n* ceimiceán **chemical weapons** airm cheimiceacha

chemist *n* ceimiceoir, **(pharmacist)** poitigéir

chemistry *n* ceimic

chemotherapy *n* ceimiteiripe

cheque *n* seic

chequebook *n* seicleabhar

chequered *adj* seicear

cherish *v* caomhnaigh, muirnigh

cherry *n* silín

chess *n* ficheall

chessboard *n* clár fichille

chessmen *n* fir fhichille

chest[1] *n* araid, cófra **chest of drawers** cófra tarraiceán, **treasure-chest** araid seod / mhaoine

chest[2] *n* (of body) ucht, cliabh, cliabhrach

chestnut *n* cnó capaill, (edible) castán

chew *v* cogain, mungail **to chew the cud** athchogain

chewing gum *n* guma coganta

chic *adj* faiseanta

chicken *n* sicín, (meat) circeoil

chickenpox *n* deilgneach

chicory *n* siocaire

chief *n* ceann, taoiseach

chief *prefix* ard-, príomh-

chief of staff *n* ceann foirne

chiffon *n* sreabhann

chieftain *n* ceann fine

chilblain *n* fochma, fuachtán

child *n* gasúr, garsún, leanbh, paiste, tachrán **children** clann, **have you any children?** an bhfuil cúram ar bith ort?

child abuse *n* íde ar pháistí, mí-úsáid ar pháistí

child-care unit *n* aonad cúraim leanaí

child sexual abuse *n* mí-úsáid ghnéis ar pháistí

childhood *n* leanbaíocht

childish *adj* leanbaí, páistiúil

childishness *n* leanbaíocht, páistiúlacht

childlike *adj* leanbaí, naíonda

chill *v* fuaraigh

chilly *adj* dearóil

chime *n, v* cling

chimes *pl* clingíní

chimney *n* simléar

chimpanzee *n* simpeansaí

chin *n* smig

China *n* an tSín

Chinese *adj, n* Síneach, (language) an tSínis

chip *n* sceallóg, scealp, slis, sliseog, **chips** sceallóga (prátaí)

chipmunk *n* iora talún

chiropody *n* cosliacht

chiropodist *n* coslia

chiropractor *n* círichleachtóir

chirp *n* bíog, gíog

chisel *n* siséal

chit-chat *n* clabaireacht

chivalrous *adj* cúirtéiseach

chivalry *n* ridireacht

chive *n* síobhas

chlorine *n* clóirín

chloroflurocarbon (CFC) *n* clórafluaracarbón (CFC), **CFCs** CFCanna

chloroform *n* clóraform

chocolate *n* seacláid

choice[1] *n* rogha, togha, toghadh, scoth, roghnú **the choicest of food and drink** togha gach bia agus rogha gach dí

choice[2] *adj* tofa, scothúil

choir *n* claisceadal, cór

choke[1] *v* tacht

choke[2] *n* (in car) tachtaire

cholera *n* calar

cholesterol *n* colaistéaról

choose *v* roghnaigh, togh

chop *n* (meat) gríscín *v* mionghearr **lamb chops** gríscíní uaineola

choppy *adj* corraithe

chopsticks *pl* cipíní itheacháin

choral *adj* córúil

chord *n* corda

choreography *n* córagrafaíocht

chorus *n* cór, curfá

Christ *n* Críost

Christian *adj* Críostúil *n* Críostaí

Christianity *n* an Chríostaíocht

Christmas *n* an Nollaig **Christmas cracker** pléascóg Nollag, **Christmas tree** crann Nollag, **Christmas Eve** Oíche Nollag, **Christmas Day** Lá Nollag, **Little Christmas** Nollaig na mBan, Nollaig Bheag, **Happy Christmas!** Nollaig Shona! Nollaig faoi shéan is faoi mhaise duit/daoibh! **Christmas decorations** maisiúcháin/rudaí na Nollag

chrome *n* cróm

chromium *n* cróimiam

chromosome *n* crómasóm

chronic *adj* ainsealach **becoming chronic** ag dul in ainseal, chun ainsil

chronicle *n* croinic

chronological *adj* cróineolaíoch

chubby *adj* beathaithe **chubby face** aghaidh phlucach

chuckle *n* maolgháire

chum *n* compánach

chunk *n* canta, alpán

church *n* eaglais, teampall

churchyard *n* cill

churl *n* aitheach

churlish *adj* doicheallach, cantalach

churn *n* cuinneog *v* maistrigh

churning *n* maistreadh

chutney *n* seatnaí

cider *n* ceirtlis

cigar *n* todóg

cigarette *n* toitín

cinema *n* **(place)** pictiúrlann, **(art)** cineama

cinnamon *n* cainéal

cipher *n* rúnscríbhinn

circle *n* ciorcal, fáinne *v* ciorclaigh

circuit *n* ciorcad, timpeall **closed circuit television** teilifís chiorcaid iata

circuitous *adj* timpeallach

circular[1] *adj* ciorclach

circular[2] *n* imlitir, ciorclán

circulate *v* cuir timpeall, scaip

circulation *n* cúrsaíocht

circumcise *v* timpeallghearr

circumcision *n* imghearradh, timpeallghearradh

circumference *n* compás, imlíne

circumflex *n* cuairín

circumscribe *v* imscríobh, cuimsigh

circumspect *adj* aireach

circumstance *n* cúinse, toisc **under no circumstances** ar aon chúinse, **unforeseeable circumstances** imthosca nárbh fhéidir a thuar

circumstantial *adj* imthoisceach

circus *n* sorcas

citizen *n* cathróir, saoránach

citizenship *n* cathróireacht, saoránacht

citrus *n* citreas **citrus fruit** toradh citris

city *n* cathair **city centre** lár na cathrach

civic *adj* carthartha

civics *n* saoránaíocht

civil *adj* carthartha, sibhialta **civil war** cogadh cathartha

civil servant *n* státseirbhíseach

civil service *n* státseirbhís

civilian *adj* sibhialtach

civility *n* sibhialtacht

civilisation *n* sibhialtacht

claim *n* éileamh, teideal *v* maígh, éiligh

claimant *n* éilitheoir

clairvoyance *n* fiosaíocht

clamour *n* callán

clamp *n* clampa, teanntán *v* clampáil

clan *n* clann, treibh

clandestine *adj* folaitheach

clap *n* bualadh bos *v* bosa a bhualadh

clapperboard *n* (in film-making) clabaire

Clare *n* an Clár Co. Clare Co. an Chláir

claret *n* clairéad

clarification *n* léiriú, soiléiriú

clarinet *n* cláirnéid

clarify *v* soiléirigh

clarity *n* glinne, réaltacht

clasp *n* claspa, greamán

class *n* aicme, grád, rang *v* grádaigh

classic(al) *adj* clasaiceach

classification *n* aicmiú, aicmiúchán, rangú

classify *v* aicmigh, rangaigh

clatter *n* clag, cleatar

clattering *n* clagarnach

clause *n* clásal

claustrophobia *n* clástrafóibe, uamhan clóis

claw[1] *n* crúb, ionga

claw[2] *v* crúbáil

clay *n* cré, créafóg

clean *adj*, *v* glan

cleaner *n* glantóir

cleanliness *n* glaine

cleanse *v* glan

clean-shaven *adj* glanbhearrtha

clear *adj* follasach, geal, glan, gléineach, glinn, léir, soiléir *v* réitigh to clear your throat do scornach a réiteach

clearance *n* réiteach

clemency *n* trócaire

clergy *n* cléir

clerical *adj* cléiriúil

clerical officer *n* oifigeach cléireachais

clerk *n* cléireach

clever *adj* aibí, cliste, gasta, glic

cleverness *n* clisteacht, gastacht, gliceas

cliché *n* sean-nath

click *v* smeach

client *n* cliant

clientele *n* cliantacht

cliff *n* aill cliffs aillte, to fall off / down a cliff titim le haill

cliffhanger *n* (film) scannán bíse

climate *n* aeráid climate conditions dálaí aeráide

climax *n* buaicphointe

climb *v* dreap

climber *n* dreapadóir

climbing *n* dreapadóireacht

cling (to) *v* greim a choinneáil ar

cling film *n* scannán cumhdaithe

clinic *n* clinic

clinical *adj* cliniciúil

clip *n* fáiscín crocodile, hair, paper clip fáiscín crogaill, gruaige, páipéir

clique *n* baicle

cloak *n* clóca, fallaing

cloakroom *n* seomra cótaí

clock *n* clog alarm clock clog aláraim

clocking in / out *n* clogáil isteach/ amach

clocking hen *n* cearc ar gor

clockwise *adj* deiseal

clod *n* dairt

clodhopper *n* cábóg

cloister *n* clabhstra

clone *n* clón

cloning *n* clónáil

close[1] *adj* dlúth, docht, lom, (of weather) meirbh *prefix* neas-, dlúth- close intimacy dlúthchaidreamh

close[2] *v* dún, druid, iaigh close the window dún an fhuinneog

closed *adj* druidte, dúnta, iata

closed circuit television *n* teilifís chiorcaid iata

close-up *n* gar-amharc

closing-down sale *n* reic clabhsúir

closure *n* clabhsúr, dúnadh, iamh

clot *n* téachtán *v* téacht **blood clot** téachtadh fola, cnapán fola

cloth *n* ceirt, éadach

clothe *v* gléas

clothes *pl* éadach, éide

cloud *n* néal, scamall

cloudburst *n* maidhm bháistí

cloudy *adj* néaltach, scamallach

clove *n* clóbh

clover *n* seamair

clown *n* áilteoir, cábóg

clowning *n* áilteoireacht

clownish *adj* cábógach

club[1] *n* **(cards)** triuf

club[2] *n* cumann, club **night / youth club** club oíche/óige

club[3] *n* **(stick)** smachtín

clubhouse *n* clubtheach

clue *n* leid **I haven't a clue** níl tuairim dá laghad agam

clump *n* tortán

clumsy *adj* anásta, ciotach, ciotrúnta, liobarnach, místuama, **(with feet)** spágach

cluster *n* triopall, **(of stars)** réaltbhraisle

clustered *adj* triopallach

clutch *n* **(mechanical)** crág *v* beir greim air **clutch failure** teip chráige

clutter *n* tranglam

coach[1] *n* **(vehicle)** cóiste

coach[2] *v* traenáil

coach[3] *n* **(sports)** traenálaí

coached *adj* traenáilte

coaching *n* traenáil, oiliúnú

coagulate *v* téacht

coal *n* gual **Coalisland** Oileán an Ghuail

coal pit *n* sloc guail

coalition *n* comhrialtas

coarse *adj* garbh

coarse angling *n* garbhiascaireacht

coast *n* cósta

coastguard *n* garda cósta

coastline *n* líne an chósta, imeallbhord

coat *n* cóta, **(of animal)** clúmh, fionnadh *v* cuir brat ar **coat of arms** armas

coating *n* scraith, coirt

coax *v* meall

cobalt *n* cóbalt

cobbler *n* caibléir

cobble *n* duirleog *v* pábháil le duirleoga

cobra *n* cobra

cobweb *n* líon damháin alla

cocaine *n* cócaon

cock[1] *n* coileach

cock[2] *v* **(gun)** cocáil

cockle *n* ruacan

cockpit *n* **(in aeroplane)** cábán píolóta

cockroach *n* ciaróg dhubh

cocktail *n* manglam

cocky *adj* sotalach

cocoa *n* cócó

coconut *n* cnó cócó

cocoon *n* cocún

cod *n* **(fish)** trosc

code *n* cód **dialling code** cód diailithe

codify *v* códaigh

co-educational *adj* comhoideachasúil

coerce *v* cuir iallach air

coffee *n* caife

coffee table *n* bord íseal

coffin *n* cónra

cog *n* fiacail

cog-wheel *n* roth fiaclach

cognac *n* coinneach

cohabitation *n* aontíos

coherent *adj* loighiciúil

coil *n* corna *v* corn

coin box *n* bosca airgid

coincide (with) *n* comhtharlaigh (le)

coincidence *n* comhtharlú

colander *n* síothlán

cold[1] *adj* fuar *n* fuacht **cold war** cogadh fuar, **to give somebody the cold-shoulder** an tsúil a dhúnadh ar dhuine

cold[2] *n* slaghdán **to catch a cold** slaghdán a tholgadh

coleslaw *n* cálslá

colic *n* coiliceam

collaborate *v* comhoibrigh

collapse *n* cliseadh *v* tit, clis

collapsible *adj* infhillte

collar *n* coiléar, bóna

collarbone *n* dealrachán

collate *v* cuir i gcomórtas

collateral *n* **(security)** cúlbhannaí

colleague *n* comhghleacaí

collect *v* cnuasaigh, cruinnigh, tiomsaigh

collection *n* cnuasach, conlán, díolaim, teaglaim

collective *adj* comh-

college *n* coláiste

collide *v* buail faoina chéile

collision *n* imbhualadh

colloquial *adj* **(speech)** coitianta

collusion *n* claonpháirteachas

colon[1] *n* **(physiology)** drólann

colon[2] *n* **(punctuation)** idirstad

colonel *n* coirnéal

colonial *adj* coilíneach

colonialism *n* coilíneachas

colonise *v* coilínigh

colonist *n* coilíneach

colonnade *n* colúnáid

colony *n* coilíneacht

colophon *n* colafan

colossal *adj* ábhalmhór

colour *n* dath, **(of complexion)** lí *v* dathaigh

colour-blind *adj* dathchaoch, dathdhall

coloured *n* daite

colourful *adj* dathannach, dathúil, péacach

colouring *n* dathú

colourless *adj* éadathach

colt *n* bromach, **(gun)** gunnán Chólt

column *n* colún

columnist *n* colúnaí

comb *n* cíor *v* cíorláil, spíon

combat *n* coimheascar, comhrac

combination *n* comhcheangal

combine *v* comhcheangail

combine harvester *n* comhbhuainteoir

come *v* tar, gabh **come here** tar i leith, gabh i leith

come apart *v* tit ó chéile

come down *v* tar anuas

come up *v* tar aníos

comedian *n* fuirseoir, aisteoir coiméide

comedy *n* coiméide

comely *adj* cumtha

comet *n* cóiméad

comfort *n* compord, sócúlacht, sólás *v* sólásaigh

comfortable *adj* sócúlach, teolaí, compordach, seascair, sóúil

comic *n* **(children's comic paper)** greannán

comical *adj* ait

comma *n* camóg

command[1] *n* ceannas, ceannasaíocht **the Southern Command** Ceannasaíocht an Deiscirt

command[2] *n* **(order)** ordú

commander *n* ceannasaí, ceannfort

commanding *adj* ceannasach

commandment *n* aithne **the Ten Commandments** na Deich nAithne

command post *n* post ceannais

commemorate *v* cuimhnigh, ceiliúir i gcuimhne...

commemoration *n* cuimhneachán, ceiliúradh cuimhne

commence *v* tosaigh

commend *v* mol

commendable *adj* inmholta

commendation *n* moladh

commensurate (with) *adj* comhthomhaiseach (le)

comment *n* léirmheas *v* trácht

commentary *n* tráchtaireacht

commentator *n* tráchtaire

commerce *n* tráchtáil

commercial *adj* tráchtála

commercialised *adj* tráchtálaithe

commission *n* coimisiún *v* coimisiúnaigh

commissioner *n* coimisinéir **the Data Protection Commissioner** an Coimisinéir Cosanta Sonraí

commit *v* (crime) déan (coir)

commitment *n* ceangal, ceangaltas

committee *n* coiste

commodity *n* tráchtearra

common *adj* coiteann, coitianta **in common** comónta

common-law wife *n* bean chéile faoin dlí coiteann

Common Market *n* Cómhargadh

commonplace *adj* gnách

commonwealth *n* comhlathas

commotion *n* caismirt, clampar, (rírá agus) ruaille buaille

communal *adj* comhchoiteann

commune *n* común

communicate *v* cumarsáid a dhéanamh

communication *n* cumarsáid

communication skills *pl* scileanna cumarsáide

communion *n* comaoineach **Holy Communion** an Chomaoineach Naofa

communism *n* cumannachas

communist *adj* cumannach *n* cumannaí

communistic *adj* cummanaíoch

community[1] *n* tionól, (religious) comhthionól, pobal **the local community** an pobal áitiúil

community[2] *n* comhphobal **the European Community** an Comhphobal Eorpach

community awareness *n* pobalfheasacht

community school *n* pobalscoil

commuter *n* comaitéir

compact *adj* comhdhlúth, dlúth *v* comhdhlúthaigh

compact disc *n* dlúthdhiosca

compact disc player *n* seinnteoir dlúthdhioscaí

compactness *n* dlús

companion *n* compánach

companionable *adj* caidreamhach

company[1] *n* (social) comhluadar, cuideachta

company[2] *n* (business) comhlacht, cuideachta **limited company** comhlacht teoranta

company[3] *n* (theatre) compántas

company[4] *n* (army) complacht

company car *n* gluaisteán cuideachta

comparable (to) *adj* inchurtha (le)

comparative *adj* coibhneasta, comparáideach *n* breischéim

compare (to, with) *v* cuir i gcomórtas, i gcomparáid (le)

comparison *n* comórtas, comparáid

compartment *n* urrann

compass *n* compás

compassion *n* taise, trócaire

compassionate *adj* taisiúil, trócaireach

compatibility *n* comhoiriúnacht

compatible *adj* comhoiriúnach

compatriot *n* comhthíreach

compel *v* cuir iallach air

compendium *n* achomaireacht

compensate *v* cúitigh

compensating *adj* cúiteach

compensation *n* cúiteamh

compete (with) *v* dul in iomaíocht (le)

competent *adj* inniúil

competition *n* comórtas, coimhlint, iomaíocht **music competition** comórtas ceoil, **free competition** saoriomaíocht

competitive *adj* coimhlinteach, iomaíoch

competitiveness *n* acmhainn iomaíochta, cumas iomaíochta

competitor *n* iomaitheoir

compile *v* tiomsaigh

compilation *n* díolaim, teaglaim

complacent *adj* bogásach

complain *v* gearán a dhéanamh

complainer *n* béalchnáimhseánaí

complaining *adj* casaoideach, clamhsánach *n* ceasacht, cnáimhseáil

complaint *n* casaoid, clamhsán, gearán

complement *n* comhlánú *v* comhlánaigh

complementary *adj* comhlántach

complete *adj* críochnaithe, déanta *v* comhlánaigh, críochnaigh

completely *adv* ar fad

completion *n* críoch, críochnú, slánú

complex *adj* casta *n* coimpléasc

complexion *n* lí, snua

complexity *n* castacht

complicate *v* cuir trí chéile

complication *n* fadhb

complicity *n* comhpháirteachas

compliment *n* moladh *v* mol **with compliments** le dea-mhéin

complimentary *adj* moltach

comply *v* déan de réir

component *n* comhpháirt

compose *v* cum

composed *adj* socair

composer *n* cumadóir

composition *n* aiste, **(artistic)** ceapachán, cumadóireacht, **(make)** comhdhéanamh, deachtú

compost *n* múirín

composure *n* guaim, suaimhneas

compound *n* cumasc, **(enclosure)** bábhún

compound word *n* comhfhocal

comprehend *v* tuig, cuimsigh

comprehensible *adj* sothuigthe

comprehensive *adj* cuimsitheach, uileghabhálach

compress *v* comhbhrúigh

comprise *v* cuimsigh

compromise *n* comhréiteach, *v* comhréitigh

compulsory *adj* riachtanach, éigeantach

compute *v* ríomh

computer *n* ríomhaire **lap top computer** ríomhaire glúine

computer graphics *pl* ríomhghrafaic

computer programmer *n* ríomhchláraitheoir

computer science *n* ríomheolaíocht, ríomhaireacht

computerise *v* ríomhairigh

comrade *n* comrádaí

comradeship *n* comrádaíocht

concave *adj* cuasach

conceal *v* ceil

concealment *n* ceilt

concede *v* géill
conceited *adj* leitheadach
conceive *v* (**scheme**) beartaigh
concentrate *v* cruinnigh
concentration *n* dianmhachnamh
concentration camp *n* sluachampa géibhinn
concept *n* coincheap
conception *n* (**mind**) tuairim, (**body**) giniúint
concern[1] *n* cúram, imní, (**business**) gnó **it is my greatest, least concern** is é an chloch is mó, is lú ar mo phaidrín é
concern[2] *v* bain (le)
concerned *adj* imníoch
concerning *prep* i dtaobh
concert *n* ceolchoirm, coirm cheoil
concerto *n* coinséartó
concession *n* deonú
conciliate *v* tabhair chun síochána
concise *adj* achomair
conciseness *n* achomaireacht
conclude *v* cuir críoch le **to conclude** mar fhocal scoir
conclusion *n* conclúid
conclusive *adj* críochnúil
concoct *v* comhbhruith
concoction *n* comhbhruith
concrete[1] *n* coincréit **reinforced concrete** coincréit threisithe, **concrete block** bloc coincréite
concrete[2] *adj* coincréiteach, nithiúil
concussion *n* comhtholgadh
condemn *v* cáin, daor **she was condemned to death** daoradh chun báis í
condemnation *n* cáineadh
condense *v* comhdhlúthaigh
condensation *n* comhdhlúthú
condescending *adj* uiríseal
condiment *n* blastán

condition[1] *n* caoi, cruth, riocht **it is in good condition** tá caoi mhaith air, tá slacht air
condition[2] *n* cúinse, coinníoll, acht, agó, dáil, dóigh, cuntar, toisc **on condition that** ar acht go, ar chuntar go, ar an gcúinse go, **conditions (terms)** coinníollacha, tosca, **climatic conditions** dálaí aeráide
condition[3] *v* riochtaigh
conditional *adj* coinníollach
condolence *n* comhbhrón **to give one's condolences to somebody** comhbhrón a dhéanamh le duine
condom *n* coiscín
condone *v* maith (do)
conduct *n* iompar *v* treoraigh, stiúir
conduction *n* (**electricity**) seoladh
conductor *n* stiúrthóir, (**of electricity**) seoltóir
cone *n* coirceog
confectioner *n* sólaisteoir
confectionery *n* milseogra
confer *v* bronn
conference *n* comhdháil
confess *v* admhaigh
confession *n* admháil, (**to priest**) faoistin
confessor *n* anamchara
confetti *pl* coinfití
confide (in) *v* lig rún le
confidence *n* muinín **in confidence** i modh rúin
confident *adj* muiníneach
confidential *adj* rúnda, faoi rún
confine (to) *v* connigh
confined *adj* teoranta
confirm[1] *v* (**sacrament**) cóineartaigh
confirm[2] *v* (**fact, thing, etc**) dearbhaigh, cinntigh
confirmation[1] *n* (**sacrament**) cóineartú

confirmation[2] *n* (of fact, thing, etc) cinntiú, dearbhú

confirmed *adj* cinntithe

confiscate *v* coigistigh

confiscation *n* coigistiú

conflict *n* caismirt in conflict i dtreis

conflicting needs *pl* riachtanais chontrártha

conform *v* déan de réir

confront *v* seas ar aghaidh duine amach, tabhair aghaidh ar

confuse *v* cuir trína chéile

confused *adj* corrabhuaiseach, trí chéile, suaite

confusion *n* corrabhuais, dallamullóg, meascán mearaí

congeal *v* oighrigh

congenital disease *n* galar broinne

congested *adj* plódaithe

congestion *n* plódú **traffic congestion** plódú tráchta

conglomerate *n* ilchuideachta

congratulate *v* tréaslaigh **to congratulate somebody** rud a thréaslú le duine, comhghairdeas a dhéanamh le duine

congratulations! *excl* comhghairdeas (leat/libh)! go maire tú/sibh an lá!

congregate *v* comhchruinnigh

congregation *n* pobal (Dé)

congress *n* comhdháil

coniferous woodland *n* coillearnach bhuaircíneach

conjugate *v* réimnigh

conjugation *n* réimniú

conjunction *n* cónasc

conjunctive *n* (grammar) cónascach

conjunctivitis *n* toinníteas

conjurer *n* asarlaí

conjuring tricks *n* asarlaíocht

Connaught *n* Connachta (the province of) Connaught Cúige Connacht

Connaught person *n* Connachtach

connect *v* cónaisc

connecting *adj* cónascach

connection *n* ceangal, cónasc

connector *n* cónascaire

connive *v* cúlcheadaigh

connivance *n* cúlcheadú

conquer *v* cloígh

conquest *n* concas

conscience *n* coinsias

conscientious *adj* coinsiasach

conscientious objection *n* diúltú coinsiasach

conscious *adj* comhfhiosach

consciousness *n* comhfhios

conscript *n* coinscríofach

consecrate *v* coisric

consecration *n* coisreacan

consensus *n* comhaontú

consent *n* deoin *v* deonaigh, toiligh

consequence *n* deasca, iarmhairt in consequence of de dheasca

conservation *n* caomhnú

conservative *adj, n* coimeádach

conservatory *n* teach gloine

conserve *v* caomhnaigh **conserving water** ag caomhnú uisce

consider *v* machnaigh (ar), smaoinigh (ar)

considerable *adj* fiúntach **a considerable amount** cuid mhaith

consideration *n* machnamh **they have no consideration for anybody** is cuma leo faoi aon duine

consign *v* coinsínigh

consignment *n* coinsíniú

consistency *n* comhsheasmhacht, seasmhacht

consistent *adj* de réir a chéile, seasmhach

consolation *n* sólás

console[1] *v* sólásaigh

console[2] *n* (computer) consól

consolidated *adj* comhdhlúite

consonant *n* consan

conspiracy *n* comhcheilg, uisce faoi thalamh

constable *n* constábla

constabulary *n* constáblacht **Royal Irish, Ulster Constabulary** Constáblacht Ríoga na hÉireann, Uladh

constant *adj* seasmhach

constancy *n* seasmhacht

constantly *adv* de shíor

constellation *n* réaltbhuíon

constipated *adj* iata

constipating *adj* stolpach

constipation *n* iatacht

constituency *n* dáilcheantar

constituent *n* toghthóir

constitute *v* comhdhéan

constitution *n* comhdhéantús, bunreacht **the Irish Constitution** Bunreacht na hÉireann

constraint *n* sriantacht

constrict *v* cúngaigh

construct *v* tóg, déan

construction *n* foirgníocht

constructive *adj* cuiditheach

constructive criticism *n* léirmheastóireacht chuiditheach

constructivism *n* tógálachas

consul *n* consal

consulate *n* consalacht

consult (with) *v* ceadaigh (le), téigh i gcomhairle (le)

consultant *n* comhairleach

consultative *adj* comhairleach

consume *v* caith, ídigh, díscigh

consumed *adj* caite, ídithe, díscithe

consumer *n* caiteoir, tomhaltóir

consumer price index *n* treoiruimhir praghsanna do thomhaltóirí

consumption *n* **(of petrol)** ídiú (peitril)

contact *n* tadhall

contact lenses *pl* lionsaí tadhaill

contagion *n* tadhlacht

contagious *adj* tógálach, tadhaill

contagious disease galar tadhaill / tógálach

contain *v* coinnigh

container *n* árthach, gabhdán, soitheach

contamination *n* salú

contaminate *v* salaigh

contemplate *v* machnaigh ar

contemporaries *pl* **my contemporaries** lucht mo chomhaimsire / chomhaoise

contemporary *adj* comhaimseartha, comhshaolach

contempt *n* dímheas, díomas, tarcaisne

contempt of court *n* díspeagadh cúirte

contemptible *adj* suarach

contemptuous *adj* dímheasúil, tarcaisneach, beagmheastúil

contend *v* troid

content[1] *n* lucht

content[2] *adj* sásta **to be perfectly content** bheith ar do sháimhín só

contention *n* cointinn, dréim, amarrán

contentment *n* sástacht

contest coimhlint, comhlann

contestant *n* iomaitheoir

context *n* comhthéacs

continent *n* ilchríoch, **(of Europe)** mór-roinn

continental *adj* ilchríochach

continental drift *n* gluaiseacht ilchríochach

contingency *n* teagmhas

contingent *adj* teagmhasach

continual *adj* buan

continue *v* coinnigh ar bun, lean

continuity *n* leanúnachas

continuous *adj* leanúnach

contort *v* freang

contortion *n* freanga

contour *n* comhrian

contraband *n* contrabhanna

contraception *n* frithghiniúint

contraceptive *adj, n* frithghiniúnach

contract[1] *n* conradh

contract[2] *v* tolg **to contract a disease** galar a tholgadh

contractor *n* conraitheoir

contradict *n* bréagnaigh

contradiction *n* trasnaíocht, trasnú

contradictory *adj* bréagnaitheach

contrary *adj* codarsnach, contráilte, contrártha

contrast[1] *n* contrárthacht **in contrast with** i gcontrárthacht le

contrast[2] *n* frithshuí *v* frithshuigh

contravene *v* cuir in aghaidh

contribute *v* cuir le, **(payment)** do chion féin a íoc

contribution *n* ranníocaíocht

contrive *v* cum, ceap

control[1] *v* smachtaigh

control[2] *n* rialtán, smacht, smachtú, urlámhas **in control** i gceannas, **driving controls** rialtáin tiomána

controller *n* ceannasaí

control lever *n* luamhán stiúrtha

controversial *adj* conspóideach

controversy *n* conspóid

convalesce *v* téarnaigh

convalescence *n* téarnamh

convalescent home *n* teach téarnaimh

convection *n* comhiompar

convene *v* tionóil

convenience *n* áis, áisiúlacht, caoithiúlacht **at your convenience** ar do chaoithiúlacht

convenient *adj* áisiúil, cóngarach, caoithiúil

convent *n* clochar

convention *n* coinbhinsiún, dáil **social conventions** comhghnás

conventional *adj* coinbhinsiúnach, comhghnásach

converge *v* comhchlaon

convergence *n* comhchlaontacht

conversant *adj* taithíoch (ar)

conversation *n* comhrá **continuing the conversation** ag leanúint den chomhrá

conversational *adj* comhráiteach

conversationalist *n* comhráití

converse (with) *v* déan comhrá (le)

conversion *n* iompú

convert *n* iompaitheach *v* iompaigh

converter *n* tiontaire **catalytic converter** tiontaire catalaíoch

convex *adj* dronnach

convey *v* tabhair le, cuir in iúl

conveyor-belt *n* crios/banda iompair

convict *n* daoránach *v* ciontaigh, teilg, daor

conviction *n* ciontú

convince *n* cuir ina luí

convivial *adj* cuideachtúil

convoluted *adj* casta

convulsion *n* arraing **in convulsions with laughter** in arraingeacha ag gáire

cook *n* cócaire *v* cócaireacht a dhéanamh

cooker *n* cócaireán

cookery *n* cócaireacht

cooking *n* cócaireacht

cool[1] *adj* fionnuar

cool[2] *v* fionnuaraigh

cooler *n* fuaraitheoir

cool-headed *adj* fuarintinneach

cooling system *n* córas fuaraithe

coolness *n* fionnuaire

coop *n* cúb

co-operate *v* comhoibrigh

co-operation *n* comhar, comhoibriú **to co-operate with somebody** dul i gcomhar le duine

co-operative *adj* comhoibritheach *n* comharchumann

co-ordinate *v* comhordaigh

co-ordinates *pl* comhordanáidí

cope *v* déileáil

copier *n* cóipire

copious *adj* flaithiúil, fras

copper *n* copar

copulate *v* déan comhriachtain, cúpláil

copulation *n* comhriachtain

copy[1] *n* cóip, macasamhail **to make a copy of something** cóip a dhéanamh de

copy[2] *v* athscríobh, cóipeáil

copybook *n* cóipleabhar

copying *n* cóipeáil

copyright *n* cóipcheart

coracle *n* curach

coral *n* coiréal

coral reef *n* sceir choiréil

cord *n* sreang, corda, téad **umbilical cord** sreang imleacáin, **(the) vocal cords** téada an ghutha

corduroy *n* corda an rí

cordial *n* coirdial

core *n* ceartlár, cuilithe

Cork *n* Corcaigh **Cork city** cathair Chorcaí

cork *n* corc

corkscrew *n* corcscriú

corn[1] *n* **(on foot)** fadharcán

corn[2] *n* **(grain)** arbhar

cornea *n* coirne

corner[1] *n* cúinne, cearn, cúil, coirnéal, **(kick)** cúinneach **blind corner** coirnéal caoch, **every corner of the world** gach ccarn den domhan

corner[2] *v* teanntaigh

corner-stone *n* cloch choirnéil

cornet *n* coirnéad

corn flakes *pl* calóga arbhair

cornflour *n* gránphlúr

Cornwall *n* Corn na Breataine

coronary *adj* corónach

coronation *n* corónú

coroner *n* cróinéir

coroner's inquest *n* coiste cróinéara

corporal *n* ceannaire

corporal punishment *n* pionós corportha

corporate *adj* corparáideach

corporation *n* cuallacht, bardas **Dublin Corporation** Bardas Átha Cliath

corps *pl* cór **diplomatic corps** cór taidhleoireachta

corpse *n* corp, corpán, marbhán

corpulent *adj* beathaithe

corral *n* banrach

correct *adj* ceart, cruinn *v* ceartaigh

correction *n* ceartúchán

correlation *n* comhghaol

correspond *n* comhfhreagair

correspondence *n* comhfhreagracht, **(of letters)** comhfhreagras

correspondent *n* comhfhreagraí **sports correspondent** comhfhreagraí spóirt

corridor *n* pasáiste, conair

corroborate *v* comhthacaigh (le)

corrode *v* cnaígh, creim

corroded metal *n* miotal cnaíte

corrupt *adj* truaillithe *v* truailligh

corset *n* cóirséad

Corsica *n* an Chorsaic

cosmetic *adj* maisitheach *n* cosmaid

cosmic *n* cosmach

cosmopolitan *adj* iltíreach

cosmos *n* cosmas

cost *n* costas *v* cosain

cost of living n costas maireachtála
costly adj costasach
costume n bréagéide
cosy adj seascair
cottage n teachín, iostán
cotton n cadás
cotton wool n olann chadáis, flocas cadáis
couch n tolg
cough n casacht v casacht a dhéanamh
coughing n casachtach
council n comhairle
councillor n comhairleoir
counsel n comhairle
counsellor n comhairleoir
count[1] n comhaireamh, cuntas, (title) cunta the first count (after election) an chéad chomhaireamh
count [2] v áirigh, comhair
countenance n cuntanós
counter[1] prefix ath-
counter[2] n (in shop) cuntar
counteract v cuir bacainn air
counteraction n frithghníomh
counterblow n athbhuille
counterfeiter n falsaitheoir airgid
counterfoil n comhdhuille
counterpart n macasamhail
countersign v comhshínigh
countess n cuntaois
counting n áireamh, comhaireamh
countless adj gan áireamh
country n tír, tuath
countryside n taobh tíre, tuath in the country faoin tuath
county n contae
county council n comhairle contae
couple n cúpla, lánúin v cúpláil engaged couple lánúin, a couple of people cúpla duine
couplet n leathrann
coupon n cúpón

courage n misneach, sprid, uchtach, ugach
courageous adj misniúil
courgette n cúirséad
courier n teachtaire
course n cúrsa the course of the sun cúrsa na gréine, one year, two year, three year course cúrsa bliana, dhá bhliain, trí bliana
coursing n cúrsáil
court n cúirt the Four Courts na Ceithre Cúirteanna, juvenile court cúirt d'aosánaigh, squash court cúirt scuaise
courteous adj síodúil
courtesy n cúirtéis
courtier n cúirteoir
courting n cúirtéireacht, suirí
court-martial n armchúirt to court-martial a soldier armchúirt a chur ar shaighdiúir
court-yard n clós
cousin n first cousin col ceathrair, second cousin col seisir, third cousin col ochtair
cove n cuas
covenant n cúnant
cover[1] n coim, clúdach under the cover of darkness faoi choim na hoíche
cover[2] v clúdaigh, cumhdaigh
coverage n tuairisciú
covering n cumhdach, scraith
covet v santaigh
covetous adj antlásach
covetousness n antlás
cow n bó
coward n cladhaire, meatachán
cowardice n claidhreacht, meatacht
cowardly adj cladhartha, meata
cowboy n buachaill bó
cower v cúb
cowhouse n bóitheach
cowl n cochall

cowslip *n* bainne bó bleachtáin

crab *n* portán

crack[1] *n* scoilt, gág, cnag, **(fun)** craic

crack[2] *v* cnag

cracker *n* pléascóg

crackle *n* cnagarnach

cradle *n* cliabhán

craft[1] *n* **(boat etc)** árthach

craft[2] *n* ceardaíocht

craftsperson *n* ceardaí, saor

craftsmanship *n* saoirseacht

craftwork *n* ceardaíocht

crafty *adj* cleasach, glic

crag *n* creig

cram *v* brúigh, pulc

cramp *n* crampa

cramped *adj* craptha

cranberry *n* mónóg

crane[1] *n* **(bird)** corr mhóna

crane[2] *n* **(building)** crann tógála

crash[1] *n* **(sudden)** plimp, tuairt, **(financial)** tobthitim

crash[2] *v* tuairteáil **the car crashed into a tree** bhuail an carr crann

crash-helmet *n* clogad cosanta

crate *n* cis

crater *n* cráitéar

cravat *n* carbhat

crave *v* cuir dúil chráite i rud

craving *n* andúil **craving for tobacco** gabhair thobac

crawl *n, v* snámh

crawling *n* lámhacán

crayfish *n* cráifisc, piardóg

crayon *n* crián

craze *n* dúil, tóir

craziness *n* mearaí

crazy *adj* ar mire, ar buile, as do mheabhair

crazy golf *n* galf mearaí

crazy person *n* gealt

creak *n* díoscán *v* díosc

creaking *n* díoscán

cream[1] *n* smearadh, uachtar **sun cream** smearadh gréine, **ice-cream** uachtar reoite

cream[2] *adj* **(colour)** bánbhuí

creamy *adj* uachtarúil

crease *n* filltín *v* filltíní a chur i rud

creased *adj* rocach

create *v* cruthaigh

creation *n* cruthú

creative *adj* cruthaitheach

creator *n* cruthaitheoir

creature *n* créatúr

crèche *n* naíolann (lae)

credentials *pl* dintiúir

credible *adj* sochreidte

credit *n* creidiúint, creidmheas, cairde, sochar **on credit** ar cairde, **she got no credit for her work** ní bhfuair sí aon chreidiúint dá hobair

credit card *n* cárta creidmheasa

creditable *adj* creidiúnach

creditor *n* creidiúnaí

creed *n* cré

creek *n* góilín

creep *v* téaltaigh, sleamhnaigh

creeper *n* **(plants)** athair

cremate *v* créam

cremation *n* créamadh

crematorium *n* créamatóiriam

crescent *n* corrán **crescent moon** corrán gealaí

crest *n* cíor, mullach

crestfallen *adj* maolchluasach

crevice *n* scáine

crew *n* criú, foireann **film crew** foireann scannáin

crib *n* cruib, mainséar

cricket[1] *n* **(game)** cruicéad

cricket[2] *n* **(insect)** criogar

crime *n* coir

criminal *adj* coiriúil *n* coirpeach

crimson *adj* corcairdhearg

cripple *v* craplaigh

crisis *n* géarchéim, **(medical)** aothú

crisp *adj* briosc

crisps *pl* brioscáin (phrátaí)

criss-cross *v* trasnaigh a chéile

criterion *n* slat tomhais, critéar

critic *n* criticeoir, léirmheastóir

critical *adj* criticiúil

critical analysis *n* léirmheastóireacht

critical awareness *n* feasacht chriticiúil

criticise *v* cáin

criticism *n* cáineadh, léirmheastóireacht, lochtú

croak *n* grág *v* grágaíl a dhéanamh

crochet *n* cróise

crocodile *n* crogall

crocodile clip *n* fáiscín crogaill

croft *n* crochta

crook[1] *n* **(of shepherd)** caimín crúca, bachall

crook[2] *n* **(person)** caimiléir

crooked *adj* bachallach, cam

crop *n* barr

crop rotation *n* uainíocht na mbarr

cross[1] *n* croch, cros **the sign of the cross** comhartha na croise, **the Red Cross** an Chros Dhearg

cross[2] *v* trasnaigh, crosáil

cross[3] *adj* cancrach, cantalach

crossbar *n* trasnán

crossbreed *v* cros-síolraigh

crossbreeding *n* cros-síolrú

cross-channel calls *pl* glaonna thar chaolmhuir, **(from Ireland to Britain)** glaonna chun na Breataine

cross-examine *v* croscheistigh

crossfire *n* croslámhach

crossing *n* trasrian, crosaire **pedestrian crossing** trasrian coisithe

cross-legged *adj* an dá chos trasna ar a chéile

cross-question *n* croscheist *v* croscheistigh

cross-reference *n* crostagairt

crossroads *n* crosaire, crosbhealach, crosbhóthar

cross-section *n* trasghearradh

crossword *n* crosfhocal

crotch *n* gabhal

crow *n* préachán

crowbar *n* gró

crowd *n* slua, scata *v* plódaigh

crowded *adj* plódaithe

crown *n* coróin *v* corónaigh

crozier *n* bachall

crucifix *n* cros chéasta

crucify *v* céas

crude *adj* amh, tútach

crude oil *n* amhola

cruel *adj* cruálach, danartha

cruelty *n* cruálacht, danarthacht

cruise *n*, *v* cúrsáil **cruise boat** bád chúrsála

cruiser *n* cúrsóir, long chúrsála

crumb *n* grabhróg **crumbs** mionbhruar

crunch *n* cnagarnach *v* cnag **when it comes to the crunch** nuair a théann sé go cnámh na huillinne

crunching *n* cnagadh

crush *n* plódú *v* brúigh

crushing *n* mionbhrú, meilt

crust *n* crústa

crusty *adj* faoi chrústa, **(of person)** cancrach

crutch *n* maide croise

cry *n* faí *v* caoin

crying *n* gol **crying over spilt milk** ag gol in áit na maoiseoige

crystal *n* criostal

crystallise *v* criostalaigh

cubby-hole *n* caochóg

cube *n* ciúb *v* ciúbaigh
cubic *adj* ciúbach **cubic foot** troigh chiúbach
cubicle *n* cillín
cuckoo *n* cuach
cucumber *n* cúcamar
cuddle *v* muirnigh, fáisc
cudgel *n* lorga
cue *n* **(snooker)** cleathóg
cuff *n* **(dress)** cufa
culminate *v* tar chun buaice
culprit *n* coirpeach
cult *n* cultas
cultivate *v* saothraigh
cultivation *n* saothrú
cultural affairs *pl* cúrsaí cultúir
culture *n* cultúr
cultured *adj* cultúrtha
cunning *adj* glic
cup *n* corn, cupán **the McCarthy Cup** Corn Mhic Cárthaigh
curable *adj* inleigheasta
curate *n* séiplíneach
curb *n* srian *v* srian, ceansaigh
cure *n, v* leigheas
curfew *n* cuirfiú
curiosity *n* fiosracht
curious *adj* fiosrach
curl *n* **(of hair)** coirnín
curlew *n* crotach
curly *adj* catach, coirníneach
currach *n* curach, naomhóg
currant *n* cuirín
currency *n* airgead reatha, airgeadra, cúrsaíocht
current affairs/events *pl* cúrsaí reatha
curriculum *n* curaclam
curry *n* curaí
curse *n* cascaine, mallacht *v* eascainigh
cursor *n* **(computer)** cursóir
curtail *v* cuir teorainn le
curtain *n* cuirtín

curve *n, v* cuar
cushion *n* adhartán, cúisín *v* plúch
custard *n* custard
custodian *n* caomhnóir, coimeádaí
custody *n* coimeád
custom *n* gnás, gnáth, nós
custom-built *adj* saincheaptha
customary *adj* gnách
customer *n* custaiméir
customs *pl* custam **customs officer** oifigeach custaim, **the Customs House** Teach an Chustaim, **Customs and Excise** Custam agus Mál
cut *n* gearradh *v* ciorraigh, gearr
cut-back *n* gearradh siar
cut fine *v* mionghearr
cut-throat competition *n* deargiomaíocht
cutlery *n* sceanra
cutting *n* **(newspaper)** gearrthán
cutlet *n* gearrthóg
cyanide *n* ciainíd
cycle *n* timthriall *v* rothaigh **planetary cycle** timthriall pláinéadach
cycle track *n* raon rothar
cyclic *adj* timthriallach
cycling *n* rothaíocht
cyclist *n* rothaí
cyclone *n* cioclón
cylinder *n* sorcóir **gas cylinder** sorcóir gáis
cymbal *n* ciombal
cynic *n* cinicí
cynicism *n* ciniceas
cynical *n* ciniciúil
Cyprus *n* an Chipir
cypress *n* **(tree)** cúfróg
cyst *n* cist
czar *n* sár
Czech[1] *n* **(language)** an tSeicis
Czech[2] *adj, n* Seiceach

D

dab *n* daba

dad *n* daid

daddy *n* daidí

daddy-long-legs *n* snáthaid an phúca, Pilib an gheataire

daffodil *n* lus an chromchinn

dagger *n* miodóg

Dáil Deputy *n* Teachta Dála

Dáil sitting days *pl* laethanta suí na Dála

daily *adv* go laethúil

dainties *pl* billíní beadaí

dainty *adj* beadaí

dairy *n* déirí

dairying *n* déiríocht

daisy *n* nóinín

dale *n* gleanntán

dam *n* damba *v* dambáil

damage *n* damáiste, díobháil, dochar *v* damáiste a dhéanamh do rud, dochar/díobháil a dhéanamh do dhuine

damages *pl* damáistí

damn *v* damnaigh **damn you!** drochrath ort!

damnation *n* damnú

damned *adj* damanta, damnaithe

damp *adj* tais *n* taisleach

dampen *v* taisrigh

dampness *n* taise

dance *n* damhsa, rince *v* damhsaigh, rinc

dancer *n* rinceoir, damhsóir

dancing *n* damhsa, rince

dandelion *n* caisearbhán

dandruff *n* sail chnis

Dane *n* Danmhargach, (historical) Danar

danger *n* contúirt, dainséar, gábh, guais, baol

dangerous *adj* contúirteach, guaiseach, baolach

Danish *adj* Danmhargach *n* (language) an Danmhairgis

dangle *v* croith

dangling *adj* ar bogarnach

dare *v* I dare you to do it! do dhúshlán é a dhéanamh!

daring *adj* dána

dark *adj* diamhair, dorcha, dubh, ciar, modartha

darken *v* dall, doiléirigh, dorchaigh, dubhaigh, teimhligh

darkness *n* dorchacht, dubh

darling! *n* a stór! a mhuirnín! a thaisce! a rún! a chuisle! a ansacht!

darn *v* dearnáil

darning *n* dearnáil, cliath

dart *n* dairt

dash *n* sciuird *v* rop, sciurd

dashboard *n* painéal ionstraimí

dashing *adj* rábach

data *pl* sonraí **data processing** próiseáil sonraí, **Data Protection Act** an tAcht um Chosaint Sonraí

data-base *n* bunachar sonraí

date[1] *n* dáta

date[2] *v* to date somebody siúl amach le duine

dative *adj, n* tabharthach

daughter *n* iníon

daughter-in-law *n* banchliamhain

daughter house *n* craobhtheach

dawn *n* breacadh an lae

day *n* lá **St Patrick's Day** Lá Fhéile Pádraig

day after tomorrow *adv* anóirthear, amanathar

day-break *n* camhaoir, amhscarthanach

day-dreaming *n* taibhreamh na súl oscailte, aislingeacht

daylight *n* solas an lae

dazzle *v* caoch

dead *adj* marbh, ar shlí na fírinne

deadline *n* spriocdháta, sprioclá

deadlock *n* sáinn

deadly *adj* marfach

dead person *n* marbh, marbhán

deaf *adj* bodhar

deafness *n* bodhaire **feigned deafness** bodhaire Uí Laoire

deal *n* margadh *v* déileáil **(cards)** déan **it's a deal** bíodh sé ina mhargadh

dealer *n* díoltóir, déileálaí

dealing *n* déileáil

delay *n* moill *v* moilligh

dean *n* déan

dear[1] *adj* daor, costasach

dear[2] *adj* dil, dílis **dear mother** a mháthair dhílis

Dear Madam / Sir A Chara

dearest *adj* ansa

death *n* éag, bás

debar *v* coisc, toirmisc

debase *v* truailligh, ísligh

debate *n* díospóireacht *v* pléigh

debauchery *n* drabhlás

debit *n* dochar **direct debit** dochar díreach

debris *n* smionagar, bruscar

debt *n* comaoin, fiach

debtor *n* féichiúnaí, fiachóir

debug *v* dífhabhtaigh

decade *n* deich mbliana, **(of rosary)** deichniúr

decadent *adj* meatach

decaffeinated *adj* **(coffee)** (caife) saor ó chaiféin

decapitate *v* dícheann

decathlon *n* comórtas deich mír

decay *n* léig, lobhadh *v* feoigh, dreoigh, meath, lobh

decayed *adj* dreoite

decaying *adj* meatach

decease *v* éag, bás

deceased *adj* nach maireann, marbh, básaithe

deceit *n* cealg, calaois

deceitful *adj* calaoiseach

deceive *v* cealg, meall **to deceive somebody** cluain a chur ar dhuine

deceiver *n* cluanaire

December *n* Nollaig, mí na Nollag

decency *n* cneastacht

decent *adj* cuibhiúil, modhúil

decentralised *adj* díláraithe

deception *n* dallamullóg, cluain, mealladh

deceptive *adj* mealltach

decibel *n* deicibeil

decide *v* cinn

decided *adj* dearfa, cinnte, beartaithe

deciduous *adj* duillsilteach

deciduous tree *n* crann duillsilteach

decimal *adj* deachúlach *adj, n* deachúil

decimal point *n* pointe deachúil

decipher *v* imscaoil

decision *n* cinneadh

decision-making *n* cinnteoireacht

decisive *adj* cinntitheach

decisiveness *n* diongbháilteacht

deck *n* deic **cassette deck** deic caiséad, **flight deck** deic eitilte

declaration *n* dearbhú, fógairt

declare *v* fógair, admhaigh, dearbhaigh

declension *n* díochlaonadh

decline[1] *v* **(grammar)** díochlaon

decline[2] *n* meathlú, trá *v* meath, tráigh

declining *adj* meatach
decode *v* díchódaigh
decompose *v* dreoigh, dianscaoil
decontaminate *v* díshalaigh
decorate *v* maisigh
decoration *n* maisiú, maisiúchán
decorative *adj* maisiúil
decorous *adj* cuibhiúil
decorum *n* cuibhiúlacht
decrease *n* laghdú, maolú *v* laghdaigh, maolaigh
decrepit *adj* díblí
dedicate *v* tíolaic, tiomnaigh, toirbhir
dedication *n* tiomnú, toirbhirt, dúthracht
deduce *v* asbheir, tuig as
deduct *v* bain de, bain as
deduction *n* asbhaint, tátal
deed *n* gníomh, gníomhas
deep *adj* domhain, duibheagánach
deep freezer *n* domhainreoiteoir
deer *n* fia **red deer** fia rua
deface *v* mill
defamation *n* aithisiú, clúmhilleadh
defamatory *adj* aithiseach, clúmhillteach
defame *v* aithisigh, clúmhill
default *n* loiceadh, faillí
defeat *n* coscairt, díomua *v* cloígh
defeated *adj* cloíte
defect *n* fabht
defective *adj* éalangach, easpach
defence *n* cosaint **defence forces** fórsaí cosanta
defend *v* cosain
defendant *n* cosantóir
defender *n* cosantóir, **(sports)** cúlaí
defensive *adj* cosantach **defensive features (of walls etc)** córacha cosanta
defer *v* cuir siar
defiant *adj* dúshlánach

deficiency *n* easpa, uireasa
deficient *adj* easnamhach, uireasach
defile *v* salaigh, truailligh
define *v* sainmhínigh, sonraigh, sainigh
definite *adj* dearfa, deimhin
definition *n* sainmhíniú
definitive *adj* deifinídeach
deflate *v* díbholg
deflation *n* **(money)** díbhoilsciú
deforestation *n* díchoilltiú
deform *v* díchum
deformed *adj* míchumtha
deformity *n* cithréim
defrost *v* díshioc
deft *adj* deaslámhach
defunct *adj* as feidhm
defy *v* dúshlán duine a thabhairt
degrade *v* díspeag
degrading *adj* táireach
degree *n* céim **7 degrees** seacht gcéim
de-ice *v* dí-oighrigh
de-icer *n* dí-oighreán
deity *n* dia
dejected *adj* gruama, atuirseach
dejection *n* atuirse
delay *n, v* moill
delaying *adj* moillitheach *n* moilleadóireacht
delegate *n* toscaire
delegation *n* toscaireacht
delete *v* bain amach
deliberate *v* déan machnamh ar
deliberately *adv* d'aon ghnó, d'aon turas, d'aon aidhm
delicacies *pl* sólaistí
delicacy *n* fíneáltacht
delicate *adj* cigilteach, leochaileach
delicious *adj* caithiseach, dea-bhlasta
delight *n* aoibhneas, gliondar *v* cuir aoibhneas/gliondar ar

delightful *adj* álainn, aoibhinn
delinquent *n* ciontóir
delirious *adj* rámhailleach
deliver *v* seachaid, toirbhir
delivery *n* seachadadh, toirbhirt
  cash on delivery (c.o.d.) íoc ar
  sheachadadh (í.a.s.)
delude *v* meall
deluge *n* díle
delusion *n* seachrán, siabhrán
delusion of grandeur *n* siabhrán
  mórgachta
demand *n* éileamh, ráchairt *v* éiligh
  tickets are in demand tá éileamh
  ar thicéid, **to demand** rud a
  éileamh
demand and supply *n* éileamh agus
  soláthar
demanding *adj* éilitheach
demarcation *n* críochú
demented *adj* néaltraithe
democracy *n* daonlathas
democrat *n* daonlathaí
democratic *adj* daonlathach
demolish *v* scartáil
demon *n* deamhan
demonstrate *v* **(political)** léirsigh,
  léirigh
demonstration *n* léirsiú, léiriú
demonstrator *n* léirsitheoir
demonstrative *adj* taispeántach
demotion *n* céim síos
demure *adj* stuama
den *n* prochóg
denationalise *v* dínáisiúnaigh
denial *n* ceilt, séanadh
denigrate *v* aithisigh
denigratory *adj* aithiseach
denim *n* deinim
Denmark *n* an Danmhairg
denomination *n* sainchreideamh
denote *v* comharthaigh

denounce *v* cáin
dense *adj* dlúth
density *n* dlús
dent *n*, *v* ding
dental *adj* déadach
dental floss *n* flas fiacla
dental health *n* sláinteachas fiacla
dentist *n* fiaclóir
dentistry *n* fiaclóireacht
deny *v* diúltaigh, séan
deodorant *n* díbholaíoch
depart *v* imigh
department *n* roinn **state**
  departments ranna stáit,
  Government departments ranna
  rialtais **department store** siopa /
  stór ilranna
departmental *adj* rannach
departure *n* imeacht
departure lounge *n* tolglann
  imeachta
depend (on) *v* braith ar
dependable *adj* muiníneach
dependant *adj* spleách
dependence *n* muinín, tuilleamaí
depending on (somebody,
  something) i dtuilleamaí (duine,
  ruda)
depict *v* léirigh
deplete *v* ídigh
deplore *v* cásaigh
depose *v* athrígh, cuir as oifig
deposit *n* éarlais *v* taisc **to put a**
  deposit on something éarlais a
  chur i rud
depot *n* stóras
depreciate *v* **the house**
  depreciated thit luach an tí
depress *v* ísligh, domheanma a chur
  ar
depression *n* lionndubh, néal
deprive *v* bain de
deprivation *n* díth

depth n doimhneacht, domhain, duibheagán **depth gauge** tomhsaire doimhneachta

deputy n teachta, toscaire

deputy- prefix leas-

derail v cuir de na ráillí

derange v mearaigh

deranged adj seachránach

derangement n seachrán

deride v fonóid a dhéanamh faoi

derision n scigmhagadh

derisive adj magúil, scigiúil

derisory adj fonóideach

derivative adj díorthach n fréamhaí

dermatitis n deirmitíteas

derogatory adj dímheasúil

Derry n Doire

descend v tuirling **descend from** síolraigh ó

descendant n sliochtach, sliocht

descent n tuirlingt

describe v cuir síos air

description n comhairthaí súirt, cur síos

desert[1] n fásach

desert[2] v tréig

deserve v tuill

design[1] v dear

design[2] n dearadh, patrún

designer n dearthóir

desirable adj inmhianaithe, meallacach

desire n mian, toil v santaigh, togair, toil

desist v scoir

desk n deasc

desk publishing n (**desktop publishing**) foilsiú deisce

desolate adj bánaithe, dearóil

despair n éadóchas

despairing adj éadóchasach

despicable adj suarach, táir

despise v díspeag

despite prep d'ainneoin, in ainneoin

dessert n milseog

destination n ceann cúrsa, ceann scríbe

destined adj i ndán

destiny n cinniúint

destitute adj dealbh, dealúsach

destitution n dealús

destroy v scrios

destroyer n díothóir

destruction n díothú, léirscrios, milleadh, scrios

destructive adj millteach, scriosach

detach v scoir

detail n sonra, sonrú

detailed adj mion **detailed account** miontuairisc, cur síos mion

detain v coimeád, coinnigh

detainee n géibheannach

detect v braith, fionn

detective n lorgaire, bleachtaire

detective novel n úrscéal bleachtaireachta

detector n brathadóir **lie detector** brathadóir bréige

detention n coimeád, coinneáil

deter v coisc

detergent n glantach

deteriorate v claochlaigh, meath

determination n cinntiú, diongbháilteacht

determined adj daingean, diongbháilte

deterrent n cosc

detest v fuathaigh **I detest them** is fuath liom iad

detestable adj fuafar

detonate v maidhm

detonating adj maidhmitheach

detonating fuse n aidhnín maidhmitheach

detonation *n* maidhm

detonator *n* maidhmitheoir

detour *n* cor bealaigh

detract *v* bain ó chlú duine

detriment *n* aimhleas, dochar

detrimental *adj* díobhálach

deuce *n* dias

devaluation *n* díluacháil

devalue *v* díluacháil

devastation *n* léirscrios, slad

develop *v* forbair, (a film) réal

development *n* forbairt, forás

deviate *v* claon ó

device *n* áis, gléas, sás, seift tapping device gléas cúléisteachta

devil *n* diabhal, púca na mbeann, an tAinspiorad

devise *v* cum, seiftigh

devolution *n* déabhlóid

devote (to) *n* toirbhir do

devoted *adj* díograiseach

devour *v* alp

dew *n* drúcht

diabetes *n* diaibéiteas

diabetic *n* diaibéiteach

diagnose *v* fáthmheas

diagnosis *n* fáthmheas, diagnóis

diagnostician *n* diagnóiseoir

diagonal *adj* fiar *n* trasnán

diagram *n* léaráid

dial *n* diail *v* diailigh

dialect *n* canúint

dialogue *n* agallamh (beirte)

diameter *n* lárlíne, trastomhas

diamond *n* diamant, (cards) muileata

diaphragm *n* scairt

diarrhoea *n* buinneach, rith buan, scaoilteacht

diary *n* dialann, cín lae

dice *n* dílse, díslí

dictaphone *n* deachtafón

dictate *v* deachtaigh

dictating machine *n* gléas deachtaithe

dictation *n* deachtú

dictator *n* deachtóir

diction *n* urlabhra

dictionary *n* foclóir

die *v* éag, síothlaigh he died cailleadh é, fuair sé bás

diesel *n* díosal

diet *n* réim bia, aiste bia balanced diet réim/aiste chothrom bia

dietary fibre *n* snáithín cothaitheach

dietician *n* bia-eolaí

difference *n* difear, difríocht

different *adj* difriúil, éagsúil

differentiate *v* idirdhealaigh

differentiation *n* idirdhealú

difficult *adj* deacair, doiligh, duaisiúil

difficulty *n* cruachás, deacracht

diffident *adj* cotúil

diffuse *adj* spréite *v* réscaip

dig *v* rómhair, tóch, tochail

dig in *v* talmhaigh

digest *v* díleáigh

digestion *n* díleá

digestive system *n* córas díleáite

digging *n* tochailt

digit *n* méar, digit

digital *adj* digiteach, uimhriúil

dignified *adj* maorga, státúil

dignity *n* dínit

digress *v* dul ar seachmall ó

dilapidated *adj* ainriochtach, díblí

dilation *n* leathadh

dilemma *n* to be in a dilemma bheith idir dhá thine Bhealtaine

diligence *n* dúthracht

diligent *adj* dúthrachtach, saothrach

dilute *v* caolaigh, tanaigh

diluted *adj* tanaí

dilution *n* tanú

dim *adj* doiléir

dimension *n* toise, buntomhas

diminish *v* laghdaigh

diminutive *adj* mion *n* díspeagadh

din *n* fothram

dining room *n* seomra bia, seomra itheacháin

dinner *n* dinnéar

dinosaur *n* dineasár

diode *n* dé-óid

dip *n* tumadh *v* fothraig, tum

diphthong *n* défhoghar

diploma *n* dioplóma

diplomacy *n* taidhleoireacht

diplomat *n* taidhleoir

diphtheria *n* diftéire

dipping tank *n* dabhach dhipeála

dire *adj* tubaisteach

direct *adj* díreach *v* treoraigh, stiúir

direct debit mandate *n* mandáid dírdhochair

direction[1] *n* aird, seol, treo, treoir from all directions as gach aird

direction[2] *n* stiúradh

directive *n* treoir

director *n* stiúrthóir Director of Public Prosecutions (DPP) Stiúrthóir Ionchúiseamh Poiblí

directory *n* eolaí, eolaire

dirt *n* sail, salachar

dirty *adj* salach, cáidheach *v* salaigh

disability *n* míchumas

disabled *adj* míchumasach

disadvantage *n* míbhuntáiste

disadvantaged *adj* faoi mhíbhuntáiste

disadvantageous *adj* míbhuntáisteach

disagree *v* easaontaigh

disagreeable *adj* míthaitneamhach

disagreement *n* easaontas

disappear *v* imigh as radharc

disappoint *v* meall

disappointed *adj* díomách I am disappointed tá díomá orm

disappointment *n* díomá

disapproval *n* míshástacht

disapprove *v* cuir in aghaidh ruda, drochbharúil a bheith agat de rud

disarm *v* dí-armáil

disarmament *n* dí-armáil multilateral, unilateral disarmament dí-armáil iltaobhach, aontaobhach

disaster *n* tubaiste

disastrous *adj* tubaisteach

disbelief *n* díchreideamh

discarded *adj* caite i dtraipisí

discerning *adj* tuisceanach

discharge *n* sceitheadh, sileadh *v* díluchtaigh, sceith, scaoil ear discharge sileadh cluaise

disciple *n* deisceabal

discipline *n* disciplín, smacht there can be no success without discipline ní bhíonn an rath ach mar a mbíonn an smacht

disclose *v* foilsigh, nocht

disclosure *n* nochtadh

disco *n* dioscó

discomfort *n* míchompord

disconcert *v* duine a bhaint dá threoir

disconnect *v* scoir

discontent *n* míshásamh

discontinue *v* éirigh as

discount *n* lacáiste, lascaine

discourage *v* drochmhisneach a chur ar dhuine

discouragement *n* drochmhisneach

discourteous *adj* míchúirtéiseach

discover *v* fionn

discovery *n* fionnachtain

discredit *n* míchreidiúint
v drochtheist a chur ar dhuine

discreet *adj* discréideach, foscúil, fothainiúil

discrepancy *n* difríocht

discretion *n* discréid

discretionary expenditure *n* caiteachas roghnach

discriminate *v* idirdhealaigh

discrimination *n* idirdhealú, leithcheal

discus throwing *n* caitheamh na teisce

discuss *v* pléigh **to discuss the question** an cheist a phlé

discussion *n* díospóireacht, cíoradh, plé, caibidil **under discussion** faoi chaibidil

disdain *n* drochmheas

disdainful *adj* dímheasúil

disease *n* aicíd, galar **to catch a disease** galar a tholgadh, **sexually transmitted disease** galar gnéas-tarchurtha

disembark *v* dul i dtír

disengage *v* scaoil

disentangle *v* réitigh

disfigure *v* máchailigh

disfigurement *n* ainimh

disgrace *n* aithis

disgruntled *adj* míshásta

disguise *n* bréagriocht, cur i gcéill *v* cuir bréagríocht ar, ceil

disgust *n* déistin, samhnas, gráin, múisc **you disgust me!** cuireann tú déistin orm!

disgusting *adj* déistineach, samhnasach

dish *n* mias, soitheach

dishevelled *adj* aimhréidh, gliobach

dishonest *adj* mímhacánta, mí-ionraic

dishonesty *n* caimiléireacht, mí-ionracas, mímhacántacht

dishonour *n* easonóir *v* easonóraigh

dishwasher *n* miasniteoir

disillusion *n* oscailt súl

disinfect *v* dífhabhtaigh

disinfectant *n* dífhabhtán

disinherit *v* duine a chur as oidhreacht

disintegrate *v* tit ó chéile

disinterested *adj* neamhchlaonta, neamh-fhéinchúiseach

disjointed *adj* curtha as alt, scaipthe

disk *n* diosca **hard disk** cruadhiosca

disk drive *n* dioscthiomáint

disk jockey (dj) *n* ceirneoir, diosceachaí

diskette *n* discéad

dislike *n* míthaitneamh *v* **I dislike them** ní maith liom iad, ní thaitníonn siad liom

dislocate *v* asaltaigh

dislodge *v* asáitigh

disloyal *adj* mídhílis, mídhlisteanach

dismal *adj* duairc, dubh, dubhach

dismantle *v* díchóimeáil

dismay *n* anbhá

dismiss *v* dífhostaigh, caith as do cheann **to dismiss something** spior spear a dhéanamh de rud

dismount *v* tuirling

disobedience *n* easumhlaíocht

disobedient *adj* easumhal

disobey *v* bheith easumhal do

disorder *n* ainghléas, ainriail, tranglam

disorderly *adv* clamprach

disown *v* séan

disparage *v* tarcaisnigh

disparaging *adj* tarcaisneach

dispatch *n* seoladh *v* seol

dispel *v* scaip

dispensary *n* íoclann

disperse *v* scaip, spréigh

dispersion *n* scaipeadh

displace *v* díláithrigh

display *n* taispeáint *v* taispeáin **on display** ar taispeáint

displease *v* diomú a chur ar dhuine

displeased *adj* míshásta

displeasure *n* míshásamh

disposable *adj* indiúscartha **disposable income** ioncam indiúscartha

disposal *n* diúscairt **waste disposal** diúscairt dramhaíola

dispose *v* srathnaigh, socraigh

disposition *n* aigne

dispossess *v* díshealbhaigh

dispossession *n* díshealbhú

disproportionate *adj* díréireach, éaguimseach

disprove *v* bréagnaigh

dispute *n* aighneas, argóint, caingean, iomarbhá *v* pléadáil

disputation *n* allagar, pléadáil

disqualify *v* dícháiligh

disregard *n* neamhshuim *v* neamhshuim a dhéanamh de

disreputable *adj* míchlúiteach

disrepute *n* míchlú

disrespect *n* dímheas, easurraim

disrespectful *adj* easurramach, beagmheastúil

disrupt *v* réab

dissatisfied *adj* míshásta

disseminate *v* craobhscaoil

dissemination *n* craobhscaoileadh

dissimilar *adj* neamhchosúil

dissent *n* easaontas *v* easaontaigh

dissipated *adj* drabhlásach

dissociate (from) *v* scar (ó)

dissolute *adj* réiciúil, scaoilteach

dissolve *v* díleáigh, scaoil, tuaslaig

dissuade *v* áitigh ar dhuine gan

distance *n* achar

distant *adj* i bhfad, coimhthíoch

distaste *n* drochbhlas, gráin

distasteful *adj* déistineach

distil *v* driog

distiller *n* stiléir

distillery *n* drioglann

distilling *n* stiléireacht

distinct *adj* léir, glinn, soiléir

distinction *n* céimíocht

distinctive *adj* sainiúil, suaithinseach

distinguish *v* dealaigh

distinguished *adj* céimiúil

distort *v* cam, athchum

distortion *n* athchuma, díchumadh

distract *v* aire duine a bhaint de rud

distraction *n* caitheamh aimsire, seachrán

distress *n* géibheann, gátar, anacair, angar, anó, deacracht

distressed *adj* anacrach, anróiteach

distressing *adj* anacrach

distribute *v* dáil, riar, roinn

distribution *n* dáileadh

district *n* ceantar, limistéar

distrust *n* drochiontaoibh, mímhuinín **to distrust somebody** drochmheas a bheith agat ar dhuine

disturb *v* cuir isteach ar

disturbance *n* suaitheadh, achrann

disturbed *adj* suaite

disunion *n* easaontas

disuse *n* léig *v* dul as feidhm, dul i léig

disused *adj* ar ceal

DIT (Dublin Institute of Technology) *n* Institiúid Teicneolaíochta Bhaile Átha Cliath

ditch *n* clais, díog

dive *n* tumadh *v* tum

dive-bomber *n* buamadóir scuibe

diver *n* tumadóir

diverse *adj* ilghnéitheach

diversify *v* éagsúlaigh

diversion *n* atreorú

divert *v* cuir ar mhalairt slí

divide *v* deighil, roinn

dividend *n* díbhinn

divine *adj* diaga

diving *n* tumadóireacht

divinity *n* diagacht

division *n* deighilt, roinnt

divorce *n* colscaradh *v* scar

divorced *adj* scartha

divulge *v* sceith

dizziness *n* meadhrán, mearbhall

dizzy *adj* meadhránach

do *v* déan **doing** ag déanamh, **to be done for** do chuid aráin a bheith ite

docile *adj* ceansa, macánta

dock[1] *n* **(law)** gabhann

dock[2] *n* **(harbour)** duga

dock[3] *n* **(plant)** copóg

dock[4] *v* teacht chun duga/cé

docket *n* duillín

dockyard *n* longlann

doctor *n* dochtúir **doctor on call** dochtúir ar fáil

document *n* cáipéis, doiciméad, **(written)** scríbhinn *v* doiciméadaigh

documentary *adj* cáipéiseach *n* clár faisnéise

documentary sources *pl* foinsí doiciméadacha

documentation *n* doiciméadú

dodge *v* seachain

doe *n* eilit

dog *n* gadhar, madra

dog-eared *adj* catach

dogmatic *adj* dogmach

dole *n* dól

doll *n* bábóg **rag doll** bábóg éadaigh

dollar *n* dollar

dolphin *n* deilf

dome *n* cruinneachán

domestic *adj* intíre **domestic animals** ainmhithe clóis

domicile *n* áitreabh

dominate *v* smacht a choinneáil ar

dominant *adj* ceannasach

domineering *adj* mursanta, tiarnúil, máistriúil

domino *n* dúradán

donate *v* bronn

donation *n* tabhartas, bronntanas

Donegal *n* Dún na nGall, Tír Chonaill

donkey *n* asal

donor *n* deontóir **blood donor** deontóir fola

doom *n* léirscrios

doomsday *n* lá an Luain, lá an bhrátha

door *n* doras

doorstep *n* leac an dorais

doorkeeper *n* doirseoir

doorway *n* doras

dormant *adj* codlatach

dormitory *n* suanlios

dormouse *n* dallóg fhéir, luch chodlamáin

dose *n* dáileog **overdose** ródháileog

dot *n* ponc *v* poncaigh

dote *n* peata

double *adj* dúbailte *v* dúbail

double bass *n* olldord

double-cross *v* feall ar

double glazing *n* gloiniú dúbailte

doubt *n* dabht, amhras, agó *v* bheith in amhras **without doubt** gan amhras, **to have doubts** bheith in amhras, **without a doubt** gan aon agó, **the benefit of the doubt** sochar an amhrais

doubtful *adj* amhrasach

dough *n* taos

doughnut *n* taoschnó

dour *adj* dúr

dove *n* colm, colmán

dovetail *n* déadalt *v* luigh le chéile

Down *n* an Dún **Co. Down** Co. an Dúin

down *adj* síos, thíos, anuas **the price is going down** tá an praghas ag dul síos/ag titim, **put it down** cuir síos é, **he is down in the kitchen** tá sé thíos sa chistin, **to come down** teacht anuas, **lay it down on the table** leag anuas ar an mbord é

down and out *adj* ar an mblár folamh

downpour *n* duartan, stealladh

downstairs *adj* thíos staighre **to go down stairs** dul síos staighre

downstream *adv* síos an abhainn

dowry *n* spré

doze *n* sámhán **she dozed off** thit néal uirthi

dozen *n* dosaen

draft *n* dréacht *v* dréachtaigh

drag *v* streachail, srac **to drag the story out** paidir chapaill a dhéanamh de

dragon *n* dragan

drain *n* draein *v* diurnaigh, draenáil, diúg, síothlaigh

drainage *n* draenáil

draining *n* diúgaireacht

draining-board *n* raca silte

drainpipe *n* gáitéar, draeinphíobán

dram *n* dram

drama *n* drámaíocht

dramatic *adj* drámata

dramatist *n* drámadóir

dramatise *v* drámaigh

draught *n* séideadh

draughts *pl* táiplis (bheag)

draughtsman / draughtswoman *n* línitheoir, dréachtóir

draw[1] *n* **(in game)** comhscór

draw[2] *v* dear, línigh, tarraing

draw near *v* taobhaigh, druid le

drawer *n* drár, tarraiceán

drawing *n* líníocht, tarraingt

drawing-pin *n* tacóid ordóige

dread *n* imeagla, uamhan *v* imeagla/uamhan a bheith ort roimh

dreadful *adj* uafar

dream *n* aisling, taibhreamh *v* taibhrigh

dregs *pl* deasca, dríodar, moirt

drenched *adj* fliuch báite **she's drenched** tá sí ina líbín báite

dress *n* gúna, culaith *v* cóirigh, deasaigh, gléas **evening dress** culaith thráthnóna

dressed *adj* gléasta

dressing *n* anlann **salad dressing** anlann sailéid

dressing gown *n* fallaing folctha

dressing room *n* seomra gléasta

dressmaker *n* gúnadóir

dribble *n* ronna

drift *n* síobadh *v* dul le sruth

driftwood *n* adhmad raice

drill[1] *n* druil **fire drill** druil dóiteáin

drill[2] *n* **(tool)** druilire **power drill** druilire cumhachta, **electric drill** druilire leictreach

drill[3] *v* druileáil

drilling platform *n* ardán druileála

drink *n* deoch *v* diúg, ól

drinking *n* ólachán, diúgaireacht, fliuchadh na seamróige

drip *n* sileadh *v* sil

drive *n* tiomáint *v* tiomáin

drive away *v* ruaig

driver *n* tiománaí

driving test *n* tástáil tiomána

drizzle *n* ceobhrán

droll *adj* barrúil

drone *n* **(of bagpipes)** dos , crónán, dord, dordán

drop[1] *n* deoir, **(of spirits)** glincín
drop[2] *v* tit **drop in** buail isteach
drought *n* triomach
drown *v* báigh
drowning *n* bá
drowsy *adj* codlatach
drowsiness *n* múisiam
drug *n* druga *v* drugáil
drug addiction *n* andúil i ndrugaí, andúilíocht drugaí
drug dealer *n* díoltóir drugaí
drug-pushing *n* mangaireacht drugaí
drug-pusher *n* mangaire drugaí
drug-trafficking *n* gáinneáil drugaí
druid *n* draoi
drum *n* druma
drunk[1] *n* druncaeir
drunk[2] *adj* óltach, ar meisce
drunkard *n* meisceoir, pótaire
drunkenness *n* pótaireacht, meisce
dry[1] *v* triomaigh **dry up** díscigh, tráigh
dry[2] *adj* tur, tirim
dry-clean *v* tirimghlan
dry-cleaner *n* tirimghlantóir
dry-cleaning *n* tirimghlanadh
dryer *n* triomadóir
drying *n* triomach
dryness *n* dísc
dual *adj* déach
dubbing *n* athghuthú, **(technical process)** dubáil
dubious *adj* amhrasach
Dublin Bay prawn *n* cloicheán Bhá Bhaile Átha Cliath
duck *n* lacha *v* crom, **(in water)** tum
due *n* cóir, dleachtach, ceart **give her her due** tabhair a ceart di, **it is overdue** is mithid é
duel *n* comhrac aonair
duet *n* díséad

dug-out *n* **(sport)** cró folaigh
dulse *n* duileasc
dumb *adj* balbh
dump *n* carn fuílligh *v* dumpáil
dumping *n* dumpáil
dumpling *n* domplagán
dune *n* dumhach
dung *n* aoileach
dungeon *n* doinsiún
dunghill *n* carn aoiligh
duplicate *n* dúblach *v* dúbail
duplicity *n* caimiléireacht
durable *adj* buanseasmhach, buanfasach
durability *n* buanfas
duration *n* achar
during *prep* ar feadh, le linn, i rith, i gcaitheamh
dusk *n* contráth
dust *n* deannach, dusta, smúit *v* dustáil
dustbin *n* bosca bruscair
duster *n* ceirt deannaigh
dusty *adj* deannachúil
Dutch *adj, n* Ollanach
duty *n* dleacht, diúité, dualgas **on duty** ar diúité, ar dualgas
duty free *adj* saor ó dhleacht
dwarf *n* abhac, lucharachán
dwell *v* cónaigh
dwelling *n* cónaí
dwindle *v* mionaigh, laghdaigh ar
dye *n* dath *v* dathaigh
dyed *adj* daite
dynamic *adj* dinimiciúil
dynamite *n* dinimít
dynamo *n* dineamó
dysentery *n* dinnireacht
dynasty *n* ríshliocht
dyspepsia *n* dispeipse

E

each *adj* gach

eager *adj* cíocrach, díbhirceach, díocasach, fonnmhar **eager for** tnúthánach

eagle *n* iolar, fiolar

ear *n* cluas

earache *n* tinneas cluaise

earl *n* iarla **the Flight of the Earls** Teitheadh na nIarlaí

earliness *n* luaithe

early *adj* luath, moch

early Christian Ireland *n* Éire luath-Chríostaí

earmuffs *pl* cosaint cluas

earn *v* gnóthaigh, saothraigh, tuill

earnest *adj* dáiríre, dícheallach

earnings *pl* saothrú, tuilleamh

earphone *n* cluasán **earphones** cluasáin

ear-ring *n* fáinne cluaise

earth¹ *n* cré, grabhar, ithir, talamh

earth² *n* **(world)** domhan

earth³ *n* **(electricity)** talmhú *v* talmhaigh

earthenware *n* cré-earraí, earraí cré

earthly *adj* saolta

earthquake *n* crith talún

earwig *n* gailseach, Síle an phíce

ease *n* suaimhneas *v* tabhair suaimhneas do, **(pain)** maolaigh

easily *adv* gan stró, go héasca

east *n* oirthear, thoir **on the east side** lastoir, **to the east** soir, **from the east** anoir, **the east wind** an ghaoth anoir, **eastern** thoir, **eastwards** soir, **going east** ag dul soir, **coming east** ag teacht aniar

Easter *n* Cáisc

Easter egg *n* ubh Chásca

eastern *adj* oirthearach

eastwards *adv* soir

easy *adj* éasca, moiglí, réidh, sámh, saoráideach, sócúlach, furasta **more easily than...** níos fusa ná...

easy-going *adj* réchúiseach

eat *v* ith

eating *n* itheachán

eavesdropping (on) *n* cúléisteacht (le)

ebb *n* trá *v* tráigh

ebb tide *n* taoide thrá

ebony *n* éabann

eccentric *adj* aisteach, ait

ecclesiastical *adj* eaglasta

echelon *n* eisliún

echo *n* macalla

eclipse *n* urú, éiclips

eclipsis *n* **(grammar)** urú

ecocentrism *n* éicealárnachas

ecological crisis *n* géarchéim éiceolaíoch

ecological disaster *n* tubaiste éiceolaíochta

ecology *n* éiceolaíocht

economic(al) *adj* eacnamaíoch, geilleagrach, coigilteach, tíosach

economics *n* eacnamaíocht

economist *n* eacnamaí

economise *v* coigil

economy *n* eacnamaíocht, geilleagar

ecosystem *n* éiceachóras

Ecstasy *n* **(drug)** Eacstais

ecu *n* **(European Currency Unit)** eacú

eczema *n* eachma

eddies *pl* guairneáin

edge *n* dreapa, colbha, ciumhais, faobhar, imeall **edge of the road** colbha an bhealaigh

edible *adj* inite

edifice *n* foirgneamh

Edinburgh *n* Dun Eideann

editing *n* eagarthóireacht

edition *n* eagrán

editor *n* eagarthóir

editorial *n* eagarfhocal, príomhalt

educate *v* oil

educated *adj* eolach, oilte

education *n* léann, oideachas

eel *n* eascann

eerie *adj* aduain, diamhair, uaigneach

effect *n* éifeacht, tionchar **he / it had an effect on me** bhí tionchar aige orm

effective *adj* cumasach, éifeachtach

effectiveness *n* éifeacht

effects *pl* deasca

efficiency *n* éifeachtacht

efficient *adj* éifeachtach

effluent *n* eisilteach

effort *n* iarracht **to make an effort** iarracht a dhéanamh

effortless *adj* gan stró

effusive *adj* pléascánta

egg *n* ubh

egg case *n* (of squid etc) sparán na caillí

egg mayonaise *n* ubh faoi mhaonáis

eggcup *n* ubhchupán

eggshell *n* blaosc uibhe

egg-shaped *adj* ubhchruthach

egotism *n* féinspéis, féinspéiseachas

egotist *n* féinspéisí

egotistic *adj* féinspéiseach

Egypt *n* an Éigipt

eight *adj* ocht **eight people** ochtar

eighteen *adj* ocht déag

eighth *adj, n* ochtú

eightieth *adj, n* ochtódú

eighty *adj* ochtó

either *adj* ceachtar **either of them** ceachtar acu

eject *v* díchuir, caith amach

eke (out an existence) *v* greim do bhéil a bhaint amach

elaborate *v* cuir le

elastic *adj* leaisteach *n* leaistic

elated *n* ardmheanmnach

elbow *n* uillinn

elder *n* seanóir, saoi

elderly *adj* cnagaosta

eldest *adj* is sine

elect *v* togh

election *n* toghchán **general election** olltoghchán **election campaign** feachtas toghchánaíochta

electioneering *n* toghchánaíocht

elector *n* toghthóir

electorate *n* toghthóirí

electric *adj* leictreach

electric blanket *n* blaincéad leictreach

electrical *adj* leictreach

electrician *n* leictreoir

electricity *n* leictreachas, aibhléis

electrify *v* leictrigh

electrocute *v* maraigh le leictreachas

electronic *adj* leictreonach

electronic surveillance *n* faire leictreonach

electronics *n* leictreonaic

elegance *n* sciamhacht

elegant *adj* galánta, sciamhach, snasta

elegy *n* caoineadh, marbhna

element *n* eilimint

elephant *n* eilifint

elevate *v* ardaigh

elevation *n* ardú

elevator *n* ardaithcoir

eleven *adj* aon déag

elf *n* lucharachán

eligible *adj* incháilithe, inphósta

eliminate *v* díothaigh
eliminator *n* díothóir
elm *n* leamhán
elocution *n* deaslabhra
elongated *adj* fadaithe
elope *v* éalaigh
eloquent *adj* deaslabhartha
else *adv* eile **or else she's mad** sin nó as a meabhair atá sí
elsewhere *adv* i mball eile
elucidate *v* soiléirigh
elude *v* seachain, éalaigh
elusive *adj* éalaitheach, seachantach
emaciated *adj* caite
e-mail *n* ríomhphost
emancipate *v* fuascail
embargo *n* (trade) trádbhac
embark *v* téigh ar bord
embarrass *v* náire chur ar
embarrassment *n* aiféaltas, náire **to embarrass somebody** aiféaltas / náire a chur ar dhuine
embassy *n* ambasáid
embed *v* leabaigh
embers *pl* aibhleoga
embitter *v* searbhaigh
emblem *n* suaitheantas
embody *v* inchollaigh, foirm a thabhairt do
embrace *n* barróg **they embraced each other** rug siad barróg ar a chéile
embroider *v* bróidnigh
embryo *n* suth
emerge *v* teacht chun solais
emergency *n* éigeandáil, géarchéim
emergency powers *pl* cumhachtaí éigeandála
emigrant *n* eisimirceach, imirceach, imirceoir
emigrate *v* dul ar imirce
emigration *n* eisimirce, imirce
eminent *adj* uasal

emotion *n* mothúchán
emotional *adj* mothúchánach **deeply emotional** tochtmhar
emperor *n* impire
emphasis *n* béim
emphasise *v* cuir béim air
emphatic *adj* tréan, diongbháilte
empire *n* impireacht
employ *v* fostaigh
employee *n* fostaí
employer *n* fostóir
employment *n* fostaíocht, fostú
empower *v* cumasaigh
empty *adj* folamh *v* folmhaigh
emulate *v* dul in iomaíocht le
emulsion *n* eibleacht
enable *v* cumasaigh
enact *v* achtaigh
enamel *n,v* cruan
enchant *v* draíocht a chur ar
encircle *v* ciorclaigh, timpeallaigh
enclave *n* iamhchríoch
enclose *v* fálaigh, loc **enclosed** faoi iamh
enclosure *n* bábhún
encompass *v* iaigh, timpeallaigh
encore¹ *n* athghairm
encore!² *excl* arís!
encounter *n* teagmháil *v* cas ar, comhraic, dáil
encourage *v* misnigh, spreag **to encourage someone** uchtach a thabhairt do dhuine
encouragement *n* spreagadh, uchtach, ugach, misneach
encouraging *adj* spreagúil
encroach *v* cúngú ar
encumber *v* ualaigh
encyclopedia *n* ciclipéid
end¹ *n* ceann, deireadh, foirceann **journey's end** ceann cúrsa, **the end of the month** deireadh na míosa, **to the bitter end** go bun an angair

end[2] v críochnaigh, cuir deireadh le

endanger v cuir i mbaol

endear v éirigh ceanúil ar

endeavour n iarracht v iarracht a dhéanamh rud a dhéanamh

ending n deireadh

endless adj gan chríoch, gan deireadh

endorse v formhuinigh

endorsement n formhuiniú

endow v maoinigh

endure v fulaing

enduring adj fulangach

enemy n namhaid **public enemy** namhad an phobail, púca na n-adharc

energetic adj fuinniúil

energy n fuinneamh

enforce v cur i bhfeidhm

engagement n **(to marry)** gealltanas pósta, **(with enemy)** comhrac

engine n inneall **fire engine** inneall dóiteáin

engineer n innealtóir

engineering n innealtóireacht

England n Sasana

English adj, n Sasanach n **(language)** Béarla

Englishperson n Gall

engrave v grean

engraving n greanadóireacht

engrossed adj sáite i

engulf v slog

enhance v barr maise a chur ar

enigma n dubhfhocal

enigmatic adj dothuigthe

enjoy v bain ceol/súp/sult as

enjoyable adj pléisiúrtha, sultmhar

enjoyment n sult, taitneamh, spraoi, pléisiúr

enlarge v méadaigh

enlargement n méadú

enlighten v soilsigh

enlist v liostáil

enmity n naimhdeas

enormous adj ábhalmhór, millteanach (mór), ollmhór

enough adj, n dóthain, sáith

enquire v fiafraigh **to enquire about somebody** tuairisc duine a chur

enquiry n fiosrú, fiosrúchán

enrage v fearg a chur ar

enrich v saibhrigh

enslave v daor

ensure v cinntigh

entail v **it entails difficulties** tá deacrachtaí ag roinnt leis

entangle v cuir in aimhréidh

entangled adj achrannach, aimhréidh

enter v iontráil

enterprise n fiontar, fiontraíocht, treallús

enterprise zone n crios fiontraíochta

enterprising adj fiontrach, tionscantach, treallúsach

entertain v sult a dhéanamh do

entertainer n siamsóir

entertainment n siamsa, siamsaíocht, craic

enthusiasm n díograis

enthusiastic adj díograiseach

entice v meall

enticing adj mealltach

entire adj iomlán, uile

entirely adv go hiomlán, go huile

entrails pl ionathar

entrance v bheith faoi dhraíocht ag

entrance fee n táille isteach, táille iontrála

entrant n iontrálaí

entreat v impigh

entreaty n impí

entry n iontráil

enumerate v ríomh

enumeration n áireamh

envelop *v* fill, imchlúdaigh

envelope *n* clúdach litreach

envious *adj* éadmhar

environment *n* timpeallacht, imshaol

environmental diversity *n* ilchineálacht timpeallachta

environmentalism *n* imshaolachas

environmentally friendly product *n* earra atá neamhdhíobhálach don timpeallacht

envoy *n* toscaire, (of poem) ceangal

envy *n* éad, formad, tnúth

ephemeral *adj* gearrshaolach

epic *n* eipic

epicentre *n* airmheán

epidemic *adj* eipidéimeach *n* eipidéim

epidemiologist *n* eipidéimeolaí

epigram *n* burdún

epilepsy *n* titimeas, eipileipse

epileptic *adj, n* titimeach

epilogue *n* iarfhocal

episode *n* eachtra

epitaph *n* feartlaoi

equal[1] *n* cómhaith, cothrom, leithéid, macasamhail

equal[2] *adj* inchurtha, cothrom le, ionann

equal[3] *v* bheith cothrom le

equal opportunities employer *n* fostóir comhionannais deiseanna

equalise *v* comhardaigh

equality *n* comhionannas, ionannas

equate *v* ionannaigh

equation *n* cothromóid

equator *n* meánchiorcal

equestrian *adj* eachrach

equilibrium *n* cothromaíocht

equinox *n* cónacht

equip *v* feistigh, trealmhaigh

equipment *n* cóir, airnéis, trealamh, gléasadh office equipment trealamh oifige

equipped *adj* trealmhaithe

equivalent *adj* coibhéiseach

equivocal *adj* déchiallach

era *n* ré

eradicate *v* díothaigh

erase *v* scrios

eraser *n* scriosán

erect *v* tóg

erection *n* tógáil

ermine *n* eirmín

erode *v* creim

erosion *n* creimeadh

erotic *adj* anghrách

errand *n* teachtaireacht running errands timireacht

erratic *adj* taomach

erroneous *adj* earráideach, seachrán

error *n* earráid, botún typing error earráid chló

erudite *adj* foghlamtha

erupt *v* brúcht

eruption *n* maidhm

escalation *n* géarú

escalator *n* staighre beo

escape *n* éalú, teitheadh *v* éalaigh

escapism *n* éalúchas

escort *n* garda *v* tionlaic

especially *adv* go háirithe

espionage *n* spiaireacht

esker *n* eiscir

essay *n* aiste

essence *n* úscra

establish *v* bunaigh

established *adj* bunaithe, socraithe

establishment *n* bunú, bunaíocht

estate *n* eastát industrial estate eastát tionsclaíoch, housing estate eastát tithíochta

esteem *n* ardmheas *v* ardmheas a bheith agat ar

esteemed *adj* gradamach

estimate *v* meas *n* meastachán

estimated income *n* ioncam measta

estrangement *n* eascairdeas

estuary *n* inbhear

et cetera (etc) agus araile (srl)

eternal *adj* síoraí

eternally *adv* go síoraí

eternity *n* síoraíocht

ethereal *adj* neamhshaolta

ethical *adj* eiticiúil

ethics *pl* eitic

ethnic *adj* eitneach **ethnic cleansing** glanadh eitneach

etiquette *n* dea-bhéas

ethnologist *n* eitneolaí

etymology *n* sanasaíocht

Europe *n* an Eoraip

European *adj* Eorpach **Member of the European Parliament** Feisire Eorpach, **European Union (EU)** an tAontas Eorpach (AE)

European Monetary Fund (EMF) *n* an Ciste Airgeadaíochta Eorpach (CIAE)

European Monetary System (EMS) *n* an Córas Airgeadaíochta Eorpach (COAE)

eulogy *n* adhmholadh

euphemism *n* sofhriotal

euphoria *n* meidhréis

euthanasia *n* eotanáis

evacuate *v* aslonnaigh

evacuation *n* aslonnú

evade *v* seachain

evaluate *v* meas

evaluation *n* meastóireacht

evangelical *adj* soiscéalach

evangelist *n* soiscéalaí

evaporate *v* galaigh

evasion *n* seachaint **tax evasion** imghabháil cánach

evasive *adj* seachantach

eve *n* **eve of festival** oíche chinn féile, **Christmas Eve** Oíche Nollag, **New Year's Eve** Oíche Chinn Bliana

even[1] *adj* cothrom, *v* cothromaigh

even[2] *adv* féin, fiú amháin **even so** mar sin féin

evening *n* tráthnóna

evenness *n* cothroime, cothromaíocht

event *n* eachtra **events** imeachtaí

eventful *adj* eachtrúil

ever *adv* choíche, riamh **more than ever** níos mó ná riamh, **ever since** ó shin

ever- *prefix* síor-

evergreen *adj* síorghlas

everpresent *adj* uileláithreach

every *adj* gach, gach uile (= chuile), gach aon

everybody / everyone *n* gach duine, cách

everything *pron* gach (aon) rud, chuile rud

everywhere *adv* gach áit, chuile áit

evict *v* díshealbhaigh

eviction *n* díshealbhú

evidence *n* fianaise

evidence of purchase *n* fianaise ar cheannach

evident *adj* follasach, léir **it is evident that** is léir go

evil *adj* olc, dona *n* olcas *prefix* droch- mí-

evocative *adj* allabhrach

evoke *v* dúisigh

evolution *n* éabhlóid

evolve *v* ceap, beartaigh

exacerbate *v* géaraigh

exact *adj* cruinn, baileach *v* bain de **to exact revenge** díoltas a bhaint amach

exactly! *excl* go díreach

exaggerate *v* áibhéil a dhéanamh ar

exaggerated *adj* gáifeach, aibhéileach
exaggeration *n* áibhéil
exaltation *n* ardú meanman
exalted *adj* ardaithe
exam(ination) *n* scrúdú **oral exam** scrúdú cainte, **medical examination** scrúdú dochtúra
examine *v* scrúdaigh, taiscéal
examiner *n* scrúdaitheoir
example *n* sampla, eiseamláir, solaoid
excavate *v* tochail
excavation *n* tochailt
excavation site *n* láithreán tochailte
exceed *v* téigh thar
exceedingly *adv* rí-
excel *v* sáraigh
excellence *n* feabhas
excellent *adj* thar barr, tharr cionn, ar fheabhas, sármhaith *prefix* sár- **excellent game** sárchluiche
except *prep* ach (amháin)
exception *n* eisceacht **to make an exception** eisceacht a dhéanamh
exceptional *adj* eisceachtúil
excerpt *n* sliocht
excess *n* iomarca, breis
excessive *adj* iomarcach **excessive drinking** póit
exchange *n* malairt, malartú, (office) malartán *v* babhtáil, malartaigh **foreign exchange** malairt eachtrach, (office) malartán eachtrach, **stock exchange** stocmhalartán
exchange rate *n* ráta malairte
exchequer *n* státchiste
excise *n* mál
excision *n* eisceadh
excitable *adj* sochorraithe
excite *v* spreag
excited *adj* corraithe, sceitimíneach, tógtha
excitement *n* corraí, sceitimíní
exciting *adj* corraitheach

exclaim *v* gáir
exclamation *n* uaillbhreas
exclude *v* fág as
exclusion *n* leithcheal
exclusive *adj* eisiach, leithleach
excommunicate *v* coinnealbháigh
excommunication *n* coinnealbhá
excrete *v* cac, eisfhear
excrement *n* cac, cisfhearadh
excruciating *n* cráite
excursion *n* turas
excusable *adj* inmhaite
excuse *n* leithscéal *v* leithscéal a ghabháil
execute *v* (plan) comhlíon, (kill) cuir chun báis
execution *n* cur chun báis
executive *adj* feidhmitheach, feidhmiúcháin
exemplary *adj* eiseamláireach
exemplify *v* eiseamláirigh
exempt *v* **I was exempted from the duty** saoradh ar an dualgas mé
exemption *n* saoirseacht, díolúine
exercise *n* aclaíocht, ceacht, cleachtadh *v* aclaíocht a dhéanamh
exert *v* saothar a chur ar
exertion *n* saothar
exhale *v* asanálaigh
exhaust[1] *v* traoch, spíon
exhaust[2] *n* sceitheadh
exhaust pipe *n* píobán sceite
exhausted *adj* cloíte, cortha, spíonta, traochta, tugtha
exhibit *v* taispeáin
exhibition *n* taispeántas
exhilarating *adj* spreagúil
exhort *v* spreag
exhortation *n* spreagadh, aitheasc
exile *n* deoraíocht, (person) deoraí *v* díbir
exist *v* bheith ann
existentialism *n* eiseachas

exit *n* bealach amach

exodus *n* imeacht

exotic *adj* coimhthíoch, andúchasach

expand *v* leathnaigh

expansion *n* leathnú

expect *v* dréim **expecting something** ag dréim le rud

expectant *adj* tnúthánach

expectation *n* dóchas, dréim, tnúth

expedient *adj* caothúil

expedition *n* sluaíocht turas **(military)**

expel *v* díbir

expend *v* caith, ídigh

expenditure *n* caiteachas

expense *n* costas

expensive *adj* daor

experience *n* cleachtadh, eispéireas, taithí, *v* taithigh, cleacht

experienced *adj* cleachtach

experiment *n* turgnamh

experimental *adj* trialach

expert *n* saineolaí, saoi

expertise *n* saineolas

expire *v* éag

explain *v* léirigh, mínigh

explanation *n* míniú, míniúchán

explanatory *adj* mínitheach

explode *v* pléasc

exploit *n* gaisce, éacht *v* bain sochar as, saothraigh, tar i dtír ar

exploitation *n* dúshaothrú

exploration *n* taiscéalaíocht

explore *v* taiscéal

explorer *n* taiscéalaí

explosion *n* maidhm, pléasc, pléascadh

explosive *adj* pléascach *n* pléascán **high explosive material** ábhar tréanphléascach, **high explosives** tréanphléascáin

export *n* onnmhaire *v* easpórtáil, onnmhairigh

exporter *n* easpórtálaí, onnmhaireoir

expose *v* nocht

exposed land *n* talamh rite / sceirdiúil

exposure *n* nochtadh **indecent exposure** nochtadh núgheanasach

express *v* cuir in iúl

express train *n* traein luais

expression *n* dreach, **(phrase)** leagan cainte

expressive *adj* lán de bhrí

expulsion *n* ruaigeadh, díbirt

exquisite *adj* fíorghleoite

extend *v* sín

extended *adj* sínte

extension *n* **(telephone)** folíne, sciathán, síneadh, fairsingiú

extensive *adj* fairsing, leathan

extensiveness *n* forleithne

extent *n* fairsinge, méid

exterior *adj* amuigh

exterminate *v* díothaigh

extermination *n* díothú

external *adj* eachtrach, seachtrach

external examiner *n* scrúdaitheoir seachtrach

extinct *adj* in éag, ídithe

extinction *n* imeacht in éag

extinguish *v* múch

extinguished *adj* múchta

extinguisher *n* múchtóir **fire extinguisher** múchtóir dóiteáin

extort *v* bain de, srac

extortion *n* cíos dubh

extra *n* breis

extra-marital *adj* seachphósta

extract *n* **(from literature)** sliocht *v* stoith **to extract a tooth** fiacail a stoitheadh

extradite *v* eiseachaid

extradition *n* eiseachadadh

extraordinary *adj* neamhghnách, iontach

extravagance *n* diomailt, rabairne

extravagant *adj* diomailteach

extreme *adj* fíor-, rí-, as cuimse, antoisceach **it is extremely heavy** tá sé fíorthrom

extremely *adv* fíor-, iontach

extremist *n* antoisceach

extrovert *adj* eisdíritheach *n* eisdíritheoir

exuberance *adj* spleodar

exuberant *adj* spleodrach

exultation *n* lúcháir

eye *n* súil, rosc **bull's eye** súil sprice

eyeball *n* mogall súile

eyebrow *n* mala

eyecream *n* uachtar súl

eyelash *n* fabhra

eyelid *n* caipín súile

eye-opener *n* oscailt súl

eyepiece *n* súilphíosa

eyeshield *n* clipéad

eyesight *n* radharc na súl

eyesore *n* rud gránna

eyewitness *n* finné súl

eyrie *n* nead

F

fable *n* fabhal, fabhalscéal

fabled *adj* fabhlach

fabric *n* fabraic

fabricate *v* cum

fabrication *n* cumadóireacht

fabulous *adj* iontach, dochreidte, abhlach

face *n* aghaidh, ceannaghaidh, gnúis **face to face** aghaidh ar aghaidh, **to face something** aghaidh a thabhairt ar rud

face mask *n* (surgical) masc máinliachta, (cosmetic) masc aghaidhe

facelift *n* (surgical) teannadh cnis, (improvement) cruth nua

facial *adj* **facial nerve** néaróg éadain

facial toner *n* tonóir éadain

facilitate *v* éascaigh

facility *n* áis, saoráid **credit facilities** áiseanna creidmheasa

facing *prep* ar aghaidh

facsimile *n* macasamhail

fact *n* fíric, fíoras

fact finding *n* aimsiú fíricí/fíoras

faction *n* faicsean **faction fighting** i faicseanaíocht

factor *n* toisc **limiting factors** tosca teorantacha

factory *n* monarcha

faculty *n* (in university) dámh

fade *v* ceiliúir

fail *v* clis, teip **my memory failed me** chlis an chuimhne orm

failure *n* cliseadh, loiceadh, meath, teip **power failure** cliseadh cumhachta

faint[1] *n* fanntais **to faint** titim i bhfanntais

faint[2] *adj* fann

fair[1] *n* aonach **at the fair** ar an aonach

fair[2] *adj* (middling) cuibheasach

fair[3] *adj* (just) cothrom, féaráilte

fair[4] *adj* (colour) fionn, fionnbhán

fairly *adj* measartha, sách **fairly high** sách ard

fairness *n* cothrom **fair play** cothrom na Féinne

fairy *n* sióg

fairy host *n* slua sí
fairy mound *n* sí
fairy-tale *n* síscéal
faith *n* **(belief)** creideamh, **(trust)** muinín
faithful *adj* dílis
faithfulness *n* dílseacht
fake *v* falsaigh
fake money *n* airgead bréige
falcon *n* fabhcún
fall *n* titim *v* tit
fallacy *n* fallás
falling *n* titim
falling star *n* réalta reatha
fallow *n* branar
false *adj* falsa, tacair, bréige, lochtach
falsehood *n* bréag
falseness *n* bréige, falsacht
false pretences *pl* dúmas bréige
falsify *v* falsaigh
falter *v* tuisligh **her voice faltered** tháinig snag ina glór
fame *n* cáil, clú
familiar *adj* aithnidiúil, taithíoch
family *n* cúram, clann, muintir, muirear, teaghlach
family tree *n* craobh ghinealaigh
famine *n* gorta **the Great Famine** an Drochshaol
famished *adj* stiúgtha
famous *adj* cáiliúil, clúiteach
fan *n* fean *v* gaothraigh
fans *pl* lucht leanúna
fanatic *n* fanaiceach
fanatical *adj* fanaiceach
fancy *n* nóisean **to take a fancy to someone** taitneamh a thabhairt do dhuine
fancy dress party *n* cóisir bhréagéide
fang *n* starrfhiacail
fantastic *adj* fantaiseach

fantasy *n* fantaisíocht
far *adv* i bhfad, i gcéin
faraway *adj* i gcéin, imigéiniúil
farce *n* **(theatre)** fronsa, scigdhráma
fare *n* táille
farewell *n* slán
farm *n* feirm *v* feirm a shaothrú / oibriú
farmer *n* feirmeoir
farming *n* feirmeoireacht
farmyard manure *n* aoileach
far-reaching *adj* fadiarmhartach
farrier *n* crúdóir
farther *adj* níos faide
fascinate *v* cuir faoi dhraíocht
fascist *adj* faisisteach *n* faisistí
fascism *n* faisisteachas
fashion *n* faisean **in fashion** san fhaisean, **out of fashion** as faisean
fashionable *adj* faiseanta
fast[1] *adj* pras, sciobtha, tapa, mear, gasta
fast[2] *n* troscadh *v* troisc
fast food chain *n* sreang mhearbhia, comhlacht sreangshiopaí mearbhia
fast food shop *n* siopa mearbhia
fasten *v* greamaigh
fastener *n* fáiscín
fastidious *adj* nósúil
fasting *n* troscadh
fat *adj* ramhar, geir, úsc
fatal *adj* cinniúnach, marfach
fatalism *n* cinniúnachas
fatality *n* timpiste mharfach
fate *n* cinniúint, dán
fateful *adj* cinniúnach
father *n* athair
father-in-law *n* athair céile
fatherly *adj* aithriúil, athartha
fathom *n* feá *v* tomhais
fatigue *n* tuirse
fatigued *adj* tuirseach

fatness *n* raimhre

fatten *v* ramhraigh

fatty *adj* sailleach, úscach

fatuous *adj* baoth

fault *n* locht *v* lochtaigh **it's not my fault** ní ormsa atá an locht

fault-finding *n* lochtú

faulty *adj* fabhtach, lochtach

favour *n* aisce, comaoin, fabhar, gar **do me a favour** déan gar dom

favourable *adj* fabhrach

favourite *n* peata **my favourite film** an scannán is fearr liom

favouritism *n* fabhraíocht

fawn *n* oisín

fax *n* facs *v* facsáil

fear *n* critheagla, eagla, faitíos, uamhan *v* eagla / faitíos / uamhan a bheith ort roimh

fearful *adj* eaglach, imeaglach

fearless *adj* neamheaglach

feasible *adj* indéanta

feasibility *n* féidearthacht

feasibility study *n* staidéar féidearthachta

feast *n* féasta

feast day *n* féile

feat *n* éacht

feather *n* cleite

feathers *pl* cluimhreach, clúmh

features *pl* ceannaghaidh, comharthaí sóirt

February *n* Feabhra

federal *adj* cónascach **Federal Republic of Nigeria** Poblacht Chónaidhme na Nigéire

federation *n* cónaidhm

fed up *v* **to be fed up with somebody, something** bheith bailithe de dhuine, rud

fee *n* táille

feeble *n* fann

feed[1] *n* **(printer)** fotha **face down / up feed** fotha aghaidh faoi/in airde

feed[2] *v* cothaigh, fothaigh, beathaigh

feeder buses *pl* busanna friothála

feedback *n* aischothú, aiseolas

feel *v* airigh, mothaigh **I feel peckish** tá goin ocrais orm

feeling *n* mothú, mothúchán

feigned deafness *n* bodhaire Uí Laoire

feigned sickness *n* tinneas muice

fell *v* **(tree)** leag

fellowship *n* comhaltacht

felon *n* feileon

felt *n* feilt

female *adj* baineann *n* baineannach

feminine *adj* banda, baininscneach

feminist *adj* feimineach *n* feiminí

fence *n* claí, fál, sconsa *v* pionsóireacht a dhéanamh

fencing *n* pionsóireacht

Fenian *n* Fínín

Fenianism *n* Fíníneachas

Fermanagh *n* Fear Manach **Co. Fermanagh** Co. Fhear Manach

ferment *v* coip

fern *n* raithneach

ferocious *adj* fíochmhar

ferret *n* firéad

ferry *n* bád farantóireachta

ferrying *n* farantóireacht

fertile *adj* aruil, torthúil

fertilise *v* leasaigh

fertiliser *n* leasachán, leasú

fervent *adj* díochra, díograiseach

fervour *n* díograis

fester *v* ábhraigh

festival *n* féile, feis, fleá

festive *adj* féiltiúil

festivity *n* fleáchas

fetch *v* dul faoi choinne

fetish *n* feitis

fetter *n* árach, cuibhreach, geimheal, laincis

feud *n* fíoch
feudal *adj* feodach
fever *n* fiabhras
feverish *adj* fiabhrasach
few *adj* cúpla, beagán **a few books** cúpla leabhar
fiasco *n* praiseach
fibre *n* snáithín
fibreglass *n* gloine snáthíní
fickle *adj* guagach
fiction *n* ficsean, finscéal, finscéalaíocht
fictional *adj* finscéalach
fictitious *adj* bréagach, cumtha
fiddle *n* fidil *v* bheith ag méirínteacht
fiddler *n* fidléir
fiddling *n* méirínteacht
fidelity *n* dílseacht
fidget *v* fútráil
fidgeting *n* fútráil
fidgety *adj* corrthónach
field *n* faiche, gort, páirc **playing field** páirc imeartha, **theme park** páirc théama
fieldwork *n* obair allamuigh
fiend *n* diabhal
fierce *adj* fíochmhar
fierceness *n* fíochmhaireacht, fraoch
fiery *adj* lasánta, teasaí
FIFA (Federation of International Football Associations) *n* Comhaontas Idirnáisiúnta na gCumann Sacair
fifteen *adj* cúig déag
fifth *adj, n* cúigiú
fiftieth *adj, n* caogadú
fifty *adj* caoga
fig *n* fige
fight *n* comhrac, troid *v* troid
fighter *n* trodaí
figment *n* samhlaíocht
figurative *adj* fáthchiallach

figure *n* amhlachas, deilbh, figiúr
filament *n* ribe
file[1] *n* comhad **back-up file** comhad cúltaca
file[2] *n* **(for nails etc)** líomhán *v* líomh
file[3] *v* comhad a chur i dtaisce
file protection *n* comhadchosaint
file manager *n* comhadbhainisteoir
filename *n* ainm comhaid
filing cabinet *n* comhadchaibinéad
fill *v* líon
fillet *n* filléad
filly *n* cliobóg
film *n* scannán *v* scannánaigh
film library *n* leabharlann scannán
film star *n* réalta/réiltín scannán
filter *n* scagaire *v* scag
filtering *n* scagadh
filth *n* bréantas, salachar
filthy *adj* bréan
fin *n* eite
final[1] *adj* críochnaitheach, deireanach
final[2] *n* cluiche ceannais **All-Ireland final** cluiche ceannais na hÉireann
final product *n* táirge deiridh
finance *n* airgeadas *v* maoinigh
financier *n* airgeadaí
financial *adj* airgeadúil
Financial Services Centre *n* Lárionad Seirbhísí Airgid
find *n* aimsiú, éadáil *v* aimsigh
finding *n* aimsiú
fine[1] *adj* mín, fíneálta, mion
fine[2] *v,n* fineáil
finery *n* callaí
fine spell (between showers) *n* aiteall
finger *n* méar *v* méaraigh **the index finger** an mhéar thosaigh, **the middle finger** an mhéar láir, **the ring finger** méar an fháinne, **the little finger** an mhéar bheag, an lúidín
fingerprint *n* méarlorg

finish *n* slacht *v* críochnaigh

finished *adj* críochnaithe, ullamh
finished product táirge deiridh

finite *adj* finideach

Finland *n* an Fhionlainn

Finn *n* Fionlannach

Finnish *adj* Fionlannach
n (language) an Fhionlannis

fir *n* giúis

fire[1] *n* tine, dóiteán bonfire tine
chnámh

fire[2] *v* gríosaigh

fire[3] *v* (pottery) bácáil

fire alarm *n* aláram dóiteáin

firearm *n* arm lámhaigh

fire-ball *n* caor thine

firebrand *n* aithinne

fire brigade *n* briogáid dóiteáin

fire extinguisher *n* múchtóir dóiteáin

fire-fighter *n* comhraiceoir dóiteáin

fire-fighters *n* lucht múchta dóiteáin

fire-hob *n* bac tine

fireplace *n* tinteán, teallach

firing squad *n* scuad lámhaigh

firm[1] *n* comhlacht

firm[2] *adj* teann, diongbháilte

firmament *n* firmimint

firmness *n* diongbháilteacht

first *adj* aonú, céad the first day an
chéad lá, the first person an
chéad duine, the first people na
chéad daoine, at first ar dtús, i
dtosach báire

first aid *n* céadchabhair, garchabhair

first aid treatment *n* cóireáil
chéadchabhrach

fish *n* iasc *v* iascaireacht/iascach a
dhéanamh

fisherman *n* iascaire

fish finger *n* méaróg éisc

fish processing *n* próiseáil éisc

fishing *n* iascaireacht

fishing rod *n* slat
iascaigh/iascaireachta

fist *n* dorn

fisticuffs *pl* to go to fisticuffs with
dul ar na doirne le

fit[1] *adj* aclaí, scafánta

fit[2] *v* feistigh, oiriúnaigh, oir

fit[3] *n* taom fit of anger taom feirge

fitful *adj* taomach

fitter *n* feisteoir

fitting *adj* cuí *n* feisteas fittings
oiriúintí

five *adj* cúig five people cúigear

fix *n* ponc *v* cóirigh, socraigh,
ullmhaigh, to be in a fix bheith i
bponc, bheith san fhaopach

fixed *adj* socraithe, seasta fixed
interest ús seasta

fixture *n* daingneán

flabby *adj* feolmhar

flag *n* bratach

flagpole *n* crann brataí

flagstone *n* leac

flair *n* bua

flake *n* calóg corn flakes calóga
arbhair

flamboyant *adj* taibhseach

flame *n* lasair, lasán *v* splanc

flamethrower *n* teilgeoir lasrach

flaming *adj* lasánta

flamingo *n* lasairéan

flammable *adj* inlasta

flank *n* taobh, cliathán

flannel *n* flainín

flap *n* plapa, liopa *v* buail

flare *n* (signal) lasair rabhaidh

flash *n, v* splanc flash of lightning
splanc thintrí

flashback *n* iardhearcadh

flashcard *n* spléach-chárta

flash floods *pl* maidhmeanna tuile

flask *n* fleasc

flat[1] *n* árasán block of flats áraslann,
bloc árasán

flat[2] *adj* cothrom

flat[3] *adj* (of drink) rodta

flatfish *n* leathóg

flatterer *n* cluanaire, plámásóir

flattery *n* galaíocht, plámás, bladar

flaunt *v* gaisce a dhéanamh as

flavour *n* blas *v* blaistigh

flaw *n* éalang

flawed *adj* éalangach

flawless *adj* gan cháim, gan smál

flax *n* líon

flay *v* feann

flea *n* dreancaid

flea market *n* margadh na míol

fledgling *n* gearrcach, scaltán

flee *v* teith

fleece *n* lomra *v* feann

fleet *n* cabhlach

fleeting *adj* neamhbhuan

flesh *n* colainn, feoil

flex[1] *v* aclaigh

flex[2] *n* fleisc

flexible *adj* solúbtha

flick *n, v* smeach **flick of fingers** speach ghearáin

flight *n* eitilt, teitheadh

flight attendant *n* aeróstach

Flight of the Earls *n* Teitheadh na nIarlaí

flighty *adj* aerach

flimsy *adj* scagach **flimsy excuse** leithscéal agus a thóin leis

flinch *v* loic

fling *n* teilgean *v* teilg

flint *n* cloch thine

flip *n, v* smeach

flirt *n* cliúsaí *v* cliúsaíocht a dhéanamh

flirting *n* cliúsaíocht

float[1] *n* **(money)** cúlchnap

float[2]*n* snámhán, éadromán *v* snámh

flock *n* **(of sheep)** tréad, **(of birds)** ealta *v* cruinnigh/bailigh le chéile

flog *v* lasc

flood *n* díle, tuile, rabharta *v* tuil **flash flood** maidhm thuile, **flood tide** taoide thuile, **flood of speech** rabharta cainte

flooding *n* **(of land)** tuile, **(of river)** sceitheadh

floodlight *n* tuilsolas

floor *n* urlár, lár

flora *n* flóra

floral *adj* bláfar

florist *n* bláthadóir

floss *n* flas **candy-floss** flas candaí, **dental floss** flas fiacla

flotsam *n* snámhraic

flounder *n* **(fish)** leadhbóg *v* iomlaisc

flour *n* plúr

flourish *n* ornáidíocht *v* fás go maith, bláthaigh

flourishing *adj* faoi bhláth

flow *n* sní *v* seol, slaod, snigh

flower *n* plúr, bláth *v* bláthaigh

flowerbed *n* ceapach bláthanna

flu *n* fliú

fluctuation *n* luaineacht

fluctuating *adj* luaineach, malartach

fluency *n* líofacht

fluent *adj* líofa

fluff *n* clúmhach *v* botún/meancóg a dhéanamh

fluffy *adj* clúmhach

fluid *adj* silteach, líofa *n* silteach

fluorescent *adj* fluaraiseach

flush *n* **(in face)** luisne *v* **(toilet)** sruthlaigh

flushed *adj* **(face)** círíneach

fluster *n* sceitimíní *v* cuir mearbhall ar

flute *n* feadóg mhór, fliúit

flutter *n* eitilt *v* eitil

flux *n* flosc

fly *n* cuil, cuileog *v* eitil

flying[1] *n* eitilt

flying² *n* foluain **the flag is flying** tá an bhratach ar foluain

flyover *n* uasbhealach

foal *n* searrach

foam *n* coipeadh, cúr *v* coip **shaving foam** cúr bearrtha

focus *n* fócas *v* dírigh (ar) **out of / in focus** as fócas / i bhfócas

foe *n* namhaid

foetus *n* gin, suth

fog *n* ceo

foggy *adj* ceoch, ceomhar

foil¹ *n* scragall **aluminium foil** scragall alúmanaim

foil² *v* toirmisc, bac

fold¹ *n* filleadh *v* fill

fold² *n* **(sheep)** loca

folder *n* fillteán

foliage *n* duilliúr

folk *n* pobal, aos, daoine **National Folk Theatre** Siamsa Tíre

folk museum *n* daoniarsmalann

folk music *n* ceol tíre

folk park *n* daonpháirc

folk school *n* daonscoil

folklore *n* béaloideas **the Folklore Department** an Roinn Bhéaloideasa

follow *v* lean

follower *n* leantóir

following¹ *n* leanúint

following² *adj* **the following words** na focail a leanas

folly *n* amaidí

fond (of) *adj* ceanúil (ar), tugtha (do)

fondle *v* cuimil, muirnigh

fondness *n* dáimh, gean

font *n* umar

food *n* bia, beatha

food chain *n* biashlabhra

fool *n* amadán, óinmhid, pleidhce, **(female)** óinseach

foolish *adj* amaideach, leibideach, **(female)** óinsiúil

foolishness *n* díth céille, amadántacht, **(female)** óinsiúlacht

foot¹ *n* cos **on foot** de chois, de shiúl na gcos

foot² *n* **(measurement)** troigh

foot³ *v* **to foot the bill** an scór a ghlanadh, an bille a sheasamh

football *n* peil, caid **game of football** cluiche peile

footballer *n* peileadóir

footbrake *n* coscán coise

footgear *n* coisbheart

foothills *pl* bunchnoic

footnote *n* fonóta

footpath *n* cosán

footprint *n* lorg coise, rian coise

footstep *n* coiscéim

for *prep* chun, do, i gcomhair, le haghaidh *conj* mar, óir

forbear *v* staon (ó)

forbearing *adj* fulangach

forbid *v* coisc

force *n* fórsa, foréigean, teann, spionnadh *v* cuir iallach ar

forceful *adj* teann

forcible *adj* foréigneach

ford *n* áth

forebode *v* tuar

foreboding *n* tuar

forecast *n* réamhaisnéis **the weather forecast** réamhaisnéis na haimsire

forehead *n* clár éadain, éadan

foreign *adj* allúrach, coimhthíoch, eachtrannach, gallda

foreigner *n* allúrach, coimhthíoch, eachtrannach, Gall

foreign investment *n* infheistíocht choigríche

foreman *n* saoiste, maor

forensic medicine *n* dlí-eolaíocht mhíochaine

forerunner *n* réamhtheachtaí

foreshore *n* urthrá

forest *n* foraois **(tropical) rainforest** foraois (theochriosach / thrópaiceach) bháistí, **man-made forest** foraois de dhéantús an duine

forestry *n* foraoiseacht

foretell *v* tairngir

forever *adv* choíche, go deo

foreword *n* brollach

forge[1] *n* ceárta *v* gaibhnigh

forge[2] *v* **(money)** brionnaigh, falsaigh

forger *n* falsaitheoir

forgery *n* brionnú **a fine forgery** brionnú breá

forget *v* dearmad

forgetful *adj* dearmadach, dímheabhrach

forgetfulness *n* dearmad

forgive *v* maith

forgiveness *n* maithiúnas

forgiving *adj* maiteach

fork *n* forc, píce **hayfork** píce féir

form[1] *n* cló, foirm, riocht **in human form** i gcló duine

form[2] *v* foirmigh

formal *adj* foirmiúil, deasghnách

formality *n* deasghnáth

format *n* formáid *v* formáidigh **to format a disk** diosca a fhormáidiú

formation *n* foirmiú

former *adj* sean-

formidable *adj* scanrúil

formula *n* foirmle

formulate *v* foirmigh

formulation *n* foirmiú

forsake *v* tréig

fort *n* daingean, dún **ring fort** ráth

forth, and so forth agus mar sin de

fortieth *adj, n* daicheadú

fortification *n* daingniú, dún-áras

fortified milk *n* bainne treisithe

fortified town *n* baile daingean

fortify *v* daingnigh

fortnight *n* coicís

fortnightly *adj* coicísiúil *n* **(perodical)** coicíseán

fortress *n* daingean, dún

fortunate *adj* ádhúil, ámharach

fortune *n* ádh, fortún

fortune teller *n* **(female)** cailleach feasa

forty *adj, n* ceathracha, daichead **in the forties** sna daichidí

forward *adv* chun tosaigh *n* tosaí

fossil *n* iontaise

fossilise *adj* iontaisigh

fossilised *adj* iontaisithe

foster *v* altramaigh

fosterage *n* altram

foster-mother *n* máthair altrama

foul[1] *n* bréan, **(weather)** doineanta

foul[2] *n* **(sport)** calaois *v* calaois a dhéanamh ar

foul[3] *v* cuir smál ar

found *v* **(establish)** bunaigh

foundation[1] *n* fondúireacht

foundation[2] *n* **(of building)** cloch bhoinn

foundry *n* teilgcheárta

fountain *n* fuarán

four *adj* ceathair, ceithre **four people** ceathrar

fourteen *adj* ceathair déag

fourth *adj, n* ceathrú

fowl *n* éanlaith **domestic fowl** éanlaith chlóis, éanlaith tí

fox *n* madra rua, sionnach

foyer *n* forhalla   ,

fraction *n* codán

fracture *n* briseadh *v* bris

fragile *adj* sobhriste, leochaileach

fragment *n* blogh **fragments** conamar

fragrance *n* cumhracht

fragrant *adj* cumhra

frail *adj* anbhann, dearóil, leochaileach

frame *n* creat, fráma *v* frámaigh

framework *n* creatlach, frámaíocht

France *n* an Fhrainc

franchise *n* saincheadúnas

frank *adj* díreach, macánta *v* frainceáil

frantic *n* ar buile

fraternal *adj* bráithriúil

fraud *n* calaois, camastaíl

fraudulent *adj* calaoiseach

free *adj, v* saor **free of charge** saor in aisce

free- *prefix* saor

freedom *n* saoirse

free estimate *n* saormheastachán

freefone *n* saorfhón

free kick *n* saorchic

freelance *adj* saor-

freelance journalist *n* saoririseoir

free market economy *n* geilleagar saoriomaíochta

freemason *n* máisiún

free range hens, eggs *pl* cearca, uibheacha saor-raoin

free trade *n* saorthrádáil

freeze *n* sioc *v* reoigh

freezer *n* reoiteoir **deep freezer** domhanreoiteoir

freezing *adj* préachta

freezing point *n* reophointe

freight *n* lasta

freighter *n* lastóir

French¹ *n* **(language)** an Fhraincis

French² *adj* Francach

French Foreign Legion *n* Léigiún Coigríochach na Fraince

French person *n* Francach

frequency *n* minicíocht **very high frequency (VHF)** ardmhinicíocht

frequent¹ *v* gnáthaigh, lonnaigh, taithigh

frequent² *adj* minic

fresh *adj* friseáilte

freshness *n* úire

freshwater lake *n* loch fionnuisce

Freudian slip *n* sciorradh Freudach

friar *n* bráthair

friction *n* cuimilt

Friday *n* Aoine **(on) Friday** Dé hAoine, **Good Friday** Aoine an Chéasta

fridge *n* cuisneoir

fried *adj* friochta **fried rice** rís fhriochta

friend *n* cara

friendly *adj* cairdiúil, muinteartha

friendly match *n* cluiche cairdeachais

Friends of the Earth *pl* Cairde na Cruinne

friendship *n* cairdeas, muintearas

fright *n* scanradh, scaoll, scáth, scéin

frighten *v* scanraigh

frightened *adj* scanraithe, scéiniúil

frightening *adj* scanrúil

frightful *adj* scáfar

frill *n* rufa

frilled *n* rufach

fringe *n* **(hair)** frainse

frisbee *n* friosbaí

friskiness *n* giodam

frisky *adj* giodamach, macnasach, meidhreach

fritter *n* friochtóg *v* mionaigh

frivolous *adj* baoth

frog *n* frog, loscann

frogman *n* frogaire

frolicking *n* pocléimneach

from *prep* ó, as **from Scotland** as Albain, **from time to time** ó am go ham, **from the east** anoir, **from the south** aneas, **from the west** aniar, **from the north** aduaidh

front *n* aghaidh, tosach *v* tabhair aghaigh ar **front bumper** tuairteoir tosaigh, **front seat** suíochán tosaigh, **front wing** cliathán tosaigh

front bench *n* binse na nAirí

frontier *n* imeallchríoch, teorainn

frost *n* reo, siocán, sioc

frost resistance *n* sioc-obacht

frostbite *n* siocdhó

frosted *adj* sioctha

frosty *adj* siocúil

froth *n* coipeadh, cúr, sobal

frothy *adj* coipeach

frown *n* grainc *v* cuir grainc ort féin

fruit *n* toradh

fruit juice *n* sú torthaí

fruit seller *n* torthóir

fruitful *adj* torthúil

frustrate *v* sáraigh, bac

frustration *n* frustrachas

fry *v* frioch **to fry food** bia a fhriochadh

frying pan *n* friochtán

fudge *n* faoiste

fuel *n* breosla *v* breoslaigh

fugitive *n* éalaitheach, teifeach

fulfil *v* comhlíon, sásaigh

fulfilment *n* comhlíonadh, fíorú

full *adj* lán **in full swing** faoi lánseol, **at full speed** faoi lánsiúl

full-blown AIDS *n* SEIF iomlán

full-forward *n* **(sport)** lántosaí

fullness *n* iomláine

full stop *n* lánstad

full-time *n* lánaimseartha

full to the brim *adj* lán go barr/béal

full up *adj* lán go barr/béal

fully qualified *adj* láncháilithe

fumble *v* bheith ag útamáil

fumbling *adj* útamálach *n* útamáil

fume(s) *n* deatach gal, toit

fun *n* aiteas, greann, spórt, spraoi **for fun** le greann

function *n* feidhm *v* feidhmigh

functional *adj* feidhmiúil

fund *n* ciste *v* maoinigh **European Monetary Fund (EMF)** Ciste Airgeadaíochta Eorpach (CIAE)

fundamental *adj* bunúsach

funeral *n* sochraid, tórramh

fungus *n* fungas

funnel *n* tonnadóir

funny *adj* greannmhar

fur *n* fionnadh **fur coat** cóta fionnaidh

furious *adj* dásachtach, fíochmhar

furlong *n* staid

furnace *pl* foirnéis, sorn

furnish *v* soláthair, **(furniture)** trealmhaigh

furnishings *pl* feisteas

furniture *n* troscán

furrow *n* clais *v* treabh

furry *adj* clúmhach

further *adv* níos mó, a thuilleadh *v* cuir chun cinn

furthermore *adv* fós, ina theannta sin, rud eile de

fury *n* fraoch

furze *n* aiteann

fuse *n* aidhnín, fiús *v* comhleáigh, comhnasc, **(electricity)** clis **safety fuse** fiús sábháilteacha

fuselage *n* cabhail

fusion *n* comhleá

fuss *n* fuirse *v* fuirsigh

fussy *adj* pointeáilte

futile *adj* fánach

future[1] *adj, n* **(tense)** fáistineach

future[2] *n* todhchaí, an t-am atá romhainn **in the future** amach anseo, sa todhchaí

futuristic *adj* todhchaíoch

G

GAA *n* Cumann Lúthchleas Gael (CLG)

gab *n* geab

gadget *n* gaireas

Gaelic *n* **(language)** Gaeilge na hAlban

gaiety *n* scléip

gain *n* éadáil *v* gnóthaigh

Galactic System *n* Córas Réaltrach

galaxy *n* réaltra

gale *n* gála

gall bladder *n* máilín domlais

gallery *n* áiléar, gailearaí **art gallery** dánlann, **the National Gallery** an Dánlann/Gailearaí Náisiúnta

gallon *n* galún

gallop *v* dul ar cosa in airde

gallowglass *n* gallóglach

gallows *n* croch

gallstone *n* cloch dhomlais

Galway *n* Gaillimh **Co. Galway** Co. na Gaillimhe

gamble *n* fiontar *v* geall a chur

gambler *n* cearrbhach

gambling *n* cearrbhachas

gambling debts *pl* fiacha imeartha

gambolling *n* aoibheall

game¹ *n* **(shooting)** géim

game² *n* cluiche

game fishing *n* géimiascaireacht

gamma-ray *n* gáma-gha

gander *n* gandal **what's good for the goose is good for the gander** ní faide gob na gé ná gob an ghandail

gang *n* drong, buíon

ganger *n* saoiste

gangster *n* amhas, bithiúnach

gap *n* mant, bearna

gap-toothed *adj* mantach

garage *n* garáiste

garbage *n* truflais, bruscar

garden *n* gairdín, garraí

garden hose *n* píobán gairdín

garden lawn *n* faiche ghairdín

gardener *n* garraíodóir

gardening *n* garraíodóireacht

Garden of Eden *n* Gairdín Pharthais

gargle *n* craosfholcadh *v* craosfholc

garland *n* bláthfhleasc

garlic *n* gairleog **clove of garlic** ionga gairleoige

garment *n* ball éadaigh

garnish *n* gairnis *v* gairnisigh

garret *n* gairéad

garrison *n* garastún

garter *n* gairtéar

gas *n* gás *v* gásaigh

gash *n* créacht

gasket *n* gaiscéad

gas mask *n* gásphúicín

gas meter *n* gásmhéadar

gasp *n* cnead *v* cnead a ligean

gastric *adj* gastrach

gastroenteritis *n* gastaireintríteas

gate *n* geata

gatekeeper *n* geatóir

gather *v* cruinnigh, bailigh, tiomsaigh

gathering *n* tionól

gauge *n* tomhas, tomhsaire *v* tomhais **depth gauge** tomhsaire doimhneachta

gaunt *adj* lom, tarraingthe

gauze *n* uige

Gay and Lesbian Society *n* an Cumann Homaighnéasach agus Leispiach

gaze *v* stán

gazelle *n* gasail

gazetteer *n* gasaitéar

gear *n* trealamh, **(of car)** giar

gear box *n* giarbhosca

gel *n* glóthach **hair-gel** glóthach gruaige

geld *v* spoch

gelding *n* gearrán

gelignite *n* geilignít

gem *n* seoid

Gemini *n* an Cúpla

gender *n* inscne

gene *n* géin

genealogy *n* ginealach

general[1] *adj* comhchoiteann, ginearálta **in general** i gcoitinne

general[2] *adj* ard-, príomh- **General Post Office (GPO)** Ard-Oifig an Phoist

general[3] *n* **(army)** ginearál

general medical practice *n* cleachtadh ginearálta ar mhíochaine

general practitioner *n* gnáthdhochtúir, dochtúir teaghlaigh

general public *n* an pobal i gcoitinne

general purpose *adj* ilchuspóireach

generally *adv* i gcoitinne

generalise *v* **to generalise something** teoiric ghinearálta a bhaint as rud

generate *v* gin

generation *n* glúin

generation gap *n* glúinbhearna

generator *n* gineadóir

generosity *n* féile, flaithiúlacht

generous *adj* fial, flaithiúil

genetic *adj* géiniteach

genetic engineering *n* inncaltóireacht ghéiniteach

genetics *n* géineolaíocht

Geneva *n* an Ghinéiv **the Geneva Convention** Coinbhinsiún na Ginéive

genitive *adj, n* ginideach

genocide *n* cinedhíothú

gentle *adj* caoin, caomh, mánla, séimh

gentleman *n* duine uasal

genuflection *n* umhlú

genuine *adj* dílis **genuine copy** cóip dhílis

geographical *adj* geografach

geography *n* tíreolaíocht, geografaíocht

geology *n* geolaíocht

geometrical *adj* geoiméadrach

geometry *n* céimseata, geoiméadracht

geophysics *n* geoifisic

Georgian *adj* Seoirseach

geranium *n* geiréiniam

gerbil *n* geirbil

germ *n* frídín

German[1] *n* **(language)** an Ghearmáinis

German[2] *adj, n* Gearmánach

Germany *n* an Ghearmáin

germinate *v* péac

gerontologist *n* seaneolaí

gerontology *n* seaneolaíocht

gesticulate *v* gotháil

gesture *n* comhartha, geáitse, gotha *v* gotha a chur ort féin

gesturing *n* geáitsíocht

get *n* faigh **to get hold of** greim a fháil ar, **to get tired** éirí tuirseach

get over *v* **to get over something** rud a chur díot

ghastly *adj* urghránna

gheottoblaster *n* bleaistéir sráide

gherkin *n* gircín

ghetto *n* geiteo

ghost *n* púca, sprid, taibhse

ghost stories *pl* scéalta taibhsí

ghost writer *n* púca pinn

giant *n* fathach, arracht

gibberish *n* gibiris

giddy *n* aerach

gift *n* aisce, duais, bronntanas, féirín, tabhartas

gifted *adj* tréitheach

gift of the gab *n* bua na cainte

gigantic *adj* ollmhór, ábhalmhór

giggling *n* sciotaíl

gills *n* geolbhach

gilt *adj* órnite *n* órú

gin *n* jin **gin and tonic** jin agus athbhríoch

ginger *n* sinséar

giraffe *n* sioráf

girder *n* ccarchaill

girl *n* cailín, **(young)** girseach

girlfriend *n* cailín

give *v* tabhair

give in *v* géill

give way *v* géill slí

glaciation *n* oighriú

glacier *n* oighearshruth

glad *adj* gliondrach, áthasach

gladden *v* ríméad a chur ar

gladness *n* áthas

glance[1] *n* sracfhéachaint, súilfhéachaint

glance[2] *v* spléach

gland *n* faireog

glandular *adj* faireogach

glandular fever *n* fiabhras na bhfaireog

glare *n* dallrú *v* dallraigh

Glasgow *n* Glaschú

glass *n* gloine

glasses *pl* **(on face)** spéaclaí

glaze *n* **(pottery)** glónraigh, **(glass)** gloinigh

glazed *adj* **(pottery)** glónraithe, **(glass)** gloinithe

glazier *v* gloineadóir

gleam *n* **(of hope)** léaró (dóchais) *v* soilsigh

glean *v* diasraigh

gleaning *n* tacar

glee *n* spleodar

gleeful *adj* spleodrach

glen *n* gleann, **(little)** gleanntán

glider *n* faoileoir

gliding *n* faoileoireacht

glimmer *n* **(of hope)** léaró (dóchais)

glimpse *n* spléachadh

global *adj* domhanda

global warming *n* téamh aeráide

globe *n* cruinneog

gloom *n* dochma, dubhachas, gruaim, smúit

gloominess *n* duairceas, gruamacht

gloomy *adj* dubhach, gruama, smúitiúil

glorify *v* glóirigh

glorious *adj* glórmhar

glory *n* glóir *v* mórtas a dhéanamh as rud

glossary *n* gluais

gloss paint *n* peint lonrach

glossy *adj* snasta

glove *n* lámhainn

glow *n* luisne *v* luisnigh, dearg

glowing *adj* dearg

glucose *n* glúcós

glue *n* gliú *v* gliúáil

glum *adj* gruama

glutton *n* alpaire, craosaire

gnaw *v* cnaígh, creim

go *v* gabh, téigh, imigh, **to go out with somebody (in a relationship)** siúl amach le duine

go into liquidation *v* dul faoi leachtú

goad *v* prioc

goal *n* **(games)** cúl, báire, **(objective)** sprioc

goalkeeper *n* cúl báire

goalpost *n* cuaille báire

goat *n* gabhar

goatee *n* meigeall

gobble *v* smailc **to gobble food** bia a smailceadh

God *n* Dia **God save us!** Dia ár sábháil! **thank God!** buíochas le Dia! **with the help of God** le cúnamh/cuidiú Dé!

godchild *n* leanbh baistí

goddess *n* bandia

godfather *n* athair baistí

godmother *n* máthair bhaistí

godparent *n* cara (as) Críost

godsend *n* cabhair Dé

goggles *pl* gloiní cosanta

go-kart *n* cairtín

gold *n* ór

golden *adj* órga **the Golden Age** an Ré Órga

Golden Fleece *n* **(legend)** Lomra an Óir

golden syrup *n* órshúlach

goldfish *n* iasc órga

gold-plated *adj* órphlátáilte

goldsmith *n* órcheardaí

golf *n* galf

golf club *n* **(stick)** maide gailf, **(society)** club gailf

golfer *n* galfaire

gong *n* gang

good *adj* maith, múinte *n* maitheas **good-looking** dathúil, **good turn** gar, **good on you!** maith an buachaill! maith an cailín! **it will do you good** déanfaidh sé maitheas duit

goodness *n* maitheas

goods *pl* earraí, airnéis

goodwill *n* dea-mhéin

goose *n* gé **what's good for the goose is good for the gander** ní sia gob na gé ná gob an ghandail, **the Wild Geese** na Géanna Fiáine

gooseberry *n* spíonán

gore[1] *n* adharcáil

gore[2] *n* cró

gorgeous *adj* álainn, taibhseach

gorilla *n* goraille

gorse *n* aiteann

gory *adj* fuilteach

gospel *n* soiscéal, seanchas

gossip *n* cadráil, cúlchaint, **(person)** reacaire

gossiping *adj* burdach

gourmet *n* beadaí

gout *n* gúta

govern *v* rialaigh

government *n* rialtas

governor *n* gobharnóir

gown *n* gúna

grab *n* greim *v* sciob **to grab something** áladh a thabhairt ar rud, rud a sciobadh

grace *n* grásta

graceful *adj* mómhar

gracious *adj* grástúil, modhúil

grade *n* céim, grád *v* grádaigh

gradient *n* grádán

gradual *adj* de réir a chéile, céim ar chéim

gradually *adj* diaidh ar ndiaidh, de réir a chéile

graduate *n* céimí *v* bain céim amach

graft *n* nódú *v* nódaigh **skin graft** nódú craicinn

grain *n* gráinne, grán

gram *n* gram

grammar *n* gramadach

grammatical *adj* gramadúil

grand-[1] *prefix* mór-, príomh-, ard-

grand[2] *adj* ardnósach

grandad *n* daideo

grandchildren *n* clann clainne

granddaughter *n* gariníon

grandfather *n* athair críonna, athair mór, seanathair

grandma *n* mamó

grandmother *n* seanmháthair, máthair mhór, máthair chríonna

grandson *n* garmhac

granite *n* eibhear

grant[1] *v* deonaigh

grant[2] *n* deontas, deonú

granulate *v* gránaigh

granulation *n* gránú

grape *n* caor fíniúna, fíonchaor **bunch of grapes** triopall fíonchaor

grapefruit *n* seadóg

grape-vine *n* fíniúin

graph *n* graf

graphic *adj* grafach

graphic display unit *n* aonad taispeána grafach

graphics *n* grafaic

grapple *v* dul i ngreim le

grasp *n* greim *v* beir greim ar

grasping *adj* santach

grass *n* féar

grasshopper *n* dreoilín teaspaigh, críogar féir

grate[1] *n* gráta

grate[2] *v* grátáil

grateful *adj* buíoch

grating *n* díoscán, grátáil

gratitude *n* buíochas

gratuity *n* aisce

grave[1] *n* uaigh

grave[2] *adj* tromchúiseach

gravel *n* gairbhéal

graven *adj* greanta

graveyard *n* reilig

gravitate *v* imtharraing ar/timpeall

gravity[1] *n* domhantarraingt, imtharraingt

gravity[2] *n* (of situation) tromchúis

gravy *n* súlach

graze *v* gránaigh

grazing *n* iníor

grease *n* úsc

greasy *adj* úscach

great *adj* mór, mórga, mór **great courage** mórmhisneach

greater sand eel *n* corr ghainimh mhór

great-grandfather *n* sin-seanathair

great-grandmother *n* sin-seanmháthair

greatness *n* mórgacht

Greece *n* an Ghréig

greed *n* airc, ampla, antlás, cíocras, craos, saint

greediness *n* santacht

greedy *adj* amplach, antlásach, cíocrach, santach

Greek *adj* Gréagach *n* (language) an Ghréigis

green[1] *n* faiche, plásóg **St. Stephen's Green** Faiche Stiofáin

green[2] *adj* glas, uaine **green, white and orange (of Irish flag)** uaine, bán agus flannbhuí

greenery *n* duilliúr

greenhouse *n* teach gloine

greenhouse effect *n* iarmhairt cheaptha teasa

greenness *n* uaine

greet *v* beannaigh (do)

greeting *n* beannú

gregarious *adj* tréadúil

grenade *n* gránáid **hand grenade** gránáid láimhe, **live grenade** gránáid bheo, **incendiary grenade** gránáid loisceach

grey *adj* glas, liath

grey-haired *adj* ceannliath

greyhound *n* cú

grid *n* greille

grid chart *n* greillchairt

grief *n* dobrón

grievance *n* casaoid

grievance procedure *n* gnás casaoide

grieve *v* goill

grieving *adj, n* dobrónach

grievous *adj* léanmhar

grill[1] *n* greille

grill[2] *v* gríosc **to grill rashers** slisíní (bágúin) a ghríoscadh

grim *adj* dúr

grimace *n* cár, strainc **to grimace** strainc a chur ort féin

grime *n* salachar

grin *n* draid, draidgháire *v* draidgháire a dhéanamh

grind *v* cogain, meil, líomh, díosc

grinder *n* meilteoir

grinding *n* díoscán

grip[1] *n* greamán

grip[2] *v* greamaigh

grisly *adj* scanrúil

grit *n* grean

grizzly bear *n* béar liath

groan *n,v* cnead

grocer *n* grósaeir

groin *n* bléin

groom[1] *n* **(wedding)** grúm, baitsiléir

groom[2] *n* **(stable)** grúmaeir

groove *n* eitre

gross *adj* oll-, iomlán, comhlón, **(ugly)** gránna **gross profit** brabús comhlán

gross domestic product (GDP) *n* olltáirgeacht intíre (OTI)

gross national product (GNP) *n* olltáirgeacht náisiúnta (OTN)

grotesque *adj* ainspianta

grotesqueness *n* ainspiontacht

grotto *n* fochla

ground *n* fearann, talamh **to stand your ground** an fód a sheasamh

ground control officer *n* oifigeach rialúcháin ar talamh

ground floor *n* urlár na talún

grounds, on the grounds that ar an gcúis go

groundsman *n* coimeádaí páirce

group *n* dream, drong, grúpa *v* bailigh, grúpáil

grove *n* garrán

grovel *v* lútáil

grow *v* fás **to grow up** fás suas/aníos, **to grow bigger** dul i méid

growl *v* drantaigh

growth *n* fás **economic growth** fás geilleagrach

grub *n* **(insect)** cruimh

grubby *adj* salach

grudge *n* faltanas, olc *v* rud a mhaíomh ar dhuine

gruelling *adj* anróch, dian

gruff *adj* garg, giorraisc

grumble *n* casaoid *v* casaoid a dhéanamh

grumpy *adj* cancrach

grunt *n* uallfairt *v* uallfairt a ligean

guarantee *n* ráthaíocht, slánaíocht, urrús *v* ráthaigh

guaranteed *adj* **(under guarantee)** faoi ráthaíocht

guarantor *n* urra, ráthóir

guard[1] *v* caomhnaigh, fair, gardáil

guard[2] *n* garda, coimhéad **security guard** garda slándála, **on your guard** ar do choimhéad

guardian *n* caomhnóir, coimirceoir

guerrilla *n* treallchogaí

guerrilla warfare *n* treallchogaíocht

guess *n* tomhas *v* tomhais

guest *n* aoi

guidance *n* treoir, stiúir

guide *n* treoraí *v* treoraigh

guide dog *n* madra daill

guidebook *n* eolaí, treoirleabhar

guided *adj* treoraithe, faoi threorú **guided missile** diúracán treoraithe / faoi threorú

guideline *n* treoirlíne **guidelines** treoirlínte

guild *n* cuallacht

guillotine *n* gilitín *v* dicheann

guilty *adj* ciontach

guinea pig *n* muc ghuine

guitar n giotár

gulf n murascaill **the Gulf War** Cogadh na Murascaille, **the Gulf of Mexico** Murascaill Mheicsiceo

gull n faoileán

gullet n craos, góilín

gullible adj saonta

gully n clasán

gulp v slog **gulp it down** slog siar é

gum[1] n **(mouth)** drandal

gum[2] n guma **chewing gum** guma coganta

gun n gunna **hilti / soldering gun** gunna hilti/sádrála

gunner n gunnadóir

gunpowder n púdar (gunna)

gun salute n cúirtéis ghunnaí

gunshot n urchar gunna

gush n, v brúcht

gusset n asclán

gust n séideán

gut n putóg v an t-ionathar a bhaint as

gutter n gáitéar

gutter press n nuachtáin lathaigh

guzzle v alp, slog

gymkhana n giomcána

gymnasium n giomnáisiam, halla gleacaíochta

gymnast n gleacaí

gymnastics n gleacaíocht

gynaecologist n lia ban, gínéiceolaí

gynaecology n gínéiceolaíocht

gypsy n giofóg

gyrate v cas, rothlaigh

gyration n rothlú

H

haberdashery n mionéadach

habit[1] n **(dress)** aibíd

habit[2] n nós, béas **bad habit** míbhéas

habitat n gnáthóg

habitation n áitreabh

hack v ciorraigh

hacker n **(computer)** bradaí

haddock n cadóg

haemophilia n haemaifilia

haemophiliac n haemaifiliach

haemorrhage n rith fola

haemorrhoids pl daorghalar

hag n cailleach

haggard adj caite n iothlainn

haggle v margáil, stangaireacht a dhéanamh

haggler n mangaire

Hague, the n an Háig

hail n cloichshneachta

hailstones pl meallóga cloichshneachta

hailstorm n stoirm chloichshneachta

hair n gruaig, clúmh, fionnadh, **(single hair)** ribe

hairclip n fáiscín gruaige

hair conditioner n feabhsóir gruaige

haircut n bearradh gruaige

hairdresser n gruagaire

hairdressing n gruagaireacht

hairdryer n triomadóir gruaige

hairy n gruagach, ribeach

hake n colmóir

half n leath prefix leath-

half-back n **(sport)** leathchúlaí

half-breed n meascach

half-cast n meascach

half-day n leathlá

half-forward n **(sport)** leath-thosaí

half-hearted adj ar nós cuma liom/leat/leis/léi/linn/libh/leo

half-hour n leathuair (a chloig)

half-pint *n* leathphionta
half-way *n* leathbhealach
hall *n* halla
hallmark *n* sainmharc
Hallowe'en *n* Oíche Shamhna
hallucination *n* meascán mearaí
halo *n* naomhluan
halt *n* stad *v* stad, stop
halting *adj* **(speech)** stadach
halting-site *n* stadláithreán
halve *v* leath
ham *n* liamhás
hamburger *n* borgaire
hamlet *n* gráig
hammer *n* casúr *v* casúireacht a dhéanamh
hammock *n* ámóg, crandaí, leaba luascáin
hamper *n* amparán *v* bac
hand *n* lámh *v* sín (chuig), tabhair (do) **to get the upper hand** an lámh in uachtar a fháil ar dhuine, **hands on experience** taithí láimhe
handbag *n* mála láimhe
handblown glass *n* gloine lámhshéidte
handbook *n* lámhleabhar
handbrake *n* coscán láimhe
handcuffs *pl* dornaisc
handful *n* dornán, mám **a handful of money** mám airgid
handicap *n* bac, **(golf)** cis **mental handicap** bac meabhrach
handicapped *adj* faoi éalang, éalangach **mentally handicapped** faoi bhac meabhrach
handicraft *n* obair láimhe
handiness *n* deaslámhacht, áisiúlacht
handiwork *n* obair láimhe, abhras
handkerchief *n* ciarsúr **paper handkerchief** ciarsúr páipéir
handle *n* cos, crann, dorn, hanla *v* ionramháil, láimhseáil, láimhsigh

handling *n* láimhdeachas
handmade *adj* lámhdhéanta
handprint *n* lorg láimhe
handshake *n* lámhchroitheadh, croitheadh láimhe
handsome *adj* dathúil, dóighiúil
handwriting *n* lámhscríbhneoireacht
handy *adj* deaslámhach, áisiúil
hang *v* croch
hangar *n* haingear
hanger *n* crochadán
hanging *n* crochadh **hanging in the balance** idir dhá cheann na meá
hangover *n* póit
Ha'penny Bridge *n* Droichead na Leathphingine
happen *v* tarlaigh, teagmhaigh
happening *n* tarlú, teagmhas
happiness *n* áthas, aoibhneas, sonas
happy *adj* áthasach, sona **she is happy** tá áthas uirthi, tá sí sona
harass *v* ciap
harassment *n* ciapadh **sexual harassment** gnéaschiapadh
harbour *n* caladh, calafort, cuan, port *v* coinnigh, dídean a thabhairt do
hard *adj* crua, **(difficult)** deacair, dian, doiligh
hard disk *n* cruadhiosca, diosca crua
harden *v* cruaigh
hard-hat *n* clogad cruach
hardliner *n* dochtaire
hardly *adv* ar éigean
hardness *n* déine
hardship *n* cruatan, anró
hardware *n* crua-earraí
hardwood *n* crua-adhmad
hard-working *adj* dícheallach
hardy *adj* cróga, crua, miotalach
hare *n* giorria
hare-lip *n* bearna mhíl, bearna ghiorria

harm *n* aimhleas, anachain, lot, díobháil, dochar, urchóid *v* díobháil / dochar a dhéanamh do **what harm?** cén dochar / díobháil?

harmful *adj* aimhleasach, díobhálach, dochrach, urchóideach

harmless *adj* neamhdhíobhálach

harmonic *adj* armónach

harmonisation *n* **(of rules etc)** comhchuibhiú

harmonise *v* armónaigh, réitigh le

harmonium *n* armóin

harmony *n* **(music)** comhcheol, armóin

harness *n* úim

harp *n* cruit, cláirseach **Jew's harp** trumpa béil

harrow *v* fuirsigh

harsh *adj* garg, garbh

harvest *n* fómhar *v* an fómhar a dhéanamh

hashish *n* haisis

haste *n* deifir, deabhadh

hasten *v* deifrigh

hasty *adj* deifreach

hat *n* hata

hatch *n* haiste *v* gor

hatchback *n* cúlhaiste

hatchet *n* tua

hate[1] *n* fuath **I hate it** is fuath liom é

hate[2] *v* fuathaigh, an ghráin (dhearg) a bheith agat ar...

hateful *adj* fuafar

hatred *n* fuath

haughty *adj* móiréiseach

haul *n* **(of fish)** cor *v* tarraing

haulage *n* tarlú

haunt *n* gnáthóg *v* gnáthaigh

have *v* **I have ...** tá ... agam, **to have a meal** béile a chaitheamh, **to have repercussions** drochthoradh a bheith ar

havoc *n* scrios, ár

hawk *n* seabhac

hawker *n* mangaire

hawthorn *n* sceach gheal

hay *n* féar

hay fever *n* fiabhras léana

hayfork *n* féir píce

haystack *n* cruach fhéir

hazard *n* guais *v* **hazard a guess** tabhair buille faoi thuairim

haze *n* ceo

hazel *n* coll **hazel tree** crann coill

hazelnut *n* cnó coill

hazy *adj* doiléir, **(of weather)** ceobhránach

he *pron* sé, é **he talks too much** labhraíonn sé an iomarca, **he is a friend** is cara é

head *n* ceann, cloigeann, **(person in charge)** ceannaire *v* treoraigh

headache *n* tinneas cinn

headboard *n* **(of bed)** clár cinn

headgear *n* ceannbheart

headguard *n* clogad

heading *n* ceannteideal

headland *n* ros

headlight *n* ceannsolas

headline *n* ceannlíne

headmaster *n* ardmháistir

headmistress *n* ardmháistreás

headphones *pl* cluasáin

headquarters *pl* ceanncheathrú

headscarf *n* caifirín

headstrong *adj* ceanndána, ardintinneach

headword *n* ceannfhocal

heal *v* cneasaigh, leigheas

healing herbs *pl* luibheanna leighis

health *n* sláinte **health is better than wealth** is fearr an tsláinte ná na táinte

health foods *pl* slánbhianna

healthier eating habits *pl* nósanna itheacháin níos sláintiúla

healthiness *n* folláine

healthy *adj* folláin, sláintiúil

heap *n, v* carn, cnap **heap of money** cnap airgid

hear *v* airigh, clois, éist, mothaigh

hearing *n* éisteacht

hearing aid *n* áis éisteachta

hearse *n* cóiste na marbh, eileatram

heart *n* croí, **(cards)** hart **the heart of the matter** croí na ceiste

heart attack *n* taom croí

heartburn *n* daigh chroí

hearth *n* tinteán

heartily *adv* go croíúil, le croí mór

hearty *adj* croíúil, folláin

heat *n* teas *v* téigh **to heat something** rud a théamh

heater *n* téitheoir **gas, electric heater** téitheoir gáis, leictreach

heather *n* fraoch

heating *n* téamh **central heating** téamh lárnach

heatproof *adj* teasdíonach

heaven *n* na Flaithis, neamh

heavenly *adj* neamhaí

heavy metal *n* miotal trom, **(music)** ceol trom-mhiotalach

heavy-hearted *adj* tromchroíoch

heavyweight *n* trom-mheáchan

Hebrew *adj* Eabhrach *n* **(language)** Eabhrais

hedge *n* fál

hedgehog *n* gráinneog

hedge-school *n* scoil scairte

hedonism *n* héadónachas

heed *n* aird *v* aird a thabhairt ar, ceann a thabhairt de

heedless *adj* neamhairdiúil

heel *n* sáil, **(of bread)** crústa

heifer *n* bearach

height *n* ard, airde **at the height of one's career** in ard do réime

heighten *v* cur le, ardaigh

heir *n* comharba, oidhre **royal heir** rídhamhna

heirloom *n* séad fine

helicopter *n* héileacaptar, ingearán

heliport *n* héileaport

hell *n* ifreann **hell!** damnú!

hellish *adj* damnaithe

helm *n* stiúir

helmet *n* clogad **crash helmet** clogad cosanta

help *n* cabhair, cuidiú, cúnamh *v* cabhraigh, cuidigh, fóir **help! fóir orm! it can't be helped** níl leigheas/neart air

helper *n* cuiditheoir, cúntóir

helpful *adj* cabhrach, cuidiúil, cúntach

helpless *adj* gan chuidiú

hem *n* fáithim

hemisphere *n* leathsféar

hen *n* cearc

hepatitis *n* heipitíteas

her[1] *pron* í, ise, sise **do you like her** an maith leat í? **apart from her** seachas ise, **without her** gan sise

her[2] *pass adj* a **her carr** a carr **her name** a hainm

herald *n* aralt

heraldic *adj* araltach

heraldry *n* araltas

herb *n* luibh, lus

herbivore *n* luibhiteoir

herd *n* táin, tréad *v* tar/tabhair le chéile

here *adv* abhus, anseo **over here** abhus anseo, **here and there** thall agus abhus, anseo is ansiúd, **how long have you been here?** cá fhad atá tú anseo? **in here** istigh anseo

hereditary *adj* dúchasach, oidhreachtúil

heredity *n* dúchas

heresy *n* eiriceacht

heretic *adj, n* eiriceach

heritage *n* dúchas, oidhreacht

heritage centre *n* lárionad oidhreachta

hermetic(al) *adj*

hermit *n* díthreabhach

hermitage *n* díseart

hero *n* gaiscíoch, laoch

heroic *adj* gaisciúil

heroin *n* hearóin

heroine *n* banlaoch

heroism *n* laochas, gaisciúlacht

heron *n* corr, Jónaí an scrogaill

herring *n* scadán

herring-bone *n* **(clothes)** cnámh scadáin

hesitancy *n* braiteoireacht

heterosexual *adj, n* heitreaghnéasach

hibernate *v* geimhrigh

hibernation *n* geimhriú

hiccup *n* fail, snag **I've got hiccups** tá fail/snag orm

hidden *adj* i bhfolach

hide *n* seithe *v* ceil, folaigh

hideous *adj* urghránna

hiding *n* folach, folachán

hierarchy *n* cliarlathas

hieroglyphics *pl* iairiglifí

high *adj* ard, ar airde

high fibre food *n* bia le neart snáithín

high pressure *n* ardbhrú

higher *adj* níos airde

higher diploma in education (H Dip) *n* ardteastas oideachais

highlight[1] *n* buaicphointe

highlight[2] *v* cuir béim air, **(with highlighter)** aibhsigh

highlighter *n* **(pen)** peann aibhsithe

highly explosive *adj* **(material)** (ábhar) tréanphléasach

high-risk activities *pl* gníomhartha fíorchontúirteacha

high-spirited *adj* ardintinneach

high-yielding varieties *pl* cineálacha tromthoraidh

hijack *v* fuadaigh

hijacker *n* fuadaitheoir

hijacking *n* fuadú

hike *n* siúlóid *v* siúil

hiker *n* siúlóir

hilarious *adj* scléipeach

hilarity *n* scléip

hill *n* cnoc

hillock *n* cnocán, maoil, altán, alt, tulach

hilly *adj* cnocach

him *pron* é **without him** gan é, **I don't like him** ní maith liom é

hinder *v* bac

hindrance *n* bac

hindsight *n* iarghaois

hinge *n* inse

hint *n* leathfhocal, leid, nod *v* nod/leid a thabhairt

hip *n* corróg, cromán

hippopotamus *n* dobhareach

hire *n* cíos *v* **to hire a car** carr a fháil ar cíos, carr a fhruiliú

hire-purchase (h.p.) *n* fruilcheannach (f.c.)

his *poss adj* a **his car** a charr, **his name** a ainm

hissing *n* siosarnach

historian *n* staraí

historic(al) *adj* stairiúil

historical costume *n* culaithirt seanré

history *n* stair

hit *n* buille, **(on target)** aimsiú *v* buail, aimsigh

hitch *v* dul ar an ordóg

hitch-hike *v* síobshiúil

hitch-hiker *n* síobshiúlóir

HIV *n* VEID (víreas easpa imdhíonachta daonna)

hive *n* **(bees)** coirceog
hives *pl* aodh thochais
hoard *n* taisce *v* taisc
hoarse *adj* piachánach
hoarseness *n* piachán
hob *n* iarta
hobgoblin *n* púca
hockey *n* haca
hoist *n* ardaitheoir *v* ardaigh
hold[1] *v* coinnigh, coimeád **hold on to it** coinnigh greim air
hold[2] *n* greim, **(of boat)** broinn
hold up *v* **(support)** tacaigh
holder *n* **(object)** gabhdán, **(person)** sealbhóir
holding *n* gabháltas
hole *n* poll
holiday *n* saoire **package holiday** saoire láneagraithe
holiness *n* naofacht
Holland *n* an Ollainn
hollow *n* log, cuasach, toll
holly *n* cuileann
holocaust *n* uileloscadh
hologram *n* holagram
holography *n* holagrafaíocht
holster *n* curra
holy *n* naofa, beannaithe **the Holy Land** an Talamh Naofa, an Tír Bheannaithe, **holy water** uisce coisricthe, **Holy Week** Seachtain na Páise
homage *n* ómós
home *n* baile **there's no place like home** níl aon tinteán mar do thinteán féin, **at home** ag baile, sa bhaile
homelessness *n* easpa dídine
homeless person *n* díthreabhach
homely *adj* tíriúil
home-made bread *n* arán baile
homepage *n* **(internet)** leathanach baile, clár cinn

homesickness *n* cumha i ndiaidh an bhaile
homewards *adv* abhaile
homework *n* obair bhaile
homicide *n* dúnbhású
homily *n* aitheasc
homogeneous *adj* aonchineálach
homosexual *adj*, *n* homaighnéasach
honest *adj* ionraic, macánta
honesty *n* ionracas, macántacht
honey *n* mil
honeycomb *n* cíor mheala
honeymoon *n* mí na meala
honeysuckle *n* féithleog, féithleann
honorary *adj* oinigh, onórach
honour *n* onóir, urraim *v* onóraigh **honours degree** céim onóracha
honourable *adj* onórach
hood *n* cochall
hoof *n* crúb
hook *n* crúca, duán *v* crúca/duán a chur i
hooligan *n* amhas
hoop *n* fonsa
hoot *n*, *v* **(owl)** scréach
hope *n* dóchas, uchtach **I hope she's right** tá súil agam go bhfuil an ceart aici, **the Cape of Good Hope** Rinn an Dóchais
hopeful *adj* dóchasach
hopeless *adj* doleigheasta, eadóchasach
horizon *n* léaslíne, fíor na spéire
horizontal *adj* cothrománach
hormone *n* hormón
horn *n* adharc, **(drinking)** corn
horned *adj* adharcach
hornet *n* cornfhoiche
hornless *adj* maol
hornpipe *n* cornphíopa
horoscope *n* tuismeá
horrible *adj* millteach, uafar, uafásach

horrify v uafás a chur ar

horror n uafás **horror film** scannán uafáis

horse n each, capall **vaulting horse** capall maide, **on horseback** ar muin capaill

horse-chestnut n cnó capaill

horseman n marcach

horsepower n each-chumhacht

horse-radish sauce n anlann raidise fiáine

horseshoe n crú

horticulture n gortóireacht

hose n píobán **fire-hose** píobán dóiteáin

hospice n ospís

hospitable adj fáilteach

hospital n ospidéal

hospitality n ósta, féile

host[1] n **(wafer)** abhlann

host[2] n óstach

host[3] n slua **the fairy host** an slua sí

hostage n giall

hostel n brú

hostile adj naimhdeach

hostility n naimhdeas

hot adj te, teasaí

hot-press n prios aerála

hot rolled steel n cruach theorollta

hotchpotch n manglam

hotel n óstlann, óstán, teach ósta

hot-tempered adj teasaí

hound n cú

hour n uair, uair an chloig

hourly adj in aghaidh na huaire

house n teach, áras

household n comhluadar, líon tí, teaghlach

household vessels n árais tí

householder n ceann tí

housekeeper n fear/bean tí

housekeeping n tíos

housing n tithíocht **housing estate** eastát tithíochta

hovel n cró

hovering adj ar foluain

how adv conas **how are you?** conas tá tú? cén chaoi a bhfuil tú? cad é mar tá tú? **how many?** an mó? cá/cé mhéad? **how much?** cá/cé mhéad? **how often?** cé chomh minic? cá mhinice?

however adv ámh, arae, áfach

howl n glam v glam a ligean

huddle n gróigeadh v gróig

huff n smut, spuaic **he's in a huff with me** tá smut air liom

huffy adj stainceach

hug n barróg **to hug somebody** barróg a thabhairt do/a bhreith ar dhuine

huge adj ollmhór

hull n cabhail

hum n crónán, dord, dordán v crónán a dhéanamh

human adj daonna **the human race** an cine daonna, **human nature** daonnacht, **human being** daonnaí, neach daonna

humane adj daonnachtúil

humanist n daonnachtaí

humanitarian adj daonchairdiúil

humanity n daonnacht

humanise v daonnaigh

humble adj uiríseal, uirísligh, umhlaigh **humble person** umhal

humid adj tais

humidifier n taisire

humiliate v uirísligh

humiliation n uirísliú

humility n umhlaíocht

humorous adj greannmhar

humour[1] n giúmar, greann

humour[2] n **(bodily)** lionn

hump n cruit, dronn

humped adj dronnach

hunchback *n* cruiteachán

hunchbacked *adj* cruiteach

hundred *n* céad **in (their) hundreds** ina gcéadta

hundredth *adj, n* céadú

hunger[1] *n* ocras, gorta **great hunger** airc, ampla

hunger[2] *v* **to hunger for something** cíocras a bheith ort chuig rud

hungry *adj* ocrach, gortach, amplach **I'm hungry** tá ocras orm

hunkers *pl* **on one's hunkers** ar do ghogaide

hunt *n, v* fiach, seilg

hunter *n* fiagaí, ruagaire, sealgaire

hunting *n* sealgaireacht

hurdle *n* cliath

hurl *v* rad, iomáin

hurler *n* iománaí

hurling *n* iománaíocht, iománt

hurricane *n* hairicín

hurried *adj* deifreach

hurry *n* deabhadh, deifir *v* deifrigh, brostaigh

hurt[1] *v* goill, loit, gortaigh

hurt[2] *adj* gonta

hurtful *adj* dochrach

husband *n* fear céile

hush! *excl* fuist!

husk *n* crotal

husky *n* huscaí

hustle *n* brú *v* brúigh

hut *n* bothán

hydraulic *adj* hiodrálach

hydroculture *n* hidreashaothrú

hydroelectric *adj* hidrileictreach

hydro-electric power *n* cumhacht hidrileictreach

hydrogen *n* hidrigin

hydraulic *adj* hiodrálach

hydraulics *pl* hiodrálaic

hyena *n* hiéana

hygiene *n* sláinteachas

hygienic *adj* sláinteach

hymn *n* iomann

hyphen *n* fleiscín

hypnotise *v* hiopnóisigh

hypnotism *n* hiopnóiseachas

hypnotist *n* hiopnóisí

hypocrisy *n* fimíneacht, béalchrábhadh

hypocrite *n* fimíneach

hypocritical *adj* fimíneach, béalchrábhadh

hypothesis *n* hipitéis

hysteria *n* histéire

hysterical *adj* histéireach

I

I *pron* mé, mise **I sold it** dhíol mé é

ice *n* oighear *v* oighrigh

ice-age *n* oighearaois

iceberg *n* cnoc oighir

ice-cream *n* uachtar reoite

ice-cube *n* ciúb oighir

Iceland *n* an Íoslainn

ice-pop *n* líreacán reoite

icing *n* reoán

icing sugar *n* siúcra reoáin

ICU (intensive care unit) *n* aonad dianchúraim

icy *adj* oighreata

idea *n* idé, smaoineamh

ideal *adj* idéalach *n* idéal

idealism *n* idéalachas

idealist *n* idéalaí

identical *n* comhionann

identification *n* aitheantas **identity papers** páipéir aitheantais

identify *v* aithin

identity *n* céannacht

identity card (i.d.) *n* cárta aitheantais

ideology *n* idé-eolaíocht

idiocy *n* amaideacht

idiom *n* nath cainte, cor cainte

idiosyncrasy *n* aisteachas

idiot *n* amadán

idiotic *adj* amaideach

idle *adj* díomhaoin, neamhghnóthach **an idle day** lá faoin tor

idleness *n* díomhaointeas

idol *n* íol

idolise *v* adhair

if *conj* má, dá **if I were you** dá mba mise thusa, **if not** mura, murach, **if he told you so** má dúirt sé leat é

ignite *v* adhain

ignoble *adj* anuasal

ignore *v* scaoil thar **ignore him / it** ná tabhair aon aird air

ignoramus *n* ainbhiosán

ignorance *n* ainbhios, aineolas

ignorant *adj* ainbhiosach, aineolach

ill *adj* breoite, tinn

illegal *adj* mídhleathach

illegible *adj* doléite

illegitimate *adj* mídhlisteanach

illiteracy *n* neamhlitearthacht

illiterate *adj* neamhliteartha

ill-mannered *adj* drochmhúinte, míbhéasach

illness *n* tinneas, breoiteacht

illuminate *v* soilsigh

illumination *n* soilsiú

illusion *n* seachmall

illusionism *n* meabhlachas

illustrate *n* léirigh, maisigh

illustration *n* léaráid, samhlaoid

illustrator *n* maisitheoir leabhar

image *n* íomhá, samhlaoid

imagery *n* samhlaoidí

imaginary *adj* samhailteach

imagination *n* samhlaíocht

imaginative *adj* samhlaíoch **imaginative reconstruction** athchruthú samhlaíoch

imagine *v* samhlaigh

imbalance *n* éagothroime

imitate *v* aithris a dhéanamh ar

imitation *n* aithris, scigaithris

imitation leather *n* leathar tacair

immaculate *adj* gan smál

immaterial *adj* neamhábhartha

immature *adj* neamhaibí, anabaí

immaturity *n* anabaíocht

immeasurable *adj* domheasta

immediate *adj* láithreach, gar- **immediate environment** garthimpeallacht

immediately *adj* ar an toirt, láithreach, bonn

immense *adj* ollmhór

immerse *v* tum

immersion *n* tumadh, bá

immersion heater *n* tumthéitheoir

immigrant *adj, n* inimirceach

immigration *n* inimirce

immoderate *adj* ainmheasartha

immoderation *n* ainmheasarthacht

immodest *adj* mímhodhúil

immoral *adj* mímhorálta

immorality *n* mímhoráltacht

immortal *adj* neamhbhásmhar

immortality *n* neamhbhásmhaireacht

immune *adj* imdhíonach

immunity *n* díolúine, **(health)** imdhíonacht

impact *n* turraing

impair *v* loit

impartiality *n* neamhchlaontacht

impassable *adj* dothrasnaithe
impassive *adj* dochorraithe
impatience *n* mífhoighne
impatient *adj* mífhoighneach
impede *v* bac
impediment *n* constaic
impenetrable *adj* dophollta
imperative *adj* fíorphráinneach
  adj, n **(grammar)** ordaitheach
imperceptible *adj* do-bhraite
imperfect *adj* neamhfhoirfe
imperial *adj* impiriúil
imperialism *n* impiriúlachas
impermanent *adj* neamhbhuan
impermeable *adj* díonach,
  neamhscagach
impersonal *adj* neamhphearsanta
impersonate *v* pearsanaigh
impertinent *adj* deiliúsach
imperturbable *adj* fuarchúiseach
impetuous *adj* spadhrúil
impetus *n* spreagadh
impinge *v* teagmháil le
implacable *adj* doshásta
implement *n* giuirléid
implicate *v* cuir cuid den mhilleán
  ar
implicit *adj* intuigthe
implore *v* achainnigh
imply *v* ciallaigh
impolite *adj* mímhúinte
import *n* allmhaire *v* allmhairigh
importance *n* tábhacht
important *adj* tábhachtach
importer *n* allmhaireoir
impose *v* forchuir
impossible *adj* dodhéanta
impotence *n* éagumas
impotent *adj* éagumasach
impound *v* gaibhnigh
impoverish *v* bochtaigh
impoverishment *n* bochtú

impractical *adj* neamhphraiticiúil
imprecise *adj* neamhchruinn
impress *v* cuir ina luí ar, téigh i
  bhfeidhm ar
impression *n* imprisean
impressionist *n* impriseanaí
impressive *adj* sonrach
imprint *n* cló, inphrionta
imprison *v* cuir i bpríosún
improbable *adj* andóch
improbability *n* andóigh
improve *v* feabhsaigh
improvement *n* feabhas
improvisation *n* seiftiú
improvise *v* seiftigh
impudence *n* deiliús, soibealtacht,
  athchaint
impudent *adj* deiliúsach, soibealta
impulse *n* ríog, tallann
impulsive *adj* ríogach, tallanach
impure *adj* neamhghlan
in[1] i, isteach **in the first instance** ar
  an gcéad ásc, **come in** tar isteach,
  in Derry i nDoire
in-[2] *prefix* neamh-, mí-, do-
in-company training *n* oiliúint i
  gcuideachta
in-thing *n* tóir-rud, rud a bhfuil tóir
  air
in-word *n* tóirfhocal, focal a bhfuil
  tóir air
inability *n* míchumas
inaccurate *adj* míchruinn
inactive *adj* neamhghníomhach
inadequate *adj* uireasach
inanimate *adj* neamhbheo
inappropriate *adj* neamh-oiriúnach
inarticulate *adj* dothuigthe
inarticulateness *n* amhlabhra
inattention *n* neamhaird
inattentive *adj* neamhairdiúil
inaudible *adj* dochloiste
inborn *adj* dúchasach

incapable *adj* éagumasach, míchumasach, neamhábalta

incapacity *n* éagumas

incarnate *adj* i gcolainn dhaonna *v* cuir i gcrích

incarnation *n* ionchollú

incendiary device *n* gaireas loisceach

incense *n* túis

incentive *n* dreasacht, spreagadh

incessant *adj* síoraí

incest *n* ciorrú coil

inch *n* orlach **seven inches** seacht n-orlaí

incident *n* teagmhas

incidental *adj* teagmhasach

incite *v* saighid

inclement *adj* anróiteach

inclination *n* claonadh, luí, slios

incline *n* fána *v* claon **to be inclined (to do something)** claonadh a bheith ionat (rud a dhéanamh)

include *v* áirigh, cuir san áireamh

inclusive *adj* cuimsitheach

income *n* fáltas, ioncam, teacht isteach

incoming tide *n* taoide thuile

incompatibility *n* neamh-chomhoiriúnacht

incompatible *adj* neamh-chomhoiriúnach

incompetent *adj* neamhéifeachtach

incomplete *adj* neamhiomlán

incomprehensible *adj* dothuigthe

inconclusive *adj* éiginntitheach

incongruous *adj* mífhreagrach

inconsiderate *adj* neamhthuisceanach

inconsistent *adj* neamhsheasmhach

inconspicuous *adj* neamhfheiceálach, neamhshuntasach

incontinence *n* neamhchoinneálacht

inconvenience *n* aistear, míchaothúlacht

inconvenient *adj* mí-áisiúil, míchaothúil, **(of place)** aistreach

incorporate *v* ionchorpraigh

incorrect *adj* mícheart

increase *n* méadú, ardú *v* ardaigh, méadaigh

increasing *adj* méadaitheach

incredible *adj* dochreidte

increment *n* incrimint

incriminate *v* ciontaigh, rud a chur síos do dhuine, rud a chur i leith duine

incubate *v* gor

incubation *n* gor

incubator *n* goradán

incurable *adj* doleigheasta

indecent *adj* mígheanasach **indecent exposure** nochtadh mígheanasach

indecision *n* éiginnteacht

indeed *adv* ambaiste, go deimhin, leoga

indefinite *adj* éiginnte

indemnity *n* slánaíocht

indent *v* eangaigh

indentation *n* eang

indented *adj* eangach

independence *n* neamhspleáchas **the War of Independence** Cogadh na Saoirse

independent *adj* neamhspleách, saor

indescribable *adj* do-inste

indestructible *adj* doscriosta

index *n* innéacs, **(number)** treoiruimhir *v* innéacsaigh **consumer price index** treoiruimhir praghsanna do thomhaltóirí

index finger *n* an mhéar thosaigh

India *n* an India

Indian *adj, n* Indiach **West-Indian** Iar-Indiach

indicate *v* comharthaigh

indication *n* tásc

indicative *adj* táscach

indicator *n* táscaire

indict *v* díotáil

indictment *n* díotáil

indifference *n* neamhshuim

indifferent *adj* leathmheasartha **to be indifferent** bheith ar nós cuma liom

indigestion *n* mídhíleá, tinneas bhéal an ghoile

indignant *adj* díomúch, feargach

indignation *n* díomua, fearg

indignity *n* easonóir

indigo *n* plúirín

indigo-blue *adj* plúiríneach

indirect *adj* indíreach

indiscreet *adj* béalscaoilte

indiscriminate *adj* gan idirdhealú

indispensable *adj* éigeantach, riachtanach

indisputable *adj* dobhréagnaithe

indistinct *adj* doiléir

individual *adj* aonair **individual skills** scileanna aonair

individuality *n* indibhidiúlacht

Indo-European *adj* Ind-Eorpach *n* **(language)** Ind-Eorpais

indolent *adj* leisciúil

indoor *adj* (taobh) istigh

induce *v* meall, spreag

inductor *n* ionduchtóir

indulge *v* luí isteach air

industrial *adj* tionsclaíoch

industrial estate *n* eastát tionsclaíochta

industrialisation *n* tionsclaíocht

industrialise *v* tionsclaigh

industrialist *n* tionsclaí

industrious *adj* tionsclach, treallúsach

industriousness *n* treallús

industry *n* tionscal **service industry** tionscal seirbhíse

inedible *adj* do-ite

inefficient *adj* mí-éifeachtach

inept *adj* mí-oiriúnach

inequality *n* éagothroime, leatrom, neamhionannas

inertia *n* marbhántacht

inescapable *adj* dosheachanta

inevitable *adj* dosheachanta

inexact *adj* míchruinn

inexhaustible *adj* do-ídithe

inexpensive *adj* neamhchostasach

inexperience *n* easpa taithí

infallible *adj* do-earráide

infamous *adj* mícháiliúil

infancy *n* naíonacht

infant *n* naí, naíonán **newborn infant** naíonán nuabheirthe

infantry *n* cos-slua

infantryman *n* coisí

infatuation *n* saobhghrá

infect *v* ionfhabhtaigh

infection *n* ionfhabhtú

infectious *adj* ionfhabhtaíoch, tógálach

inferior *adj* íochtarach *n* íochtarán

inferior goods *pl* earraí lagmheasa

infernal *adj* ifreanda

infertile *adj* neamhthorthúil

infidelity *n* mídhílseacht

infinite *adj* infinideach, neamhtheoranta

infinity *n* neamhtheorantacht, infinideacht

infirm *adj* easlán

infirmary *n* otharlann

infirmity *n* cróilí

inflame *v* las

inflamed *adj* athlasta

inflammable *adj* inlasta

inflammation *n* athlasadh

inflatable *adj* inséidte

inflate *v* séid

inflation *n* séideadh, **(monetary)** boilsciú

inflexible *adj* dolúbtha

inflict a penalty on *v* pionós a ghearradh ar

inflow of cash *n* insreabhadh airgid

influence *n* tionchar

influenza *n* fliú

inform *v* rud a chur in iúl

inform on *v* sceith ar

informal *adj* neamhfhoirmiúil

informant *n* faisnéiseoir

information *n* eolas, faisnéis, fios, tuairisc

information technology *n* teicneolaíocht (an) eolais, ríomhaireacht

informative *adj* faisnéiseach

informer *n* sceithire

infrastructure *n* bonneagar

infrequent *adj* annamh

infringe *v* sáraigh

infringement *n* sárú

infuriate *v* cuir le buile

ingenuity *n* gliceas, beartaíocht

ingratiating *adj* plásánta

ingratitude *n* míbhuíochas

ingredient *n* comhábhar

ingrowing toenail *n* ionga i bhfeoil

inhabit *v* áitrigh

inhabitant *n* (of house) áitreabhach, áitritheoir, (of country) dúchasach

inhale *v* ionanálaigh

inherent *adj* dúchasach

inherit *v* rud a fháil le hoidhreacht

inheritance *n* oidhreacht

inhibit *v* rud a chrosadh ar

inhospitality *n* doicheall

inhuman *adj* mídhaonna

initial *adj* tionscantach *n* iniseal

initiate *v* tosaigh, tionscain

initiative *n* tionscnamh

initiator *n* tionscnóir

inject *v* insteall

injection *n* instealladh

injunction *n* foláireamh

injure *v* gortaigh, loit

injured *adj* gortaithe

injury *n* gortú, máchail

injustice *n* éagóir

ink *n* dúch *v* cuir dúch ar

inland *adj* intíre

inlet *n* góilín

inmate *n* príosúnach

inn *n* teach ósta

innate *adj* dúchasach

innocence *n* (of crime) éigiontacht, soineantacht

innocent *adj* (of crime) éigiontach, neamhchiontach, soineanta

innovation *n* nuáil

innumerable *adj* dí-áirithe

inoffensive *adj* neamhurchóideach

inopportune moment *n* antráth

input *n* ionchur

inquest *n* coiste cróinéara

inquire *v* fiosraigh

inquiry *n* fiosrú

inquisitive *adj* fiosrach, caidéiseach

inquisitiveness *n* caidéis

insane *adj* as do mheabhair, as a mheabhair, as a meabhair…

insanity *n* gealtacht, mearadh

inscribe *v* inscríobh, grean

inscription *n* inscríbhinn

insect *n* feithid, míol

insecticide *n* feithidicíd

insect-pollinated *adj* feithidphailnithe

insect repellent *n* ruagaire feithidí

insecure *adj* éadaingean

insecurity *n* (sense of) (mothú) neamhdhiongbháilteacht(a)

insensitive *adj* neamh-mhothálach

inside *adj, adv* istigh, laistigh, taobh istigh

inside out *adj* an taobh tuathail amach

insider trading *n* trádáil taobh istigh

insight *n* léargas

insignificant *adj* neamhshuimiúil

insincere *adj* éigneasta

insistent *adj* seasmhach

insoluble *adj* **(of problem)** doréitithe, **(chemistry)** dothuaslagtha

insolvent *adj* dócmhainneach

insomnia *n* easuan, neamhchodladh

inspect *v* iniúch, déan cigireacht ar

inspection *n* iniúchadh, cigireacht

inspector *n* cigire

inspire *v* spreag

inspiration *n* spreagadh, inspioráid

inspiring *adj* spreagúil

install *v* insealbhaigh, cuir isteach

installation *n* suiteáil **gas installation** suiteáil gáis

instant *n* meandar

instantly *adv* láithreach bonn

instead of *prep* in ionad, in áit

instep *n* droim

instinct *n* instinn

institute *n* foras, institiúid *v* tionscain

institution *n* institiúid

instruct *v* deachtaigh, teagasc

instruction *n* múineadh, oideas, teagasc

instructor *n* teagascóir

instrument *n* ionstraim, uirlis, gléas

insufficient *adj* easnamhach

insular *adj* oileánach

insulate *v* insligh, teasdíon

insulation *n* insliú, teasdíonadh

insulator *n* inslitheoir

insulin *n* inslin

insult *n* achasán, masla, tarcaisne *v* maslaigh, tarcaisnigh **to insult someone** achasán a chaitheamh le duine

insulting *adj* maslach, tarcaisneach

insurance *n* árachas **fire / life insurance** árachas tine/saoil, **third-party insurance** árachas tríú páirtí

insure *v* árachaigh **to insure something** árachas a chur ar rud, rud a árachú

intact *adj* slán

intangible *adj* do-bhraite

integrate *v* comhtháthaigh

integrated rural development *n* forbairt chomhtháite na tuaithe

integration *n* imeascadh **monetary integration** imeascadh airgeadaíochta

integrity *n* ionracas

intellect *n* intleacht

intellectual *adj, n* intleachtach

intelligence[1] *n* intleacht, meabhraíocht **artifical intelligence** intleacht shaorga

intelligence[2] *n* **(information)** faisnéis

intelligence officer *n* oifigeach faisnéise

intelligence testing *n* tástáil éirime

intelligent *adj* éirimiúil, meabhrach

intelligibility *n* intuigtheacht

intend *v* bheith ar aigne / de rún / ar intinn agat...

intense *adj* dearg-, dian-, géar

intensify *v* géaraigh

intensity *n* déine

intensive *adj* dian **intensive course** dianchúrsa

intensive care unit (ICU) *n* aonad dianchúraim

intent *n* rún

intention *n* intinn, rún

interactive *adj* idirghníomhach

interchange *n* idirmhalartú

interchangeable *adj* inmhalartaithe

intercom *n* idirchum

intercontinental ballistic missiles *pl* diúracáin bhalaistíocha idirilchríochacha

interest[1] *n* spéis, suim

interest[2] *n* **(money)** ús

interest rate *n* ráta úis

interesting *adj* suimiúil, inspéise, spéisiúil

interface *n* comhéadan

interfere *v* cuir isteach ar

interference *n* trasnaíocht

interfix *n* idirnasc

interim *adj* eatramhach

interior *adj* intíre

interior decorator *n* maisitheoir istigh

interlock *v* comhghlasáil

interlude *n* eadarlúid

intermediate *adj* meán-

intermission *n* idirlinn, sos

intern *v* imtheorannaigh

internal *adj* inmheánach **internal call** glao inmheánach

international *adj* idirnáisiúnta

International Olympic Committee *n* Coiste Idirnáisiúnta na gCluichí Oilimpeacha

internet *n* idirlíon

internment *n* imtheorannú

interpret *n* ciall a bhaint as

interpretation[1] *n* léamh

interpretation[2] *n* **(of map etc.)** léirléamh, **interpretation (of data)** léirmhíniú (sonraí)

interpreter *n* ateangaire

interpretive centre *n* lárionad léirithe

interrelated *adj* comhghaolmhar

interrogate *v* ceistigh

interrogation *n* ceistiú

interrupt *v* trasnaigh, cuir isteach ar

intersect *v* trasnaigh

intertwine *v* figh

interval *n* eatramh, idirlinn

intervention *n* eadráin, idirghabháil

interview *n* agallamh

interviewee *n* agallaí

interviewer *n* agallóir

interwoven *adj* fite fuaite

intestine *n* putóg, stéig

intimacy *n* **(close)** dlúthchaidreamh

intimate *adj* dlúth

intimidate *v* scanraigh

in-thing *n* tóir-rud, rud a bhfuil tóir air

into *prep* isteach

intolerant *adj* éadulangach

intoxicated *adj* ar meisce

intoxicating *adj* meisciúil

intoxication *n* meisce

intransitive *adj* neamh-aistreach

intravenous injection *n* instealladh infhéitheach

intrepid *adj* neamheaglach

intricate *adj* casta

intrigue *n* cluainíocht

introduce *v* **(people)** cuir in aithne dá chéile, **(subject)** tarraing anuas

introduction *n* **(of book)** réamhaiste, réamhrá, **(to somebody)** cur in aithne

introductory *adj* réamh-

introspective *adj* inbhreathnaitheach

introvert *n* indíritheoir

intrude *v* brúigh isteach ar

intruder *n* foghlaí

intuition *n* iomas

intuitive *adj* iomasach

inundate *v* báigh, plúch

invade *v* ionradh a dhéanamh ar

invader *n* ionróir

invalid[1] *n* easlán, othar

invalid[2] *adj* neamhbhailí

invalidate *v* neamhbhailigh

invaluable *adj* fíorluachmhar

invasion n ionradh

invent v ceap, cum

invention n cumadóireacht, fionnachtain

inventive adj airgtheach

inventory n liosta, fardal

inversion n aisiompú

invert v aisiompaigh, iompaigh

invest v infheistigh

investigate v scrúdaigh

investigation n fiosrú, (police) imscrúdú

investment n infheistíocht

invigorate v beoigh

invigorating adj athbhríoch

invincible adj dochloíte

invisible adj dofheicthe

invitation n cuireadh

invite v tabhair cuireadh (do)

invoice n sonrasc v sonraisc

invoke v toghair

involuntary n éadoilteanach

involve v baint a bheith (agat) le

involved adj bainteach le, páirteach i

invulnerable adj doghonta

in-word n tóirfhocal, focal a bhfuil tóir air

iodine n iaidín

ionosphere n ianaisféar

IOU dlitear duit uaim (DDU)

Ireland n Éire from / in Ireland ó/in Éirinn, the people of Ireland muintir na hÉireann

iris¹ n (of eye) imreasc

iris² n (flower) feileastram

Irish¹ n (language) Gaeilge, Irish-speaker Gaeilgeoir

Irish² adj Éireannach, Gaelach the Irish Sea Muir Éireann, an Mhuir Mheann

Irish-language school n Gaelscoil

Irishman / Irishwoman n Gael, Éireannach

Irish Republican Brotherhood (IRB) n Bráithreachas Phoblacht na hÉireann

iron¹ n iarann iron ore amhiarann

iron² n iarnáil, smúdáil

ironic adj íorónta

ironing n iarnáil, smúdáil

irony n íoróin

irrational v éigiallta

irregular adj aimhrialta, neamhrialta

irrelevant adj neamhábhartha

irresponsible adj místuama

irrigation n uisciú

irrigate v uiscigh

irritate v griog

irritating pain n griog

Islam n Ioslamachas

island n oileán, inis

islander n oileánach

isle n inis

Isle of Man n Oileán Mhanann

isolate v aonraigh, leithlisigh

isolated adj aonarach, iargúlta, leithliseach

isolation n (of patient) leithlis

isolation ward n barda leithlise

Israel n Iosrael

Israeli adj, n Iosraelach

issue¹ n ceist

issue² n eisiúint v eisigh

it pron sé, sí, é, í it fell thit sé/sí, hit it with the hurley buail leis an gcamán é/í

Italian adj, n Iodálach n (language) Iodáilis

italics pl cló iodálach

Italy n an Iodáil

itch n tochas

itchy adj tochasach

itinerant n bean/fear siúil

itinerary n cúrsa taistil

ivory n eabhar

ivy n eidhneán

J

jack¹ *n* (car) seac
jack² *n* (cards) cuireata
jackal *n* seacál
jackdaw *n* cág
jacket *n* casóg, seaicéad, (of book) forchlúdach
jack-of-all-trades *n* gobán
jackpot *n* pota óir
jagged *adj* spiacánach
jail *n* príosún, carcair
jam *n* subh
jammed *adj* sáinnithe
January *n* Eanáir
Japan *n* an tSeapáin
Japanese *adj, n* Seapánach *n* (language) an tSeapáinis
jar *n* crúsca, próca
jargon *n* béarlagair
jaundice *n* buíochán
javelin *n* sleá
jaw *n* giall, corrán géill
jazz *n* snagcheol
jealous *adj* éadmhar
jealousy *n* éad
jeep *n* jíp
jeer *v* fonóid a dhéanamh faoi
jelly *n* glóthach
jellyfish *n* smugairle róin
jeopardise *v* cuir i mbaol
jerk *n* sracadh *v* srac
jersey *n* geansaí
Jesus *n* Íosa
jet *n* scaird
jet plane *n* scairdeitleán
jet lag *n* scairdtuirse
jet-black *adj* daoldubh
jetty *n* lamairne
Jew *n* Giúdach

Jew's harp *n* trumpa béil
jewel *n* seoid
jeweller *n* seodóir
jewellery *n* seodra
Jewish *adj* Giúdach
Jigsaw (puzzle) *n* míreanna mearaí
jingle *n* ceoilín
job *n* jab, post
job description *n* jobthuairisc
job sharing *n* postroinnt, páirtiú in obair
job safety *n* jabshábháilteacht
jockey *n* jacaí disk jockey ceirneoir, diosccachaí
jog *n* bogshodar
jogger *n* bogshodaire
jogging *adj* ar bogshodar
join *v* snaidhm, comhcheangail
joiner *n* siúinéir
joinery *n* siúinéireacht
joint¹ *n* alt out of joint as alt
joint² *n* (meat) spóla
joint responsibility *n* freagracht chomhpháirteach
joint undertaking *n* gnóthas comhpháirteach
jointed *adj* altach
jolly *adj* áthasach
joke *n* magadh what starts as a joke can end up being serious tagann an magadh go leaba an dáiríre
joker *n* (cards) Fear na gCrúb
journal *n* iris
journalism *n* iriseoireacht
journalist *n* iriseoir
journey *n* turas, triall, aistear *v* triall journey in vain turas in aisce
jovial *adj* soilbhir
joy *n* áthas, ríméad, gliondar, gairdeas, suáilce

joyful *adj* aiteasach, áthasach, suáilceach

joyous *adj* lúcháireach, gliondrach

joyrider *n* spraoithiománaí, bradmharcach

joystick *n* luamhán stiúrtha

jubilant *adj* lúcháireach

jubilation *n* lúcháir, ollghairdeas

jubilee *n* iubhaile

judicial *adj* dlíthiúil, breithiúnach

judge *n* breitheamh *v* breith a thabhairt ar

judo *n* júdó

jug *n* crúsca, crúiscín

juggernaut *n* arracht

juggle *v* cleas na n-úll a dhéanamh le

juggler *n* lámhchleasaí

juice *n* sú **orange, tomato, fruit juice** sú oráistí, trátaí, torthaí

juicy *adj* súmhar

July *n* Iúil

jumbo-jet *n* ábhalscaird

jump *v* léim, (fright) clis

jumper *n* geansaí

jumping *n* léimneach, (startle) cliseadh

junction *n* gabhal **Limerick Junction** Gabhal Luimnigh

June *n* Meitheamh

jungle *n* dufair

junior *adj* sóisearach *n* sóisear

junk *n* mangarae

junk yard *n* clós mangarae

junket *n* juncaed

jurist *n* dlí-eolaí

juror *n* giúróir

jury *n* giúiré, coiste

just *adj* ceart, cóir

just now *adv* díreach anois, anois díreach

justice cóir **justice and injustice** cóir agus éagóir

justify *v* fírinnigh

juvenile *n* aosánach **juvenile delinquent** ógchiontóir, **juvenile court** cúirt d'aosánaigh, cúirt na n-aosánach

juxtaposition *n* in **juxtaposition** le hais a chéile

K

kangaroo *n* cangarú

karate *n* karaté

kebab *n* ceibeab

keel *n* cíle

keen *adj* faobhrach

keep *v* coinnigh, coimeád **to keep an account** cuntas a choinneáil, **keep going** coinnigh ort, **keep quiet!** bí i do thost!

keeper *n* coimeádaí

keeping *n* in **safe keeping** ar lámh shábháilte

keepsake *n* cuimhneachán

kennel *n* conchró

kerb *n* colbha

kernel *n* eithne

Kerry *n* Ciarraí **Co. Kerry** Co. Chiarraí

kettle *n* citeal **to put the kettle on** an citeal a chur síos

key *n* eochair

keyboard *n* eochairchlár, méarchlár

keyhole *n* poll na heochrach

keynote *n* gléasnóta

khaki *adj*, *n* caicí

kick *n* cic, speach *v* ciceáil **horse's kick** speach chapaill, **kick of a gun** speach ghunna **free kick** cic saor

kid *n* **(goat)** meannán

kidnap *v* fuadaigh

kidnapper *n* fuadaitheoir

kidnapping *n* fuadú

kidney *n* duán, ára

Kildare *n* Cill Dara **Co. Kildare** Co. Chill Dara

Kilkenny *n* Cill Chainnigh **Co. Kilkenny** Co. Chill Chainnigh

kill *n* maraigh

killer *n* marfóir

killing *n* marú

kiln *n* áith

kilogram *n* cileagram

kilometre *n* ciliméadar

kilowatt *n* cileavata

kilt *n* filleadh beag

kind[1] *adj* carthanach, cineálta, lách

kind[2] *n* sórt, cineál, saghas

kindergarten *n* naíonra

kind-hearted *adj* dea-chroíoch

kindle *v* adhain, fadaigh

kindly *adj* cineálta

kindness *n* cineáltas

kindred *adj* gaolta

kinetic *adj* cinéiteach

king *n* rí

kingdom *n* ríocht

kingfisher *n* cruidín, rí-iascaire

kinship *n* gaol, muintearas

kiosk *n* both

kiss *n* póg **kiss of life** análú tarrthála

kitchen *n* cistin **kitchen unit** aonad cistine

kite *n* eitleog

kitten *n* piscín

kiwi *n* cíbhí

knead *v* fuin

knee *n* glúin

kneecap *n* caipín glúine, gealacán, pláitín

kneecapping *n* glúinmhilleadh

kneel *v* sléacht, umhlaigh

knickers *n* brístí

knife *n* scian **carving knives** sceana feola, **blade of knife** lann scine

knight *n* ridire

knighthood *n* ridireacht

knit *v* cniotáil, **(of bone, wound, etc)** snaidhm

knitting *n* cniotáil, **(of bone, wound, etc)** snaidhmeadh

knob *n* **(handle)** murlán **knob of butter** meall ime

knock *v* cnag **to knock on** cnag a bhualadh ar

knock down *v* leag

knocking *n* cnagadh

knocking down *n* leagan

knot *n* **(of hair)** dual, **(in rope)** snaidhm, **(in wood)** alt

knotty *adj* altach

know *v* **to know somebody** aithne a bheith agat ar dhuine, **to know something** eolas a bheith agat ar rud, a fhios a bheith agat faoi rud, **I know you to see** tá súilaithne agam ort, **I know this road very well** tá eolas maith agam ar an mbóthar seo, **I don't know** níl a fhios agam, n'fheadar

know-how *n* fios (do) c(h)eirde

knowledge *n* eolas, fios, iúl **the way to knowledge is to question** doras feasa fiafraí

knowledgeable *adj* eolach

knuckle *n* alt

L

label *n* lipéad

laboratory *n* saotharlann **language laboratory** teanglann

laborious *adj* sclábhúil

labour *n* obair, saothar **in labour** i luí seoil, **the Labour Party** Páirtí an Lucht Oibre

labourer *n* oibrí, saothraí, sclábhaí

labyrinth *n* cathair ghríobháin

lace[1] *n* (of shoe) iall *v* iallacha do bhróg a cheangal

lace[2] *n* lása *v* cuir lása ar

lacerate *v* stiall

lack *n* díth, éagmais, easpa, uireasa

lacking *adj* uireasach

lacquer *n* laicear

ladder *n* dréimire

laden *adj* faoi ualach

ladies and gentlemen! *excl* a dhaoine uaisle!

ladle *n* liach, ladar

lady *n* bean uasal, bantiarna

ladybird *n* bóín Dé, bóín samhraidh, cearc Mhuire

lager *n* lágar

lager louts *pl* bodaigh bheorach

lagging jacket *n* saicéad fálaithe

lagoon *n* murlach

lair *n* gnáthóg

lake *n* loch

lamb *n* uan, (meat) uaineoil

lame *adj* bacach **lame person** bacach, **lame excuse** leithscéal agus a thóin leis

lament *n* caoineadh, olagón *v* caoin

lamentable *adj* cásmhar

laminate *v* lannaigh

laminated *adj* lannach

lamp *n* lampa, lóchrann

lampoon *n* aoir

lampooner *n* aorthóir

lance *n* sleá, lansa *v* lansaigh

land[1] *n* dúiche, fearann, talamh

land[2] *n* (country) tír

land[3] *v* tuirling

landing *n* tuirlingt, teacht i dtír

landlady *n* bean tí

land-locked *adj* talamhiata

landlord *n* tiarna talún

landmark *n* críoch-chomhartha

landowner *n* úinéir talún

landscape *n* amharc tíre, tírdhreach

landslide *n* maidhm thalún

lane *n* lána, cabhsa

language *n* teanga **native language** teanga dhúchais

language laboratory *n* teanglann

languid *adj* meirbh

lantern *n* lóchrann

Laois *n* Laois **Co. Laois** Co. Laoise

lap *n* ucht

Lappland *n* an Laplainn

lap top computer *n* ríomhaire glúine

larch *n* learóg

larceny *n* gadaíocht **petty larceny** mionghadaíocht

large *n* mór **large scale** mórscála

lark *n* fuiseog

laryngitis *n* laraingíteas

larynx *n* laraing

laser *n* léasar

laser printer *n* printéir léasair, léasarphrintéir

lash *v* lasc

last[1] *adj* deireanach **last night** aréir, **last year** anuraidh, **at (long) last** ar deireadh/faoi dheireadh (thiar), **last but not least** an meall mór ar deireadh

last[2] *v* mair

lasting *adj* marthanach

latch *n* laiste *v* cuir laiste ar

late *adj* antráthach, déanach, deireanach, mall **late last night** go deireanach/déanach aréir

lately *adv* le déanaí/deireanas

lateness *n* déanaí, deireanas

lathe *n* deil

lather *n* coipeadh, sobal *v* sobal a dhéanamh

Latin *adj* Laidineach *n* (language) Laidin

latitude *n* domhanleithead

laudable *adj* inmholta

laugh *n* gáirc *v* gáir

laughable *adj* áiféiseach

laughing stock *n* ceap magaidh, staic áiféise/mhagaidh

laughter *n* gáire **fit of laughter** taom/racht gáire, **hysterical laughter** saobhgháire

launch¹ *n* lainseáil, seoladh *v* lainseáil, seol **book launch** lainseáil/seoladh leabhair

launch² *v* (of missile) diúraic

launching pad *n* ceap lainseála

launder *v* (money) sciúr

laundry *n* (place) neachtlann, (of clothes) níochán

laurel *n* labhras

lava *n* laibhe

lava flow *n* sreabh laibhe

lavender *n* labhandar

lavish *adj* fial, flaithiúil

law *n* dlí, reacht **common law** dlí coiteann

lawful *adj* dleathach, dleachtach, dlisteanach, dlíthiúil

lawless *adj* aindlíthiúil

lawn *n* faiche, plásóg

lawnmower *n* lomaire faiche

law suit *n* cúis dlí

lax *adj* scaoilte

laxative *adj* scaoilteach

lay¹ *n* cuir, leag

lay² *n* (poem) laoi

lay-by *n* leataobh

layer *n* ciseal, sraith **the ozone layer** ciseal (an) ózóin

laying *n* cur, leagan

layperson *n* tuata

laziness *n* leisce

lazy *adj* leisciúil

lazybones *n* giolla na leisce

lead¹ *n* luaidhe

lead² *prefix* príomh- *v* treoraigh **in the lead** chun tosaigh, **lead singer** príomhamhránaí, **lead guitarist** príomhghiotáraí

leader *n* ceann feadhna, ceannaire, taoiseach

leadership *n* ceannasaíocht

leaf *n* duilleog

league *n* conradh, (sport) sraithchomórtas, comórtas sraithe **the Gaelic League** Conradh na Gaeilge, **league match** cluiche sraithe

leak *n* deoir anuas *v* lig uisce isteach / anuas

lean¹ *v* claon

lean² *adj* **lean meat** feoil thrua

leap *n, v* léim

learn *v* foghlaim

learned *adj* foghlamtha, léannta

learner *n* foghlaimeoir

learning *n* éigse, foghlaim, léann, saíocht

lease *n* léas *v* léasaigh

leash *n* iall

least *n* an ceann is lú **it's the least you might do** is é is lú is gann duit é, **last but not least** an meall mór ar deireadh

leather *n* leathar

leave¹ *v* cead, fág **leave it aside** fág uait é

leave² *n* saoire

leaving *n* imeacht

Leaving Certificate *n* Ardteist(iméireacht)

Lebanon *n* an Liobáin

lecherous *adj* drúisiúil

lecture *n* léacht *v* léacht a thabhairt

lecturer *n* léachtóir

lectureship *n* léachtóireacht

lecturing *n* léachtóireacht

ledge *n* aragail

Lee *n* an Laoi

leech *n* diúgaire, súmaire

leek *n* cainneann

leek and potato soup *n* anraith cainneann agus prátaí

left *adj, n* clé **on the left** ar clé, **the left** an eite chlé, **'no left turn'** 'ná castar ar clé', **on the left hand side** ar thaobh na láimhe clé

left-hand *n* ciotóg

left-handed *adj* ciotach

left-handed person *n* ciotóg

leg *n* cos **leg of mutton** ceathrú caoireola

legacy *n* oidhreacht

legal *adj* dlíthiúil, dleathach **legal tender** dlíthairiscint

Legal Aid Board *n* an Bord um Chúnamh Dlíthiúil

legalise *v* dlí a dhéanamh de, rud a fhágáil dleathach

legend *n* finscéal

legible *adj* soléite

legion *n* léigiún **the French Foreign Legion** Léigiún Coigríochach na Fraince

legislate *v* reachtaigh

legislation *n* reachtaíocht

legitimate *adj* dlisteanach

Leinster Laighin **(the province of) Leinster** Cúige Laighean, **native of Leinster** Laighneach

leisure *n* fóillíocht

leisure centre *n* sólann

Leitrim *n* Liatroim **Co. Leitrim** Co. Liatroma

lemon *n* líomóid

lemonade *n* líomanáid

length *n* fad

lengthen *v* fadaigh

lengthy *adj* fada

lenition *n* séimhiú

lenient *adj* bog, trócaireach

lens *n* lionsa

Lent *n* an Carghas **I have given up sweets for Lent** táim ag déanamh an Charghais ar mhilseáin

lentil *n* piseánach

Leo *n* an Leon

leopard *n* liopard

leotard *n* culaith ghleacaíochta

leper *n* lobhar

leprosy *n* lobhra

lesbian *adj, n* leispiach

less *n* lúide

lessen *v* laghdaigh

lesson *n* ceacht

let *v* lig **let her alone** ná bac léi, **let down** lig síos

let it rip! let it loose! scaoil amach an bobailín

lethal *adj* marfach

lethargic *adj* spadánta

lethargy *n* spadántacht

letter *n* litir

letter-box *n* bosca litreacha

lettering *n* scríbhneoireacht

lettuce *n* leitís

leukaemia *n* leoicéime

level[1] *adj* cothrom, réidh **level space** léibheann, **level place** plás

level[2] *n* leibhéal

level[3] *v* cothromaigh

level of activity *n* leibhéal gníomhaíochta

levelness n réidhe

lever n luamhán

levy n tobhach

lewd adj graosta

lewdness n graostacht

liability n dliteanas, fiachas

liable adj freagrach

liaise v ceangail

liaison n ceangal

liar n bréagadóir

libel n leabhal

liberal adj liobrálach n liobrálaí

liberalise v liobrálaigh

liberate v saor, fuascail

liberation n saoradh, fuascailt

liberator n fuascailteoir

liberty n saoirse **the Liberties** na Saoirsí, na Libirtí

Libra n an Mheá

librarian n leabharlannaí

library n leabharlann

licence n ceadúnas **driving licence** ceadúnas tiomána

licence plate n uimhirchlár

license v ceadúnaigh

licensed adj ceadúnaithe

lick v ligh

lid n clár

lie[1] n bréag, éitheach **to lie** éitheach / bréag a insint

lie[2] v luigh **lie down** luigh síos

lie detector n brathadóir bréige

lieutenant n leifteanant

life n beatha, anam, saol **to lay down one's life** d'anam a thabhairt, **life sentence** príosún saoil

life-belt n crios tarrthála

life-boat n bád tarrthála

life-guard n maor snámha, garda coirp

life jacket n seaicéad tarrthála

lifeless adj díbheo, neamhbheo

lifelike adj beoga

lifelong friend n cara saoil

life-style n nós maireachtála

life support machine n meaisín tacaíochta beatha

lifetime n saol, linn, ré **in my lifetime** le mo ré

Liffey n an Life

lift[1] n ardaitheoir v ardaigh, tóg

lift[2] n (in car etc) marcaíocht, síob

lifter n tógálaí, ardaitheoir

lifting n tógáil

light[1] v (of cigarettes) dearg **light up** gcal

light[2] adj éadrom

light[3] n solas **to bring something to light** rud a thabhairt chun solais

light aircraft n eitleán beag

light-coloured adj fionnbhán

lighten v éadromaigh, laghdaigh

light-hearted adj aerach

lighthouse n teach solais

lighting n lasadh, soilsiú

light milk n bainne caol

lightness n éadroime

lightning n tintreach, splancacha **thunder and lightning** splancacha agus toirneach

lightweight adj éadrom n éadrom-mheáchan

light-year n bliain solais

like[1] n leithéid, macasamhail **I like it** taitníonn sé liom, is maith liom é, **our likes will not be here again!** ní bheidh ár leithéidí arís ann! **to like someone** bá a bheith agat le duine

like[2] adj cosúil **you are very like her** tá tú an-chosúil léi

like[3] prep amhail, mar, ar nós **a person like him** duine mar é, duine ar a nós

likeable adj taitneamhach

likelihood n dóchúlacht

likely *adj* dócha, dóchúil **it is likely (that)** is dócha (go), **as likely as not** chomh dócha lena athrach / mhalairt, **not likely!** beag an baol!

likeness *n* cosúlacht, samhail

likewise *adv* freisin, mar an gcéanna

liking *n* dúil, bá

lilac *adj* liathchorcra

lily *n* lile

limb *n* géag

lime[1] *n* aol

lime[2] *n* **(tree)** teile

limelight *n* **in the limelight** os comhair an phobail

Limerick *n* Luimneach **Co. Limerick** Co. Luimnigh

limerick *n* luimneach

limestone *n* aolchloch

lime-white *adj* aolmhar

limit *n* críoch, foirceann, teorainn **speed limit** teorainn luais

limited *adj* teoranta

limiting *adj* teorantach

limiting factors *pl* tosca teorantacha

limp *adj* bacach

limping *n* bacadaíl

line *n* líne *v* líneáil **fishing line** dorú, **on line** ar líne

lineage *n* ginealach

lined *adj* línithe

linen *n* línéadach, líon

linesman *n* taobhmhaor

lingerer *n* leadránaí

lingerie *n* éadaí cnis

linguist *n* teangeolaí

linguistic *adj* teangeolaíoch

linguistics *n* teangeolaíocht

lining *n* líneáil

link[1] *n* ccangal, nasc **cable link** nasc cábla

link[2] *v* ceangail, nasc

lino *n* líonóil

linseed *n* ros

lion *n* leon

lip *n* liopa, **(of plate)** faobhar **lips** beola

lip-service *n* béalghrá

lipstick *n* béaldath

liqueur *n* licéar

liquid *adj* leachtach *n* leacht

liquidate *v* leachtaigh

liquidator *n* leachtaitheoir

liquidity *n* leachtacht

liquid hydrogen *n* hidrigin leachtach

liquidise *n* leachtaigh

liquidiser *n* leachtaitheoir

liquid manure *n* múnlach

liquify *v* leachtaigh

liquorice *n* liocras

list *n* liosta *v* liostaigh

listen *v* éist

listener *n* éisteoir

listless *adj* díbheo

literacy *n* litearthacht

literal *adj* liteartha

literary *adj* liteartha

literate *adj* liteartha

literature *n* litríocht

litre *n* lítear

litter[1] *n* **(animals)** ál, cuain

litter[2] *n* árach

little *adj* beag

little finger *n* an mhéar bheag, lúidín

live *adj* beo *v* mair

livelihood *n* slí bheatha

liveliness *n* beochan, bríomhaireacht, anam

lively *adj* anamúil, beoga, bríomhar

liven *v* spionnadh a chur i rud

liver *n* ae

Liverpool *n* Learpholl

living *n* maireachtáil **cost, standard of living** costas, caighdeán maireachtála

living room n seomra teaghlaigh
lizard n earc, laghairt
load n lód, ualach v lódáil, luchtaigh, ualaigh
loaf n (bread) bollóg, builín
loan n iasacht, airleacan
lobby n forsheomra v brústocaireacht a dhéanamh
lobbying n brústocaireacht
lobe n (ear) maothán
lobster n gliomach
lobster pot n pota gliomaigh
local adj áitiúil **local government** rialtas áitiúil, **the local people** muintir na háite
locate v (find) aimsigh, (situate) suigh
location n suíomh
lock n glas, (on canal) loc v glasáil
locker n taisceadán
locket n loicéad
lockjaw n teiteanas
locksmith n glasadóir
lode n lód
lodge n lóiste v lóisteáil, taisc
lodgement n taisce
lodger n aoi, lóistéir
lodgings pl lóistín
loft n lochta
log n (mathematics) logartam, (tree) lomán
loganberry n lóganchaor
logic n loighic
logical adj loighciúil
log in / on v log ann
log out / off v log as
loin n (food) luan **loins** ára
loiter v máinneáil
loitering n máinneáil
lollipop n líreacán
London n Londain **London Bridge** Droichead Londan

lone adj aonarach
loneliness n cumha, uaigneas
lonely adj uaigneach
long adj fada **a long story** scéal fada
long for v tnúth le
long-distance call n cianghlao
long-lived adj fadsaolach
long-sighted adj fadradharcach
long-suffering adj fadfhulangach
long-term adj fadtéarmach, fadtréimhseach
long-winded adj fadchainteach
Longford n an Longfort
longing n tnúth **longing for Christmas** ag tnúth leis an Nollaig
longitude n domhanfhad
look n amharc, féachaint, dearcadh v dearc, breathnaigh, féach **look at** féach ar, amharc ar, **good looks** dathúlacht
look-out n faire
look-out post n (military) post faire
looking glass n scáthán
loom n seol v taibhsigh
loop n lúbóg v lúb
loophole n poll éalaithe
loose adj scaoilte
loosen v scaoil
loot n slad v creach
lopsided adj leataobhach, ar sceabhadh
lord n tiarna
lord mayor n ardmhéara
lordship n flaith, tiarnas
lore n seanchas
lorry n leoraí
lose v caill **to lose weight** meáchan a chailleadh
loser n cailliúnaí
loss n caill, díobháil, díth
lost adj caillte

lot *n* crann **to cast lots for something** rud a chur ar chrainn

lotion *n* lóis **sun lotion** lóis ghréine

lottery *n* crannchur **the National Lottery** an Crannchur Náisiúnta

loud *adj* glórach

loudspeaker *n* callaire

lough *n* loch **Lough Dan** Loch Deán, **Lough Dubh** Dúloch, **Lough Feeagh** Loch Fíodh, **Lough Inagh** Loch Eidhneach, **Loughinisland** Loch an Oileáin, **Lough Sillan** Loch Saileán

lounge (bar) *n* tolglann **departure lounge** tolglann imeachta

louse *n* míol

lousy *adj* míolach

Louth *n* Lú **Co. Louth** Co. Lú

love *n* cion, gean, grá, searc *v* gráigh

Love Spell *n* Ortha na Seirce

lover *n* leannán

loving *adj* ceanúil

low *adj* íseal **low spirits** lagmhisneach

lower *adj* íochtarach *v* íslígh

lower part *n* íochtar

lowering *n* ísliú, leagan

low-fat milk / skim milk *n* bainne bearrtha

lowly *adj* uiríseal

loyal *adj* dílis

loyalist *n* dílseoir

loyalty *n* dílse

lozenge *n* losainn

LP (long-playing record) *n* fadcheirnín

lubricant *n* bealadh

lubricate *v* bealaigh

lubricating oil *n* ola bhealaithe

lucid *adj* glé **he is perfectly lucid** tá a chiall is a chéadfaí aige

luck *adj* ádh **good luck** ádh mór ort, go n-éirí leat

lucky *adj* ádhúil, ámharach, amhantrach **you are lucky, lucky you!** is méanar duit, **to be lucky** an t-ádh a bheith ort/leat, **to be very lucky** seamróg na gceithre gcluas a bheith agat, an tseamair Mhuire a bheith agat

ludicrous *adj* áiféiseach

luggage *n* bagáiste

lukewarm *adj* fuarbhruite, patuar, alabhog

lull *n* eatramh *v* **(to sleep)** cealg

lullaby *n* seoithín seó, suantraí

lumbago *n* lumbágó

luminous *adj* lonrach

lump *n* ailp, meall, cnap, alpán, cnapán *v* carn **lump sum** cnapshuim, **lump sugar** cnapshiúcra

lumpy *adj* cnapach

lunacy *n* gealtachas

lunar probe *n* taiscéalaí na gealaí

lunatic *n* gealt

lunch *n* lón

lunchtime *n* am lóin

lung *n* scamhóg

lung cancer *n* ailse (na) scamhóg

lunge *n* áladh, scuib *v* **to lunge at somebody** áladh a thabhairt ar rud

lurid *adj* scéiniúil

lust *n* drúis

lustful *adj* adharcach, drúisiúil **lustful person** adharcachán

lusty *adj* fuinniúil

Luxembourg *n* Lucsamburg

luxuriant *adj* uaibhreach

luxury *n* só

luxury apartment / flat *n* só-árasán

luxury goods *pl* só-earraí

lyric *adj* liriceach *n* liric

lyrical *adj* fileata, liriceach

M

macaroni *n* macarón

machine *n* inneall, meaisín **machine gun** meaisínghunna, **life support machine** meaisín tacaíochta beatha

machinery *n* innealra

machinist *n* meaisíneoir

mackerel *n* maicréal, murlas, ronnach

mad *adj* ar buile **mad dog** madra dúchais, **he is madly in love with her** tá a chroí istigh inti, **he is stark raving mad** tá sé glan as a mheabhair, tá sé ar mire

mad cow disease (BSE) *n* galar na bó buile

madness *n* mire

magazine[1] *n* iris

magazine[2] *n* (military stores) armlann, (cartridges) piléarlann

magazine rack *n* raca irisí

maggot *n* cruimh

magic *n* asarlaíocht, draíocht

magician *n* asarlaí, draoi

magistrate *n* giúistís

magnanimous *adj* móraigeanta

magnet *n* maighnéad

magnetic *adj* maighnéadach

magnificent *adj* taibhseach

magnification *n* formhéadú, formhéadúchán

magnify *v* formhéadaigh

magnifying glass *n* gloine formhéadúcháin

magpie *n* snag breac, pocaire / preabaire na mbánta

mahogany *n* mahagaine

maid *n* cailín aimsire

maiden *n* maighdean

mail *n* post *v* postáil

mailing list *n* liosta poist

maim *v* martraigh

main *adj* mór-, ceann-, príomh-

mainland *n* míntír, mórthír, tír mór

mainlining *n* (drug addiction) féithiú

main road *n* príomhbhóthar

mains (electricity) *pl* príomhlíonra, príomhphíopa

mainstay *n* crann taca

main street *n* príomhshráid

maintain *v* coimeád, coinnigh

maintenance *n* coinneáil, coimeád, cothabháil

majestic *adj* mórga

majesty *n* mórgacht

major *adj* mór- *n* maor

majority *n* formhór, móramh, tromlach

make *v* déan **to make somebody do something** iallach a chur ar dhuine rud a dhéanamh

make-believe *n* cur i gcéill

maker *n* déantóir **decision maker** cinnteoir

makeshift *adj* tacair

make-up *n* smideadh

make-up artist *n* ealaíontóir smididh

malaria *n* maláire

male *adj* fearga, fireann *n* fireannach

malevolent *adj* droch-chroíoch

malice *n* mailís, mioscais, urchóid

malicious *adj* mailíseach

malign *adj* dochrach *v* caith anuas ar

malignancy *n* mailís, urchóid

malignant *adj* mailíseach, urchóideach

mallet *n* máilléad

malnutrition *n* míchothú

mammal *n* mamach, sineach

mammary *adj* mamach

mammography *n* x-ghathú cíche

mammoth *n* mamat

mam(my) *n* mam(aí)

man *n* duine, fear **good man!** maith an fear! bulaí fir! togha fir! **the man in the street** Tadhg an mhargaidh

manage *v* láimhseáil, riar

manageable *adj* soláimhsithe

management *n* bainistíocht **management information system (MIS)** córas eolais bhainistíochta

managerial approach *n* cur chuige bainistiúil

managing director *n* stiúrthóir bainistíochta

Manchester *n* Manchain

mandarin orange *n* mandairín

mandate *n* sainordú, mandáid

mandatory *adj* sainordaitheach

mandatory sentence *n* pionós sainordaitheach

mane *n* moing

manger *n* mainséar, **(Xmas crib)** beithilín

mango *n* mangó

mangy *adj* clamhach

man-hole cover *n* clúdach dúnphoill

manhood *n* feargacht

mania *n* máine

maniac *n* máineach

manic depression *n* máindúlagar

manicure *n* lámh-mhaisiú

manifesto *n* forógra

manipulate *v* cúbláil, ionramháil, láimhsigh

manly *adj* fearga

manmade *adj* saorga, de dhéantús an duine

mannequin *n* mainicín

manner *n* caoi, dóigh **manners** béasa

mannerism *n* nósúlacht

mannerly *adj* modhúil

manoeuvre *n* **(military)** inlíocht *v* ainligh

manor house *n* mainéar

mansion *n* teach mór

manslaughter *n* dúnorgain

mantelpiece *n* matal

manual *n* lámhleabhar **manual labour** obair láimhe

manual training *n* lámhoiliúint

manufacture *n* déantús **manufacture of arms** armadóireacht

manufacturer *n* déantóir

manure *n* leas, leasú, aoileach *v* leasaigh

manuscript *n* lámhscríbhinn

Manx *n* **(language)** Manainnis

Manxperson *n* Manannach

many *adj*, *n* mórán, iomaí, iomad

many happy returns! *excl* gurab amhlaidh duit!

map *n* cairt, léarscáil, mapa *v* mapáil

maple *n* mailp **maple tree** crann mailpe

marathon *n* maratón

marble *n* marmar, **(toy)** mirlín

March *n* Márta

march *n*, *v* máirseáil

marcher *n* máirseálaí

mare *n* láir

margarine *n* margairín

margin *n* ciumhais

marginal *adj* imeallach

mariculture *n* muirshaothrú

marijuana *n* marachuan

marina *n* muiríne

marine *adj* muirí

marital *adj* pósta

maritime *adj* muirí

mark[1] lorg, marc, smál **question mark** comhartha ceiste, **quotation marks** comharthaí athfhriotail

mark[2] v marcáil

market n margadh v margaigh **free / unrestricted market** margadh neamhshrianta, **the black market** an margadh dubh

marketing n margaíocht, margú

market price n margadhphraghas

market value n margadhluach

marksman n aimsitheoir

marmalade n marmaláid, subh oráistí

maroon n (colour) marún

marquee n ollphuball

marriage n pósadh

married adj pósta

married couple n lánúin (phósta)

marrow[1] n (vegetable) mearóg

marrow[2] n (bone) smior

marry v pós

Mars n Mars

marsh n riasc, seascann

martial adj míleata

martial arts pl ealaíona míleata

martin n gabhlán **house martin** gabhlán binne

martyr n mairtíreach

martyrdom n mairtíreacht

marvel n iontas v iontas a dhéanamh de

marvellous adj iontach

Marxism n Marxachas

Marxist adj, n Marxach

marzipan n prásóg

mascara n mascára

masculine adj fearga, (grammar) firinscneach

masculinity n feargacht

mask n masc v folaigh

mason n (saor) cloiche, (freemason) máisiún

masonry n saoirseacht (chloiche)

Mass[1] n Aifreann **funeral Mass** Aifreann na marbh, **to attend Mass** an tAifreann a éisteacht

mass[2] cnap, toirt **mass production** olltáirgeadh

massacre n ár v ár a dhéanamh ar

massage n suathaireacht v suaith

masseur n suathaire

massive adj fíormhór

mast n crann, crann seoil

master n máistir v sáraigh

masterful adj máistriúil

mastering n máistreacht

mastermind v tionscain

masterpiece n sárshaothar

mastery n máistreacht

mat n mata

match[1] n (marriage) cleamhnas v meaitscáil

match[2] n (sports) cluiche

match[3] n cipín, lasán

mate[1] n (bird) leathéan v cúpláil

mate[2] n (sailor) máta

material adj ábhartha n ábhar

materialism n ábharachas

materialise v **to materialise** teacht i gcrích

maternal adj máthartha

maternity n máithreachas

maternity hospital n ospidéal máithreachais

maternity leave n saoire mháithreachais

mathematical adj matamaiticiúil

mathematician n matamaiticeoir

mathematics n matamaitic

maths n mata

matron n mátrún

matter n ábhar, damhna **matters** cúrsaí, **it doesn't matter** is cuma faoi

mattress n tocht

mature *adj* aibí, críonna *v* aibigh

maturity *n* críonnacht

mausoleum *n* másailéam

maximum *n* uasmhéid, uas-

May[1] *n* Bealtaine

may[2] *v* it may be too late b'fhéidir gur ródhéanach atá sé, may the devil choke you! go dtachta an diabhal thú!

maybe *adv* b'fhéidir

Mayo *n* Maigh Eo Co. Mayo Co. Mhaigh Eo

mayonnaise *n* maonáis

mayor *n* méara

maze *n* lúbra, cathair ghríobháin

me *pron* mé, mise she kissed me phóg sí mé, it wasn't me ní mise a bhí ann

meadow *n* móinéar, cluain

meagre *adj* gann

meal *n* proinn, béile oatmeal min choirce

mean[1] *adj* ainnis, sprionlaithe, suarach, gortach

mean[2] *v* ciallaigh

meaning *n* ciall, brí

meanness *n* ainnise, suarachas

means *pl* acmhainn, caoi, deis means of transport deis iompair

meanwhile *adv* idir an dá linn

measles *n* bruitíneach

measly *adj* suarach

measure[1] *n* líon, tomhas *v* tomhais to measure something rud a thomhas

measure[2] *n* miosúr

measurement *n* miosúr, tomhas, toise

meat *n* feoil

Meath *n* an Mhí Co. Meath Co. na Mí

mechanic *n* meicneoir

mechanical *adj* meicniúil

mechanics *n* meicnic

mechanised *adj* meicnithe

mechanism *n* meicníocht

medal *n* bonn

meddle *v* drann le

media *pl* na meáin

mediate *v* eadráin a dhéanamh

mediator *n* eadránaí, idirghabhálaí

medical practice *n* cleachtadh míochaine

medical practicioner *n* lia, cleachtóir míochaine

medical scanning *n* scanadh míochaine

medication *n* cógas

medicine *n* leigheas, míochaine

medieval *adj* meánaoiseach

mediocre *adj* lagmheasartha

meditate *v* machnaigh

meditation *n* machnamh

Mediterranean *n* (Sea) an Mheánmhuir

Mediterranean countries *pl* tíortha na Meánmhara

medium[1] *n* meán the (communications) media na meáin (chumarsáide)

medium[2] *adj* meán-

medium[3] *adj* (cooking) scothbhruite

medium red *adj* meándearg

medley *n* meascra

meek *adj* ceansa

meet *v* cas le, buail le, cas ar to go to meet a person dul in airicis duine, dul chun bualadh le duine

meeting *n* cruinniú, dáil

megaphone *n* stoc fógartha

melancholy *adj* dubhach *n* lionn dubh

mellow[1] *v* séimhigh

mellow[2] *adj* séimh

melodious *adj* siansach

melodrama *n* méaldráma

melody *n* fonn, siansa

melon *n* mealbhacán

melt *v* leáigh

melting-point *n* leáphointe

member *n* comhalta, ball

membership *n* comhaltas, ballraíocht

member state *n* ballstát

memoirs *n* cuimhní cinn

memorandum *n* meabhrán, meamram

memorial *n* leacht cuimhneacháin

memorise *v* cuir de ghlanmheabhair

memory *n* cuimhne, meabhair

mend *v* cóirigh, deisigh

menial *adj* uiríseal

meningitis *n* meiningíteas

menstruate *v* míostraigh

menstruation *n* míostrú, fuil mhíosta, bláthscaoileadh

mental strain *n* tuirse intinne

mentality *n* meon, dearcadh

mental handicap *n* bac meabhrach

mental hospital *n* ospidéal meabhairghalair

mention¹ *n* iomrá, tagairt, lua, trácht not to mention gan trácht ar

mention² *v* luaigh, tagair

menu *n* biachlár

MEP *n* TPE (Teachta Pharlaimint na hEorpa)

mercenary *n* amhas

merchandise *n* marsantacht

merchant *n* ceannaí

merciful *adj* trócaireach

merciless *adj* éadrócaireach, míthrócaireach

Mercury *n* Mearcair

mercury *n* mearcair

mercy *n* trócaire

merge *v* comhtháthaigh, cónaisc

merger *n* cumasc

merging traffic *n* (roadsign) cumar tráchta romhat

meringue *n* meireang

merit *n* fiúntas *v* gnóthaigh

mermaid *n* maighdean mhara, murúch

merry *adj* súgach, subhach

mesh *n* mogall

mess¹ *n* prácás, praiseach *v* praiseach a dhéanamh de rud, salaigh they had the place in a complete mess bhí an áit ina chíor thuathail acu

mess² *n* (soldiers) cuibhreann the officers' mess cuibhreann na n-oifigeach

message *n* teachtaireacht

messenger *n* teachtaire, timire

Messiah *n* Meisias

messing *n* pleidhcíocht, méiseáil

messy *adj* cáidheach, salach

metal *n* miotal

metallic *adj* miotalach

metamorphosis *n* claochlú

metaphor *n* meafar

metaphorical *adj* meafarach

metaphysics *n* meitifisic

meteor *n* dreige

meteorology *n* meitéareolaíocht

meter *n* méadar

method *n* modh, slí, dóigh

methodical *adj* críochnúil

Methodist *n* Modhach

methylated *adj* meitileach

meticulous *adj* mionchúiseach

metre¹ *n* (verse) meadaracht

metre² *n* méadar

metric *adj* méadrach

mettle *n* miotal

metropolis *n* ceannchathair, ardchathair

Mexican *adj, n* Meicsiceach
Mexico *n* Meicsiceo
mews *pl* stáblaí
miaowing *n* meamhlach
micro- *prefix* micri- micrea-
microbe *n* miocrób
microchip *n* micrishlis
microfilm *n* micreascannán
microphone *n* micreafón
microscope *n* micreascóp
microwave *n* micreathonn
microwave oven *n* oigheann micreathonnach
mid- *prefix* idir-, meán-
mid-afternoon *n* ardtráthnóna
midday *n* meán lae
middle[1] *n* meán
middle[2] *adj* meán-, meánach
Middle Ages *n* an Mheánaois
middle age *n* meánaois
middle-aged *adj* meánaosta
middle-class *adj* meánaicmeach
middle finger *n* an mhéar láir
middleman *n* meáncheannaí
middleweight *n* meánmheáchan
middling *adj* cuibheasach
midge *n* corrmhíol, míoltóg
midlands *n* lár na tíre
midnight *n* meán oíche
midsummer day *n* Féile Eoin
midsummer eve *n* Oíche Sin Seáin
midwife *n* bean chabhrach, bean ghlúine
mighty *adj* tréan
migraine *n* mígréin
migrant *adj* imirceach
migrate *v* imirce a dhéanamh
migration *n* imirce
migratory *adj* imirceach migratory bird éan imirce, migratory labourer spailpín
mild *adj* cineálta, cneasta, éadrom, séimh

mildew *n* coincleach
mildewed *adj* clúmhúil
mildness *n* cneastacht
mile *n* míle
mileage *n* míleáiste
milestone *n* céim, cloch mhíle
militant *adj, n* míleatach
military *adj* míleata
milk *n* bainne *v* crúigh, bligh super milk, fortified milk bainne treisithe
milky *adj* bainiúil the Milky Way Bealach na Bó Finne, Eireaball na Lárach Báine, claí mór na réaltaí
mill *n* muileann
millennium *n* mílaois
miller *n* muilleoir
milligram *n* milleagram
millimeter *n* milliméadar
million *n* milliún
millionaire *n* milliúnaí
mime *n, v* mím
mimic *n* aithriseoir
mimicry *n* aithris, aithriseoireacht, athmhagadh
mince *v* mionaigh
mincemeat *n* mionfheoil, mionra
mincer *n* miontóir
mind *n* aigne, intinn, meabhair what's on your mind? cad é atá ar d'aigne? I don't mind ní miste liom, don't mind them ná bac leo
mindful *adj* aireach, meabhrach
mine *n* mianach landmine mianach talún, gold mine mianach óir
mine field *n* log mianach
miner *n* mianadóir
mining *n* mianadóireacht
mineral *adj* mianrach *n* mianra
mineral water *n* uisce mianrach
mingle *v* measc
miniature *n* (model) mionsamhail
minibus *n* mionbhus
mini-golf *n* mionghalf

minimalism *n* íostachas

minimum *adj* íos-, íosta, **(amount)** íosmhéid

minimum fee *n* táille íosta

minimum wage *n* íosphá

mining *n* mianadóireacht

miniskirt *n* mionsciorta

minister *n* **(church)** ministir, **(government)** aire

ministry *n* **(Government)** aireacht, ministreacht

mink *n* minc

minor *adj* mion- *n* mionúr

minor detail *n* mionsonra

minor key *n* mionghléas

minority *n* mionlach

minstrel *n* oirfideach

mint *n* miontas

minus *prep* lúide *n* **(sign)** míneas

minute[1] *n* nóiméad, bomaite

minute[2] *adj* bídeach

minutes **(of meeting)** *pl* miontuairiscí

miracle *n* míorúilt

miraculous *adj* míorúilteach

mirage *n* mearú súl, meabhalscáil

mire *n* láib

mirror *n* scáthán

mirth *n* subhachas

mis- *prefix* mí-

misappropriate *v* cúbláil

misbehaviour *n* mí-iompar, drochiompar

miscalculation *n* mí-áireamh

miscellaneous *adj* ilghnéitheach, il-

miscellany *n* meascra

mischance *n* anachain

mischief *n* diabhlaíocht, drochobair

mischievous *adj* diabhalta

misconduct *n* mí-iompar **serious misconduct** mí-iompar tromchúiseach

misdemeanour *n* anghníomh, oilghníomh

miser *n* sprionlóir

miserable *adj* ainnis, scallta

miserly *adj* sprionlaithe

misery *n* ainnise, donas

misfortune *n* donas, mí-ádh, mífhortún, amarrán

misgiving *n* drochamhras

misguided *adj* seachránach

mishap *n* míthapa, taisme, timpiste

misinterpret *v* míchiall a bhaint as

misinterpretation *n* míchiall

mislead *v* duine a chur amú

mismanagement *n* míriar

misprint *n* dearmad cló

miss[1] *v* **I miss him** braithim / mothaím uaim é, crothnaím é

miss[2] *v* caill **she missed the bus** chaill sí an bus, **I missed the target** theip orm an sprioc a aimsiú, níor éirigh liom an sprioc a aimsiú

miss[3], **Miss O'Connor** Iníon Uí Chonchúir

mis-shapen *adj* anchumtha

missile *n* diúracán **guided missile** diúracán treoraithe/faoi threorú

missing *adj* ar lár

mission *n* miseán

missionary *n* misinéir

mist *n* ceo, smúit

mistake *n* dearmad, iomrall **mistaken identity** iomrall aithne

mistletoe *n* drualus

mistress *n* máistreás, **(lover)** bean leapa

mistrust *v* drochiontaoibh a bheith agat as

misty *adj* ceobhránach, ceoch

misunderstanding *n* míthuiscint

misuse *n* mí-úsáid

mite *n* fríd

mitten *n* miotóg

mix[1] *v* measc, suaith **to mix cement** suimint a shuaitheadh

mix² *n* suaitheadh

mix up *n* meascán

mixed *adj* ilchineálach, measctha

mixer *n* meascthóir

mixture *n* meascán

moan *n, v* éagaoin

moat *n* móta

mob *n* gramaisc *v* plódaigh

mobile *adj* soghluaiste, gluaisteach

mobile (tele)phone *n* (teilea)fón gluaisteach, (teilea)fón póca, guthán gluaisteach, guthán póca

mobilise *v* slóg

mock¹ *adj* tacair, bréag- **moch exam** bréagscrúdú

mock² *v* magadh/fónóid a dhéanamh faoi **don't mock her** ná bí ag magadh/fonóid fúithi

mockery *n* magadh, fonóid

mocking *adj* magúil, fonóideach

mode *n* modh

mode of production *n* córas táirgeachta

model¹ *n* (**art**) cuspa

model² *adj* eiseamláireach *n* eiseamláir, samhail

model³ *n* (**fashion**) mainicín

modelling *n* mainicíneacht

moderate *n* measartha, réasúnta

moderation *n* measarthacht

modern *adj* nua-aoiseach **modern language** nuatheanga

modernisation *n* nuachóiriú

modernise *v* nuachóirigh

modest *adj* modhúil, náireach

modesty *n* modhúlacht, náire

modify *v* modhnaigh

modulate *v* modhnaigh

module *n* modúl

mohair *n* móihéar

moist *adj* maoth, tais

moisten *v* maothaigh

moistness *n* taise

moisture *n* taisleach

moisturiser *n* taisritheoir

molar *n* cúlfhiacail

mole *n* (**animal**) caochán, (**on skin**) ball dobhráin

molecule *n* móilín

molest *v* cuir isteach ar dhuine, déan dochar do

moment *n* nóiméad

momentary *adj* gearrshaolach

momentous *adj* tábhachtach

momentum *n* móiminteam

Monaghan *n* Muineachán **Co. Monaghan** Co. Mhuineacháin

monarch *n* monarc

monarchy *n* monarcacht

monastery *n* mainistir

monasticism *n* manachas

Monday *n* Dé Luain **on Monday** Dé Luain

money *n* airgead **my money** mo chuid airgid, **pocket money** airgead póca

money lender *n* fear gaimbín

mongrel *n* bodmhadra

monitor *n* monatóir *v* monatóireacht a dhéanamh ar

monk *n* manach

monkey *n* moncaí

monkey-puzzle *n* (**tree**) arócar

mono- *prefix* aon-

monogamous *adj* monagamach

monogamy *n* aonchéileachas

monolithic *adj* monailiteach

monologue *n* monalóg

monopoly *n* monaplacht

monosyllable *n* aonsiolla

monotone¹ *n* aonton

monotone² *adj* aontonach

monotonous *adj* aontonach

monoxide *n* aonocsaíd **carbon monoxide** aonocsaíd charbóin

monsoon *n* monsún

monster *n* arracht, ollphéist

monstrous *adj* anchúinseach

month *n* mí

monthly¹ *n* **(journal)** míosachán

monthly² *adj* míosúil

monument *n* séadchomhartha

mood *n* aoibh, fonn **quiet mood** sáimhín

mood music *n* ceol atmaisféir

moody *adj* taomach

mooing *n* géim, géimneach

moon *n* gealach, ré

moor¹ *v* **(boat)** feistigh

moor² *n* móinteán

moose *n* mús

mop¹ *n* **(of hair)** mothall

mop² *n* mapa *v* mapáil

moral *adj* morálta

morale *n* meanma

morality *n* moráltacht

morbid *adj* duairc

more *adj* breis, níos mó, tuilleadh **there were more than a thousand people there** bhí breis agus míle duine ann, **will you have more?** an mbeidh níos mó/tuilleadh agat? **more or less** a bheag nó a mhór

moreover *adv* thairis sin

morgue *n* marbhlann

Mormon *n* Mormannach

morning *n* maidin

morose *adj* modartha

morphine *n* moirfín

Morse code *n* cód Morse

morsel *n* ruainne

mortar *n* **(cement)** moirtéal

mortgage *n* morgáiste *v* morgáistigh

mosaic *n* mósáic

Moscow *n* Moscó

moss *n* caonach **peat moss** caonach móna **a rolling stone gathers no moss** ní thagann caonach ar chloch reatha

most beloved *adj* **my most beloved (one)** an (ceann) is ansa liom

moth *n* leamhan, féileacán oíche

mother *n* máthair **mother tongue** teanga mháthartha

motherhood *n* máithreachas

mother-in-law *n* máthair chéile

motherly máithriúil

motion *n* gluaiseacht, **(of debate)** rún **in motion** faoi shiúl

motionless *adj* gan chorraí

motivate *v* spreag

motivated *adj* spreagtha

motive *n* réasún, bunchúis

motor *n* mótar

motor- *prefix* mótar-

motorbike *n* gluaisrothar

motorboat *n* mótarbhád

motor car *n* mótar, carr, gluaisteán

motorcyclist *n* gluaisrothaí

motorist *n* gluaisteánaí

motorway *n* mótarbhealach

motto *n* mana

mould¹ *n* **(growth)** coincleach

mould² *n* múnla *v* múnlaigh, fuin

mound *n* tulach

mount *v* dul in airde

mountain *n* sliabh **mountain range** sliabhraon

mountaineer *n* sléibhteoir

mountaineering *n* sléibhteoireacht

mountainous *adj* sléibhtiúil

mounting board *n* cairtchlár gléasta

mourn *v* caoin

mourner *n* caointeoir

mouse *n* luch, **(computer)** luchóg

mouse-trap *n* sás luiche

moustache *n* croiméal

mouth *n* béal *v* labhairt (amach) go gáifeach

mouthpiece *n* béalóg

mouthwash *n* folcadh béil

movable *adj* inaistrithe, sobhogtha, aistritheach, athraitheach

move *n* **(house)** aistrigh, corraigh, gluais

movement *n* gluaiseacht

movie *n* scannán

mow *v* lom

MP *n* feisire

Mr Ryan an tUasal Ó Riain

Mr So-and-So Tadhg Ó Rudaí

much *adj* go leor, mórán, a lán **there is much work to be done** tá a lán oibre le déanamh, **we don't have much time** níl mórán ama againn, **much ado about nothing** mórán cainte ar bheagán cúise

Mrs Bean (Uí)

muck *n* láib

mucus *n* múcas

mud *n* clábar, draoib, lábán, láib, pluda, puiteach

muddle *n* meascán *v* meascán a chur ar

muddy *adj* lábánach, pludach, draoibeach

mudguard *n* pludgharda

muesli *n* múslaí

mug *n* muga *v* ionsaigh

mulberry *n* maoildearg

mule *n* miúil

multicoloured *adj* dathannach, ildathach

multidenominational *adj* ilchreidmheach

multilaterisation *n* iltaobhú

multimedia *adj* ilmheánach

multinational *adj* ilnáisiúnta

multiple *adj* iolrach

multiple choice *adj* ilroghnach

multiple sclerosis *n* scléaróis iolrach

multiplication *n* iolrú

multiplicity *n* iolracht, iliomad

multiply *v* iolraigh

multiracial *adj* ilchiníoch

multistory *adj* ilstórach

multistory carpark *n* carrchlós ilstórach

mum *n* mamaí

mumble *v* mungail

mummy *n* seargán

mumps *n* leicneach, plucamas

mundane *adj* domhanda, leamh

municipal *adj* cathrach

Munster *n* Mumhain **(the province of) Munster** Cúige Mumhan

Munster person *n* Muimhneach

mural *n* múrmhaisiú **murals** múrmhaisithe

murder *n* dúnmharú *v* dúnmharaigh

murderer *n* dúnmharfóir

murky *adj* modartha

murmur *n* monabhar *v* monabhar a dhéanamh

muscle *n* féitheog, matán **cardiac muscle** matán cairdiach

muscular *adj* féitheogach

museum *n* iarsmalann, músaem **the National Museum** an tArd-Mhúsaem

mushroom *n* fás aon oíche, muisriún

music *n* ceol

musical *adj* ceolmhar

musical instrument *n* uirlis cheoil, léas ceoil

musician *n* ceoltóir

Muslim *adj, n* Moslamach

muslin *n* muislín

mussel *n* diúilicín

mustard *n* mustard

muster *n* tóstal *v* tionóil

musty smell *n* seanbholadh

mute *adj* balbh *n* balbhán

mutilate *v* ciorraigh

mutinous *adj* ceannairceach
mutiny *n* ceannairc *v* dul chun ceannairce
mutton *n* caoireoil
mutual *adj* cómhalartach, araon
muzzle *n* béalóg, puslach, soc
my *poss adj* mo, mo chuid
mysterious *adj* diamhair, mistéireach, rúndiamhrach

mysteriousness *n* diamhracht
mystery *n* mistéir, rúndiamhair
mystic *adj* misteach
mystify *v* mearaigh
myth *n* miotas
mythical *adj* miotasach
mythology *n* miotaseolaíocht

N

nail[1] *n* **(of finger)** ionga **ingrowing toenail** ionga i bhfeoil
nail[2] *n* **(metal)** tairne *v* tairneáil
naive *adj* saonta, soineanta
naked *adj* nocht **naked person** nocht
name *n* ainm **by his name** ina ainm, **what's your name?** cad is ainm duit? **Christian name** ainm baiste
nameless *adj* gan ainm
nameplate *n* **(street)** ainm chláir
namesake *n* comhainmneach
nap *n* néal, támh chodlata
napkin *n* naipcín
nappy *n* clúidín
narcissism *n* naircisíocht
narcissus *n* nairciseas
narcossis *n* támhshuan
narcotic *adj* támhshuanach
narrate *v* aithris, eachtraigh
narration *n* insint, aithris
narrative *n* scéal
narrator *n* scéalaí
narrow *adj* cúng *v* caolaigh
narrow-minded *adj* cúngaigeanta, caolaigeanta
nasal *adj* srónach
nasty *adj* gránna

nation *n* náisiún **the United Nations** na Náisiúin Aontaithe
national *adj* náisiúnta
national convention *n* ardfheis
National Council for Curriculum and Assessment *n* an Chomhairle Náisiúnta Curaclaim agus Measúnachta
nationalism *n* náisiúnachas
nationalist *n* náisiúnaí
nationalistic *adj* náisiúnaíoch
nationality *n* náisiúntacht
nationalisation *n* náisiúnú
nationalise *v* náisiúnaigh
native *adj* dúchais, dúchasach
Native American *n* Meiriceánach Dúchasach
native country *n* tír dhúchais
natural *adj* nádúrtha
natural gas pipline *n* píblíne gháis nádúrtha
natural resources *pl* acmhainní nádúrtha
naturalism *n* nádúrachas
naturalist *n* nádúraí
nature *n* dúlra, nádúr **from nature** ó nádúr, **nature is stronger than nuture** is treise dúchas ná oiliúint

nausea *n* masmas, múisiam, samhnas
nauseating *adj* masmasach
nautical *adj* farraige, muir-
naval *adj* muirí
nave *n* corp eaglaise
navel *n* imleacán
navigable *adj* inseolta
navigate *v* stiúir, loingsigh
navigation *n* loingseoireacht
navvy *n* sclábhaí
navy *n* cabhlach
Nazi *adj* Naitsíoch *n* Naitsí
Nazism *n* Naitseachas
neap tide *n* mallmhuir
near *adj* in aice (le), cóngarach, gairid, gar (do)
near- *prefix* neas-
nearly *adv* beagnach, nach mór / beag
near-sighted *adj* gearr-radharcach
neat *adj* deismir, néata, ordúil, piocúil, slachtmhar
neatness *n* deismireacht, néatacht, ord, piocúlacht, slacht
necessary *adj* riachtanach
necessity *n* riachtanas
neck *n* muineál **long thin neck** scrogall
necklace *n* muince
need *n* call, díth, gá, gátar, riachtanas **to need something** rud a bheith de dhíth ort, **you don't need to go** ní gá duit imeacht, **in time of need** in am an ghátair
needy *adj* anásta, gátarach
needle *n* snáthaid
needlework *n* fuáil, bróidnéireacht
negative[1] *adj* diúltach
negative[2] *n* (photo) claonchló
neglect *n* léig, neamart, neamhchúram, siléig **to neglect things** do mhaidí a ligean le sruth

neglectful *adj* neamartach
negligence *n* neamart
negligent *adj* neamhchúramach
negotiable *adj* inaistrithe
negotiate *v* idirbheartaíocht a dhéanamh
negotiation *n* idirbheartaíocht
negotiations *pl* comhchainteanna
negotiator *n* idirbheartaí
neighbour *n* comharsa
neighbourhood *n* comharsanacht
Neighbourhood Watch Area *n* Ceantar Faire
neighbourly *adj* comharsanúil
neighing *n* seitreach
neither *adv* ceachtar
neon *n* neon **neon lights** soilse neoin
nephew *n* nia
nepotism *n* finíochas
nerve éadan, néaróg
nervous *adj* neirbhíseach
nervous breakdown *n* cliseadh néaróg
nervous system *n* néarchóras
nervousness *n* neirbhís
nest *n* nead *v* neadaigh
nest-egg *n* ubh fáire
nestle *v* neadaigh
nestling *n* scalltán
net *n* eangach, líon
Netherlands *n* an Ísiltír
netting *n* cangach
nettle *n* neantóg
network *n* gréasán, líonra **computer network** líonra ríomhairí, **data network** líonra sonraí
networking *n* líonrú
neurology *n* néareolaíocht
neurotic *adj* néaróiseach
neurosis *n* néaróis
neuter *adj* neodrach *v* coill, neodraigh

neutralise *v* neodraigh

neutrality *n* neodracht

never *adv* choíche, go deo, riamh **I'll never talk to them again** ní labhróidh mé leo go deo / choíche arís, **I was never there** ní raibh mé riamh ann, **better late than never** is fearr déanach ná go brách/ródhéanach, más mall is mithid

never-ending *adj* síoraí

new *adj* úr, nua **new year** athbhliain

New Grange *n* Slí an Bhrú

New Year's Day *n* Lá Caille

New Year's Eve *n* Oíche Chinn Bliana

New York *n* Nua-Eabhrac

New Zealand *n* an Nua-Shéalainn

New Zealander *n* Nua-Shéalannach

newborn *adj* nuabheirthe

newcomer *n* núíosach

new-fashioned *adj* nuanósach

newly- *prefix* nua-

news *n* nuacht, scéala

newsagent *n* nuachtánaí

newsletter *n* nuachtlitir

newspaper *n* nuachtán

newsprint *n* nuachtpháipéar

newt *n* earc luachra

next *adj* **the next thing that happened** an chéad rud eile a tharla

next-door neighbour *n* comharsa bhéal dorais

next-of-kin *n* neasghaol

nibble *n, v* gráinseáil

nibbling (at food) *n* blaistínteacht (ar bhia)

nice *adj* deas

niceties *pl* deismíneachtaí

niche *n* almóir

nickel *n* nicil

nickname *n* leasainm

nicotine *n* nicitín

niece *n* neacht

night *n* oíche **during the night** i rith na hoíche

night club *n* club oíche

night cream *n* smearadh oíche

nightdress *n* léine oíche

nightfall *n* crónachan, titim na hoíche

nightingale *n* filiméala

nightmare *n* tromluí

night-visiting *n* airneán

nil *n* neamhní

nimble *adj* luaineach

nine *adj* naoi **nine red cars** naoi gcarr dhearga, **nine sweet apples** naoi n-úll mhilse, **nine people** naonúr

ninetieth *adj, n* nóchadú

ninety *adj* nócha

ninth *adj, n* naoú

nip *n* liomóg, **(in the air)** goimh

nipple *n* dide, sine, ballán cíche

nitrogen *n* nítúighn

no[1] *adv* **to say no you give the negative form of the verb: are you well? no** an bhfuil tú go maith? níl, **did you get a drink? no** an bhfuair tú deoch? ni bhfuair, **is that so? no** an ea? ní hea, **an mar sin é?** ní hea

no[2] *adj* aon, **ai bidh he has no sense** níl aon chiall aige, níl ciall ar bith aige

nobility *n* uaisleacht

noble *adj, n* ard, uasal **nobles** uaisle

nobody *pron* aon duine, duine ar bith *n* neamhdhuine

nocturnal *adj* oíchí

nod *n* sméideadh *v* sméid **a nod is as good as a wink** is leor nod don eolach

noise *n* callán, torann, tormán, trup **background noise** torann cúlra

noisy *adj* callánach, clamprach, tormánach

nominal *adj* ainmniúil

nominate *v* ainmnigh, ceap

nomination *n* ainmniúchán

nominative *adj, n* ainmneach

nominator *n* moltóir

nominee *n* ainmnitheach

non- *prefix* neamh-

non-absorbent *adj* neamhshúiteach

non-alcoholic *adj* neamh-mheisciúil

none *pron* aon duine, aon rud

nonentity *n* neamhdhuine

non-biodegradable *adj* do-bhithmhillte

non-fiction *n* neamhfhicsean

non-native *adj* andúchasach

non-political *adj* neamhpholaitiúil

non-renewable *adj* neamh-inathnuaite

nonsense *n* amaidí, raiméis, seafóid **it's nothing but nonsense** níl ann ach amaidí

nonsensical *adj* seafóideach

non-stop *adj* síoraí

nook *n* clúid, cúil, cúinne

noon *n* nóin

noose *n* dol, **(of hangman)** sealán

nor *conj* ná

normal *adj* nádúrtha, normálta, gnách **normally** de ghnáth, **it is normal to…** is gnách…

Norman *adj, n* Normannach

Normandy *n* an Normainn

north *n* tuaisceart **to the north** ó thuaidh, **from the north** aduaidh, **North America** Meiriceá Thuaidh, **the north wind** an ghaoth aduaidh

north-east *n* oirthuaisceart **to the north-east** soir ó thuaidh, **from the north-east** anoir aduaidh

north-eastern *adj* thoir thuaidh

northern *adj* tuaisceartach

northener *n* tuaisceartach

North Pole *n* an Mol Thuaidh

northwards *adv* ó thuaidh

north-west *n* iarthuaisceart **to the north-west** siar ó thuaidh, **from the north-west** aniar aduaidh

north-western *adj* thiar thuaidh

Norway *n* an Iorua

Norwegian *adj, n* Ioruach *n* **(language)** Ioruais

nose *n* srón, caincín, gaosán

nostalgia *n* cumha

nostril *n* polláire

nosy *adj* caidéiseach, fiosrach

notable *adj* nótáilte

notary *n* nótaire

notepaper *n* páipéar litreach

notch *n* eang

note *n* nóta *v* nótáil

nothing *n* dada, náid, faic, neamhní **there is nothing left** níl dada fágtha, **nothing at all** faic na fríde, **to make nothing of something** spior spear a dhéanamh de rud

notice *n* fógra

noticeable *adj* sonraíoch, suntasach

notify *v* fógair, cuir in iúl

notion *n* nóisean

notorious *adj* iomráiteach

nought *n* náid

noun *n* ainmfhocal **verbal noun** ainm briathartha

nourish *v* cothaigh

nourishing *adj* cothúil

nourishment *n* cothú

novel *adj* úr *n* úrscéal

novelist *n* úrscéalaí

November *n* Samhain, mí na Samhna

now *adv* anois **now and then** anois is arís, **right now** anois díreach

nowhere *adv* in aon áit, áit ar bith

nozzle *n* soc

nuclear *adj* eithneach, núicléach

nuclear energy *n* fuinneamh eithneach

nuclear free seas *pl* farraigí neamhnúicléacha

nuclear non-proliferation treaty *n* conradh in aghaidh iomadú núicléach

nuclear reactor *n* imoibreoir núicléach

nucleus *n* eithne, núicléas

nude *adj* nocht

nudist *n* nochtach

nudity *n* nochtacht

nuisance *n* núis

numb *adj* marbh

number *n* líon, uimhir *v* uimhrigh even number ré-uimhir, whole number slán uimhir, odd number corruimhir, there was a great number of people there bhí líon mór daoine ann

number-plate *n* uimhirphláta

numerical *adj* uimhriúil

numerous *adj* líonmhar

nurse *n* banaltra, (male) altra *v* aire a thabhairt do

nursery[1] *n* (infants) naíolann

nursery[2] *n* (botanic) plandlann

nursing *n* altranas

nursing home *n* teach altranais

nurture *n* oiliúint *v* oil nature is stronger than nurture is treise dúchas ná oiliúint

nut *n* cnó

nutcracker *n* cnóire

nutmeg *n* noitmig

nutrient *n* cothaitheach

nutrition *n* cothú, scamhard

nutritionist *n* saineolaí cothúcháin

nutritious *adj* beathúil, scamhardach

nutshell *n* blaosc cnó, crotal cnó

nylon *n* níolón

O

oak *n* dair oak tree crann darach

oar *n* maide rámha, rámh

oasis *n* ósais

oath *n* mionn

oath of allegiance *n* mionn dílseachta

oatmeal *n* min choirce

oats *pl* coirce

obdurate *adj* dígeanta

obedience *n* umhlaíocht

obedient *adj* umhal

obey *v* umhlaigh (do), géill (do)

object[1] *n* (purpose) cuspóir, (thing) rud

object[2] *v* cuir i gcoinne, cuir in aghaidh

objection *n* cur i gcoinne, cur in aghaidh

objective *adj* oibiachtúil *n* aidhm, cuspóir, sprioc

objector *n* agóideoir

obligation *n* cuing, comaoin, dualgas

oblige *v* iallach a bheith ar

obliged *adj* I'm obliged to you tá mé faoi chomaoin agat

obliging *adj* garach

oblique *adj* fiar

oblivion *n* díchuimhne

oblivious (of) *adj* dímheabhrach (ar)

obnoxious *adj* déistineach

oboe *n* óbó

obscene *adj* graosta, gáirsiúil

obscenity *n* graostacht, gáirsiúlacht

obscure *adj* doiléir, dorcha

observance (of law) *n* coinneáil (dlí)

observant *adj* géar, grinn

observatory *n* réadlann

observe *v* breathnaigh, **(of law)** coimeád, fair, coinnigh

observer *n* féachadóir, breathnóir

obsess *v* **to be obsessed with something** rud a bheith ag luí ar d'intinn

obstacle *n* bac, bacainn, constaic

obstinate *adj* ciotrúnta, ceanntréan, ceanndána, stuacach

obstruct *v* bac, toirmisc

obtain *v* gnóthaigh

obtrusive *adj* treallúsach

obvious *adj* follasach, sofheicthe, soiléir

obviousness *n* soiléireacht

occasion *n* ócáid, uain, turas **on this occasion** an turas seo

occasional *adj* fánach, ócáideach

occasionally *adv* corruair, uaireanta

occupation *n* **(career)** slí bheatha, **(of place)** lonnú

occupier *n* sealbhóir, áititheoir

occupy *v* sealbhaigh, áitigh

occur *v* tarlaigh

occurrence *n* tarlú

ocean *n* aigéan **the Pacific Ocean** an tAigéan Ciúin

o'clock a chlog

October *n* Deireadh Fómhair

octopus *n* ochtapas

odd *adj* aisteach, ait, corr **oddly enough** aisteach go leor, **doing odd jobs** ag timireacht

oddness *n* aiteacht

odds *pl* corrlach

odour *n* boladh

of *prep* as, de, ó **they are out of their minds** tá siad as a meabhair, **that's only part of the story** níl ansin ach cuid den scéal, **free of tax** saor ó cháin

of late *adv* le déanaí, ar na mallaibh

off *adj*, *adv* **off you go!** bailigh leat! **well off** go maith as, **it smells off** tá drochbholadh uaidh, **turn off the light** múch an solas

Offaly *n* Uíbh Fhailí

offence *n* cion, coir

offend *v* ciontaigh, maslaigh

offender *n* coireach, ciontóir

offensive *adj* tarcaisneach

offer *v* ofráil, tairg

offering *n* ofráil, íobairt

office *n* oifig, cúram **to take office** teacht i réim, **the post office** oifig an phoist

office equipment *n* trealamh oifige

officer *n* oifigeach

official[1] *n* feidhmeannach

official[2] *adj* oifigiúil

off-licence *n* eischeadúnas

off-licence shop *n* siopa eischeadúnais

off-shore oil-gas exploitation platform *n* ardán saothraithe ola agus gáis ar muir

offspring *n* sliocht

often *adv* go minic

ogham *n* ogham

oil *n* ola

oil storage tank *n* umar stórála ola

oilfield *n* olacheantar

oil rig *n* rige ola

oilskins *pl* aidhleanna

oil-tanker *n* tancaer ola

oily *adj* olúil, olach, úscach

ointment *n* ungadh

old *adj* sean, aosta **old age** seanaois, ársaíocht, **old man** seanfhear, **old person** seanduine, **the Old-Testament** an Sean-Tiomna, **to**

be your old self again bheith ar do sheanléim arís

old-age pension *n* pinsean seanaoise

old-age pensioner *n* pinsinéir seanaoise

old-fashioned *adj* seanaimseartha, seanfhaiseanta

old-timer *n* seanfhondúir

olive *n* ológ

Olympic *adj* Oilimpeach **the Olympic Games** na Cluichí Oilimpeacha, **International Olympic Committee** Coiste Idirnáisiúnta na gCluichí Oilimpeacha

ombudsman *n* ombudsman, fear an phobail

omelette *n* uibheagán

omen *n* comhartha, tuar

ominous *adj* tuarúil

omission *n* faillí

omit *v* fág amach, fág ar lár

omnivore *n* uiliteoir

on *prep* ar **on time in am, on demand** ar éileamh

on-line *adj* ar líne

once *adv* uair amháin **once a month** uair sa mhí, **once he had left** a luaithe a bhí sé ar shiúl

one *adj* aon, ceann, amháin **one by one** ceann ar cheann, **one night** oíche amháin

one eye *n* leathshúil

one-parent family *n* clann le tuismitheoir amháin

one-sided *adj* leataobhach

onion *n* oinniún

onlooker *n* féachadóir, breathnóir

only *adj* aon-, aonair **an only child** páiste aonair, **only for** murach

onslaught *n* imruathar

onus *n* dualgas, freagracht

ooze *v* úsc

opaque *adj* teimhneach

open *adj* oscailte *v* oscail

opening *n* oscailt **the opening verse** an véarsa tosaigh

openly *adv* os comhair an tsaoil, os ard, go hoscailte

opera *n* ceoldráma, **(general)** ceoldrámaíocht

operate *v* oibrigh, feidhmigh, cuir faoi scian

operatic *adj* ceoldrámach

operating system *n* **(computer)** córas oibriúcháin

operating theatre *n* obrádlann

operation *n* feidhmiú, oibriú, **(medical)** obráid **to have an operation** dul faoi scian

operator *n* oibreoir

opinion *n* dearcadh, tuairim

opinion poll *n* pobalbhreith

opium *n* codlaidín **opium den síbín codlaidín**

opponent *n* céile comhraic

opportune *adj* tráthúil

opportunist *n* brabúsaí

opportunity *n* áiméar, caoi, faill, uain, deis **to seize the opportunity** an t-áiméar a fhreastal, **to grasp an opportunity** deis a thapú

oppose *v* cuir i gcoinne

opposing *adj* freasúrach

opposite *adj* codarsnach, contrártha, os comhair, ar aghaidh

opposition *n* freasúra

oppress *v* cos ar bolg a imirt ar

oppression *n* cos ar bolg, leatrom

oppressive *adj* leatromach

optic *adj* optach

optical *adj* optúil, radharcach

optician *n* radharceolaí

optics *pl* optaic, radharceolaíocht

optimism *n* soirbhíochas

optimist *n* soirbhíoch

optimistic *adj* dóchasach

option *n* rogha

optional *adj* roghnach

opus *n* saothar

or *conj* ná, nó

oracle *n* aitheascal

oral exam *n* scrúdú cainte

orange *adj* (colour) flannbhuí, oráiste **green, white and orange** uaine, bán agus flannbhuí (**Irish flag**)

orange(ade) *n* deoch oráistí

Orangeman *n* Oráisteach, fear buí

orator *n* óráidí

oratory *n* (church) aireagal, (speech) óráidíocht

orb *n* cruinne

orbit *n* fithis *v* fithisigh

orchard *n* úllord, úllghort

orchestra *n* ceolfhoireann

orchid *n* magairlín

ordain *v* oirnigh, ceap

order[1] *n* eagar, ord **in order that** ionas go, **in order of priority** de réir tosaíochta

order[2] *v* ordaigh

order[3] *n* ordú **postal order** ordú poist

ordinary *adj* coitianta

ordination *n* oirniú

ordnance *n* ordanás **the Ordnance Survey** an tSuirbhéireacht Ordanáis

organ *n* orgán **mouth organ** orgán béil, **vital organs** baill bheatha

organic *adj* orgánach

organist *n* orgánaí

organisation *n* eagraíocht, eagras, eagrú

organise *v* eagraigh

organiser *n* eagraí, timirc

orgasm *n* súnás

Orient *n* an tOirthear, an Domhan Thoir **in the Orient** san Oirthear

oriental *adj,* *n* oirthearach

orienteering *n* treodóireacht

origin *n* bunús

original *adj* bun- *n* bunchóip

originally *adv* ó bhunús

Orion's Belt *n* an Bhanlámh

ornament *n* ornáid

ornamental *adj* ornáideach

ornithologist *n* éaneolaí

orphan *n* dílleachta

orphanage *n* dílleachtlann

orthodox *adj* ceartchreidmheach

orthopaedic *adj* ortaipéideach **orthopaedic bed** leaba ortaipéideach

oscillate *v* luascadh

oscillation *n* luascaire

ostentation *n* buaileam sciath

ostentatious *adj* gáifeach

ostrich *n* ostrais

other *adj* eile **any other business** aon ghnó eile

otherwise *adv* ar chaoi eile, ar chuma eile

otter *n* dobharchú, madra uisce, cú dobhráin

ounce *n* unsa

our *poss adj* ár

ourselves *pers pron* muid féin, sinn féin

out *adv* amach **the way out** an bealach amach, **the outgoing mail** na litreacha amach, **out in the open** amuigh faoin spéir, **get out!** amach leat! **out of date** as dáta, **out of school educational activity** gníomhaíocht oideachasúil lasmuigh den scoil, **to be out of bed** bheith i do shuí, **to go out with somebody** siúl amach le duine

outburst *n* racht

outcast *n* díbeartach

outcome *n* toradh

outcry *n* gáir, agóid

outdoors *adv* lasmuigh

outer *adj* amuigh

outfit *n* feisteas

outgrow *v* fás as

outlandish *adj* aisteach, coimhthíoch

outlaw *n* eisreachtaí, meirleach
v eisreachtaigh

outline[1] *n* imlíne *v* imlínigh

outline[2] **(idea)** *n* cur síos garbh
v cuir síos go garbh

outlook *n* dearcadh

outnumber *v* bheith níos
líonmhaire ná

out-patient *n* othar seachtrach

outpost *n* urphost

output *n* táirgeacht, aschur **national
output** aschur náisiúnta

outrage *n* scannal

outrageous *adj* scannalach

out-right *adv* amach is amach, scun
scan

outset *n* tús

outside *prep* amuigh, lasmuigh,
taobh amuigh

outside broadcast *n* craoladh
seachtrach

outsider *n* éan corr

outspoken *adj* neamhbhalbh

outstanding *adj* suntasach, **(of debt)**
le híoc

outstanding person *n* duine tofa

outstretched *adj* sínte

outward *adj* amach, amuigh

outwit *v* an ceann is fearr a fháil ar

oval *adj* ubhchruthach *n* ubhchruth

ovary *n* ubhagán

ovation *n* gártha molta

oven *n* oigheann **microwave oven**
oigheann micreathonnach

over[1] *prep* thar, os **all over the place**
ar fud na háite

over[2] *adv* anonn, sall, thall **she went
over to Scotland** chuaigh sí

anonn / sall go hAlbain, **over
there** thall ansin

overalls *pl* forbhríste

overboard *adv* thar bord

overcast *adj* modartha

overcoat *n* cóta mór

overcome *v* sáraigh, cloígh

overdose *n* ródháileog

overdose of drugs *n* ródháileog
drugaí

overdraft *n* rótharraingt

overdrawn *adj* rótharraingthe

overdue *adj* thar téarma, mall

overfishing *n* ró-iascaireacht

overflow *v* sceith

overgrowth *n* fásach

overhaul *n* deisiú *v* deisigh

overhead *adv* lastuas, lasnairde

overhead cable *n* cábla lasnairde

overhead light *n* solas anuas

overhead projector *n* osteilgeoir

overheads *pl* forchostais

overjoyed *adj* ríméadach

overland *adv* thar tír

overlap *n* forluí *v* forluigh

overload *v* anluchtaigh, róluchtaigh

overlook *v* dearmad

overnight *adv* thar oíche

overpower *v* cloígh

overpowering *adj* cloíteach

overrule *v* rialú in aghaidh, **(in
court)** cuir ar neamhní

overrun (with) *adj* ar snámh (le)

overseas *adv* thar lear, thar sáile

overseas surface mail *n* post de
mhuir is de thalamh

overshadow *v* an solas a bhaint de

oversight *n* dearmad

overtake *v* dul thar

overthrow *v* treascair

overtime *n* ragobair

overture *n* réamhcheol

overview *n* forbhreathnú
overwhelm *v* cloígh, báigh
overwhelming *adj* coscrach
overwork *v* an iomarca oibre a thabhairt do
ovulation *n* ubhsceitheadh
owe *v* airgead a bheith ag duine ort
owl *n* ulchabhán

own *v* do you own it? an leat é?
owner *n* úinéir
ownership *n* úinéireacht
ox *n* damh
oxygen *n* ocsaigin
oyster *n* oisre
ozone *n* ózón **the ozone layer** ciseal an ózóin

P

pace *n* luas
pacemaker *n* séadaire
pacifism *n* síochánachas
pacifist *n* síochánaí
pacify *v* ceansaigh, suaimhnigh
pacifying *adj* suaimhnitheach
pack *n* paca *v* pacáil
package *n* pacáiste
package holiday *n* saoire láneagraithe
packet *n* paicéad
packing *n* pacáil
pad *n* ceap, pillín *v* stuáil **brake pads** pillíní coscáin
padding *n* stuáil
paddle *n* céasla *v* céaslaigh
paediatrics *n* péidiatraic
paedophile *n* péidifíle
paedophilia *n* péidifilia
pagan *adj* págánta *n* págánach
page *n* leathanach
pageant *n* tóstal
pager *n* glaoire
paid *adj* íoctha
pain *n* pian, arraing *v* gortaigh, goill ar **acute pain** scoilteach
painful *adj* goilliúnach, nimhneach, peannaideach, pianmhar
painkiller *n* pianmhúchán

paint *n* péint *v* dathaigh, péinteáil
painter *n* péintéir
painting *n* péinteáil, (art) péintéireacht, pictiúr
paint roller *n* péintrollóir
pair *n* dís, péire
palace *n* pálás
palatable *adj* so-bhlasta, taitneamhach
palatalise *v* caolaigh
Pale[1] *n* an Pháil
pale[2] *adj* mílítheach
Palestine *n* an Phalaistín
Palestinian *adj, n* Palaistíneach
pallet *n* pailléad
palm *n* (of hand) dearna, bos
palm tree *n* pailm
palpitation *n* athbhuille, líonrith **palpitations** buailtí croí **to have / get palpitations** athbhuille / líonrith a bheith ar do chroí
pamphlet *n* paimfléad
pan *n* (frying) friochtán
pancake *n* pancóg **Pancake Tuesday** Máirt na hInide
pancreas *n* paincréas
panda *n* panda
pane *n* pána **window pane** pána fuinneoige
panel *n* clár, painéal **instrument panel** painéal ionstraimí

panel-beater *n* buailteoir painéil

pang *n* daigh

panic *n* anbhá, líonrith, scaoll, sceimhle

panicky *adj* scaollmhar

pant *n, v* cnead

pantheism *n* paindiachas

panther *n* pantar

panties *n* brístín

pantomime *n* geamaireacht

papacy *n* pápacht

papal *adj* pápach

paper *n* páipéar **wallpaper** páipéar balla, **toilet paper** páipéar leithris

paperback *n* leabhar faoi chlúdach bog

paperclip *n* fáiscín páipéir

parable *n* fáthscéal, parabal

parachute *n* paraisiút

parade *n* paráid *v* máirseáil

paradise *n* parthas

paradox *n* frithchosúlacht, paradacsa

paradoxical *adj* frithchosúil, paradacsúil

paraffin *n* pairifín

paragraph *n* paragraf, alt

parallel *adj* comhthreomhar *n* pairaléal

paralyse *v* pairilis a chur ar

paralysis *n* pairilis

paralytic *adj* pairiliseach

paramedic *n* paramhíochaineoir

paramilitary *adj, n* paraimíleatach

paranoia *n* paranóia

paranoid *adj* paranóiach

paraphrase *n* athleagan

parasol *n* parasól, scáth gréine

parboiled *adj* cnagbhruite

parcel *n* beart

parched *adj* spallta, stiúgtha

parchment *n* pár

pardon *n* maithiúnas, pardún *v* maith **pardon me!** gabhaim pardún (agat)!

parent *n* tuismitheoir

Paris *n* Páras

parish *n* paróiste

park *n* páirc *v* páirceáil

parking *n* páirceáil, locadh

parliament *n* parlaimint, dáil **European Parliament** Parlaimint na hEorpa

parliamentary *adj* parlaiminteach

parlour *n* parlús

parochial *adj* paróisteach

parody *n* scigaithris

parole *n* parúl **on parole** ar parúl

parrot *n* pearóid

parsley *n* peirsil **parsley and thyme** persil agus tím

parsnip *n* meacan bán

part[1] *n* comhpháirt, cuid, páirt **to take something in good part** rud a ligean ar ghreann

part[2] *v* scar

partake *v* bheith rannpháirteach i, (béile) a ghlacadh

partaking *adj* rannpháirteach

partial *adj* claonta, taobhach, páirt-

partial eclipse *n* páirtéiclips

partiality *n* lé

participate *v* páirt a ghlacadh i

participating *adj* páirteach

participation *n* páirteachas, rannpháirteachas

particle *n* cáithne, cáithnín, páirteagal, **(grammar)** mír

particular *adj* sonrach, áirithe, pointeáilte

parting *n* scaradh, **(in hair)** stríoc

partisan *adj* páirtíneach

partition *n* **(of country)** deighilt, críochdheighilt, **(building)** spiara, landair

partner *n* páirtí
partnership *n* páirtíocht
partridge *n* patraisc
part-time *adj* páirtaimseartha
party[1] *n* cóisir
party[2] *n* páirtí **interested party**
  páirtí leasmhar
pass[1] *n* **(mountain)** mám
pass[2] *v* seachaid, pasáil
pass[3] *n* pas
pass away *v* síothlaigh
passage *n* fithis, pasáiste
passenger *n* paisinéir
passenger terminal *n* port na
  bpaisinéirí
passion *n* páis, paisean
passion fruit *n* páiseog
passionate *adj* díochra, paiseanta
passive *adj* síochánta, éighníomhach
passive role *n* páirt
  neamhghníomhach
passive smoking *n* caitheamh gan
  toil
passport *n* pas
password *n* pasfhocal
past *adj* caite, thart
pasta *n* pasta
paste *n* leafaos, taos
pasteurised milk *n* bainne
  paistéartha
pastille *n* paistil
pastime *n* caitheamh aimsire
pastor *n* aoire
pastry *n* taosrán **pastries** cácaí milse
pasture *n* féarach
password *n* pasfhocal
pat *v* slíoc
patch *n* paiste *v* paisteáil **patchwork**
  obair phaistí
patched *adj* píosáilte
patchy *adj* sceadach
patent *n* paitinn *v* paitinnigh

paternal *adj* aithriúil, athartha
paternity *n* atharthacht
path *n* cabhsa, cosán
pathetic *adj* truamhéalach
pathology *n* paiteolaíocht
pathological *adj* paiteolaíoch
patience *n* foighne
patient[1] *adj* foighneach, fulangach
patient[2] *n* othar
patriot *n* tírghráthóir
patriotic *adj* tírghrách
patriotism *n* tírghrá
patrol *n* patról
patron *n* caomhnóir, coimirceoir,
  éarlamh, pátrún
patronage *n* coimirce, pátrúnacht
patronise *v* uasal le híseal a
  dhéanamh ar dhuine
pattern *n* patrún
pause *n* sos
pave *v* pábháil
pavement *n* cosán sráide
pavilion *n* pailliún
paving *n* pábháil
paw *n* lapa *v* crúbáil
pawn *n* **(chess)** ceithearnach
pawnbroker *n* geallearbóir
pay *n* pá *v* íoc, díol
pay packet *n* pacáiste pá, fáltas pá
pay offer *n* páthairiscint
payable *adj* iníoctha
PAYE ÍMAT (Íoc Mar A Thuillir)
payee *n* íocaí
payer *n* íocóir
payment *n* díolaíocht, íocaíocht
payphone *n* táillefón
payroll *n* párolla
pea *n* pis
peace *n* síocháin, suaimhneas
peaceful *adj* síochánta, suaimhneach
peach *n* péitseog

peacock *n* péacóg

peak *n* stuaic **to be at your peak** bheith i mbarr do réime

peaked *adj* stuacach

peak-hour traffic *n* trácht buaicuaire

peak viewing-time *n* buaic-am féachana

peanut *n* pis talún

peanut butter *n* im piseanna talún

pear *n* piorra

pearl *n* péarla **pearl bracelet** bráisléad péarlaí

peasant *n* tuathánach

peat *n* móin

pebble *n* méaróg, póirín cloiche, púrog

peculiar *adj* aisteach, leithleach, sonraíoch

peculiarity *n* aiste, sonraíocht, leithleachas

pedal *n* troitheán *v* na troitheáin a oibriú

pedantic *adj* saoithíneach

peddlar *n* mangaire

peddle *v* reic

pedestrian *n* coisí

pedestrian crossing *n* trasrian coisithe

pedicure *n* cosmhaisiú

pedigree *n* ginealach, pórtheastas

pedigree dog *n* madra folaíochta

peel *n* craiceann *v* scamh

peering *n* gliúcaíocht

peg *n* pionna **clothes peg** pionna éadaigh

pelican *n* peileacán

pellet *n* piollaire

pelt[1] *v* clag

pelt[2] *n* craiceann

pelvis *n* peilbheas

pen[1] *n* (for animals) cró *v* loca, loc

pen[2] *n* (writing) peann

penal *adj* peannaideach

penal law *n* péindlí **the Penal Laws** na Péindlíthe

penalise *v* pionósaigh

penalty *n* pionós

penance *n* aithrí

pencil *n* peann luaidhe, pionsail

pendant *n* siogairlín

pendulum *n* luascadán

penetrating *adj* toltannach

pen-friend *n* cara cleite, cara pinn

penguin *n* piongain

penicillin *n* peinicillin

peninsula *n* leithinis **the Dingle Peninsula** Leithinis an Daingin

penis *n* bod, pilibín, péineas

penitent *adj*, *n* aithríoch

penniless *adj* gan phingin, ar phócaí folmha

penny *n* pingin

pension *n* pinsean

pensioner *n* pinsinéir

pensive *adj* smaointeach

pentagon *n* peinteagán

pentathlon *n* peinteatlón

penthouse *n* díonteach

people *pl* aos, daoine, muintir, pobal

pepper *n* piobar

perceive *v* airigh

percentage *n* céatadán

perception *n* aireachtáil, mothú

perceptive *adj* braiteach, mothaithcach

perceptual skills *pl* scileanna aireachtála

perch *n* péirse

percolate *v* síothlaigh

percolator *n* síothlán

perennial *adj* ilbhliantúil

perfect *n* foirfe, idéalach *v* foirfigh **perfect!** faoi mar a chacfadh an t-asal é

perfection *n* foirfeacht

perforate *v* poll
perforation *n* polladh
perform *v* (work) déan, (duty) comhlíon, (music) seinn, (play) léirigh
performance *n* (work) déanamh, (duty) comhlíonadh, (music) seinm, (play) léiriú
performer *n* aisteoir, (of music) seinnteoir
perfume *n* cumhrán
perhaps *adv* b'fhéidir
peril *n* contúirt, priacal
perimeter *n* imlíne, peiriméadar
period[1] *n* aga, linn, tréimhse
period[2] *n* daonnacht, fuil mhíosta **I'm having my period** tá daonnacht orm, tá an fhuil mhíosta orm
periodic *adj* tréimhsiúil
periodical *n* tréimhseachán
peripheral *adj* forimeallach
periscope *n* peireascóp
perish *v* bás a fháil
perishable goods *pl* earraí meatacha
perjure *v* mionn éithigh a thabhairt
perjury *n* mionn éithigh, éitheach
perky *adj* bíogúil
perm *n* (in hair) buantonn
permanent *adj* buan, marthanach
permeate *v* leath ar fud
permissible *adj* ceadaithe, ceadmhach
permission *n* cead
permissive *adj* ceadaitheach
permit *n* cead, ceadúnas *v* ceadaigh
permitted *adj* ceadaithe
perpendicular *adj* ingearach *n* ingear
perplexed *adj* **he was completely perplexed** thit an lug ar an lag aige
persecute *v* céas
persecution *n* géarleanúint
Persian *adj*, *n* Peirseach **the Persian Gulf** Murascaill na Peirse

persist *v* lean ar, mair
persistent *adj* leanúnach, seasmhach
person *n* duine, neach, pearsa
personal *adj* pearsanta
personality[1] *n* pearsantacht
personality[2] *n* (well known person) duine aithnidiúil
personify *n* pearsantaigh
personification *n* pearsantú
personnel *n* pearsanra
perspective *n* peirspictíocht
perspire *v* allas a chur
perspiration *n* allas
persuade *v* áitigh ar **to persuade someone** áitiú ar dhuine
persuasive *adj* áititheach
pervade *v* leath tríd, téigh ar fud
perverse *adj* saofa
perversion *n* saobhadh
pessimism *n* duairceas
pest *n* lotnaid, (of person) plá
pet *n* peata *v* slíoc
pet child *n* maicín
pet day *n* peata lae, lá idir dhá shíon
petal *n* piotal
petition *n* achainí, iarratas
petrify *v* clochraigh **she was petrified** rinneadh staic di
petrol *n* artola, peitreal
petroleum *n* peitriliam
petrol tank *n* umar peitril
pettiness *n* suarachas
petty *adj* suarach
petty bourgeois *adj* leath-mheánaicmeach
petty officer *adj* mionoifigeach
pewter *n* péatar
phantom *n* taibhse
pharmacist *n* cógaiseoir
pharmacy *n* cógaslann
phase *n* céim, pas **the phases of the moon** céimeanna na gealaí

pheasant *n* piasún
phenomenon *n* feiniméan
philanthropy *n* daonchairdeas
philosopher *n* fealsamh
philosophical *adj* fealsúnach
philosophy *n* fealsúnacht
phlegm *n* réama
phobia *n* fóibe
phone *n* fón, guthán **mobile phone** fón gluaisteach, fón póca, guthán gluaisteach, guthán póca
phonecard *n* cárta gutháin
phonetics *n* foghraíocht
photocopier *n* fótachóipire, meaisín fótachóipeála
photocopy *n* fótachóip
photograph *n* grianghraf, fótagraf
photographer *n* grianghrafadóir
photography *n* grianghrafadóireacht
phrase *n* frása
physical *n* fisiciúil, fisiceach
physical education *n* corpoiliúint
physician *n* lia
physicist *n* fisicí
physics *n* fisic
physiotherapy *n* fisiteiripe
pianist *n* pianódóir
piano *n* pianó **piano tuner** tiúnadóir pianó, **grand piano** mórphianó
pick[1] *v* pioc, roghnaigh
pick[2] *n* piocadh **the pick of the bunch** sméar mhullaigh an chnuasaigh
pickaxe *n* piocóid
picket *n* picéad *v* picéadaigh **all-out picket** picéad glan amach
picking *n* piocadh
pickle *n, v* picil
pickpocket *n* peasghadaí
picnic *n* picnic
picture *n* pictiúr
picturesque *adj* pictiúrtha

pie *n* píóg **apple pie** píóg úll
piebald *adj* alabhreac
piece *n* giota, píosa
pie chart *n* píchairt
pie diagram *n* píléaráid
pierce *v* poll, toll
piercing *adj* polltach, tolltach
piety *n* cráifeacht
pig *n* muc **'on the pigs back'** ar mhuin na muice
pigeon *n* colúr **homing pigeon** colúr frithinge
piglet *n* banbh, arcán
pigsty *n* cró muice
pigtail *n* trilseán
pike *n* **(fish)** liús
pilchard *n* pilscár
pile *n, v* carn, cruach
piles *pl* **(illness)** daorghalar, fíocas
pilgrim *n* oilthreach
pilgrimage *n* oilithreacht
pill *n* piollaire
pillar *n* colún, piléar
pillory *n* piolóid
pillow *n* adhairt, ceannadhairt, piliúr
pillow-talk *n* cogar an philiúir
pilot *n* píolóta, luamhaire
pilot scheme *n* treoirscéim, scéim phíolótach
pimple *n* goirín
pin *n* pionna
pinafore *n* pilirín
pincers *n* pionsúr, teanchair
pinch *n* liomóg, **(of salt)** grainnín **to pinch somebody** liomóg a bhaint as duine
pine[1] *n* giúis
pine[2] *v* cumha a bheith agat i ndiaidh ruda
pineapple *n* anann
pink *adj, n* bándearg
pin-point *v* aimsigh

pint *n* pionta

pioneer *n* ceannródaí

pious *adj* diaganta

pip *n* síol

pipe[1] *n* píb **bagpipes** píb mhála, **uilleann pipes** píb uilleann

pipe[2] *n* **(smoking)** píopa

piped television *n* teilifís chábla

pipeline *n* píblíne

piper *n* píobaire

piping *n* píobaireacht

pirate *n* foghlaí

Pisces *pl* na hÉisc

pistol *n* piostal

pit *n* **(mine)** sloc, coire

pitch[1] *n* **(music)** airde

pitch[2] *n, v* pic

pitch and putt *n* galf dhá mhaide

pitch-black *adj* dubh dorcha

piteous *adj* truamhéalach

pith *n* laíon

pitiful *adj* truamhéalach

pitiless *adj* éadruach

pity *n* trua **it's a pity you didn't talk to me** is trua nár labhair tú liom

pizza *n* pizza

placard *n* fógra

place[1] *n* áit, ionad, láthair, log, plás **parking place** ionad páirceála, **dwelling place** áit chónaithe, **Fitzwilliam Place** Plás Mhic Liam

place[2] *v* cuir

place-name *n* logainm

placid *adj* moiglí, réchúiseach

plague[1] *n* plá

plague[2] *v* pláigh

plaice *n* leathóg

plain[1] *n* má, machaire

plain[2] *adj* soiléir

plaintiff *n* éilitheoir, gearánaí

plaintive *adj* caointeach

plait *n* trilseán *v* cuir trilseán i

plan[1] *n* plean, scéim

plan[2] *v* pleanáil

plane[1] *n* **(aeroplane)** eitleán

plane[2] *n* plána *v* plánáil

planet *n* pláinéad, rinn

planetary cycle *n* timthriall pláinéadach

planner *n* pleanálaí

planning *n* pleanáil **family planning** pleanáil chlainne

plant[1] *n* lus, planda *v* cuir, plandaigh, plandáil

plant[2] *n* **(factory)** monarcha

plantation *n* plandáil **the Plantation of Munster** Plandáil na Mumhan

plaster *n* **(sticking)** greimlín, plástar *v* plástráil **plaster of Paris** plástar Pháras

plasterboard *n* plástarchlár

plastic *adj* plaisteach

plasticine *n* marla

plate *n* pláta **armour plate** pláta armúir

plateau *n* ardchlár

platform *n* ardán, léibheann

platinum *n* platanam

plausible *adj* dealraitheach **the story seems plausible** tá dealramh na fírinne ar an scéal

play[1] *n* **(theatre)** dráma, **(fun)** spraoi

play[2] *n* imeartas **word play** imeartas focal

play[3] *v* imir, **(music)** seinn

playboy *n* buachaill báire

player *n* imreoir, **(of music)** seinnteoir

playful *adj* macnasach, spraíúil

playfulness *n* spraoi, macnas

playground *n* faiche imeartha

playgroup *n* naíscoil, grúpa súgartha

playing *n* imirt, súgradh **playing field** páirc imeartha

playschool *n* naíscoil

playwright *n* drámadóir

plea *n* achainí, pléadáil

plead *v* agair, pléadáil

please[1] le do thoil, más é do thoil é
please God le cúnamh/cuidiú Dé

please[2] *v* sásaigh

pleased *adj* sásta

pleasant *adj* séimh, soilbhir, sultmhar, pléisiúrtha, aiteasach, aoibhiúil, ait

pleasantness *n* aiteas, taitneamh

pleasing *adj* taitneamhach

pleasure *n* sult, aiteas, pléisiúr, taitneamh

pleat[1] *n* pléata

pleat[2] *v* pléatáil

plebiscite *n* pobalbhreith

pledge *n* dílse, gealltanas

plentiful *adj* flúirseach, rábach

plenty *n* neart, dalladh **plenty of money** dalladh airgid, neart argid

pliable *adj* solúbtha

pliers *n* greamaire, teanchair

plight *n* caoi, bail

plot[1] *n* **(conspiracy)** comhcheilg, snaidhm **the unravelling of the plot** scaoileadh na snaidhme

plot[2] *n* **(land)** gabháltas, plota

plough *n* céachta *v* treabh

ploy *n* cleas

pluck *v* stoith, cluimhrigh, pioc

plug *n* plocóid, pluga, stopallán **three pin plug** plocóid trí phionna

plum *n* pluma

plumb *adj* ceartingearach

plumber *n* pluiméir

plumbing *n* pluiméireacht

plummet *v* tum

plump *v* beathaithe

plunder *n* creachadh *v* creach

plunderer *n* foghlaí

plunge *n* tumadh *v* tum

plunger *n* suncaire

plural *n* iolra **the plural** an uimhir iolra

pluralism *n* iolrachas

plus *n* **(sign)** plus *prep* móide

plywood *n* sraithadhmad

pneumatic *adj* aer-oibrithe

pneumatic tyres *pl* boinn aeir

pneumonia *n* niúmóine

poach *v* scall **poached egg** ubh scallta

poacher *n* póitseálaí

poaching *n* póitseail

pocket *n* póca **to be out of pocket** bheith ar phócaí folmha

pod *n* faighneog

poem *n* dán, duan, laoi

poet *n* file

poetic *adj* fileata

poetry *n* filíocht, éigse

poignant *adj* géar

point *n* **(games)** cúilín, pointe, **(tip)** rinn, **(dot)** ponc *v* dírigh **(ar) to be on the point of doing something** bheith ar tí rud a dhéanamh

point to point races *pl* rásaí ó phointe go pointe

pointed *adj* rinneach, stuacach

pointer *n* treoir, snáthaid

pointless *adj* gan éifeacht

poison *n* nimh *v* nimhigh

poisoning *n* nimhiú

poisonous *adj* nimhiúil

poke *n* sonc *v* prioc

poker[1] *n* **(game)** pócar

poker[2] *n* priocaire

Poland *n* an Pholainn

polar *adj* polach

polarise *v* polaraigh

polarised *adj* polaraithe

Pole[1] *n* Polannach

pole[2] *n* crann, cuaille, polla

pole³ *n* pol **the south pole** an pol theas, **the north pole** an pol thuaidh

police *n* póilíní, péas *v* póilínigh

policeman / woman *n* póilín, garda, póilín, péas

policy *n* polasaí, beartas **insurance policy** polasaí árachais, **fiscal policy** beartas fioscach

polio *n* polaimiailíteas

Polish *adj* Polannach *n* **(language)** an Pholainnis

polish *n* snas, snasán *v* líomh

polished *adj* snasta

polite *adj* múinte, nósmhar

politeness *n* múineadh

political *adj* polaitiúil

politician *n* polaiteoir

politics *n* polaitíocht

poll *n, v* vótáil **to go to the poll** dul ag vótáil

pollen *n* pailin

pollute *v* truailligh

polluted *adj* truaillithe

pollution *n* **(of the environment)** truailliú (na timpeallachta)

polo *n* póló

polygon *n* polagán

polygamy *n* ilphósadh

pomegranate *n* pomagránait

pomp *n* poimp

pompous *adj* mustrach, ardnósach, poimpéiseach

pond *n* linn, lochán

ponder *v* smaoinigh

pony *n* pónaí, capaillín

pony trekker *n* fálróidí ar chapaillín

ponytail *n* **(in hair)** pónaí

poodle *n* púdal

pool *n* linn **swimming pool** linn snámha

poor *adj* bocht, daibhir, dearóil

poorish *adj* leathmheasartha

pop music *n* popcheol

popcorn *n* poparbhar

pope *n* pápa

poplar *n* poibleog

poppy *n* poipín

popular *adj* coitianta

population *n* daonra, pobal **shifting population** daonra aistritheach

porcelain *n* poirceallán

porch *n* póirse

porcupine *n* torcán craobhach

pore *n* **(skin)** piochán

pork *n* muiceoil **pork chop** gríscín muiceola

pornography *n* pornagrafaíocht

porous *adj* póiriúil, scagach

porpoise *n* muc mhara

porridge *n* leite, brachán

port¹ *n* calafort, port

port² *n* **(wine)** pórtfhíon

portable *adj* inaistrithe, iniompartha

portable television *n* teilifíseán iniompraithe

porter *n* doirseoir, **(beverage)** pórtar

portfolio *n* punann

portion *n* cuid, mír, sciar

portly *adj* toirtiúil

portrait *n* portráid

portray *v* léirigh

Portugal *n* an Phortaingéil

Portuguese *adj* Portaingéalach *n* **(language)** Portaingéilis

Portuguese man-of-war *n* smugairle an tseoil

posing *adj* gothach

position *n* cúram, áit, ionad *v* ionadaigh

positive *adj* dearfach, diongbháilte, deimhneach

posse *n* díorma

possess *v* sealbhaigh, rud a bheith agat **he is possessed by the devil** tá an diabhal ann possession *n* seilbh possession(s) sealúchas

possessive *adj* sealbhach

possibility *n* féidearthacht

possible *adj* it is possible that is féidir go

possibly *adv* b'fhéidir, seans

post[1] *n* (stake) cuaille, staic

post[2] *n* post the postal service an Post, free post saorphost, postman fear poist

post[3] *n* (job) post

post[4] *v* postáil

postage *n* postas

postbox *n* bosca poist

postcard *n* cárta poist

poster *n* póstaer

postgraduate *adj* iarchéime *n* iarchéimí

postman *n* fear poist

postmark *n* postmharc

post-mortem *n* scrúdú iarbháis

postpone *v* cuir ar athlá

postponement *n* cur siar

postscript *n* aguisín, iarscríbhinn

posy *n* pósae

pot *n* corcán flower-pot próca

pot-oven *n* bácús

potato *n* práta, fata small potato póirín

poteen *n* poitín

potential *n* acmhainn

pothole *n* coirín, linntreog

potter *n* potaire pottering gíotáil

potterer *n* potrálaí

pottery *n* potaireacht

potting compost *n* múirín potaithe

pouch *n* mealbhóg, púitse, spaga

poultry *n* éanlaith chlóis, éanlaith tí

pound[1] *v* tuargain

pound[2] *n* (money, sugar, etc) punt

pour *v* doirt

pouring *n* doirteadh pouring rain ag stealladh báistí

pout *n* pus, smut

pouting *adj* pusach

poverty *n* bochtanas, bochtaineacht

powder *n* púdar baking powder púdar bácála, washing powder púdar níocháin, gunpowder púdar gunna

powdered *adj* mion

powdery *adj* púdlach

power *n* cumhacht to come into power teacht i gcumhacht, in power i dtreis

power station *n* stáisiún cumhachta

powerful *adj* cumhachtach

practicable *adj* indéanta

practical *adj* fóinteach, praiticiúil

practicality *n* praiticiúlacht

practice *n* cleachtadh, taithí out of practice as cleachtadh

practise *v* cleacht, taithigh

practitioner *n* cleachtóir

pragmatic *adj* pragmatach

pragmatics *n* pragmataic

praise *n* moladh *v* mol

pram *n* naíchóiste, pram

prance *v* pramsáil

prank *n* cleas

prawn *n* cloicheán, piardán

pray *v* guigh

prayer *n* guí, urnaí, paidir

praying guíodóireacht, urnaí

pre- *prefix* réamh-

pre-Christian Ireland *n* Éire réamh-Chríostaí, Éire roimh theacht na Críostaíochta

pre-Raphaelites *pl* réamh-Rafaeilitigh

preach *v* craobhscaoil preaching ag seanmóireacht

preacher *n* soiscéalaí, seanmóirí

precaution *n* réamhchúram

precedence *n* tosaíocht

precept *n* aithne, teagasc

precious *adj* lómhar, luachmhar
precious stone cloch lómhar

precipice *n* aill

precise *adj* beacht, cruinn

precocious *adj* seanchríonna

precondition *n* réamhchoinníoll

predecessor *n* réamhtheachtaí

predicament *n* cruachás **in a predicement** i gcruachás, idir dhá thine Bhealtaine

predict *v* tuar, tairngir **he predicted that...** thuar sé go...

predominant *adj* ardcheannasach

predominate *v* smacht a bheith agat ar

pre-eminent *adj* gradamach

preen *v* cluimhrigh, pioc

prefabricated *adj* réamhdhéanta

preface *n* réamhrá

prefect *n* maor

prefer *v* **I prefer** is fearr liom

preference *n* tosaíocht

preferable *adj* le moladh thar

prefix *n* réimír

pregnant *adj* torrach **I am pregnant** tá mé ag iompar clainne

prejudice *n* claontacht

prejudiced *adj* claonta

preliminary *adj* tosaigh, réamh-

premature *adj* anabaí, roimh am

premier *n* **(of play)** céadléiriú, **(of government)** príomh-aire, taoiseach

premises *n* áitreabh

premium *n* préimh **insurance premium** préimh árachais

prepaid *adj* réamhíoctha

preparation *n* ullmhú, ullmhúchán

prepare *v* ullmhaigh, réitigh

prepared *adj* ullamh

prepay *v* réamhíoc

preposition *n* réamhfhocal

preposterous *adj* áiféiseach

prerogative *n* pribhléid, sainchumas

Presbyterian *adj, n* Preispitéireach

prescribe *v* ordaigh

prescription *n* oideas (dochtúra)

presence *n* teacht i láthair

present[1] *n* féirín, bronntanas

present[2] *adj* i láthair **at present** faoi láthair

present[3] *v* cuir in aithne, bronn

presentable inchaite

presentation *n* toirbirt

preservation *n* caomhnú

preservative *n* leasaitheach

preserve *v* caomhnaigh

preserved *adj* **(of food)** leasaithe

presidency *n* uachtaránacht

president *n* uachtarán **the president of Ireland** Uachtarán na hÉireann

press[1] *n* cófra

press[2] *n* preas **press conference** preasagallamh, **press release** préaseisiúint

press[3] *v* preasáil, brúigh

pressing *adj* cruógach

pressure *n* brú

pressure cooker *n* bruthaire brú

pressure group *n* brúghrúpa

pressure switch *n* brúlasc

pressurise *v* brú a chur ar

prestige *n* ardcháil

presume *v* talamh slán a dhéanamh de rud, leomh

presumption *n* andóchas, dánacht

pretence *n* cur i gcéill

pretend *v* lig ar

pretext *n* cúinse

pretty *adj* gleoite

prevalent *adj* ceannasach

prevent *v* coisc

prevention *n* cosc
preventive *adj* coisctheach
preview *n* réamhthaispeántas
previous *adj* roimhe, roimh ré
prey on *v* seilg
price *n* praghas
price list *n* praghasliosta
price war *n* praghaschoimhlint
prick *n* priocadh *v* prioc
pride *n* mórtas, móráil, mórchúis, uabhar
priest *n* sagart
priesthood *n* sagartacht
primary *adj* príomha, príomhúil, bun-
prime *adj* príomh-
prime minister *n* taoiseach, príomh-aire
primeval *adj* cianaosta
primitive *adj* scanársa, primitíveach
primrose *n* sabhaircín
prince *n* flaith, prionsa
princess *n* banphrionsa
principal[1] *adj* príomh-
principal[2] *n* (school) príomhoide
principle *n* prionsabal
print[1] *n* cló, prionta out of print as cló
print[2] *v* clóbhuail, clóigh
printer *n* (machine) printéir, (person) clódóir
printing *n* clódóireacht
print-out *v* ríomhphrionta, asphrionta
priority *n* tosaíocht in order of priority de réir tosaíochta
prison *n* carcair, príosún
prisoner *n* cime, príosúnach
prison warder *n* bairdéir príosúin
privacy *n* príobháid
private *adj* príobháideach
privatise *v* príobháidigh
privatisation *n* príobháidiú

privilege *n* pribhléid
prize *n* duais
prizewinner *n* duaiseoir
pro- *prefix* ar thaobh
probability *n* dóchúlacht
probable *adj* dócha
probation *n* promhadh
probe *n* tóireadóir lunar probe taiscéalaí na gealaí
problem *n* fadhb to solve a problem fadhb a réiteach
procedure *n* nós imeachta, modh
proceed (with) *v* lean (le)
proceeds *pl* fáltais
process *n* próiseas *v* próiseáil
processing[1] *n* próiseáil word-processing próiseáil focal
processing[2] *n* (of film) réaladh
processor *n* próiseálaí word-processor próiseálaí focal
procession *n* mórshiúl
proclaim *v* fógair
procure *v* soláthair
prod *n* priocadh *v* prioc
produce *n* táirge *v* gin, léirigh, táirg agricultural produce táirgí talmhaíochta
producer *n* léiritheoir, táirgeoir
product *n* táirge final / finished product táirge deiridh
production *n* (theatre) léiriú, (of produce) táirgeacht, táirgeadh
productive *adj* táirgiúil
productivity *n* táirgiúlacht
profess *v* maígh
profession *n* gairm
professional *adj* gairmiúil, proifisiúnta *n* gairmí, proifisiúnaí
professor *n* ollamh
professorship *n* ollúnacht
proficiency *n* oilteacht
proficient *adj* oilte (ar)
profile *n* próifíl

profit n fáltas, sochar, brabús, tairbhe

profit sharing n páirtiú i mbrabús

profitable adj tairbheach

profound adj domhain

profuse adj flúirseach, raidhseach

profusion n raidhse

prognosis n tátal, prognóis

programmable adj in-ríomhchláraithe

programme[1] n clár

programme[2] n (computer) ríomhchlár v ríomhchláraigh

programmer n (of computers) ríomhchláraitheoir

progress n dul chun cinn, forás **in progress** idir lámha

progression n seicheamh

progressive adj forásach

prohibit v coisc, cros **to prohibit something** rud a chosc

prohibition n cosc, toirmeasc

project n tionscadal

projection n teilgean

projector n teilgeoir

proletariat n prólatáireacht

prolific adj rafar

prologue n brollach

prolong n fadaigh

promenade n promanád

promiscuity n saorchumasc

promise n, v geall **he promised her the world** gheall sé na hoirc is na hairc di

promote v cuir chun cinn

promoter n tionscnóir

promotion n ardú céime, (of product) tionscnamh

prompt adj pras v leid a thabhairt

prone (to) adj tugtha (do)

pronoun n forainm

pronounce v fuaimnigh, fógair

pronunciation n fuaimniú

proof n cruthú, cruthúnas, (editing) profa, (science) promhadh

proofreading n léamh profaí

prop n taca v teannaigh

propaganda n síolteagasc

propagate n craobhscaoil, póraigh

propagation n craobhscaoileadh

propel v tiomáin

propellant n tiomántán

propeller n lián

proper adj ceart, cuibhiúil, cóir, dílis **proper name / noun** ainm dílis

properly adv mar is cóir

property n airnéis, maoin, sealúchas, (of substance) airí

prophecy n fáidheadóireacht, fáistine, tairngreacht

prophesy v tairngir

prophet n fáidh

prophetic adj fáidhiúil

proportion n cionmhaireacht, coibhneas, comhréir

proportional adj cionmhar, comhréireach **proportional (with)** i gcomhréir (le)

proposal n moladh, togra, tairiscint

propose v tairg, mol

proposer n moltóir

proposition n tairiscint

proprietor n dílseánach

proscribe v (outlaw) eisreachtaigh

prose n prós

prosecute v cúisigh

prosecution n cúiseamh, ionchúiseamh **Director of Public Prosecutions** Stiúrthóir Ionchúiseamh Poiblí

prosecutor n cúisitheoir, ionchúisitheoir

prospect n ionchas

prospector n taiscéalaí

prosper v rathaigh

prosperity n rath, rathúnas

prosperous *adj* rathúil

prostitute *n* striapach, meirdreach, bean choitinn

prostitution *n* striapachas

protect *v* caomhnaigh, cumhdaigh, díon, scáthaigh

protection *n* caomhnú, coimeád, coimirce

protective *adj* cosantach, díonach

protector *n* caomhnóir, cosantóir

protein *n* próitéin

protest *n* agóid *v* agóid a dhéanamh

Protestant *adj, n* Protastúnach

Protestantism *n* Protastúnachas

protester *n* agóideoir

protocol *n* comhghnás, prótacal

protract *v* fadaigh

protracted *adj* fada, sínte

protrude *v* gob amach

proud *adj* mórálach, uaibhreach

prove *v* promh, cruthaigh

proved *adj* dearfa

proven *adj* cruthaithe

proverb *n* seanfhocal

provide *v* soláthair **to provide a service to somebody** seirbhís a sholáthar do dhuine

provided (that) ar choinníoll (go)

province *n* cúige

provincial *adj* cúigeach

provision *n* riar, **(of treaty, act, etc)** foráil

provisional *adj* sealadach **the Provisionals** na Sealadaigh

provisions *pl* lón

provocative *adj* gríosaitheach

provoke *v* spreag, saighid

prowess *n* gaisce

prowl *v* bheith sa tseilg ar, bheith ag smúrthacht thart

proximity *n* foisceacht, cóngar

prudence *n* stuaim

prudent *adj* stuama

prune[1] *n* **(dried plum)** prúna

prune[2] *n* bearraigh

psalm *n* salm

pseudonym *n* ainm cleite

psychoanalysis *n* síocanailís

psychoanalyst *n* síocanailísí

psychological *adj* síceolaíoch

psychologist *n* síceolaí

psychology *n* síceolaíocht

pub *n* tábhairne

puberty *n* caithreachas

public *adj* poiblí **public relations** caidreamh poiblí, **Public Relations Officer (PRO)** Oifigeach Caidrimh Phoiblí (OCP)

public enemy *n* púca na n-adharc, namhaid an phobail

publican *n* tábhairneoir

publication *n* foilseachán

publicity *n* poiblíocht

publicise *v* poibligh

publicly *adv* os comhair an tsaoil, go poiblí

publish *v* foilsigh

publisher *n* foilsitheoir

publishing *n* foilsitheoireacht

puce *adj, n* **(colour)** ruachorcra

puck *n* poc **free puck** poc saor

pudding *n* putóg, maróg **Christmas pudding** maróg Nollag, **black pudding** putóg dhubh

puddle *n* linntreog

puff *n* **(of wind)** puth, séideog *v* **(cigarette)** smailc

pull[1] *n* smailc **to take a pull of a cigarette** smailc a bhaint as toitín

pull[2] *v* tarraing

pulley *n* roithleán

pulp *n* laíon

pulpit *n* puilpid

pulsar *n* pulsár

pulse[1] *n* cuisle, bíog **to feel a pulse** cuisle a bhrath

pulse² *n* piseánach

pump *n* caidéal, **(bicycle)** teannaire *v* caidéalaigh, pumpáil **petrol pump** caidéal peitril

pumping *v* pumpáil

pumpkin *n* puimcín

pun *n* imeartas focal

punch¹ *n* dorn **a punch in the face** dorn san aghaidh

punch² *n* **(drink)** puins

punctual *adj* poncúil, tráthúil

punctuality *n* poncúlacht

punctually *adv* go tráthrialta

punctuation *n* poncaíocht

puncture repair kit *n* fearas deisithe poill

punish *v* cuir pionós air

punishment *n* pionós

punk rock *n* punc-rac

punt *n* **(boat)** punta

pupil¹ *n* **(of eye)** mac imrisc

pupil² *n* dalta

puppet *n* puipéad

puppet government *n* rialtas soip

puppy *n* coileán

purchase *n* ceannach *v* ceannaigh

purchased item *n* ceannachán

purchaser *n* ceannaitheoir

pure *adj* fíor-, glan, íon

pure mathematics *n* glanmhatamaitic

pure white *adj* gléigeal

purgatory *n* purgadóir

purge *n* purgóid

puritan *adj, n* piúratánach

purple *adj* corcra

purpose *n* aidhm, cuspóir **on purpose** d'aon turas, d'aon ghnó, d'aon aidhm

purring *n* crónán

purse *n* spaga, sparán

pursue *v* tóraigh

pursuit *n* leanúint, tóir, tóraíocht **they are in pursuit of you** tá siad sa tóir ort

pus *n* angadh

push *n* brú *v* brúigh

push-button *n* brúchnaipe

pussy cat *n* puisín

put *v* cuir **to put off something to another day** rud a chuir ar athlá, **put up with** cuir suas le

putty *n* puití

puzzle *n* dúcheist *v* mearbhall a chur ar dhuine

pyjamas *pl* pitseámaí

pylon *n* piolón

pyramid *n* pirimid

Pyrenees *pl* na Piréiní

Q

quack *n* potrálaí

quadrangle *n* **(of school)** cearnóg, **(of shape)** ceathairuilleog

quadrant *n* ceathramhán

quadruple *v* méadaigh faoi cheathair

quagmire *n* criathar, scraith ghlugair

quaint *adj* barrúil

quake *v* crith

Quaker *n* Caecar, ball de Chumann na gCarad

qualification *n* agús, cáilíocht

qualified *adj* cáilithe

qualify *v* cáiligh

quality *n* cáil, cáilíocht, tréith, ardchaighdeán **good qualities** dea-thréithe, **a quality service** seirbhís ardchaighdeáin, seirbhís

den scoth, **quality of life**
caighdeán/cáilíocht na beatha
quantity n cainníocht, méid
quarantine n coraintín
quarrel n achrann, maicín, troid
v troid
quarrelsome adj achrannach,
cointinneach
quarry n **(stone)** cairéal
quart n cárt
quarter n ceathrú **a quarter of an
hour** ceathrú uaire, **a quarter
past six** ceathrú i ndiaidh/tar éis
a sé, **a quarter to five** ceathrú
chun a cúig
quarterly adj ráithiúil
quartz n grianchloch
quaver n **(music)** camán
quay n cé
queen n ríon
queen bee n cráinbheach
queer adj ait
queerness n aiteacht, aiteas
quench v múch **quenching of thirst**
bá tarta
query n ceist v ceistigh
question n ceist v ceistigh
questionnaire n ceistiúchán

question time n tráth na gceist
queue n scuaine v dul i scuaine
quibble n imearthas focal, argóint
quick adj gasta, mear, tapa
quickly adv go gasta, go tapa
quickness n luaithe, tapa, tapúlacht
quicksand n gaineamh súraic,
súmaire gainimh, gaineamh beo
quiet[1] adj ciúin, socair, suaimhneach
stay quiet! fan(aigí) socair
quiet[2] n ciúnas, suaimhneas **on the
quiet** faoi choim
quieten v suaimhnigh
quietness n ciúnas, suaimhneas
quill n cleite
quilt n cuilt
quinine n quinín
quintet n cúigréad
quip n ciúta
quit v éirigh as
quite adv ar fad, glan, amach is amach
quiver n creathán, crith, **(for
arrows)** bolgán saighead
quiz n tráth na gceist v ceistigh
quorum n córam
quota n cuóta
quotation n athfhriotal
quote n sliocht v luaigh

R

rabbi n raibí
rabbit n coinín
rabble n conairt, daoscarshlua
rabid adj confach
rabies n confadh
race[1] n **(of people)** cine
race[2] n rás v rith **relay race** rás
sealaíochta
racecourse n ráschúrsa
racehorse n capall rása

racial adj ciníoch
racism n ciníochas
racist n ciníochaí
rack n raca
racket[1] n **(noise)** racán, ruaille
buaille
racket[2] n raicéad **tennis racket**
raicéad leadóige
racketeer n cambheartaí
racketeering n cambheartaíocht

radar *n* radar
radar-controlled *adj* radar-rialaithe
radiance *n* dealramh, léas
radiant *adj* lonrach
radiate *v* gathaigh
radiation *n* gathaíocht, radaíocht
radiator *n* radaitheoir
radical *adj* radacach
radio *n* raidió
radio transmission mast *n* crann tarchurtha raidió
radioactive *adj* radaighníomhach
radioactive fallout *n* radachur
radiography *n* radagrafaíocht
radiotherapy *n* radaiteiripe
radish *n* raidis **horseradish sauce** anlann raidise fiáine
radius *n* ga
raft *n* rafta
rafter *n* rachta
rag *n* ceirt, giobal, leadhb
rage *n* cuthach
ragged *adj* gioblach
raid *n* táin, ruathar
rail *n* ráille
railing *n* ráille
railroad *n* iarnród
rain *n* báisteach, fearthainn **it's raining** tá sé ag cur fearthainne / báistí
rainbow *n* tuar ceatha, bogha báistí, bogha ceatha, bogha síne
raincoat *n* cóta báistí
rainfall *n* báisteach, fliuchras
rainforest *n* foraois bháistí **tropical rainforest** foraois theochriosach / thrópaiceach bháistí
raise *v* ardaigh, tóg **to raise one's voice** do ghlór a ardú
raised *adj* crochta
raisin *n* rísín
raising *n* tógáil
rake *n* (**gardening**) ráca *v* rácáil

rally *n* slógadh *v* cruinnigh
ram *n* (**animal**) reithe
ramble *n* spaisteoireacht
rambler *n* fánaí
ramp *n* fánán, rampa
rampart *n* múr (cosanta)
ranch *n* rainse
rancour *n* mioscais
random *adj* fánach, randamach
range *n* raon, réimse *v* rangaigh **out of range** as raon
rank *n* céim, céimíocht
ransack *v* ransaigh
ransom *n* fuascailt *v* fuascail, dúchíos a bhaint de dhuine
rap *n*, *v* cniog
rape[1] *n* **crop** ráib
rape[2] *n* banéigean, éigean *v* éignigh **statutory rape** banéigean reachtúil
rapid *adj* tapa, sciobtha
rapist *n* éigneoir
raptures *pl* sceitimíní
rapturous *adj* sceitimíneach
rare *adj* annamh
rascal *n* alfraits
rash *adj* tobann *n* (**on skin**) gríos
rasher *n* slisín
raspberry *n* sú craobh **raspberries** sútha craobh
rat *n* francach, luch mhór/fhrancach
rate *n* ráta *v* grádaigh
ratify *v* daingnigh
rating *n* grádú
ratio *n* cóimheas
ration *n* ciondáil
rational *adj* réasúnach
rationalise *v* réasúnaigh
rationalism *n* réasúnachas
rat poison *n* nimh francach
rattle *n* (**for infant**) gligín
rattlesnake *n* nathair shligreach

rattling *adj* gliograch
ravage *v* slad a dhéanamh ar
rave music *n* réamhcheol
raven *n* fiach
ravenous *adj* cíocrach
ravine *n* altán, cumar
raving *n* rámhaille
ravishing *adj* aoibhinn
raw *adj* amh, **(of wound)** dearg
raw material *n* amhábhar
rawlplug *n* ráldallán
ray *n* ga, **(fish)** roc
razor *n* rásúr
reach *v* sroich, bain amach
react *v* imoibrigh
reaction *n* frithghníomh, imoibriú
  chain reaction imoibriú slabhrúil
reactionary *adj* frithghníomhach
  n frithghníomhaí
reactor *n* freasaitheoir
read *v* léigh
readable *adj* soléite
reader *n* léitheoir
reading *n* léamh, léitheoireacht
readjust *v* athchóirigh
read-out *n* asléamh
ready *adj* réidh, ullamh
ready-made *adj* réamhdhéanta
reaffirmation *n* athdhearbhú
real *adj* dearg, fíor, nithiúil, réadach
real estate *n* eastát réadach
realisation *n* réadú **realisation of**
  assets réadú sócmhainní
realise *v* **(assets etc)** réadaigh
realism *n* réalachas
realist *n* réalaí
realistic *adj* réadúil, réalaíoch
reality *n* réaltacht
really *adv* ambaiste, dáiríre, leoga
  really? gan bhréag? dáiríre?
realm *n* ríocht
reanimate *v* athbheoigh

rear[1] *n* deireadh
rear[2] *v* oil, tóg
rearguard *n* cúlgharda
rear-view mirror *n* scáthán
  cúlradhairc
rearing *n* oiliúint, tógáil
rearrange *v* athchóirigh
reason[1] *n* fáth, réasún **it stands to**
  reason luíonn sé le réasún
reason[2] *v* réasúnaigh
reasonable *adj* ciallmhar
reasoning *adj* réasúnaíocht
reassurance *n* athdhearbhú
reassure *v* athdhearbhaigh, duine a
  chur ar a shuaimhneas
rebel *n* ceannairceach *v* éirigh amach
rebellion *n* éirí amach, reibiliún
rebellious *adj* ceannairceach,
  reibiliúnach
rebound *n, v* athléim
rebuild *v* atóg
recalculate *v* athchomhair
recall *v* athghlaoigh, **(remember)**
  cuimhnigh
recapitulate *v* achoimre a thabhairt
recapture *n* athghabháil *v* athghabh
recede *v* cúlaigh, tráigh
receipt *n* admháil
receive *v* faigh, glac
receiver *n* faighteoir, glacadóir
recent *adj* úrnua, deireanach
recently *adv* le déanaí, ar na
  mallaibh, le gairid
reception *n* fáiltiú
receptionist *n* fáilteoir
recess *n* ascaill
recession *n* trá, meathlú **economic**
  recession meathlú geilleagrach,
  eacnamaíochta
recipe *n* oideas
recipient *n* faighteoir
reciprocal *adj* cómhalartach
reciprocate *v* cómhalartaigh

recital *n* aithris, **(of music)** ceadal

recitation *n* aithriseoireacht

recite *v* aithris **to recite a poem** dán a aithris

reciter *n* aithriseoir

reckless *adj* rábach

reckon *v* áirigh, meas **what do you reckon?** cad é/céard é do mheas?

reckoning *n* áireamh

reclaim *v* **(land etc)** tabhair chun míntíreachais

reclamation *n* **(of land)** míntíreachas

recluse *n* díthreabhach

recognise *v* aithin

recognised *adj* aitheanta

recognition *n* aitheantas, aithne **to gain recognition** aitheantas a fháil

recoil *v* aisléim, athscinn

recollect *v* **I don't recollect that** ní cuimhin liom é sin

recollection *n* cuimhne

recommend *v* mol

recommendation *n* moladh, teist

recompense *n* cúiteamh *v* cúitigh

reconcile *v* athmhuintearas a dhéanamh, tabhair le chéile

reconciliation *n* athchairdeas

reconnaissance *n* taiscéalaíocht

reconnoitre *v* taiscéal

reconstruct *v* athchum, atóg

reconstruction *n* athdhéanamh **(imaginative) reconstruction of events** athchruthú (samhlaíoch) imeachtaí

record[1] *n* **(music)** ceirnín, **(account)** cuntas **to keep a record of something** cuntas a choinneáil ar rud

record[2] *n* **(sport)** curiarracht **in record time** i gcuriarracht ama, **record holder** curiarrachtaí

record[3] *n, v* taifead

recorder *n* **(musical instrument)** fliúit Shasanach, **(for taping)** taifeadán

recording *n* taifeadadh

recount *v* athchomhair

recoup *v* aisíoc, cúitigh

recover[1] *v* faigh ar ais, **(convalesce)** téarnaigh

recover[2] *v* **(possession)** athghabh

recovery *n* athghabháil, **(convalescing)** téarnamh

recreation *n* caitheamh aimsire, siamsaíocht

re-creation *n* athchruthú

recreational areas *pl* achair chaithimh aimsire

recruit *n* earcach *v* earcaigh

rectangle *v* dronuilleog

rectangular *adj* dronuilleogach

rectify *v* ceartaigh

recuperate *v* téarnaigh

recur *v* atarlaigh, athfhill

recurrence *n* atarlú

recurrent *adj* athfhillteach

recurring *adj* athfhillteach, timthriallach

recycle *v* athchúrsáil

red[1] *adj* dearg **red hot** dearg te

red[2] *adj* rua **red hair** gruaig rua, **the Red Sea** an Mhuir Rua

redden *v* dearg

reddish *adj* scothdhearg

redeemer *n* slánaitheoir

redeeming *adj* **(of qualities)** cúiteach

redeploy *v* athdháil

redirect *v* athdhírigh

redistribute *v* athdháil

redo *v* athdhéan

redress *n, v* leigheas *v* ceartaigh

reduce *v* laghdaigh

reduction *n* laghdú

redundancy *n* iomarcaíocht

redundant *adj* iomarcach **he was made redundant** chaill sé a phost de bharr na hiomarcaíochta

reed *n* giolcach

reef *n* sceir **coral reef** sceir choiréil, **barrier reef** sceir bhacainneach

reek *n* géarbholadh

reel *n* **(dance)** cor, ríl

re-establish *v* athbhunaigh

re-establishment *n* athbhunú

refer (to) *v* tagair (do)

referee *n* **(sport)** réiteoir, **(for C.V.)** moltóir

reference *n* tagairt

reference book *n* leabhar tagartha

referendum *n* reifreann

refill *n* athlíonadh *v* athlíon

refine *v* **(metal)** athleáigh

refined *adj* caoin, deismíneach, snasta

refinement *n* deismíneacht

refinery *n* scaglann

reflect *v* frithchaith, **(think)** machnaigh, smaoinigh

reflection[1] *n* athmhachnamh, machnamh **on reflection** ar athmhachnamh

reflection[2] *n* scáil

reflective *adj* machnamhach

reflector *n* frithchaiteoir

reflex action *n* gníomhú athfhillteach, frithluail

reflexive *adj* athfhillteach

reflexology *n* freagreolaíocht

refold *v* athfhill

reform[1] *v* leasaigh

reform[2] *n* leasú

Reformation *n* an Reifirméisean

reforming *adj* leasaitheach

refract *v* athraon

refraction *n* athraonadh

refrain *n* **(song)** loinneog

refrain from *v* staon ó

refresh *v* úraigh

refreshing *adj* fionnuar

refreshment *n* fionnuarú

refrigerator *n* cuisneoir

refuge *n* dídean

refugee *n* dídeanaí

refund *n, v* aisíoc

refurbishment *n* athchóiriú

refusal *n* diúltú, eiteach

refuse[1] *v* diúltaigh, eitigh **to refuse someone** duine a eiteach

refuse[2] *n* dramhaíl **refuse disposal** diúscairt dramhaíola, **refuse collection** bailiúchán dramhaíola

regain *v* athghnóthaigh **regain one's composure** greim a fháil ort féin

regal *adj* ríoga

regard *n* meas **I have great regard for her** tá an-mheas agam uirthi

regarding *prep* maidir le, mar gheall ar

regardless of *adj* beag beann ar

régime *n* réim

regiment *n* reisimint

region *n* ceantar, dúiche, réigiún

regional *adj* réigiúnach

regional technical college (RTC) *n* ceardcholáiste réigiúnach, coláiste teicniúil réigiúnach (CTR)

register *n* rolla *v* cláraigh

registered *adj* cláraithe

registrar *n* cláraitheoir

registration *n* clárú

registration number *n* uimhir chláraithe

registry *n* clárlann

regression *n* cúlú, aischéimniú

regressive *adj* cúlaitheach

regret *n* aiféala, aithreachas, cathú **I regret it** tá aiféala orm

regular *adj* rialta

regularity *n* rialtacht

regularly *adv* go tráthrialta, go rialta

regulate *v* rialaigh

regulation *n* rialú

rehabilitate *v* athshlánaigh

rehabilitation *n* athshlánú

rehearsal *n* cleachtadh

rehearse *v* cleacht

reheat *v* atéigh

reign[1] réimeas, ré **Reign of Terror** Ré an Uafáis

reign[2] *v* rialaigh

reimburse *v* aisíoc

rein *n* srian

reindeer *n* réinfhia

reinforce *n* treisigh, cuir i bhfeidhm arís

reinforced concrete *n* coincréit threisithe

reinforcement *n* athneartú

reiterate *v* athluaigh

reiteration *n* athrá

reject *v* diúltaigh do

rejection *n* diúltú, obadh

rejoinder *n* athfhreagra

rejuvenate *v* athnuaigh

rejuvenation *n* athnuachan

rejoice *v* gairdeas a dhéanamh

rejoin *v* athcheangail

relapse *n* atitim, athbhuille

relate *v* **(a story etc)** aithris, inis

related *adj* gaolmhar, muinteartha

relation *n* gaol

relations *pl* caidreamh, daoine muinteartha

relationship *n* cumann, coibhneas, gaol

relative[1] *adj* **(grammar)** coibhneasta

relative[2] *n* gaol

relax *v* lig scíth **to relax oneself** do scíth a ligean, **relax! tóg go bog é! déan go réidh!**

relaxation *n* faoiseamh, scíth

relaxing *adj* suaimhnitheach

relay *n* **(sport)** sealaíocht *v* leaschraol

relay race *n* rás sealaíochta

release *n* fuascailt, scaoileadh, eisiúint *v* scaoil, fuascail **recent release** eisiúint le déanaí, **press release** preaseisiúint

relent *v* bog

relentless *adj* neamhthrócaireach, buan

relevant *adj* ábhartha

reliable *adj* **(of source)** údarásach, **(of person)** iontaofa

relic *n* iarsma

relief *n* faoiseamh, rilíf, maolú

religion *n* creideamh, reiligiún

religious *adj* cráifeach, reiligiúnach

relish[1] *n* anlann

relish[2] *v* **I don't relish the idea** ní thaitníonn an smaoineamh liom

relocate *v* **(find)** athaimsigh, **(move)** athlonnaigh

reluctance *n* doicheall, drogall

reluctant *adj* drogallach, leasc **I was reluctant ...** bhí drogall orm..., ba leasc liom...

rely (on) *v* braith (ar)

remain *v* fan

remainder *n* fuílleach

remains *pl* fuílleach, iarsmaí

remake *n* athdhéanamh *v* athdhéan

remand[1] *v* athchur

remand[2] *n* **on remand** ar coimeád

remark *n* focal **hurtful remark** goineog

remarkable *adj* suntasach

remedial teaching *n* teagasc feabhais

remedy *n, v* leigheas

remelt *v* athleáigh

remember *v* cuimhnigh **I remember...** is cuimhin liom...

remind *v* meabhraigh (do), cuir i gcuimhne (do)

reminisce *v* athchuimhnigh

reminiscence *n* athchuimhne

remission *n* loghadh

remit *n* cumhacht *v* maith, suim airgid a íoc

remittance *n* seoltán

remnant *n* fuílleach

remorse *n* doilíos

remorseful *adj* doilíosach

remote *adj* scoite, iargúlta

remote-controlled *adj* cianrialaithe

remote control *n* cianrialú, (device) cianrialtán

removal *n* aistriú

remove *v* cealaigh, bain as, aistrigh

remunerate *v* luach saothair a thabhairt

remuneration *n* luach saothair

renaissance *n* athbheochan the Renaissance an Athbheochan Léinn

rendering *n* (of music) seinm

rendezvous *n* coinne

renegade *n* séantóir

renew *v* athnuaigh

renewable resource *n* acmhainn in-athnuaite

renewal *n* athnuachan

renewed vigour *n* athbhrí

renounce *v* diúltaigh do, séan

renovate *v* athchóirigh, athnuaigh

renovation *n* athchóiriú, deisiú

renown *n* clú

renowned *adj* clúiteach

rent *n* cíos

renunciation *n* diúltú

repair *n* cóiriú, deisiú *v* cóirigh, deisigh

reparation *n* díol, cúiteamh

repay *v* aisíoc, cúitigh

repayment *n* aisíoc

repeal *n* aisghairm (history) reipéil *v* aisghair

repeat[1] *n* athchraoladh, atarlú

repeat[2] *v* repeat after me abair i mo dhiaidh

repel *v* ruaig

repellent *adj*, *n* ruaigtheach

repent *v* aithreachas a dhéanamh

repentance *n* aithreachas, aithrí

repercussion *n* frithbhualadh, (of action) toradh

repetition *n* athrá, athsheinm

repetitive strain injury *n* stróghalar athfhillteach

replace *v* athchuir, cur ar ais

replacement *n* athchur

replant *v* athchuir, athphlandaigh

replay *n* athimirt, athsheinm

replenish *v* athlíon, athsholáthair

reply *n* freagra *v* freagair

report *n* tuairisc tuarascáil *v* tuairiscigh **annual report** tuairisc bhliantúil

reporter *n* tuairisceoir, tuarascálaí

repose *n* suaimhneas

represent *v* ionadaigh

representation *n* ionadaíocht

representative *n* ionadaí

repression *n* cos ar bolg

reprieve *n* faoiseamh

reprimand *v* casaoid a thabhairt do

reproach *n* aithis

reproduce *v* atáirg, síolraigh

reproduction *n* atáirgeadh

reproductive *adj* atáirgeach

reproductive organs *pl* baill ghiniúna, orgáin atáirgthe

reptile *n* péist, reiptíl

republic *n* poblacht the Republic of Ireland Poblacht na hÉireann

republican *adj*, *n* poblachtach **republican movement** gluaiseacht na poblachta

republicanism *n* poblachtachas

repugnant to *adj* aimhréireach le

repulsive *adj* gránna

reputable *adj* creidiúnach

reputation *n* ainm, cáil, clú, teist

request *n* achainí *v* iarr

require *v* what do you require? cad é/céard atá ag teastáil uait?

requirement *n* coinníoll, riachtanas

rescue *n, v* sábháil, tarrtháil

rescuer *n* tarrthálaí

research *n* taighde **research work** obair thaighde

resemblance *n* dealramh

resemble *v* cosúlacht/dealramh a bheith ag rud/duine le rud/duine

resent *v* olc a ghlacadh le

reservation¹ *n* agús **to make a reservation** rud a chur in áirithe / áirithint

reservation² *n* tearmann (nature, Native American, etc)

reserve¹ *n* cúlchiste, cúltaca, dúnáras

reserve² *v* **to reserve two seats** dhá shuíochán a chur in áirithe

reserved *adj* dúnárasach, in áirithe

reservoir *n* taiscumar

reshuffle *n* athshuaitheadh

reside *v* cónaigh

residence *n* cónaí

resident *adj* cónaitheach *n* cónaitheoir

residue *n* fuíoll

resign *v* éirigh as

resilience *n* teacht aniar

resilient *adj* acmhainneach

resin *n* roisín

resist *v* cuir in aghaidh

resistance *n* cur in aghaidh, (electricity) friotaíocht

resolute *adj* diongbháilte

resolution *n* fuascailt, rún

resolve *v* réitigh

resort *n* (holiday) ionad saoire

resonance *n* athshondas

resonant *adj* athshondach

resource *n* seift, acmhainn

resourceful *adj* seiftiúil

respect *n* meas, ómós, urraim **I have great respect for Cathal** tá anmheas agam ar Chathal

respectable *adj* fiúntach

respectability *n* measúlacht

respectful *adj* measúil, ómósach, urramach

respiration *n* análú

respirator *n* análaitheoir

respite *n* cairde

respond *v* freagair

response *n* freagairt, freagra

responsibility *n* cúram, freagracht

responsible *adj* freagrach

responsive *adj* freagrach, mothálach

rest *n* sos, taca, scíth, suaimhneas, suan

restage *v* athléirigh

restart *v* atosaigh

restaurant *n* bialann, teach itheacháin

restitution *n* aiseag, aisíoc, leorghníomh

restless *adj* corrthónach, míshuaimhneach

restlessness *n* anbhuain

restoration *n* athbhunú, athchóiriú

restore *v* athbhunaigh, athchóirigh

restrain *v* cuir srian ar

restrained *adj* srianta

restraint *n* srian, (self-restraint) araíonacht

restrict *v* cúngaigh

restriction *n* cúngú

result *n* iarmhairt, toradh **it will only result in…** ní bheidh de thoradh air ach go…

resume *v* atosaigh

resumption *n* atosú

resurgence *n* aiséirí

resurrection *n* aiséirí

resuscitate *v* athbheoigh

retail *v* miondíol
retailer *n* miondíoltóir
retain *v* coimeád, coinnigh
retake[1] *v* atóg
retake[2] *n* **(of film)** téic eile
retention *n* coinneáil
retentive *adj* coinneálach
reticent *adj* dúnárasach
reticence *n* dúnáras
retina *n* reitine
retire *v* tarraing siar, éirigh as
retreat[1] *n* dul ar gcúl, cúlú,
  teitheadh *v* cúlaigh
retreat[2] *n* **(place)** díseart
retort *n* aisfhreagra
retransmit *v* athchraol
retribution *n* cúiteamh
retrieval *n* aisghabháil
retrieve *v* aisghabh
retrogression *n* céim siar
retro-rockets *pl* roicéid mhoillithe
retrospect *n* cúlamharc **in
  retrospect** ag féachaint siar air
return *n* filleadh, **(on keyboard)**
  aisfhilleadh *v* fill
return ticket *n* ticéad fillte
return button *n* **(on keyboard)**
  cnaipe aisfhillte
returns *pl* tuairisceáin, sochair
reunion *n* athaontú, teacht le chéile
reunite *v* athaontaigh
reuse *v* athúsáid
reveal *v* tabhair chun solais, nocht
revelation *n* nochtadh, taispeánadh
revelry *n* pléaráca, ragairne
revenge *n* díoltas **to take revenge
  on** díoltas a imirt ar
revenue *n* ioncam, teacht isteach
Revenue Commissioners *pl* na
  Coimisinéirí Ioncaim
reverberate *v* aisfhuaimnigh
reverend *adj* oirmhinneach

reverend person *n* urramach
reverent *adj* ómósach
reversal *n* aisiompú
reverse *v* **(car)** cúlaigh, aisiompaigh
reversed *adj* drom ar ais
reversible *adj* iniompaithe
review[1] *n* athbhreithniú
  v athbhreithnigh
review[2] *n* léirmheas
reviewer *n* léirmheastóir
revise *v* athbhreithnigh
revision *n* athbhreithniú, dul siar
revisionism *n* athbhreithniú staire
revival *n* athbheochan
revive *v* athbheoigh
revolt *n* ceannairc, éirí amach **you
  revolt me!** cuireann tú déistin
  orm!
revolting *adj* déistineach
revolution *n* réabhlóid, muirthéacht
  the French Revolution Réabhlóid
  na Fraince
revolutionary *adj* réabhlóideach
  n reabhlóidí
revolver *n* gunnán
revolving *adj* rothlach **revolving
  door** doras rothlach
revulsion *n* col
reward *n* duais *v* tabhair duais /
  luach saothair do
rewind *v* cúlchas
rewrite *v* athscríobh
rhetoric *n* reitric
rheumatics *n* scoilteacha
rheumatism *n* daitheacha,
  réamatacht
rhino *n* srónbheannach
rhubarb *n* biabhóg, purgóid na
  manach
rhyme *n* rím *v* rím a dhéanamh le
rhythm *n* rithim
rib *n* easna **rib-vaulted ceiling** síleáil
  bhoghta easnacha

ribbing *n* (knitting) rigín

ribbon *n* ribín

rice *n* rís

rich *adj* saibhir

riches *pl* maoin, saibhreas

rid *v* **to rid yourself of something** rud a chur díot

riddle *n* dúcheist, tomhas

ride *n* marcaíocht, síob *v* marcaigh

rider *n* marcach

ridge *n* droim, iomaire

ridicule *v* fonóid a dhéanamh faoi

ridiculous *adj* áiféiseach, seafóideach

riding *n* marcaíocht

rife *adj* forleathan

riff-raff *n* gramaisc

rifle *n* raidhfil

rift *n* scoilt

rig *n* rige *v* rigeáil

rigging *n* rigín

right[1] *adj* ceart, cóir *n* ceart, cóir, ceartas *v* cuir i gceart **right and wrong** ceart agus éigeart, **by right** de cheart, **to be right** an ceart a bheith agat, **civil rights** cearta sibhialta, **right of way** ceart slí, **you are right** is fíor duit, tá an ceart agat

right[2] *adj* deas **the right hand** an lámh dheas, **the right-hand side** an taobh deas, **to turn right** casadh ar dheis, **at God's right hand** ar dheis Dé

righteous *adj* fíréanta

rightful *adj* ceart, dlisteanach

rigid *adj* dolúbtha, docht

right wing *n* eite dheas

right-handed *adj* deaslámhach

rigmarole *n* deilín

rigorous *adj* dian

rile *v* cuir fearg ar

rim *n* fóir, imeall, faobhar

rind *n* crotal

ring *n* cró, fáinne **circus ring** cró sorcais, **the ring finger** méar an fháinne

ringleader *n* ceann feadhna

ringlet *n* bachall

ringleted *adj* bachallach

ring road *n* cuarbhóthar

rink *n* rinc **skating rink** rinc scátála

rinse *n* sruthlú *v* sruthlaigh

riot *n* círéib *v* círéib a thógáil

riotous *adj* círéibeach

rip *n* roiseadh *v* rois

ripe *adj* aibí

ripen *v* aibigh

ripple *n* cuilithín

rise *v* éirigh **rise again** aiséirigh

rising *n* éirí, éirí amach **the Easter Rising** Éirí Amach na Cásca

risk *n* fiontar, priacal **baggage at owner's risk** bagáiste ar phriacal an úinéara, **to run / take a risk** dul sa seans

risky *adj* amhantrach, priaclach

rissole *n* riosól

ritual *n* deasghnáth

rival *n* céile comhraic

rivalry *n* coimhlint, iomaíocht

river *n* abhainn

road *n* bóthar, ród

roadblock *n* bacainn bhóthair

road show *n* seó bóthair

roadsign *n* comhartha / sín bóthair

roaming *adj* siúlach

roar *n, v* búir

roast *n* rósta *v* róst

roasted *adj* rósta

rob *v* robáil

robber *n* robálaí

robbery *n* robáil

robe *n* róba

robin *n* spideog

robot *n* robat

robotics *n* róbaitic

robust *adj* urrúnta

rock *n* carraig **Blackrock** an Charraig Dhubh

rockery *n* creig-ghairdín

rocket *n* roicéad

rock-garden *n* creig-ghairdín

rock pool *n* **(by the sea)** lochán carraige

rocky *adj* carrach, creagach

rod *n* slat **fishing-rod** slat iascaigh / iascaireachta

rodent *n* creimire

roe *n* **(in fish)** eochraí

rogue *n* cneámhaire, rógaire

role *n* páirt, ról

role-playing *n* páirtghlacadh, rólghlacadh

roll[1] *n* corna *v* corn

roll[2] *n* rolla *v* roll **toilet roll** rolla leithris, **bread roll** rollóg

roll on-roll off jetty (Ro Ro) *n* cé róró

roll about *v* iomlaisc

roller *n* rollóir

roller-skates *n* scátaí rothacha

rolling movement *n* únfairt

Roman *adj, n* Rómhánach

romance *n* rómánsaíocht

Romania *n* an Rómáin

Romanian[1] *n* **(language)** Rómáinis

Romanian[2] *adj, n* Rómánach

romantic *adj* rómánsach

Rome *n* an Róimh **Rome wasn't built in a day** de réir a chéile a thógtar na caisleáin

roof *n* ceann, díon

rook[1] *n* **(chess)** caiseal

rook[2] *n* **(bird)** préachán

room *n* áit, spás, seomra

roomy *adj* fairsing

root *n* fréamh, rúta

rope *n* rópa, téad

rope ladder *n* dréimire rópa

rosary *n* Coróin Mhuire

rosary beads *n* paidrín

Roscommon *n* Ros Comáin

rose *n* rós

rosebud *n* cocán róis

rosebush *n* rósóg

rose-garden *n* rósarnach

roster *n* uainchlár

rostrum *n* ardán, rostram

rosy *adj* rósach

rot *n* lobhadh *v* lobh

rota *n* róta, uainchlár

rotate *v* rothlaigh

rotating *adj* rothlach

rotation *n* rothlú, sealaíocht, uainíocht

rotatory *adj* rothlach

rotten *adj* lofa

rough *adj* garbh **rough sea** farraige ard

roughage *n* gairbhseach

roughly *adv* go garbh

roulette *n* rúiléid **Russian roulette** rúiléid Rúiseach

round[1] *adj* cruinn, cuar

round[2] *adv* thart

round[3] *n* **(sport)** dreas

roundabout *adj* timpcallach *n* timpeallán

roundabout way *n* aistear

roundness *n* cruinne

rouse *v* múscail

rout *n, v* ruaig

route *n* bealach, slí

routine *adj* gnáth- *n* gnáthamh

rove *v* dul ag fánaíocht

roving *adj* **(of person)** aistreach

row[1] *n* sraith

row[2] *v* rámhaigh

row[3] *n* achrann **to cause a row** raic a thógáil

rowdy *adj* racánach *n* racánaí
rower *n* iomróir
rowing *n* iomramh, rámhaíocht
royal *adj* ríoga
royal heir *n* rídhamhna
royal jelly *n* glóthach ríoga
royalty[1] *n* **(of book, film)** dleacht
royalty[2] *n* ríochas
rub *n* cuimilt *v* cuimil
rub out *v* scrios
rubber *n* cuimleoir, scriosán, rubar
rubber band *n* banda rubair
rubbish *n* truflais
rubble *n* spallaí, brablach
ruby *n* rúibín
ructions *n* ruaille buaille, míle murdar
rucksack *n* mála droma
rudder *n* stiúir
rude *adj* drochbhéasach, drochmhúinte, mímhúinte, míshibhialta
rudiment *n* buntús
ruffian *n* ruifíneach
rug *n* ruga, súsa
rugby *n* rugbaí
rugged *adj* garbh
ruin[1] *n* fothrach
ruin[2] *v* mill, scrios
ruination *n* creachadh
ruinous *adj* scriosach
rule *n* riail, rialú *v* rialaigh
ruled *adj* línithe
ruler *n* **(person)** rialtóir, **(tool)** rialóir
ruling *adj* ceannasach
rum *n* rum
rumble *n* **(of stomach)** geonaíl
ruminate *v* athchogain
ruminant *adj, n* athchogantach
rummage *v* fuirsigh, ransaigh

rumour *n* gáir, iomrá, luaidreán, ráfla
rump *n* prompa
rumpus *n* racán, scliúchas
run[1] *v* **(of exercise)** rith **to go on the run** dul ar ar do theitheadh
run[2] *v* **(business)** reáchtáil
run[3] *n* sraith, rith
run away *n* teifeach
rung *n* runga
runner *n* reathaí
runners *pl* bróga reatha
running *n* **(of business)** reáchtáil, **(exercise)** rith
running errands *n* timireacht
runway *n* rúidbhealach
rupee *n* rúipí
rupture *n* maidhm sheicne
rural *adj* **(community)** (pobal) tuaithe
rush[1] *n* fuadar, ruathar, sciuird, práinn *v* sciurd
rush[2] *n* **(plant)** feag
Russia *n* an Rúis
Russian[1] *n* Rúisis **(language)**
Russian[2] *adj, n* Rúiseach
rust *n* meirg *v* meirgigh
rustic *adj* tuathúil
rusting *n* meirgiú
rustle *n* siosarnach
rustling *n* siosarnach
rust-proof *adj* meirgdhíonach
rusty *adj* meirgeach
rut *n* **to be in a rut** bheith ag gabháil don rud céanna i gcónaí, bheith ag treabhadh an iomaire chéanna i gcónaí, **to get out of a rut** do dhroim a thabhairt don ghnáth
ruthless *adj* neamhthrócaireach
rye *n* seagal

S

sabbath *n* sabóid
sabbatical *adj* sabóideach
sabotage *n* sabaitéireacht
saccharine *n* siúicrín
sachet *n* saicín
sack *n* mála, sac *v* an bóthar a thabhairt do dhuine
sacrament *n* sacraimint
sacred *adj* naofa, beannaithe
sacrifice *n* íobairt *v* íobair
sad *adj* faoi chian, brónach, gruama
sadden *v* dubhaigh
saddle *n* diallait *v* diallait a chur ar
sadist *n* sádach
sadistic *adj* sádach
sadness *n* cian, brón
safe[1] *adj* sábháilte, slán **safe sex** gnéas sábháilte
safe[2] *n* taisceadán
safety *n* sábháilteacht
safeguard[1] *n* **(financial)** ráthaíocht
safeguard[2] *n* **(in general)** cosaint *v* cosain
saga *n* sága
sage[1] *n* **(herb)** sáiste
sage[2] *n* saoi
Sahara *n* **(desert)** an Sahára
sail *n* éadach, seol *v* seol **under full sail** faoi iomlán éadaigh/seoil
sail-cloth *n* anairt
sailing *n* seoladh, seoltóireacht
sailing boat *n* bád seoil
sailor *n* mairnéalach, seoltóir
Saint *n* naomh, San **Saint Brigid** Naomh Bríd, **Saint Francis** San Proinsias, **St Valentine's Day** Lá Fhéile Vailintín, **St Stephen's Day** Lá an Dreoilín, Lá Fhéile Stiofáin
sake *n* **for the sake of...** as ucht..., **for God's sake** as ucht Dé, **for your own sake** ar mhaithe leat féin

salad *n* sailéad
salary *n* tuarastal
sale *n* díol, reic
sale of work *n* díolachán earraí
salesperson *n* díoltóir
saliva *n* seile
salmon *n* bradán **the salmon of knowledge (in stories of the Fianna)** eo fis
salon *n* salón **hair salon** salón gruaige
saloon *n* salún
salt *n* salann *v* saill
salt cellar *n* sáiltéar
salted *adj* goirt
salted meat *n* saill
salt water *n* uisce goirt, sáile
salty *adj* goirt
salute *n* beannú, **(military)** cúirtéis *v* beannaigh
salvage *n, v* tarrtháil
salvation *n* slánú **Salvation Army** Arm an tSlánaithe
same *adj* céanna **at the same time** san am céanna
sample *n* sampla *v* sampláil
sanctimonious *adj* béalchráifeach
sanction *n* **(permission)** cead, **(restriction)** smachtbhanna *v* ceadaigh **economic sanctions** smachtbhannaí eacnamaíocha
sanctuary *n* tearmann
sand *n* gaineamh
sandal *n* cuarán
sandbank *n* oitir, banc gainimh
sandblasting *n* greanroiseadh
sander *n* greanóir
sandpaper *n* greanpháipéar
sandstone *n* gaineamhchloch
sandwich *n* ceapaire

sandwich man *n* fógróir dhá chlár

sandy *adj* **(colour)** fionnrua, gainmheach

sane *adj* slánchéillí

sanitary towel *n* súitín sláintíoch, tuáille sláintíochta

sanitation *n* sláintíocht

sanitorium *n* slánlann

sanity *n* slánchiall

Santa Claus *n* San Nioclás, Daidí na Nollag

sap *n* sú, súlach

sapphire *n* saifir

sarcastic *adj* searbhasach

sarcasm *n* searbhas

sardine *n* sairdín

sash *n* sais

satchel *n* tiachóg

satellite *n* satailít **telecommunications satellite** satailít teileachumarsáide

satellite dish *n* mias satailíte

satellite photograph *n* fótagraf satailíte

satin *n* sról

satire *n* aoir

satirical *adj* aorach

satirise *v* aor

satirist *n* aorthóir

satisfaction *n* sásamh, sástacht

satisfactory *adj* sásúil

satisfied *adj* sách, sásta

satisfy *v* sásaigh

saturate *v* sáithigh

saturation *n* sáithiú, sáithiúchán

Saturday *n* Satharn, Dé Sathairn **on Saturday** Dé Sathairn

sauce *n* anlann

saucepan *n* sáspan

saucer *n* fochupán, sásar

Saudi Arabia *n* an Araib Shádach

sauntering *n* fálróid

sausage *n* ispín **I couldn't give a sausage!** is cuma liom sa sioc!

savage *adj* fiáin *n* duine fiáin

save *v* sábháil, spáráil

saving *n* sábháil

saviour *n* slánaitheoir

savoury *adj* blasta

saw *n, v* sábh

sawdust *n* min sáibh

sawmill *n* muileann sábhadóireachta

saxophone *n* sacsafón

say *v* abair **said** arsa

saying *n* ráiteachas **old saying** seanrá

scab *n* gearb

scabbard *n* truaill

scabby carrach

scaffold *n* scafall

scaffolding *n* scafalra

scald *n* scall

scale[1] *n* **(fish)** gainne, lann

scale[2] *n* scála **on a large scale** ar an mórchóir, **scales** meá, **scale of charges** réim praghsanna

scallop *n* muirín, scolb

scam *n* camscéim

scan *n* scan

scandal *n* scannal

scandalise *v* scannal a thabhairt do

scandalmonger *n* béadánaí

scandalous *adj* scannalach

Scandinavia *n* Críoch Lochlann

Scandinavian *adj, n* Lochlannach

scanner *n* scanóir, gléas scanála **bar-code scanner** scanóir barrachód

scanning *n* scanadh, scanáil **ultrasound scanning** scanadh ultrafhuaime

scanty *adj* scáinte

scapegoat *n* ceap milleáin

scar *n* colm *v* fág colm i

scarce *adj* scáinte, gann, tearc

scarcely *adv* ar éigean

scarcity *n* gainne, ganntanas, gannchuid

scare *n* scanrú *v* scanraigh

scarecrow *n* fear bréige, babhdán

scarf *n* scairf

scarlet *adj* scarlóideach

scary *adj* scanrúil

scathing *adj* nimhneach, géar

scatter *v* scaip, spréigh

scattered *adj* scaipthe

scavenger *n* scroblachóir

scene *n* amharc, (in play) radharc

scenery *n* radharc tíre, (in play) radharcra

scenic *adj* sciamhach

scent *adj* boladh *v* bolaigh

sceptic *n* sceipteach

scepticism *n* sceipteachas

sceptical *adj* amhrasach, sceiptiúil

schedule *n* clár ama, amchlár, sceideal

scheme *n* scéim

schemer *n* scéiméir

scheming *n* scéiméireacht

schism *n* siosma

scholar *n* scoláire

scholarly *adj* scolártha

scholarship *n* scoláireacht

school *n* scoil

schooling *n* scolaíocht

science *n* eolaíocht

scientific *adj* eolaíoch

scientist *n* eolaí

scissors *n* siosúr

scissors-like *adj* siosúrtha

scold *n* báirseach *v* scioll

scone *n* toirtín

scoop *n* scúp

scooter *n* scútar

scope *n* scóip

scorch *v* ruadhóigh

scorched *adj* ruadhóite

score *n* scór *v* scóráil

scorn *n* tarcaisne *v* drochmheas a chaitheamh ar

Scorpio *n* an Scairp

scorpion *n* scairp

Scot *n* Albanach

Scotland *n* Albain

Scottish *adj* Albanach

Scottish Highlands *pl* Garbhchríocha na hAlban

scoundrel *n* alfraits

scour *n* sciúradh *v* sciúr

scourge *n* sciúirse *v* sciúrsáil

scourging *n* sciúrsáil

scout *v* gasóg, scabhta

scout around *v* scabhtáil

scowl *n* púic, púicín

scramble *v* scrobh

scrambled egg *n* ubh scrofa

scrape *v* gránaigh, scríob

scratch *n* scríobadh *v* tochais, scríob

scrawl *n*, *v* scrábáil

scream *n*, *v* scread **he's a scream!** is mór an fear seoigh é!

screech *n*, *v* scréach

screen *n* scáileán, scáthlán *v* criathraigh

screw *n* sciú *v* scriúáil

screwdriver *n* scriúire

scribble *n*, *v* scrábáil

scribe *n* scríobhaí

script *n* script

scripture *n* scrioptúr

scroll *n* scrolla

scrounger *n* súmaire

scrounging *n* súmaireacht

scrub *v* sciomair

scrum(mage) *n* clibirt

scruple *n* scrupall

scrupulous *adj* scrupallach

scrutinise *v* grinnigh, mionscrúdaigh

scullery *n* cúlchistin

sculptor *n* dealbhóir, snoíodóir

sculpture *n* dealbhóireacht, snoíodóireacht *v* snoigh

scum *n* coirt, screamh

scurrilous *adj* graosta

scythe *n* speal

sea *n* farraige, lear, muir **the open sea** an fharraige mhór, **at sea** ar muir, **deep sea** duibheagán

sea anemone *n* sine bó leid

sea bream *n* garbhánach

seaboard *n* imeallbhord

seafaring *n* maraíocht

seafood *n* bia mara

seagull *n* faoileán

seal[1] *n* séala

seal[2] *v* séalaigh

seal[3] *n* **(animal)** rón

seam *n* uaim, séama

séance *n* séans

seaplane *n* muireitleán

seaport *n* calafort

search *n* cuardach *v* cuardaigh

searchlight *n* tóirsholas

seashore *n* cladach

seasickness *n* tinneas farraige, muirghalar

season *n* ráithe, séasúr *v* blaistigh

seasonal *adj* séasúrach

seat *n* suíochán

seat belt *n* crios sábhála

seawater *n* sáile

seaweed *n* feamainn

secateurs *n* deimheas crann

secluded *adj* cúlráideach

seclusion *n* **in seclusion** ar an gcúlráid

second[1] *adj* dóú, dara, ath- *v* cuidigh **the second woman** an dara bean

second[2] *n* **(of time)** soicind

secondary *n* tánaisteach, meán- **secondary school** meánscoil

seconder *n* cuiditheoir

second-hand *adj* athláimhe

second-hand dealer *n* athcheannaí

secrecy *n* rúndacht

secret *n* rún **in secret** faoi rún, go rúnda

secretariat *n* rúnaíocht

secretary *n* rúnaí

secretive *adj* rúnda, rúnmhar

secretly *adv* faoi cheilt, faoi rún

sect *n* seict

sectarian *adj* seicteach

sectarianism *n* seicteachas

section *n* alt, rannóg

sector *n* teascóg, earnáil **the public, private sector** an earnáil phoiblí, phríobháideach

secular *adj* tuata

secure *n* daingean, slán *v* daingnigh, feistigh

security *n* slándáil, **(guarantee)** urrús

sedation *n* suaimhniú

sedative *n* suaimhneasán, suanán

sediment *n* deasca, dríodar

seduce *v* meall

seductive *adj* mealltach

see *v* féach, feic **see you later** feicfidh mé ar ball thú, **see overleaf** féach lastall/an taobh eile

seed *n* pór, síol

seedling *n* síolphlanda

seedy *adj* síolach

seek *v* cuardaigh

seem *v* dealraigh, taibhsigh **it seems to me** feictear dom, taibhsítear dom

seemly *adj* cuibhiúil

seemliness *n* cuibhiúlacht

seep *v* úsc, sil

seesaw n crandaí bogadaí

segment n teascán

segregate v leithscar

seize v forghabh, tapaigh, urghabh
seize the opportunity tapaigh an deis

seizure n taom

seldom adj annamh

select adj tofa v togh, roghnaigh

selection n toghadh, rogha, roghnú

selection process n próiseas roghnúcháin

selective adj roghnach

self- prefix féin-

self-assertion n treallús

selfish adj leithleach

selfishness adj leithleachas

self-confidence n féinmhuinín

self-control n féinsmacht, stuaim

self-defence n féinchosaint

self-employed adj féinfhostaithe

self-important adj mórchúiseach

self-pity n féintrua

self-righteous adj ceartaiseach

self-sacrifice n féiníobairt

self-service n féinseirbhís

self-service station n stáisiún féinseirbhíse

sell v díol, reic

sell-by date n dáta díola is deireanaí

seller n díoltóir, reacaire

sellotape n seilitéip

semantic adj séimeantach

semantics n séimeantaic

semen n síol, seamhan

semi- prefix leath

semicircle n leathchiorcal

semicolon n leathstad

semi-detached adj leathscoite

semifinal n cluiche leathcheannais

seminar n seimineár

semi-state body n comhlacht fo-stáit/leathstáit

senate n seanad

senator n seanadóir

send v cuir chun bealaigh, seol

sender n seoltóir

senility n meath seanaoise

senior adj sinsearach n sean, sinsear

seniority n sinsearacht

sensation n mothú

sensational adj éachtach

sensationalism n gáifeachas

sense n céadfa, ciall v mothaigh, airigh have a bit of sense bíodh ciall agat, common sense réasún

senseless adj díchéillí

sensible adj céillí, ciallmhar, stuama

sensitive adj goilliúnach, íogair

sensitivity n íogaireacht

sensory adj céadfach

sensual adj collaí

sensuous adj collaí

sentence n abairt, (penalty) pionós

sentiment n mothúchán, muoithneachas

sentimental adj maoithneach

sentimentality n maoithneachas

sentry n fairtheoir

separate v scar, deighil, dealaigh

separate(d) adj scartha

separation n scaradh, deighilt

September n Meán Fómhair

septic adj seipteach septic tank umar seipteach

sequel n clár leantach

sequence n seicheamh, sraitheog
slow-motion sequence sraitheog moillithe

serenade n saranáid

serene adj sámh

sergeant n sáirsint

serial n sraithscéal

serial number n sraithuimhir

serialise v srathaigh

series n sraith

serious[1] *adj* dáiríre **you're not serious!** níl tú dáiríre

serious[2] *adj* **(grave)** tromchúiseach

serious misconduct *n* mí-iompar tromchúiseach

seriousness[1] *n* dáiríreacht

seriousness[2] *n* **(gravity of situation)** tromchúis

sermon *n* seanmóir

serpent *n* nathair

serrated *adj* cíorach

servant *n* searbhónta, seirbhíseach

serve *v* dáil, fóin, freastail ar, riar, seribhísigh

service *n* fónamh, freastal, riar, seirbhís **secret service** rúnseirbhís, **the service industry** an tionscal seirbhíse

serviette *n* naipcín boird

servile *adj* sclábhánta

servitude *n* braighdeanas

session *n* seisiún, suí

set *n* foireann, láithreán, **(mathematics)** tacar *v* cuir, ullmhaigh

set dance *n* rince seit

settee *n* tolg

setting *n* suíomh, **(of sun)** dul faoi na gréine

settle *v* cónaigh, lonnaigh, socraigh

settled *adj* socraithe, socair

settlement *n* socrú, **(dwelling)** lonnaíocht

seven *adj, n* seacht **seven people** seachtar

seventeen *adj, n* seacht déag

seventh *adj, n* seachtú

seventieth *adj, n* seachtódú

seventy *adj, n* seachtó

sever *v* teasc

several[1] *adj* éagsúla, a lán

severe *adj* daor, dian, feannta, anróiteach

severity *n* déine, dianas

sew *v* fuaigh

sewage *n* camras

sewerage *n* séarachas

sewing *n* fuáil

sex *n* gnéas

sex discrimination *n* leithcheal ar bhonn gnéis

sexist *adj* gnéasaíoch

sexual *adj* collaí, gnéasach

sexual harassment *n* gnéaschiapadh

sexually transmitted disease *n* galar gnéas-tarchurtha

shabby *adj* smolchaite

shack *n* seantán

shackle *n* geimheal

shade *n* scáil, scáth *v* scáthaigh

shaded *adj* scáthlínithe

shadow *n* scáth

shady *adj* foscúil, scáthach

shaft *n* crann, seafta, **(of mine)** sloc

shaggy *adj* mothallach

shake *n* creathán *v* croith **milk shake** creathán bainne

shaky *adj* creathach

shallow *adj* éadomhain, tanaí

shallowness *n* éadoimhneacht

sham *n* cur i gcéil

shambles *pl* seamlas

shame *n* aiféala, náire *v* náirigh **shame on you!** mo náire thú!

shameful *adj* náireach, aithiseach

shameless *adj* mínáireach

shampoo *n* foltfholcadh, seampú

shamrock *n* seamróg

shandy *n* seandaí

Shannon *n* an tSionainn

shape[1] *n* cló, múnla, cruth, cuma, riocht, deilbh **to take shape** teacht i gcruth

shape[2] *v* múnlaigh

shapeless *adj* éagruthach

shapely *adj* dea-chumtha

share *n* sciar, cion, cionmhaireacht, cuid, roinn, **(of company)** scair

shareholder *n* scairshealbhóir

sharing *adj* páirteach

shark *n* siorc

sharp *adj* feannta, géar, **(of tongue)** siosúrtha

sharp-edged *adj* faobhrach

sharpen *v* líomh, faobhraigh, géaraigh

sharpener *n* bioróir

sharpened *adj* líofa **sharpened blade** lann líofa

sharpening *n* géarú

sharp-eyed *adj* géarshúileach

sharpness *n* géire

shatter *v* coscair, réab

shave *v* bearr

shawl *n* seál

she *pron* sí, í, sise, ise **did she hit you?** ar bhuail sí thú? **who is she?** cé hí sin? **she is to blame** ise is cúis leis, **she was there before us** bhí sise ann romhainn

sheaf *n* punann

shear *v* lom

shearer *n* lomaire

shears *n* deimheas

sheath *n* truaill

shebeen *n* síbín

shed *n* bothán, scid *v* doirt **shedding tears** ag doirteadh fola

sheep *n* caora

sheep dog *n* madra caorach

sheepish *adj* maolchluasach

sheep market *n* margadh caorach

sheet *n* leathán, leathanach **sheet of ice** leac oighir

sheik *n* síc

shelf *n* seilf

shell *n* sliogán, faighneog

shelter *n* díon, foscadh, dídean **to give shelter to someone** dídean a thabhairt do dhuine

shepherd *n* aoire, tréadaí *v* treoraigh

sheriff *n* sirriam

sherry *n* seiris

shield *n* sciath, armas *v* cosain

shift[1] *v* aistrigh, athraigh, corraigh

shift[2] *n* **(of work)** seal

shiftwork *n* sealobair, uainobair

shilling *n* scilling

shimmer *v* crithlonraigh

shin *n* lorga

shine *n* taitneamh, dealramh *v* dealraigh, lonraigh, soilsigh

shin-guard *n* loirgneán

shining *adj* lonrach, taitneamhach, dealraitheach

ship *n* long, soitheach

shipment *n* lastas

shipper *n* lastóir

shipping *n* loingeas

shipwreck *n* longbhriseadh

shipwrecked *adj* longbhriste

shipyard *n* longcheárta, longchlós

shirt *n* léine

shiver *v* crith

shoal *n* ráth

shock *n* geit, turraing **electric shock** turraing leictreach

shoe[1] *v* **(a horse)** crúigh

shoe[2] *n* bróg

shoemaker *n* gréasaí

shoneen *n* seoinín

shoot[1] *n* **(plant)** péacán

shoot[2] *v* scaoil urchar le, lámhach

shooting *n* lámhach

shooting star *n* réalta reatha

shoot-out *n* tréanbhabhta lámhaigh

shop *n* siopa

shopkeeper *n* siopadóir

shopping *n* siopadóireacht **shopping centre** lárionad siopadóireachta

shore *n* cladach

short *adj* gairid, gearr, sciotach

shortage *n* easnamh, ganntanas

short-circuit *n* gearrchiorcad

shortcut *n* aicearra, cóngar **to take a shortcut** aicearra a ghabháil

shorten *v* giorraigh

shorthand *n* luathscríbhinn

short-list *n* gearrliosta

short-lived *adj* gearrshaolach

shortly *adv* ar ball beag

shortness of breath *n* gearranáil

shortsighted *adj* gearr-radharcach

shot *n* **(of bullet)** urchar, **(of film)** seat **film shots** seatanna scannáin, **aerial shot** seat ón aer

shot-gun *n* gunna gráin

should *v* **what should be done** an rud ba cheart a dhéanamh, **you shouldn't have done this** níor cheart duit é seo a dhéanamh

shoulder *n* gualainn *v* guailleáil

shoulderblade *n* slinneán

shout *n,v* scairt, béic

shouting *n* scairteadh

shovel *n* sluasaid *v* sluaisteáil

show *n* seó, taispeántas *v* taispeáin **on show** ar taispeáint, **road show** seó bóthair, **talk show** seó cainte

shower[1] *n* **(bathroom)** cithfholcadán

shower[2] *n* cith, fras

shower(ing) *n* cithfholcadh, radadh

showy *adj* feiceálach

shrapnel *n* srapnal

shred *n* ruainne **there's not a shred of truth in it** níl ruainne den fhírinne ann, **in shreds** ina ribeoga

shrewd *adj* géarchúiseach, críonna

shrewdness *n* géarchúis, críonnacht

shriek *n, v* scréach

shrill *adj* caolghlórach

shrimp *n* ribe róibéis

shrine *n* scrín

shrink *v* crap

shrinkage *n* crapadh

shrivel *v* searg

shroud *n* taiséadach *v* ceil

Shrovetide *n* an Inid

shrub *n* tom, tor

shrubbery *n* rosán

shudder *n* fionnachrith **he shuddered** ghabh fionnachrith é

shun *v* seachain

shut *adj* dúnta *v* druid, dún

shut up! éist do bhéal!

shutter *n* comhla

shuttle *n* tointeálaí **shuttle service** seirbhís tointeála

shuttlecock *n* cearc cholgach

shuttling *n* tointeáil

shy *adj* cúlánta, cúthail, faiteach

shyness *n* cúthaileacht, cotadh, faitíos

sick *adj* tinn, breoite **I'm sick and tired of it** tá mé tinn tuirseach de

sicken *v* breoigh **it would sicken you** chuirfeadh sé déistin ort

sickle *n* corrán

sickly *adj* meata

sickness *n* tinneas, breoiteacht **feigned sickness** tinneas muice

side[1] *n* cliathán, colbha, sciathán, slios, taobh

side[2] *v* taobhaigh **to side with somebody** taobhú le duine

side street *n* taobhshráid

sideboard *n* cornchlár

sidelight *n* taobhsholas

sideline *n* taobhlíne, **(business)** fo-ghnó

sideshow *n* fothaispeántas

sideways *adj* cliathánach

siege *n* léigear **the Siege of Derry** Léigear Dhoire

sieve *n* criathar *v* criathraigh

sift *v* criathraigh

sigh *n* osna *v* osna a ligean

sight *n* amharc, léargas, radharc out of sight as amharc, ó léargas, in sight ar amharc

sightseeing *n* fámaireacht

sign[1] comhartha, fíor the sign of the cross fíor na croise, there was no sign of him ní raibh tásc ná tuairisc air

sign[2] *v* saighneáil, sínigh

signpost *n* craobh eolais

signal *n* comhartha, comhairc

signature *n* síniú

significance *n* éifeacht, tábhacht

significant *adj* tábhachtach

signify *v* ciall, comharthaigh

silence *n* ciúnas, tost

silent *adj* ciúin, tostach

silhouette *n* scáthchruth

silk *n* síoda you can't make a silk purse out of a sow's ear cuir síoda ar ghabhar agus is gabhar i gcónaí é

silky *adj* síodúil

silver *n* airgead

silver-plated *adj* airgeadaithe

silversmith *n* gabha geal

silvery *adj* airgeadúil

similar *adj* comhchosúil, cosúil

simile *n* samhail

simmer *v* suanbhruith simmering ar meathbhruith

simple *adj* simplí

simpleton *n* simpleoir

simplicity *n* simplíocht

simplify *v* simpligh

simultaneous *adj* comhuaineach, in éineacht le

sin *n* peaca *v* peacaigh original sin peaca an tsinsir, mortal sin peaca marfach

since *conj* nuair, ó since then ó shin

sincere *adj* macánta

sincerity *n* macántacht

sinew *n* féitheog

sinewy *adj* féitheogach

sinful *adj* peacach, peacúil

sing *v* abair, can, cas

singe *v* barrdhóigh, barrloisc

singed *adj* barrdhóite, barrloiscthe

singer *n* amhránaí

singing *n* amhránaíocht singing ag gabháil fhoinn, ag canadh

single *adj* aonarach, singil, aonta

single-barrelled gun *n* gunna aonbhairille

Single European Act *n* an Ionstraim Eorpach Aonair

single-handed *adj* i d'aonar

singsong *n* deilín

singular *adj* uatha

sink[1] *n* doirteal

sink[2] *v* dul go tóin poill

sinner *n* peacach

sinus *n* cuas

sip *n* súimín, súimóg

siphon *n* siofón

sipping *n* súimíneacht

SIPTU (the Services, Industrial, Professional and Technical Union) *n* an Ceardchumann Seirbhísí, Tionsclaíoch, Gairmiúil agus Teicniúil

siren *n* bonnán

sister *n* deirfiúr, (religious) siúr

sister-in-law *n* deirfiúr chéile

sit *v* suigh

site *n* suíomh, láithreán

sitting *n* suí, tionól she is sitting there since twelve tá sí ina suí ansin óna dódhéag

sitting-room *n* seomra suí

situated *adj* suite

situation *n* suíomh

six *adj, n* sé people seisear

sixteen *adj, n* sé déag
sixth *adj, n* séú
sixtieth *adj, n* seascadú
sixty *adj, n* seasca
size *n* méid, toisc
skate[1] *n* scáta *v* scátáil **roller skates** scátaí rothacha
skate[2] *n* (fish) sciata
skateboard *n* clár scátála
skater *n* scátálaí
skating *n* scátáil
skeleton *n* cnámharlach, creatlach
sketch *n* sceitse *v* sceitseáil
sketchy *adj* scáinte
skewer *n* bior
ski *n* scí *v* sciáil
skid *n* sciorradh *v* sciorr
skier *n* sciálaí
skiing *n* sciáil
skilful *adj* deaslámhach, ealaíonta, sciliúil, stuama
skill *n* ealaín, oilteacht, scil, stuaim
skilled *adj* saoithiúil, oilte
skim *v* scimeáil
skim milk *n* bainne bearrtha
skimpy *adj* sciotach
skin *n* cneas, craiceann, (of animal) seithe
skin graft *n* nódú craicinn
skip *n* foléim *v* léim
skipper *n* captaen
skipping *n* téadléimneach
skirmish *n* scirmis
skirt *n* sciorta *v* sciortáil
skittle *n* scidil **skittles** cluiche scidilí
skull *n* cloigeann, blaosc
skunk *n* scúnc
sky *n* spéir
skylark *n* fuiseog
skylight *n* fuinneog dín
skyscraper *n* teach spéire, ilstórach
slab *n* leac

slack *adj* scaoilte
slacken *n* scaoil
slackening *n* maolú
slam *n, v* plab
slander *n* clúmhilleadh, athiomrá
slant *n* fiar, sceabha *v* cuir ar fiar
slap *n* greadóg *v* greadóg a thabhairt
slash mark *n* slais
slate *n* scláta, slinn
slaughter *n* ár, coscairt *v* ár a dhéanamh ar, coscair
slaughterhouse *n* seamlas
slave *n* daor, sclábhaí
slavery *n* daoirse, daorsmacht, sclábhaíocht
slay *v* maraigh
sledge *n* carr sleamhnáin
sledgehammer *n* ord
sleek *adj* slíoctha, slítheánta, slim
sleep[1] *n* codladh, suan, támh **to be asleep** bheith i do chodladh, **to go to sleep** dul a chodladh, **to sleep in** codladh go headra, **he / it would put you to sleep** chuirfeadh sé chun suain thú
sleep[2] *v* codail
sleeper *n* (rail) trasnán
sleeping-bag *n* mála codlata
sleepwalker *n* suansiúlaí
sleepy *adj* codlatach
sleet *n* flichshneachta
sleeve *n* muinchille
sleigh *n* carr sleamhnáin
slender *adj* leabhair, seang, slim
slice *n* canta, slios, slis, sliseog
slick *n* (oil) doirteadh ola
slide *n* sleamhnán *v* sciorr, sleamhnaigh
sliding door *n* comhla shleamhnáin
sliding scale *n* scála aistritheach
Sligo *n* Sligeach **Co. Sligo** Co. Shligigh
slim *adj* seang, slim

slime *n* ramallae
slimy *adj* ramallach
sling *n* tabhall
slink *v* téaltaigh
slip[1] *n* foghúna, slis
slip[2] *n* sciorradh *v* sleamhnaigh
Freudian slip sciorradh Freudach
slip of the pen *n* sciorradh pinn
slip of the tongue *n* sciorradh focail
slipper *n* slipéar
slippery *adj* sciorrach, sleamhain
slipshod *adj* amscaí
slit *n* gearradh, scoilt *v* gearr
slither *v* sleamhnaigh
slob *n* slabaire
sloe *n* airne
slogan *n* mana
slops *pl* dríodar
slope *n* claon, fána *v* claon
sloping *adj* claonta
sloppy *adj* amscaí
slot *n* sliotán
sloth *n* spadántacht
slouch *n* sleabhac
slovenly *adj* maolscríobach
slow *adj* mall, lcasc
slow-coach *n* malltriallach
slow-motion sequence *n* sraitheog moillithe
slow-moving *adj* malltriallach
slow-witted *adj* mallintinneach
sluggish *adj* spadánta
slum *n* sluma, (district) plódcheantar, (house) plódteach
slumber *n* suan *v* codail
slump *n* (financial) tobthitim
slur *n* aithis *v* aithisigh
slush *n* coscairt
slut *n* sraoilleog
sly *adj* glic
smack *n* greadóg *v* greadóg a thabhairt

small *adj* beag, mion-
smallness *n* laghad
smallpox *n* bolgach
smart *adj* cliste, piocúil
smart card *n* cárta cliste
smash *v* smiot, tuairteáil
smear *n* smearadh *v* smear
smell *n* boladh *v* bolaigh
smile *n* aoibh, meangadh (gáire), miongháire *v* miongháire a dhéanamh
smiling *adj* aoibhiúil
smith *n* gabha
smithereens *pl* smidiríní
smock *n* forléine
smog *n* toitcheo
smoke *n* deatach, gal, smúit, toit *v* (fish) deataigh to smoke tobac a chaitheamh
smoked *adj* deataithe
smoker *n* caiteoir tobac
smoke-free zone *n* ionad gan cead caite
smokeless zone *n* ceantar saor ó thoit
smoky *adj* smúitiúil, toiteach
smooth[1] *adj* mín, réidh, plásánta, slim, sleamhain
smooth[2] *v* mínigh
smoothed *adj* snoite
smoothness *n* réidhe
smother *v* múch
smothered *adj* múchta
smudge *n* smearadh *v* smear
smug *adj* bogásach
smuggle *v* smuigleáil
smuggler *n* smuigléir
smuggling *n* smuigléireacht
smut *n* smúiteán
snack *n* smailc
snag *n* fadhb
snail *n* seilide

snake *n* nathair **poisonous snake** nathair nimhe, **rattlesnake** nathair shligreach

snap *n* smeach **snap of fingers** speach ghearáin

snapshot *n* grianghraf (mear)

snare *n* dol, gaiste

snarl *n* drannadh *v* drann

snatch *v* sciob

sneaky *adj* fáilí

sneer *n* fonóid *v* fonóid a dhéanamh

sneeze *n* sraoth *v* sraoth a ligean

sniff *n* boladh *v* smúr

snigger *n* seitgháire *v* seitgháire a dhéanamh

snipe *n* naoscach

sniper *n* **(shooting)** naoscaire, lámhachóir fadraoin

snobbery *n* baothghalántacht

snobbish *adj* ardnósach

snooker *n* snúcar

snooping *n* smúrthacht

snooze *n* néal

snore *n, v* srann

snorkel *n* aerphíobán

snot *n* smuga

snout *n* pus, smut, soc

snow *n* sneachta *v* sneachta a chur

snowblindness *n* daille sneachta

snowdrift *n* ráth sneachta

snowflake *n* cáithnín sneachta, calóg shneachta

snowman *n* fear sneachta

snowy *adj* sneachtúil

snub-nosed *adj* geancach

snuff *n* snaoisín

snug *adj* seascair, teolaí

snuggle *v* **to snuggle up to** luí isteach le

so *adv* chomh, mar sin, amhlaidh **the baby is so big now** tá an leanbh chomh mór sin anois, **why do you talk to me so?** cén fáth a labhraíonn tú mar sin liom? **if so**

más amhlaidh, **so be it** bíodh amhlaidh, **so much / so many** an oiread sin

soak *v* maothaigh

soak up *v* súigh

soaking wet *adj* fliuch báite, báite fliuch

soap *n* gallúnach

soap opera *n* gallúntraí

sob *n* snag *v* bheith ag snagaíl

sober *adj* sóbráilte

so-called *adj* mar dhea

soccer *n* sacar

sociable *adj* cuideachtúil

social *adj* sóisialta

social partners *pl* comhpháirtithe sóisialta

social security *n* leas sóisialta

social welfare *n* leas sóisialta **social welfare benefits** sochair leasa shóisialaigh

socialism *n* sóisialachas

socialist *adj* sóisialach *n* sóisialaí

society *n* sochaí, pobal

sociology *n* socheolaíocht

sock *n* stoca

socket *n* cró, logall, **(electrical)** soicéad

sod *n* fód

soda *n* sóid

soda water *n* uisce sóide

sofa *n* tolg

soft *adj* maoth, bog, moiglí

soft-boiled *adj* scothbhruite

soften *v* maothaigh

software *n* bogearraí **system software** bogearraí córais, **applications software** bogearraí feidhmiúcháin

soil *n* ithir, úir *v* salaigh

solace *n* sólás

solar *adj* grian-

solar battery *n* griancheallra

solder *n* sádar *v* sádráil

soldering *n* sádráil

soldier *n* saighdiúir

sole[1] *n* **(fish)** sól **lemon sole** sól sleamhain

sole[2] *adj* amháin

sole[3] *n* **(shoe)** bonn

solemn *adj* sollúnta

sole-trader *n* trádálaí aonair

solicit *v* meall (chun peaca)

solicitor *n* aturnae

solid *adj* cruánach, daingean, soladach *n* solad

solidity *n* tathag

solidarity *n* dlúthpháirtíocht, comhghuaillíocht

solitary *adj* uaigneach, aonarach, aonraic

solitary person *n* aonarán

solitude *n* uaigneas

solo *adj* aonair *n* **(music)** aonréad

soloist *n* aonréadaí

solstice *n* grianstad

soluble *adj* **(chemistry)** intuaslagtha

solution *n* **(of problem)** réiteach, **(chemistry)** tuaslagán

solve *v* fuascail, réitigh

solvent[1] *adj* **(finance)** sócmhainneach

solvent[2] *n* **(chemistry)** tuaslagóir

sombre *adj* dorcha

some *adj* éigin **some day** lá éigin, **some distance from home** tamall ó bhaile, **some people** roinnt daoine

somebody *n* duine éigin

somehow *adv* ar chaoi éigin

something *n* rud éigin

sometime *adv* uair éigin

sometimes *adv* uaireanta, scaití

somewhat *adv* cineál **somewhat strange** cineál ait

somewhere *adv* áit éigin

son *n* mac

son-in-law *n* cliamhain

song *n* amhrán, **(of bird)** ceiliúr **give us a song!** croch suas é!

songbird *n* éan ceoil

soon *adv* go luath, gan mhoill

soot *n* súiche

soothe *v* suaimhnigh

soother *n* **(of baby)** gobán súraic

soothing *adj* suaimhneach

sophisticated *adj* sofaisticiúil

soprano *n* soprán

sorcerer *n* asarlaí

sorcery *n* asarlaíocht

sordid *adj* táir

sore *adj* pianmhar *n* cneá

sorrow *n* doilíos, dólás, mairg

sorrowful *adj* doilíosach

sorry *adj* **I'm sorry** tá brón orm, tá mé buartha, tá aiféala orm, **sorry!** gabh mo leithscéal! **I'm sorry for your trouble** is trua liom do chás

sort *n* saghas, sórt *v* sórtáil

soul *n* anam **upon my soul!** ar m'anam féin

sound[1] *n* **(strait)** bealach

sound[2] *n* foghar, fuaim, glór, torann **sound barrier** fuaimbhac, **sound technician** teicneoir fuaime

sound[3] *v* fuaimnigh **that sounds terrible** tá cuma uafásach air sin

sound[4] *adj* slán

soundproof *adj* fuaimdhíonach

sound-track *n* fuaimrian

soup *n* anraith, sú, súp **cream of vetetable soup** anraith glasraí le huachtar, **chicken soup** sú circe, **mutton soup** súp caoireola

sour *adj* searbh

source *n* foinse

south *n* deisceart **to the south** ó dheas, **from the south** aneas, **South America** Meiriceá Theas, **the south wind** an ghaoth aneas

south-east *n* oirdheisceart **to the south-east** soir ó dheas, **from the south-east** anoir aneas, **South-East Asia** Oirdheisceart na hÁise

south-eastern *adj* thoir theas, soir ó dheas

southern *adj* deisceartach

southwards *adv* ó dheas

south-west *n* iardheisceart **to the south-west** siar ó dheas, **from the south-west** aniar aneas

south-western *adj* thiar theas, siar ó dheas

souvenir *n* cuimhneachán

sovereignty *n* ceannas, flaitheas

sow[1] *n* cráin (mhuice)

sow[2] *v* cuir

sowing *n* cur

soya sauce *n* anlann soighe

spa *n* spá

space *n* spás *v* spásáil

spacecraft *n* spásárthach

space probe *n* taiscéalaí spáis

space shuttle *n* spástointeálaí

spacesuit *n* culaith spáis

spacing *n* spásáil

spacious *adj* áirgiúil, fairsing

spaciousness *n* fairsinge

spade[1] *n* rámhainn, spád

spade[2] *n* **(cards)** spéireata **call a spade a spade** ná baintear an t-ainm den bhlonag

Spain *n* an Spáinn

span *n* réise **wing-span** réise sciathán

Spaniard *n* Spáinneach

spaniel *n* spáinnéar

Spanish *adj* Spáinneach *n* **(language)** an Spáinnis

spanner *n* castaire

spare *adj* spártha *v* spáráil

spare wheel *n* roth breise

spark *n* aithinne, drithleog, spréach

spark-plug *n* spréachphlocóid

sparkle *n* glioscarnach *v* drithligh

sparkling *adj* drithleach

sparrow *n* gealbhan

sparse *adj* gann

spartan *adj* spartach

spasm *n* freanga, ríog

spate *n* roiseadh **spate of talk** roiseadh cainte

spatial distribution *n* dáileadh spásúil

spawn *n, v* sceith **frog spawn** sceith fhroig

spawning bed *n* áth

speak *v* can, labhair

speaker *n* **(person)** cainteoir, **(loudspeaker)** callaire **a native speaker** cainteoir dúchais

speaking *n* labhairt

spear *n* ga, sleá

special *adj* speisialta, sain-

special interest groups *pl* grúpaí sainleasa

specialisation *n* speisialtóireacht

specialise *v* speisialaigh

specialist *n* speisialtóir

speciality *n* speisialtacht

species *n* cineál, gné, speiceas

specific *adj* sainiúil, sonrach

specification *n* sonrú, sonraíocht **built to specification** tógtha de réir sonraíochta

specify *v* sonraigh

specimen *n* sampla

speck *n* dúradán

spectacles *pl* spéaclaí

spectacular *adj* mórthaibhseach

spectators *pl* lucht féachana

spectre *n* arracht

spectrum *n* speictream

speculate *v* amhantraíocht a dhéanamh

speculation *n* amhantraíocht

speculative *adj* amhantrach

speculator *n* amhantraí

speech *n* aitheasc, caint, óráid, urlabhra

speech therapist *n* teiripí urlabhra

speech therapy *n* teiripe urlabhra

speechless *adj* he was left speechless fágadh ina stangaire é

speed *n* luas to reduce speed luas a mhaolú, at full speed faoi lánsiúl

speed boat *n* bád luais

speediness *n* tapúlacht

speed limit *n* teorainn luais

speedometer *n* luasmhéadar

speedy *adj* luath, tapa

spell[1] *n* seal, uain, dreas

spell[2] *n* to cast a magic spell over somebody duine a chur faoi dhraíocht

spell[3] *v* litrigh

spelling *n* litriú

spend *v* caith to spend the night an oíche a chaitheamh

spender *n* caiteoir

spending *n* caitheamh

spent *adj* caite

sperm *n* speirm, síol

spew *v* sceith

sphere *n* sféar

spice *n* spíosra

spick and span *adj* pioctha bearrtha

spicy *adj* spíosrach

spider *n* damhán alla

spike *n* spíce

spill *n* doirteadh *v* doirt oil spill doirteadh ola

spilling *n* doirteadh

spin *v* rothlaigh, (weave) sníomh

spinach *n* spionáiste

spine *n* cnámh an droma, dromlach

spineless *adj* cladhartha

spinning-wheel *n* tuirne

spiral *adj* bíseach *n* bís spiral staircase staighre bíse

spire *n* spuaic, stuaic

spirit *n* aigne, meanma, spiorad, sprid

spirited *adj* aigeanta, anamúil, meanmnach, spridiúil

spiritual *adj* spioradálta

spiritual adviser *n* anamchara

spit *n* smugairle, seilc *v* seile a chaitheamh

spite *n* faltanas, gangaid, mioscais, naimhdeas, olc

spiteful *adj* gangaideach, miascaiscach

spitroast *v* bior-róst

spittle *n* seile

splash *n, v* steall, steanc

splashing *n* slaparnach

splendid *adj* ar fheabhas

splendour *n* breáthacht

splint *n* (surgical) cléithín

splinter *n* scealp, scolb

split *n, v* scoilt

spoil *v* mill

spoilt child *n* maicín

spoke *n* spóca

spokesperson *n* urlabhraí

sponge *n* spúinse *v* diúg, spúinseáil

sponger *n* diúgaire

spongy *adj* spúinseach

sponsor *n* urra *v* urraigh sponsored by... urraithe ag...

sponsorship *n* urraíocht

spontaneous *adj* spontáineach

spooky *adj* uaigneach spooky place áit uaigneach

spool *n* spól

spoon *n* spúnóg

sporadic *adj* treallach

sport *n* spórt, áineas

sports centre *n* lárionad spóirt

sportsman *n* fear spóirt

sportswoman *n* bean spóirt

sporty *adj* spórtúil

spot *n* **(pimple)** goirín

spotless *adj* gan smál

spotlight *n* spotsolas

spotty *adj* goiríneach

spouse *n* céile, nuachar

spout *n, v* scaird

sprain *n* leonadh *v* leon

spray *n* cáitheadh, sprae *v* spraeáil

spread *n* forleathadh, **(of butter)** smearadh *v* leath, spréigh

spring[1] *n* **(metal)** tuailm, sprionga *v* eascair

spring[2] *n* **(water)** fuarán

spring[3] *n* **(season)** earrach

spring back *v* athscinn

springboard *n* preabchlár

spring tide *n* rabharta

springtime *n* earrach

springwater *n* fíoruisce

sprinkle *n* croitheadh *v* croith

sprinkler *n* spréire

sprinkling *n* croitheadh

sprint *n* ráib, ruthag

sprout[1] *n* bachlóg, péacán **Brussels sprouts** bachlóga Bhruiséile

sprout[2] *v* péac

spruce[1] *n* sprús

spruce[2] *adj* pioctha

spur[1] *n, v* spor

spur[2] *n* **on the spur of the moment** ar ala na huaire

spy *n* spiaire

spying *n* spiaireacht

squabble *n* achrann

squad *n* scuad **firing squad** scuad lámhaigh

squalid *adj* suarach

squadron *n* scuadrún

squander *v* diomail

square *adj* cearnach *n* cearnóg *v* cearnaigh **Merrion Square**

Cearnóg Mhuirfean, **four square metres** ceithre mhéadar chearnacha, **square root** fréamh chearnach

squash[1] *v* brúigh

squash[2] *n* **(sport)** scuais

squat *v* suí ar do ghogaide

squatter *n* suiteoir

squeal *v* **to squeal on somebody** sceitheadh ar dhuine

squeamish *adj* lagáiseach

squeeze *n* fáisceadh *v* fáisc, teann

squint *n* fiarshúil *v* claonamharc a thabhairt

squirrel *n* iora **red squirrel** iora rua

squirt *n, v* scaird, steanc

stab *n* sá, ropadh *v* sáigh, rop **to stab somebody** duine a shá, duine a ropadh

stabbing pain *n* arraing

stability *n* cobhsaíocht

stabilise *v* cobhsaigh

stabiliser *n* cobhsaitheoir

stabilisation *n* cobhsú

stable[1] *n* stábla

stable[2] *adj* cobhsaí

stack *n, v* cruach

stadium *n* staid

staff *n* foireann, **(stick)** bachall

stag *n* carria, fia beannach

stage[1] *n* ardán, stáitse *v* stáitsigh

stage[2] *n* **(period)** céim

stage-hand *n* giolla stáitse

stagger *n* tuisle *v* tuisligh

stagnant *adj* marbhánta **stagnant pond** lochán marbh

stagnate *v* éirigh marbhánta

straighten *v* dírigh

stain *n* smál, ruaim *n* smálaigh, ruaimnigh

stainless steel *n* cruach dhosmálta

staircase *n* staighre

stairs *n* staighre

stake *n* cuaille

stalactite *n* aolchuisne

stalagmite *n* aolchoinneal

stale *adj* stálaithe **stale milk** bainne géar

stalemate *n* **(in chess)** leamhsháinn

stalk *n* gas *v* duine a leanúint

stallion *n* stail

stamina *n* teacht aniar

stammer *n* stad cainte

stamp *n* stampa *v* stampáil

stamp album *n* albam stampaí

stampede *n* táinrith *v* dul chun scaoill

stance *n* seasamh **to adopt a fighting stance** gothaí troda a chur ort féin

stand[1] *v* seas **to stand a drink** deoch a sheasamh, **I can't stand them** ní féidir liom iad a sheasamh

stand[2] *n* ardán, seastán **the Hogan Stand** Ardán Uí Ógáin

standard[1] *n* caighdeán, **(flag)** meirge

standard[2] *adj* caighdeánach

standard of living *n* caighdeán maireachtála

standardise *v* caighdeánaigh

stand-in *n* aisteoir ionaid

standing *adj* seasta *n* seasamh

stand-offish *adj* doicheallach

stanza *n* ceathrú

staple *n* stápla *v* stápláil

stapler *n* stáplóir

star *n* réalta **shooting star** réalta reatha, **guiding star** réalta eolais, **small star** réaltóg, **film star** réalta/réiltín scannán

starboard *n* deasbhord

starch *n* stáirse

stare *n* stánadh *v* stán

starfish *n* crosóg mhara

stark *adj* lom

stark naked *adj* lomnocht, tarnocht

starlit *adj* spéirghealaí

starling *n* druid

starry *adj* réaltach

start[1] *v* tosaigh, **(machine)** dúisigh

start[2] *n* tosaigh, tosú, tús

starter[1] *n* **(of machine)** dúisire

starter[2] *n* **(of meal)** cúrsa tosaigh

startle *v* **he was startled** baineadh geit as

starve *v* bás a fháil den ocras

starving *adj* stiúgtha **I am starving** tá mé stiúgtha leis an ocras

state[1] *v* maígh, sonraigh

state[2] *n* staid, riocht, bail, stát **the United States** na Stáit Aontaithe, **member state** ballstát

stately *adj* maorga, státúil

statement *n* maíomh, ráiteas

statesman *n* státaire

stateswoman *n* státaire

static *adj* statach

station *n* stáisiún **power, fire, petrol, train station** stáisiún cumhachta, doiteáin, peitril, traenach, **Garda station** stáisiún na nGardaí

stationary *adj* ina stad

stationer *n* stáiseanóir

stationery *n* páipéarachas, stáiseanóireacht

statistic *n* staitistic **statistics** staidreamh, staitisticí

statistical *adj* staitistiúil

statue *n* dealbh

status *n* stádas

status symbol *n* siombail céime

statute *n* reacht

statutory *adj* reachtúil

staunch *adj* diongbháilte

staunchness *n* diongbháilteacht

stay *v* fan

steadfast *adj* seasmhach

steady *adj* socair *v* daingnigh

steak *n* stéig

steal *v* goid **he'd steal the shirt off your back** ghoidfeadh sé an earra ón seangán

stealthy *adj* fáilí

steam *n* gal *v* galbhruith

steam-engine *n* galinneall

steaming *adj* galach

steed *n* each

steel *n* cruach **stainless steel** cruach dhosmálta

steep[1] *adj* crochta, rite, géar

steep[2] *v* **to steep something** rud a chur ar maos

steeple *n* spuaic

steepness *n* riteacht

steer *v* stiúir

steering *n* stiúradh

stem *n* gas

stencil *n* stionsal

stenographer *n* luathscríobhaí

stenography *n* luathscríbhneoireacht

step *n* céim **step by step** céim ar chéim

step- *prefix* leas-

stepbrother *n* leasdeartháir

stepdaughter *n* leasiníon

stepfather *n* leasathair

stepmother *n* leasmháthair

stepladder *n* dréimire taca

stepsister *n* leasdeirfiúr

stepson *n* leasmhac

stereo *n* steiréafón

stereo system *n* córas steiréafóin

stereo (cassette, cd) player *n* steiréisheinnteoir (caiséad, dlúthdhioscaí)

stereo *adj* steiréafónach

sterile *adj* aimrid

sterilise *v* aimridigh

sterling *adj* dea-mhiotail *n* punt Sasanach

stern[1] *n* **(boat)** deireadh

stern[2] *adj* dian, crua

stew *n* stobhach *v* stobh

steward *n* maor, reachtaire

stewardship *n* maoirseacht, reachtas

stick[1] *v* greamaigh

stick[2] *n* maide

stick out *v* gob amach

sticker *n* greamaitheoir

sticky *adj* greamaitheach, **(situation)** achrannach

stiff *adj* righin

stiffen *v* righnigh

stifling *adj* plúchtach

stigma *n* stiogma

still[1] *n* **(for distilling whiskey, poitín, etc)** stil

still[2] *adj* fós, go fóill, i gcónaí

still-born child *n* marbhghin

still life *n* **(art)** ábhar neamhbheo

stilts *pl* cosa fuara

stimulant *n* spreagthach

stimulate *v* spreag

stimulating *adj* spreagthach, spreagúil

stimulus *n* spreagadh

sting *n* cealg, goimh *v* cealg, loisc

stinginess *n* sprionlaitheacht

stinging *adj* goimhiúil

stinging pain *n* gradfach

stingy *adj* sprionlaithe, gortach

stipulate *v* éiligh

stipulation *n* cuntar

stir *v* corraigh

stir-fry *n* suaithfhriochadh, béile suaithfhriochta

stirrup *n* stíoróip

stitch[1] *n* arraing **to have a stitch (in one's side)** arraing a bheith ionat

stitch[2] *n* **(sewing)** lúb, **(in wound)** greim *v* fuaigh

stoat *n* easóg

stock *n* stoc

stockbroker *n* stocbhróicéir

stock exchange *n* stocmhalartán

stock market *n* stocmhargadh **stockmarket prices** praghsanna stocmhargaidh, **the world's stockmarkets** stocmhargaí an domhain

stocking *n* stoca

stocklist *n* stocliosta

stockpile *n* stocthiomsú *v* tiomsaigh

stockpot *n* stocphota

stocktaking *n* stocáireamh

stocky *adj* suite

stodgy *adj* stolpach

stolid *adj* spadánta, dochorraithe

stomach *n* goile, bolg *v* **to stomach something** rud a sheasamh

stone *n* cloch

stone dead *adj* chomh marbh le hart

stonemason *n* saor cloiche

stone wall *n* claí cloch

stool *n* stól

stoop *v* crom

stooped *adj* crom

stop *n*, *v* stop, stad **the bus stop** stad an bhus

stoppage *n* stopadh, stad **stoppage of work** stopadh oibre, stad oibre

stopper *n* stopallán

stopwatch *n* staduaireadóir

storage *n* stóráil, **(computers)** stóras

store *n* stór, taisce *v* cnuasaigh **department store** stór ilrannach

stored energy *n* fuinneamh taiscthe

storeroom *n* stóras

storey *n* stór, urlár **ten storey building** foirgneamh deich stór

stork *n* corr bhán

storm *n* anfa, doineann, stoirm

stormy *adj* stoirmeach

story *n* scéal **short story** gearrscéal, **that's another story** sin scéal eile

storyteller *n* scéalaí, seanchaí

storytelling *n* scéalaíocht, seanchaíocht, seanchas

stout[1] *n* **(drink)** leann dubh

stout[2] *adj* téagartha

stove *n* sornóg

stow away *v* fanacht i bhfolach

stowaway *n* folachánaí

straddle *n* srathair *v* dul ar scaradh gabhail

straggling *adj* streachlánach

straight *adj* díreach **straight line** líne dhíreach, **straight across** díreach anonn

straighten *v* dírigh

straightforward *adj* ionraic, díreach

strain[1] *v* **(liquid)** síothlaigh, **(ankle)** leon, teann

strain[2] *n* teannas

strained *adj* **(relations)** cascairdiúil

strainer *n* síothlán

strait *n* caolas **the Strait of Gibraltar** Caolas Ghiobráltar

strand[1] *n* **(of rope)** dual, **(of hair)** ribe

strand[2] *n* **(beach)** trá

stranded *adj* ar an trá fholamh

strange[1] *adj* aduain, anaithnid, coimhthíoch, deoranta, strainséartha

strange[2] *adj* **(weird)** ait, aisteach, anaithnid

stranger *n* strainséir

strangle *v* tacht

strap *n* iall

strapping *adj* scafánta

stratum *n* stratam

strategic *adj* straitéiseach

strategy *n* straitéis

stratosphere *n* strataisféar

straw *n* tuí **drinking straw** sop

strawberry *n* sú talún **strawberries** sútha talún

stray *n* ainmhí seachráin *v* dul ar strae

straying *n* seachrán, strae

streak *n* stríoc

streaked *adj* riabhach

stream *n* sruth, sruthán

streamer *n* sraoilleán

streamlet *n* altán

streamlined *adj* sruthlíneach

street *n* sráid **O'Connel Street** Sráid Uí Chonaill

strength *n* neart, láidreacht, tathag, arrachtas

strengthen *v* láidrigh, daingnigh, neartaigh, treisigh

strenuous *adj* fuinniúil

stress *n* strus, teannadh

stretch *v* sín, searr **to stretch oneself** tú féin a shearradh

stretcher *n* sínteán

stretching *n* searradh, síneadh

strict *adj* docht

stride *v* céimnigh

strife *n* imreas

strike *n* stailc, buille *v* buail, stríoc

striker *n* stailceoir, buailteoir **hunger striker** stailceoir ocrais

string *n* sreang, corda, téad

stringed *adj* sreangach

stringy *adj* sreangach

strip *n* leadhb, straidhp, stráice, stiall **strip of paper** leadhb pháipéir, **airstrip** aerstráice

stripe *n* stríoc

striped *adj* riabhach

strive *v* troid

stroke *n* **(medical)** stróc, slíoc, stríoc

strolling *n* spaisteoireacht

strong *adj* láidir, neartmhar, teann, tréan

stronghold *n* daingean, dún

structural *adj* struchtúrach

structure *n* comhdhéanamh, foirgneamh, struchtúr **cross-border structures** struchtúir trasteorann

struggle *n* streachailt *v* streachail

stubble *n* coinleach

stubborn *adj* cadránta, ceanndána, stuacach

stubbornness *n* ceanndánacht

stud[1] *n* **(farm)** graí, **(horse)** graíre

stud[2] *n* stoda

student *n* **(second level)** dalta, **(third level)** mac léinn

studio *n* stiúideo

studious *adj* staidéartha, staidéarach

study *n* staidéar, **(room)** staidéarlann *v* staidéar a dhéanamh (ar)

stuff *n* stuif *v* stuáil

stuffing *n* stuáil, búiste

stuffy *adj* plúchtach

stumble *n* turraing, tuisle *v* tuisligh

stump *n* grágán, stumpa

stun *v* néal a chur ar dhuine/ainmhí

stunt[1] *n* éacht

stunt[2] *v* crandaigh

stunted *adj* cranda

stuntman / stuntperson *n* éachtóir

stupendous *adj* iontach, ar fheabhas

stupid *adj* dúr **stupid fellow** gamal

style *n* stíl

stylish *adj* faiseanta, stíleach

suave *adj* síodúil

subconscious *adj* fo-chomhfhiosach *n* fo-chomhfhios

subdue *v* cloígh

subdued *adj* cloíte, maolchluasach

subheading *n* fotheideal

subject[1] *n* ábhar **subject to** faoi réir

subject[2] *n* **(person)** géillsineach

subjective *adj* suibiachtúil

subjunctive *adj, n* foshuiteach

sublet *v* folig

submarine *n* fomhuireán

submerged *adj* tumtha, báite

submission *n* géilleadh, umhlú, umhlaíocht

submissive *adj* géilliúil, umhal

submit *v* umhlaigh, géill, cuir isteach

subnormal *adj* fonormálta

subordinate *adj* íochtaránach *n* íochtarán

subscribe *v* foscríobh, taobhaigh le

subscriber *n* (to magazine etc) síntiúsóir

subscription *n* síntiús

subsequent *adj* iartheachtach

subsequently *adv* ina dhiaidh sin

subside *v* tráigh

subsidiary *n* fochuideachta

subsidy *n* fóirdheontas

subsist *v* mair

subsistence *n* cothú, maireachtáil

substance *n* substaint, taithag

substantial *adj* fuaimintiúil, substaintiúil, téagartha

substitute *n* ionadaí *v* rud a chur in ionad ruda eile

subtitle *n* fotheideal

subtle *adj* caolchúiseach

subtract *v* dealaigh **subtract from** dealaigh ó

subtraction *n* dealú

suburb *n* fo-bhaile, bruachbhaile

subvert *v* treascair

subway *n* fobhealach

succeed *v* éirigh le **if we succeed** má éiríonn linn

success *n* conách, rath

successful *adj* rathúil

succession *n* comharbas

successor *n* comharba

succulent *adj* súmhar

such, such a fool a leithéid d'amadán, **such is life** sin é an saol, **such as** ar nós

suck *v* diúl, súraic

sucker *n* súiteoir, súmaire

sucking *n* súmaireacht

suction *v* sú, súmaireacht, súrac

sudden *adj* tobann

suddenly *adv* de sciotán, go tobann

sue *v* agair, an dlí a chur ar

suede *n* svaeid

suffer *v* fulaing

suffering *adj* fulangach *n* fulaingt

suffice *v* **that will suffice** is leor sin, déanfaidh sé sin cúis

sufficiency *n* sáith, dóthain

sufficient *adj* leor

suffix *n* iarmhír

suffocate *v* plúch

suffocation *n* múchadh, plúchadh

suffragette *n* sufraigéid

sugar *n* siúcra *v* siúcraigh

suggest *v* mol

suggestion *n* moladh

suicide *n* féinmharú **he committed suicide** chuir sé lámh ina bhás féin

suit¹ *n* culaith

suit² *v* feil, oir, fóir (do)

suitability *n* oiriúint, oiriúnacht

suitable *adj* feiliúnach, fóirsteanach, oiriúnach

suitcase *n* mála taistil

suitor *n* suiríoch

sulk *n* stuaic *v* dul chun stuaice

sulky *adj* stuacach

sullen *adj* dúr

sulphur *n* sulfar

sultan *n* sabhdán

sultana *n* sabhdánach

sultry *adj* meirbh

sum *n* suim

summarise *v* achoimrigh, coimrigh

summary *n* achoimre

summer *n* samhradh

summit *n* mullach

summon *v* toghair

summons *n* scairt, toghairm

sun *n* grian

sunbathe *v* tú féin a ghrianadh

sunbeam *n* ga gréine

sunburn n dó gréine
sunburst n scal ghréine
suncream n smearadh gréine
Sunday n Domhnach, Dé Domhnaigh
   on Sunday Dé Domhnaigh
sundial n clog gréine
sunflower n lus na gréine
sunglasses n spéaclaí gréine
sunlight n solas na gréine, grian
sun lotion n lóis ghréine
sunny adj grianmhar
sunrise n éirí (na) gréine
sunset n luí (na) gréine
sunshine n dealramh gréine
sunstroke n béim ghréine
sun-tan n griandath
suntanned adj griandaite
super- prefix sár-
superb adj ar fheabhas
superficial adj éadrom
superfluous adj iomarcach
superimpose v forshuigh
superintendent n ceannfort
superior adj uachtarach n uachtarán
superiority complex n coimpléacs
   uaisleachta
superlative n sárchéim
supermarket n ollmhargadh
supermilk n bainne treisithe
supernatural adj osnádúrtha
superpower n sárchumhacht
superstition n piseog
superstitious adj piseogach
supervise v stiúir
supervision n feitheoireacht,
   stiúradh
supervisor n feitheoir, maoirseoir,
   stiúrthóir
supervisory position n post
   maoirseachta
supper n suipéar
supplement n (newspaper)
   forlíonadh v cuir le

supplier n soláthraí
supply v soláthair
supply and demand n soláthar agus
   éileamh
support n taca, tacaíocht v tacaigh
   le, taobhaigh le, treisigh le
supporter n tacaí **supporters** lucht
   tacaíochta
suppose v cuir i gcás
supposition n cur i gcás
suppress[1] v cuir faoi chois
suppress[2] n (of noise) sochtaigh
supremacy n ardcheannas
supreme adj ard-, sár-
Supreme Being n Ard-Bheith
Supreme Court n Ard-Chúirt
sure adj deimhin **to make sure of**
   something deimhin a dhéanamh
   de rud
surety n go surety for urraigh
surf n (on sea) bruth
surface n dromchla, brat **to surface**
   a road brat/craiceann (nua) a
   chur ar bhóthar
surf-board n clár toinne
surfing n seoltóireacht toinne
surge n borradh v borr
surgeon n máinlia **heart surgeon**
   máinlia croí
surgery n (profession) máinliacht,
   (place) áit mháinliachta
surgical adj máinliach
surname n sloinne
surpass v sáraigh
surpassing n sárú **it can't be**
   surpassed níl a shárú ann
surplus n fuíoll
surprise n ábhar iontais
surprising adj aisteach
surrealism n osréalachas
surrealist adj osréalach
surrender v géill
surround v timpeallaigh
surroundings n timpeallacht

surtax *n* forcháin
surveillance *n* faire **electronic surveillance** faire leictreonach
survey *n* suirbhé, suirbhéireacht **the Ordnance Survey** an tSuirbhéireacht Ordanáis
surveyor *n* suirbhéir
survive *v* mair, téarnaigh
survivor *n* marthanóir
susceptible *adj* braiteach
suspect *n* díol amhrais *v* bheith san amhras ar dhuine/rud, amhras a chaitheah ar dhuine/rud **I suspected just as much** níor mheath mo bharúil orm
suspend *v* croch
suspenders *pl* crochóga
suspension *n* fionraí **to suspend someone** duine a chur ar fionraí
suspicion *n* amhras **to cast suspicion on someone** amhras a chaitheamh ar dhuine
suspicious *adj* amhrasach
sustain *v* cothaigh
sustained *adj* marthanach **sustained attack** amas/ionsaí marthanach
swallow[1] *n* **(bird)** fáinleog
swallow[2] *n* bolgam *v* alp, slog
swamp *n* séascann
swan *n* eala
swarm *n* scaoth, saithe **swarm of bees** scaoth/saithe beach
swarming (with) *adj* dubh (le)
swarthy *adj* ciar
swastika *n* svaistice
swaying *n* longadán
swear *n* eascaine *v* eascainigh **to swear in a jury** coiste a mhionnú
sweat *n* allas **sweating profusely** ag bárcadh allais, **she broke into a cold sweat** tháinig allas fuar léi
sweatshirt *n* geansaí spraoi
sweaty *adj* allasúil
swede *n* svaeid
Sweden *n* an tSualainn

Swedish *adj* Sualannach *n* **(language)** an tSualainnis
sweep *v* scuab
sweet[1] *adj* milis
sweet[2] *n* milseán
sweeten *v* milsigh
sweetheart *n* cuisle mo chroí
sweetness *n* milseacht
swell *n* **(at sea)** borradh *v* at
swelling *n* at
swift *adj* mear, luath *n* **(bird)** gabhlán gaoithe
swim *n*, *v* snámh
swimmer *n* snámhóir
swimming pool *n* linn snámha
swimsuit *n* culaith shnámha
swing *v* luasc *n* luascadh, luascán **in full swing** faoi lánseol
swing door *n* luascdhoras
swinging *adj* luascach
swipe *v* sciob
Swiss *adj*, *n* Eilvéiseach
switch *n* lasc *v* cas **to switch off** múch, **switched off** múchta
switchboard *n* lasc-chlár
Switzerland *n* an Eilvéis
swoon *n* fanntais, támhnéal *v* tit i bhfanntais
swop *n*, *v* babhtáil
sword *n* claíomh
swordfish *n* colgán
sycamore *n* seiceamar
syllable *n* siolla
syllabus *n* siollabas
symbol *n* samhailchomhartha, siombail
symbolic *adj* siombalach
symbolise *v* siombalaigh
symbolism *n* siombalachas
symmetrical *adj* siméadrach
symmetry *n* siméadracht
sympathetic *adj* cásmhar, tuisceanach

sympathise *v* comhbhrón a dhéanamh le, taobhaigh le
sympathy *n* bá, comhbhá, trua **I sympathise with you** tuigim duit
symphonic *adj* siansach
symphony *n* siansa
symptom *n* airí
synagogue *n* sionagóg
syndicate *n* sindeacáit
syndrome *n* siondróm
synod *n* sionad
synonym *n* comhchiallach
synopsis *n* achoimre

syntactic(al) *adj* comhréireach
syntax *n* comhréir
synthesis *n* sintéis
synthetic *adj* sintéiseach **synthetic fibres** snáithíní sintéiseacha
syphilis *n* sifilis
syringe *n* steallaire
syrup *n* síoróip
system *n* córas **decimal system** córas deachúlach
system software *n* bogearraí córais
systematic *adj* córasach
systems analyst *n* anailísí córas

T

tab *n* cluaisín, (computer) táb *v* tábáil
table[1] *n* (of contents) clár
table[2] *n* bord, tábla
table tennis *n* leadóg bhoird
tablecloth *n* éadach boird
tablet *n* taibléad
tabloid *adj* tablóideach **tabloid newspaper** nuachtán tablóideach
taboo *n* geis
tabulate *v* táblaigh
tacit *adj* tostach
taciturn *adj* tostach
tack *n* (nail) tacóid, greim
tackle *n* fearas, tácla *v* tabhair faoi **fishing tackle** fearas iascaireachta, **lifting tackle** tácla ardaithe
tact *n* tuiscint
tactful *adj* tuisceanach
tactics *n* oirbheartaíocht
tactless *adj* tuathalach
tadpole *n* torbán
tag *n* cluaisín
tail *n* eireaball
tailor *n* táilliúir
tailoring *n* tailliúireacht

take[1] *v* tóg **take it away with you** ardaigh/tabhair leat é, **it will take me a day** tógfaidh sé lá orm, **to take something for granted** talamh slán a dhéanamh de rud
take[2] *n* (of film) téic
take after *v* **she takes after her mother** téann sí lena máthair
talcum *n* talcam **talcum powder** púdar talcaim
tale *n* scéal
talent *n* tallann
talented *adj* éirimiúil, tréitheach
talk *n* caint, (loud) allagar *v* labhair **talks** comhchainteanna
talkative *adj* cainteach
talk show *n* seó cainte
tall *adj* ard **to be six feet tall** bheith sé troithe ar airde
tame *adj* ceansa *v* ceansaigh
tamper (with) *v* gabháil de rud
tampon *n* súitín sláintíoch
tangent *n* tadhlaí
tangerine *n* tainséirín
tangible *adj* inbhraite
tangle *adj* achrann, gréasán **it's in a tangle** tá sé ina ghréasán

tank[1] *n* umar **septic tank** umar seipteach, **oil storage tank** umar stórála ola

tank[2] *n* tanc

tanker *n* tancaer

tantalise *v* griog

tap *n* sconna, buacaire, tapa

tape *n* téip, ribín *v* taifead

tape recorder *n* téipthaifeadán

tape recording *n* téipthaifeadadh

tape measure *n* ribín tomhais

taper *n* fáideog

tapestry *n* taipéis

tapping device *n* gléas cúléisteachta

tar *n* tarra *v* tarra a chur ar

target *n* sprioc, targaid

tariff *n* taraif **tariff agreements** comhaontuithe taraifí

tariff barrier *n* bacainn chustaim, bacainn taraifí

tarnish *v* téimhligh

tart *n* toirtín

task *n* tasc

task force *n* tascfhórsa

tassel *n* scothóg

taste *n* blas *v* blais, tástáil **everybody has his own taste** beatha (do) dhuine a thoil

tasteless *adj* leamh

tasty *adj* blasta, dea-bhlasta, so-bhlasta

tattered *adj* liobarnach

tattoo *n* tatú *v* tatúáil

tattooed *adj* tatúch

Taurus *n* an Tarbh

taut *adj* teann

tautness *n* teannas

tautology *n* athluaiteachas

tax *n* cáin **inclusive of tax** cáin san áireamh, **to tax** cáin a ghearradh ar, **value-added tax (VAT)** cáin bhreisluacha (CBL), **income tax** cáin ioncaim

taxation *n* cánachas

tax-free *adj* saor ó cháin

tax-free allowance *n* liúntas saor ó cháin

taxpayer *n* íocóir cánach, cáiníocóir

taxi *n* tacsaí

tea *n* tae

teabag *n* máilín tae

tea break *n* sos tae

teach *v* múin, teagasc

teacher *n* múinteoir, oide

teaching *n* múineadh, múinteoireacht, teagasc

Teaching English as a Foreign Language (TEFL) Ag Múineadh an Bhéarla mar Theanga Iasachta

tea cosy *n* púic tae

teak *n* téac

team *n* foireann

teamwork *n* obair foirne, comhar

teapot *n* taephota

tear[1] *n* deoir

tear[2] *n* stróiceadh, roiseadh *v* (rip) srac, stróic

tearful *adj* deorach

tear gas *n* deoirghás

tease *v* griog, spíon, spoch

teaspoon *n* taespúnóg

teat *n* (infant's bottle) dide, sine

technical *adj* teicniúil

technical drawing *n* líníocht theicniúil

technicality *n* teicniúlacht

technician *n* teicneoir **sound technician** teicneoir fuaime

technique *n* teicníc, teicníocht

technological *adj* teicneolaíoch

technology *n* teicneolaíocht

tedious *adj* fadálach, leadránach, liosta

teenager *n* déagóir

teens *pl* déaga

teetotaller *n* lánstaonaire, staonaire

telecommunications *n* teileachumarsáid

telecommunications satellite *n* satailít teileachumarsáide

telegram *n* teileagram

telepathy *n* teileapaite

telephone *n* teileafón, guthán **telephone number** uimhir theileafóin/ghutháin, **mobile telephone** teileafón/guthán gluaisteach, teileafón/guthán póca

telephonist *n* teileafónaí

telescope *n* teileascóp

teletext *n* teilitéacs

televise *v* teilifísigh

television *n* teilifís, **(set)** teilifíseán **cable television** teilifís chábla, **closed circuit television** teilifís chiorcaid iata

telex *n* teiléacs

tell *v* abair (le), inis (do) **tell me this** abair an méid seo liom, **tell us a funny story** inis scéal grinn (dúinn)

teller *n* airgeadóir

telltale *n* sceithire

temper *n* cuthag (feirge)

temperament *n* meon

temperamental *adj* spadhartha

temperate *adj* measartha

temperature *n* teocht

tempestuous *adj* stoirmeach, fiáin

temple[1] *n* **(of the head)** ara, uisinn

temple[2] *n* teampall

temporal *adj* saolta

temporary *adj* sealadach

tempt *v* cathaigh **to tempt someone** cathú a chur ar dhuine

temptation *n* cathú

ten *adj, n* deich **ten people** deichniúr, **ten o'clock** a deich a chlog

tenacious *adj* righin

tenacity *n* righneas

tenancy *n* tionóntacht

tenant *n* tionónta

tend *v* freastail (ar), claonadh a bheith agat rud a dhéanamh

tendency *n* claon, claonadh

tender *adj* leochaileach, maoth, tláith

tenement *n* tionóntán

tennis *n* leadóg

tenor *n* teanór

tense[1] *n* **(grammar)** aimsir **the future tense** an aimsir fháistineach

tense[2] *adj* rite, ar bís

tension *n* teannas

tent *n* puball

tentacle *n* adharcán

tentative *adj* trialach

tenth *adj, n* deichiú

tenuous *adj* caol

tenure *n* sealbhaíocht

term *n* téarma

terminal *n* críochfort

terminal illness *n* galar báis

terminate *n* cuir deireadh le

termination *n* críoch, deireadh

terminology *n* téarmaíocht

terrace *n* **(of houses)** sraith (tithe)

terrain *n* tír-raon

terrestrial *adj* domhanda

terrible *adj* damanta, uafásach, millteanach

terrific *adj* iontach

terrified *adj* critheaglach

terrifying *adj* scanrúil

territory *n* críoch, limistéar

terror *n* sceimhle, scéin, anfa, uafás

terrorise *v* sceimhligh

terrorism *n* sceimhlitheoireacht

terrorist *n* sceimhlitheoir

terse *adj* gonta

test *n* promhadh, tástáil, triail **aptitude test** tástáil inniúlachta *v* promh, tástáil, triail

test ban treaty *n* conradh coiscthe trialacha

test match n (cricket) cluiche idirnáisiúnta (cruicéid)

testament n tiomna, uacht

tester n tástálaí **lipstick tester** tástálaí béaldatha

testicle n magairle

testify v fianaise a thabhairt

testimony n fianaise, teist, teistiméireacht

test-tube n promhadán

test-tube baby n leanbh promhadáin

testy adj cantalach

tetanus n teiteanas

text n téacs

textbook n téacsleabhar

texture n uigeacht

than conj ná **bigger than** níos mó ná

thank v buíochas a ghabháil le **thank you (very much)** go raibh (míle) maith agat, go bhfága Dia agam thú

thankful adj buíoch

thankless adj gan bhuíochas

thanksgiving n altú

that[1] rel part, rel pron see **a**[5] and **ar**[3] in Irish-English section

that[2] conj see **go**[3], **gur**, **nach**[2] in Irish-English section

that[3] pron sin, siúd, úd **that cat** an cat sin, **that guy!** é siúd! **that house over there** an teach úd thall

thatch n tuí

thatched house n teach ceann tuí

thaw n coscairt v coscair, leáigh **it thawed** tháinig an choscairt

the def art an indef art na **the boat** an bád, **the boats** na báid, **the step** an chéim, **the steps** na céimeanna, **it's 'the' show** is é an seó is fearr amuigh é

theatre n amharclann, (operating) obrádlann

theft n gadaíocht, goid

their(s) poss adj **their house** a dteach, **their name** a n-ainm, **it's theirs** is leo é

them pron iad **I like them** is maith liom iad

theme n téama

then adv ansin **even then** ansin féin

theological adj diaga

theology n diagacht

theorem n teoirim

theoretical adj teoiriciúil

theory n teoiric

therapy n teiripe **speech therapy** teiripe urlabhra

there adv ann, ansin, ansiúd **he was there** bhí sé ann, **over there** thall ansin, **it's there** tá sé ansin

thereabouts adv timpeall (ar)

thereby adv dá bharr sin, ar an gcaoi sin

therefore adv ar an ábhar sin

thermal adj teirmeach

thermometer n teirmiméadar

thermostat n teirmeastat

thesaurus n stórchiste (focal)

these pron iad seo

thesis n tráchtas

they pron siad

thick adj tiubh, (stupid) dúr

thicken v tiubhaigh

thickness n téagar, tiús

thief n gadaí

thigh n ceathrú, más

thimble n méaracán

thin adj caol, lom, tanaí v tanaigh

thing n ní, rud

think v ceap, machnaigh, síl, smaoinigh **what do you think?** cad a cheapann tú? céard a shíleann tú? **to think of something** machnamh / smaoineamh ar rud

think-tank n buíon (na) smaointe

thinker n smaointeoir

third adj tríú

thirst n tart

thirsty *adj* tartmhar **I'm thirsty** tá tart orm

thirteen *adj* trí déag

thirtieth *adj, n* tríochadú

thirty *adj, n* tríocha

this *pron* seo **this one** an ceann seo, **this is it** seo é

thistle *n* feochadán

thorn *n* dealg

thorn bush *n* sceach

thorny *adj* deilgneach

thorough *adj* críochnúil

thoroughbred *adj* folúil *n* ainmhí folaíochta

thoroughfare *n* bealach

those *pron* iad sin

though *conj* cé go

thought *n* cuimhneamh, machnamh, smaoineamh

thoughtful *adj* machnamhach, maranach, smaointeach

thoughtless *adj* místuama

thoughtlessness *n* místuaim

thousand *n* míle **a thousand times** míle uair

thousandth *adj, n* míliú

thrash *v* leadair

thread *n* snáithe, snáth

threadbare *adj* smolchaite

threat *n* bagairt

threaten *v* bagair

three *n* trí **three people** triúr

three-dimensional *adj* tríthoiseach

three-legged *adj* tríchosach

threshold *n* tairseach

thrift *n* tíos

thrifty *adj* tíosach

thrill *n* corraíl

thriller *n* **(book, film)** scéinséir

thrilling *adj* corraitheach

thrive *v* rathaigh

thriving *adj* rafar

throat *n* scornach, sceadamán

throb *n, v* preab

thrombosis *n* trombóis

throne *n* ríchathaoir

throng *n* slua *v* cruinnigh, plódaigh

throttle *n, v* scóig

through *prep* trí

throughout *prep* ar fud, i rith

throw *n* caitheamh *v* caith, teilg **throw up** caith aníos

thrush *n* **(infection)** béal salach, truis, **(bird)** smólach

thrust *n* sá, ropadh *v* rop, sáigh

thud *n* tuairt

thug *n* maistín

thuggery *n* maistíneacht

thumb *n* ordóg **under her thumb** faoi ghad aici

thump *n* tailm *v* tuairteáil

thunder *n* toirneach **thunder and lightning** toirneach agus splancacha

thunderbolt *n* caor thine

thunderclap *n* rois toirní

thunderstorm *n* spéirling

thundery *adj* toirniúil

Thursday *n* Déardaoin **on Thursday** Déardaoin

thus *adv* mar seo, amhlaidh

thyme *n* tím

tick[1] *n* **(blood-sucking)** sceartán

tick[2] *n* tic *v* **tick the appropriate box** cuir tic sa bhosca cuí

ticket *n* ticéad

tickle *n* cigilt *v* cigil

ticklish *adj* cigilteach

tidal *adj* taoidmhear **tidal wave** tonn taoide

tide *n* taoide

tidings *n* scéala

tidy *adj* deismir, slachtmhar, triopallach **to tidy up** slacht a chur ar

tie[1] *n* ceangal *v* ceangail

tie[2] *n* carbhat **bow tie** carbhat cuachóige

tied *adj* ceangailte

tier *n* sraith

tiger *n* tíogar

tight *adj* docht, teann **tight grip** greim an fhir bháite

tights *pl* riteoga

tighten *v* teann

tightness *n* teannas

tightrope *n* téad rite

tightrope walker *n* téadchleasaí

tile *n* slinn, tíl

till[1] *v* saothraigh **to till the land** an talamh a shaothrú

till[2] *n* **(cash)** scipéad

till[3] *prep* go **to fight till death** troid go bás

tilt *n* claonadh *v* claon

timber *n* adhmad

time *n* am, aimsir, aga, uain, tráth, taca *v* tomhais **the time** an t-am, **what time is it?** cén t-am é? **teatime** am tae, **bedtime** am luí, **quitting time** am scoir, **on time** in am, **at the proper time** in am trátha, **pastime** caitheamh aimsire, **I spent some time there** chaith mé seal ann, **by this time** faoin am seo, **to kill time** am a mheill, **time up!** tá an t-am istigh! **a word in time** focal i dtráth, **when you get time for it** nuair a gheobhaidh tú aga/uain chuige, **about this time last year** um an dtaca seo anuraidh

time-limit *n* teorainn ama

timely *adj* tráthúil

timer *n* amadóir

timetable *n* clár ama, amchlár

timid *adj* faiteach, scáfar

tin *n* stán **tin can** canna stáin

tinge *n* imir *v* cuir imir i

tingle *n* drithlín

tinkle *n, v* cling

tinned *adj* stánaithe **tinned food** bia stánaithe

tin-opener *n* stánosclóir

tinsel *n* tinsil

tint *n* imir *v* cuir imir i

tiny *adj* bídeach

tip[1] *n* **(peak)** rinn

tip[2] *n* **(money)** síneadh láimhe, seachadadh láimhe **tips** síntí / seachadtaí láimhe

tip[3] *v* buail go héadrom, **(rubbish)** dumpáil

Tipperary *n* Tiobraid Árann **Co. Tipperary Co.** Thiobraid Árann

tipsy *adj* súgach

tire *v* tuirsigh

tired *adj* tuirseach **I'm tired** tá tuirse orm

tiredness *n* tuirse

tireless *adj* dothuirsithe

tiresome *adj* tuirsiúil

tiring *adj* tuirsiúil

tissue *n* fíochán, uige, **(paper)** ciarsúr páipéir **a tissue of lies** gréasán bréag

tit *n* **(bird)** meantán

title *n* teideal

to *prep* go (dtí), chuig, chun, do **she went to the pictures** chuaigh/d'imigh sí go dtí an phictiúrlann, chuig an bpictiúrlann, chun na pictiúrlainne, **I gave it to you already** thug mé cheana duit é

toast[1] *n* **(cheers)** sláinte

toast[2] *n* **(bread)** tósta *v* tóstáil

toaster *n* tóstaer

tobacco *n* tobac

tobacconist *n* tobacadóir

toboggan *n* carr sleamhnáin

today *adv* inniu

toddler *n* lapadán, tachrán

toe *n* méar coise, ladhar **little toe** lúidín, **big toe** ordóg na coise, an ladhar mhór

toffee *n* taifí

together *adv* in éineacht, le chéile

toil *n* dua *v* saothraigh

toilet *n* leithreas, teach an asail

token *n* éarlais **book token** éarlais leabhair

tolerance *n* lamháltas

tolerant *adj* fulangach

tolerate *v* fulaing

toll *n* dola **toll bridge** droichead dola

tomato *n* tráta

tomato juice *n* sú trátaí

tomb *n* tuama

tomboy *n* cailín báire, Muireann i mbríste

tombstone *n* tuama, leac uaighe

tomorrow *adv* amárach **tomorrow morning** maidin amárach, **the day after tomorrow** amanathar, arú amárach

ton *n* tonna

tone *n* ton

tongs *n* teanchair, tlú

tongue *n* teanga **she was tongue-tied** ramhraigh an teanga ina béal

tongue-twister *n* rabhlóg

tonic *adj, n* athbhríoch **gin and tonic** jin agus athbhríoch

tonight *adv* anocht **tonight's programmes** cláir na hoíche anocht

tonsil *n* céislín

tonsilitis *n* céislínteas

too *adv* (**also**) leis, freisin, fosta, (**too much**) ró- **too much / many** an-iomad, an-iomarca, barraíocht

tool *n* uirlis, acra

tooth *n* déad, fiacail **false teeth** fiacla bréige

toothache *n* tinneas fiacaile

toothpaste *n* taos fiacla

top *n* barr, mullach, uachtar **on top of one another** i mullach a chéile

topic *n* ábhar

topical *adj* ábhartha, comhaimseartha

torch *n* tóirse

torment *n* ciapadh, crá *v* ciap, cráigh

tormented *adj* ciaptha, céasta, cráite

tornado *n* tornádó

torpedo *n* toirpéad

torpedo boat *n* bád toirpéid

torrent *n* caise

torso *n* cabhail

tortoise *n* toirtís

torture *n* céasadh *v* céas

toss *n* caitheamh san aer *v* caith san aer

total *adj* iomlán

totally *adv* go huile (is go hiomlán)

touch *n* tadhall *v* teagmhaigh do **touch of humour** iarracht den ghreann, **to put the finishing touches to something** an dlaoi / dlaíóg mhullaigh a chur ar rud

touch-down *n* (**landing**) tuirlingt, (**sport**) talmhú

touching *adj* corraitheach

touchy *adj* goilliúnach, nimhneach, tógálach

tough *adj* righin

toughen *v* righnigh

toughness *n* righneas

tour *n* turas

tourism *n* turasóireacht

tourist *n* cuairteoir, turasóir

tournament *n* ilchomórtas

towards *prep* chun, i dtreo, faoi dhéin

towel *n* tuáille

tower *n* túr *v* seas go hard (os cionn)

town *n* baile mór

townland *n* baile fearainn

toxic *adj* tocsaineach **toxic waste** dramhaíl thocsaineach

toxin *n* tocsain

toy *n* bréagán, áilleagán *v* bheith ag súgradh le rud

toyboy *n* staillín

trace *n* lorg, rian *v* rianaigh

tracer bullet *n* rianphiléar

tracing-paper *n* rianpháipéar

track *n* lorg, raon *v* dul sa tóir ar

tracksuit *n* raonchulaith

traction *n* tarraingt

tractor *n* tarracóir

trade *n* **(profession)** ceird, tráchtáil, trádáil *v* trádáil

trade-in *n* trádáil isteach **to trade in** trádáil isteach

trade-mark *n* trádmharc

trader *n* trádálaí

trading *n* trádáil **insider trading** trádáil taobh istigh

tradition *n* nós, traidisiún **oral tradition** *n* traidisiún béil

traditional *adj* traidisiúnta **traditional unaccompanied singing** amhránaíocht ar an sean-nós

traffic *n* trácht **peak-hour traffic** trácht buaicuaire

traffic jam *n* plódú tráchta

trafficker *n* gáinneálaí

trafficking *n* gáinneáil **drug-trafficking** gáinneáil drugaí

traffic-lights *pl* soilse tráchta

traffic warden *n* maor tráchta

tragedy *n* tragóid, **(theatre)** traigéide

tragic *adj* taismeach, tragóideach

trail *n* rian

trailer *n* leantóir

trailing *adj* streachlánach

train[1] *n* sraith, **(locomotive)** traein

train[2] *v* traenáil, oil

trained *adj* oilte, traenáilte

trainee *n* foghlaimeoir

trainer *n* traenálaí

training *n* oilteacht, traenáil

train station *n* stáisiún traenach

trait *n* tréith

traitor *n* fealltóir, tréatúir

tram *n* tram

tramp *n* fear siúil *v* siúil go trom (ar)

trample *n* satail

trampoline *n* trampailín

trance *n* támh, támhnéal **he is in some sort of trance** tá sé i dtámh éigin, **I was put in a trance** cuireadh i dtámhnéal mé

tranquil *adj* suaimhneach

tranquility *n* suaimhneas

tranquilliser *n* suaimhneasán, suanán

transaction *n* beart, idirbheart

transatlantic *adj* trasatlantach

transcribe *v* athscríobh

transfer *n* aistriú *v* aistrigh

transformation *n* athchuma

transformed *adj* athraithe

transformer *n* claochladán

transfusion *n* **(blood)** fuilaistriú

transgress *v* sáraigh

transient *adj* neamhbhuan

transistor *n* trasraitheoir

transit *n* **in transit** faoi bhealach

transition *n* athrú

transitional *adj* idirthréimhseach

transition year *n* idirbhliain **transition year options** roghanna na hidirbhliana

transitive *adj* aistreach

translate *v* tiontaigh, aistrigh

translation *n* aistriú, aistriúchán

translator *n* aistritheoir

transmission *n* tarchur

transmission breakdown *n* teip tarchuir

transmit *n* tarchuir **sexually transmitted disease** galar gnéas-tarchurtha

transmittor *n* tarchuradóir

transparency *n* trédhearcacht

transparent *adj* trédhearcach

transpire *v* tit amach

transplant *n* nódú *v* athphlandaigh, nódaigh

transport *n* iompar *v* iompair

trap *n* sás, gaiste *v* sáinnigh **mouse-trap** sás luiche

trap-door *n* comhla thógála

trappings *pl* feisteas

trauma *n* tráma

traumatic experience *n* eachtra thrámach

travail *n* tiaráil

travel *n* taisteal *v* triall, taistil

traveller *n* taistealaí

travelling *n* taisteal **the Travelling Community** an Lucht Taistil

trawler *n* trálaer

tray *n* tráidire

treacherous *adj* cealgach, fealltach

treachery *n* tréatúireacht, cealg, feall

treacle *n* triacla

tread *v* siúil

treason *n* tréatúireacht, tréas

treasonable *adj* tréasach

treasure *n* ciste, stór, taisce

treasure chest *n* araid seod / mhaoine

treasure hunt *n* tóraíocht taisce

treasurer *n* cisteoir, sparánaí

treasury *n* ciste an stáit

treat *n* féasta *v* **she treated me well** chaith sí go maith liom

treatment *n* cóireáil **medical treatment** cóir leighis, cóireáil mhíochaine

treaty *n* conradh

tree *n* crann **evergreen tree** crann síorghlas

tree trunk *n* lomán

trek *n* aistear

tremble *n* creathán *v* crcatlınaigh, crith

trembling *adj* creathánach

tremendous *adj* ar fheabhas, iontach

tremor *n* creathán

trench *n* díog, trinse

trend *n* nós, treocht

trespass *n* treaspás *v* treaspás a dhéanamh

trespassers *pl* lucht treaspáis

tress *n* cuach, trilseán

trial *n* tástáil, triail

triangle *n* triantán

triangular *adj* triantánach

tribe *n* treibh

tribulation *n* dólás

tribunal *n* binse fiosraithe **the Beef Tribunal** Binse Fiosraithe na Mairteola, **the Payments to Politicians Tribunal** an Binse Fiosraithe um Íocaíochtaí do Pholaiteoirí

tributary *n* craobh-abhainn

tribute *n* ómós

trick *n* cleas **to play a trick on** cleas a imirt ar

trickery *n* cleasaíocht

trickster *n* cleasaí

tricky *adj* cleasach, casta

tricolour *adj, n* trídhathach

tricycle *n* trírothach

trifle[1] *n* mionrud

trifle[2] *n* **(dessert)** traidhfil

trigger *n* truicear

trilogy *n* triólóg

trim *adj* slachtmhar *v* bearr

trimmings *n* **(cooking)** anlann

trinket *n* áilleagán

trio *n* tríréad

trip[1] *v* tuisligh **to trip someone** tuisle a bhaint as duine

trip[2] *n* **(journey)** geábh, turas

triple *adj* triarach

triplet *n* trírín

tripod *n* tríchosach

triumph *n* bua *v* buaigh

triumphant *adj* caithréimeach

trivial *adj* suarach, neafaiseach

triviality *n* suarachas, neafais

trolley *n* trucail, tralaí

trombone *n* trombón

troop *n* díorma, trúpa

trophy *n* comhramh, trófaí

tropic *n* trópaic **the Tropics** an Teochrios, na Trópaicí

tropical *adj* teochriosach, trópaiceach

tropical rainforest *n* foraois theochriosach/thrópaiceach bháistí

trot *n* sodar *v* bheith ag sodar

trouble *n* trioblóid *v* buair

troubled *adj* buartha, imníoch

troublemaker *n* clampróir

troublesome *adj* crosta, trioblóideach

trough *n* losaid, trach, umar

trousers *n* bríste, treabhsar, triús

trout *n* breac

trowel *n* lián

truant *n* múitseálaí **to play truant** múitseáil a dhéanamh

truce *n* sos cogaidh

truck *n* trucail **articulated truck** trucail altach

truculent *adj* colgach

trudge *v* spágáil

true *adj* fíor

truly *adv* go fíor

trump *n* **(card)** mámh

trumpet *n* trumpa

trunk *n* cabhail, trunc

trust *n* iontaoibh, muinín, **(legal)** iontaobhas **I don't trust them** níl aon mhuinín/iontaoibh agam astu

trustee *n* iontaobhaí

trusting *adj* muiníneach

trustworthy *adj* iontaofa

truth *n* fíor, fírinne **the truth hurts** bíonn an fhírinne searbh

truthful *adj* fírinneach

try[1] *n* **(rugby)** úd

try[2] *v* triail **I'm trying to concentrate** táim ag iarraidh m'aigne a chruinniú

trying *adj* duamhar

T-shirt *n* T-léine

T-square *n* T-chearnóg

tub *n* dabhach, tobán

tube *n* feadán, píobán, tiúb **fallopian tube** feadán fallópach

tube repair *n* tiúbdheisiú

tube repair patch *n* paiste tiúbdheisithe

tuberculosis (TB) *n* eitinn

tuberous root *n* meacan

Tuesday *n* Máirt, Dé Máirt **on Tuesday** Dé Máirt

tuft *n* dlaoi, dos, dual, tom

tug *n* **(boat)** tuga

tug of war *n* tarraingt téide

tuition *n* teagasc

tulip *n* tiúilip

tumble *n* titim *v* tit

tumbler *n* **(glass)** timbléar

tumbler drier *n* triomadóir rothlaim

tumult *n* callán

tumultuous *adj* callánach

tuna *n* truinnín

tune *n* fonn, port, tiúin **signature tune** port aitheantais, **to be in tune with** bheith i dtiúin le

tuneful *adj* ceolmhar

tuner *n* tiúnóir

tunic *n* tuineach

tunnel *n* tollán

turbulence *n* sruthlam

turbulent *adj* sruthlamach

turf *n* móin

Turkey *n* an Tuirc

turkey *n* turcaí

Turkish *adj* Turcach *n* **(language)** an Tuircis

turmoil *n* racán

turn *n* casadh, iompú, tiontú *v* cas, iompaigh, tiontaigh **to turn around** casadh/iompú/tiontú timpeall, **it's your turn** is é do sheal/d'uain é, **we'll take it in turns** déanfaimid sealaíocht/uainíocht air/leis

turning *n* tiontú

turnip *n* tornapa

turnover *n* láimhdeachas **stock turnover** láimhdeachas stoic

turntable *n* caschlár

turpentine *n* tuirpintín

turquoise *n* turcaid

turtle *n* turtar

tusk *n* starrfhiacail

tussle *v* **to tussle with somebody** dul i ngleic le duine

tutor *n* oide, teagascóir *v* teagasc

tutorial *n* rang teagaisc

tweed *n* bréidín

tweezers *n* pionsúirín

twelve *adj* dó dhéag

twentieth *adj, n* fichiú

twenty *n* fiche, scór

twice *adv* dhá uair, faoi dhó

twilight *n* clapsholas, coineascar

twin *n* leathchúpla **twins** cúpla

twine *n* sreangán

twinge *n* daigh

twinkle *n* drithliú *v* drithligh

twist *n* casadh *v* cas

twitch *n* freanga **twitches of pain** freangaí tinnis

two *adj* dhá *n* dó **two people** beirt, **two black cats** dhá chat dhubha, **number two** uimhir a dó

two-faced person *n* Tadhg an dá thaobh

two-way traffic *n* trácht dháthreo

tycoon *n* **(business)** toicí

tympanum *n* tiompán

type[1] *n* cló *v* clóscríobh

type[2] *n* **(kind)** cineál, saghas, sórt

typescript *n* clóscríbhinn

typewriter *n* clóscríobhán

typewriting *n* clóscríbhneoireacht

typewritten *adj* clóscríofa

typical *adj* samplach, tipiciúil

typify *v* léirigh

typing *n* clóscríbhneoireacht

typist *n* clóscríobhaí

tyranny *n* anlathas, aintiarnas, ansmacht, tíorántacht

tyrannical *adj* anlathach, tíoránta, aintiarnúil

tyrant *n* aintiarna, tíoránach

tyre *n* bonn

Tyrone *n* Tír Eoghain **Co. Tyrone** Co. Thír Eoghain

U

ubiquitous *adj* uileláithreach

udder *n* úth

UFO *n* úfó, réad eitilte gan aithint **UFOs** úfónna

ugliness *n* gránnacht

ugly *adj* gránna, gráiniúil, míofar

uilleann pipes *pl* píb uilleann

ulcer *n* othras

Ulster *n* Ulaidh **(the province of) Ulster** Cúige Uladh

Ulster epic cycle *n* an Rúraíocht

ultimate *adj* deireanach

ultra- *prefix* ultra-

ultrasound *n* ultrafhuaim

ultrasound scanning *n* scanadh ultrafhuaime

ultraviolet *adj* ultraivialait

umbilical cord *n* sreang imleacáin

umbrella *n* scáth báistí, scáth fearthainne

umpire *n* moltóir, réiteoir

un- *prefix* mí-, neamh-, do-

unable *adj* neamhábalta

unacceptable *adj* nach féidir glacadh le

unaccompanied *adj* gan tionlacan

unaccustomed *adj* neamhchleachtach

unaffected *adj* simplí

unanimous *adj* d'aon ghuth

unanimity *n* aontacht

unanimously *adv* d'aon ghuth

unattractive *adj* míthaitneamhach, gránna, míofar

unauthorised *adj* neamhúdaraithe

unavoidable *adj* dosheachanta

unbalanced *adj* míchothrom

unbearable *adj* dofhulaingthe

unbeatable *adj* dosháraithe

unbelievable *adj* dochreidte

unbeliever *n* neamhchreidmheach

unbelieving *adj* neamhchreidmheach

unbreakable *adj* dobhriste

uncanny *adj* diamhair

uncertain *adj* éiginnte, neamhchinnte

uncertainty *n* éiginnteacht, neamhchinnteacht

uncharitable *adj* neamhcharthanach

uncle *n* uncail

unclean *adj* neamhghlan

uncomfortable *adj* míchompordach

uncommon *adj* neamhchoitianta, neamhghnách

uncompromising *adj* neamhghéilliúil

unconscious *adj* neamhaireachtálach

unconcerned *adj* neamhchúiseach

unconditional *adj* neamhchoinníollach

uncontrollable *adj* doshrianta, dosmachtaithe

uncooked *adj* amh

uncouth *adj* cábógach

undecided *adj* idir dhá chomhairle

undeniable *adj* doshéanta

under *prep* faoi **under discussion** idir chamáin, **under arms** faoi arm

undercoat *n* **(painting)** fo-bhrat

undercurrent *n* foshruth

undergraduate *n* fochéimí

underground *adv* faoi thalamh

undergrowth *n* scrobarnach

underhand dealings *pl* uisce faoi thalamh

underline *v* líne a chur faoi

undermine *v* bain faoi (rud), bonn a bhaint ó (rud)

underpants *pl* fobhríste

underpass *n* fobhealach

understand *v* tuig **easily understood** sothuigthe, **it's difficult to understand them** is deacair iad a thuiscint, tá sé doiligh iad a thuigbheáil

understandable *adj* intuigthe

understanding *adj* tuisceanach *n* tuiscint

undertake *v* tabhair faoi, tóg ar **to undertake to do something** rud a thógáil ort féin

undertaker *n* adhlacóir

undertaking *n* gnóthas **joint undertaking** gnóthas comhpháirteach

underwater *adj* faoi uisce **underwater shooting (of filming)** scannánú faoi uisce

underwear *n* fo-éadach

underwriter *n* frithgheallaí

undeveloped *adj* neamhfhorbartha

undivided *adj* gan roinnt

undoubtedly *adv* gan amhras

undress *v* éadach a bhaint

undulating *adj* droimneach, tonnúil, altach

unearthly *adj* neamhshaolta

unease *n* anbhuaine

uneasy *adj* míshocair

unemployed *adj* dífhostaithe **the unemployed** lucht dífhostaíochta

unemployment *n* dífhostaíocht

unending *adj* gan deireadh

uneven *adj* éagothrom, anacair

unevenness *adj* éagothroime, anacair

unexpectedly *adv* gan choinne, go tobann

unfair *adj* éagothrom

unfaithful *adj* mídhílis

unfeeling *adj* fuarchroíoch

unfinished *adj* neamhchríochnaithe

unfold *v* oscail amach, tar chun solais

unforeseeable circumstances *pl* imthosca narbh fhéidir a thuar

unforeseen *adj* gan choinne, gan súil (leis)

unforgettable *adj* dodhearmadta

unforgivable *adj* do-mhaite

unfortunate *adj* mí-ámharach, mífhortúnach

unfortunately *adv* ar an drochuair

unfriendly *adj* eascairdiúil, míchairdiúil

ungainly *adj* liopasta

ungrateful *adj* míbhuíoch, neamhbhuíoch

unhappiness *n* míshonas

unhappy *adj* míshona

unhealthy *adj* mífholláin

uni- *prefix* aon-

unicorn *n* aonbheannach

uniform[1] *adj* aonfhoirmeach, aonghnéitheach

uniform[2] *n* **(school)** éide

unify *v* aontaigh

unilateral *adj* aontaobhach

unimportant *adj* neamhthábhachtach

uninhabited *adj* neamháitrithe

unintelligible *adj* dothuigthe

uninteresting *adj* neamhshuimiúil, neamhspéisiúil

union *n* aontacht, aontas, ceardchumann **union dues** dleachtanna ceardchumainn, **the European Union (EU)** an tAontas Eorpach (AE)

unionist *n* aontachtaí

unique *adj* uathúil

uniqueness *n* uathúlacht

unisexual *adj* aonghnéasach

unit *n* aonad **Intensive Care Unit (ICU)** Aonad Dianchúraim

unite *v* aontaigh

united *adj* aontaithe **the United States** na Stáit Aontaithe

unity *n* aontacht

universal *adj* uilechoiteann, uilíoch **universal decimal classification** aicmiú deachúil uilíoch

universe *n* cruinne

university *n* ollscoil **University College, Dublin** an Coláiste Ollscoile, Baile Átha Cliath

university education *n* ollscolaíocht

unjust *adj* éagórach

unkind *adj* míchineálta

unknown *adj* anaithnid

unlawful *adj* mídhleathach

unleaded *adj* saor ó luaidhe

unless *conj* mura **unless I am mistaken** mura bhfuil dearmad orm, **unless it was that one** murabh é an ceann sin é

unlike *adj* neamhchosúil

unlikely *adj* neamhdhóchúil

unload *v* díluchtaigh

unlucky *adj* mí-ámharach
unmanageable *adj* docheansaithe
unnatural *adj* mínádúrtha
unnecessary *adj* neamhriachtanach, gan ghá
unobtainable *adj* do-fhaighte
unofficial *adj* neamhoifigiúil
unpleasant *adj* míthaitneamhach
unprofitable *adj* éadairbheach
unqualified *adj* neamhcháilithe
unravel *v* scaoil, réitigh, rois
unravelling *n* scaoileadh the
  unravelling of the plot scaoileadh na snaidhme
unreal *adj* bréagach
unreasonable *adj* míréasúnta
unreliable statement *n* ráiteas gan údar
unrest *n* neamhshocracht, **(trouble)** achrann
unripe *adj* neamhaibí, anabaí
unruly *adj* doriartha, mírialta
unsafe *adj* contúirteach, baolach
unsatisfactory *adj* míshásúil
unscrupulous *adj* neamhscrupallach
unselfish *adj* neamhleithleach
unsettled *adj* corrach, **(of person)** aistreach
unsightly *adj* gránna
unsociable *adj* dochaideartha
unspeakable *adj* dolabhartha
unstable *adj* míshocair, éagobhsaí
unsteady *adj* corrach, neamhsheasmhach
unsuitable *adj* mí-oiriúnach, mífheiliúnach
unsuccessful *adj* mírathúil
untameable *adj* docheansaithe
untidy *adj* liopasta, míshlachtmhar, sraoilleach, amscaí
until *prep* go, go dtí
untimely *adj* antráthach, míthráthúil
untold *adj* do-inste

untrue *adj* bréagach
unused *adj* díomhaoin
unusual *adj* éagoiteann, iontach, neamhghnách, annamh
unwelcoming *adj* doicheallach
unwell *adj* breoite, gan a bheith ar fónamh
unwilling *adj* neamhthoilteanach
unwise *adj* éigríonna
unworkable *adj* do-oibrithe
unworldly *adj* neamhshaolta
unworthy *adj* neamhfhiúntach
unyielding *adj* dolúbtha
up *adv* thuas, suas, aníos **she is up in the attic** tá sí thuas sa lochta, **to go up a ladder** dul suas dréimire, **to come up the stairs** teacht aníos an staighre
upbringing *n* tógáil
upper *adj* uachtarach
upper class *adj* uasaicmeach *n* uasaicme
upper part *n* uachtar
upright *adj* ionraic
uprising *n* éirí amach **the Easter Rising** Éirí Amach na Cásca
uproar *n* raic, rírá
uproot *v* stoith
upset *adj* suaite *n* múisiam **it upset me greatly** ghoill sé go mór orm
upstairs *adv* thuas (an) staighre **to go upstairs** dul suas (an) staighre
upstart *n* fáslach
upwards *adv* aníos, suas, in airde
urban *adj* uirbeach
urge *n* fonn *v* spreag
urgency *n* práinn
urgent *adj* práinneach **most urgent need** an gad is gaire don scornach
urinate *v* mún
urine *n* fual, mún
urn *n* próca
us *pron* muid, muidne, sinn, sinne

use *n* feidhm, gar *v* ídigh, úsáid **to use something** feidhm a bhaint as rud, úsáid a bhaint as rud, **in use** in úsáid, **there's no use in complaining** níl gar i ngearán

useful *adj* áisiúil, tairbheach, úsáideach

usefulness *n* úsáidí

useless *adj* gan mhaith, gan tairbhe, beagmhaitheasach

user *n* úsáideoir

user friendly *adj* feidhmchúntach

U-shaped *adj* U-chruthach

usual *adj* iondúil, nósmhar

usually *adv* de ghnáth, go hiondúil

usurpation *n* anlathas

utensils *pl* acraí

uterus *n* útaras

utility *n* fóntas, áisiúlacht **public utility** fóntas poiblí

utopia *n* útóipe

utter[1] *adj* dearg **utter shame** deargnáire

utter[2] *v* **don't utter a word** ná habair focal

U-turn *n* U-chasadh

V

vacancy *n* folúntas

vacant *adj* folamh

vacate *v* éirigh as

vacation *n* saoire

vaccination *n* vacsaíniú

vaccine *n* vacsaín

vacuum *n* folús

vacuum-cleaner *n* folúsghlantóir

vagabond *n* ruagaire reatha

vagina *n* faighin

vagrant *n* seachránaí, fánaí

vague *adj* éiginnte, doiléir

vagueness *n* éiginnteacht, doiléire

vain *adj* baoth **in vain** in aisce

vale *n* gleann

valentine *n* vailintín **valentine card** cárta lá Fhéile Vailintín, **St Valentine's Day** Lá Fhéile Vailintín

valiant *adj* galach, gaisciúil

valid *adj* bailí

validity *n* bailíocht

valley *n* gleann

valour *n* gaisce, gal, laochas

valuable *adj* luachmhar

valuation *n* luacháil

value *n* luach *v* luacháil

valve *n* comhla **safety valve** comhla sceite

vampire *n* vaimpír

van *n* veain

vandal *n* loitiméir

vandalism *n* loitiméireacht

vanguard *n* urgharda

vanilla *n* fanaile

vanish *v* dul as radharc, ceiliúir

vanity *n* díomhaointeas, móráil

vapour *n* gal

variable *adj* claochlaitheach *n* athróg **variable component** comhpháirt inathraithe

variant *adj* athraitheach *n* athróg

variation *n* athrúchán

varicose *adj* borrtha **varicose vein** féith bhorrtha

varied *adj* ilchineálach

variety *n* éagsúlacht

various *adj* éagsúil

varnish *n* vearnais

vary *v* athraigh, éagsúlaigh

vase *n* vása
vasectomy *n* feadánghearradh
vaseline *n* veasailín
vast *adj* uafásach **vast amount (of people)** an t-uafás (daoine)
vat *n* dabhach
VAT *n* CBL (cáin bhreisluacha)
Vatican *n* an Vatacáin
vault *n* tuama
veal *n* laofheoil
veer *n* fiar *v* claon
vegetable *n* glasra
vegetal *adj* plandúil
vegetarian *adj* feoilséantach *n* feoilséantóir, veigeatóir
vegetarian diet *n* aiste bia fheoilshéantaigh
vegetarianism *n* veigeatóireachas
vegetation *n* fásra
vehicle *n* feithicil
veil *n* caille
vein *n* cuisle, féith
velvet *n* veilbhit
vending machine *n* meaisín díola
vendor *n* díoltóir, reacaire
veneer *n* athchraiceann
venerate *v* tabhair urraim do
vengeance *n* díoltas
vengeful *adj* díoltasach
Venice *n* an Veinéis
venison *n* fiafheoil, oiseoil
venom *n* goimh, nimh
venomous *adj* goimhiúil
vent *n* gaothaire *v* **to vent one's feelings** do racht a ligean amach
ventilation *n* aeráil
ventilator *n* aerálóir
ventriloquist *n* bolgchainteoir
venture *n* fiontar, amhantar *v* tabhair faoi
venue *n* ionad
Venus *n* Véineas

vernacular *adj* dúchasach *n* teanga dhúchais
verb *n* briathar
verbal *adj* briathartha
verbose *adj* briathrach
verdict *n* breithiúnas
verge *n* bruach, imeall
verification *n* fíorú
verify *v* fíoraigh
vermin *n* míolra
versatile *adj* ildánach, iltréitheach
verse *n* rann, véarsa, **(in general)** véarsaíocht
version *n* leagan
versus *prep* i gcoinne, in aghaidh
vertebral *adj* veirteabrach **vertebral column** colún veirteabrach
vertical *adj* ingearach, ceartingearach *n* ingear
vertiginous *adj* meadhránach
vertigo *n* meadhrán
very *adj* fíor-, iontach, an-, rí-
very high frequency (VHF) *n* ardmhinicíocht
vessel *n* soitheach, árthach
vest *n* veist **bullet-proof vest** veist philéardhíonach
vestige *n* rian
vet *n* tréidlia
veteran *n* seanfhondúir, seansaighdiúir
veterinary medicine *n* tréidliacht
veterinary surgeon *n* tréidlia
via *prep* bealach **via Dundrum** bealach Dhún Droma
viable *adj* inmharthana
viaduct *n* tarbhealach
vibrant *adj* tonnchreathach, **(of colour)** glé
vibrate *v* tonnchrith
vibrating *adj* creathach
vibration *n* tonnchrith
vicarious *adj* ionadach

vice[1] n **(immoral)** duáilce, **(tool)** bís **hand vice** bís láimhe

vice[2] *prefix* leas **vice-president** leasuachtarán

vice grip n teanchair bísghreama, bísghreamán

viceroy n leasrí

vicinity n comharsanacht

vicious *adj* drochmhúinte **vicious animal** ainmhí mallaithe

vicious circle n ciorcal lochtach

victim n **(of sacrifice)** íobartach

victor n buaiteoir

victory n bua

video n **(tape)** fístéip

video camera n físcheamara

video(cassette) recorder n fístaifeadán

videoconferencing n físchomhdháil

video film n fís-scannán

Vietnam n Vítneam **the Vietnam War** Cogadh Vítneam

Vietnamese *adj, n* Vítneamach n **(language)** an Vítneamais

view n amharc, radharc, **(outlook)** dearcadh v breathnaigh

vigilant *adj* airdeallach

vigorous *adj* fuinniúil

vigour n athbhrí, spionnadh, fuinneamh

Viking *adj, n* Lochlannach

vile *adj* táir

village n sráidbhaile

villain n cladhaire

vindictive *adj* díoltasach

vine n fíniúin

vinegar n fínéagar

vineyard n fíniúin, fíonghort

vinyl n vinil

viola n vióla

violate v éignigh, réab, sáraigh

violator n éigneoir

violence n foréigean, forneart

violent *adj* foréigneach

violet *adj, n* **(colour)** corcairghorm n **(flower)** sailchuach

violin n veidhlín

violinist n veidhleadóir

virgin n maighdean, ógh

virginity n maighdeanas, ócht

Virgin Mary n an Mhaighdean Mhuire

Virgo n an Mhaighdean

virile *adj* fearúil

virtual reality n réaltacht fhíorúil

virtue n suáilce

virtuous *adj* suáilceach

virulent *adj* nimhiúil

virus n víreas

visa n víosa

visa card n cárta víosa

visibility n infheictheacht, léargas

visible *adj* infheicthe, sofheicthe

vision n aisling, fís, radharc

visionary *adj* aislingeach

visit n cuairt v cuairt a thabhairt

visiting n cuartaíocht

visitor n cuairteoir

visor n scáthlán **sun visor** scáthlán gréine

visual *adj* radharcach

visualise v samhlaigh

vital *adj* riachtanach

vitality n beogacht

vitals *pl* baill bheatha

vitamin n vitimín

vivacious *adj* bíogúil

vivid *adj* glé

vivisection n beodhioscadh

vocabulary n foclóir

vocal cords *pl* téada an ghutha

vocation n gairm

vocational *adj* gairmiúil, gairm-

vocational education n gairmoideachas

vocational school n gairmscoil

vocative adj, n gairmeach

vodka n vadca

voice n glór, guth, **(grammar)** faí
v nocht

voice mail n glórphost

void adj ar neamhní n folús

volatile adj luaineach

volcano n bolcán **active volcano**
bolcán beo, **extinct volcano**
bolcán marbh, **passive volcano**
bolcán suaimhneach, **dormant**
volcano bolcán suanach

volley n **(sport)** eitleog, **(bullets)** rois

volleyball n eitpheil

volt n volta

voltage n voltas

voltmeter n voltmhéadar

voluble adj líofa

volume[1] n **(of book)** imleabhar

volume[2] n **(mass)** toirt, **(of noise)**
airde

voluntary adj deonach, toilteanach

volunteer[1] n óglach **the Irish**
Volunteers Óglaigh na hÉireann

volunteer[2] n **(worker)** oibrí
deonach

voluptuous adj macnasach

vomit n urlacan, múisc, aiseag
v urlaic, cuir amach

voracious adj alpach

voracity n ampla

vortex n cuilithe

vote n vóta v vóta a chaitheamh
casting vote vóta réitigh

voter n vótálaí

voting n vótáil

voucher n dearbhán **luncheon**
voucher dearbhán lóin

vow n móid v móidigh

vowel n guta

voyage n aistear farraige

vulgar adj gáirsiúil, graosta

vulnerable adj soghonta

vulture n badhbh, bultúr

W

wade v siúil

wafer n abhlann

wag v croith **wagging its tail** ag
croitheadh a eircabaill

wage[1] n pá **wages** pá

wage[2] v fear

wager n geall

wagon n vaigín

wagtail n glasóg

wail n olagón v olagón a dhéanamh

waist n coim

waistcoat n vástchóta, veist

wait n feitheamh v fan **wait for** fan le

waiter n freastalaí

waiting-list n liosta feithimh

waiting-room n seomra feithimh

waive v tarscaoil **to waive your**
rights do chearta a tharscaoileadh

wake[1] v dúisigh, múscail

wake[2] n faire, tórramh

Wales n an Bhreatain Bheag

walk n siúl, siúlóid v siúil

walker n siúlóir

walkie-talkie n siúlscéalaí

walk-in centre n ionad siúil isteach

wall n balla, claí, múr **stone wall** claí
cloch

walled adj caisealta **walled**
enclosure bábhún

wall-cupboard n almóir

wallet *n* tiachóg

wallow *v* iomlaisc

wallowing *n* únfairt

walnut *n* gallchnó

walrus *n* rosualt

waltz *n* válsa *v* válsáil

wand *n* slat draíochta

wandering *adj* strae, fánach
n fánaíocht

want[1] *n* uireasa, ceal

want[2] *v* teastaigh **what does she
want?** cad a theastaíonn uaithi?
céard atá uaithi? **I don't want any
more** níl a thuilleadh uaim

wanting *adj* in easnamh, uireasach

wantonness *n* macnas

war *n* cogadh

war-cry *n* rosc catha

ward[1] *n* (law) coimircí

ward[2] *n* barda, aireagal

warden *n* maor

wardrobe *n* vardrús

warehouse *n* trádstóras **wholesale
warehouse** trádstóras mórdhíola

warfare *n* cogaíocht

wariness *n* airdeall, faichill

warm *adj* te *v* téigh **to warm
yourself** do ghoradh a dhéanamh

warming *n* goradh

warmth *n* teas

warn *v* fainic a chur ar dhuine

warning *n* rabhadh, foláireamh,
fainic

warning signal *n* rabhchán

warp *n* freangadh *v* stang, freang

warrant *n* barántas **arrest warrant**
barántas gabhála

warranty *n* barántas **three-year
warranty** barántas trí bliana

warren *n* coinicéar

warrior *n* laoch, gaiscíoch

warship *n* long chogaidh, soitheach
cogaidh

wart *n* faithne

wary *adj* airdeallach, seachantach

wash *n* folcadh *v* nigh **mouth-wash**
folcadh béil

washable *adj* in-nite

washbasin *n* doirteal

washer *n* niteoir

washing *n* ní, níochán, **washing
machine** meaisín níocháin,
washing powder púdar níocháin

wasp *n* foiche, beach chapaill, beach
ghabhair

waste *n* diomailt, fuíoll, fuíollábhar
v diomail, meil, vástáil **to waste
time** am a chur amú

waste away *v* snoigh

wasted *adj* amú

wasted away *adj* snoite

wasteful *adj* diomailteach

waste-pipe *n* píobán fuíollábhair

waster *n* diomailteoir

watch[1] *n* faire, coimhéad, féachaint
v fair (ar), coimhéad, féach ar
watching television ag faire /
féachaint ar an teilifís, **to watch
over something** rud a choimhéad

watch[2] *n* uaireadóir

watcher *n* feighlí

watchfulness *n* fuireachas

watchman *n* fear faire

water *n* uisce *v* uiscigh

watercolour *n* uiscedhath

watercress *n* biolar

watered whiskey *n* Seán báite

waterfall *n* eas

Waterford *n* Port Láirge **Co.
Waterford** Co. Phort Láirge

watering can *n* fraschanna

waterproof *adj* uiscedhíonach

water-skiing *n* sciáil ar uisce

waterspout *n* sconna

waterway *n* uiscebhealach

watery *adj* uisciúil

watt *n* vata

wave[1] *n* tonn

wave[2] *v* lámh a chroitheadh chuig / le duine

wavelength *n* tonnfhad

wavy *adj* tonnúil

wax *n* céir *v* cuir céir ar

way[1] *n* caoi, dóigh **in a bad way** in anchaoi, i ndroch-chaoi, **you can't have it both ways** ní féidir leat an dá thrá a fhreastal

way[2] *n* bealach, slí **you're in my way** tá tú sa tslí orm, **the Milky Way** Bealach na Bó Finne

we *pron* muid, muidne, sinn, sinne

weak *adj* lag, lagbhríoch, tláith, anbhann

weak tea *n* anglais tae, tae tanaí

weaken *v* lagaigh

weakling *n* meatachán

weakness *n* éalang, lagar, laige

wealth *n* saibhreas, conách, éadáil, maoin, ollmhaitheas, rachmas

wealthy *adj* saibhir, rachmasach

weapon *n* arm **automatic weapon** arm uathoibreach

wear *v* caith

wear out *v* spíon, traoch

wearer *n* caiteoir

weariness *n* atuirse

weary *adj* tuirseach, atuirseach

weasel *n* easóg

weather *n* aimsir, uain **bad weather** síon, drochaimsir, doineann

weave *v* figh, sníomh

weaver *n* fíodóir

web *n* gréasán, líon, uige **worldwide web** an gréasán domhanda

web-page *n* leathanach gréasáin

website *n* láithreán gréasáin

wedding *n* bainis, pósadh **wedding ring** fáinne pósta

wedge *n*, *v* ding

wedlock *n* cuing an phósta

Wednesday *n* (Dé) Céadaoin **Ash Wednesday** Céadaoin an Luaithrigh, **on Wednesday** Dé Céadaoin

weedkiller *n* fiailnimh

weed(s) *n*, *pl* fiaile, luifearnach

week *n* seachtain **two weeks** dhá sheachtain, **three weeks** trí seachtaine

weekend *n* deireadh seachtaine

weekly *n* seachtainiúil, **(paper)** seachtanán

weep *v* caoin

weeping *n* ag sileadh (na n)deor, gol

weft *n* inneach

weigh *v* meáigh

weight *n* meáchan, tromán

weir *n* cora

weird *adj* aisteach, ait

welcome *n* fáilte *v* fáiltigh **welcome!** fáilte romhat! fáilte romhaibh!

welcoming *n* fáilteach

weld *v* táthaigh

welder *n* táthaire

welded *adj* táite

welfare *n* leas, sochar **social welfare** leas sóisialta, **social welfare benefits** sochair leasa shóisialaigh

well[1] *n* tobar

well[2] *adj* **I am not well** níl mé ar fónamh

well-appointed *adj* áirgiúil

well done! *excl* maith thú! togha fir! togha mná! bulaí fir! bulaí mná!

well-fed *adj* beathaithe

well-known *adj* clúiteach, aithnidiúil

well-mannered *n* dea-mhúinte

well off *adj* go maith as

well-wishing *adj* dea-mhéineach

west *adv* thiar, iarthar **to the west** siar, **from the west** aniar, **the west wind** an ghaoth aniar, **going**

west ag dul siar, **coming west** ag teacht anoir, **the West of Ireland** Iarthar na hÉireann

western *adj* iartharach, thiar

Westmeath *n* an Iarmhí **Co. Westmeath** Co. na hIarmhí

westwards *adv* siar

wet *adj* fliuch

Wexford *n* Loch Garman **Co. Wexford** Co. Loch Garman

whale *n* míol mór

wharf *n* cé

what *interrogative* cad? céard? cén? cé na?

whatever *pron* cibé, pé

wheat *n* cruithneacht

wheel *n* roth **spare wheel** roth breise

wheelbarrow *n* bara rotha

wheelchair *n* cathaoir rothaí

wheeziness *n* carsánacht

wheezy *adj* cársánach

when *conj* nuair *interrogative* **when?** cathain? cá huair? cén uair?

whenever *adv* pé uair, cibé uair

where *interrogative* cá? cén áit? **where is she going?** cá bhfuil a triall? cá bhfuil / cá háit a bhfuil sí / sé ag dul?

whether *conj* pé, cé acu **whether he likes it or not** pé olc maith leis é, **whether...or...** cé acu...nó...

which *interrogative* cé? cén? cé na?

whichever *adv* cibé, pé

while *n* scaitheamh, tamall, seal **for a while** ar feadh tamaill, **after a while** tar éis/i ndiaidh scaithimh, **she won't be here for another while** ní bheidh sí anseo go ceann tamaill eile

whin *n* aiteann

whine *n* geonaíl *v* geonaíl a dhéanamh

whinging *n* gluaireán

whip¹ *n* **(politics)** aoire

whip² *n* fuip, lasc *v* fuipeáil

whirlpool *n* coire guairneáin

whirlwind *n* gaoth ghuairneáin, cuaifeach

whisk *n* greadtóir *v* gread

whiskers *pl* féasóg leicinn, guairí cait

whiskey *n* fuisce, uisce beatha

whisper *n* cogar *v* rud a rá i gcogar le duine

whispering *n* cogarnach

whispering sound *n* siosarnach, seoithín

whistle *n* fead, **(instrument)** feadóg *v* fead a ligean

whistling *n* feadaíl

white *adj* bán, geal, fionn *n* **(of egg, eye)** gealacán

whiten *v* geal

whitewash *n* aoldath *v* aol

whiting *n* **(fish)** faoitín

who *interrogative* cé? *rel* a

whoever *pron* cibé ar bith, pé duine

whole *adj* iomlán, uile

wholemeal *n* caiscín

wholesale *n* mórdhíol

wholesaler *n* mórdhíoltóir **cash and carry wholesaler** mórdhíoltóir íoc is iompair

wholesome *adj* folláin

wholesomeness *n* folláine

whom *pron* cé

whooping cough *n* triuch

whose *interrogative* cé leis?

why *adv* cad ina thaobh? cad chuige? cén fáth?

wick *n* fáideog

wicked *adj* olc, mallaithe

Wicklow *n* Cill Mhantáin **Co. Wicklow** Co. Chill Mhantáin

wide *adj* fairsing, leitheadach, scóipiúil **wide open** ar leathadh

widen *v* leathnaigh

widening *n* leathnú

widespread *adj* forleathan

widow *n* baintreach

widower *n* baintreach fir

width *n* leithead

wife *n* bean (chéile)

wig *n* folt bréige

wild *adj* allta, fiáin

wilderness *n* fásach, fiántas

wildlife *n* fiadhúlra

wildness *n* alltacht, fiántas

will[1] *n* uacht, **(law)** tiomna **she left me her car in her will** d'fhág sí a carr le huacht agam

will[2] *n* toil, deoin **of her own free will** dá deoin féin

willing *adj* deonach, toilteanach, ullamh

willingness *n* toilteanas

willow *n* saileach **willow tree** crann sailí

win *v* buaigh

winch *n* cráncaid

wind[1] *v* cas, tochrais

wind[2] *n* gaoth **the east wind** an ghaoth anoir, **the west wind** an ghaoth aniar, **the north wind** an ghaoth aduaidh, **the south wind** an ghaoth aneas, **it's an ill wind that blows nobody good** is olc an ghaoth nach séideann do dhuine éigin

windfall *n* amhantar

winding *adj* casta

windmill *n* muileann gaoithe

window *n* fuinneog

windpipe *n* sciúch, sceadamán

windscreen *n* gaothscáth

windscreen wipers *pl* cuimilteoirí gaothscátha

windy *adj* gaofar

wine *n* fíon **a glass of wine** gloine fíona

wine cellar *n* siléar fíona

wineglass *n* fíonghloine

wing *n* eiteog, eite, sciathán **the Left wing** an eite chlé, **wings (of theatre)** cliatháin amharclainne

wing mirror *n* scáthán cliatháin

wing-span *n* réise sciathán

winger *n* **(sport)** cliathánaí

wink *n* caochadh *v* sméid, caoch

winner *n* buaiteoir

winter *n* geimhreadh

wipe *v* cuimil

wiper *n* cuimilteoir

wire *n* sreang, **(telegram)** sreangscéal *v* sreangaigh

wire brush *n* sreangscuab

wiring *n* sreangra, sreangú

wisdom *n* eagna, gaois, saíocht **the Book of Wisdom** Leabhar na hEagna

wisdom tooth *n* fiacail forais

wise *adj* críonna **the Three Wise Men** na Trí Fáithe

wise person *n* saoi

wish *n* toil, mian

wisp *n* dlaíóg, dlaoi, dual, sóp

witch *n* bean feasa

witchcraft *n* draíocht

with *prep* le

withdraw *v* aistarraing

withdrawal *n* aistarraingt

wither *v* feoigh

withered *adj* feoite, dóite, dreoite

withhold *v* coinnigh siar, ceil

within *adv* laistigh, istigh

without *prep* gan **without further delay** gan a thuilleadh moille

withstand *v* seas

witness *n* finné

witticism *n* léaspairt

witty *adj* deisbhéalach

wizard *n* draoi

woe *n* mairg

wolf *n* mac tíre

wolfhound *n* faolchú

woman *n* bean **good woman!** maith an bhean! togha mná! bulaí mná! **two women** beirt bhan, **three women** triúr ban

womanly *adj* banúil

womb *n* broinn **in the womb** in áras an chléibh

wonder *n* ionadh, iontas **I wonder** n'fheadar, ní mé, **no wonder** ní nach ionadh

wonderful *adj* iontach, seoigh

wood¹ *n* **(general)** adhmad

wood² *n* **(forest)** coill

Wood Quay *n* an Ché Adhmaid

wooded *adj* coillteach

wooden *adj* adhmadúil

woodpecker *n* cnagaire

woodwind *n* **(instrument)** gaothuirlis

woodwork *n* adhmadóireacht

woodworm *n* réadán

wool *n* olann

woollen *adj* olla **woollens** éadaí olla

word *n* focal

word-processing *n* próiseáil focal

word-processor *n* proiseálaí focal

work *n* obair, saothar *v* oibrigh, saothraigh **at work / working** ag obair, **field work** obair allamuigh, **construction work** obair thógála, **Office of Public Works** Oifig na nOibreacha Poiblí, **working the land** ag saothrú na talún, **working away** ag treabhadh ar aghaidh, ag obair leat

workable *adj* inoibrithe

workforce *n* líon saothair

work sheets *pl* bileoga saothair

worker *n* oibrí **social worker** oibrí sóisialta

working party *n* meitheal

working class *n* lucht oibre

workmate *n* comhoibrí

workshop *n* ceardlann

worktop *n* cuntar oibre

world *n* domhan, saol **all over the world** ar fud an domhain, **in this world** sa saol seo

world champion *n* curadh / seaimpín an domhain

worldly *adj* domhanda, saolta

worldwide *adj* domhanda

worldwide web *n* an gréasán domhanda

worm *n* péist **the worm turning** casadh na péiste

worn *adj* caite

worn down *adj* snoite

worn out *adj* athchaite, seanchaite, spíonta, traochta

worried *adj* imníoch

worry *n* imní

worse *adj* níos measa

worship *n* adhradh *v* adhair

worst *adj* díogha, is measa

worth *n* fiú, fiúntas

worthless *adj* beagmhaitheasach **it's worthless** ní fiú faic/tada é

worthwhile *adj* **it's not worthwhile** ní fiú é

worthy *adj* fiúntach

wound *n* cneá, goin *v* leon, cneáigh **war wounds** gonta cogaidh

wounded *adj* gonta

wrap *v* clúdaigh, cuach

wrapper *n* cumhdach

wreath *n* fleasc

wreck *n* raic

wreckage *n* raic

wren *n* dreoilín

wrench *n* rinse

wrestler *n* gleacaí, iomrascálaí

wrestling *n* gleacaíocht, iomrascáil

wretch *n* ainniseoir, trua

wretched *adj* ainniseach, aimlithe, dearóil

wretchedness *n* ainnise, dearóile

wring *v* fáisc
wrinkle *n, v* roc
wrinkled *adj* rocach
wrist *n* caol na láimhe
write *v* scríobh
writer *n* scríbhneoir

writing *n* scríbhneoireacht, scríbhinn **creative writing** scríbhneoireacht chruthaitheach
wrong *adj* cearr, contráilte, éagórach, mícheart, seachránach **something is wrong with it** tá rud éigin cearr leis, **the wrong side** an taobh contráilte

X

X-chromosome *n* X-chrómasóm
X-ray *n* (ray) x gha, (photo) x-ghathú

Y

yacht *n* luamh
yachting *n* luamhaireacht
yachtsman *n* luamhaire
Yank *adj, n* Poncánach
yard[1] *n* (measurement) slat
yard[2] *n* (area) clós **school yard** clós scoile
yarn[1] *n* abhras, snáth
yarn[2] *n* (story) scéal
yawn *n* méanfach
Y-chromosome *n* Y-chrómasóm
year *n* bliain **two years** dhá bhliain, **three years** trí bliana, **eight years** ocht mbliana, **during the year** i rith na bliana, **years ago** blianta ó shin
yearly *adj* bliantúil
yearn *v* tnúth (le)
yeast *n* deasca, giosta
yell *n, v* scairt
yellow *adj* buí
yelping *n* sceamháil
yes, to say **yes** the positive answer to the question is given i.e. **will you be here tomorrow? yes** an mbeidh tú anseo amárach? beidh, **do you like brown bread? yes** an maith leat

arán donn? is maith, **is that so? yes** an mar sin é? / an ea? is ea
yesterday *adv* inné
yet *adv* fós, go fóill
yew *n* iúr
Yiddish *n* an Ghiúdais
yield *n* tál *v* géill, stríoc
yoga *n* ióga
yogurt *n* iógart
yoke *n* cuing *v* cuingigh
yolk *n* buíocán
yonder *adv* ansiúd, úd thall
yore, of yore anallód
you *pron* tú, sibh, tusa, sibhse
young *adj* óg
youngster *n* malrach, aosánach
yourself *pron* tusa **it's yourself!** tú féin atá ann!
youth[1] *n* macaomh, óganach, gasúr, aosánach **youths** macra
youth[2] *n* (general) óige
youth club *n* club óige
youthful *adj* óigeanta
youth hostel *n* brú óige**

Z

zeal *n* díbhirce, díograis, dúthracht

zealous *adj* díbhirceach, díograiseach, dúthrachtach

zebra *n* séabra

Zen Buddhism *n* Búdachas Zen

zero *n* náid, nialas

zest *n* fonn chun ruda

zigzag *n* fiarlán

zinc *n* sinc

zip *n* sip, sipdhúntóir

Zodiac *n* Stoidiaca

zone *n* crios **buffer zone** crios deighilte, **enterprise zone** crios fiontraíochta

zoo *n* zú

zoology *n* zó-eolaíocht